GLOBALIZATION

GLOBALIZATION

PEOPLE, PERSPECTIVES, AND PROGRESS

William H. Mott IV

Westport, Connecticut
London

Library of Congress Cataloging-in-Publication Data

Mott, William H.
    Globalization : people, perspectives, and progress / William H. Mott IV.
      p.   cm.
    Includes bibliographical references and index.
    ISBN 0–275–97917–2 (alk. paper)
    1. Globalization.   I. Title.
  JZ1318.M67   2004
   303.48′2—dc22   2003060154

British Library Cataloguing in Publication Data is available.

Library of Congress Catalog Card Number: 2003060154
ISBN: 0–275–97917–2

First published in 2004

Praeger Publishers, 88 Post Road West, Westport, CT 06881
An imprint of Greenwood Publishing Group, Inc.
www.praeger.com

Printed in the United States of America

The paper used in this book complies with the
Permanent Paper Standard issued by the National
Information Standards Organization (Z39.48–1984).

10 9 8 7 6 5 4 3 2 1

CONTENTS

PREFACE

After months of frustrating reviews of contemporary commentaries on globalization, any explanations or opinions seemed either impossibly unclear or simplistically narrow. I reread Ralph Waldo Emerson's elegant admonition of the scholar's duties. Emerson reminds us that scholarship uncovers the "facts amidst appearances" through patient "observation . . . [by] cataloguing obscure and nebulous stars of the human mind." The scholar must be "self-relying and self-directed. . . . He is the world's eye. He is the world's heart." His is to communicate "the conclusions of history. Whatsoever oracles the human heart, in all emergencies, in all solemn hours, has uttered as its commentary on the world of actions—these shall he receive and impart. And whatsoever new verdict Reason from her inviolable seat pronounces on the passing men and events of today—this he shall hear and promulgate. . . . Let him hold by himself; add observation to observation . . . [and] satisfy himself alone that this day he has seen something truly. . . . The world is his who can see through its pretension."[1] Any explanation of globalization must account for, but not rely on, the commentaries on today's passing world of actions and current events. It must include the conclusions of history, the heartbeat of humanity, and also people's observations.

Within the historical perspective, globalization has been in the heart and eye of humanity since before Aristotle focused both on the good life. Aristotle focused the human mind on globalization when he identified as the fundamental question of public life the ordering of communal society around the good life. As "the chief end, both for the community as a whole and for each of us individually," the good life became synonymous with globalization.[2] In seeking an answer to Aristotle's question, Ibn Khaldun developed the Science of Civilization (al-'Emran) to explain a current situation and also to suggest a broad pattern for any future order.[3] The complex, integrative approach of al-'Emran reflects St. Thomas Aquinas's premise that truth is a multilayered, multifaceted phenomenon that human beings can discover in many ways and in many places. Like Aquinas's treatises, Ibn Khaldun's Science of Civilization recognizes that each of the exclusionary paths to truth —religion, speculation, observation, insight, logic, reason, and others—presents a single one-dimensional face. Each narrow perspective presents some valuable insight for the complex reality of the human condition and the civilizations that humans construct for themselves. Understanding all of these faces in a multidimensional global perspective concentrates the spirit of Emersonian scholarship. The global perspective exposes an understanding of human civilizations and the globalization that has brought humanity from the past into the present and continues into the future.

The European Renaissance, the Enlightenment, and modernity itself eclipsed Aristotle's project and the Science of Civilization for several centuries. Only in the last few years of the twentieth century did Dean Jack Galvin introduce *The Global Perspective* at the Fletcher School of Law and Diplomacy while I was a student there (1991-1996). It is probably too much to create some direct link between Aristotle, Aquinas, Ibn Khaldun, Emerson, and Jack Galvin. Their several concepts—pursuit of the good life, *al-Emran*, principles to replace polemic, and the global perspective—form the essence of globalization. They embody the complex, integrative approach that I attempt to use to continue the Aristotelian quest within the global perspective.

The technologies of the Industrial Revolution and the information revolution have established coherent telecommunications and transportation networks that encircle the planet. People can take a global view across several dimensions and even integrate them over time for a holistic view of life and living. Explanations of human behavior must be likewise richer in dimensions and perspectives that standard narrow-perspective social science or philosophies neglect. They must consider not only the costs and benefits of economic integration but also the political and cultural dimensions of glolbalization beyond the national perspectives of foreign policy. Complex social interactions arise from deep individual and communal motives that transcend the various aspects of *homo—homo sapiens, homo emptor, homo bellicus, homo politicus, homo faber*, and many others. For most of us, the invigorating freshness of the global perspective not only reveals unnoticed faces of globalization but invites us to participate in globalization as a process and enjoy it as a condition.

Technology has brought some understanding of the condition of the planet and exposed it as an archetype of what Roger Lewin, Murray Gell-Mann, and others have called complex systems. The complex system is at the heart of the globalist schools of international relations and political economy, which recognize that politics and economics themselves form complex, historical systems. Globalization has repeatedly synthesized humanity's previous civilizations, world visions, and value systems into novel historical systems. Each cycle preserved a few more elements of a potential global civilization as its legacy to a global commonwealth of humanity within the global perspective.

Technology and knowledge have brought the processes of biological, cultural, cognitive, and spiritual evolution so far that humanity now confronts immensely complex ecological, political, economic, and social problems. These complex problems, which globalization has created and is exposing, may be beyond the capacity of any narrow perspective to comprehend. They are certainly beyond the ability of any single scholarly discipline, any one narrow perspective, or even any concentration of political power or economic wealth to resolve.

Understanding the human condition, like that of the planet, requires a holistic approach, as envisioned by Aristotle, organized by Aquinas, formulated by Ibn Khaldun, and resurrected by Jack Galvin. The holistic approach embraces civilization as the unit of study and analysis. Dominant within the narrow, industrial-modern perspective, the sovereignty-bound state wrapped in political institutions, military power, and cultural exclusivity is only one element of the mysterious paradox that is globalization. Despite its salience and ubiquity, the capitalist, free-market economy is merely one feature of many within the global perspective.

The continuing, emotional debate between globalizers and antiglobalists makes it prudent to avoid powerful polemic and to project an Emersonian objectivity and scholarly neutralism. Any such prudence necessarily constrains any serious consideration of many interesting questions that become significant and accessible to objective analysis within the global perspective. Although the tenor and scope of this book do not lend themselves to detailed analysis of narrow, specific issues, they offer a philosophical platform and historicist foundation to those who will eventually deal with them.

NOTES

1. See Ralph Waldo Emerson, "The American Scholar," in *Essays and Lectures*, edited and notated by Joel Porte, 51–72 (New York: Literary Classics of the United States, 1983), 63–66.

2. Aristotle, "Politics" in *The Works of Aristotle*, Vol. 2, Great Books of the Western World (Chicago: Encyclopædia Britannica, 1952), 1278b.

3. Ibn Khaldun, *The Muqaddimah: An Introduction to History*, tr. Franz Rosenthal, 3 vols. (New York: Pantheon, 1958), vol. 1, 83–84.

ACKNOWLEDGMENTS

This book has emerged over several years through discussions with many colleagues and students and support from numerous people and institutions. The deficiencies, controversies, or oversights that readers will find in my premises, analyses, or presentation have emerged through my own faults and negligence. My themes and the book's conclusions reflect and include the work of many scholars, managers, diplomats, and students. Over the several years spent in developing my concepts into coherent perceptions of globalization, the endurance, regard, and understanding of my mentors, students, family, and friends have been indispensable. Many gracious colleagues—diplomatic, commercial, and academic—and students have patiently heard, read, and examined my ideas and analyses, and the conclusions in the book. Many have provided useful, undiscovered references, as well as much-needed criticism and focus. Some of my students have adapted one or another of my themes to their own work in different fields and have introduced me to their own novel ideas and insights.

The staffs of the Ginn Library of the Fletcher School of Law and Diplomacy and the Tisch Library of Tufts University have been of immeasurable assistance and support. Not only have they tolerated my unusual research habits, but enthusiastically sought—and found—the arcane references and information that I persisted in demanding. I owe special thanks to Karen Coppock and Ted Johnson, who read the chapters as I constructed them.

My family tolerated my endless papers, notes, and books as I tried to organize what seems to many to be an impossibly complex set of ideas, events, and impressions. The result of an invaluable and very special person, this book is dedicated to my wife, Donna, who has given and tolerated far much more than I have deserved.

1

KNOWLEDGE, PERSPECTIVES, AND PEOPLE

Globalization has become . . . the most important, economic, political, and
cultural phenomenon of our time.[1]

So important is this controversial phenomenon that people cannot afford to
misunderstand globalization and the broad, global perspective that it has
opened to all people everywhere. In the train of the global economy and
unfamiliar forms of global governance is a new global culture: a consumer
society with a panorama of goods and services, transnational fashions and art,
and cosmopolitan personal relationships. New technologies are creating new
products, new markets, and new industries and changing the nature of work
as production becomes global, telecontrolled, and virtual.[2] The proliferation of
instant telecommunication and public fascination with global media events
threaten to create Marshall McLuhan's global village.[3] People redefine culture
itself as a source of *both* individual *and* social identities, as computer networks
circulate ideas, information, and images throughout the world.[4] Whereas
cosmocrats construct a global information superhighway, many global villagers
condemn, resist, and attack a new wave of media-based cultural imperialism.

Although few may appreciate the dimensions of globalism, most people
alive today have experienced a personal epiphany in the last few decades when
globalization became either frighteningly solid or reassuringly real. For many,
connection to the networks of globalization is an empowering experience that
enhances the glory and pleasure of living in a globalizing world. These
cosmocrats lead growing numbers of carriers in expanding social reality from
narrow, local perspectives to a global perspective of life and living. Outside the
charmed circle of the few-score million people connected to global
telecommunication networks, however, even the idea of globalization seems
disempowering. To the unconnected, globalization brings cynicism and
hopelessness in the feeling that inexorable market forces cannot be guided by
people, regulated by the state, or controlled by God. For many, globalization

brings despair in the loss of dual personal and social identity in the global market of and for everything. For some it simply replaces trans-Atlantic political imperialism with the even more powerful hegemony of global capital.[5]

As *both* a current process *and* an eternal human condition, globalization rests on the powers of ideas and art embodied in globalism. Swelling on the underside of globalization, globalism recognizes the influence of events in one perspective on perceptions in another perspective, but avoids absolute priorities of one narrow, functional perspective over another. Globalism expands human interests and concerns beyond lives and living to embrace a universal or global perspective that transcends and includes the other narrow perspectives. Rejecting Parsonian claims for the predominance of culture, globalism also obscures Marxian assertions of economic foundations for all politics and all culture and invalidates realist convictions of the absolute power of politics.

Some consequences and paradoxes of globalization—empowering in some perspectives or frightening in others—have spawned active, antiglobalist reactions. Abrupt dislocations in the international division of labor have started disturbing migrations. Chaotic interpenetration of cultures with the fearsome, or friendly, penumbra of a dominant, if inchoate, global culture has become widespread anti-Americanism. Intractable ethical concerns have arisen around the huge consumption of resources and rampant pollution by the rich in juxtaposition with insufficient resources and minimal waste among the poor.

Such controversial issues bring political challenges to traditional values and institutions. Compressions of space and time in all aspects of living have created new lifestyles and social standards. Economic inequality has increased dramatically as markets and firms have expanded into conflict-ridden Africa and Eastern Europe, but also in more peaceful Latin America and Asia.[6] Rapid industrialization has brought environmental degradation and ethnic conflict in West Africa, popular protest and government regulation in Europe, and political debate in North America. In Central Asia, however, industrial pollution energized ethnic conflict that quickly submerged any environmental concern beneath local hopes for the economic benefits of globalization.[7]

Although neither globalism nor globalization embodies any normative premises, any ideological or philosophical notions can establish an attitude towards both. Neither globalists nor antiglobalists have any qualms about appending or detaching ideologies, moralities, or ethics to support their positions. The globalization-globalism debate not only has become controversial but has often aligned single-issue antiglobalists against narrow-perspective globalizers in awkwardly shallow, *ad hoc* coalitions of convenience.

THEMES

This book revolves around three primary themes and their interconnections—knowledge, perspective, and progress. The first is the wonderful capacity of people to create and use knowledge. The second is the broad power of perspective and the specific power of the global perspective. The third is the persistence of humanity in pursuing progress. Within the lens of historicism, globalization has never been anything more or less than the progressive expansion of human knowledge towards the global perspective.

Knowledge and People

Knowledge has occupied the center of people's perspectives from the first civilizations' beginnings. Thinkers, politicians, jurists, traders, and ordinary people have faced changing contexts for their lives. Many approached changes less as problems demanding solutions than as opportunities to create new knowledge. They found themselves creating knowledge that relieved stresses, shifted perspectives, and transformed firms, polities, economies, cultures, civilizations, and, most significantly, their perceptions of themselves. Their shifts in perspective and the new knowledge that they created transformed worlds of crisis, stress, and disorder into new realities of hope and promise.

Between transformations that were often catastrophic, people expanded knowledge and diffused it through innovation, conversion of skill and experience—tacit knowledge—and learning.[8] People developed knowledge incrementally in a continual dialogue across a train of ideas, innovations, and theories and a succession of observations, discoveries, and facts. Whereas new theories have often resolved current problems, they invariably generated new questions by changing the constraints on answers. The new unknown answers and the problems still unsolved remain globalization's invitations to progress.

Problem solving and cognitive knowledge have never been enough for people unless they also provided normative meaning for living and existence. "In this predicament, action, with its involvement and commitment, its being *engagé*, seemed to hold out the hope, not of solving any problems, but of making it possible to live with them."[9] Creating new knowledge, integrating it with old wisdom, and understanding the product are essential human tasks and missions. The intense urge of people everywhere and always to know remains the timeless stimulus for progress within and across every perspective.

Perspective

Beyond the technical definitions of art, people understand many things within the term *perspective*—discipline, profession, philosophy, attitude, natural and social science, ideology, prejudice, culture, common sense, job, belief, branches of learning, and others. Whatever fashion chooses to call them, people's perspectives on life and living are sets of "cognitive and moral maps that orient an actor within a policy sphere."[10] When people combined values with knowledge, they discovered or created narrow, functional perspectives on social reality that organized and focused their thoughts and motivations on economics, politics, science, or culture as foundations for action.[11]

With clear, functional focus—politics, economics, culture, or something else—perspectives organize knowledge, identify problems, specify people's interests, and prioritize purposes and goals around their values. They bring people to normative judgments about what to do and how to behave, lead them into particular paths of thought and courses of action, and reinforce their decisions to take a particular approach to an issue. Perspectives are useful in situations with less than complete information, since they narrow the scope of the relevant and allow experience, precedent, and prejudice to influence decisions. The utility of perspectives arises from the regularity of the natural universe and the limits on personal human experience. Over history, people have become very clever in merging them into understandings of the past, useful systems of present reality, and self-satisfying predictions of the future.

As cognitive maps, perspectives include definitions and contexts that translate observations and prior knowledge into understanding. By focusing people's attention and interest, they exclude what people determine to be irrelevant, trivial, confusing, or untrue. Perspectives enable people to answer the general question, What is it that's going on here?[12] They allow people to make sense of what they observe in complicated situations and ignore what does not make sense. They also answer specific questions and provide standards about a particular issue or concern. Analogies, metaphors, and symbols provide languages for interpreting events and prescribing action.[13]

As moral maps, perspectives assign values and social, political, or economic meaning to ideas, people, institutions, and actions. Perspectives translate these negative or positive connotations and images and implications into moral indignation at injustices or proud righteousness over heroism. People with different perspectives have different moral reactions to the same situation. Perspectives vest certain people or ideas with moral authority to represent a group of people who share a perspective, to prescribe moral orthodoxy, or to organize information and interpret reality within the perspective.

People can revise their prior understandings of the world quickly by expanding or contracting a perspective simply by refining a definition, changing a metaphor, recognizing new knowledge, or adding or omitting a value. A change in perspective does not require any admission that a prior perspective was wrong or flawed but justifies any expansion or contraction by recognizing a change in the situation. People have commonly expanded their perspectives on social reality without abandoning the moral traditions, social norms, cultures, institutions, or knowledge inherited from prior civilizations. Instead, they recognized some new facts, created some new knowledge to explain those facts, and shifted to some new, expanded perspectives.

Although people could define any number of narrow perspectives and adopt a different perspective for every thought, modern perceptions of globalization are focused in three broad, less-than-global perspectives: politics, economics, and culture. Even recognizing that these perspectives are neither mutually exclusive nor comprehensive, ordinary people, well-informed economists, and politicians with global responsibilities routinely adopt only one perspectives in assessing globalization and determining how to deal with it. Whether finding economic benefit, political failure, or cultural tragedy in globalization, most perceptions of it remain within a single economic, political, or cultural perspective. Even the carriers of globalism and barriers to globalization often do not extend to the global perspective.

Historical Lenses

People perceive nature and reality within their particular perspectives through lenses of understanding, knowledge, values, and belief. Although history is replete with contractions and shifting of perspectives, globalization seems consistently to have expanded narrow perspectives as new knowledge refocused these lenses. At several times over history, humanity has undertaken momentous projects—*pax Romana*, the Renaissance, the Enlightenment, modernity, and possibly postmodernity—to grind new lenses for its current assortment of perspectives on life, living, time, the world, and the universe.

The lenses used by Renaissance thinkers looked backwards in time and inwards in space to rediscover the speculative wisdom of Athens and Rome. Premodern lenses focused people on the tradition of the past, historical systems, physical survival in the present, and God in the hereafter. The Enlightenment lens shifted people's narrow perspectives towards the rational certainty of science in the present as the premise to truth in the future and exposed a broad, global perspective. Instead of introspection, thinkers looked beyond themselves in rational observation of the natural world and invited humanity to understand itself and its world through its own reason and spirit.

The hastily crafted lens of modernity blurred the Enlightenment image of universal understanding through reason and revelation. Although the emergence of time consciousness was sharpening temporal perspectives, and technology was expanding spatial perspectives as the Enlightenment faded, human understanding remained a congeries of narrow, functional perspectives. Labored reworkings of the modern lenses has converged cultural, political, and economic perspectives on living into an emphasis on quality of living, self-expression, and sociopolitical participation. The congeries of attitudes, thought patterns, theories, and movements that meet at the postmodern focal point does not itself, however, project a coherent or cohesive perspective.

Historicism

The complex lens of historicism expands all human perspectives to embrace *both* space *and* time. Historicism is "most fundamentally an acute awareness of the past as moving in the present, a sense of the historicity, the historical nature and context, of the here and now. Human existence is a living whole across the generations, change and continuity together."[14]

Through the historicist lens, knowledge connects the past to the present and shapes the future. Neither absolute nor static, knowledge is universally and eternally relative, incomplete, and dynamic. The historicist expansion of knowledge that has accompanied the expansion of human perspectives on life and living has energized and continues to sustain globalization. Through the historicist lens, globalization is clearly a knowledge-based, permanently emergent condition, not merely a process with a beginning and an end.

Globalization has been concurrent with human evolution since primal humans expanded their perspectives to discover the world outside themselves. Like Darwinian evolution, globalization is not a directional, linear, historical process with a beginning and an end but temporal expansion of human consciousness into *both* the past *and* the future. Neither does it converge to any singular condition or final destination for social change.[15] Through the historicist lens, "globalization is therefore not an inexorable, exogenous process, a march to a higher—or indeed lower—form of civilization. It is a path-dependent process, rooted in real historical decisions, nondecisions, and conjunctural turning points."[16] Less a chronological history of change than a reflexive pattern of human will, it expands people's *a priori* ideas, beliefs, and values about reality and living. In so doing, globalization alters itself.

Understanding globalization through the historicist lens exposes not only the present but also the past—the necessary and contingent conditions that historically launched each of globalization's many, successive waves. Globalization evolves from and through all past civilizational structures, which may continue their own local histories while embedded in an evolving global pattern of governance. Emerging from, but not defined by or beginning in, the past, globalization exposes and limits but does not determine the future.

The Idea of Progress

Most people believe in progress, the notion that things will somehow get better. More than hope or desire, progress elicits the confidence of scientific prediction based on trends, laws of history, or the certainty of human nature.[17] So deeply embedded in people's lives is the idea of progress that most accept it unconsciously and unquestioningly. Few indeed are those who doubt the progress that science has brought through improvements in technology.

Only slightly less broad is the economic perspective within which technological improvement also leads to greater wealth and better material conditions of living. Beyond the economic perspective, considerably fewer people, perhaps only a minority, adopt the political perspective. For them, progress refers primarily to improvements in social and political institutions or better governance. Political progress, which globalization may bring in the future, would promise greater justice, wider freedom, more equality, and predictable stability. Confronted with persistent economic inequality and political instability, many people doubt that globalization has brought real progress within these perspectives. Reminding themselves that people are motivated by personal experience and self-interest, some people mistrust globalization to improve things and adopt an antiglobalist perspective.

Fewer people still are persuaded that globalization brings progress in controlling and managing institutions or that human nature is improving. Little evidence of cultural improvement has emerged from the historical perspective of globalization. Neither the economic nor the political perspective offers much support to faith in a kinder, gentler, better-natured humanity. Among these few faithful are the very few—known as idealistic or mad—who confidently predict that economic, political, and cultural progress will improve humanity itself in physical, spiritual, and intellectual ways.

As humanity has matured, "the area over which man has sought to obtain control has changed with his changing powers and his changing active role in a developing human society, and today it is extending to new dimensions."[18] Despite any aggregate progress that change may bring, within each narrow, individual perspective, globalization creates unstable chaos as new facts expose uncertainties that tradition cannot explain. Transcending narrow perspectives, however, the idea of progress provides the moral and philosophical stability that people crave in a world of permanent change. Although "observed progress is mainly technical, whereas believed progress is mainly spiritual," for most people, progress—observed and believed—"is a truth that lies somewhere near the roots of our religion."[19] The idea of progress links the eternal past of observed reality through the urgent present to the infinite future of belief.

GLOBALIZATION: THE GLOBAL PERSPECTIVE

Fashionable debate often confuses globalization, which has accompanied history for millennia, with the current project of imposing a global version of liberal, capitalist democracy. Within the historicist pattern of globalization, the current wave is only beginning and extends far beyond a narrow, economic perspective. Like globalization, the global perspective is multidimensional and encompasses all narrow perspectives—functional, spatial, and temporal. Along its functional dimension, the global perspective embraces the narrow perspectives that focus human prospects on life and living—economic, political, scientific, or cultural. Along its spatial dimension, the global perspective includes all people and the groups to which they belong. Along the temporal dimension, the historicist lens expands the spatial and functional perspectives to encompass the past, the present, and also the future. Through the historicist lens, the temporal and spatial dimensions of the global perspective show that the relationships among functional perspectives vary over time and space.

Process and Condition

With due respect to the salience of economics and commerce for modern people, globalization is not only, or even primarily, economic. Neither is it focused in any geographical dimension or unique to modernity. Transcending the ideologies that bind humanity to its own experience, the series of human transformations of its own social reality is the *process* of globalization linking the remembered past through the urgent present to the impenetrable future. The process is not without a past and seems to have occurred—or at least begun—many times as people repeatedly transformed their social realities into something new.[20] Each historical transformation has launched a wave of globalization that expanded people's perspectives beyond those of earlier societies. Globalization is "a complex set of distinct but related processes —economic, cultural, social, and also political and military—through which social relations have developed towards a global scale and with global reach, over a long historic period."[21] As these multiple processes continue towards their appointed goals within some civilizational context, they integrate and fragment, create opportunities and pose problems, centralize power and diffuse knowledge. Successive, cumulative expansions of knowledge, through innovation and diffusion as advanced technology, have each, in turn, stimulated and carried incremental progress within every perspective of living. Along its functional dimensions, the process has expanded the spatial dimensions of living and changed globalization itself. Within this broader perspective, globalization implies "the intensification of worldwide social relations which link distant realities in such a way that local happenings are shaped by events occurring many miles away and vice versa."[22]

Nonlinear, irregular, flexible, path-dependent, contingent on place and time, and directed by people themselves, globalization has also been a human *condition* through history. Within every narrow, brief historical perspective bounded by the here and now, globalization appears a process. Through the eternal lens of historicism, globalization is a condition of human life and living. People seem instinctively addicted to expanding their perspectives, gaining new understanding, and making progress. Although knowledge creation is defined by its historical, spatial, and human context, the dynamic permanence of the process—in some form of globalization—has been and is the nucleus and essence of the human condition in all times and in all places.

Expanding Perspectives

The global perspective and globalism expand knowledge to include belief, insight, visions, care, love, trust, ideals, and the many other thoughts that humans have and know. Globalization introduces people to new ways of doing and living as they create new knowledge and have novel thoughts. Just as some transforming, new knowledge and its applications have energized each successive wave of globalization, the power of information technologies to compress time and space is the engine of the current wave.

The global perspective expands understanding beyond the political perspectives of high politics and international relations, beyond economic perspectives of low politics and commerce, and beyond narrow ethnic or religious perspectives. Expansion into the global perspective congeals the many sorts and levels of flows and exchanges of products, ideas, information, people, and technology in a comprehensive set of human relationships. Embracing the entirety of human life and thought, the global perspective exposes the disjunctions and anomalies between narrow perspectives, as well as opportunities for resolving them through expanding perspectives.[23]

As each person recognizes the world beyond the immediate reach of the physical human senses, globalization not only expands the perspectives of humanity as a whole but also transforms the life of every individual. Nor is globalization primarily geographic, since it extends across time as well as space. The global perspective expands human perspectives on life and living through interconnections of experience and knowledge across disparate eras of time. Beneath the many features and effects of globalization lie the dual negative notions of *delocalization* and *detemporalization*: the expansion of ideas and relationships from local traditions and cultures and current concerns to a global, ageless context. In all its guises across all perspectives, globalization transforms people, their thoughts, and the social reality in which they live.

Expanding narrow perspectives into the global perspective exposes cultural trauma, the search for identity, and intense, emotional resistance. Within their primal, self-centered perspectives, people naturally feel responsibility to and for themselves, their welfare, and their personal behaviors. Expansion of self into the global perspective exposes and even stimulates feelings of compassion for other people who are beyond the familiarities of local communities. A broader social or global self expands individual responsibility to families, companies and professions, communities, political parties and churches, geographic areas, countries, and nations. Globalization through pervasive and ubiquitous networks among people living *de facto* a single global destiny expands human and even individual "accountability to and responsibility for the world."[24]

Global Governance and Values

Exposing much more than simply a global mode of production, the global perspective expands human compassion and accountability to broader processes and deeper structures: global governance and human values. A pattern of global governance includes institutions, rules, and practices that form the context for global relationships. A set of simultaneous human values, attitudes, beliefs, and behaviors embedded in the contemporary structure of global governance imposes the limits on those relationships.

Although common usage often interchanges the terms *government* and *governance* as synonyms, it is useful to differentiate between government as a structural notion and governance as a process. Beyond the traditional, personal reciprocities and hierarchic relationships preserved as government in the Westphalian nation-state, the processes of governance embody the expansive and dynamic properties of knowledge and information technology. Rather than a simple extension of traditional notions of state-centered government, global governance contains nonstate and transnational relationships in the infinitude of reciprocal interrelationships that information technology has made possible. The power concentrated in government takes public decisions by enacting laws, promulgating policies, establishing and enforcing regulations, allocating public expenditures and investments, and providing incentives to prefer some behaviors and discourage others. Beyond government, governance also includes a social mechanism to adapt the rules—legislation, adjudication, enforcement, and influence—of its political community to people's changing perspectives of social reality in event time. Governance explicitly includes the penetration of civil society and the public sphere into the political process.

Globalization has transformed any meanings of *both* governance *and* government through information technologies, which have mobilized capital and multiplied global liquidity through instantaneous financial transfers and arbitrage. Beyond physical, national locations, the global economy and any global polity are also deeply embedded in various electronic spaces that transcend familiar jurisdictions for conventional government or regulation. Because globalization and governance are deeply embedded *both* in information technologies *and* in physical places, they extend into and through the state and beyond most notions of state-centered systems of government.

Among emerging global values are the prevalence of dialogue and mutual understanding to replace competitive conflict; personal acceptance of a portion of global responsibility; and the legitimacy of multiple civilizational contexts. Globalization transforms individual knowledge and values into global norms and practices, which appear to people as intuitively obvious or natural, because they are effective in providing security, prosperity, and justice. Such transformations have included—but are not limited to—the expansion of rationality after the Enlightenment, recognition of technology as a major force behind progress, or acceptance of the value of the individual as legitimate features of human existence. Modern transformations have brought free trade, peaceful dispute resolution, individual ownership of property and wealth, and balance between rights and duties. In relieving the stresses of society, transformations of social reality have brought recognition of human rights and reliance on science rather than tradition or belief in making decisions. Not simply the replacement of politics with economics or culture, globalization is reconstructing the fundamental norms, practices, and institutions that have historically separated the domains of private living, public life, and human justice. Global governance is extending, with increasing legitimacy, beyond politics and economics into social, judicial, and cultural affairs.

Knowledge and Learning

A major focus of the global perspective is a postrational concept of learning that is "not merely acquiring information . . . nor is it merely improving one's mind; it is learning to recognize some specific invitations to encounter particular adventures in human self-understanding."[25] Globalization challenges the Enlightenment conclusion that scientific-technical reason was the single reliable basis for determining the proper means for achieving separate political, economic, or ethical ends. Including the Enlightenment's prescriptions of rationality and optimal utility, the global perspective places them in tandem with human values, ethics, and moralities as sources for knowledge, truth, and goodness. Globalization expands the role and scope of knowledge beyond explaining the world as it appears to be to determining the aims of societies—how the world ought to be.

Within the global perspective, globalization promises neither utopia nor catastrophe. It does promise a transformation of social reality, introduce a novel system of governance, and provide humanity a platform from which to launch a new civilization with its own new set of challenges, values, and visions. In either the spatial or the temporal dimension alone, globalization is uneven, contradictory, often unbalanced, and usually confusing. Pervading space, time, and the human spirit, globalization affects all of humanity, every individual, every corner of the earth, the present and the future, and synthesizes the legacies of the past into a new system of social reality. As people learn old information and create new knowledge, globalization exposes the unknown by expanding human perspectives, even as it erodes the foundations of the comfortable world of modernity and shatters the traditions that support them. Presenting the specter of fear as well as the promise of hope, the global perspective remains humanity's eternal challenge.

NOTES

1. John Micklethwaite and Adrian Wooldridge, *A Future Perfect: The Challenge and Hidden Promise of Globalization* (New York: Random House–Crown Business, 2000), xvi.

2. See David Morley and Kevin Robbins, *Spaces of Identity* (London: Routledge, 1995); David Harvey, *The Condition of Postmodernity: An Enquiry into the Origins of Social Change* (Oxford: Blackwell, 1989).

3. See Marshall McLuhan, *Understanding Media* (London: Routledge, 1964); Marshall McLuhan, *The Global Village: Transformations in World Life and Media in the 21st Century* (New York: Oxford University Press, 1989); McKenzie Wark, *Virtual Geography: Living with Global Media Events* (Bloomington and Indianapolis: Indiana University Press, 1994).

4. See Bill Gates, *The Road Ahead* (New York: Viking, 1995).

5. See Paul Hirst and Grahame Thompson, *Globalization in Question: The International Economy and the Possibilities of Governance* (Cambridge: Polity, 1996).

6. See Paul Collier and Anke Hoeffler, "On Economic Causes of Civil War," *Oxford Economic Papers* 50(4) (October 1998): 563–573; Juan Luis Londoño, *Poverty, Inequality, and Human Capital Development in Latin America, 1950–2025* (Washington, D.C.: World Bank, 1996).

7. See Jane I. Dawson, *Eco-Nationalism: Anti-Nuclear Activism and National Identity in Russia, Lithuania, and Ukraine* (Durham: Duke University Press, 1996).

8. The idea that knowledge is crucially important for firms, countries,and regions and for human progress is so widely accepted that it may seem trivial. See, among others, Alvin Toffler, *Powershift, Knowledge, Wealth, and Violence at the Edge of the 21st Century* (New York: Bantam, 1990); Robert B. Reich, *The Work of Nations: Preparing Ourselves for 21st Century Capitalism* (London: Simon and Schuster, 1991); Peter F. Drucker, *Post-Capitalist Society* (New York: HarperCollins, 1993); Michael Gibbons, Camille Limoges, Helga Nowotny, Simon Schwartzman, Peter Scott, and Martin Trow, *The New Production of Knowledge* (Beverly Hills, California: Sage, 1994), 24–26.

9. Hannah Arendt, *Between Past and Future: Six Exercises in Political Thought* (New York: Viking, [1954] 1961), 9.

10. Erik Bleich, "Integrating Ideas into Policymaking Analysis: Frames and Race Policies in Britain and France," *Comparative Political Studies* 35(9) (November 2002): 1054–1076; 1063.

11. Political science and economics adopted the term *worldview* to capture the ability of a perspective to connect people to the real world through lenses of values and knowledge. More recent jargon has replaced both terms with the recondite phrase *cognitive frame*.

12. Erving Goffman, *Frame Analysis: An Essay on the Organization of Experience* (Cambridge: Harvard University Press, 1974), 25.

13. Aquatic metaphors of waves, streams, or floods of immigrants, capital, goods, foreign cultures, or something else have often been used to justify turning off the taps or closing the valves to avoid swamping or flooding. See Yuen Foong Khong, *Analogies at War* (Princeton: Princeton University Press, 1992), 20–21, 26–29.

14. Claes G. Ryn, "Defining Historicism," *Humanitas* 11(2) (Spring-Summer 1998): 86–101; 89. Available from http://www.nhinet.org/ryn-rob.htm. National Humanities Institute, Washington, D.C. [cited 5 June 2002].

15. See David Held, David Goldblatt, Anthony McGrew, and Jonathan Peraton, "The Globalization of Economic Activity," *New Political Economy* 2(2) (July 1997): 257–277; 258. See also David Held, David Goldblatt, Anthony McGrew, and Jonathan Peraton, *Global Flows, Global Transformations: Concepts, Theories, and Evidence* (Cambridge: Polity, 1997).

16. Philip G. Cerny, "Restructuring the Political Arena: Globalization and the Paradoxes of the Competition State," in *Globalization and Its Critics*, edited by Randall D. Germain, 117–138 (New York: St. Martin's, 2000), 121.

17. These ideas are expanded in, among others, Sidney Pollard, *The Idea of Progress* (New York: Basic Books, 1968), v-vii.

18. Pollard, *The Idea of Progress*, 200.

19. Gilbert Murray, *Essays and Addresses* (London: G. Allen and Unwin, 1921), 19.

20. Emma Rothschild, "Globalization and the Return of History," *Foreign Policy* 115 (Summer 1999): 106–116; 107.

21. Martin Shaw, "The State of Globalization: Towards a Theory of State Transformation," *Review of International Political Economy* 4(3) (Autumn 1997): 497–513; 498.

22. Anthony Giddens, *The Consequences of Modernity* (Cambridge: Polity, 1990), 64.

23. See Douglas Kellner, *Critical Theory, Marxism, and Modernity* (Cambridge and Baltimore: Polity and Johns Hopkins University Press, 1989).

24. Vaclav Havel, "Faith in the World," *Civilization* 5(2) (April-May 1998): 51–53; 52.

25. Michael Oakeshott, *The Voice of Liberal Learning* (New Haven: Yale University Press, 1989), 29.

2

KNOWLEDGE AND KNOWLEDGE CREATION

Knowledge "represents the capacities or capabilities of an individual or social group. These capacities are multifaceted and span the cognitive or holistic processes associated with meaning and understanding, as well as the abilities to organize, interpret, and assess information."[1] Through the broad lens of historicism, knowledge, its creation, its expansion and diffusion, and its accumulation appear within the global perspective as the primary dynamics of globalization. Transcending all of the narrow perspectives, knowledge creation focuses progress, animates transformation, relieves social stress, and forms the stimulus for action. As globalization and revolutions were transforming the Enlightenment into modernity, Anne-Robert-Jacques Turgot may have glimpsed the timeless, distinctively human process of creating knowledge:

> To discover and verify the truth, it is no longer a question of establishing a small number of simple principles and then merely allowing the mind to be borne along by the current of their consequences. . . . Ideas emerge and are assembled in our minds almost without our knowing it. . . . Little by little we learn to distinguish between them, less by reference to what they are in themselves than by reference to their relation to our habits and needs. . . . This chaotic blend of ideas and expressions grows and becomes more complex all the time; and when man starts to seek for truth, he finds himself in the midst of a labyrinth which he has entered blindfold.[2]

"Revolutions in science often give rise to revolutions in thought, after which the earlier understanding comes to seem naïve and the new conception intuitively obvious."[3] During the Enlightenment, when revolutions were rapidly changing science and philosophy, the knowledge base was neither well expressed nor widely diffused. Because the interactions between science, philosophy, and knowledge were inherently incomplete and idiosyncratic for different individuals in different societies, people created knowledge in the uncertainty and unpredictable chaos of Turgot's labyrinth. Knowledge itself experienced a severe revolution as Francis Bacon sought "a total reconstruction of sciences, arts, and all human knowledge, raised upon the proper foundation . . . [and took] all knowledge to be my province."[4]

Some thinkers have described globalization as "a knowledge revolution, an acceleration in the pace of generation of new ideas and of the decline in the cost of disseminating these ideas."[5] Arising from Bacon's audacious globalization of knowledge, the knowledge revolution gained momentum as science insisted on rejecting tradition and received wisdom without empirical confirmation. Globalization embodies continuous creation of new knowledge that destroys old orthodoxy, creates a new universe and way of living, and transforms social reality. Knowledge creation has repeatedly transformed the institutional and hierarchical contexts around each wave of globalization.

Merging economics, politics, culture, and science, the most important force behind globalization is people's collective ability to create new knowledge and refine old knowledge continuously from current capabilities.[6] Constructed on existing rational knowledge and built of new cognitive knowledge, globalization includes, and is bounded by, identifiable hierarchies of values and beliefs—normative knowledge—that people can be expected to change at will.[7] The depth and breadth of the stock of human knowledge, what people know—the knowledge base—are merely interesting origins.[8]

BACON'S IDOLS

Francis Bacon (1561–1626) identified four types of impediments to creation of new knowledge or expansion of humanity's store of knowledge. He christened them idols of the human mind and its thought: *idola specus* (idols of the cave), *idola fori* (idols of the forum), *idola theatri* (idols of the theater), and *idola tribus* (idols of the tribe). Bacon's idols, despite recognition only at the dawn of the Enlightenment, have constrained human thought since the first humans realized that they could think, and the idols hobble human creativity today. The most salient of these idols have taken the contrasting forms of what David Riesman has called tradition-direction (*idola theatri*), inner-direction (*idola specus*), and other-direction (*idola fori*).[9]

The Idols in Profile

Bacon's *idola specus* recall Plato's shadows of reality as individual idiosyncrasies of judgment, fears, illusions, or fallacies. These are the idols of self-identity, inner-direction, character, belief, and passion. They appear as private habits, prejudices, or desires, learned from parents, teachers, and experience, and often don the armor of tradition. These idols operate through the ingenuity of each mind in perceiving reality, discerning its own emotions, and creating self-centered order within familiar, comfortable perspectives. The *idola specus* use the powers of ignorance, fear of the unknown, and self-satisfaction to create personal resistance to change or expanding perspectives. They force people to justify learning and change instead of challenging ignorance and stagnation. Even when defeated by objectivity or rationality, these idols are quick to create new prejudices and mind-sets.

Idola fori impose limits through the inability of human languages, symbols, and cultures to express or even formulate novel ideas or new knowledge outside narrow perspectives of existing knowledge. These idols use the power of words and symbols to induce belief in ideas and things that exist not in objective reality but only in the human mind. They establish credibility by denying the existence of things that language cannot express or describe. The *idola fori* incite specialized thinkers to concoct distinct jargons of words, meanings, premises, logic, abstractions, and symbols that are largely untranslatable into the languages of other people or even into other specialized jargons. Bacon demanded that rational thinkers "banish all logical tricks of wishful thinking, all verbal absurdities of obscure thought. We must put behind us all those majestic deductive systems of philosophy which proposed to draw a thousand eternal verities out of a few axioms and principles."[10] Exposure of the *idola fori* was not enough, however, since they simply changed shape. New knowledge presented the dilemmas of inventing new expressions, adding novel content and meanings to old ones, or appending modifiers. In 1804, British physician James Parkinson recognized the power of these idols to prevent proper explanation, or even conceptions, of anything beyond people's current perspectives. "Whilst endeavoring to find appropriate terms, a considerable difficulty arose; language not possessing a sign to represent that idea, which the mind of man had not till now conceived."[11] Ludwig Wittgenstein recognized the power of Bacon's *idola fori* in his admonition not to speak about the unspeakable.[12] These idols force people to create novel nomenclatures and languages to express any new knowledge that they create and describe any innovations that they invent or discover.

Bacon conceived *idola theatri* as the time-honored limits of orthodoxy, custom, or belief that exclude unacceptable ideas or facts. Worshipers of these idols are the skeptics who doubt the validity of any claims to knowledge beyond a particular, narrow truth, while accepting without question the philosophies and demonstrations within that truth as absolute. The medieval world evinced no clear notion of tradition as distinct from daily living, which involved little beyond tradition. As they gradually identified it with dogma and ignorance, Enlightenment thinkers developed the notion of tradition embodied in Bacon's *idola theatri*, which prevented people from expanding the new knowledge that rationality discovered. Bacon's *idola theatri* thrive on ritual and repetition and are most comfortable in communities or collectivities that seek a social identity beyond self. The *idola theatri* distinguish themselves by defining truth. "For someone following a traditional practice, questions do not have to be asked about alternatives. However much it may change, tradition provides a framework for action that can go largely unquestioned."[13]

Idols of the tribe (*idola tribus*) transcend individuals, cultures, and even history in what people have come to know as human nature. Still faithfully worshiped some four centuries after Bacon exposed his idols, human nature has become recognizable as "the sum of the behavior and characteristics that are typical of the human species, arising from genetic rather than environmental factors."[14] Bacon found two tribal idols—both of which ignore facts that do not emerge from direct observation—particularly hostile to expansion of knowledge: anthropocentrism and hypergeneralization. The tendency to explain everything in terms of personal experience was expressed by the Greek Sophist Protagoras, "Man is the measure of all things." The propensity to generalize from single observations to universal truths has been reduced to the all-encompassing Latin phrase *ceteris paribus*.[15] Many modern philosophers would add another powerful idol of Bacon's tribe: "the urge to form strong attachments to groups, ranging from the family, through gangs, tribes, organizations, ethnic, religious and linguistic groups, to nations."[16] Despite their manifesto of universal order not only in human nature but in the chaos of environmental nature and the disorder in human behaviors, Bacon's *idola tribus* have lost credibility. Rationality has convinced people that the imaginations of one generation have been less than competent to deal with the challenges of succeeding generations. History has taught them to distrust the claims of *idola tribus* that human nature is a universal, timeless absolute value. Human nature has, in fact and history, changed dramatically over time,

Dealing with the Idols

Although the Enlightenment had permanently expanded the scope of knowledge and exposed the global perspective, rationalism did not depose the idols. Despite his own deep faith, Enlightenment rationalism expanded Bacon's insights to embrace religion and emotions and sought to depose the idols' legitimacy and replace them with rationality: "Let men's minds be filled with true ideas; let their reason be cultivated; let justice govern them; and there will be no need of opposing to the passions, such a feeble barrier as a fear of the gods. . . . In vain should we attempt to cure men of their vices, unless we begin by curing of them of their prejudices. . . . Let the vain chimeras of men be removed, and reasonable opinions will soon come of themselves, into these heads which were thought to be forever destined to error."[17]

As modernity learned to coexist with the idols, the *idola theatri* repeatedly refined and reinvented themselves by resurrecting old traditions in a surge of fundamentalism or simply inventing new ones. People's efforts towards progress have often featured compromises with the tribal idols. As Bacon presciently observed, people have remained comfortable in measuring everything in terms of themselves, simplifying every contrast to a dichotomy, or generalizing universality from narrow sets of biased data. Bacon's idols led Renaissance scholars to take pains to unite their own direct observations with classical wisdom. With similar diligence, modern thinkers relate new ideas to universal common sense or the intuitively obvious through the tribal idols in universal concepts explained by simplistic examples.

Beyond crippling compromises, challenges to the idols have generated self-defeating controversies within constraints imposed by the *idola tribus*. Decisionmakers and ordinary people struggle to decide among many eminently sensible alternative perspectives, all claiming truth within their different contexts of facts and relevant observations. Scientists and philosophers balance knowledge and understanding between orthodoxy (*idola theatri*), observation (*idola specus* and *idola fori*), and insight (*idola tribus*). Despite heroic human efforts, Bacon's idols retain much of their attraction and power through their ability to procreate and adapt as people create and accumulate knowledge.

Subduing the Idols

Across every perspective of philosophy and science, these compromises and controversies about progression from narrow experience to broad understanding have introduced new and fundamental questions. The answers —often neither simple nor dichotomous—have emerged gradually through creation of new knowledge that eventually shattered Bacon's *idola theatri*, one by one, at the feet of the crumbling *idola tribus*. The impediments of language and culture (*idola fori*) present formidable barriers to learning, creating new knowledge, and even solving basic problems. Even in a context of fluid communication, the ubiquitous *idola specus* ensure that consensus congeals only slowly around any new knowledge that displaces old truth. Even, however, as old theories (*idola theatri*) yield to new understanding and people can disregard the instinctive biases of human nature (*idola tribus*), the idols' phoenixlike power of self-regeneration gives them new life in new contexts.

Bacon's pantheon of idols continues to restrain people's efforts to create and expand knowledge and seems to reside deep within human culture. Although the idols conspire to convert the search for understanding into a Sisyphean ordeal, they have not contained humanity's need for knowledge. Another trait, also deep in human nature, seems persistently to vanquish them: the drive to ask and to know. The unremitting pressure towards universal understanding and truth provides the fascination, frustration, and faith that energize human progress. This indefatigable curiosity has expanded human understanding from gods, magic, and demons to black holes, to quarks and chromodynamics, back to the big bang, and forward to the nature of God.

CREATION OF KNOWLEDGE

More than accumulating skills and information, knowledge is autocatalytic (self-driving), autogenous (self-starting), and self-generative. People who know can create new knowledge and generate new information from existing knowledge. Beginning with contradictions and opposites, "knowledge creation is a process of synthesizing such opposites by transforming and uniting them to transcend the existing self. Contradiction is a necessity, not an obstacle, for creation. By trying to synthesize the contradictions, one can transcend the existing optimal balance and create new reality."[18]

Since knowledge has no boundaries, people can create new knowledge in any form from insanity or whimsy through rational pragmatism to artistic insight and divine inspiration. Social existence, however, constrains knowledge creation within boundaries of relevance. Describing society's structure and domain, its legacy of knowledge synthesizes a society's absolute values, which are not affected by current conditions, with people's relative values in the here and now. Since the evolution of a society and the projects that its people undertake emerge from its base of existing knowledge and system of values, knowledge creation is necessarily path-dependent, although not predetermined.

The accumulation of knowledge as people create it is a uniquely human experience whereby understanding realizes possibilities and also exposes new possibilities in expanded perspectives. Holders of knowledge can adapt themselves and their knowledge to new information and to the effects of using their knowledge as new interpretations of old facts shift narrow perspectives, synthesize new knowledge, and refine comprehensive explanations. By converting "techniques, methods, and designs that work in certain ways and with certain consequences, even when one cannot explain exactly why" into explicit facts that explain things and information that they can learn, people can diffuse and exchange knowledge.[19] "New knowledge—often in the form of new technology—brings new capabilities to observe additional facts . . . and to construct different or new systems to explain phenomena."[20]

When faced with complexity, shifting or hazy perspectives, and new facts, people have instinctively sought to simplify or reconcile their views of living within their own perspectives. Instead of drawing on the huge store of knowledge available to society at large, people rely heavily and primarily on the information that surrounds them to understand how the world works. Neither do people aggressively seek new facts or observations that disturb familiar ideas. To avoid disrupting their patterns of living, many people interpret new facts loosely or flexibly to accommodate existing notions.

Although most individuals can simply learn more old knowledge—which is new within their narrow personal perspectives—when faced with the unknown, societies and civilizations must absorb new facts into old perspectives and stores of knowledge. Least disruptive has been expansion of useful, old knowledge through the alternative processes of knowledge conversion and diffusion—societal learning by doing. Broadly unstructured and unsystematic, these simple types of learning opportunistically absorb whatever the context of social reality presents. Especially within the modern industrial-economic perspective, people have expanded these simplistic notions of learning by doing to learning through innovation.[21]

More than sophisticated learning, innovation involves creation of the new knowledge that has always been a prominent feature of globalization. By "proposing explanatory theories based on some alternative, coherent system of structures, institutions, and processes," people could create new knowledge in small increments through innovation as predicted by the Enlightenment. The continuing emergence of new facts, however, eventually forced people into "developing comprehensive explanations of the universe, life, and humanity into which the new facts fit neatly"—experiment and scientific method. Since each fed on the other, when *both* science *and* insight reached the limits of knowledge, people learned to construct "novel, coherent structural, universal systems for interpreting *both* social reality *and* novel events and phenomena" —intuition, inspiration, and art. Strictly intertwined and complementary, each way of creating new knowledge involved expanding interactions among individuals and organizations with different types and contents of knowledge.[22]

Conversion and Diffusion

Although learning and innovation can also be nonlinear, knowledge conversion is explicitly linear: teachers convert observations or skills directly to information and data that people can learn. Each bit of information contains a quantum of novelty, which learners convert into knowledge through interpretation and classification. Learned knowledge confronts faith and wisdom, which encompass beliefs and judgments, and learners resolve the confrontation with another quantum of new knowledge. Knowledge conversion to expand the quality and quantity of knowledge has occurred regularly in most narrow perspectives and also within the global perspective.[23]

Whether reduced to writing, translated into a routine, or programmed into a machine, the cumulative conversion and expansion of knowledge change the form and structure of social reality gradually through diffusion. As knowledge "is explored, used, and better understood, less of it remains idiosyncratic to a person or few people, and more of it is transformed into some systematic form."[24] A continuing role for modern firms is converting and diffusing knowledge through systematic transfers of information and skills on organizing and operating firms to perform the economic functions of global business. Although firm-specific conversion and diffusion occur within a deliberately constructed, narrow, economic perspective, the dual process accelerates social diffusion and stimulates innovation and creation of new knowledge.

Knowledge diffusion is a primary stimulant for functional specialization within narrow perspectives through *both* conversion *and* innovation. Diffusion can occur, however, only within a stable system of people who understand the vocabulary, standards, and processes of conversion and are connected in some communication network. Since all people may not be connected or know the conversion languages, the processes of knowledge conversion and diffusion are both necessarily path-dependent within some narrow perspective.

Innovation

Innovation is the new combination of existing ideas, knowledge, and processes.[25] Modernism narrowed the focus of knowledge creation to innovation within a technological, economic context.[26] Commonly seeking a solution to a specific problem, innovation operates exclusively on information and knowledge. Original thought by an innovator or entrepreneur provides energy and focus. In addition to observations, any objective stimulus can start the process as an innovator interprets it in the dual context of already known knowledge and some personal world vision that embraces faith and belief. The process of innovation is better suited than knowledge conversion or diffusion to developing and refining complex systems, products or social structures.

Innovation seems tightly linked to the context of social reality, perspectives, and relationships in which people are embedded. Strong, interactive, reciprocal ties of community and family—oversocialization—inhibit and restrain innovation through social pressures to conform. Weaker, trusting relationships with little intimacy or emotional commitment across a loose, diverse array of acquaintances that serve primarily as sources of information —undersocialization—stimulate and sustain innovation.[27] Not necessarily a linear process in any context, innovation occurs in various ways.

Innovative Learning

Through innovation, people combine narrow, experiential learning and observation with broader insight, intuition, and experiment to produce a new result that contributes to solving a particular problem. New learning often stimulates the innovative inspiration that becomes new knowledge. People with substantial stocks of knowledge are good learners who can readily correlate old knowledge in new ways as innovation that appears as useful, new knowledge. Since the content of innovated new knowledge depends on *both* the depth and scope of old knowledge *and* the context from which it is drawn, innovative learning is path-dependent and specific to different social contexts. Although learning by doing continues between and through innovations, each innovation is a unique event of *both* learning old information *and* creating new knowledge. Innovative learning includes the many different ways in which people learn and their reliance on the many sources of knowledge that are deeply embedded in social, organizational, and institutional structures.

Incremental Innovation

Unlike nonlinear, random, innovative learning, incremental innovation is an orderly, sequential process that refines scientific discoveries through research, engineering, and conversion of skills and processes into useful devices that meet specific requirements.[28] Often, as when Charles Goodyear invented the industrial process for making rubber, innovation has been the result of a happy accident.[29] Beginning with a specific problem, incremental innovation adds new facts to old knowledge. People with narrow expertise are effective as collaborators in the process, which is complete when the innovator interacts with other people in diffusion, application, or transfer of new knowledge. Many innovators and inventors "fail to reap the rewards of their ideas since the very qualities that make them so creative—original thinking, obsessive concentration on one goal, detachment from everyday concerns—make it difficult for them to deal with the real, often cruel, world."[30] Individual innovators often become enmeshed in litigation over patent rights or government agencies over the effects of new technologies on public welfare.

Individual Knowledge Creation

The unique individual ability to create knowledge seems durably confined within narrow perspectives and bound by intellectual property rights to local institutions. Beyond learning old information, during formal education students create new knowledge by converting common knowledge—cultural preferences, moral attitudes, or ideologies—into personal identity patterns. Within narrow perspectives, individuals can create specific knowledge alone —in forms of data, designs and specifications, a scientific formula, experimental results, technologies, patents, and other explicit information. Other than artistic creativity, new knowledge that individuals create is rarely global in scope or historic in depth. New work skills or project-specific research results are usually formed within the narrow perspective of a job or market. "These institutions are themselves less globalizable because they are deeply embedded within nationally specific cultures."[31] Even though that knowledge may have global effects through products that are sold and distributed worldwide, through global communication, or cultural globalization, individuals create specific knowledge at home or at work within some narrow perspective.

Collective Knowledge Creation

The Enlightenment promoted the concept of the single, heroic inventor or discoverer as the champion of rationality. Modernity recognized that entrepreneurial consortia often undertake innovation and project teams frequently generate new knowledge. Although only individuals can know or understand in an intensely personal and private experience, *both* individuals *and* groups can create new knowledge. Collective knowledge creation seems to occur either within particular, narrow space-time perspectives, in which exclusive inward-facing groups create specific knowledge, or across several perspectives in which many people create global knowledge. Engineers, technicians, entrepreneurs, politicians, and many other people create new knowledge in project teams or discussion groups within narrow perspectives to solve immediate problems or to deal with urgent contingencies. Modern corporations focus this extension of incremental innovation through intensive programs of research and development and embody its results in new technologies protected by institutional rights to intellectual property.[32]

Within the global perspective, the dynamic interactions among several individuals with each other and with their environment in ways that transcend self and social institutions create new, global knowledge. Scholars, scientists, artists, philosophers, and others create new knowledge in outward-facing social structures that often do not reflect the current exigencies of the world. Instead of solving problems, "they are supposed to provide ways of doing things in the real world, of reweaving the great seamless causal web so that various human purposes might be accomplished."[33] In an essential contrast to the specific knowledge created by individual or corporate innovators, creation of global, social knowledge necessarily embodies some expansion of social trust beyond an innovator's primary group. Although technology continues to have important effects on all societies, the expansion of perspectives and social relationships through the new knowledge of expanding interpersonal and systemic trust transforms social reality itself.

Collective transformation of social reality by knowledge creation is not simply division of labor to increase productivity or concentration of votes to build consensus. Groups of people who create global knowledge do much more than process information, solve problems, or negotiate to agreement. Since they need not even constitute a proper organization, they often cannot have in mind an *ex ante* result, solution, or even a set of alternatives. Nor can humanity or any group of humans ever have any confidence about what needs to be known or even what someone ought to know.

THE CONTEXT OF KNOWLEDGE CREATION

Within the global perspective, this collective creation of new knowledge occurs within a dynamic, self-locating, synchronic context (*basho*) in dynamic space-time—a shared context of cognition and action in motion.[34] This continually reemerging, self-determining context shared by many minds moving together through space and time while interacting with each other and with their common environment to create, share, and use new knowledge is *basho*. Although Bacon's idols have persistently conspired to contain knowledge within narrow perspectives, it is the nature of *basho* to expand irresistibly towards the global perspective and into the eternal.

The Stimulus

Globalization has historically presented arrays of contradictions that eventually accumulate into explosive social stresses. As deepening social stresses penetrate within and across societies, *basho* begins to emerge in efforts by individuals and groups to resolve contradictions and relieve social stresses with existing knowledge and capabilities. Although *basho* begins in unbounded contradictions and stress, it brings people to share multiple contexts around a shared context within some boundary on the knowledge to be created and relevant contexts to be shared. Emerging from a legacy of prior knowledge, a dominant cultural system of values determines what kinds of knowledge people need to create. The constraints of institutional norms and current fashions limit the contexts and shared content and set a boundary for interactions among participants in *basho*, although the boundary of *basho* remains open and creates its own unbounded context and content.

When the pressures of social stresses stabilize the boundaries of context, value-based knowledge, and shared content as a self-organizing space-time place with its own intention, direction, and mission, *basho* forms. The multiple perspectives of many participants provide many contexts, and social stresses form a universal, shared context. Cultural values focus and direct the creation and application of new knowledge, and society's base of knowledge establishes a boundary that is path-dependent yet not deterministic.

The Locus

Embedded in the self-determining here and now, *basho* is temporal-in-spatial and spatial-in-temporal. Neither static nor stable, *basho* is an existential place—or, in the Internet age, a virtual place—that may, but need not, be geographically physical or temporally limited. More than a meeting, a conference, or a communication network, *basho* is not "a fixed set of surrounding conditions, but a wider dynamical process of which the cognition of an individual is only a part."[35] Constantly moving in all of its dimensions, fluid, and continually forming and reforming, *basho* transcends the individual human self and the social reality in which people formed it. Social reality and *basho* are constantly coevolving as they affect, change, and reify each other and new knowledge transforms both into the future.

Within *basho* are places for the silence of individual inspiration—artistic sanctuaries—and for dense concentrations of thinkers—cognitive islands—that stimulate innovations, intuitions, and insights that challenge orthodoxy. Directed, personal exchanges of knowledge within webs of weak ties among sanctuaries and islands flow freely within *basho* through spatial-temporal places for communal discourse, intense communication, and debate. Well-suited *both* for innovating within narrow perspectives *and* for creating new knowledge *sui generis* within cognitive islands and sanctuaries, insular thinkers or reclusive artists complement public personalities and civil society in *basho*.

Many-In-One

More than simply a place in space-time, *basho* is an interactive, social process and context that involves far more than simple transfer of information or even teaching and learning within an epistemic community of scholars and experts. *Basho* almost always acts through and on individuals. Among competing people, individuals less than well suited to their communities or societies are more likely than conformists to explore unconventional thinking and find themselves in *basho*. Firmly embedded in social reality and cultural context, every *basho* operates to connect people through collective, random interaction to interpret information, which gains new, additional meanings to become new knowledge within a new context. Embodying the new knowledge that the many individuals in *basho* have created, a transformed social reality creates new meanings for life and living around new identities. As new knowledge diffuses, erstwhile conformists either adapt or fade into history as former misfits survive, flourish, and the nature of society changes.[36] The multiple people in *basho* form the nucleus of a global community that constantly refines, expands, and reifies those human values on which the being and well-being of humankind depend.[37]

This nucleus of a multiplicity of intellectually inventive and aesthetically creative individuals determining themselves in time, knowledge, and space emerges as the self-determination of an infinitely creative reality. "The multiplicity is not a simple numerical many, but a many-in-one. The multiplicity of individuals comes into being as individuals only when they are joined as one while at the same time remaining absolutely independent of one another . . . only when they are mediated by the universal of unmediated mediation (or world as place). This is why the world as place maintains its self-identity in the midst of its infinite creative dynamism. It is the self-identity that makes creation possible and *vice versa*."[38]

The cultural context in which *basho* is embedded determines the form of those relationships, the depth and breadth of trust, and the extent of disparate sources of useful knowledge. Individual thinkers in *basho* who are deeply embedded in their own cultures, experience, and perspectives are often predictable, whereas interactions with less embedded participants bring novelty to knowledge creation. These interactive, organic *basho* and the cohesion of the people participating in them must be supported and sustained by trustful sharing and continual exchanges of knowledge. Without trust and interaction, *basho* disappear. "Through such interactions those who participate in *basho* and the context itself evolve through self-transcendence to create knowledge. . . . *basho* is an emerging relationship among individuals and between an individual and the environment."[39]

The Process

Within and across all perspectives, *basho* collect and mobilize existing information, apply people's new knowledge from narrow perspectives, and integrate both with human thought and inspiration. The context of *basho* accommodates personal insight, collective reflection or speculation, discursive explanation, unifying existing knowledge, or simply awareness of alternatives for explication. Beyond personal discovery and intuition, "new knowledge is created out of existing knowledge through the change of the meanings and the contexts."[40] Individual experience and prior knowledge, the benefits and costs of change, and the dynamics of the participants form the structure and foundation for knowledge creation. Human will provides the energy and direction for *basho*. Human interactions use that energy to convert information, reason, and inspiration to new knowledge to relieve social stress in social transformation and begin incremental innovation, globalization, and progress into the future.[41] Simply "making knowledge explicit is in itself an act of human and social progress and enlightenment."[42]

Directed by the interests, preoccupations, and moralities of their societies, people experience in *basho* "moments in history when events suddenly allow us to see the challenges ahead with a degree of clarity previously unimaginable."[43] Current problems to be solved, preconceptions of solution strategies, and the physical and temporal setting focus knowledge creation and subsequent incremental innovation. Especially in narrow-perspective *basho*, the prevailing balance of power and control of knowledge are constraints on knowledge creation.[44] Despite, however, any constraints, the art, science, and interaction within *basho* are "marked by those moments of dazzling illumination and shared recognition that characterize insight in all domains of human endeavor. Advance in any field has always been preceded by a sudden leap of the imagination, which is recognized for its brilliance by the participating group, and galvanizes them in their turn into further activity."[45]

The Effects

From *basho*, people disperse and apply new knowledge as solutions or innovations that relieve social stresses, but most significantly as transformations of social reality. Individual creation of new knowledge on a cognitive island or sanctuary in *basho* "can commence an evolutionary process of successful outward spread from the initial site. In some cases, such outward spread may culminate in complete takeover."[46] Broad bodies of standard thinking induce broader diffusion of current knowledge within and beyond *basho*.[47] Faced with the new knowledge created in *basho* and a new social reality, Bacon's idols lose much of their power. Since their traditional institutions of social reality and culture form the structure of new knowledge and the new social reality, the idols quickly begin rebuilding the social stresses that transformation has just relieved.

Within and beyond *basho*, much of what people already know loses relevance as they discover new facts and generate new thoughts that relegate old knowledge and former thoughts to remembrance. In a perhaps counterintuitive way, *basho* also stimulate the loss of knowledge that has become obsolete or superseded by new knowledge. New knowledge often replaces or inactivates concepts that have lost their roles in human living, and allowing them to be forgotten and eventually lost.

GLOBAL KNOWLEDGE

Within the global perspective, new knowledge emerging from *basho* embraces art, philosophy, and science, separately and in combination; it is global knowledge. The active process of knowledge-based globalization exposes and merges the effects of narrow-perspective *basho* and innovation across many perspectives in global *basho* where people create global knowledge.

The Content

The ancient etymology of art focuses on putting things together, assembling disparate things and thoughts and information into some unitary whole. Whereas art simplifies the complex, science suggests cutting things into pieces. Science analyzes things and reduces information, thoughts, and observations to their component elements. Art transfers living into the global perspective by putting things together; science dissects life into excruciating detail by breaking things apart. Although as antithetical forms of knowledge they are permanently in tension, art and science are complementary and necessary for the global understanding that new knowledge brings. "Without intellect, our intuition may drive us unchecked into emotional chaos. Without intuition, we risk failing to resolve complex social dynamics and moral dilemmas."[48] Within global *basho*, people resolve the tension and create the balance between them that energizes progress through global knowledge.

Within the global perspective, knowledge expands beyond the explicit information and data of traditional, functional, narrow perspectives. Global knowledge is normative, subjective, and experiential—procedures, processes, skills, routines, patterns of action. It includes art, belief, insight, intuition, models, visions, other forms described only as genius, and also care, love, trust, ideals, and the many thoughts and feelings that people have and know. Global knowledge accepts that people can know without knowing that they know and expands the human capacity for direct knowledge with people's intuition, insight, and inspiration without direct observation or rational thought.

People everywhere can readily share, transfer, or expand this broad, global knowledge but can capture it outside *basho* only with difficulty. As a counterpart of the explicit intellectual property rights common in narrow perspectives, global knowledge is inherently a public good with no identifiable private-property rights. Intangible and transcendent across time and space, global knowledge loses its identity when captured within a single discipline or perspective. Not merely something to be learned and then taught, global knowledge is a dynamic, human, reiterative condition of forming, refining, and justifying personal and social belief towards some not-yet-known truth.[49]

Globalization expands the success of the natural sciences in understanding the physical world into the social sciences and the humanities as *basho* dissolves the discontinuities across discrete cognitive perspectives. As an integral part of globalization, "the expansion of consilient cause-and-effect explanation outward from the natural sciences towards the social sciences and humanities is calling the traditional division of knowledge into question."[50] The ability of art to unify human perspectives and spiritual insights with cognitive rationality reminds people that understanding and thought itself are results of personal creativity. Global knowledge extends beyond cognitive rationality into the entire scope of human living and beyond the present into *both* the eternal past *and* the unknowable future.

Creating Global Knowledge

Collocated and organically connected with narrow-perspective *basho* within the global perspective is global *basho*, where and when people transfigure human nature, shatter Bacon's idols, and transform social reality with new, global knowledge. As narrow-perspective *basho* transform local, functional reality, the knowledge-creation process amplifies, aggregates, and expands into global *basho*. Chronically unstable, global *basho* involve fluid interfaces with narrow-perspective *basho* that evolve indeterminedly as knowledge diffuses and evolves through trusting human interactions.

Unlike the Enlightenment or the modern perspectives, knowledge creation within the global perspective is not limited to inductive research programs, hypothesis testing, the scientific method, or even rationality. The global *basho* formulates and defines human thought and science itself; identifies goals and prioritizes values; and reconfigures the intellectual and spiritual foundations of human life itself. Instead of simply manipulating facts or processing information, as suggested by modern knowledge theory, within the global perspective, knowledge creation creates new meaning, new identities for individuals, and a new collective self for humanity.

Within the global perspective, knowledge creation never ends; humanity's purpose is never achieved. Equilibrium and stability are at best transient, functional, and local. Progress begins anew with every narrow-perspective *basho* that expands to the global perspective. As the primary dynamic of globalization, knowledge creation relates things, ideas, facts, people, and their perspectives to each other in a universal social reality that is explicitly and inclusively humanistic, rather than merely rational. An individual mind to which all facts, ideas, and feelings were simultaneously known would have no need for new knowledge. Because this perfect knowledge is beyond the capability of a single mind, people create knowledge through the interactions of multiple minds, each of which possesses only partial knowledge, in *basho*. An aggregate of narrow-perspective transformations of new knowledge within a global *basho* has launched each wave of globalization as humanity struggled to stabilize the new social reality within a new civilizational context.[51]

To create the global knowledge that transforms social reality, people, firms, governments, and cultures must integrate themselves, assess risk and cost, and interact globally in *basho*. For innovation and applications to benefit people in the here and now, they must fit into local contexts. Not cosmetic or limited to democratic elections, racial nondiscrimination, religious tolerance, market penetration, or production, this dual-focus for human evolution is a prominent feature of *both* the process *and* the condition of globalization. Energized by the normative knowledge held within epistemic communities and professional networks, knowledge creation not only reflects cognitive rationality and normative morality but rests on personal relationships based on mutual trust.[52] The knowledge that only people can create is *both* a self-organizing system *and* an emergent property. "Self-organization and emergence arise out of complex systems that grow and learn as they change."[53] Knowledge itself—cognitive and normative—confers these properties on the social systems that people construct on and from knowledge.

NOTES

1. Patrick Cohendet and W. Edward Steinmueller, "The Codification of Knowledge: A Conceptual and Empirical Exploration," *Industrial and Corporate Change* 9(2) (June 2000): 195–210; 204.

2. Anne-Robert-Jacques Turgot, "A Philosophical Review of the Successive Advances of the Human Mind," in *Turgot on Progress, Sociology, and Economics*, edited and translated by Ronald L. Meek, 41–59 (Cambridge: Cambridge University Press, 1973), 44–45.

3. Richard Panek, "And Then There Was Light," *Natural History* 111(9) (November 2002): 46–51; 46.

4. Francis Bacon, *The Letters and Life of Francis Bacon, Including All His Occasional Works*, edited by James Spedding, 7 vols. (London: Longman, Green, Longman, and Roberts, [1862–1874] 1890), 1: 108. See also John Aubrey, *Minutes of Lives*, edited as *Aubrey's Brief Lives* by Oliver L. Dick (Ann Arbor: University of Michigan Press, [1813] 1957), 130.

5. Joseph E. Stiglitz, "Knowledge for Development: Economic Science, Economic Policy, and Economic Advice," in *Annual World Bank Conference on Development Economics 1998*, edited by Boris Pleskovic and Joseph E. Stiglitz, 9–58 (Washington, D.C.: World Bank, 1999), 11.

6. Although global knowledge creation extends well beyond the theory of the firm, much theoretical and empirical work in the context of the firm as a knowledge-creating group addresses organizational knowledge creation. See, among others, Ikujiro Nonaka and Noboru Konno, "The Concept of Ba: Building a Foundation for Knowledge Creation," *California Management Review* 40(3) (Spring 1998): 40–55; Robert M. Grant, "Toward a Knowledge-Based Theory of the Firm," *Strategic Management Journal* 17 (Special Issue) (Winter 1996): 109–122; 113–119; Richard M. Cyert and James G. March, *A Behavioral Theory of the Firm* (Englewood Cliffs, New Jersey: Prentice-Hall, 1963), 99–113; Daniel Levinthal and Jennifer Myatt, "Coevolution of Capabilities and Industry: The Evolution of Mutual Fund Processing," *Strategic Management Journal* 15 (Special Issue) (Winter 1994): 45–62; 49.

7. Cognitive knowledge is explicit and tacit. Explicit knowledge forms the familiar sets of facts and information that explain things and events. Tacit knowledge, or skill, comprises techniques and methods that work in certain ways and with certain

consequences. Normative knowledge guides people in deciding whether and how to transform tacit knowledge into explicit knowledge and in creating new knowledge.

8. The knowledge base includes individual units of knowledge, functional facts, elemental technologies, primal principles, and other explicit learning. The structure of knowledge includes linkages and patterns among units of knowledge and humanity's priorities for applying knowledge. The dynamics of knowledge is the interaction between the knowledge base and the knowledge structure, communication between functional groups of humans, processes and techniques for combining and applying units of knowledge, and the capabilities for creation of new knowledge.

9. Riesman found the sources of human behaviors, attitudes, and feelings in social and personal traditions (tradition-direction), the individual self (inner-direction), and the need to conform (other-direction). See David Riesman, with Nathan Glazer and Reuel Denney, *The Lonely Crowd: A Study of the Changing American Character* (New Haven: Yale University Press, [1950] 1967), ch. 1.

10. Will Durant and Ariel Durant, *The Story of Civilization*, vol. 6, *The Age of Reason Begins* (New York: Simon and Schuster, 1961), 175.

11. James Parkinson, *Organic Remains of a Former World: An Examination of the Mineralized Remains of the Vegetables and Animals of the Antediluvian World, Generally Termed Extraneous Fossils, the First Volume; Containing the Vegetable Kingdom*, (London: J. Robson, 1804), 32.

12. *Wovon man nicht sprechen kann; darüber muss man zweigen.* Ludwig Wittgenstein, *Tractatus Logico-Philosophicus* (London: Routledge and Kegan Paul, [1921] 1961), statement 7, p. 150.

13. Anthony Giddens, *Runaway World: How Globalization Is Reshaping Our Lives* (London: Profile, 1999), 41.

14. Francis Fukuyama, *Our Posthuman Future: Consequences of the Biotechnology Revolution* (New York: Farrar, Straus, and Giroux, 2001), 130.

15. Stephen Jay Gould, "Bacon, Brought Home," *Natural History* 108(5) (June 1999): 28–33, 72–78; 30.

16. Herbert A. Simon, "We and They: The Human Urge to Identify with Groups," *Industrial and Corporate Change* 11(3) (June 2002): 607–610; 607.

17. Paul Henri Thiery Holbach, *Common Sense: or Natural Ideas Opposed to Supernatural* (New York: N.p., 1795), 7–9.

18. Ikujiro Nonaka and Ryoko Toyama, "A Firm as a Dialectical Being: Towards a Dynamic Theory of a Firm," *Industrial and Corporate Change* 11(5) (November 2002): 995–1009; 999–1000.

19. Nathan Rosenberg, *Inside the Black Box: Technology and Economics* (Cambridge: Cambridge University Press, 1982), 143. See also Jacqueline Senker, "Tacit Knowledge and Models of Innovation," *Industrial and Corporate Change* 4(2) (June 1995): 425–447; 426.

20. James Burke, *The Day the Universe Changed* (London: British Broadcasting Corporation, 1985), 11.

21. The enormous business literature on learning and innovation may have begun with Edith T. Penrose, *The Theory of the Growth of the Firm* (Oxford: Blackwell, 1959), 76–80. See also, among others, Richard R. Nelson and Sidney G. Winter, *An Evolutionary Theory of Economic Change* (Cambridge: Harvard University Press, 1982), 74–95; Coimbatore K. Prahalad and Gary Hamel, "The Core Competence of the Corporation, " *Harvard Business Review* 68(3) (May-June 1990): 79–91; 82; Giovanni Dosi and Luigi Marengo, "Some Elements of an Evolutionary Theory of Organizational

Competences," in *Evolutionary Concepts in Contemporary Economics*, edited by Richard W. England, 157–178 (Ann Arbor: University of Michigan Press, 1994), 166–178.

22. See Burke, *The Day the Universe Changed*, 11.

23. See Ikujiro Nonaka and Hirotaka Takeuchi, *The Knowledge-Creating Company* (New York: Oxford University Press, 1995); Ikujiro Nonaka, *Chishiki-Souzou no Keiei* [A Theory of Organizational Knowledge Creation] (Tokyo: Nihon Keizai Shimbun-sha, 1990) (in Japanese, paraphrases translated by author).

24. Edwin Hutchins, *Cognition in the Wild* (Cambridge: MIT Press, 1995), xiii.

25. See Joseph A. Schumpeter, *The Theory of Economic Development* (Cambridge: Harvard University Press, [1911] 1934), 65–68; Nelson and Winter, *An Evolutionary Theory of Economic Change*, 277–281.

26. See, among others, Nathan Rosenberg, *Perspectives on Technology* (Cambridge: Cambridge University Press, 1976); Rosenberg, *Inside the Black Box*; Eric von Hippel, *The Sources of Innovation* (Oxford: Oxford University Press, 1988); Giovanni Dosi, "The Nature of the Innovative Process," in *Technical Change and Economic Theory*, edited by Giovanni Dosi, Christopher Freeman, Richard R. Nelson, Gerald Silverberg, and Luc Soete, 221–238 (London: Pinter, 1988); Stephen J. Kline, "Innovation Styles in Japan and the United States: Cultural Bases; Implications for Competitiveness," the 1989 Thurston Lecture, Report INN-3 (Stanford: Department of Mechanical Engineering, Stanford University, 1990); Ikujiro Nonaka, "Managing Innovation as an Organizational Knowledge Creation Process," paper prepared for *Tricontinental Handbook of Technology Management* (Tokyo: Institute of Business Research, Hitotsubashi University, 1992); Roy Rothwell, "Successful Industrial Innovation: Critical Factors for the 1990s," *R&D Management* 22(3) (July 1992): 221–239; Wendy Faulkner, "Conceptualizing Knowledge Used in Innovation," *Science, Technology, and Human Values* 19(4) (Autumn 1994): 425–458.

27. See Mark S. Granovetter, "The Strength of Weak Ties," *American Journal of Sociology* 78(6) (May 1973): 1360–1380; 1367–1368; Mark S. Granovetter, "Economic Action and Social Structure: The Problem of Embeddedness," *American Journal of Sociology* 91(3) (November 1985): 481–510; 483–487; Max Weber, *Economy and Society: An Outline of Interpretive Sociology*, edited by Guenther Roth and Claus Wittich (New York: Bedminster, [1924] 1968), 321–323; Martin Ruef, "Strong Ties, Weak Ties, and Islands," *Industrial and Corporate Change* 11(3) (June 2002): 427–449; 429–433.

28. For a discussion of the leading models of innovation, see Senker, "Tacit Knowledge and Models of Innovation."

29. In 1839, Charles Goodyear mixed rubber with sulphur and white lead. When a bit of the mixture fell onto the kitchen stove, instead of melting, it hardened. This accident led him eventually to the right combination of rubber, solvent, sulphur, and white lead that became an effective industrial process.

30. John Steele Gordon, "Pioneers Die Broke," *Forbes* 170(13) (23 December 2002): 258–264; 262.

31. Jonathan West, "Limits to Globalization: Organizational Homogeneity and Diversity in the Semiconductor Industry," *Industrial and Corporate Change* 11(1) (February 2002): 159–188; 183.

32. Like individual innovators, corporations sometimes are so focused on their primary, current businesses that they fail to exploit the new knowledge that their project teams, research groups, and development budgets create. The classically famous prototype of such corporate conservatism remains the failure of Xerox to profit from internal inventions—graphical user interface, the computer desktop model, electronic

organization of data, WYSIWYG word processing, the laser printer, and the multifunction mouse-pointer—that emerged from Xerox laboratories in the 1970s.

33. Richard Rorty, "Against Unity," *Wilson Quarterly* 22(1) (Winter 1998): 28–38; 30–31.

34. The Japanese philosopher Nishida Kitarō (1870–1945) introduced the concept of *basho* and the related copulative relationship between the individual and the world as a shared, synchronic, spatial context in motion through time experienced by a momentary social community. Although Plato, Heidegger, Husserl, and Whitehead also emphasized the importance of place in human cognition and action, Fernand Braudel has probably come closest to Nishida's concept of *basho* with his concept of *conjonctures* at which humanity conjoins the various narrow perspectives of living and thinking briefly to transform them all into a novel social reality. See Nishitani Keiji, *Nishida Kitarō*, translated by Yamamoto Seisaku and James W. Heisig (Berkeley: University of California Press, 1991), 67–68, 192–198, 202–205, 227; Nishida Kitarō, "The Logic of the Place of Nothingness and the Religious Worldview," *Last Writings: Nothingness and the Religious Worldview*, translated by David A. Dilworth (Honolulu: University of Hawaii Press, 1987), 47–124; Nishida Kitarō, *An Inquiry into the Good* (New Haven: Yale University Press, [1921] 1990); Nishida Kitarō, *Fundamental Problems of Philosophy: The World of Action and the Dialectical World* (Tokyo: Sophia University Press, 1970).

35. Hutchins, *Cognition in the Wild*, xiii.

36. The notion of knowledge creation in *basho* and the roles of diffusion and innovation as vehicles of human progress is clearly an extension of the still controversial ideas of Charles Darwin in his theories of natural selection of species through the seminal thought of Stephen Jay Gould. See Charles Darwin, *On the Origin of Species* (New York: Heritage, [1859] 1963), 63, 73, 77–88, 97–104; "Evolution: The Grand View," reviewing *The Structure of Evolutionary Theory*, by Stephen Jay Gould (Cambridge: Belknap Press of Harvard University Press, 2002), *The Economist* 365(8302) (7 December 2002): 82.

Whereas Darwinian natural selection of organisms and species promotes individuals that are best suited to their environments, *basho* stimulates less-suited individuals to change the environments of their societies. Darwin aggregated microevolution of individuals over long periods of time and expanses of space into macroevolutionary patterns of the history of life revealed by the fossil record. Similarly, *basho* operates over years, decades, and generations through aggregating individual human thoughts and ideas into coherent, cohesive new knowledge that gradually and incrementally transforms social reality. Darwin suggested that natural selection built novelty and change incrementally if variation were abundant and variation in one characteristic were independent of variation in other characteristics. In an analogous syllogism, *basho* depends on diffusion of new knowledge and incremental innovation by individuals to change social realities. Just as Darwin insisted on explicit conditions for variation to explain biological change, *basho* requires conducive political and economic contexts. Before the technical possibilities and modern understandings of paleobiology, Darwin could only speculate that the amounts and kinds of variation were such as to explain the evolutionary transformations of biological evolution. Modern science has shown, not without controversy, that Darwin was not quite right. Just as natural constraints on biological variation seem to have stimulated some types of variation and hindered others, so social constraints guide diffusion and focus innovation. The biological story of life and the epistemological story of thought alike show *both* great innovation *and* great conservativeness.   Like the relationships between evolution in particular populations and the macroevolution shown in the history of life, the complex interdependence between *basho*, learning, and innovation is not well understood and remains open to controversy and skepticism.

37. Jacob Bronowski, *Science and Human Values* (New York: Harper Colophon, [1956] 1975), 58–71.

38. Keiji, *Nishida Kitarō*, 202.

39. Ikujiro Nonaka, Ryoko Toyama, and Akiya Nagata, "A Firm as a Knowledge-Creating Entity: A New Perspective on the Theory of the Firm," *Industrial and Corporate Change* 9(1) (March 2000): 1–20; 8–9.

40. Nonaka, Toyama, and Nagata, "A Firm as a Knowledge-Creating Entity," 8–9. These authors use the simpler term *ba*, instead of Kitarō's original term *basho*.

41. See Nonaka and Konno, ""The Concept of Ba."

42. Björn Johnson, Edward Lorenz, and Bengt-Åke Lundvall, "Why All the Fuss about Codified and Tacit Knowledge?" *Industrial and Corporate Change* 11(2) (April 2002): 245–262; 256.

43. Thomas E. White, "The Army Is Dedicated to Delivering Victory," *Army* 52(10) (October 2002): 15–22; 15.

44. See Michel Foucault, "Truth and Power," in *Power/Knowledge: Selected Interviews and Other Writings 1972–1977*, edited and translated by Colin Gordon (New York: Pantheon, 1980), 111–112, 131–133.

45. Lisa Jardine, *Ingenious Pursuits: Building the Scientific Revolution* (New York: Talese, Doubleday, 1999), 5.

46. In a sociological context, Scott A. Boorman introduces the metaphor of social islands as the origins of diffusing social traits.   See Scott A. Boorman, "Island Models for Takeover by a Social Trait Facing a Frequency-Dependent Selection Barrier in a Mendelian Population," *Proceedings of the National Academy of Sciences* 71(5) (May 1974): 2103–2107; 2104.

47. See David Strang and John W. Meyer, "Institutional Conditions for Diffusion," *Theory and Society* 22(4) (August 1993): 487–511; 493–494.

48. Michael Shermer, "The Captain Kirk Principle," *Scientific American* 287(6) (December 2002): 39.

49. See Nonaka and Takeuchi, *The Knowledge-Creating Company*; Nonaka, Toyama, and Nagata, "A Firm as a Knowledge-Creating Entity," 2–4.

50. Edward O. Wilson, "Resuming the Enlightenment Quest," *Wilson Quarterly* 22(1) (Winter 1998): 16–27; 17.

51. See Friedrich A. von Hayek, "The Use of Knowledge in Society," *American Economic Review* 35(4) (September 1945): 519–530; 529–530; Hutchins, *Cognition in the Wild*, xiii; Edward S. Casey, *The Fate of Place: A Philosophical History* (Berkeley: University of California Press, 1997), 16.

52. For a discussion of the four-level structure of knowledge see Bernard Ancori, Antoine Bureth, and Patrick Cohendet, "The Economics of Knowledge: The Debate about Codification and Tacit Knowledge," *Industrial and Corporate Change* 9(2) (June 2000): 255–288; 265–270.

53. Michael Shermer, "Digits and Fidgets," *Scientific American* 288(1) (January 2003): 35.

3

THE POWER OF PERSPECTIVE

Economists agonize about capital flows but often overlook the social disruptions, cultural clashes, or political changes that globalization brings. Radicals conjure visions of capitalism gone mad, while merging cultural norms escape their notice. Cyberprophets dream of unifying the world in webs of copper and fiber optics or networks of cell phones and spot beams but remain blissfully unaware of trends in global migration. Governments are chained to the national interest and power and miss the rise of global civil society. The surviving dot-coms and multinationals are so self-absorbed in technology and turnover that they miss the grandeur and power of globalization. Emanating from a clutter of narrow, functional, personal perspectives, the loud, emotional debate about globalization features poignant, "searing images of broken homes and closed factories" balanced by "ponderous examinations of trade flows," with digressions into human rights and depletion of resources, and a "dire catalogue of winners and losers."[1] Lost in the narrow-perspective clamor for attention is the global perspective on humanity and the world that it inhabits.

People began to understand the notion of perspective late in the tenth century. The Arab mathematician abu-'Ali ab-Hasan ibn-al-Haytham (939?–?1039) first recognized that objects radiate light to the eye in cones emanating from each point of the object. The larger angles subtended by the cones of light from near objects obscure those from farther objects within the cone of sight (perspective) of the viewer. The effect of bringing objects nearer is that of narrowing the visual perspective of the viewer. This notion of a cone of light rays emanating from each point of an object is the foundation of the idea of perspective. Perspective moved visual art into the third dimension, lent mobility to music, and projected thought across space and time. Although art and science quickly translated perspective into technology and technique, more profound was the change in human attitudes towards living and existence. Perspective challenged people's self-perceptions as fixed objects manipulated in some cosmic scheme of absolute, eternal truth and perfect order. They began to realize that only the here and now, this particular location and this fleeting moment, were fixed: a point of view and its perspective in time and space. Most important was that each individual chose a personal perspective on life and living. Perspective is not a static point of view with a single, unchanging prospect; it is a continuing, willed action of creating successive perspectives in time and space. People could choose to open their eyes from *any* point of view *anywhere* within *any* perspective. Determined by thought, understanding became a cumulative process of catching the shifting perspectives of several moments as a trace in cognitive space.

As understanding expanded across space and over time, the power of perspective became a basic pattern of human thought and relationships. "The facts as known to and by people determine people's views of the world and their perspectives on the world."[2]   Rather than referring to any universal, infinite truth or objective reality, people focus their perspectives and remodel their views from private perceptions, familiar ideas, and self-assembled collages of symbolism. Although no individual perceives total reality or possesses full knowledge, everyone uses the power of perspective to construct a coherent social reality within some personal perspective: a personal universe. Since each perspective can accommodate only a slice of reality and each person's position in space-time is unique, each personal perspective is different from every other perspective. "It's a beautiful thought: we each have our own universe."[3]

Individual, narrow-perspective views into the past and across the present determine whether people's lives and—through generalization or contrast—the plight of humanity are improving, stagnating, or deteriorating. The power of perspective transforms these views through *tunnel vision*, *dogma*, or *mind-set* into flexible, path-dependent, individual approaches to the future. Narrow perspectives are generally unidimensional—the human condition appears as only economic, only political, only religious, only rational, only cultural, or only something else. Separated by perceptions of mutual exclusivity, each narrow perspective exposes a different notion of truth—liberalism, racism, poverty, management, crime, and many others. Each uses a distinct language that is often not translatable into those of other perspectives. With different ways of knowing different sorts of knowledge, the each narrow perspective subordinates the others in a discontinuous hierarchy of knowledge.

The discontinuities across various, narrow perspectives are "neither an intrinsic barrier between the great branches of learning nor a Hadrian's Wall protecting humanistic studies and high culture from reductionistic barbarians, but rather a subject of extraordinary potential awaiting cooperative exploration from both sides."[4]   Constantly flitting to and fro through time and across space, conscious thought and its powerful partner, emotion, re-create each individual's self and its social reality as they construct and remodel perspectives. Oblivious to discontinuities, the fresh individual identities and social realities that emerge and vanish through the power of perspective embody personal values, social goals, and recalled memories of past realities.

The power of perspective accommodates new knowledge and novel feelings and anchors people's identities of self and society within broader perspectives that embrace narrow perspectives without eclipsing them. Globalization has historically expanded and integrated traditional, narrow perspectives towards a transcendent, global perspective that expands space to every corner of the globe and extends the present into the future as well as the past. The power of this historicist, global perspective suggests that every civilization may have experienced at least one wave of globalization that expanded its perspectives beyond what social reality could explain or understand. "As a result of these successive expansions of particular civilizations, the whole habitable world has now been unified into a single great society. . . . [Modern globalization, however,] has merely completed the unification of the world and has not been the agency that has produced more than the last stage of the process."[5] The power of expanding perspectives over vast stretches of time, across innumerable insights of many thinkers, and through many people's observations is the essence of globalization.

THE LENSES OF HISTORY

The power of perspective operates through the particular lenses of values, knowledge, understanding, and beliefs that people use to interpret what lies within their narrow perspectives. The lenses that people use focus their identities, their characters, and their personalities and provide their notions of progress and meaning. Whereas their perspectives determine what they perceive, the lenses create context for attitudes and will for actions. Beyond expanding perspectives with new knowledge and discoveries, globalization has realigned people's lenses several times to bring an accumulated broadening of perspective into focus. For most of history, people peered through the lenses of history and civilizations and explained the present in narrow terms of the past. Later historical lenses resolved people into separate identities—premodern tradition-directed, the Enlightenment's inner-directed, or a modern other-directed—that adjusted themselves to a static social reality.

The Enlightenment lens replaced visions of tradition-directed identities with self-reliant, purposeful, inner-directed "character types who can manage to live socially without strict and self-evident tradition-direction. . . . *The source of direction for the individual is inner in the sense that it is implanted early in life and directed towards generalized but nonetheless inescapablly destined goals.*"[6] Through this new lens, education, technology, industrialization, and urbanization were deliberate, human creations and expansions of knowledge. Science perceived laws of nature that would allow people to assess and even manipulate the risks of a worldly future. Philosophy discoverd a universal morality to guide people in their confusing lives. The differences among people exposed by the Enlightenment lens led to a broad politics of exclusion as humanity segregated itself into races, cultures, classes, and countries.

The lens of modernity inverted the Enlightenment politics of exclusion into visions of inclusive global citizenship. Within the global perspective, people sought to absorb the new knowledge that confronted them by locating themselves in the global context, despite the absence of a global structure that could replace the nation-state as a source of communal identity. In contrast to the Enlightenment's inner-directed personality, industrial modernity and technological globalization introduced "other-directed types, who were brought up to rely upon the cues of others, particularly peer groups, coworkers, and the mass media, in addition to parents, to find their ways in the world."[7] Although the lens of modernity resolved *both* inner-directed *and* other-directed personalities coexisting comfortably, it also resolved a social reality that accommodated reason, morality, and the broad expanse of the human soul.[8]

The twentieth-century obsession with self-realization rejected any form of direction and focused the modern lens on a conspicuous self-autonomy that concentrated identity in self. Not among history's heroes, "the autonomous person, living like everyone else in a given cultural setting, employs the reserves of his character and station to move away from the adjusteds of the same setting." Autonomy from *both* inner-direction *and* other-direction left people lost in freedom and equality and alone in the crowd on the far side of tradition and culture. "The idea that men are created free and equal is both true and misleading: men are created different; they lose their social freedom and their individual autonomy in seeking to become like each other."[9]

Through the dialectical optics of the historicist lens, thinkers perceive a collective understanding of the dual identities of self and society within an eternal, global context. Historicism unifies experience, consciousness, and will longitudinally through time and expands people's perspectives laterally across a contemporary present. Unlike the classical historical lenses, historicism perceives history as a sequence of unique, willed choices, each contingent on all previous choices and conditioning subsequent choices. Narrow perspectives and distinct contexts merge over time in historicism as change and continuity become indistinguishable in the broad context of eternal, universal humanity.

Historical Systems and Civilizations

To understand their social realities and to explain expanding knowledge and continuous change, people organized themselves into complex cultures, polities, and economies.[10] These historical systems often developed around sensitive balances of inherited wisdom, direct experience, values, and faith into civilizations. Common usage of the term *civilization* includes some sense of a large population grouping several cultures around cumulative traditions and values in a broad geographic area. Intrinsically inclusive, although historically less than global, civilization embodies *both* the process of becoming civilized *and* the condition of being civilized. Beyond sophisticated intellectual, artistic, and scientific traditions, civilizations have embodied durable "political, social, and economic institutions that have developed sufficiently to conquer at least some of the problems of order, security, and efficiency in a complex society."[11] Beneath the political functions of the *polis* and the narrow business of an economy, a civilization provides ethical standards of value and some practical *modus operandi* for living. "Civilizations are ways of being, ways of understanding the world, ways of acting upon that understanding. They shape people's perceptions and thus how they react to events."[12]

As some historical systems matured into durable stability or a semblance of permanence, they developed the future-oriented vision and some ethical-moral structure that distinguished them as civilizations. Balancing past, present, and future, civilization's orientation towards the future has stabilized change in a subjective sense of meaning for individuals and for the peoples embraced by the civilization. The essential meaning that civilizations have imparted to life and living transcends politics, economics, and culture, which have been historically shared among contemporary and successive civilizations, and provides a functional balance and cognitive focus for existence.

Civilizations balanced the demands of the past imposed by people's insistence on legitimacy, the urgency of the present, and the promise of the future that lies in technology and rationality. When civilizations lost their balance across time or space, they lost the capacity to meet the demands of the present for power, wealth, culture, and justice and have uniformly declined.[13] Each civilizational balance generated nonlinear, uneven progress within a few narrow perspectives as emerging values appealed to successive generations and gradually synthesized past systems into definitive cultures and institutions.

Intrinsically cohesive across interconnected societies and cultures, most civilizations have tolerated cultural identities within some central world vision embodied in a hierarchical, political-economic structure. Purposeful human will and intensive involvement in civilizations generated social innovation as people adapted to economic, political, and cultural environments. As social innovation led people to create more new knowledge, increasingly complex civilizations became the archetypes of contemporary human florescence, thought, and effort. Each civilization has been a unique historical system that synthesized previous systems in a coherent world vision, expanded traditional perspectives, and established a code for people's behavior beyond self-interest.

The historical lenses have presented spatial globalization and the flow of time into the future as a single, linear dynamic with three alternate processes —catastrophism, determinism, and incrementalism. Catastrophists appreciate the role of accidents in focusing globalization and determining the future. Incrementalists recognize that "some ideas and discoveries have come down through the centuries with no change except in the direction of improvement. . . . Many elements of the old cultures survived, but they were frequently modified or woven into quite different patterns."[14] Determinism pushes humanity slowly into a path-dependent future on the wings of globalization, although inevitable clashes between civilizations occlude a global perspective.

Catastrophism

The eruption of Mt. Vesuvius in A.D. 79, which occurred as polytheism was beginning to yield to monotheism, recalled ancient mythic predictions of a catastrophic end of time and humanity. Observations by Pliny the Elder (23–79), whom it killed, and Pliny the Younger (61–113) may have inspired the resignation to catastrophe that dominated Europe until the Enlightenment. After Mt. Vesuvius erupted again in 1631, Athanasius Kircher's (1601–1680) report of his descent into its active caldera led him, like Pliny, to extrapolate from a direct observation of volcanic eruption to a globally catastrophic end of time: "that the history of our planet must be ruled by sudden cataclysms that rupture episodes of quiescence and mark the dawn of a new order."[15]

Like medieval pessimists, Renaissance thinkers generalized geological catastrophism into a broader perspective of historical progress, which Bacon's idols transformed into directionalism and eventually into determinism. Catastrophists concluded that this world and its people were not random, meaningless accidents but integral parts of something mysteriously progressing in some linear direction. The sources, direction, and purpose—and the implied complex of moral imperatives—of whatever was happening were beyond imperfect human understanding without the intervention of divine revelations.

Narrow, polytheistic perspectives had embraced globalization as normal, unexplainable progress towards the unknown and unknowable. Within the linear, catastrophist Renaissance perspectives, the globalization carried by the voyages of discovery was part of the global paroxysm of the Enlightenment. The emergence of national consciousness, the rise of capitalism, and resentment against papal taxation formed the causal swarm of social catastrophes that converged in globalization and revolution. Geological catastrophism linked episodic volcanoes and earthquakes to cooling of the earth over geologic time and consequent crustal collapse. In analogy, the social version found comfort in Smith's invisible hand, which mystically brought social prosperity, and Hobbes's vision of people leaving the state of nature to create Leviathan, which clearly linked wars and crises to their primal nature.[16] Little more than normal operation of the cosmic train lurching towards perfection, catastrophic globalization led people from the Renaissance through rationalism to individualism and communalism. Linear globalization led the Hobbesian nation-state through nationalism and regionalism to globalism; the invisible hand of Smithian capitalism to liberal, capitalist democracy; and the visible hand of Marxist materialism to socialism and social democracy.

Incrementalism

For most of history, individuals have observed things, interpreted their observations to other people, and ignored things that happened outside their own narrow perspectives on life. Shifts and expansions of perspective, which were difficult, traumatic, and distressing, began not with catastrophic turmoil but with proposals for reforms in conventional thinking to accommodate any new observations and facts. The proposals of Martin Luther in 1517 to correct the abuses of the Roman Catholic Church fomented a century-long Reformation that gradually pushed people into the Enlightenment. Those of Jean-Baptiste Lamarck in the 1790s to correct the standard linear taxonomies of life developed by Carolus Linnaeus a half century earlier brought one century of incremental knowledge creation and another of controversy.[17]

Operating on even longer scales than the expansion of knowledge, civilizations rose and fell over generations or centuries in a loose series of incremental periods.[18] The stimuli for the rises and declines of civilizations were cultural factors—war, religion, trade, intrigue, or corruption in a complex web of social interactions—rather than climate changes, volcanoes, plagues, or earthquakes. The results of these ponderous, incremental expansions of perspective accumulated in each civilization's fund of common knowledge. As people learned, they not only coped with catastrophe but accepted, believed, and relied on common knowledge, despite their own observations of different evidence within their own narrow perspectives. Because life was too short to test everything personally, people came to believe some things blindly in a mystical, collective delusion that overwhelmed observation and memory and formed their faiths in the future. So long as civilization was expanding and progressing towards current and future-oriented values, observation of local, immediate reality within each narrow perspective could reinforce comfortable civilizational beliefs through faith in the future. The placid momentum of a civilization's incremental rise and fall focused its knowledge within a few narrow perspectives that often excluded much of social reality.

Incrementalism reached its climax in 1793, when Marie-Jean-Antoine-Nicolas de Caritat, marquis de Condorcet, dismissed Bacon's idols in an awesome, global perspective that unified a complex world controlled by identifiable, Newtonian laws. Condorcet portrayed a sweepingly broad perspective of cosmic purposes known only to God that resurrected Aristotelian visions of incremental, linear progress. Beckoning from the haze of future perfection and completely open to rational observation, Condorcet's vision accommodated the determinism and unity of monotheism, the Enlightenment's faith in reason, and the certainty of ancient catastrophism:

> No bounds have been fixed to the improvement of the human species: the perfectibility of man is absolutely indefinite; the progress of this perfectibility . . . has no other limit than the duration of the globe upon which nature has placed us. . . . This course of this progress may doubtless be more or less rapid, but it can never be retrograde. . . . All the intellectual occupation . . . concurred in the progress of human reason. It is the same with the entire system of the labor of men as with a well-composed work; of which the parts, though methodically distinct, must, nevertheless, be closely connected to form one single whole, and tend to one single object. . . . [Condorcet envisioned humanity] advancing with a firm and indeviate step in the paths of truth . . . as part of the eternal chain of the destiny of mankind.[19]

Determinism

Although historians debate the origins and declines of civilizational systems, they generally recognize that civilizations have emerged, thrived, and competed when people created opportunities for exchanging ideas, knowledge, and goods with each other. Although neither logic nor history can impute a direction of causality, civilizations have not often risen and flourished in remote isolation with no possibilities to expand their narrow, local perspectives to embrace novel skills, processes, values, attitudes, or cultures. Each of the twenty to thirty civilizations that people have created has begun with cultural mixing and expansion of one culture to absorb others in broadly uniform, predictable patterns that have varied only in the detailed legacies from which they arose. The rise of a young civilization has inevitably brought the decline of either its decrepit predecessor or a weaker neighbor.

Nascent civilizations have almost always expanded or displaced geographically through intensifying and expanding exports of their cultures, even though technology did not allow them to expand to global scales until modernity. Arising from contacts, globalization has brought conflicts between civilizations since at least neolithic eras, as all civilizations have tended to expand by extending political control to adjoining territory, resources, and people. Eventually, the peripheries of expanding civilizations reversed the force and flow of struggle, challenged the cores, generated intracivilizational or class conflict, and reduced the rates of expansion. As civilizations began to decline, rigid institutionalism recalled people to fundamentalism, pessimism, superstition, and otherworldliness within traditional, narrow perspectives in their efforts to preserve individual and civilizational identities. As decline became decay, civilizations lost the ability to defend and justify themselves and were eventually conquered and replaced by other young civilizations, perhaps arising within themselves. A deterministic cycle of rise, expansion, contact, conflict, and decline not only links the future to the past but has seemed to determine the fates and futures of *both* civilizations *and* people. The rational context of modern waves of globalization has refined the notion of civilizational clashes as an inevitable precursor of cyclical, civilizational decline into the idea of clashes of civilizations as determinants of progress and change.[20]

Change and Progress

Catastrophic change that brought new knowledge and novel ideas occurred in rare, unpredictable, explosive episodes of global paroxysm. Subject to unknown and unknowable forces beyond human understanding, these abrupt bursts of chaotic progress quickly subsided into routine, incremental, linear progress. Globalizing societies and the people in them changed "*not* by global creep forward, inch by subsequent inch, but rather in rushes or whooshes, usually following the removal of some impediment or the discovery of some facilitating device, either ideological or technological."[21]

Incremental change and progress occurred gradually over lifetime, and accumulated over the histories of civilizations as reality slowly evolved around new knowledge. Only as orthodoxy proved too rigid or narrow to ignore accumulations of inconsistencies could new knowledge force people to expand their perspectives. Although progress operated through people as knowledge expanded, change was the result of inspiration, divine guidance, or natural law.

Determinism found the engines of progress and globalization not in volcanoes, earthquakes, plagues, or extinctions or even in the gradual accumulation of knowledge over generations. Change emerged in inventions, discoveries, innovations, and insights, or wars and revolutions, deliberately done *by people*, not *to them*. Although incremental progress might slowly satisfy any preconditions for progress, or catastrophic changes might destroy civilizations unpredictably, the parents of change and progress were people. Progress, change, and globalization were deliberate and reversible.

Until the lens of global historicism transcended all perspectives, Bacon's idols presented each engine of progress—catastrophism, incrementalism, and determinism—as *both* ultimate truth *and* the impossibility of understanding any truth. The controversy and confusion penetrated all perspectives of thought, faith, and civilization. Although the historical lenses clearly showed social progress and change, the constraining powers of perspective and Bacon's idols obscured more than their enticing outlines in a blur of globalization.

The Enlightenment

After the Renaissance recalled the proud, metaphysical certitude that people were the crown of creation, the Enlightenment expanded understandings of life and living from monotheist determinism to a more secular notion of the perfectibility of human nature. "Enlightenment is man's emergence from his self-imposed immaturity. Immaturity is the inability to use one's understanding without guidance from another. This immaturity is self-imposed when its cause lies not in lack of understanding, but in lack of resolve and courage to use it without guidance from another."[22] As a few Europeans were beginning to question the norms of life and living that had guided them within their many narrow perspectives for millennia, immaturity blossomed into rationalism. At the end of the sixteenth century, Francis Bacon (1561–1626), Galileo Galilei (1564–1642), and René Descartes (1596–1650) laid the European foundations for a global transformation in thought and knowledge. Although globalism was not yet even a gleam in the eyes of its scientific parents, the next wave of globalization was arising imperceptibly within new and unclear perspectives in China, Europe, and the Americas.

Bacon's magisterial program of reason transformed the Renaissance dogmas of unified knowledge in the service of divine truth into the particular functions of science and philosophy in pursuing global understanding and human progress. Beyond revising the role of knowledge, "rationalism assumes the existence of an *a priori* knowable external reality which is true at all times and in all places and which is the highest grade of knowledge. Such knowledge does not need to be justified by any sensory experience."[23]

Escaping from the Procrustean need to fit new knowledge to doctrine and dogma, Galileo Galilei (1564–1642) expanded the scope of new knowledge beyond the limits of personal experience. His two expansions of observation —the telescope and the microscope—and insistence on direct observation stimulated scientists to combine observation with insight in their search for knowledge. Galileo and Bacon shifted the understanding of knowledge "as a cumulative process of discovery, propelled by processing sensory data about the external world through the reasoning powers of the human brain."[24]

Descartes's technique of reducing objects and ideas to the sum of their parts—reductionism, introduced over the years 1637–1649—promised deeper understanding within the global perspective. Respecting Bacon's concessions to religion and Galileo's insistence on empirical observation, Descartes's philosophy effectively deanimized thought. Descartes's rational perspective was "uninhabited by occult forces, among animals and plants unequipped with souls, where the only ground of certainty lay in the thinking self."[25]

The rational perspective, which the Enlightenment lens eventually overlaid on all of the narrow premodern perspectives, was the collective discovery of these thinkers. Bacon and Galileo symbolize the expansive shift of perspective away from the past and towards the Enlightenment vision of disciplined, general learning as the path to a better future. Descartes expanded cause and effect through the implacable logic of mathematics from physics to metaphysics, medicine, and morality in a system of interconnected truths. As Bacon investigated the philosophical and psychological barriers to expansion of thought beyond people's own narrow perspectives, Galileo shifted the focus of natural science towards external reality. Descartes illuminated the duality of mind and matter in "a complex architecture built of social constraint, historical circumstance, and psychological hope—as well as nature's factuality, seen through a glass darkly."[26] In a counterpoint to Descartes's dualism and Galileo's empiricism, Bacon's philosophical perspective on knowledge anticipated Edward O. Wilson's idea of the consilience of knowledge.

Multiple Perspectives

The scientists and philosophers who lived and thought early in the Enlightenment were never able to expand objectively into the global perspective. Their expansiveness was limited to focusing the powers of science and reason on the confusing world as seen through the Renaissance lens that focused life and living into an infinity of paired dichotomies. People understood life and living in two perspectives that split everything into a simple choice between good and evil, large and small, the planets and the molecule; the infinite and the infinitesimal; the mind and the body; or the spirit and the intellect. The same lens focused most Enlightenment thought within two philosophical perspectives—reason and religion—that were fundamentally distinct with a few common points that made them mutually supplementary rather than mutually exclusive. Secular knowledge was firmly unified within the perspective of reason, just as divine truth was solidly within the perspective of faith. Many new notions—human rights, tolerance, freedom, democracy, and indefinite but inevitable human progress—seemed beyond *both* reason *and* faith. Images of the state as a legal-mechanical contrivance for keeping civil order, natural law, and some sort of secular justice linked to divine morality appeared confusingly in both perspectives.

Bacon's Inductive Method. In his *Novum Organum*, Bacon rejected *both* the scholastic satisfaction in accumulating and conserving old knowledge *and* the Renaissance view of the past as perfection. He found in knowledge the power that could merge human understanding in a continuing pageant of progress. His innovative method of inductive reasoning broadened the perspective of science from Aristotelian deduction and syllogism to the study of nature through observation, insight, experience, and experiment. His ultimate aim was to apply his rigorous inductive method of science to the analysis of human instincts and emotions and a resolute remolding of human character.

Persistent in his own faith, Bacon acknowledged that "all knowledge is to be limited by religion."[27] In the tradition of Thomas Aquinas (1225–1274) and William of Ockham (1300–1349), he separated religious truth from scientific or philosophical truth, although, unlike Galileo, he did not confront the contradictions between them. With theological certainty, he accepted that faith offered truths that science and philosophy could not discern and subordinated secular knowledge to morality. Admitting that pragmatic reality justified moderation of religious zeal, Bacon excepted political states from the moral codes of their citizens, and considered successful wars to be self-justifying.[28]

Galileo's Dual Perspective. Within the rational perspective, Federico Cesi, duke of Aquasparta, may have realized with Francis Bacon in 1603 that understanding demands more than simply acute observation within a single, narrow, focused perspective. In some anticipation of Descartes's confident introspection of his own thinking self, Cesi sought deeper insight into the mental structures and strictures that limited that scientific perspective when he named Europe's first scientific society for the Lynx.[29] Galileo's telescope and microscope expanded the narrow perspectives of sixteenth-century Europe beyond the abilities of the Lynxes to understand what they saw. Galileo and the Lynxes combined the expanding perspectives of observation and the narrow perspectives of knowledge-based insight in a new pair of dual scientific perspectives. Rational understanding emerged as a pattern of truths interconnecting *both* observation *and* insight. Truth emerged expansively across several narrow perspectives only when *both* reason *and* faith could abstract and express it in first premises and mathematics as a unified whole of objective reality, knowable cause, and rational effect. Alongside the powerful, but unknowable, certainty of religion, the broad perspective of rigorous, austere, natural science promised an orderly, understandable universe.

Descartes's Universal System.   Instead of starting with Galileo's observations, and studiously ignoring Bacon's idols, Descartes began from only the first principles that the thinking self could rationalize. Assuming God to be rational, he proved God's existence and constructed the only kind of universe that God could rationally create. His absolute conception of the world marked the ambition of science to provide a picture of reality undistorted by any particular perspective. Descartes's systematic universe explained everything from the infinite cosmos to the nature and workings of the human mind, body, and spirit: ultimate and absolute truth. It collided, however, with the inescapable perspectival limits of moral thinking. He never resolved the dilemma that people could also find outside science objective truths like those found within science. Although parts of his system were incomplete and could not account for several salient bits of observed reality —planetary motions or biological evolution—it opened a new perspective on social and natural reality. The Cartesian system established the existence of, and exposed tantalizing glimpses of, an exciting global perspective in which mind and body were separate but inseparable. Material bodies were hard things that filled space, had color and texture, and could be cut, measured, or divided; living bodies were mobile and mortal. The mind was an indivisible, immaterial thing that transcended space, a thinking soul, potentially immortal, that learned, used, and created knowledge. People lived on two planes: one physical plane shared with other beings and bodies and a second mental-spiritual plane of perception, thought, and passion occupied only by humans. Although Descartes's dichotomous universe simply confused most people, the ensuing work of Isaac Newton (1642–1727) made the universe not only orderly but also intelligible. Newton thrust humanity unceremoniously into the global perspective where "at least a part of God's grand design could be written with a few lines on a piece of paper."[30]

Voltaire's Perspective.   Beyond its focus on rationality, the Enlightenment was uncertain about how to deal with metaphysical reality, values, human destiny, or justice. Expanding the human condition beyond rationality, universalism, and deism, many thinkers explored a third perspective: emotion, sentiment, and the swarm of thoughts that were neither reasonable nor religious. François Marie Arouet Voltaire (1694–1778) found himself within this untidy, third perspective as his society shifted from hierarchic status and Christian values to rational contract around science and truth. Refining *both* logic *and* faith, Voltaire unified third-perspective thought around psychology and empiricism based on a deep commitment to the values of civilization and progress. As revolution threatened to destroy the past and create a new present, he fought on the side of the future with tactics of practical gradualism. "He believed in small steps rather than great leaps forward because he understood the difficulties and the risks of social change and did not want a whole way of life to be suddenly engulfed in a diluvial disaster."[31]

Voltaire's scientific humanism integrated Bacon's deist induction, Galilean deduction, and Cartesian universalism. His cosmopolitan patriotism embodied logical reason, literary art, equivocal sentiment, and practical morality in a constructive appreciation of every aspect of the human condition—*l'esprit humain*. "Reason persuaded him that all nations can have but one legitimate aim—world progress, humanity. . . . Universally applicable principles of justice in human relations is less a national issue than an ethical obligation towards mankind."[32] Within this third perspective, Voltaire recognized the need for order as the foundation for earthbound human living and the certainty of knowledge for understanding destiny. With an implicit preference for scientific methods, Voltairist thought was a manifold of ideas across *both* Cartesian universalism *and* Galilean-Newtonian rationalism.

Troubled with Bacon's deism, Voltaire was a freethinker, neither agnostic nor atheist. Voltaire's God, however, regulated the universe through natural law without capricious intervention to answer prayers or perform miracles. Possessing free will, people were active instruments for developing virtuous civilizations around moral principles provided by God. Visibly and palpably imperfect, nature, law, and will were the art of God, the Master Artificer. Although Voltaire never resolved this paradox of an imperfect God, his legacy carried notions of a limited God. Coeternal with mind, body, and matter, Voltaire's God ordered the world as best he could under the conditions of history, time, and space as the premise of a deist ethic linking human will with God. Voltaire's thought extended beyond Bacon, Galileo, and Descartes by linking human will to freedom through human action. For Voltaire, freedom was the ability to perform willed actions, but whatever people willed was the inevitable result of an antecedent cause: God's intention for human progress within natural law. Beyond the powers of *both* God *and* man, within this third perspective "all citizens cannot be equally powerful, but they can all be equally free. . . . Freedom means being dependent only on the law."[33]

Uniformitarianism

The collision of incrementalism, catastrophism, and determinism left people unsure about where and when they were and how and why they had gotten there, although *both* current opinion *and* ancient wisdom agreed that the future would be better. Even as humanity was stumbling into a paroxysm of revolution, social stress, and transformation, modern hubris exposed a final vision of the global perspective perceived through rational direct observation.

In his cosmic alternative to Condorcet's progressive incrementalism, geologist Charles Lyell (1797–1875) razed another Baconic idol: catastrophism. Lyell's doctrine of static-cyclical uniformitarianism replaced catastrophism as the explanation for changes in the physical world and in human perspectives of it. Within Lyell's perspective, "currently observable processes, operating at characteristically gradual rates, could explain the full pageant of planetary history without any invocation of episodic global paroxysms or early periods of tumultuous planetary change superseded by the staid global maturity of our own time."[34] Although inspired as a theory of geology, Lyell's revitalization of incrementalism explained global catastrophes—volcanoes, earthquakes, wars, epidemics, depressions, genocides, extinctions, or others—as the explosions of small changes that accumulated incrementally over historic time.

Lyell, however, almost incidentally, implicated people as agents of calamity and change and noted that the greatest dangers emerged not from natural catastrophes but from preventable human violence and venality:

> The inhabitants [of Campania, the site of Vesuvius], indeed, have enjoyed no immunity from the calamities which are the lot of mankind; but the principal evils which they have suffered must be attributed to moral, not to physical, causes—to disastrous events over which man might have exercised a control, rather than to inevitable catastrophes which result from subterranean agency. When Spartacus encamped his army of ten thousand gladiators in the old extinct crater of Vesuvius [in 73 B.C.], the volcano was more justly a subject of terror to Campania than it has ever been since the rekindling of its fires.[35]

The logical conclusion of Lyell's uniformitarianism was a steady-state, nondirectional, trendless, homeostatic world, in which observation of the present reflected images of the past and visions of the future. Anticipating the media focus on the spectacular, uniformitarianism recognized that any evidence of incremental change languished generally unrecorded and unnoticed in the penumbra of hugely visible catastrophes. Over sufficiently long periods, catastrophic events, manifested primarily in fleeting, local effects, blended the flow of history into stasis or some cyclic pattern of recurrent incremental change and balancing variations. The future was simply the past revisited. Historic, uniform, global change never slowed, accelerated, reversed, ceased, paused, or offered choices. There were no such things as progress or perfection, only existence and life, both fully observable and understandable.

Although Lyell's uniformitarianism effectively silenced Bacon's *idola theatri* of catastrophism, many modern thinkers remained firmly within the incrementalist perspective. With the connivance of the irrepressible *idola specus*, their narrow focus on personal, rather than civilizational, progress became an incremental determinism in the autosuggestive mantra of Couéism: "Every day, in every way, I'm getting better and better."[36] By the mid-twentieth century, incremental determinism had expanded to a collective form. Its climax in the era of mass production may have been the Japanese *kaizen* system of incremental improvement, which Toyota pioneered in the 1970s to improve productivity. *Kaizen* encouraged individual workers to make tiny, self-determined, incremental changes in whatever they did, while managers set broad production targets and provided minimal instructions. By the late 1990s, self-deterministic, *kaizen* incrementalism was becoming a modern, industrial mantra to complement the consumer cultures that were constructing personal prosperity through incremental accumulation of personal possessions.

The End of Enlightenment

As the Enlightenment irreversibly transformed social reality and exposed the global perspective to everyone, rationality challenged tradition in every perspective. People could not or would not ignore Bacon's idols—especially the religious *idola theatri*—trust Galileo's science, recognize Descartes's novel universalism, understand Newton's calculus, or to accept Voltaire's humanism. Believers rejected the rational dream of merging philosophy, science, and faith within a greater vision of morality. Political, economic, and cultural elites remained perversely within their narrow perspectives and stressed national security, commerce, industry, or religion as the proper activities of humanity.

As people realized their own complexity, they refined rationality into as many versions as the pragmatic needs that demanded responses. The contemplative philosophers—Plato, John Locke, or René Descartes—sought to explain and improve the human condition by questioning it through logic, speculation, or observation explored the possibilities of scientific rationality. Even revolutionaries—Oliver Cromwell, Thomas Paine, or Karl Marx—whose only aim was change exercised a positive rationality that has contributed much to understandings of the condition, nature, and behavior of humanity. To explain the human condition within the global perspective, Ibn Khaldun's science of civilization accommodated several forms of rationality as contraries that "pose sharp differences . . . but never allow the contrast to exclude the possibility of rapprochement and even, from time to time, inversion."[37]

From Rationality into Reality. By the end of the Napoleonic Wars, the Enlightenment image of universal understanding through reason and revelation was blurring into a new social reality. Intellectuals were losing faith in science while scientists distrusted philosophers, clerics rejected them all, and confused commoners did not care. As politicians rearranged geography around political-military power, businesses were expanding commerce under their respective flags of sovereignty and accumulating the wealth that would bring prosperity. Science focused on inventing technological devices and the world's religions rebuilt their shattered idols in fundamentalism and missionary zeal.

Hyperrationality. Progressive thinkers pushed rationality to excess in a hyperrationality of oversimplification, maximization, and natural selective rationalization. Although rationality sought the single best solution, the rational spirit did not preclude several alternatives that may all work in some situations. Neither does rationality specify that the maximum—especially in economic contexts—is always the best result.[38] Although, in competitive environments, the relatively fitter usually survive, rationality could not justify supposing that the survivors were the fittest to survive. The excesses of hyperrationality reflected the persistent power of Bacon's *idola specus* of *ceteris paribus*. Its limits became clear in its fascination with unrealistic assumptions —perfect and equal knowledge, unlimited human intelligence, universal human rights and freedoms, complete absence of self-interest, or others.

Normative Rationality.   As Ibn Khaldun realized, within the global perspective, rationality could take normative forms that included religious and moral standards without the stigma of heresy. The religious thoughts of St. Augustine (354–430), Abu al-Nasr Al-Farabi (870–950), St. Thomas Aquinas (1225–1274), John Calvin (1509–1564), and many others were clearly rational. Their moral rationalities were different from Hugo de Grotius's (1583–1645) rational legalism, Voltaire's scientific humanism, or Jeremy Bentham's (1748–1832) utilitarian rationality. These sorts of normative rationality generated the moral serenity and stable individual identities that returned a sense of meaning to life and living, a certainty about what ought to be done and how to do it, and a predictability and faith in the future. From "the moment [when] people come to form communal life and, particularly, the highest form of such life—a civilization—they require a balanced mix of all three. A successful civilization needs each type of rationality to manifest itself and play its proper role."[39]

The splendid spirit of the Enlightenment survived in the minds of a few enlightened thinkers and idealists, who sharpened the legacies of Bacon, Galileo, Cesi, Descartes, Voltaire, Condorcet, Benedict Spinoza, Jean-Jacques Rousseau, Thomas Hobbes, John Locke, and others. Rather than the broad, universalist, global perspective, however, their new schools of thought focused in specific, narrow perspectives—free-market economics (Adam Smith and David Ricardo), utilitarianism (Jeremy Bentham and John Stuart Mill), materialism (Karl Marx and Friedrich Engels), pragmatism (Charles Pierce, William James, or John Dewey), or nationalism (Alexander Hamilton or Giuseppe Mazzini). "But the grand conception that had riveted thinkers during the previous two centuries lost most of its credibility."[40]

Transformations of Modernity

As people transformed the nature of rationality, Cartesian reductionism deepened to a concentrated effort to understand the world without recourse to chaos, uncertainty, ambivalence, ambiguity, morality, deism, or theism.[41] The world slid away from the noble conviction that reason could ultimately understand everything within a single global perspective. At the bottom of the slippery slope lay a set of simple, clear, homogeneous patterns of structural order within multiple narrow, discontinuous perspectives. Modernity relegated science, philosophy, reason, and religion to their own concerns within their own narrow disciplinary perspectives. People focused ordinary living within functional, economic, political, and cultural perspectives, which they could understand completely without either rationality or morality.

Rumblings of political and industrial revolutions led to a boundless confidence in people's ability eventually to understand *both* the universe *and* the world within narrow, functional perspectives. Expanding Galileo's principles of direct observation and knowledge-based insight as the universal scientific method shifted people's attention away from Bacon's philosophy,

Galileo's science, Descartes's first premises, and Voltaire's humanism. Descartes's dualism led natural science along his narrow path of material reductionism towards pragmatic explanations of how things worked. Logical positivism pulled the social and behavioral sciences along his other path of introspective insight into their own fragmented and narrow perspectives in emulation of the natural sciences. To clarify this kaleidoscopic view, people transformed the global, absolute truth sought by Enlightenment thinkers to a mosaic of narrow, functional perspectives, each with its own truth.

Relative Truths

Through the lens of modernity, absolute truth resolved into true belief justified by empirical observation, which could be deduced through reasoning from known axioms, laws, and theories. Because universal first principles remained beyond human understanding, modern thinkers transformed knowledge and the truth that it embodied into specific orthodoxies within narrow Procrustean disciplines. Unwilling or unable to rely on the will of God to justify multiple truths, modernity found morality in a narrow, secular logic of relativism. Focusing John Stuart Mill's greatest happiness principle within each narrow perspective transformed moral behavior into benefiting as many people as possible and harming as few as possible. Depending not on absolute truth, observed reality, or universal principles but on subjective feeling, relativist morality concluded "that actions are right in proportion as they tend to promote happiness, wrong as they tend to produce the reverse of happiness."[42]

Through the lens of modernity, what had seemed universal within premodern perspectives became parochial and explainable in less-than-global perspectives. Whatever could not be explained became the victim of a modern self-delusion that concealed uncertainty in hopes that additional information or better insight would clarify everything. By the Cold War, the various perspectives had collected mutually exclusive artistic and scientific cultures, which were prisoners of Bacon's *idol fori*, unable to communicate with each other.[43] Humanity had forgotten, or lost interest in, the global perspective conceived by Bacon and Descartes and limned by Condorcet and Marx.

Positivism

Merging Galileo's empiricism with Cartesian dualism in the economic imperatives of capitalist industry, logical positivism found meaning for knowledge and value for truth in converting them to useful technology embodied in devices to address people's demands. Capturing the essence of knowledge in the form of statements about the natural, observable universe —premises, laws, theories, or technology—became a prominent aim of the positivist sciences. Bacon's idols focused the positivist transformation of knowledge into technology with the vision that people could not only design the future with science but could construct social reality with technology.

To coopt Bacon's *idola fori*, positivism transformed functional focus and pragmatic relativism into the ubiquitous liberal arts education with its focus on science and mathematics. Multidisciplinary education around a broadly scientific curriculum stressed diffusion, rather than creation, of knowledge. With epistemological universality, positivism sought to preempt the *idola fori* by merging them into an absolute, universal language of knowledge based on mathematics. Converting skill, information, and pure science to objective technology and humanly useful devices would not only vanquish the *idola fori*, but also weaken the hold of tradition, the *idola theatri*, on knowledge itself.

More interested in immediate concerns—prosperity and security—than in global understanding or universal knowledge, social positivism combined politics and economics in a hazy, composite perspective: international political-economy. Many positivist approaches focus technology through a global political-economy in a logical, materialist design for a perfect global culture. Applying positivist, market-mediated innovation to human behaviors could establish, or even impose, a technology-intensive, global civilization.

Positivism has been unable to overcome the *idola specus*, individuality, or the *idola tribus*, human nature, that dominate cultural living. It has focused knowledge on material plenty, political order, and technological progress. Neither has positivism merged Galileo's objectivity with the subjectivity of Bacon or found any role for Descartes's insight beyond technological innovation. Positivism cannot agree on the "distinctions between fact and concept, between generalization and mathematical truth, or between theory and speculation. . . . [or] to arrive at an invariant and fundamental difference between scientific and nonscientific statements. . . . Neither philosophers nor scientists who attacked the problem could explain the physical acts of observation and reasoning in other than highly subjective terms."[44]

Freedom

The social transformations that modern globalization has brought have not only relieved contemporary social stresses, but refined and expanded people's notions of freedom. For liberal thinkers of the Enlightenment, the essences of freedom involved civic rights, political independence, democracy, and the rule of law. Individual freedom emerged from and around the relationship between citizens and their Westphalian governments. Differences in freedom across various polities were legitimate and even acceptable. The transformations into modernity split individual freedom into two types —economic and political. Political freedom included civic rights for some people and also a group of civil rights of individuals. Economic freedom encompassed individual rights to work for a living, to earn a living wage, and to pursue prosperity. The conjunctural *basho* and the transformations of twentieth-century globalization created the ideas of state's rights and freedoms as new knowledge. The Westphalian criteria for statehood appeared as state's freedoms validated by international law.

The wave of globalization launched by World War II expanded human perspectives on freedom. After the Atlantic Charter created the rights of peoples to self-determination, the United Nations expanded and combined the civic and civil rights of people to universal human rights. Freedom, as transformed by the new knowledge of the 1970s wave of globalization, has merged state's rights and human rights in a trilogy of global freedom, social freedom, and individual freedom. Beyond the legacy freedoms of the past, global freedom "encompasses at least two other broad imperatives: maximizing opportunities for the creation of wealth and removing whatever impediments remain to confine the sovereign self. Freedom has come to mean treating the market and market values as sacrosanct (the economic agenda of the Right) and celebrating individual autonomy (the cultural agenda of the Left)."[45]

Economic Priorities

By the 1970s, with the maturity of modernity and the political stability of Cold-War mutual deterrence, economic globalization had taken its place among Bacon's idols and was focusing much of people's attention and efforts within the narrow economic perspective. Modern globalization transformed an expanding materialism into a social obsession with prosperity and economic growth and the conviction that economic prosperity deserved first priority among people's many social concerns. Modern economic globalization expanded the Enlightenment stress on improving people's material circumstances through rationality to modern social reliance on technology-intensive, mass production of goods for consumption by prosperous citizens.

Within the political perspective, people transformed Hobbes's leviathan into the welfare state to ensure societal welfare by redistributing wealth. As globalization introduced new knowledge, welfare states expanded beyond redistribution to a reliance on technological innovation to improve the quality of citizens' lives. Globalization transformed European notions of welfare-state politics to a natural or divine mission of enlightened states to globalize and develop the rest of the world through the power of prosperity.[46] Expansion of wealth and understanding through development and globalization implied restructuring not only political and economic relationships but also cultural perspectives. Beyond diplomacy and politics or business and trade, these restructurings are promoting "ideas of a global civil society, the decline of the national community and regulatory powers of the state, information overload, and the destruction of a mass culture based on conformity. However, . . . processes of instrumental reason, capitalist economics, world regional power, and national cultures remain major structuring forces."[47]

Braudel's Triple Perspective

Nearly four centuries after Bacon and Galileo, Fernand Braudel reformulated Bacon's idols in his triple perspective on the domains of human economic life: material life, the market economy, and global capitalism.[48] Bacon's idols operated in each domain as what Braudel called *mentalités*, imperfectly rendered in English as attitudes towards living, or in American as *mind-sets* or *prejudices*. The pervasive *mentalités* linked people to the past through various legacies of received wisdom—economic organization, social norms, political institutions, language, and others. *Mentalités* defined the traditional patterns of social behaviors, set each individual's place in society, and changed only very slowly and under duress. Bacon's *idola theatri* or *idola tribus* dominated Braudel's domains of individual material life and the market economy as subjective limits of perspectives. As capitalism penetrated the market economy, Bacon's *idola specus* and *idola fori* narrowed people's economic *mentalités* to individuals' mental horizons. Although Braudel's triple perspective integrated politics, economics, and culture, it could not eliminate Bacon's idols, simply by changing their names from Latin to French.

Dominated by Bacon's *idola specus*, Braudel's primal domain—material life—comprises "the routines and rituals that both govern [people's] daily relationships and inform the way [in which they] characterize [their] environment."[49] Beyond economic or political influences, these behaviors are shaped by personal desires, identities, environments, and cultures. Especially for poor people, the domain of material life is little more than the struggle for physical—not just economic—survival. For others it involves improvements in broad styles of living, and for a few it focuses on accumulation of wealth.

Braudel's second perspective—the open market economy—appeared in the misty dawn of history as societies formed and interacted in supply-and-demand markets focused on simple, direct returns.[50] Broader than material life, the market economy is less constrained by Bacon's *idola fori* and *idola theatri*. Operating through something like Adam Smith's invisible hand, the *mentalité* of the market diffuses knowledge about prices, costs, and the mechanisms of exchange and idealizes transparent or equal knowledge of market conditions. Under the influence of globalization, "the market economy is the realm in which most basic needs are expressed and met, and around which the fabric of daily life is most tightly woven. From this perspective, it is perhaps not too much to say that in the contemporary period the market economy is the basic substratum of society."[51] With a primary focus on goods and services for the domain of material life, the open-market-economy *mentalité* permeates the global consumer market in what has come to be the consumer culture.

The third perspective—risk-acceptant, global capitalism—appeared with modernity and includes the stable, riskless open-market economy. Energized by the restless power of risk, the global capitalist perspective embraces exchanges built on judgments and risk assessment rather than on transparent or equal knowledge. The contingency and risk of unequal exchanges lead to speculation, discontinuity, and turbulence, as a new generation of aggressive shareholders shifts the primary motives for investments and exchanges from direct profit to dividends, interest, and capital accumulation. "This is the *capitalisme sauvage* that so upsets the French."[52] Whereas the open-market economy remembers the past and seeks stability of the material life within a parent society, global capitalism "embeds itself in the future by calculating future profit and loss, and therefore risk, as a continuous process."[53] Although the global capitalist *mentalité* complements the *mentalités* of material life and the open market, the powerful link between risk and reward excludes much of the narrower domains and exposes them to low-risk, capitalist predation.

Modernity has expanded the economic perspective well beyond Braudel's political-economic domains into all perspectives of thought and living through a pervasive global consumer culture. Within the global perspective, all of Braudel's domain of global capitalism, much of the open-market economy, and some of material life form a coherent, single market for goods, labor, and capital. Despite exposing only parts of human activity and ignoring any nonmaterial, political, or sociocultural perspectives, Braudel's triple perspective forms a foundation for understanding the entire range of human living.

Permanent, Directed Change

As globalization transformed the narrow perspectives within which most people spent their lives, the social stresses of technology and entrepreneurship brought a "state of perpetual revolution, [of] continual effort to produce radically new ideas and institutions."[54] Increasing technical ability to manage and systematize globalization has established social purposes to create revolutionary change in knowledge, perspective, institutions, and values. Embedded in globalization and in thrall to Bacon's *idola fori*, "modern technology is directed toward producing the means and instruments of constant change, [which inevitably produces] a consequent instability. Modern societies stress change, replacement of obsolete institutions, development of new social values around technological change and unstable perspectives of the universe, and creation of new systems and structures, as human perspectives of [life] expand into infinite diversity."[55] The compromise between experience and people's need to know has become a continuing condition of change whose attendant trauma and uncertainty expose the ineptitude of Bacon's idols and institutional tradition in managing nontraditional circumstances.

Despite the dominance of natural changes, the technical ability to change the earth and its environment continues to increase people's power to manipulate *both* globalization *and* evolution towards their own preferences. At the intersections of globalization and evolution with daily routine, winners self-select, and losers self-destroy. Human manipulation and directed change force other systems—human and natural—to adapt and adopt, to reform or revolt, simply to survive, much like Alice's hopeless position in the Red Queen's race, running ever faster just to stay in the same place.[56]

In the company of the winners but not delayed by the losers, human will and technology direct globalization, focus change, and guide progress within a particular, narrow perspective—economic, cultural, political, or something else. In the non-Darwinian world of directed globalization and focused change, civilizations, societies, species, ideas, knowledge, and people become Darwin's organisms that evolve or die. Paradoxically, as in Darwin's undirected, evolutionary world, *"only those organisms best suited to making a living, to coping with the very factors that limit population size will, on average, be the ones that survive and reproduce.* Those that are successful, . . . will tend to pass along those very traits that were the ingredients for success."[57]

Creative Destruction

In expanding the economic perspective to embrace entrepreneurial, economic growth as a form of social transformation, Joseph Schumpeter introduced the notion of creative destruction. Originally a narrow, economic insight based on technological change in modern industry, Schumpeter's idea combined and expanded the alternative, narrow perspectives of catastrophism and incrementalism to replace uniformitarianism. In Schumpeter's broadened perspective, instead of random events, repetitive cycles, or unpredictable natural catastrophes, it was focused entrepreneurship in pursuit of specific aims that replaced an obsolete past with progress. Instead of the manipulations by Adam Smith's invisible hand or the ineluctable current towards perfection, progress was the product of inspired decision and willed intervention.

In a context of permanent change and creative destruction, the struggle for survival and fame in artistic and cultural modernism followed the reductionist pattern of science and technology. Creative destruction appeared as an obsessive drive to create the novel, controversial, and even provocative and destroy, or at least displace, the traditional. The modernist cult of celebrity captured artists, scientists, scholars, and entrepreneurs alike in their searches for the novelty and change that brought fame and wealth. Whereas science was constrained by experience and stabilized around fact, philosophy and literature could experiment with new forms of truth and simply abandon all received wisdom. Art could self-consciously shatter tradition and even reality, as technology made all things and thoughts possible.

Creative-destructive modernism seems to have forgotten the Baconian and Cartesian strictures about religion and morality and has shifted a significant segment of scientific, philosophical, and artistic attention from society to self. Bacon's idols have proudly replaced the Renaissance and Enlightenment traditions—knowledge, thought, beauty, sentience, justice, and even truth— with modern concepts of order, well-being, meaning, and identity. In increasingly strident calls for change, modern humanism has claimed political, economic, and cultural attention for humanity itself. The humanist focus for logical rationality and compassionate insight alike is on the increase in material inequality that technology and globalization have brought.

Transformation of Time

Modernity introduced several irreversible transformations of people's perspectives on time and its relationships with their lives and destinies. With modernity, people transferred the foundations of their time consciousness from nature to culture and intruded time into their systems of values. "The way members of a culture perceive and use time reflect's their society's priorities and even their own worldview."[58] With the Enlightenment idea of progress, people colonized the future with the expectation that the human condition *should* become better as the present faded into the past and became the future.

The Passage of Time. Modern rationality confirmed the division of time into three parts. The past has slipped away out of existence, and the future is a shadowy shape of unformed details. Rationality associated only the present with reality in two alternate metaphors: the arrow or the fabric of time. In one perspective, time was a metaphorical arrow flying into the future carrying time with it in a flow that people could feel. "In this simple picture, the *now* of our conscious awareness glides steadily onward, transforming events that were once in the unformed future into the concrete but fleeting reality of the present, and thence relegating them to the fixed past."[59] Despite the comfortable attraction and simplicity of this view, many people conceive time as a fabric, similar to Islam's tapestry of time, on which the events of past, present, and future are located. This alternative metaphor of time does not identify the present as a particular, distinctive moment and omits any process that systematically converts future events into present, and then past, events. Instead of experiencing the passage or flow of time, people observe that the future, which they do not remember, differs from the past, which they can recall. The fabric reflects not the passage of time but its asymmetry.

Compression of Time and Space. Premodern civilizations bound time and space tightly to each individual's immediate location as a stable feature of social reality. Modernity unceremoniously *separated* all three, compressed time, shrank space, and expanded place, although at different rates. "Time-space compression involves a shortening of time and a shrinking of space —progressively, the time taken to do things reduces and this [reduction] in turn reduces the experiential distance between different points in space."[60]

People's perspectives of the time-space relationship changed permanently when increases of early industrial productivity generated an economic crisis of overaccumulation in the 1840s. Unification of European capital and credit markets after the collapse of credit in 1847–1848 began the compression of time, which continues today, as the telegraph shifted capital and credit more quickly. In parallel, investment in transportation and telecommunications began to shrink space as Europeans colonized the planet's entire surface. The spread of railways, the invention of mass production, and introduction of air travel in the twentieth century further compressed space-time within global systems of distribution. Global financial stability based on the British pound-sterling and the designedly universal political system of the League of Nations compressed *both* space *and* time in a global political-economy. As in the 1850s, the overaccumulation crisis of the 1970s brought another burst of space-time compression. The introduction of fiber optics, satellite communications, and the Internet as communications media made possible instantaneous economic transactions, financial arbitrage, diplomacy, and political interactions. In the twenty-first-century social reality of space-time compression and technological capability to manipulate the environment, the past fades into irrelevance. For those who are connected to the global web of information, the instantaneous present becomes life itself, and the future becomes an artifact of human will.

Event Time and Progress. At the beginning of the second Industrial Revolution in the late nineteenth century, Henri Bergson introduced the notion of time as a unique, subjective human experience. What he called *durée* comprised willful reasoning, acting, choosing—freedom—and resisting pressures on action and choice—the constraints of Bacon's idols—through individual will. Merging past, present, and future within individual consciousness, Bergson's *durée* extended beyond and within the uniform measurement of the sequence of events, which correlated space and time—*event time*. Bergson's *durée* was not, however, simply the duration of a series of events but, rather, the instantaneous, cognitive union of cause and effect, past and future, act and thought. Every individual experienced *durée* as a solitary moment of freedom to choose within personal perception of present social reality when the memory of the past is merged with present action into anticipation of the future.[61] From Bergson's focus on the individual, Fernand Braudel later expanded *durée* into periods of collective, social experience between what he called *conjonctures*, which marked and focused social progress. Varying in pattern across functional perspectives—politics, economics, culture, technology, or language—and in pace over event time, social progress came to represent the flexible unit of an additional level of time—*social time*. Beyond the familiar event time that organizes routine living within the narrow perspectives of the here and now, social time embraced each of people's individual perspectives, including time, within the global perspective of social progress.

For centuries, the constraining factor on progress was information. With few observations and little knowledge and unable to share it, people were neither certain nor confident about the operation of the universe or their places and roles in it. Progress seemed a simple function of event time as it flowed smoothly into the future, carrying people with it. "Today, virtually everyone in the developed world has access to an infinity of books. Everyone can be surrounded by music every moment of the day, or religious sermons, or news, or gossip, or whatnot."[62] No longer a constraint, instant, universal abundance of information has revealed that progress is not simply the arrival of the future but something that people actively create. As the pace of progress increases in event time, it is time itself that seems to constrain progress. Each day has a fixed amount of time to accomplish all of the day's work before the arrow of time flies into the future. As gathering, sorting, and interpreting information consume more time in communication, people have less time for creating and using knowledge for production, for human interactions, for progress, and for whatever else they have always done. Unlike other types of globalization that expand perspectives, the globalization of time narrows people's temporal focus and constrains progress within time itself.

Social Time and Transformation. The *durée*, which Bergson had envisioned as a momentary feature of individual psychology in the context of uniform measures of chronological, event time, became the foundation of social time, an expansive feature of social reality and transformation. Bergson glimpsed and Braudel envisioned something like the global perspective that encompassed *both* space *and* time. Social time is the temporal medium within which humanity repeatedly reinvents the future as the limits of the possible expand within the global perspective. Although the social time does not resolve the contradictions and stresses that vex all of people's narrow perspectives, it carries transformations of social reality that may banish them to the past and render them unimportant in the present and irrelevant in the future.

Measuring incremental progress in rigid, physical units, the familiar instantaneity and seriality of event time are both firmly embedded in social time. Social time, however, measures temporal units of human understanding —the span of an economic cycle, the length of a political crisis or social age, the continuity of a populist movement, the duration of an ideology or scientific paradigm. Progress from one social-time unit to the next occurs at logical climaxes of understanding, changes in values or norms, or shifts and expansions of perspectives—transformations of social reality. Constrained within the narrow limits of human knowledge, premodern social times were long and the few transformations were slow. The expansion of knowledge through modern globalization has compressed social times as people increase their collective capabilities to transform the ways in which they live.

Social Trust

Premodern peoples found social and personal confidence within their own local, primary social groups—families, tribes, villages, or local cultures—their physical senses, and their own personal experiences. Trade-based globalization brought extended, artificial groups together in systems of collective sanctions to punish violators of commercial codes that applied to entire groups. Patently unfair by modern standards, such systems created the trust "under which interstate trading could flourish, since it obliged trading communities to enforce internal discipline to encourage fair dealing."[63] From this commercial origin, intragroup trust has remained the foundation of social living in the twenty-first century. Modern technologies extended the temporal and spatial distances over which social relationships could form and operate beyond local interactions based on intimate familiarity and personal trust. The new idea of trust was explicitly impersonal. Globalization formed relationships across large, even global distances as people interacted beyond their own narrow, self-based perspectives without any direct contact. Based on evolving notions of systemic trust that were replacing personal consanguinity and friendship, these extended relationships imperceptibly transformed people's notions of self and locality.

The emergence of law and capitalism reflected the expansion of trust with expanding knowledge as Enlightenment rationalism began to emphasize individual responsibility as the foundation of interpersonal relationships, especially commerce. People learned to have confidence in money—currency, financial instruments, and credit—which transfers value over great distances and long times. Societies developed social trust in expert systems—software, legal codes, or bureaucracies—that guarantee expectations across all contexts, times, and distances. The paradoxical power of new knowledge embodied in expanding trust, however, instead of deepening people's perceptions of risk and threat, has generally reinforced their attitudes of trust.

Risk Consciousness

Whereas natural risks have not changed significantly over the eons of history, human-manufactured risk seems to have increased in parallel with intensifying globalization. The balance of risks has also changed; human-manufactured risks that globalization has created—the risks of misplaced trust or incomplete knowledge—are often more threatening than natural risks have always been. Focused on human risk, modern risk consciousness paradoxically balances the hubris of universal trust with self-doubt. Ready to trust their lives, prosperities, securities, and futures to impersonal flows of capital and expertise, people cannot overcome the universal self-doubt that forces them to assess and insure against risk. Even in a context of trust, people constantly watch each other, seek information about the value of goods, labor, and money, and question the validity of expertise.

Natural Risk. Modernity shifted people's attention from primal fears of natural risk to themselves towards concerns about what people have done, and were doing, to nature. As new knowledge provided relief from poor harvests, bad weather, floods, plagues, famines, and other things that nature could do to them, people expanded their risk perspectives. Modern prospects of risk encompass not merely the physical environment or even the biosphere but human nature, society and culture, physiology, and spirituality. "The struggle for one's daily bread has lost its urgency as a cardinal problem . . . For many people problems of overweight take the place of hunger. . . . Parallel to that, the knowledge is spreading that the sources of wealth are polluted by growing hazardous side effects."[64] Despite the progress of science and technology, human ability to manipulate the natural, external risk imposed upon people by the insistence of Bacon's idols or by nature itself remains feeble.

Man-made Risk. A risk that modern society seems to have created for itself is that of not knowing what to do, since every human behavior involves obtaining knowledge and guidance from some expert system through books, communication, software, expert consultants, or teachers. Although learning itself is as old as humanity, the risk that knowledge is not current or that an individual is trusting a flawed or obsolete expertise is distinctly modern. In some contrast to the continuing inability to command the power of nature, technology has provided a determining ability to control the risks created by people's knowledge and actions, which ultimately affect human social realities.

Reflexive Risk. Within the global perspective, risk is reflexive through people's growing awareness of it. The technologies of modernity and globalization have led people to recognize risks from radioactivity, toxins, or pollutants that, although not perceptible to unaided human senses, have always caused irreversible or invisible damage. Although reductions in economic growth or extinction of languages, species, and social identities have occurred for millennia, globalization has alerted people to them as the direct, unavoidable risks of industrialization and modernization. These risks reflect not scarcity of resources, inadequacy of technology, or even ignorance but the social stresses of globalization, overproduction, imbalanced overpopulation and distribution, and uncertainty about justice or morality. Increasing awareness of these threats acts reflexively through modern risk-consciousness to increase broader social, economic, and political risks. Since people have not learned how to relieve the stresses of modernization and globalization except by going to war or by transforming social reality, risk-consciousness simply increases human risk. In a context of risk-consciousness, the expansion of reflexive threats through globalization of high-risk industries and activities has made rational assessment of risk, its costs, and its consequences impossible.

Global Risk. Globalized risk universalizes threat, equalizes its effect across any distance and over long periods, and ignores political borders. Globalization of risk expands consciousness towards the global perspective, which increases awareness of risk with recognition that the only risk-reduction techniques are global. The global perspective diffracts risk consciousness, acceptance, and aversion across many narrow perspectives. Poor societies can convert economic handicap into risk disadvantage and purchase economic growth by accepting global risk as dangerous, dirty, profitable industries migrate out of rich, regulated countries. In a perplexing paradox of risk, as globalization compresses the rich and the poor into the same global neighborhood, "the multiplication of risks causes the world society to contract into a community of danger."[65]

Living with Risk. Since the Enlightenment, people have learned to use risk to assess, regulate, and determine a probabilistic future without rational certainty. People with the risk-inclusive perspective that emerged with modernity focus their attention on "different points in the space-time scale in which we all dwell. They differ in the factors [that] they take into account in forecasting the state of the world, how far they look into the future, and how much they care about nonhuman life."[66] Risk-consciousness permits a probabilistic choice between risk and something else in allocations resources and knowledge across the various perspectives that demand political attention.

HISTORICISM

Although historians lament the lack of historical perspective in economics, politics, and sociology, scientists—natural and social—express frustration with the inability of the historical perspective to generate explanatory models and test hypotheses. Politicians and bureaucrats often have little patience with history or science, since "history's lessons are too specific to their subjects' times and places to inform today's actions. And economics leans so heavily on simplifying assumptions and formal modeling that its conclusions cannot easily be related to policymakers' concerns."[67] Despite the scientific search for universal propositions and historians' stress on particularities, careful thinking and understanding require some synthesis of the historical and the scientific.

The lens of historicism focuses scientific models on finding similarities and regularities and relies on the historians' skill to explain anomalies over time and across space. Historicism expands the particularism of the historian through the models of the scientist into a perspective on human living that is global in spatial expanse and timeless in temporal depth. Unifying the insight of philosophy with the logic of reason, historicism recognizes knowledge and knowledge creation as the willed use of philosophical reason to transform present social reality into a path-dependent, yet indeterminate, future.

The Rise of Historicism

Explicitly modern, but with no direct intellectual parentage, the spirit of historicism informed the ancient Chinese notion of *Tao*, may have inspired St. Thomas Aquinas, and stirred Voltaire's concerns about *l'esprit humain*. Historicism began to congeal between Kant's categorical imperative and Burke's historically informed understanding. So powerful was Enlightenment expansion that by the 1750s, Anne-Robert-Jacques Turgot was anticipating historicism with the Enlightenment's broad, global, temporal perspective:

> All the ages are bound up with one another by a sequence of causes and effects which link the present state of the world with all those that have preceded it. The arbitrary signs of speech and writing, by providing men with the means of securing the possession of their ideas and communicating them to others, have made of all the individual stores of knowledge a common treasure-house which one generation transmits to another, an inheritance which is always being enlarged by the discoveries of each age. Thus, the human race, considered over the period since its origin, appears to the eye of a philosopher as one vast whole.[68]

From Turgot's insight, the shift from exclusive social arrangements to social inclusivity condensed a vision of global civilization linked by knowledge and will to its own past. This same legacy of knowledge harbored the germs of humanity's common future and human will had the responsibility of nurturing them into social progress. The social inclusivity of liberalism and socialism focused Turgot's temporal unity in the present as the nexus between the past and the future. As the post–1815 Industrial Revolutions transformed social reality, people's narrow perspectives expanded beyond politics and economics to aggregate sociocultural concerns about justice. The historic socioeconomic exclusivities protected by Bacon's idols began to lose credibility as political participation in Europe expanded after the liberal uprisings of 1830–1848. Throughout the world, the emergent societies of the early twentieth century "took their form after the expansion of participation and the extension of compulsory education in the 1880s. . . . The postwar capitalist industrial societies were typically even more inclusive with reallocative market economies and strong welfare states."[69]

Borrowing from *both* liberalism *and* positivism, historicism merges human history laterally with natural law and unifies human experience from the eternal past longitudinally across a contemporary present into an unknown future. Whereas culture and spirit bind experience into a noncognitive pillar of humanity, civilization, and even individuality, historicism blurs autobiographic knowledge of experience into self-awareness for *both* individuals *and* societies. "Perceiving the unity of the universal and the particular through concrete thought, philosophical reason has as its criterion of reality the historical self-awareness of the will."[70] Unifying the universal and the particular exposed an insidious idol that Bacon failed to recognize: moral inertia or deistic obsession with absolute truth in the form of perfect good. Human nature—at once self-regarding and bound by experience but also searching the cosmos for truth—is crippled by the moral tension of eternal fragmentation between particular experience and promises of universal truth.

To relieve this chronic tension between morality and practicality, historicism recognizes the power of humanistic self-control exercised through human will to resolve the paradox of the particular and the universal and the mysteries of the one and the many. "Life does not give here an element of oneness and there an element of change. It gives a *oneness that is always changing.*"[71] An eternal unity of opposing inclinations and understandings, humanity is compulsively drawn into socially destructive impulses but is able, *under the power of human will*, to transform destruction of the individual past into creation of the communal future. The combination of direct experience with human insight through the historicist lens with a focus on willpower stabilized and matured around twentieth-century aesthetics in a merger of art and reason. The lens of historicism resolved human will, rationality, art, and spirit into creative action as they matured around the intuition, and aesthetics of Benedetto Croce, Irving Babbitt's notion of a will to civilization, and Kitaro Nishida's conceptions of dynamic, cohesive place, *basho*, in space-time.

Particular Universality: The Condition of Globalization

Historicism understands particular identity, ecumenical unity, and social diversity together in a balanced relationship of mutual implication: particular universality. Within the global perspective, the lens of historicism unites the universal with the particular, the active with the rational, and the moral with the willed in an eternal, human condition of globalization. The transformation at the heart of every wave of globalization arises in a universal, civilizational freedom that is inseparable from *both* particular institutions of place and time *and* particular sets of personal and social identities. Each transforming wave of globalization not only relieves current social stresses but also adjusts the freedom, order, universality, and particularity to the circumstances of time and place. Accommodating each person's individuality within some particular universality, the condition of globalization recognizes people's moral goodness as a universal quality that an infinite number of particular actions may have. The expansion of individual morality to universality occurs as historically particular, willed actions to create good enter experience in event time. The moral universalism engendered by individual actions reveals itself in social time by becoming selectively immanent in historical particularity.[72] As human thought and belief converge the particular, the circumstantial, and the universal in *basho*, the consequent and continuing transformation of social reality constitutes the human condition of globalization.

The lens of historicism resolves globalization as a "relational rather than a literal term, one which expresses a relative and fluid social relationship rather than an absolute and static one."[73] Denying to the *process* of globalization any sense of predetermination or even direction, historicism relaxes the semantic expectation that the *condition* of globalization be geographically worldwide at a particular time. "Globalization today is nothing more than a form of globalized social practice inherent to a particular terrain of social activity, a terrain which, although it has expanded over the past century, remains nevertheless bound by certain constraints," the legacy of the past.[74]

The broad ideational, spatial, and temporal perspectives of historicism lead smoothly into a circumstantial universality that embodies the immanence of knowledge, will, and spirit across different circumstances. Ignorance of the past is fully compatible with a chaotic present and an unknowable future. Successive social realities expose *both* continuities *and* discontinuities. Most important for progress into the future are willed, particular action and social learning to transform past lessons through current possibilities into future realities and expand particular circumstances towards universality.[75]

Within the historic parade of progress the lens of historicism resolves not only political groups and social classes but also individual heroes—good or evil—and their feats as carriers of globalization. Just as Odysseus and Achilles were globalizing heroes in Homeric Greece, so Lech Walesa and Nelson Mandela are heroes of post–Cold-War globalization. Within the global perspective the historicist lens extends thought into unity beyond rationality, faith, or art into the spirit, the soul, and the compassion that ennoble humanity without losing particularity. Historicist science, art, and philosophy extend understanding from the particular past through a circumstantial present into a predictable, universal future. People find identities within themselves and within multiple communities as rational individuality concentrates, combines, and transcends self in accordance with deliberate human will.

The Power of Willed Action

In discounting *both* philosophical rationality *and* Voltaire's metaphysics as the royal road to truth, historicism celebrates willpower as the anchor for *both* rationality *and* spirituality in the reality of the here and now. The tradition of natural law presents the universal, the good, and progress as logical results from principles of reason explored by St. Thomas Aquinas and refined by Francis Bacon. Derived from Thomistic doctrine, historicism concentrates the universal, the selfish, and the normative in a will that is *both* universal *and* particularistic. Within the global perspective, the historicist lens shifts the Thomistic focus from rationally discovering and complying with divine will to defining a higher—but not exclusively divine—will. In its humanistic, rather than religious, manifestation, this higher, universal will energizes not only natural events but also *deliberate humanly willed acts of creation and destruction*.

Spanning the endlessly diverse desires and perspectives of human nature within the global perspective, "the authority to which man ultimately defers is not a set of conceptual propositions but a special power of will which finally transcends efforts at exhaustive intellectual definition, . . . an unvarying sense of higher moral purpose which transcends all particular impulses. The same in all men, this sense harmonizes the individual circumstances of each . . . [and] brings men together at a common center of value."[76] The lens of historicism resolves this moral ordering of living and action through the human actions of will as the eternal, moral, civilizing force that unifies globalization and progress.

Moral Imperative

Although rationality and religion have been content to exhort people to *be* good in ways prescribed by cultural interpretations of divine scriptures, the lens of historicism resolves the opportunity to *create* good beyond the individual. Historicist morality is the act of creating human will around the legacy of experience—knowledge, religion, historical insight, or cultural tradition—in the context of social reality. People bring good into the world not by following momentary impulse, by complying atomistically with the dictates of scriptural truth, or by exercising pure rationality, nor even by spreading spiritual revelation. Good emerges not spontaneously but instead deliberately through creation and exercise of human will to transform the immoral and painful of the past to the moral and good of the future.

The moral dimensions of rationality, prudence, politics, and economics all lie beyond discovered, preconceived rules, or social relations. The moral face of rationality appears in a moral imperative or will towards "that eternal, immutable law in which will and reason are the same."[77] This human will to restrain crass, atomistic desires and pursue a deeper, socializing, and satisfying moral imperative lies at the center of social consciousness but beyond social context. Individually particular and transient in event time, this morally imperative will is universal, suprasocial, and immutable as it pulls people towards the special qualities of living that satisfy their deepest yearnings to do good and to know truth.[78] In expanding from particular, undersocialized desire to universal, oversocialized will, people unify their atomistic personalities and move into knowledge-creating communion with others: *basho*. They "do not behave or decide as atoms outside a social context, nor do they adhere slavishly to a script written for them by the particular intersections of social categories that they happen to occupy. Their attempts at purposive action are instead embedded in concrete, ongoing systems of social relations."[79] The eternal human will focuses the rational capability to transform social reality—a distinct concatenation of people, policies, relationships, cultures, and attitudes at a particular time—in knowledge creation. The convergence of eternal will and rationality in historicist *basho* generates the transformations that propel humanity along historically conditioned, but not predetermined, trajectories.[80]

Will to Civilization

The embodiment of morality, "civilization is something that must be deliberately willed; it is not something that gushes up spontaneously from the depths of the unconscious. Furthermore, it is something that must be willed first of all by the individual in his own heart."[81] In a social context of past realities, this eternal will to civilization congeals in *basho* around the principle of moral order that resides within the human soul, acts through the human mind, and focuses *both* rationality *and* morality in creating new knowledge. Outside and before *basho*, the "minds of the individuals who can be said to have willed civilization are minds filled with a great variety of objects of will, according to place, time, and individual constitution."[82] In *basho*, the will to civilization brings unity among a multiplicity of minds and individual activities and creates *both* new knowledge *and* morality. Spanning the many perspectives of individual minds with the will to order and civilization, the progress carried by new knowledge into transformed social reality focuses human action on the ultimate moral ends of truth, goodness, and civilization.

Creative Action

The philosophical fulcrum of historicism is a primal kind of knowledge that extends below and beyond rational thought. Beyond observations of the here and now, it includes each person's autobiographic knowledge of its own personal experience, which in *both* the individual self *and* aggregate humanity is *human consciousness*. In merging will, values, rationality, and spirit, consciousness is permanently active, since the primal acts of being aware of self or knowing the present add these experiences to historical knowledge of the past. For human consciousness, the crux of reality is not simply discovery of rational truth about the good, but the freedom to act on whatever insight, impressions, and knowledge that people may have. Choosing the content of the future and determining its value—good or bad—through awareness of legacies of past knowledge, present morality, and self-awareness through consciousness comprise the active affirmation of will that creates reality.

The lens of historicism exposes the inadequacy of mere hope, thought, desire, or legacies of morality and goodness alone to generate progress. "We do not desire things because we know them to be good or useful; but we know them to be good and useful because we desire them. . . . Practical action is preceded by knowledge, or rather, knowledge of the practical: to obtain this, we must first have practical action."[83] Only as people convert past knowledge, learning, and experience into new knowledge in conscious, willed, creative action can they brighten the light of eternal, universal social reality and transform it into a circumstantial future. "The final reply to all the doubts that torment the human heart is not some theory of conduct, however perfect, but the man of character," the person of good action, who willfully embodies itself and its creative action in the reality of the eternal.[84]

The present action of creating new knowledge carries self, society, civilization, and people into the future. Although individual action is often instinctive, invisible, routine, and instantaneous, societies' creative actions occur naturally and sporadically in *basho* in flexible social time. Individuals and societies alike deliberate among competing perspectives, contexts, disparate knowledge, and feelings in choosing and in bestowing value on their choices. Whether in private thoughts and dreams or in open *basho*, "presiding over the deliberation is a will, either moral or merely economic, which prefers this and rejects that incipient action. Preferring is bestowing value on what is preferred in the very creation of the act. Rejecting is bestowing negative value, or antivalue, on an incipient action and thereby eliminating it from possible future existence."[85] Although people can expand the deliberation indefinitely in space and time, any deliberative context is, itself, another act of creating new knowledge with intrinsic determination of value. Both active decisions emerge from the same complicated sets of volitions, knowledge legacies, and larger contexts that form current reality. Both are as value-bestowing and knowledge-creating as the thoughtless, spontaneous actions of daily living or the great, civilizational transformations that destroy and create global reality.

Self-Directed Evolution

Historicism offers an alternative to the views that human events are the results of ponderous, immutable, impersonal forces—capital, labor, power, fate, demography, technology, or globalization—that obey laws with predictable results. Whereas the laws of nature are immutable for nature, they are constraining, lawlike regularities within the historicist perspective of human living and evolution. Although nature does affect human events, history has shown that "unforeseen upheavals—the end of apartheid, the collapse of communism, or the wars of Yugoslav succession—have shaken confidence in a purely long view of human events. It is no longer convincing to treat history as slow and implacable, like the shifting of the earth's tectonic plates: chance counts and accidents matter; individuals do make a difference."[86] Rather than a series of evolutionary epochs neatly arranged in event time, historicism depicts human progress in modest increments of dynamism in social time.

The historicist lens shows humanity, with its knowledge and reason, its philosophy and will, and its values and attitudes, as the director of its own evolution through a series of social realities, not the divinely inspired object or purpose of predestined maturation. Individuals, classes, cultures, societies, and even civilizations are irretrievably embedded not in an incomprehensible skein of divine law but in a broad, self-constructed, social reality that gives moral, intellectual, and spiritual form to historical existence and progress. Historicism does not limit knowledge creation to converting, combining, or integrating existing knowledge or even to incremental innovation within narrow perspectives. Just as knowledge is not fixed in space or time, knowledge creation transcends space and time through transformation of both through evolution of its creators.[87] Extending well beyond technology and process, knowledge creation changes self and others alike, reifies perspectives and space-time itself, and transforms social reality into what people make of it. The human processes of creating new knowledge provide the force and direction for progress within narrow, functional perspectives and also for humanity's collective journey into a future that it creates for itself.

The Unity of Been, Being, and Becoming

Since all objects and thoughts are historical insofar as the realities in which they were created and to which they belong are in the past, consciousness of their meanings in the present embodies a consciousness of time. Modern time consciousness expanded people's present awareness of everything through rationality to include awareness and consciousness of the past. Current consciousness and reality merge in a flow of past human experiences, all concentrated in the present. Expanding into the future, historicism exposes an infinite, unfinished series of future meanings for present knowledge and events, which have themselves emerged from the past.[88]

Historicism not only expands time consciousness but recognizes the unity of being, knowledge, consciousness, and time. Time, however, is not simply a succession of experiences—Bergson's *durée*—that all occur in the present and immediately become part of the past.[89] "It is clear that the past is, like thought, a 'now' [and] *at the same time* a 'no more' like a memory; the future, a 'now' [and] at the same time a 'not yet.' From that, one cannot say that time flows *in* consciousness; it is, to the contrary, consciousness that, starting from its own now, unfolds or constitutes time."[90] Consciousness and being are not bound within an individual or its particular present but spread across all time and distribute experience and thought into the past, the present, or the future according to the knowledge that they embody. The present appears, for a society, as a culture, a polity, an economy, and, for people, as a moment in the continuing triple processes of being, becoming, and creating. The new knowledge created in the present does not show the truth as a contradiction of the historical past or the unknowable future but rather shows the open door to the truth of eternal becoming. Consciousness and knowledge are eternal, transcendent, and universal, *both* containing *and* contained by time and *both* unified *and* discontinuous.

In a future that is *both* path-dependent *and* unspecified, historicism completes the syllogism of continuity from the past into the future. Remembering what the past might have become, historicist imagery merges it with what people are doing in present reality. People can use the same imagery to project the merger into what they will do and can become in the future. Historicism finds meaning in human progress and expansion of consciousness, despite here-and-now skepticism about any coherent continuity between a past with many interpretations and a future with no knowable goal or end state.[91] Through the lens of historicism within the global perspective, meaning lies in creating the process of becoming. People transform becoming into progress not because they believe in any absolute meaning embracing the process but because in the process of living their individual lives together, they create that meaning.[92] The future remains forever open, unknown, and unknowable, because the possibilities of becoming, although many, are finite and determined by the past and the present. By becoming their own future, people create it.

Knowing as Being

Historicism recognizes knowledge as neither absolute nor static, but universally and eternally relative, incomplete, dynamic, and global. Neither does historicism connect knowledge explicitly or exclusively with rationality or cognition, but recognizes artistic creation, literary inspiration, entrepreneurial innovation, intellectual insight, religious revelation, or mythical-magical vision as useful and real forms of knowledge. The broad, global expanse and historicist spread of knowledge transcend narrow perspectives and specific facts and also all dimensions of time and space. Historicist, global knowledge embraces individual human beings and groups of people—dynamic, social, competitive, and innovative—interacting with each other and with the world in which they live.

Whereas the rationalism of the Enlightenment and modernism conceived knowledge as intrinsically individual, historicism recognizes knowledge as *both* personal *and* collective. Individuals learn and accumulate personal knowledge from the collective knowledge and beliefs held by some larger community —socialized paradigms or Bacon's *idola theatri*—in which they are embedded. When they create new knowledge through individual insight, innovation, or experience, that new knowledge cannot remain personal so long as the individual remains embedded in society. Even scientific, personal, objective reasoning can divorce itself only slowly from traditional, communal understandings about how the world works, learned from society and other people.[93] Civilizations, societies, and formal organizations—governments, firms, churches, associations, interest groups, and others—are protective and conservative depositories for collective knowledge of all types.[94] Every social individual simultaneously and continuously learns from and contributes to social knowledge. Global historicism symbiotically merges the uniqueness of individuality and personal experience with shared humanity, conserved knowledge, preserved history, and social meaning in a collective, global knowing. Historicism is the sum of innovation plus conservatism and the product of individuality times collectivity.

Historicism, Globalism, and the Global Perspective

Global historicism takes a situational view of *both* people with their ideas *and* civilizations with their historical events in a context of unity and continuity beyond chronological time. Emerging from the past as social legacy, institutions and values establish the dimensions and patterns of human relationships and choices and provide stability and cultural continuity across the transformations that change, destroy, and create civilizations. Within the broad scope and depth of the global perspective, historicism projects a world reconstructed by people's choices at every transformation of social reality: a "bounded social totality exhibiting a strong sense of organic coherence."[95]

In contrast to the premodern, narrow, historical perspectives, the lens of historicism does not reveal the ultimate meaning of life or even of history. Unlike faith- or reason-based perspectives, historicism does not dismiss the present as merely a conditioned extension of the past and therefore transitory. The dynamic perspective of historicist globalism perceives living as a deep, complex web of willed, human relationships that link people, natural structures and processes, cultural values, and individual actions. The decisions that people make reflect the social reality in which they live. As small, incremental changes occur, people begin to make different choices in different ways. Good times generate expansion of perspectives, personal ambition, risk acceptance, and the scope of interest and activity. Bad times focus attention, will, and action narrowly on survival. The choices that people make "are made not entirely or even primarily for reasons that can be explained in material terms, but because of changes in cultural mood and expectation."[96] The historicist recognitions of will and the freedom of choice invalidate the absolute universalisms of medieval Christendom and Islam and of ancient Chinese thought and discredit the determinist overtones of Renaissance classicism, Enlightenment rationalism, and modernist positivism.

Time Perspectives

Within the global, historicist perspective, the distinctive details of events, their special circumstances, and their inner complexities explain those events in the chronological time measured by human perception and mechanical clocks—event time. Understanding social change requires more than historical generalization of small, short events into large, long ones. A time perspective across generations extends beyond any sequence of events into a distinct level or dimension of social time as a unit of progress. The *longue durée*, where all history is one great fact about which no generalization is possible, requires not generalization but aggregation for any appreciation of the human condition.

Event Time and Chaos

What Ray Kurzweil has called the Law of Time and Chaos operates most visibly in event time within people's narrow perspectives, although it penetrates deeply into the global perspective as people expand into it. "In a process, the time interval between salient events (that is, events that change the nature of a process or significantly affect the future of the process) expands or contracts along with the amount of chaos."[97] As chaos exponentially increases, event time exponentially decelerates as the intervals between events increase. In a perfectly ordered universe—the instant of the Big Bang—the intervals between catastrophes are in nanoseconds. As each catastrophe complicates the universe and increases chaos, the intervals between them increase exponentially to micro- and milliseconds and eventually to billions of years.

The First Corollary. Within the historicist-global perspective, globalization operates Kurzweil's law as its own inverse corollary. As globalization increases order—and reduces chaos—in the eternal universe of human living, the interval between globally salient events decreases—salient events seem more frequent in event time. This inverse corollary to Kurzweil's law resolves biological evolution, basic scientific advance, the growth of human knowledge, and the globalization of ethical human affairs into broader perspectives of time and space. As humanity learns to understand the universe, it becomes more orderly and people seek, through Schumpeter's creative destruction, to impose even greater order through further human-directed expansion into the global perspective. Kurzweil's law predicts decreasing event-time intervals between *globally salient* events as globalization increases global order and the global perspective exposes more globally salient events.

The Second Corollary. The second corollary operates across *both* event time within narrow perspectives *and* social time within the global perspective. Within narrow perspectives, increasing global order—decreasing chaos within the global perspective—appears as decreasing order and increasing chaos in the uncertainties and unexplained anomalies exposed as narrow perspectives expand. In event time, focused specialists may perceive such uncertainties as functionally catastrophic within their narrow perspectives. Within the global perspective, however, they are little more than local perturbations in social time, rarely the salient events of Kurzweil's law.

Social Time and Order

In social time, the global perspective presents increasing order with greater human understanding and shorter social-time intervals between salient global events that change the nature of global governance and social reality. In accordance with Kurzweil's law, globalization compresses the flexible units of social time as global chaos decreases with increases in human knowledge. Modern people perceive more salient events within the world to which globalization has exposed them during their lifetimes than did earlier generations. Even as event time continues with comfortable regularity and decreasing intervals between narrow-perspective crises, fewer local crises generate transformations of global social reality.

Beneath, however, the increasing order within the global perspective in social time, globalization appears to increase chaos in more local crises of uncertainty and fewer narrow-perspective salient events in event time. Whereas historical, event time passes in uniform increments within any perspective, the units of historicist, social time differ across perspectives. Social time expands and passes in increasing intervals as chaos increases within narrow perspectives under the pressures of globalization. Within the global perspective, in contrast, social time contracts into decreasing intervals as globalization decreases chaos. The anomaly suggests that the dimensions of social time remain invisible within narrow, functional perspectives.

The Paradox of Order and Chaos

Bacon's idols concentrate the second corollary to Kurzweil's Law in the narrow economic, political, and functional perspectives with internal foci on applied technology and specific solutions. As local chaos increases with the greater uncertainties of globalization, people's efforts to understand the anomalies exposed by an expanding perspective generate new local crises that seem to demand re-establishing functional equilibrium. As increasing uncertainty shortens event-time intervals between crises, narrow-perspective specialists tinker with familiar tradition and mold it around each new anomaly into an unstable, local equilibrium, *instead of assimilating the increasing order of the global perspective.* Instead of absorbing and creating new knowledge in social transformation, Bacon's idols teach functionalists to repair traditional models of reality.

Since these local crises of uncertainty and the narrow-perspective repairs and solutions to them are only rarely the salient events that generate social transformation, they often unbalance global order in social time. As crises deepen, expand, and continue, uncertainty threatens to explode any artificial equilibrium from the present into the future. The functional difficulties of maintaining local equilibrium through event-time crisis response generate longer social-time intervals between the salient, *narrow-perspective* events that transform narrow-perspective reality. As globalization increases global order, people's efforts to reestablish local order paradoxically increase and deepen these narrow, functional crises of uncertainty that claim the attention of people bound by Bacon's idols in narrow-perspective, event time. The same mechanism that relieves social stress by reestablishing local equilibrium paradoxically increases the intervals between global catastrophes and Kurzweil's salient events as local solutions persistently blur less-than-global perspectives and inhibit global progress. Within different perspectives, the rates of significant relevant events may be not only different, but contradictory; local disorder may appear as global order; and the local pursuit of equilibrium may restrict global progress.

The Longue Durée

Historicism extends Braudelian time beneath and beyond social and chronological time with his concept of the *longue durée*. Transcending the spatial compass of the present, social time is embedded in a third level of time, the *longue durée*—also known as logical time, model time, or cosmic time. Merging the time and space of present social reality into the totality of human existence, logical time, unlike event time and social time, runs *both* into the past *and* into the future. All points and times in the *longue durée* coexist simultaneously in the mind of an observer, a philosopher-analyst, or humanity itself. The *longue durée* measures civilizatioinal transformations: the very slow shifts in Braudel's *mentalités*—Bacon's *idol specus, idola fori, idola theatri*, or *idola tribus*. Invisible in event time and only sometimes apparent in social time, these ponderous changes are clear only in the *longue durée* over generations, centuries, and millennia within the global perspective.

The a historical, chronological lens, Kurzweilian intervals of event time and the unit of social time decrease from decades to years or months with increases in knowledge. Through the historicist lens, the period of time—the *longue durée*—between civilizational transformations of global social reality decreases from millennia to centuries. Through the lens of historicism, the Law of Time and Chaos resolves any compression or expansion of event time in social time and the *longue durée* and recognizes the uneven and complex influence of triple-level time on thought, perceptions, and progress.

Conjonctures in Time

Braudel also recognized the probability that two or three of the time levels —event time, social time, and the *longue durée*—would occasionally and inevitably intersect in what he identified as *conjonctures*. Braudel's *conjonctures* expanded Bergson's individual constraints and freedoms (Bacon's *idola fori* and *idola theatri*) into the societal perspective, established the contexts for social changes, and explained their consequences. Within *conjunctures*, social choice and action have historically joined human will to resist and overcome Bacon's idols, which constrain people within narrow perspectives. This juncture has usually created *basho* to transform social reality as rising civilizations have displaced or weakened declining ones. During these transient *conjonctures*, people have expanded their perspectives and created new historical lenses by creating new knowledge, establishing new institutions, developing new values, and launching new waves of globalization. *Conjonctures* have included the replacement of the Renaissance lens by the Enlightenment lens in the seventeenth century and the shift from the international perspective to the global perspective in the 1970s. The event time taken by a *conjoncture* forms a new unit of social time, and is usually marked in history by a notable event extending over many years—the Napoleonic Wars—or a single decision —President Nixon's decision to end dollar convertibility.

Double Conjonctures. Through these sporadic intersections between human systems—societies, polities, economies, cultures, or civilizations—in event time and social time, people deliberately and rationally manipulate reality and behavior. Within the double *conjoncture* of event time and social time, people create new knowledge, expand narrow perspectives, and identify new paths for innovation. Incremental innovation emanating from the latest *conjoncture* energizes and measures progress between successive *conjonctures*, which self-selects people as winners and damages others. Human *mentalités* —Bacon's idols—mark the limits of the possible as people expand their narrow perspectives in a double *conjoncture*.

Without the linearity or cyclicity that burdened catastrophism, incrementalism, and uniformitarianism, historicist social time reveals globalizing societies progressing at different paces of social time within different perspective. Their intersection—a *conjoncture*—creates a *basho* that challenges and eventually transforms social reality through operation of a conjunctural dialectic into a new era of social time. The transformations of one distinct social reality into another form units of social time that transcend historical, event time and merge into the *longue durée*. This variable, perspective-dependent social time explains the expansion of perspectives over time in a context of *both* catastrophes *and* increments and replaces any unilinear concept of globalization with fluid expectations.[98]

Triple Conjonctures. At triple intersections between humanity and natural systems in the *longue durée*, human determination, free will, the urge to ask, and the need to answer can overpower the pressures of Bacon's idols and replace the certitudes of failed certainties with new perspectives of life, living, and the universe. Historically, the ponderous changes in human *mentalités* and civilizations have begun in, occurred between, and continued through triple *conjonctures*. Shifts in the *longue durée* have registered a broad recognition of some clear change in human nature—development of time consciousness or recognition of human rights.

Some conjunctural changes in social time consolidate, stabilize, and congeal slowly into fundamental, incremental changes of *mentalités* in the *longue durée*. Others occur as people consciously adjust their *mentalités*, shatter Bacon's idols, and expand their perspectives when all three levels of time intersect. The inevitable, but unpredictable, intersection of all three levels of time and the conjunction of contradictions and crises of uncertainty across several perspectives create a conjunctural dialectic of time. "It begins with an understanding of the contradictions and proceeds to identify the potential for transformation based on concerted action by self-conscious social forces."[99] At these conjunctural points of uncertainty and transition, historicist globalization opens the future to human creativity and will. "Fundamental change is possible, albeit never certain, and this fact makes claims on [humanity's] moral responsibility to act rationally, in good faith, and with strength, to seek a better historical system."[100]

Path Dependence

Although the path into *basho* is a well-known legacy for every society, the direction from a *conjoncture* in transforming social reality cannot be constrained by mechanical laws. The open future is immanent in every *conjoncture*, not something added. Clearly path-dependent, each social transformation of globalization generates not another predictable stage in the evolution of global society but an array of possibilities. The future is the successor of each historical *conjoncture*, which carries the essence of the transformation that society makes to relieve social stresses.[101]

Although neither predicting nor identifying causal mechanisms, path dependence implies far more than any simplistic recognition that the past matters in transforming the present into the future.[102] "Path dependence has to mean, if it is to mean anything, that once a country or region has started down a track, the costs of reversal are very high. There will be other choice points, but the entrenchments of certain institutional arrangements obstruct an easy reversal of the initial choice."[103] Historical institutions—Bacon's *idola fori* and *idola theatri*—which are themselves the results of choices made at some earlier time, create and limit the array of possibilities available to people for making choices and transforming social reality.[104] Preserving continuity with the past, stable institutions and behaviors persist through transformation as "historically changing and cross-nationally varying institutional configurations —interrelations among states and social structures. . . .[These refined values, norms, and memories] have much to do with the development and deployment of systems of ideas, including scientific ideas as well as political or moral ideologies."[105] Although the particularities of historical, social progress —catastrophic or incremental—and current crises often dominate current policies, in its institutional path-dependency, "culture is an important source for the formation and sustenance of social institutions."[106]

Within the global perspective, the path-dependent effect appears at Braudelian *conjonctures* as people conjoin the various narrow perspectives of living and thinking briefly in *basho* to transform them all into a novel social reality. The historicist global perspective exposes path dependence as a powerful conditioner and instrument of human progress, albeit neither a cause in itself nor merely an uncomplicated, vague learning technique in the narrow perspectives of politics, economics, and culture.[107] What seem to be reflexive effects of path dependence within narrow perspectives are nested within the global perspective in a larger transformation created by human will at a *conjoncture* of people's many perspectives across multiple levels of time.

Transformation of social reality does not simply replace one social reality or *modus operandi* arbitrarily with another. Human will, creativity, and knowledge create new realities that include all of humanity's eternal yesterdays in a novel, emergent present that is more effective and more relevant to contemporary living than any of the remembered yesterdays. This historicist path dependence forms the intimate connection that Edmund Burke saw between the historically developed best thoughts, insights, and achievements of humanity—"the general bank and capital of nations and ages"—and the necessary progress of humanity towards the moral good.[108]

NOTES

1. John Micklethwaite and Adrian Wooldridge, *A Future Perfect: The Challenge and Hidden Promise of Globalization* (New York: Random House–Crown Business, 2000), vii.

2. James Burke, *The Day The Universe Changed* (London: British Broadcasting Corporation, 1985), 9.

3. Amanda Gefter, "Throwing Einstein for a Loop," *Scientific American* 287(6) (December 2002): 40–41; 41.

4. Edward O. Wilson, "Resuming the Enlightenment Quest," *Wilson Quarterly* 22(1) (Winter 1998): 16–27; 17.

5. Arnold J. Toynbee, *Civilization on Trial*, in *Civilization on Trial* and *The World and the West* by Arnold J. Toynbee, (New York: Meridian, 1948), 142.

6. David Riesman, with Nathan Glazer and Reuel Denney, *The Lonely Crowd: A Study of the Changing American Character* (New Haven: Yale University Press, [1950] 1967), 15.

7. Wilfred M. McClay, "Fifty Years of *The Lonely Crowd*," *Wilson Quarterly* 22(3) (Summer 1998): 34–42; 37. See also Riesman, *The Lonely Crowd*, 22.

8. Grid-group theory has refined the dichotomy of inner- and other-direction to a four-sector grid that recognizes inner-directed individualists and degrees of other-direction in fatalists, egalitarians, or hierarchists as different cultural features. In the prespective of grid-group theory, all societies are multicultural, although a dominant, dispositional culture predisposes a society to particular forms of institutions and behaviors. For a summary analysis and bibliography on grid-group theory, see Charles Lockhart, "Cultural Contributions to Explaining Institutional Form, Political Change, and Rational Decisions," *Comparative Political Studies* 32(7) (October 1999): 862–893; 864–884.

9. Riesman, *The Lonely Crowd*, 294, 373.

10. A historical social system is a collection of groups linked together by mutual transactions and interactions and by the high probability that changes in one group will lead to changes in the others. Individuals within the system perceive it as stable and permanent within their generations. Within the system's boundaries, interdependence is high; transactions across the boundaries are independent. Political attributes of historical social systems have included nationalism, peace, law, and internal order; economic attributes have included the law of one price, external trade barriers, and systemwide tax regimes. Large historical systems—empires or countries—often comprise smaller subsystems—tribes, provinces, or cities—with different properties.

11. Edward M. Burns, *Western Civilizations* (New York: Norton, 1969), 21–22. See also Fernand Braudel, "The History of Civilizations: The Past Explains the Present," in *On History*, edited by Fernand Braudel, 177–218 (Chicago: University of Chicago Press, 1980),

177; Arnold J. Toynbee, *A Study of History*, 10 vols. (London: Oxford University Press, 1934), vol. 1, 149; Marshall G. S. Hodgson, *Rethinking World History, Essays on Europe, Islam, and World History* (New York: Cambridge University Press, 1993), 84.

12. Robert W. Cox, "Civilizations, Encounters, and Transformations," *Studies in Political Economy* 47(2) (Summer 1995): 7–31; 11.

13. See Carroll Quigley, *The Evolution of Civilizations: An Introduction to Historical Analysis* (Indianapolis, Indiana: Liberty Fund, 1961), 146.

14. Burns, *Western Civilizations*, 5.

15. Stephen Jay Gould, "Pillars of Wisdom," *Natural History* 108(3) (April 1999): 28–34, 87–89; 30.

16. See Thomas Hobbes, *Leviathan*, edited by Crawford B. Macpherson (Harmondsworth: Penguin, [1651] 1968), Book 1, ch. 13, 185–186.

17. Lamarck was already worrying about the rigidities of orthodox, Linnaean, linear evolution in 1801 when he first redefined the Linnaean system under a cautious cover of incomplete data. In 1802, he expanded the old orthodoxy into an innovative, but still linear, perspective based on additional, elegant, exploratory work of Georges Cuvier. Lamarck struggled with the fundamental inconsistencies of progressive, linear evolution for several years until in 1809 he tentatively proposed the concept of unpredictable, nonlinear evolutionary branching. Lamarck's new knowledge not only excluded any perspective of evolutionary progress towards perfection in humans but also replaced the ancient scientific ideal of lawlike predictability with an uncomfortable perspective of natural complexity. In 1820, half a lifetime after his original concerns, in his final book, *Analytic System of Positive Knowledge of Man*, Lamarck finally "advocates the same tree of life that would later become conventional through the influence of Darwin and other early evolutionists." Stephen Jay Gould, "Branching through a Wormhole," *Natural History* 108(2) (March 1999): 24–27, 84–89; 86.

18. One scientific, philosophical historian arbitrarily assigns seven stages to the rise and fall of civilizations: Cultural Mixture; Gestation; Expansion; Conflict; Empire; Decay; and Invasion. Carroll Quigley, *The Evolution of Civilizations: An Introduction to Historical Analysis* (Indianapolis, Indiana: Liberty Fund, 1961), 146. Quigley's discussion of the rise-and-fall process (ch. 5, pp. 128–166) addresses most of humanity's historical civilizations.

19. Marie-Jean-Antoine-Nicolas de Caritat, marquis de Condorcet, *Outlines of an Historical View of the Progress of the Human Mind* (London: J. Johnson, 1795), 4, 307–308, 371.

20. Refining the civilizational and cultural thought of historians or philosophers and the state-centered, territorial power politics of geostrategists, Samuel Huntington has famously transferred clashes of civilizations from the deterministic historical cycle of civilizations to the deliberate, historicist process of globalization. See Toynbee, *A Study of History*, vol. 8, 97–125; Oswald Spengler, *The Decline of the West*, 2 vols. (New York: Knopf, [1926, 1928] 1973), vol. 1, 335–355; vol. 2, 107–110, 416–431; Nikolai I. Danilevskyi, *Russland und Europa* (Osnabruck: Otto Zeller, [1888, 1920] 1965), 19–28; Halford J. Mackinder, *Democratic Ideals and Reality* (New York: Holt, [1919] 1942), 150; Nicholas J. Spykman, *America's Strategy in World Politics: The United States and the Balance of Power* (New York: Harcourt, Brace, 1942), 15–26; Nicholas J. Spykman, *The Geography of the Peace* (New York: Harcourt, Brace, 1944), 3–7, 43, 45, 55–60; Saul B. Cohen, *Geography and Politics in a World Divided* (New York: Random House, 1963), 7–16, 24–28; Samuel P. Huntington, *The Clash of Civilizations and the Remaking of World Order* (New York: Simon and Schuster, 1996), 90–91

21. Stephen Jay Gould, "On Embryos and Ancestors," *Natural History* 107(6) (July-August 1998): 20–22, 58–65; 20.

22. Immanuel Kant, "An Answer to the Question: What is Enlightenment?" in *Perpetual Peace and other Essays*, by Immanuel Kant, translated by Ted Humphrey (Indianapolis: Hackett, 1983), 41.

23. Bernard Ancori, Antoine Bureth, and Patrick Cohendet, "The Economics of Knowledge: The Debate about Codification and Tacit Knowledge," *Industrial and Corporate Change* 9(2) (June 2000): 255–288; 260.

24. Stephen Jay Gould, "Bacon, Brought Home," *Natural History* 108(5) (June 1999): 28–33, 72–78; 28.

25. Anthony Grafton, "Descartes the Dreamer," *The Wilson Quarterly* 20(4) (Autumn 1996): 36–46; 37.

26. Stephen Jay Gould, "The Sharp-Eyed Lynx, Outfoxed by Nature," *Natural History* 107(5) (June 1998): 23–27, 69–73; 72.

27. Francis Bacon, "Valerius Terminus of The Interpretation of Nature with the Annotation of Hermes Stella," in *The Works of Francis Bacon*, edited by James Spedding, Robert L. Ellis, and Douglas D. Heath, 15 vols., vol. 6, 25–76 (Cambridge, Massachusetts: Riverside Press, 1870), 28.

28. See Francis Bacon, *"De Augmentis Scientiarum,"* in *The Works of Francis Bacon*, edited by James Spedding, Robert L. Ellis, and Douglas D. Heath, 15 vols., vol. 6, 87–412, vol. 8, 395–520, and vol. 9, 13–377 (Cambridge, Massachusetts: Riverside Press, 1870), 6: 92–97, 207–214; 8: 477; 9: 308–311, 348–350; Francis Bacon, *Essays or Counsels, Civil and Moral*, "Of Truth," "Of Goodness and Goodness of Nature," "Of Empire," and "Of the True Greatness of Kingdoms and Estates," in *Selected Writings: Essays, Advancement of Learning, New Atlantic* (Franklin Center, Pennsylvania: Franklin Library, 1982), 7–9, 33–35, 50–54, 75–83.

29. In Rome in 1603, several natural philosophers founded the Society of Lynxes with Duke Cesi as patron and named for the Lynx's legendary acuity of vision, which combined sharpness of vision and depth of insight. Cesi seems to have taken the society's emblem from the title page of Giambattista della Porta's *Natural Magic* (1589), which accompanies the lynx with the motto *aspicit et inspicit*—he looks at and looks into.

30. Edward O. Wilson, *Consilience, The Unity of Knowledge* (New York: Knopf, 1998), 30.

31. William F. Bottiglia, "Introduction," in *Voltaire: A Collection of Critical Essays*, edited by William F. Bottiglia, 1–17 (Englewood Cliffs, New Jersey: Prentice-Hall, 1968), 7.

32. Constance Rowe, *Voltaire and the State* (New York: Columbia University Press, 1955), 192.

33. François Marie Arouet de Voltaire, "Government," in *Voltaire: Political Writings*, edited by David Williams, 49–62 (Cambridge: Cambridge University Press, 1994), 59. See also James Chace, "Voltaire's Coconuts—and Ours," *World Policy Journal* 16(2) (Summer 1999): 147–148; 147.

34. Gould, "Pillars of Wisdom," 31.

35. Charles Lyell, *Principles of Geology*, vol. 1, 10th ed. (London: John Murray, 1867), 654.

36. Emile Coué (1857–1926), a French pharmacist, devised this formula for autosuggestive self-improvement. This early psychological treatment was know as Couéism. The original French formula was *"Tous les jours, à tous points de vue, je vais*

de mieux en mieux."

37. Bruce B. Lawrence, *Defenders of God: The Fundamentalist Revolt Against the Modern Age* (San Francisco: Harper and Row, 1989), 17.

38. Modern economics has resolved the uncertainty of maximization with the concepts of *trade-off* and *satisficing.* "The gains from greater accuracy . . . must . . . be balanced against the costs of achieving it." Milton Friedman, *Essays in Positive Economics* (Chicago: University of Chicago Press, 1953), 17. If rational analysis can reach the same result through satisfying a lesser standard as through maximizing, and if the former is easier to implement, then thinkers and policymakers can be analytical satisficers. See Herbert A. Simon, "From Substantive to Procedural Rationality," in *Method and Appraisal in Economics,* edited by Spiro J. Latsis, 129–148 (Cambridge: Cambridge University Press, 1976), 140.

39. Farhang Rajaee, *Globalization on Trial: The Human Condition and the Information Civilization* (West Hartford, Connecticut: Kumarian, 2000), 13.

40. Wilson *Consilience,* 38.

41. The radical Enlightenment thinkers disputed the Judeo-Christian-Islamic theism of an omnipotent, ubiquitous, and omniscient God personally interested in individual human beings, as well as any nonmaterial world of heaven and hell associated with such a God. Rather, however, than endorsing atheism, which connoted cosmic chaos and human triviality, they invented a deism that conceded the existence of a divine creator whose entire nature could be known rationally through the objects and processes that he had created. See Wilson *Consilienc,* 32–33.

42. John Stuart Mill, *Utilitarianism* (Indianapolis, Indiana: Hackett, [1861] 2001), 7; See also Geoffrey Scarre, *Utilitarianism* (London: Routledge, Chapman, and Hall, 1996), 1–26.

43. See Charles P. Snow, *The Two Cultures and the Scientific Revolution* (New York: Cambridge University Press, 1959), 4–18.

44. Wilson, "Resuming the Enlightenment Quest," 27.

45. Andrew J. Bacevich, "New Rome, New Jerusalem," *The Wilson Quarterly* 26(3) (Summer 2002): 50–58; 58.

46. For a depiction of modernism as a system of world order, see Stephen E. Toulmin, *Cosmopolis: The Hidden Agenda of Modernity* (New York: Free Press, 1990), ch. 3, 89–137.

47. Nick Stevenson, "Globalization and Cultural Political Economy," in *Globalization and Its Critics,* edited by Randall D. Germain, 91–113 (New York: St. Martin's, 2000), 111.

48. See Fernand Braudel, *Capitalism and Material Life, 1400–1800,* translated by Miriam Kochan (New York: Harper & Row, 1963), xi–xv; Fernand Braudel, *Civilization and Capitalism, 15th–18th Century, Vol 3, The Perspective of the World,* translated by Siân Reynolds (London: Collins/Fontana, 1984), 630. Zygmunt Bauman referred to the Modernity project as the imperative to understand the world from a perspective that did not include chaos or ambivalence. Zygmunt Bauman, *Modernity and Ambivalence* (Cambridge, Massachusetts: Polity, 1991), 4–5, 15–16.

49. Randall D. Germain, "Globalization in Historical Perspective," in *Globalization and Its Critics,* edited by Randall D. Germain, 67–90 (New York: St. Martin's, 2000), 78.

50. See Braudel, *Civilization and Capitalism,* 457.

51. Germain, "Globalization in Historical Perspective," 82.

52. "Lots of It About," *The Economist* 365(8303) (14 December 2002): 62–63; 63.

53. Anthony Giddens, *Runaway World: How Globalization Is Reshaping Our Lives* (London: Profile, 1999), 24.

54. Anthony Grafton, "Descartes the Dreamer," *The Wilson Quarterly* 20(4) (Autumn 1996): 36–46; 40.

55. Burke, *The Day The Universe Changed*, 14.

56. After finding the Red Queen in the spacious garden of Looking Glass House, Alice was mysteriously entered into an exhausting Red Queen's Race. After catching her breath, she observed that "somehow or other, they began to run. . . . The most obvious part of the thing was that the trees and the other things round them never changed their places at all: however fast they went, they never seemed to pass anything. . . . [After the race the Red Queen explained that] it takes all the running you can do to keep in the same place. If you want to get somewhere else, you must run at least twice as fast as that." Lewis Carroll, *Through the Looking Glass and What Alice Found There* (New York: Random House, 1946), 30–32.

57. Niles Eldridge, "Evolution and Environment," in *Life in the Balance: Humanity and the Biodiversity Crisis* (Princeton: Princeton University Press, 1998) 59.

58. Carol Ezzell, "Clocking Cultures," *Scientific American* 287(3) (September 2002): 74–75; 74.

59. Paul Davies, "The Mysterious Flow," *Scientific American* 287(3) (September 2002): 40–47; 40–41.

60. Malcolm Waters, *Globalization* (London: Routledge, 1995), 55. See also David Harvey, *The Condition of Postmodernity: An Enquiry into the Origins of Social Change* (Oxford: Blackwell, 1989), 241.

61. "*La durée toute pure est la forme que prend la succession de nos états de conscience quand notre moi se laisse vivre, quand il s'abstient d'établir une séparation entre l'état présent et les états antérieurs.*" (The essence of the *durée* is the form taken by the succession of the states of consciousness when the self asserts itself and does not separate present consciousness from the past.) Henri Bergson, *Essai sur les Donnés Immédiates de la Conscience*, 144th ed. (Paris: Presses Universitaires de France, [1927] 1970), 74–75. See also 73–97, 147–149, 160, 165, 170. See also George L. S. Shackle, *Decision, Order, and Time in Human Affairs*, 2d ed. (Cambridge: Cambridge University Press, 1969), ch. 3, 14–21, 20, 38.

62. Herbert A. Simon, "Organizing and Coordinating Talk and Silence in Organizations," *Industrial and Corporate Change* 11(3) (June 2002): 611–618; 614.

63. James Surowiecki, "A Virtuous Cycle," *Forbes* 170(13) (23 December 2002): 248–256; 250.

64. Ulrich Beck, *Risk Society* (London: Sage, 1992), 20.

65. Beck, *Risk Society*, 44.

66. Edward O. Wilson, "The Bottleneck," *Scientific American* 286(2) (February 2002): 82–91; 86.

67. Robert S. Chase, "The More Things Change . . .; Learning from Other Eras of 'Unprecedented' Globalization," reviewing *Globalization and History: The Evolution of the Nineteenth Century Atlantic Economy*, by Kevin H. O'Rourke and Jeffrey G. Williamson (Cambridge: MIT Press, 1999), *SAIS Review* 20(2) (Summer-Fall 2000): 223–229; 223.

68. Anne-Robert-Jacques Turgot, "A Philosophical Review of the Successive Advances of the Human Mind," in *Turgot on Progress, Sociology, and Economics*, edited and translated by Ronald L. Meek, 41–59 (Cambridge: Cambridge University Press, 1973), 41.

69. Craig Murphy, "Globalization and Governance: A Historical Perspective," in *Globalization and Europe*, edited by Roland Axtmann, 144–163 (London: Pinter, 1998), 148.

70. Claes G. Ryn, *Will, Imagination, and Reason: Babbitt, Croce, and the Problem of Reality* (New Brunswick, New Jersey: Transaction, 1997), 144.

71. Irving Babbitt, *Rousseau and Romanticism* (Austin: University of Texas Press, 1977), 7.

72. See Joseph F. Baldacchino, Jr., "The Value-Centered Historicism of Edmund Burke," *Modern Age* 27(2) (Spring 1983), 139–145; 141–142.

73. Germain, "Globalization in Historical Perspective," 73.

74. Germain, "Globalization in Historical Perspective," 88.

75. See Steven Best, *The Politics of Historical Vision* (New York: Guilford, 1995).

76. Ryn, *Will, Imagination, and Reason*, 29–30.

77. Edmund Burke, *Reflections on the Revolution in France* (Indianapolis, Indiana: Hackett, [1790–1792] 1987), 191–192. See also 151–153, 189. Edmund Burke used these terms interchangeably. See also Edmund Burke, *The Works of Edmund Burke*, vol. 2, *Letter to the Sheriffs of Bristol* (London: Bohn's Standard Library, 1886), 7, 27.

78. See Irving Babbitt, *Democracy and Leadership* (Indianapolis, Indiana: Liberty Classics, [1924] 1979), 28.

79. Mark S. Granovetter, "Economic Action and Social Structure: The Problem of Embeddedness," *American Journal of Sociology* 91(3) (November 1985): 481–510, 487.

80. See Richard R. Nelson, "A Retrospective," in *National Innovation Systems: A Comparative Analysis*, edited by Richard R. Nelson, 505–523 (New York: Oxford University Press, 1993), 509–520.

81. Babbitt, *Democracy and Leadership*, 229.

82. Thomas S. Eliot, *Selected Essays* (New York: Harcourt, Brace, 1960), 425.

83. Benedetto Croce, *Aesthetic*, 2d rev. ed. (London: Macmillan, 1922), 49–50.

84. Babbitt, *Democracy and Leadership*, 171–172.

85. Ryn, *Will, Imagination, and Reason*, 136.

86. "Back to the Classics," *The Economist* 339(7966) (18 May 1996): 85–87; 86.

87. See Joseph A. Schumpeter, *Capitalism, Socialism, and Democracy* (New York: Harper and Brothers, 1942), ch. 7, pp. 81–86.

88. "Dire que la conscience est historique, ce n'est past seulement dire qu'il y a quelque chose, comme du temps pour elle, mais qu'*elle est temps*. Or la conscience est toujours conscience de quelque chose, et une élucidation aussi bien psychologique que phénoménologique de la conscience va mettre à jour une série infinie d'intentionalités, c'est-à-dire de consciences. . . . En ce sens la conscience est flux de vécus (Erlebnisse), qui sont tous au présent." Jean-François Lyotard, *La Phénoménologie* (Paris: Presses Universitaires de France, 1967), 94–95.

89. See Maurice Merleau-Ponty, *Phénoménologie de la Perception* (Paris: Gallimard, 1945), 472.

90. "Il est clair que le passé est comme noèse un 'maintenant' *en même temps* qu'un 'ne plus' comme noème, l'avenir un 'maintenant' en même temps qu'un 'pas encore,' et dès lors il ne faut pas dire que le temps s'ecoule *dans* la conscience, c'est au contraire la conscience qui, a partir de son maintenant, déploie ou constitue le temps." Lyotard, *La Phénoménologie*, 96.

91. See Raymond Aron, *Introduction à la Philosophie de l'Histoire* (Paris: Gallimard, 1938), 88.

92. See Lyotard, *La Phénoménologie*, 106.

93. See Paul Nightingale, "A Cognitive Model of Innovation," *Research Policy* 27(7) (November 1998): 689–709; 692; Stephen J. Gould, *The Mismeasure of Man* (New York: Norton, 1996), 25–26, 53–55.

94. See Richard R. Nelson and Sidney G. Winter, *An Evolutionary Theory of Economic Change* (Cambridge: Belknap, Harvard University Press, 1982), 99–107.

95. Braudel, *Civilization and Capitalism* 22.

96. David Hackett Fischer, *The Great Wave: Price Revolutions and the Rhythm of History* (New York: Oxford University Press, 1996), 247.

97. Ray Kurzweil, *The Age of Spiritual Machines* (New York: Viking Penguin, 1999), 29; see also Edward J. Wilkins, "The Mind Electric," *Sextant: The Journal of Salem State College* 10(2) (Spring 2000): 40–43.

98. See E. N. Helleiner, "Braudelian Reflections on Globalization: The Historian as Pioneer," in *Innovation and Transformation in International Studies*, edited by Stephen Gill and James H. Mittelman, 90–104 (Cambridge: Cambridge University Press, 1997), 93–96.

99. Robert W. Cox, "A Perspective on Globalization," in *Globalization: Critical Reflections*, edited by James H. Mittelman, 21–30 (Boulder, Colorado: Lynne Rienner, 1996), 27.

100. Immanuel Wallerstein, "The Prospect of Politics," *Civilization* 5(2) (April-May 1998): 70–77; 72.

101. "La société global qui s'en trouve affectée ne peut être cernée comme une chose évoluante selon les lois de la mécanique, et qu'à une étape de ce systéme complexe, ne succède pas *une* étape, mais un éventail d'éventualités. . . . Enfin ce futur ouvert appartient en tant qu'ouvert à la conjoncture présente ell-même, il ne lui est pas surajouté, c'est elle qui se prolonge en lui comme dans sa propre essence." Lyotard, *La Phénoménologie*, 106–107.

102. See Randall Hansen, "Globalization, Embedded Realism, and Path Dependence," *Comparative Political Studies* 35(3) (April 2002): 259–283; 270.

103. Margaret Levi, "A Model, a Method, and a Map: Rational Choice in Comparative and Historical Analysis," in *Comparative Politics: Rationality, Culture, and Structure*, edited by Mark I. Lichbach and Alan S. Zuckerman, 19–41 (Cambridge: Cambridge University Press, 1997), 27.

104. See Stephen D. Krasner, "Sovereignty: An Institutional Perspective," *Comparative Political Studies* 21(1) (February 1988): 66–94; 71–72.

105. See Dietrich Rueschemeyer and Theda Skocpol, eds., *States, Social Knowledge, and the Origins of Modern Social Policies* (Princeton: Princeton University Press, 1996), 4.

106. Lockhart, "Cultural Contributions to Explaining Institutional Form, Political Change, and Rational Decisions," 868.

107. See Krasner, "Sovereignty, 71–72; Hansen, "Globalization, Embedded Realism, and Path Dependence," 270–271; Paul Pierson, "When Effect Becomes Cause: Policy Feedback and Political Change," *World Politics* 45(4) (July 1993): 595–628; 597.

108. Burke, *Reflections on the Revolution in France*, 76.

4

THE IDEA OF PROGRESS

Within any perspective, the notion of change is implicit in any definition of globalization. Centuries of philosophy and rationality have focused most understandings of change into two broad dynamics. Unpatterned change embraces *both* stasis or the absence of change *and* change imposed by exogenous, uncontrollable forces–the gods, nature, destiny, chance, or the occult. Patterned change includes cycles of repetitive changes around static equilibrium; incremental change in some direction; and deliberate, fundamental transformation of a system from past reality to future reality.

The idea of progress captured humanity as it passed into modernity, although ancient thinkers had speculated about incremental change from at least the fourth century B.C. Whereas Aristotle and other classical philosophers thought of progress towards various ideal visions of human perfection, justice, or happiness, modernists identified progress in terms of the human condition. As modernity deepened, historians noted apparently unpredictable points when economic, political, social, and environmental systems seemed to transform themselves to relieve systemic stresses. Although stability and equilibrium seemed to persist for long periods, these transformations seemed to punctuate some undeniable, continuing improvement in the human condition. People developed a deep faith in progress, the conviction that things will surely get better.

Although the word *progress* carries a host of meanings and implications, few would quibble about its meliorative content. Whatever the past was, the future will be better! People accept the idea of progress as "directional change, that there is a progression, an identifiable sequence of alterations in the characteristics of specific entities."[1] Arising from humanity's maturing consciousness of time, the idea of progress is a theory that binds the history of the past to a prophecy of the future. The theory of progress is a strictly modern idea, depending not only on time consciousness but on the prevalence of rationality.

Faith in progress requires a deterministic confidence that the patterns of history are stable and predictable. Belief in progress contains a belief in globalization, a conviction that humanity is progressing through time towards a better future. Any variety among peoples and individuals exists only because they are at different stations on their paths of progress, which may be distinct but are definitely parallel. Unlike conflict resolution, crisis management, or problem solving, progress appears as sociocultural changes over decades and centuries rather than the volatile fluctuations in political power or wealth.

Until the Enlightenment, assertions of progress did not command general assent. Even the ubiquitous modern faith in progress often goes little deeper than confidence that technology will continue to provide prosperity to make the rich richer and the poor less miserable. Over four centuries, people have smuggled the idea of progress into every perspective of their lives and linked it firmly to knowledge and technology. Beyond an unconscious faith, however, understanding of progress remains shallow, confused, and uncertain.

PREMODERN IDEAS OF PROGRESS

Ancient civilizations were locked within various perspectives of unpatterned change, which people could not control or even understand. As societies formed, people began to observe that the texture of life was broadly stable, patterns recurred, and events repeated themselves endlessly in birth, growth, politics, economics, and death. Within the stability of living, people noticed some regularity in the patterns of variation: cycles. Social cycles appeared as the rise and decline of civilizations. Political cycles reflected shifts in hegemony or a balance of power. Economic cycles produced depressions and prosperity. With glacial slowness, some process seemed to be making life more complex and structured as repeatedly civilization recycled itself. To deal with this process, "past societies have stressed stability over time, survival of useful institutions, perpetuation of social values, and refinement of existing systemic structures as human perspectives of [life] slowly changed."[2]

Social change and the human condition were in the hands of the gods or fate, not within the power of people. With the slow evolution of thought, ancient peoples came to accept that improvement evolved gradually from constant, steady, incremental accumulation of knowledge and human learning. Although people could not create new knowledge, they could learn bits of absolute truth from nature and from God. To avoid tedious relearning from nature, people learned from human teachers what earlier people had learned before. As human knowledge accumulated, faith in progress through gradual, incremental change became "an ancient claim embodied in the victory cry of Aesop's tortoise, 'slow and steady wins the race.'"[3]

As teaching developed imperceptibly through learning, philosophers and scientists began to create new knowledge. Usually in isolated thought but occasionally in primitive *basho*, new knowledge eventually transformed the world. Innovation, discovery, and invention stimulated by the diffusion of knowledge accelerated incremental progress. Ordinary people were making their lives better with inventions that emerged from new knowledge.

Some people were deep thinkers and idealists who sought to solve the dilemma of human misery through innovations in faith, compassion, and understanding. The emergence of Asian Confucianism and Buddhism and European-Muslim monotheism introduced the ideals of perfection and human perfectibility as the goal and ultimate result of progress. Within this spiritual perspective, faith and right behavior were the preferred instruments of human perfectibility to be achieved through incremental individual and social progress.

Other people were entrepreneurs, craftsmen, and peasants who had, and developed, the "capitalist spirit [which] comprises within itself, besides the spirit of enterprise and the desire for gain, . . . the views and convictions (and of course the actions and conduct based upon them) of a respectable citizen and head of a family, no less than of an honest tradesman."[4] The continuing expansion of trade with more prosperous peoples sharpened ancient urges towards accumulation of wealth. Progress for *both* individuals *and* society appeared as much in wealth and prosperity as in human perfection. Within this materialist perspective, trade, commerce, and industry were the instruments of material progress, which could occur alongside human progress.

As more people learned more, technology, science, and philosophy expanded incremental progress into paths of materialism, scientism, and deism. An epistemological sort of globalization recalling the *basho* of the sixth century B.C., which created the new knowledge of universal unity, emerged in the late Middle Ages. The fourteenth-century *conjoncture* of humanism, scientism, and deism expanded *basho* beyond learned elites and deepened knowledge and progress to embrace *both* people *and* truth. Through incremental progress over some three centuries, this conjunctural *basho* created the new knowledge that eventually transformed the Renaissance into the Enlightenment.

Over the epochal periods of premodernity, civilizations incrementally refined institutions, ideas, and living patterns according to times, places, and perspectives. Predicted by most religions, incremental progress occurred along and within narrow perspectives—astronomy, mathematics, literature, art, politics, or economics. It gradually shaped and focused human values as civilizations progressed slowly towards perfection. Greece and the Roman republic stressed politics, whereas the Roman empire stressed order, economics, literature, and art. Ancient China stressed virtue and civil order. Medieval Europe stressed religion, while early Islam stressed science and art. After Renaissance Europe stressed prosperity and classical wisdom, the Enlightenment stressed rationality. Modernity stressed prosperity and security, while postmodernity stresses dual individual and social identities. Since, until late modernity, incremental progress was never able to expand to more than speculation about a global perspective, progress and incremental changes were narrow, local, and functional, rather than universal.

MODERN NOTIONS OF PROGRESS

By the seventeenth century, especially in Europe, merchants, entrepreneurs, peasants, and bankers were learning that the work of technicians, managers, scientists, and clerks, rather than the dreams of philosophers and priests, were making things better. The marriage of practical, industrial experience with the new knowledge of rational science spawned the idea of progress as their natural child. In Europe and Asia, both parents found the slogan of material progress useful and fruitful, while the North Americans found it natural and comfortable. Much concerned with economic and material standards of living, people associated progress with technological advance as a modern *deus ex machina* that has been onstage so long that many people forget the machinery that put it there.[5] For moderns, technology—like nature and the gods of the premodern past—became a true *deus* with its own uncontrollable and unpredictable dynamic and no need for the *machina*. For people who could not ignore the *machina*, technology was the result of new knowledge, innovation, scientific institutions, advancing along some path of progress determined by people, and the current needs and fashions of social reality.

The Darwinian theory of natural selection banished "the idea of perfection from the discussion of progress. Progress became 'greater fitness for purpose' relative to some possibly transient selection environment."[6] In the context of continuing technological innovation towards greater social utility, the continuing advances of scientific knowledge and their expansion into human and social affairs seemed to assure the inevitability of progress. Technology and the social reality that applied it were bringing people together and offering material improvements for all through globalization.

Multiple Perspectives

Despite continuing poverty, misery, oppression, and disease, people still believe powerfully in progress. Within and across their various functional perspectives, modern people use the technological idea of progress to explain the past, focus the present, and chart their paths into the future. Like their ancestors, people of the twenty-first century can perceive progress in several perspectives and through several historical lenses.

Catastrophist

Within catastrophist perspectives, *both* knowledge creation *and* progress are intrinsically unpredictable or random and depend on the institutional, natural, and human constraints in which *basho* operates and are not inevitable. Nor is does *basho* focus new scientific or philosophical principles within the narrow, functional perspectives in which people live their lives. Although the new knowledge created in *basho* transforms human social reality in social time and the *longue durée*, people live under the stresses and urgencies of event time. The essential, catastrophic process that links new knowledge to present living is innovation. Neither social transformation nor knowledge energizes progress, but the catastrophic, creative destruction of technological innovation. The technological link between social time and event time converts the catastrophic new knowledge of social transformation through innovation into incremental progress that benefits people in the here and now.

Incrementalist

Within incrementalist perspectives, the idea of progress embodies directional change, an orderly progression through a sequence of deliberate, willed alterations in something. Independent of new knowledge or *basho*, technology, discovery, and invention inspired by human will are the common carriers of progress. For Aristotle, incremental progress towards improvement in the human condition was inevitable and, like Darwinian evolution, glacially slow. Even though people might not control, do not understand, and may not even perceive the process within their narrow perspectives, they have faith that willed efforts to advance technology will inevitably generate progress. Through different logic, incrementalists reach the catastrophist conclusion about progress. Even though cosmic forces generate catastrophic events and change, the key to human progress is applied technology, not expanding knowledge to understand either those forces or any absolute truth.

Economic

The modern notion of economic progress rejects "the rightly discredited idea of progress as an intrinsic drive to perfection controlled by natural laws. Instead, whatever directional changes [that] we observe are the unintended consequences of those variation, selection, and development processes that characterize capitalism as a system."[7] Learning, innovation, and technologies link progress closely to economic prosperity. Modern understandings of history include the idea of broad material progress over an average of global humanity.[8] "Progress is associated with the expansion of the range and scale of productive opportunity and measured, albeit very imperfectly, by the growth of GDP [gross domestic product] per head over time."[9] This modern perspective relates economics to progress by relegating nonmarket activities, leisure, and public goods—law and order—to products or *outputs* of the capitalist system.[10] Even without accurate measures of progress, "one would have to be remarkably curmudgeonly to deny that an economy such as the USA [United States of America] has made progress between 1900 and 2000. . . . the extension of the expected lifespan, the decline in infant mortality, the reduction in the duration of the working life all have released the gift of time in a fundamental way. Surely that is progress."[11]

Expansive

Beyond prosperity or truth, the expansive idea of progress recognizes the growing power of knowledge and technology over the earth's environment, over the human condition, and even over life itself. Although some ideologies still proclaim revolution as a necessary process for progress, others prefer orderly reform of existing institutions. Both approaches foresee the inevitable happier future for all people, which is the ultimate aim of progress. "Observing the power of the new science and technology, and the growing social control made possible by it, they also both share the earlier faith in the growing possibility of the humanity of man towards his fellow men."[12]

Expansion of progress is natural and also desirable, and material progress is the essential precondition for its expansion into other perspectives. The modern preoccupation with material progress and the brilliant model of Euro-American prosperity have fostered the expectation that progress is predictable and orderly. Once people make certain economic and political adjustments, every society will enter the domain of self-sustaining, continuing economic development. Progress, in the form of modern economic growth, will certainly bring other improvements—democracy, education, freedom, power over the environment, and social pride—that will generate further growth. This self-sustaining cycle of expansive economic growth has become the talisman for expanding progress. Beyond mere prosperity and freedom, expansive progress promises ever more assistance for human frailties and growing opportunities for personal fulfillment and social achievement. Whether animated by the humanist optimism of Mahatma Gandhi, the materialism of Karl Marx, or self-confident American liberalism, expansive progress promises continued progress through economic growth as more things continue to improve.

Cautious

With its notoriously short memory, the public continues to doubt the reality of progress. The global media obsessions with tragedy and catastrophe generate popular misgivings that reflect current experience as spectators. The frightening experiences of current generations and the rediscovery of evil have dulled the shine of progress with the motif that human nature does not change. Something of the primitive fear of the unknown has infected the modern idea of progress. More salient, however is the fear of what is known, of what has been discovered as new knowledge. Moreover, progress seems to have increased the power of people for evil apace with the power for good. Progress itself may be inevitable, but people drive it towards good and continuing improvement or towards evil and destruction. To constrain evil and to focus progress on the good, many cautious people seek popular constraints on political and economic power. Instead of inevitable orderly progress towards improvement, skeptics conclude that orderly society and orderly change are neither natural nor normal and certainly not inevitable but are, instead, rare and precarious achievements of atypical societies.

PROGRESS THROUGH THE LENS OF HISTORICISM

Through the historicist lens, progress emerges within the global perspective from the dual processes of *both* knowledge-based change through drastic transformation *and* incremental change. A progressive society has the capacity to adjust its institutions to solve the urgent problems of the day. More important, it can generate and absorb the consequences of *both* social transformation *and* evolutionary change. Each generation also transforms its own social reality, which determines the properties and features of the next generation's perspectives on living. Drastic social transformation emerges from the new knowledge created in conjunctural *basho*, which operates to relieve the social stresses that formed *basho*. Incremental progress appears in the adaptation of a society's institutions, values, and behaviors to the context and content of new knowledge, which *both* creates the social stability necessary for distributed innovation *and* unites past to future through the present. The dynamic of progress converts new knowledge through diffusing, varying, selecting, developing, combining, and innovating into useful actions and items and for expanding it again into new knowledge. Moreover, the global perspective recognizes social progress as autogenous and self-generating.

Progress through Confusion

Confusion about progress had arisen from the Renaissance rediscovery of the rise and fall of humanity's various civilizations. History recorded long periods when civilizations were static and occupied themselves within their own narrow perspectives. Any progress appeared as incremental refinements of institutions, improved ideas and patterns of living, and occasional development of technological innovations. Novel inventions have repeatedly "remained dormant in a society until at last—usually for reasons which remain mysterious—they awaken and become active elements in the shaping of a culture to which they are not entirely novel. . . . The acceptance or rejection of an invention, or the extent to which its implications are realized if it is accepted, depends quite as much upon the condition of a society, and upon the imagination of its leaders, as upon the nature of the technological item itself."[13]

Historical confusion and disruption of social order presented opportunities for cultural innovation, adoption of dormant inventions, and diffusion of knowledge within a stable society. These periods of confusing opportunity for incremental progress were punctuated by abrupt, brief periods of catastrophic change. Social transformation multiplied confusion as new institutions, ways of thinking, and patterns of living often expanded into new civilizations. These punctuations often marked the rise and fall of particular civilizations. Despite apparent regularity, modern historians recognize "that the process is neither rigid nor single in any society, but rather that each civilization is a confused congeries of such processes in all types of human activities."[14]

Intrasocietal Innovation

Social progress intuitively involves all of the people, cultures, and elements of a civilization, inner-directed, other-directed, egalitarian, fatalistic, or idiosyncratically balanced between external prescription and group affiliation.[15] The development and sustenance of individual and human rights and market-based institutions by individualistic cultural elements within society have been crucial for progress. Inner-directed citizens armed with these rights and institutions have regularly created new knowledge and generated the innovations that have produced social progress. The market-based cultural vision that is unique to individualism launches progress from personal liberty and market efficiency towards economic prosperity.[16] Other-directed hierarchists achieve progress through remarkable feats of social mobilization through tutelary systems to create bureaucratic expertise, preserve social order, expand provision of public goods, or energize social development.[17] Hierarchists, however, find the indirection and confusion of market-based progress uncomfortable and prefer a master plan for progress.

Egalitarians within society perceive progress as creating person-respecting social solidarity and integration that reinforce individual identities but discourage alienation.[18] The stratifying effects of markets and bureaucracies become status differences that erode any senses of self-esteem, compassion, or inclusive social equality. Egalitarians unite policy and progress with ethics in their "focus on integrative systems: on processes, transactions, and institutions which promote an individual's sense of identity, participation, and community and allow him more freedom of choice for the expression of altruism and which, simultaneously, discourage a sense of individual alienation."[19]

Although change rarely emerges from them, the fatalistic corners of society form a reservoir for the social discontent and stress that launches progress in revolutionary social transformations. The interactions between all of the internal cultures and ways of living in multicultural civilizations often involve stress and conflict as distinct cultures seek to extend their preferred institutions and values and reshape society in their own images. "The inevitable result of the intercultural, but intrasocietal, conflict is social change, as issues raised by historical contingencies favor one culture and then another."[20] Stable, robust societies can often absorb such stressful changes through intrasocietal innovation, rearranging priorities, or conflict resolution. Historically, when social disruptions and stresses have stretched the fabrics of civilizations too thin, they have relieved social stresses by rending asunder in the periodic transformations of social reality that have punctuated history.

Transformations and Punctuations

The Swiss historian Jacob Burckhardt (1818–1897) may have had these punctuations in mind in his references to the rare "crises of history . . . leading to vital transformations." These critical transformations emerged from some deep, stress-laden imbalance across the various perspectives of society—for Burckhardt, the state, religion, and culture—that had lost their links with their civilizational origins. When something rends the fabric of society, "a crisis in the whole state of things is produced, involving whole epochs and all or many peoples of the same civilization, since invasions, undertaken and suffered, ensue of themselves. The historical process is suddenly accelerated in terrifying fashion." Such historical crises diffuse electrically through entire civilizations to infect unconnected individuals with the blind conviction that things must change. The result of such crises is that things do change. For Burckhardt, these critical punctuations of history, rather than the smooth rise and fall of civilizations, are the roots of progress.[21] For knowledge creation, these punctuations form the contexts of *basho* and social transformation. For people, they are the events that create and relieve the stresses of daily living.

During historical punctuations, people transformed the social reality of an old civilization into an inchoate social reality of a new—revolutionary, refined, or reformed—civilization. Beyond *sometimes* launching new civilizations, these periodic transformations have uniformly marked the expansion of people's perspectives and the creation of new knowledge in *basho*. Expansion and globalization have been only loosely coordinated with civilizational risings and fallings, whether incremental or catastrophic, but closely correlated with civilizational transformations. Beyond marking civilizational histories in social time, which may have shown incremental progress, these punctuations have launched the major waves of expansive globalization throughout history.

Confusion, Innovation, or Transformation?

In the current institutional and cultural context, the accumulation of social stresses in confusion stimulates incremental progress through innovation in event time. Human will provides the energy and direction for social transformation through *basho* in social time. Many functional transformations occur within a single, narrow perspective and outside a conjunctural intersection of event time and social time. Beyond relieving functional stress, knowledge created through these narrow-perspective *basho* has often generated incremental innovation for scientific and technological progress between *conjonctures*. Although increasing local, narrow-perspective order, these narrow-perspective transformations have paradoxically generated much of the global confusion and social stress that have led to successive civilizational crises.

To relieve cross-perspective confusion and stresses, people form global *basho* at double and triple *conjonctures*. The global knowledge that people create in these *basho* extends beyond functional science and technology and has informed humanity's progress in the arts, humanities, and philosophy. The *basho* that have emerged from global confusion in triple *conjonctures* have introduced people to the *longue durée* and the global perspective. Through the historicist lens, the triple-intersection *conjoncture* is eternal and double *conjonctures* are periodic as narrow-perspective *basho* emerge and disappear in their wakes. With each *conjoncture*, the historicist dynamic recycles and begins anew with a new *basho* in a new, transformed, social reality.

Punctuated, Parallel Progress

Neo-Platonic catastrophist and Condorcet's incrementalist perspectives excluded human direction or technology in any sort of progress, although people could learn about the process. Modern people, however, insisted on active intervention in the flows of progress and globalization to pursue deliberate aims with actions that had predictable results. The historicist perspective introduced human will, determination, and creativity but left people morally blind about what to do or create and any ultimate goal of progress. One approach has been to respond to cycles of economic forces. Another stresses the urgency of current crises, and a third allows humanity to follow several paths into the future.

Cyclical Transformation

The lens of historicism resolves Condorcet's progressive incrementalism and Lyell's static-cyclical uniformitarianism into a series of social epicycles that embody aggregate, incremental social progress. Relying primarily on economic forces, each epicycle involves a wave of globalization and a minor economic transformation that carries politics and culture along with it into the future. The rich sociological insights of Antonio Gramsci complement Karl Polanyi's perspicacious double movement—an expansion of market forces and the reactive social demands for protection against the stressful, disruptive, and polarizing effects of capitalism. Craig Murphy has melded the two concepts in a cycle of build-thrive-clash-grab-hoard.[22]

As the cycle begins, firms, governments, and people make large investments—economic, political, and psychological—in new expansive industries, regimes, and ideas beyond the narrow perspectives of contemporary orthodoxy. As a new social reality begins to thrive, these investments eventually generate broad prosperity, stability, and satisfaction that mitigate the trauma, stresses, and turmoil of change. A hubris born in thriving institutions, ideas, and markets begins to presage the *next* globalizing transformation in a widespread shift of resources to novel, high-risk, global projects. Globalization quickly exposes latent clashes—business with labor, poor countries with rich societies, ideological confrontations, struggles for power, and cultural disputes about rights or truth—as faults and gaps in prosperity, global peace, and intercultural injustice. As popular confidence wanes and social order decays into tremors of unrelieved stress, capitalists take profits, governments concentrate power, and societies consolidate cultural values in a paroxysm of international competition.

At this stage of explosive social stress, Bacon's idols celebrate pragmatism, realism, and fundamentalism as the only obvious, rational solutions to humanity's discomforts, as society fragments into conservative factions and progressive, globalizing interests.[23] Gramscians note that this reassertive antiglobalism stimulates tumultuous economic speculation throughout the world, which is transient, shallow, and irrational. Speculative bubbles inevitably burst into economic stagnation, political fragmentation, and cultural isolation. The ensuing explosion of social stress into general crisis has historically introduced Murphy's hoarding—the reactive half of Polanyi's double movement against extremist, liberal fundamentalism, or Gramsci's passive revolutions. As the antithesis of prosperity, the hoarding phase returns the cycle to the creative-destructive rebuilding of social reality that activates another cycle of globalization.[24] Whether understood as Murphy's hoarding, Polanyi's reaction, or Gramsci's revolution, accumulating social stresses generate *basho* to relieve stress with new knowledge, launch incremental innovation, and lay the foundations for the next wave of globalization.

Crisis Response

Throughout history, great minds have developed new knowledge and formulated novel perceptions of social reality in periods of confusion and uncertainty. Their knowledge transformed their epochs in broad, profound reactions to what they perceived as world-shattering social stresses, crisis, or disorder. Among the parade of ancient thinkers that expanded humanity's perspectives from crisis and destruction to hope and creation were Confucius (551–479 B.C.), Kautilya (4th century B.C.), Plato (427–347 B.C.), Jesus of Nazareth (A.D. 1–33), Augustine (354–430), and Mazdak (5th century). Thomas Aquinas (1225–1274), Ibn Khaldun (1332–1406), Macchiavelli (1469–1527), Thomas Hobbes (1588–1679), John Locke (1632–1704), and Jean-Jacques Rousseau (1712–1778) continued the pageant through premodernity.[25]

Modern thinkers, including Thomas Jefferson (1743–1826), Karl Marx (1818–1883), Woodrow Wilson (1856–1924), Franklin D. Roosevelt (1882–1945), Mahatma Ghandi (1869–1948), or Mao Tse-tung (1893–1976), have also struggled to understand the mounting disorder and spreading stresses of their societies. As civilizations have continued to develop beyond the limits of current social realities and the narrow perspectives of the past towards the global perspective, the motivation of crisis resolution has universally been to restore order to human living. The results, however, have been dramatic transformations of social reality, destruction of the old set of Bacon's idols and persistent expansion of humanity's perspectives with new knowledge.

Parallel Specialization

A powerful result of Schumpeter's creative destruction and Kurzweil's law is the possibility of parallel or divergent progress along different trajectories with increasing technological specialization over decreasing social times. "Nations can follow quite different technological trajectories, and therefore divergent development and growth paths, and yet be economically successful, . . . [in] contrast with a more established view that nations follow essentially the same path as they develop, only at different speeds."[26] National, cultural, or industrial trajectories of development and progress may diverge for prolonged periods of event time within a single era of social time. Several may converge in a successive social reality, although most will disappear in failure.

As societies specialize, transnational, technical communities and professional networks emerge as carriers of globalization and conduits for progress. Paradoxically, technical globalization stimulates and deepens national and local specialization and decentralization most saliently in the global economy. As local "entrepreneurs innovate in increasingly specialized niche markets, intense communications in turn ensure the speedy, often unanticipated, recombination of these specialized components into changing end-products. . . . [through] the speed and flexibility as well as the conceptual advances associated with the process of specialization and recombination."[27] Although innovation, specialization, and progress are possible in isolation, the technical and professional networks that pervade the global perspective deepen the social division of labor. Globalization creates new opportunities for innovation, especially in peripheral geographic areas, and stimulates specialization in an expanding self-energizing spiral of globalization that may not include local progress.

Choice and Path Dependence

Historicism understands progress as more than cyclical and deeper than learning and as autogenous or self-generating. Each unit of social time develops within itself the germ of the next, and the next, and the next. Each stage in this pattern emerges from a discrete sequence of human decisions that are contingent on previous decisions and constrained by actual and perceived social reality. Each decision becomes a part of the context for succeeding decisions. Despite active human involvement, however, the causal sequence of progress and change is not fixed, mechanical, or even stable in its determinism. Causality itself develops as a fragile chain of individual and institutional choices. The cumulative effects of choices expand in consequences that are unintended, undesired, and unpredictable. Novel patterns of change convert rational decisions and choices into social results that are irrational. The structure and dynamics of causality, like those of social reality, change from one unit of social time to the next.

For a time between *conjonctures*, the sequence of human choice and consequence develops as a trend within a stable context set by traditional culture and social reality. When the trends move beyond that narrow, socially acceptable range and appear as a new secular trend, people and institutions make different choices. Society's cultural mood changes to reflect an expanding sense of material uncertainty and moral confusion, which unbalances the entire social system. The consequent stresses on social relationships, class conflicts, and political processes lead to yet another sort of choices. People and institutions become defensive and seek protection or profit from what appear as significant changes in the conditions and circumstances of living.

With imbalance and stress, the cultural mood changes to social pessimism, a sense of the limits—even futility—of human effort. Pessimism and increasing stress create political instability, which has brought social disorder, internal violence, and interstate war. Economic activity becomes unpredictable as prices surge and decline, production and productivity decline, and markets fail to clear. The accompanying cultural instability challenges traditional norms of value and sources of identity. The youth of a society, facing the primal decisions of entering adulthood, either embrace the traditional institutions with an attitude of reform or reject them completely in a choice for revolution. The outcast and the poor are driven to despair, as individual and social choice disappear in the path-dependent flow of events.

Eventually, some triggering event, which in different circumstances might have been a minor disturbance, explodes into a major civilizational crisis that relieves the pressures and stresses and briefly reverses the prevailing trends. Many people try to recover the preceding good times and stability. Others —primarily the young—choose to carry society into the future as a new social reality begins to crystallize around novel decisions that begin to form new trends. Equilibrium and stability develop and the cultural mood shifts toward positivism. The cycle begins again in the context of a transformed social reality *which is the result of human choice in a path-dependent context.*

In social time, the structure and dynamic of this pattern have changed as institutional decisions have gained more salience in generating change. Early, premodern waves of globalization involved primarily individual choices as the pressures of population demanded more resources. Institutional choices—the development of banking and credit, recognition of risk, and the sophistication of bureaucracy—contributed to creating and resolving the global crises of the Renaissance and the Enlightenment. Modernity introduced intergovernmental institutions and later corporations as dominant sites of choice between alternative paths of progress. The information age has reversed this submersion of the individual beneath the institution and has expanded the relevance of individual decision and choice. Correspondingly, the structure and dynamics of choice have deepened and broadened into an impossibly complex global context of choices made by millions of people and thousands of institutions. With more urgency than the premodern past, in the modern institutional context, "the pace of globalization matters: A more gradual process means that traditional institutions and norms, rather than being overwhelmed, can adapt and respond to the new challenges."[28] People can also manipulate incremental change and adapt to gradual increases in social stress, whereas catastrophic transformation often sweeps them along with it. Accumulation of knowledge, human choices, and social trends are certainly not mechanical reflexes of each other. Rather, progress has reflected the broad context of civilizational conditions and choices conditioned by social reality and constrained by previous choices.

Transformation and Progress

Through the lens of historicism, progress is not some natural phenomenon that happens—incrementally or catastrophically—to people but the constructed aggregate of human creation of knowledge, willed choice, and expansion of values. Once people began creating new knowledge and transforming narrow-perspective social reality, "progress became clearly linked to the possibility of adaptive inventions and the local properties of evolutionary processes."[29] The broader historicist perspective included the promise that "gradual reform would ameliorate the inequalities of the world system. The illusion that this [progress] was possible within the framework of the system has in fact been a great stabilizing element, in that it has legitimated states in the eyes of their populations and promised them a heaven on earth in the foreseeable future."[30] Historicism recognized also the chronic irregularity of progress, which entailed *both* destruction *and* creation, and the unpredictable consequences of social transformation of knowledge, values, and institutions.

Although historicism could not expect uniform progress without relapses, neither could it expect continuous progress across transformations of social reality. It could assume, however, "that all humanity is as one life, always learning, always adding to its knowledge, and never quite forgetting the lessons of the past."[31] Progress is uneven and nonuniform "because the progress of practically useful knowledge is uneven. . . . Indeed, the pattern of the growth of knowledge depends on the pattern of its utilization."[32] Within the historicist perspective, the catastrophic social transformation embodied in the creation of new knowledge and values is inseparable from the idea of incremental expansion of knowledge.

The historicist perspective expands Schumpeter's notion of creative destruction from a functional, industrial perspective to social transformation within the global perspective. Creative social destruction implies that the decline of some social activities and institutions is necessary for the growth of others. Social activities decline through incremental progress and disappear in catastrophic transformation. When these changes occur, however, the residual pattern of social reality remains constrained by an institutional structure that has lost its *raison d'être*. It becomes a restraint on progress and a limit to human choice. People choose new social activities and values despite the absence of suitable institutions by creating new knowledge, which often becomes a destabilizing balance for institutional psychological inertia. Incremental evolution gradually replaces obsolete structures as new choices and activities construct new ones. Historicism accommodates *both* transformational catastrophism *and* evolutionary incrementalism and binds them inseparably in the willed expansion of human knowledge and perspectives. Creation of new knowledge and values transforms social reality radically and their diffusion through innovation and progress reforms systems and structures gradually.

For knowledge, as for economics, politics, ethics, morality, and culture, Braudel's *conjonctures* and Nishida's *basho* admit only one entrance—the past—and no solid center, since the present is instantaneous and ever-dissolving. Social transformation through creation of new knowledge, however, creates infinite exits into the future, all discoverable through the labyrinth of circumstance by human will and action. Even with consilience of knowledge, as E. O. Wilson has recognized, "the labyrinth of the real world is thus a Borgesian maze of almost infinite possibilities. We can never map it all, never discover and explain everything."[33] The paradox of progress is that, although expanding and unifying knowledge may infinitely expand people's perspectives and focus incremental innovation, it can never achieve the global perspective, since each *conjoncture* has more exits than its predecessor. The infinite perspective of understanding life and living does not allow people ever to know that the journey towards understanding is complete or even to have confidence that the journey even exists as a linear, knowable path. Humanity must exploit each Braudelian *conjoncture* with several dynamic *basho* in creating a world vision, a set of global values, and a body of new knowledge of what to do with the vast capabilities of technology for incremental progress along parallel paths into the future.

KNOWLEDGE-BASED PROGRESS

Through the lens of historicism, progress is not a goal or a result. Rather, it is a sequence and web of processes that create, accumulate, and diffuse knowledge within a system of institutions linked over time and across space by knowledge. "What is progressive is the processes at work. A progressive system is marked by its capacity to coadjust the economic and social institutional arrangements, to solve problems as they are generated, to adjust for the bads as well as for the goods. Progressive systems are adaptive systems and adaptive systems are evolutionary in structure."[34] Tightly bound to the conditions for creating knowledge in *basho* and diffusing it, progress is profoundly idiosyncratic within a civilizational context. Guided by people, energized by capitalism, and involving far more than science and technology, knowledge-based progress is an intrinsic, defining feature of every civilization.

Knowledge-based Institutions

Although only individuals can know, institutions stimulate and focus individual knowing through exchanging information or communicating knowledge in social processes of common understanding. Prevalent in knowledge-based civilizational systems, such processes and institutions diffuse knowledge widely across people's perspectives in what Joseph Schumpeter called vision of things.[35] A Schumpeterian vision is the essential precondition for interpreting and understanding social reality. This dynamic preknowledge cognition—Schumpeterian vision—creates a context for *basho*, activates knowledge creation, and launches the growth and expansion of knowledge along different paths within different perspectives. Knowledge creation or "analytic work begins with material provided by our vision of things, and this vision is ideological almost by necessity. It embodies the picture of things as we see them, and wherever there is any possible motive for wishing to see them in a given rather than another light, the way in which we see things can hardly be distinguished from the way in which we wish to see them."[36]

Within each narrow perspective, knowledge-based institutions store knowledge and understanding and provide the languages and opportunities for inclusive communication. As asylums for Bacon's idols, they also establish and support exclusive patterns of social interaction, which the idols have historically constrained within narrow, functional perspectives. Differing institutions and visions generate different patterns, establish different languages, and create different perceptions of social reality with an interpretive, narrow-perspective freedom described by Schumpeter as *ideology*. Within narrow perspectives, knowledge-based institutions reflect and focus the specialization of knowledge such that "expertise in some domains is a trained aptitude for ignorance in other domains."[37]

Across and beyond narrow perspectives, knowledge-based institutions compile collective knowledge and common understanding and diffuse them through civilization. These institutions establish a division of cognitive labor with a knowledge-based society such that "each individual becomes more expert in his own peculiar branch, more work is done upon the whole, and the quantity of science is considerably increased by it."[38] Beyond the influences of Bacon's idols, these broad-perspective institutions also embody the rules, values, and fashions of society that make social living possible while focusing new knowledge and constraining understanding within narrow perspectives.

Knowledge-based Capitalism

Emerging from the Renaissance and the Enlightenment as a sibling of rationalism and science, resource-based capitalism found few opportunities in economics for the controlled experiments that rational science exploits to create new knowledge. In contrast to science's search for universal, eternal understanding, resource-based capitalism deals with human behaviors and responses in a current economy of solid goods and resources. The early resource-based capitalism encouraged universal trade as an expansion of provincial markets. It demanded an expansion of trust and trustworthiness from familial contexts to global relationships with strangers and foreigners and extended economic relationships deep into the future. It shifted economic responsibility from a primary economic group—city, province, or country—to the individual who became accountable for the actions and consequences of a transaction. It demanded that people judge rationally the probabilities of risk, cost, and reward over vast distances and years into the future.

As a pragmatic counterpart to the scientific method, knowledge-based capitalism has systematized the innovation process and focused much economic activity on the production and diffusion of knowledge and information. Like natural science, modern capitalism is knowledge-based, although it uses a different knowledge basis. The chronic dynamism, social stress, and transformation that are defining features of knowledge-based capitalism reflect less either the instability of human nature or the solidity of natural resources than the nature of knowledge creation, accumulation, and diffusion. The limits of reality and the foci for innovation and progress reflect the "institutions that shape the growth and application of scientific, technological, and social knowledge in particular. Capitalism is restless because knowledge is restless."[39] The restless, irreversible turbulence of capitalism across time and space is a defining feature of Braudel's domains of global capitalism and market economy. Restless, knowledge-based capitalism and growth also reflect the erratic natures of knowledge creation and accumulation.[40] Resource-based capitalism operating in Braudel's domain of the market economy relied primarily on economic growth to contain the social pressures of globalization and modernization. Embracing *both* the market economy *and* risk-based capitalism, knowledge-based capitalism actively relieves those pressures through transformation of social reality.

Economists from Alfred Marshall to Simon Kuznets have recognized that capitalist enterprise has always absorbed and changed knowledge in some unpredictable way. Knowledge-based capitalism has exposed new possibilities for new enterprise, which again changed knowledge, *ad infinitum*.[41] It has also, however, exposed its own vulnerability to uncertainty and incomplete knowledge. Although globalization has thrust the great ideological battles into the past, the transient, incomplete nature of knowledge and people's unpredictable ability to create it ensure that knowledge-based capitalism will remain restless and unstable. It will *both* create social stresses through economic growth *and* resolve them through social transformation.

Knowledge-based capitalism is an open, self-organizing system that continually stresses itself and its environment by its own metabolic activity. It relieves the stresses that it creates by redefining itself through innovation, learning, and creation of new knowledge in a sort of progress towards some goal.[42] The evolution of knowledge-based capitalism is restlessly self-energizing within a powerful political-economic system whose dominant dynamic is change. "Every position is open to challenge, there are powerful incentives to mount those challenges, and the characteristic feature of the market mechanism is to facilitate those changes."[43] Individual decisions and political policies in such an evolutionary system are emergent, behavioral consequences of the interactions of people and processes. Not immediately or directly evident from the system's rules, these consequences emerge collectively as progress from the higher-level principles of rationality rather than from the intrinsic, systemic attributes of knowledge-based capitalism.[44]

Within the global perspective, the knowledge-based economy always shows order across the human processes of economic interaction in patterns of market-based coordination. Market operations and human interactions are simultaneously the context of order and the constraints—Bacon's idols—against which people originate disrupting challenges and imagine expansive innovations. The ordering forces of markets and coordinating institutions impose the predictability, stability, and path-dependent direction that are the *sine qua non* of creative, incremental progress. In contrast to the resource-based order imposed by homeostatic equilibrium, this spontaneous order of the *morphogenetic*, knowledge-based system continually increases the organization and power of the system.[45]

Like quantum mechanics, knowledge-based capitalism operates around a mysterious relationship called *entanglement*, which arises when people use knowledge to assemble simple, resource-based, economic units into a complex, knowledge-based creation. The economic function of resource-based units —mines, fields, factories, workers, patents, or markets—does not depend explicitly on the resource involved. Entangled inventions or innovations are independent of their resource-based components, which often lose their individualities. Only the entangling entity, as a whole, has a well-defined identity and economic function. Entangling through creating new knowledge creates a recondite, cognitive function for the group, beyond its economic role. "Entangled objects behave as if they were connected with one another no matter how far apart they are—distance does not attenuate entanglement in the slightest. If something is entangled with other objects, a measurement of it simultaneously provides information about its partners."[46] Just as the behaviors of entangled quantum systems are impossible for classical physics, the consequences of knowledge-entangled capitalism are beyond the predictions of classical economics. Like quantum-entangled physics, knowledge-based capitalism has identified a new source of energy beyond physical resources and beyond the understanding of classical resource-based economics.

Subjective exercise of individual will in interacting and choosing —freedom—in a knowledge-based, capitalist market and in resisting pressures on action and choice—equilibrium in resource-based economies—generates innovation. Patterns of material profits that arise around innovations finance the technical and institutional changes to implement them and stimulate further innovation. The union of innovation and market selection in knowledge-based capitalism creates the incentive and the adjustment processes to energize and sustain economic progress. The growth and expansion of knowledge and development of belief that are the foundations of knowledge-based capitalism ensure that equilibrium is never more than momentary. Within the global perspective of knowledge-based capitalism, human knowledge and thought seem intrinsically hostile to any notion of equilibrium.

Knowledge-based capitalism evolves, even though individuals, firms, and governments remain static, diverse, and self-identified. Knowledge evolves as capitalism extends the scope and changes the participants in economic interactions. Progress occurs as economies expand geographically from local to national to global or functionally from capital goods to consumer goods to services to information services. Instead of reconstructing identities within deconstructive or reductionist postmodern perspectives, the global, historicist perspective confirms a robust, institutional individualism in the entrepreneurial innovation that energizes and sustains knowledge-based capitalism.

The Processes

Few modern economists would argue that either progress or economic development is the simple product of the classical factors of production —capital, land, and labor. More recognize that the energy of capitalism in the global economy arises from "the generation of novelty in order and the emergence of order from novelty."[47] This sort of capitalism is based on knowledge, not resources. Its active dynamic is innovation, not investment. Its result is human progress, not just individual profit or social prosperity.

The evolutionary power of knowledge-based capitalism arises in the mutually interdependent processes of market selectivity and development of innovation systems. Market selection through competition depends less on structure or regulation than on the exposure of every market position to challenge. The unpredictable, orderly generation of novelty is the vehicle for mounting those challenges. "Innovation is an exploratory process and experimental behavior is a necessary feature of real-world competition with all the uncertainties and lack of predictability that this entails."[48] Progress through innovation occurs incrementally through objective observation, deliberate change, and recognition of the result as new knowledge. The forces that generate innovation do not act blindly. People innovate for some purpose in anticipation of some effects. Innovation occurs within the constraints of existing knowledge, design philosophies, and market selection in a multilevel diffusion guided by economic weights that people assign to alternative results.

The Institutions

The organic systems and organizations inherent to knowledge-based capitalism stimulate and focus innovation and knowledge creation. These institutions and their functions provide the context for progress. "It is the combination of institutions for selection and development that gives to capitalism its undoubted potential to change itself from within, to be, as it were, in a permanent, self-induced state of transformation."[49] Beyond these market institutions, political policymakers establish the context for innovation and promote connectivity and expansion of perspectives. Policy can have a critical role in generating collaborative innovation within preferred groups through focused incentives. National technology policies to promote innovation in national firms operate as a powerful alternative for competitive market selection.

Knowledge-based capitalism operates aggressively in an economic institutional context of markets and innovation to stimulate and sustain incremental changes to knowledge as the engine of general, social progress. Stability of specialized institutions focuses innovation into specific economic sectors as competitive capitalist national economies select alternate trajectories of development and progress.[50] Directed innovation, accumulation, and incremental change of knowledge reflect the self-organization of knowledge within the institutional market context—an essential element of evolutionary progress. These incremental changes to knowledge have historically occurred in a broader context of political institutions that coordinated and focused their effects into ordered patterns of economic development and progress.

The noneconomic institutional context of capitalism—politics, law, education, culture, and ideology—stabilizes interaction, cooperation, competition, and continuity of market and nonmarket arrangements.[51] Knowledge-based political-economies stimulate and coordinate innovation through market and nonmarket processes and institutions that are deeply embedded in social infrastructures and in formal political systems. Capitalist arrangements for generating innovation have historically been broader, more robust, and stronger than other institutions for creating new scientific, political, or social knowledge. Capitalism and the self-interest embodied in its institutions has often provided the focus for converting existing knowledge into new technologies.

The political context for knowledge-based capitalism is also ambiguous. Despite the close correlation in many prosperous, modern countries, rationality and logic have not shown that resource-based capitalism and democracy are causally or systemically linked. Knowledge-based capitalism does not rely on a necessary, direct, causal, or functional relationship with democracy but presents it as a complementary institution. The discursive social and political institutions, pluralistic check-and-balance systems on power, active political parties, popular elections, and judicial enforcement of rights typical of modern democracies, however, do seem preconditions for knowledge-based capitalism.[52]

Intellectual Property. A basic premise of knowledge-based capitalism embodies the broadly recognized proposition that society benefits most when society recognizes expressions of new knowledge, applications of technology, or diffusion of innovative ideas as intellectual property. The capitalist institution of ownership with its intrinsic right of exploitation for profit has accelerated social progress as knowledge-based capitalism has stimulated economic growth. Capitalistic society learned early to stimulate knowledge creation through a socioeconomic pact with inventors and innovators. Government would confer and protect the exclusive right of an inventor or innovator to sell any new knowledge for profit as an incentive to creativity, in exchange for sharing ideas with the public. During the Renaissance, the Venetian government institutionalized this pact in a requirement to reduce the new knowledge to actual, physical use and an explicit, fixed duration for the right to state protection of the idea. Societies have struggled ever since with determining which ideas warrant rewards and what those rewards should be.

Globalization has expanded the scope of the bargain between the creators of knowledge and society to segregate societies into net importers and exporters of ideas. Expansion of the bargain ensures that global society benefits regardless of whether people live in idea-importing or knowledge-exporting countries. The bargain offers a real incentive to create for innovators, inventors, entrepreneurs, and artists and that their new knowledge and ideas spread rapidly through the global economic market. As globalization continues to expand *both* the demands to own ideas *and* the demands for cheaper access to ideas, the capabilities to protect intellectual property are diminishing as more people learn to exploit technology to gain access to ideas and knowledge. The process itself is eroding its own foundations. Paradoxically, the same technologies and processes that are essential to robust, knowledge-based capitalism are spreading *both* technology *and* ideas to societies with weak capitalist institutions. Consumers using technology to penetrate patented and copyrighted content are eroding a fundamental prerequisite and intractable paradox of knowledge-based capitalism. Society must protect intellectual property, even as people recognize that the freedom of ideas and knowledge to mix with one another and diffuse across artificial boundaries is the energy of progress. Within knowledge-based capitalism, only the promise of profit can initiate either growth or progress.

The Firm. The commercial firm has a critical role in knowledge-based capitalism as the primary organization that can accumulate and focus the several types of knowledge that stimulate innovation. In addition to a particular set of functional capabilities, firms must assemble the many networks and knowledge-diffusion channels that form its unique external organization. Within the global perspective, firms must deliberately construct their own systems of innovation within the orderly context of knowledge-based capitalism. The aggregate of these firm-specific innovation systems starts and feeds the capitalist engine of progress, which runs, however, in both directions. Competition and capabilities generate innovation, but innovation generates further competition and new capabilities.

Firms are, however, reinforced by a wide array of other organizations and institutions that also generate, convert, interpret, diffuse, and store knowledge. Although professional societies, communities of practice, technical communities, international institutions, and individuals operate global networks for transferring information and knowledge, they are not autonomous innovation systems. Despite the ambitions of some governments to construct national innovation systems, these extrafirm channels lack the capabilities and incentives that capitalism concentrates in firms. Just as competition and cooperation are equally important in balanced operations of the capitalist engine of progress, the firms' profit incentives balance the nonprofit incentives that guide scholarly and public research. Despite the demise of central planning as a viable economic structure, knowledge-based capitalism demands continuing regulation to preserve noneconomic social values and pursue nonmarket aims. Regulation has been effective within national economies, although less so within the global economy. In analogy to economic production in the global economy, capitalism divides the complex functions of accumulating, expanding, creating, and using knowledge in a specialized, cognitive division of labor.

Equilibrium and Progress

Knowledge-based capitalism extends the notion of order beyond, below, and above equilibrium to encompass human interactions and institutional coordination to accommodate internally generated change. Despite the inherent future orientation of modernity and capitalism, classical economics used the notion of convergence towards equilibrium to explain and understand economic activity and change within less-than-global perspectives. Reminiscent of Lyell's uniformitarian epicycles, classical equilibrium was the focus for orderly, material progress as the disorder brought by innovation eventually dissipated in a new equilibrium. The new equilibrium represented movement along the path of progress. With confidence in the eventual reestablishment of equilibrium, economic rationality could rely on confident foresight as a basis for economic choices, and expect progress as natural and even inevitable.

As a knowledge-based system of socially mediated discovery and focused innovation within the global perspective, however, knowledge-based capitalism cannot rest on equilibrium. "In equilibrium, there can be no scope for entrepreneurial behavior, for entrepreneurship and equilibrium are incompatible concepts."[53] Every temporary equilibrium generates from within itself the forces to unbalance that order, primarily as society accumulates and diffuses knowledge in pursuit of innovation. Progress emerges, rather, from the order and regularity that arise from institutional coordination of diverse interactions and their individually unpredictable effects. A notion of preserving equilibrium—as a fact or as an ideal—in a social reality dominated by knowledge and belief is ultimately inconsistent with capitalism. Knowledge-based capitalism inherently generates destabilizing change from within. Economic equilibrium and political stability preclude the creation and accumulation of new knowledge that would unbalance and destabilize society.

In a context of knowledge-based capitalism, equilibrium is irreconcilable with the historicist recognition of knowledge as the link that connects the totality of humanity through time and space. In equilibrium, history either stops or repeats itself eternally. The only change possible in equilibrium is that imposed on the system itself by God, by nature, or by something else, but not by humanity within the system. This simple sort of exogenous equilibrium is outside time and human experience and does not reflect or describe knowledge-based capitalism; the best that humanity can do is to observe it. In dealing with the complex implications of static equilibrium, "it slips away from the conditions of real life. In fact we are here verging on the high theme of economic progress. . . . Though the statistical treatment alone can give us definiteness and precision of thought, and is therefore a necessary introduction to a more philosophic treatment of society as an organism, it is yet only an introduction." To understand organic growth, it is necessary to go beyond static, short-period equilibrium "to the study of progress and development of industries which show a tendency to increasing return."[54]

Inherently unpredictable, the effects of knowledge-based development are the unexpected consequences of evolutionary change and the invisible signatures of progress. Despite any reflections of incrementalist visions of ultimate human perfection, knowledge-based capitalism rejects any notion of foresight, either rationally objective or spiritually subjective. Since innovation and risk taking are possible only in a stable, malleable context, capitalism relies on informed judgments and knowledge-based imagination.

Global capitalism's efficiency in using knowledge connects variation, selection, development, and innovation in a path-dependent process of incremental, economic progress. Within the global perspective, political coordination of this economic progress can create economic order based on common expectations and shared knowledge. It does not, however, lead to stable equilibrium but follows the tendency towards "an equilibrium relative to that knowledge which people will acquire in the course of their economic activity."[55] Consistent, orderly patterns of interactions and events with predictable results according to uniform principles of interdependence arise through the creative destruction of distributed innovation. Economic coordination within the same capitalist institutions that focus knowledge in ordered patterns implies a global economic regularity that generates material progress through incessant change and unpredictable, local innovation.[56] Although markets can clear to bring instantaneous equilibrium in event time, the conditions for equilibrium are changing incrementally through progress and innovation in social time, which flows more slowly. Flowing more slowly still through the *longue durée* are the creation of new knowledge in *basho* and transformation of social reality that provides the context for all economic exchanges. Even though people are living simultaneously on all three levels of time, knowledge-based capitalism can never be at rest without internal forces of change. New knowledge created abruptly in *basho* or accumulated incrementally through innovation creates within every point of equilibrium the conditions to disrupt that order.

Economic Growth as Progress

Few modern economists would quibble with an assertion that knowledge accumulation, innovation, invention, and discovery are proximate sources of growth. Nor would many economists or philosophers exclude human capital beyond labor and financial capital as a factor of production in focusing resource-based capitalism on economic growth. An overly simplistic interpretation of the model explains economic growth through developing an educated workforce, infusing massive capital and mobilizing resources. The successful formula for sustained growth is increasing economic efficiency in combination with high levels of human and physical capital: productivity-driven growth. The growth model places a premium on particular kinds of knowledge—managerial techniques, technology, understanding of markets, a flexible ability to adapt, an innovative spirit—and de-emphasizes others as factors of production. The primacy of sustained, productivity-driven growth as a final result of resource-based capitalism leaves to knowledge and knowledge creation the role of increasing efficiency and productivity.

Many resource-based growth models include a dynamic of sustaining growth around national economic equilibrium at a steady, predictable rate to generate the economic progress desired. Classical economics expanded national growth by positing global economic growth as convergence of growing economies towards equilibrium. In contrast, knowledge-based capitalism includes growth as only one component of social progress, and knowledge-based economics precludes *both* equilibrium *and* convergence in capitalist economies. The social progress generated by knowledge-based capitalism is broader than equilibrium and deeper than growth. Understanding knowledge-based capitalism as the engine of social progress introduces a novel approach to economic growth as an engine of progress rather than the goal of progress.

Economic expectations of steady-rate growth within a knowledge-based capitalist economy rely on steady-rate growth of knowledge. History, however, confirms the uneven growth of knowledge, science, and technology over even short periods of event time. Innovations, inventions, and discoveries themselves may be transformational or incremental with ready practical applications or relevance only in social time. Neither is the human base of knowledge simply an aggregate stock of ideas and information that grows as each new bit of knowledge is added to it. Rates of knowledge growth vary unpredictably over time from nearly zero to more than exponential. The nature of knowledge creation, accumulation, and diffusion is not compatible with the notion of steady or sustained economic growth.

One stylized fact of economic growth is the accompanying structural change throughout a society. Growth does not occur without substantial changes not only in the economy but also in the political and cultural structures of a society. Nor do slow changes in macroeconomic conditions imply slow, incremental progress and change throughout society. "The empirical observation of steady, aggregate growth is invariably based on microeconomic turmoil. Such turmoil is not an inconvenience that hides all that is essential about the economic process: like the shadows on the wall of Plato's cave, *it is the process of growth.*"[57] Although knowledge-based capitalism generates *both* economic growth *and* social progress, the two results are separate. Growth occurs within the narrow perspective of economic materialism in aggregate, quantitative terms. Rather than simply the increases in material wealth of growth, progress encompasses an entire society and involves incremental, individual changes across every civilizational perspective.

Measuring growth in aggregate terms necessarily obscures and averages away the details that define social progress. The coordination of diverse processes and interactions in specific civilizational contexts and the application of new knowledge define the progress of which growth is only one consequence. In contrast to economic growth, which can be imposed from above or outside an economy, knowledge-based progress emerges within a society from below. Growth rates at different social levels and times are permanently emerging phenomena generated by new knowledge and focused by the structural changes brought by prior growth. "It is not just knowledge of production processes that matters. . . . Good institutions and effective management will not only facilitate the transfer of knowledge, but will also enhance the likelihood that such knowledge will be used effectively."[58]

The Engine of Progress

The foundations of resource-based capitalism, embodied in traditional, private enterprise, do not include standards of social welfare, principles of Pareto optimality or equity, the public good, or even a focus on economic development. Through the lens of modernity, capitalism has been purely and overtly materialistic with little scope or vision beyond the economic perspective. Within the economic perspective, resource-based capitalism has been an efficient system for accumulating wealth, increasing human productivity, and diffusing the benefits of economic growth through the markets of the world. As capitalism began to concentrate wealth and the control of resources in corporations, government regulation began to focus the power of capitalism on some notion of national progress through codes of rules on health, safety, and working hours and later nationalization of industries into public ownership.[59]

Beyond the economic perspective, through the lens of historicism, knowledge-based capitalism has been an efficient social system for focusing the accumulation and decentralizing the conversion of knowledge. Whereas the resource-based capital markets of Braudel's domain of global capitalism are ruthless in pursuing immediate or quick profits, the corporations operate in *both* the open-market economy *and* the capital markets. Beyond profits, knowledge-based capitalism requires and generates sustainable markets through social trnasformation and progress. From early in the twentieth century, the knowledge-based management profession has recognized that providing benefits to workers, suppliers, and customers, in addition to paying dividends, is a form of social progress in the ultimate interests of shareholders.

As knowledge-based corporate capitalism stimulated collective innovation and translation of specific knowledge to produce useful actions and items, managers found themselves in *basho* creating new, global, social knowledge in the form of trust. "The evolution of capitalism has been in the direction of more trust and transparency, and less self-serving behavior: not coincidentally, this evolution has brought with it greater productivity and economic growth." The development of the stable institutions of knowledge-based capitalism around the new knowledge of trust and productivity quickly diffused the immense benefits of trusting and being trustworthy as a new social reality. As corporate social franchises continue to deepen with commercial habit and globalization, the new knowledge created through experience congeals in broad, corporate and social trust. Gradually replacing the ancient truth of *caveat emptor*, knowledge-based capitalist trust and productivity allows workers, customers, suppliers, companies, and countries to survive even severe economic catastrophes. As a powerful engine of growth and progress, knowledge-based capitalism, with its institutions of innovation and trust, has "well demonstrated that flourishing economies require a healthy level of trust in the reliability and fairness of everyday transactions."[60]

With the managerial shift from resource-based capitalism to knowledge-based capitalism in the nineteenth century, trust congealed into a systemic, capitalist institution. As entrepreneurs began to realize that trustworthiness attracted customers, formal institutions appeared in civic society to nurture a social climate of trust in commercial transactions. The inherent future orientation of capitalism reinforced the shift towards trust with a modern focus on accumulation of capital over the lifetime of an individual, a project, an investment, or a company, to replace the narrow view of immediate profit. Knowledge-based capitalism perceived each transactions as a link in a longer chain of commercial ventures, rather than separate opportunities to exploit for maximum profit. Diffusion of new knowledge in the form of trust became not only the lubrication of commerce but the fuel of systemic political and cultural globalization, as people deepened trade into interpersonal and intersocietal relationships. As impersonal, systemic trust permeated not only commerce but people's noneconomic lives, capitalism itself became impersonal and transactions embodied not merely friendship or simply exchanges of resources. Commerce joined all other human relationships in each individual's search for value, satisfaction, knowledge, and progress as determined within some personal perspective.

Resource-based capitalism pursues administrative simplicity to reduce costs, responsive productive flexibility in adapting to unexpected market situations, and orderly control of innovation. Knowledge-based capitalists also continually exploit knowledge to create new opportunities to exploit yet-to-be-developed resources and to build social trust. These purely economic incentives provide the foundations for a powerful, self-induced, self-contained capacity for autogenous adaptation from within capitalism itself in the forms of enterprise and entrepreneurship. Knowledge-based capitalism continuously refines and improves its system of decentralized invention and uncoordinated innovation, which also forms the context of social trust and progress. Even as innovative change occurs, trust expands it from the domain of capitalism through the market economy into Braudel's domain of material life. A slightly altered social reality stabilizes within the order-imposing structures and institutions of market processes and creates a new context—economic and social—for further change.

An orderly system of multiple, competing initiatives linked by trust, knowledge-based capitalism derives its motives from individual self-interest and its energy from continual accumulation and expansion of knowledge. A rich, diverse context of capitalist and political institutions constrains and promotes the creation and use of new knowledge and focuses its application towards the priorities of society. The continuous institutional and structural modifications to the context and content of capitalism ensure that change never ends but that reform and incremental progress arise autogenously within capitalism itself. Knowledge-based capitalism is very efficient at diffusing, converting, and codifying knowledge for market purposes in the economic perspective and has effectively coopted political power through trust into the market process. This unique and defining combination of materialistic, human incentive in entrepreneurial enterprise and political-economic institutional process —knowledge-based capitalism—is the engine of incremental social progress.

This same engine is also, however, a powerful constraint on *basho*-created, multiperspective, new knowledge that can transform social reality.[61] Capitalism efficiently diverts human knowledge, attention, and progress away from noneconomic aims of social justice, political order, or resolving issues of cultural identities. As ironically foreseen by Karl Marx, Friedrich Engles, and others, global capitalism—resource-based or knowledge-based—concentrates wealth efficiently, but its principles and logic do "not favor social justice. Economic globalization has thus become a formidable cause of inequality among and within states, and the concern for global competitiveness limits the aptitude of states and other actors to address this problem."[62]

Resource-based capitalism generates local economic change in some form of resource-based economic development and the ensuing noneconomic effects in event time. In social time, knowledge-based capitalism energizes incremental progress, which eventually unbalances social reality to the extent that event time merges with social time in *conjoncture*. People create new knowledge and trust in *basho* as globalization expands life and living towards the global perspective and the levels of time merge in civilizational transformation of social reality. Within the historicist perspective of the *longue durée*, knowledge-based capitalism realigns incremental social progress with the human sources of the new wave of globalization, and progress continues. Knowledge-based capitalism broadens people's perspectives as it discredits notions of trusting only people in some particular groups. Knowledge-based capitalism is as essentially and expansively cosmopolitan as is the universal trust created by the social system in which it operates. Not only can people confidently trade with anyone who offers value, but they can exchange knowledge and noneconomic value with any other person, despite belonging to different groups. Capitalism —resource-based and knowledge-based—creates new knowledge in the form of trust and requires trust to operate well. It encourages people to believe that *both* economic transactions *and* interpersonal relationships will occur smoothly as expected and intended, not because of enforcement of the law or fear of collective sanctions, but because trust makes it possible for people to prosper in security and justice. When things work well, people trust each other; when people trust each other, things work well.

The capitalist incentive to action, the institutional structures of the market, the focus provided by political processes, and the power of human knowledge merge in globalization and *basho* as people gradually expand their knowledge into the global perspective. Knowledge-based capitalism makes it probable that people enmeshed in the capitalist system are also the people most likely to affect people elsewhere in the world even without any personal relationships between them. Being good, successful capitalists seems to predispose people to consider the global and historicist aspects of their actions and decisions. Like knowledge-based capitalism, universal humanitarianism invokes the conviction that all people are connected to, and even responsible for, other people in distant places or future times with no familial, cultural, political, or economic ties. Like idealistic humanitarianism, knowledge-based capitalism embodies a powerful future orientation, an embracing trust in humanity, and a conviction that people can deliberately transform social reality through progress.

NOTES

1. J. Stanley Metcalfe, "Institutions and Progress," *Industrial and Corporate Change* 10(3) (September 2001): 561–586; 564.

2. James Burke, *The Day The Universe Changed* (London: British Broadcasting Corporation, 1985), 14.

3. Stephen Jay Gould, "On Embryos and Ancestors," *Natural History* 107(6) (July–August 1998): 20–22, 58–65; 20.

4. Werner Sombart, *Quintessence of Capitalism* (New York: Dutton, 1915), 103.

5. Classical Greek and Roman plays routinely used stage machinery to introduce a god who would resolve a crisis or direct a particular course of events arbitrarily. In most such plays, the same machinery removed the god quickly after its required changes to the plot.

6. Metcalfe, "Institutions and Progress," 565.

7. Metcalfe, "Institutions and Progress," 565.

8. See Joel Mokyr, *The Lever of Riches* (Oxford: Oxford University Press, 1990), 6–8; David S. Landes, *The Wealth and Poverty of Nations* (New York: Little, Brown, 1998), 187–193, 513.

9. Metcalfe, "Institutions and Progress," 565.

10. See Simon Kuznets, *Economic Growth of Nations: Total Output and Production Structure* (Cambridge: Belknap, Harvard University Press, 1971); William Nordhaus and James Tobin, "Is Growth Obsolete?" in *Economic Growth* (New York: National Bureau of Economic Research, 1972), 4–13, 24–60.

11. 565.

12. Sidney Pollard, *The Idea of Progress* (New York: Basic Books, 1968), 184.

13. Lynn T. White Jr., *Medieval Technology and Social Change* (Oxford: Clarendon, 1962), 28.

14. Carroll Quigley, *The Evolution of Civilizations: An Introduction to Historical Analysis* (Indianapolis, Indiana: Liberty Fund, 1961), 416.

15. For inner- and other-directed people, see David Riesman, with Nathan Glazer and Reuel Denney, *The Lonely Crowd: A Study of the Changing American Character* (New Haven: Yale University Press, [1950] 1967), 15, 22; For the grid-group-theory orientations of social cultures, see Charles Lockhart, "Cultural Contributions to Explaining Institutional Form, Political Change, and Rational Decisions," *Comparative Political Studies* 32(7) (October 1999): 862–893; 864–884.

16. See Mancur Olson Jr., "Dictatorship, Democracy, and Development, " *American Political Science Review* 87(3) (September 1993): 567–576; 572–573.

17. See, among others, Charles E. Lindblom, *Politics and Markets: The World's Political-Economic Systems* (New York: Basic Books, 1977), 52–62; Chalmers Johnson, *MITI and the Japanese Miracle* (Stanford: Stanford University Press, 1982), 256, 264–271.

18. See Kenneth E. Boulding, "The Boundaries of Social Policy," *Social Work* 12(1) (January 1967): 3–11; 7.

19. Richard M. Titmuss, *The Gift Relationship: From Human Blood to Social Policy* (New York: Random House, 1971), 290.

20. Lockhart, "Cultural Contributions to Explaining Institutional Form," 869.

21. Jacob Burckhardt, *Reflections on History* (Indianapolis, Indiana: Liberty Fund, 1979), 213–252; 223–224.

22. See Craig N. Murphy, *International Organization and Industrial Change: Global Governance since 1850* (Cambridge: Polity, 1994), 26–45, 261; Antonio Gramsci, *Selections from the Prison Notebooks of Antonio Gramsci*, edited and translated by Quintin Hoare and Geoffrey Nowell Smith (New York: International, 1971), 158–175, 242–245, 275–276; Karl Polanyi, *The Great Transformation* (New York: Rinehart, 1944), 130–134.

23. For a discussion of ideological and institutional opposition in the United States and the United Kingdom to globalizing competition strategies, see Simon Reich, *The Fruits of Fascism: Postwar Prosperity in Historical Perspective* (Ithaca: Cornell University Press, 1990), 34–38.

24. For discussions of the transition to the next social reality at the end of the epicycle through the double movement or passive revolution, see David Forgacs, ed., *The Antonio Gramsci Reader* (New York: Schocken, 1988), 428; Polanyi, *The Great Transformation*, 130–134; Robert W. Cox, *Production, Power, and World Order: Social Forces in the Making of History* (New York: Columbia University Press, 1987), 343–353, 393–403; Murphy, *International Organization and Industrial Change*, 260–275.

25. See Thomas Spragens Jr., *Understanding Political Theories* (New York: St. Martin's, 1976).

26. Jonathan West, "Limits to Globalization: Organizational Homogeneity and Diversity in the Semiconductor Industry," *Industrial and Corporate Change* 11(1) (February 2002): 159–188; 159. See also Paolo Guerrieri, "Technological and International Trade Performance of the Most Advanced Countries," Berkeley Roundtable on the International Economy working paper no. 49, Berkeley, California, 1991; David R. Dollar and Edward N. Wolff, *Competitiveness, Convergence, and International Specialization* (Cambridge: MIT Press, 1993); Daniele Archibugi and Jonathan Michie, *The Globalization of Technology: Myths and Realities*, University of Cambridge Research Papers in Management Studies, 1992–1993, no. 18 (Cambridge: University of Cambridge, 1993).

27. Anna Lee Saxenian and Jinn-Yuh Hsu, "The Silicon Valley-Hsinchu Connection: Technical Communities and Industrial Upgrading," *Industrial and Corporate Change* 10(4) (December 2001): 893–920; 899–900.

28. Joseph E. Stiglitz, *Globalization and Its Discontents* (New York: Norton, 2002), 247.

29. Metcalfe, "Institutions and Progress," 565.

30. Immanuel Wallerstein, "The Prospect of Politics," *Civilization* 5(2) (April-May 1998): 70–77; 72.

31. Pollard, *The Idea of Progress*, 204.

32. Metcalfe, "Institutions and Progress," 566.

33. Edward O. Wilson, *Consilience, The Unity of Knowledge* (New York: Knopf, 1998), 67.

34. Metcalfe, "Institutions and Progress," 566.

35. Joseph Schumpeter introduced this sense of the term, *vision*, as the "pre-analytic cognitive act" by which people construe the meanings and values of the institutions of the world. See Joseph A. Schumpeter, *History of Economic Analysis* (New York: Oxford University Press, 1954), 41–42.

36. Schumpeter, *History of Economic Analysis*, 42.

37. Metcalfe, "Institutions and Progress," 569.

38. Adam Smith, *The Wealth of Nations* (New York: Modern Library, [1776] 1994), 11.

39. Metcalfe, "Institutions and Progress," 561.

40. Friedrich A. von Hayek, "Economics and Knowledge," *Economica* 4(NS 13) (February 1937): 33–54; 53. See also Brian J. Loasby, *Knowledge, Institutions, and Evolution in Economics* (London: Routledge, 1999), 21, 76–77, 108, 134.

41. Alfred Marshall, *Industry and Trade* (London: Macmillan, 1898), 99–103, 132–134, 203–205; Alfred Marshall, *Principles of Economics*, 9th ed. (London: Macmillan, 1961), 138–139; Simon Kuznets, "Two Centuries of Economic Growth: Reflections on U.S. Experience," *American Economic Review* 67(1) (February 1977): 1–14; 6–8; John Foster, "Economics and the Self-organization Approach: Alfred Marshall Revisited," *Economic Journal* 103(419) (July 1993): 975–991; 986–987.

42. Ludwig von Bertalanffy has defined a self-organizing system in its capability of "evolving from a less to a more differentiated state." Ludwig von Bertalanffy, *General System Theory: Foundation, Development, Applications* (New York: Braziller, 1968), 68.

43. Metcalfe, "Institutions and Progress," 575.

44. See Richard N. Langlois, "Systems Theory, Knowledge, and the Social Sciences," in *The Study of Information: Interdisciplinary Messages*, edited by Fritz Machlup and Una Mansfield, 581–600 (New York: Wiley, 1983), 598–599.

45. Walter Buckley has made a general distinction between morphostatic and morphogenetic systems than can and cannot change their own features. Walter Buckley, *Sociology and Modern Systems Theory* (Englewood Cliffs, New Jersey: Prentice-Hall, 1967), 58–59. The general systemic notion of morphogenesis has been more commonly known in economics as entrepreneurship through innovation—acquiring new knowledge, changing the problem, and creating a novel solution.

46. Michael A. Nielsen, "Rules for a Complex, Quantum World, *Scientific American* 287(5) (November 2002): 67–75; 73.

47. Metcalfe, "Institutions and Progress," 562.

48. J. Stanley Metcalfe, "Technology Policy in an Evolutionary World," paper presented at the second International Conference on Science and Technology Policy Research of the National Institute of Science and Technology Policy (24–26 January 1991: Oiso, Japan) *What Should Be Done? What Can Be Done? Science and Technology Policy Research: The Proceedings of the NISTEP Second International Conference on Science and Technology*, edited by Sogo Okamura, Kenichi Marakami, and Ikujiro Nonaka, 109–121 (Tokyo: Mita Press, 1991), 111.

49. Metcalfe, "Institutions and Progress," 579.

50. See Richard R. Nelson, ed., *National Innovation Systems: A Comparative Analysis* (New York: Oxford University Press, 1993).

51. See Richard R. Nelson, "National Innovation Systems: A Retrospective on a Study," *Industrial and Corporate Change* 2(2) (June 1992): 347–374.

52. See Francis Fukuyama, *The End of History and the Last Man* (New York: Free Press, 1992). For critiques of, and alternatives to, this view see Samuel Bowles and Herbert Gintis, *Democracy and Capitalism: Property, Community, and the Contradictions of Modern Social Thought* (New York: Basic Books, 1986), 3–14, 131–135; Douglas Kellner, *Television and the Crisis of Democracy* (Boulder, Colorado: Westview, 1990), 93–95; Alan Wolfe, *The Limits of Legitimacy: Political Contradictions of Contemporary Capitalism* (New York: Free Press, 1977), 7–10, 241–244.

53. J. Stanley Metcalfe, "Technology Policy in an Evolutionary World," paper presented at the second International Conference on Science and Technology Policy Research of the National Institute of Science and Technology Policy (24–26 January 1991: Oiso, Japan) *What Should Be Done? What Can Be Done? Science and Technology Policy Research: The Proceedings of the NISTEP Second International Conference on Science and Technology*, edited by Sogo Okamura, Kenichi Marakami, and Ikujiro Nonaka (Tokyo: Mita Press, 1991), 109–121; 111.

54. Marshall, *Principles of Economics*, 461.

55. Hayek, "Economics and Knowledge," 53.   See also Loasby, *Knowledge, Institutions, and Evolution in Economics*, 21, 76–77, 108, 134.

56. See Fabrizio Coricelli and Giovanni Dosi, "Coordination and Order in Economic Change and the Interpretive Power of Economic Theory," in *Technical Change and Economic Theory*, edited by Giovanni Dosi, Christopher Freeman, Richard R. Nelson, Gerald Silverberg, and Luc Soete, 124–147 (London: Pinter, 1988), 136–142.

57. Metcalfe, "Institutions and Progress," 581.

58. Joseph E. Stiglitz, "Knowledge for Development: Economic Science, Economic Policy, and Economic Advice," in *Annual World Bank Conference on Development Economics 1998*, edited by Boris Pleskovic and Joseph E. Stiglitz, 9–58 (Washington, D.C.: World Bank, 1999), 11.

59. The large U.S. industrial organizations and companies, led by the infamous *robber barons* of the nineteenth century, built much of the residential, educational, and health infrastructure of the United States as company towns.   Corporate directors accepted and implemented the premise that well-housed, well-educated, healthy workers would be more productive than ill, angry, feckless people living in slums.   Companies introduced retirement pensions and health-care systems before governments accepted the ideologies of welfare as the foundation of social democracy.   In 1915, Procter & Gamble introduced disability and retirement pensions, and, in 1918, the eight-hour workday and guaranteed work for 48 weeks each year. Heinz provided employee education in citizenship on company time.

60. James Surowiecki, "A Virtuous Cycle," *Forbes* 170(13) (23 December 2002): 248–256; 250.

61. See Richard R. Nelson, "Assessing Private Enterprise: An Exegesis of Tangled Doctrine," *The Bell Journal of Economics* 12(1) (Spring 1981): 93–111; 104–106.

62. Stanley Hoffman, "Clash of Globalizations," *Foreign Policy* 81(4) (July-August 2002): 104–115; 108.

5

THE POLITICAL PERSPECTIVE

> Let us teach ourselves and others that politics can be not only the art of the possible—especially if this means speculations, intrigues, secret deals, and pragmatic maneuvering—but also the art of the impossible, namely, the art of improving ourselves and the world. Václav Havel[1]

Many notions of globalization stress the economics of the human condition and include claims about the erosion and decreasing relevance of politics: the *end-of-politics* theme. Aristotle's (384–322 B.C.) notion that people are by nature political, however, seems unaffected by globalization and valid despite other claims about human nature. People remain prone to discourse and cooperation, competition and conflict, and "authoritative allocation of values" —economic, political, social, and cultural—to avoid feelings of exclusion within a community.[2] Historically, the nation-state has accrued a quasi-moral legitimacy through the bonds of nationalism, national identity, and individual self-sacrifice, which extends beyond the original pragmatism that was its foundation. Political globalization implies erosion of these intangible bonds between state and people and demotion of the state from a *gemeinschaft* of communal solidarity to a mere *gesellschaft* of pragmatic convenience. It also implies promotion of some global community from *gesellschaft* to *gemeinschaft*.[3]

People have used domestic politics to create and manage satisfying relationships between society, the state, and the individual and to relieve the recurring stresses that enervate their cultural, political, and economic arrangements through collective action. Without, however, the communal cohesion of a society or the rational personality of the individual, international politics has been people's preferred process to manage relationships between states. Since states have often sought to relieve internal social stresses through interstate conflict, people have used war, diplomacy, and international law *not to relieve the social stresses that generated conflict but to control states' efforts to dissipate them outside their own sovereign jurisdictions.*

Unlike local, national, or international politics, global politics must deal with issues that demand resolution of social stresses and global collective action. "Globalization has meant that there is increasing recognition of arenas where impacts are global. It is in these arenas where global collective action is required—and systems of global governance are essential."[4] Although economic globalization generated the powerful forces behind them, a set of complex, global patterns of ecological, political, and social systemic problems calls for global governance to resolve social stresses in a symphony of systems.

The swarm of unrelieved social stresses that politics has dissipated beyond national jurisdictions keeps any prospect of universal world order remote, despite globalization. People have conceived global systems of cooperation and competition to govern not only human interaction but globalization itself. Beyond dyadic governance among sovereign states, knowledge and perspectives have refined visions of a society of states. One alternative to *ad hoc* dyadic governance is the notion of world government as an extension of triadic governance systems within less-than-global political communities. Modern globalization has also exposed innovative possibilities for popular governance in one integrated world or through a global civil society. Most visions of global governance, however, do not offer credible or comprehensive resolution for the social stresses that politics has sought to relieve for millennia.

POLITICAL GLOBALIZATION

Political globalization is the expansion of the exclusive perspectives of domestic and interstate politics to inclusive global politics. Political globalism appreciates global values and concerns, deflates commitments to narrow perspectives and local interests, and seeks to relieve social stresses in human progress and new knowledge. This multidimensional expansion involves not only the geographical expansion of political ideas into foreign polities but also the expansion of political activity from narrow perspectives to broader ones.

Political Contagion

Even before the Enlightenment, political globalization had spread the sovereignty-bound, territorial state beyond Europe with its infectious ideology of nationalism and institutions of capitalism. As economic globalization increased the permeability of state borders to flows of goods, people, and information, political ideas expanded also. Although comparisons to pressure or osmosis reflect the spread of capitalism and growth through the world, the metaphor of contagion better describes the expansive force of political ideas.[5] Contagious spread of political ideas is especially virulent when people do not recognize a clear, certain course for action. They appropriate the decisions and ideas of others, usually in the past, to inform their own decision-making or problem-solving processes. Autogenously self-reproducing, political contagion involves deliberate mimicry or emulation of policies, processes, or institutions that seem to have brought rewards in other polities. The popular association of globalization with the failure of Soviet state intervention and economic regulation has spread political contagion into the economic perspective in a flurry of imitative privatization. Although cultural imitation in fashion, music, or entertainment is often benign, political contagion carries the possibilities of significant disruptions in *both* domestic society *and* international relations. Since imitators tend to be seeking practical solutions to immediate crises, political contagion often does not expand perspectives and rarely leads to new knowledge. In contrast to well-publicized economic penetrations or cultural imperialism, political globalization spreads ideas slowly and imperceptibly as political movements generate epidemics that persist for centuries.

Movements that embody universal ideas apparently applicable to all people —liberalism or communism, but not Asian values or Christian democracy—are highly contagious and spread rapidly. Ideas that promise large material or social benefits at minimal cost are very attractive—capitalism, socialism, or Keynesianism—especially to the world's poor and oppressed masses. Successful episodes involving these contagious ideas attract many imitators, which, if they also succeed, attract yet more emulation in a spiral of political globalization. Beyond this self-reflexivity, most powerful political ideas carry ideological, moral, or ethical baggage that proselytes adherents as evangelists.

The spread of political ideas within groups of like-minded people and similar societies within a single region is, not surprisingly, quicker and more likely than infection between unlike societies. Despite the insidious power of political contagion, although uncontrollable political epidemics do occur, they are historically rare. In the globalizing world, political ideas are most likely to spread through "a gradual and nearly invisible process of learning and adjustment, rather than from a sudden and dramatic transformation in an entire social order, . . . [as] the slow spread of regulatory norms over mundane issues . . . [or] the product of transnational networks of lawyers, bureaucrats, and industry lobbyists who are largely shielded from intense public scrutiny."[6]

Cultural differences seem just as effective as political dissimilarities in immunizing societies against a political movement or even an epidemic. Interdependence and power-based international politics seem to have repressed interstate political conflict beneath the universal obsession with economic growth. Globalization and political contagion seem, however, to have broadened the relationships between social stress and economic growth into the cultural perspective and deepened interstate conflict into civil war.

Social Stress and Conflict

Within the classical power-based international system, the state concentrated the several narrow-perspective stresses in its sovereignty and relieved them in interstate conflict or war. War and conflict served to diminish social stress within states as nationalism rallied societies in defense or pride, although victory or defeat served to redistribute and diffuse stress to some other society. Constrained by the threat of escalation to catastrophic, nuclear war, the power politics of international relations, with its batteries of realist and liberal control mechanisms, suppressed interstate conflict reasonably well. In deference to the pragmatic need to avoid war, societies either absorbed the social stresses of globalization, suffered civil war, or sought local relief through social transformation into welfare states. With no systemic mechanism to manage civil wars, to relieve the stresses of globalization, or the resource-intensive demands of welfare states, international politics has struggled to balance interstate harmony with expanding prosperity and intrastate wars.

Despite fashionable understandings of globalization as a powerful process converting political barriers into commercial opportunities, replacing obsolescence with modernity, and subverting state control with free markets, social reality remains stress-laden. Expanding political contagion and economic integration into the cultural perspective carry the stresses of expanding ideas through and across interdependent societies and cultures. Through contagion, new ideas and stresses that transform a society's own social reality expand to stress other societies within, perhaps, different perspectives in some socioeconomic triggering zone. The same epidemic forces also, however, spread the reductions in social stress brought through transformation of social reality and new knowledge created in *basho* within some cultural-political stress shadow.

Interstate Political Conflict

The strategic goal for interstate war has historically been "destruction of the enemy's military power."[7] With due respect for the social imperatives of resource-based growth, premodern societies limited war to violent interactions between armies and navies but did not involve the enemy's civilians or their property. As globalization introduced more economies to modern resource-based economic growth in a context of market-based competition for resources, the direct relationship between resource-based growth and conflict intensified and deepened.[8] As market competition deepened into interstate conflict, war also became resource-intensive, and the twentieth century brought a striking change within the military and economic perspectives. Until World War I, governments at war did not disturb enemy civilians, businesses, or property domiciled in their countries, so long as they refrained from political or warlike activities. World War I began the practices of internment and confiscation into government custody in wartime. In modern, resource-intensive war, there are no civilians. The paradoxical effects of this military-economic campaign may help to win a war but have significantly impaired a victor's capacity to win the ensuing postwar peace. After the destruction of every twentieth-century war, the victors have won the responsibility and the costs for reconstructing the societies of the vanquished, relieving their social stresses, and restarting resource-based growth.

In an industrial context of rising political expectations of sustained economic growth, the demands for ever more material resources translated uneven growth into social stress and interstate conflict. As people recognized the power of resources to generate growth, "the goal of warfare was redefined as destroying the enemy's potential for waging war, which meant destroying the enemy's economy."[9] Globalization and interdependence adjusted war to the realities of the global economy but have done little to replace interstate conflict as an efficient relief for the social stresses that they generate. As businesses shift from national strategies to multi- and transnational commercial models, globalization has made Bacon's idols of military-economic, interstate war irrational, unsupportable, and probably dysfunctional. The global economy of transnational production cannot operate as a wartime economy, and global governance cannot operate as a wartime government. Although within the global perspective, winning a postwar peace is more important than winning an interstate war, within the military perspective, "war is a continuation of political intercourse with a mixture of other means."[10]

Deterred from war to relieve social stress, societies and their governments find promises of stability in economic growth and social transformation. Rather than shifting the focus of international politics to global prosperity and relieving global stress, Bacon's idols continue to shape governments' foreign policies around volatile blends of geopolitical perceptions and domestic politics. "Even in undemocratic regimes, forces such as xenophobic passions, economic grievances, and transnational ethnic solidarity can make policymaking far more complex and less predictable."[11] The multipolarity implicit in the global perspective leads intuitively through nationalism and sovereignty to dour predictions of interstate conflict in unstable post–Cold-War interdependence.[12]

Intrastate Conflict and Civil War

Globalization has exposed the social stress, which is often the source of war and conflict, not "as an exogenous force that acts on states and societies from without; it derives rather from within them."[13] As new knowledge expands from *basho* in a transformed social reality through innovation, learning, and diffusion, stress inevitably accumulates as broader prespectives expose new uncertainties. Lost between past, present, and future, people struggle to create new identities, refine old values, and adapt to new truths. Torn between market forces, political sovereignty, and the international imperative towards stability, governments face cruel, impossible choices between economic competitiveness, nationalist pride, and social welfare. Since international politics has no effective control mechanisms to resolve internal conflicts or civil war, such choices in many societies chronically generate the brutal internal conflicts that invite foreign military and political intervention.

Regardless of internal trauma or transformation, political contagion and economic integration invite social stresses to migrate across political borders as stimuli for local conflicts and civil wars within amorphous triggering zones of interdependence. Cultural idiosyncracies readily transform subtle stresses in one society into cataclysmic pressures in another and explode trivial policy decisions of one government into the triggers of civil war in another polity. Actual civil war, however, seems to efface the political shadow of contagious stress reduction and demands some unique culture-specific transformation of social reality through *basho* and new knowledge. The intervention invited by interdependence and globalization parenthetically energizes a nascent international community or society of states.

Stress Triggering. Although the constraints of international politics preclude relieving stress in interstate war, since the international system has not restrained civil war, social stress congeals in domestic conflict. At least some of the social stress that globalization gradually concentrates within economic, political, or cultural perspectives can find release in civil war, *basho*, and social transformation. This social stress does not, however, simply dissipate in popular satisfaction with change; it diffuses through political contagion, economic interdependence, and cultural convergence. Globalization and interdependence have penetrated social and cultural immunities and made social stress contagiously interactive across polities with the consequences that conflict—especially civil conflict—is also contagious. The contagion of social stress inherent in globalization carries *the probability of spreading stress-related conflict through interdependence.* Known as stress triggering, this mutant of political contagion embodies the increasing responsiveness of interdependent polities and economies to subtle social stresses in neighbors.[14]

Stress Shadows. Transformation of a society's social reality—through war or *basho*—not only relieves its own stress and increases stress in societies within a stress-triggering zone but also relieves stress within some stress shadow. Although the triggering zone and stress shadow cast by each society are mutually exclusive, interdependence ensures that most societies lie in several triggering zones and stress shadows. When stress shadows coincide with triggering zones of other transformations, the effect is confused by the timing and strengths of all of the original social transformations.

Stress Fatigue. Social stress never accumulates to the point of destroying a civilization; it generates transformation through conflict or *basho* and new knowledge. Since social stress is a continuous variable, rather than a dichotomous value, social transformations, which relieve stress, generate an immediate, brief, torrent of social reactions—often civil war—that diminishes with time. Neither the originating society nor those within a triggering zone retain these high rates of stress-induced change indefinitely. In *both* parent societies *and* those that are triggered or shadowed, the rate of social change immediately falls but gradually recovers as incremental innovation diffuses new knowledge through society in new values and attitudes. Although globalization and interdependence determine the patterns of triggering and shadowing, the scope and depth of civil war and the new knowledge created in *basho* determine the duration and extent of stress fatigue.

Kurzweil's Law. Instead of stagnating or destroying society, the accumulation or dissipation of social stress alters the rate of relevant stress-related events in accordance with Kurzweil's Law of Time and Chaos. As local chaos increases within a society's narrow perspectives—with *basho*, social transformation, or conflict—contagion increases the rate of significant narrow-perspective events within a trigger zone. The First Kurzweil Corollary, operating within the global perspective through conversations between *basho*, ensures that the number of social transformations and the chaos associated with them may be decreasing in social time as stress shadows expand, merge, and stabilize. Although international politics has decreased international chaos and thereby reduced the frequency of war, by proscribing interstate conflict, globalization and interdependence have increased domestic chaos in a *de facto* convergence of political, economic, and cultural perspectives.

Fragmegration

Globalization juxtaposes a powerful trend towards integration and centralization of wealth with equally powerful pressure towards fragmentation, decentralization, and diffusion of political power. As Newtonian mechanics placed the atom and the planet as polar references for universal understanding, globalization recognized the unitary individual as the prime mover of human progress. Just as the quantum revolution is disrupting familiar relationships between atoms and planets, an *in-utero*, universal polity, and a global economy form personal and social interactions in a context of some global civilization. The *process* of globalization empowers the individual and weakens connections between individuals and groups of people but firmly integrates both within the global perspective. This is the paradox of *fragmegration*—the conjuncture of fragmentation and integration in the *condition* of globalization.[15]

As political focus fragmented across more countries, the agenda of international politics expanded across more human concerns and perspectives within the integrating penumbra of economic globalization. A global political process developed international law into a legitimate set of universal values and norms for individual and state behaviors and focused them in transnational institutions. The salience of transnational organizations and subnational movements has raised the specter of bizarre coalitions of government bureaucrats, international lawyers, demagogic radicals, and sincere individuals setting the agenda for global politics. Economic integration is shifting many of the functions of the state—security, law making and enforcement, civil administration, or infrastructual management—to international regimes and organizations that assume transfer of functional sovereignty.

Global fragmegration seems to augur a loose system of global governance surmounting a swarm of tiny, fragmented, Lilliputian municipalities as the precursor of a supranational, Leviathan state with dominant coercive, legislative, and regulatory powers.[16] Instead of an integrated symphony of integrated systems, global governance seems the repetitive canon of cultural exceptionalism swelling to engulf the entire world. This latest reiteration of Karl Polanyi's double movement paradoxically decentralizes and concentrates political power even as the global economy concentrates wealth in transnational corporations and increases global economic inequality.

As they have before, the processes of integration and fragmentation have created a Braudelian *conjoncture* as the foundation of a new fragmegrated civilization. The people who shape governments, exchange goods and services in rational markets, share remembered knowledge of the past, and create visions with faith in the future are slowly forming *basho* to guide progress into the future. Beneath the amorphous currents that force people into choices between the Charybdis of cultural homogenization and the Scylla of political fragmentation lies a novel civilization that globalization is slowly forming.

Institutions

The developing institutions of the state, a society of states, or a global community of people reflect people's expanding knowledge, changing perspectives, and evolving identities in the dynamics of politics. Premodern people found their identities in tradition and their interests in balance between people, between societies, and between humanity, God, and nature. People felt that justice was beyond human capabilities, outside politics, and best left to the gods. Societies left power politics to elites whose perspectives did not include the problems of people's lives. Political institutions embodied personalities, and policy was largely discretionary. Premodern political institutions and states embodied these values in the political goals of stability and balance.

The Enlightenment and modernity established people's identities and formed their *mentalités* around wealth, class, and culture. People found identity and direction within themselves and discovered freedom in choice, change, and progress. As democracy transformed issues into dichotomous choices, political institutions embedded personal and social priorities of security within modern ideologies—liberalism, socialism, and nationalism. Inner-directed people resolved social and economic issues in politics that involved extensive and intensive participation of self-interested individuals in civil society and a public sphere. As people sought to prosper through innovation, gain freedom, and meet moral obligations through political engagement, they associated public and private interests power. The invention of capitalism focused political processes on economic issues and prosperity as social interests shifted towards materialistic concerns. Justice in the modern world referred to achieving and protecting civil rights and freedoms through collective or triadic, impersonal political process, rather than maintaining balance or stability. With legacies of discretionary policy and exclusive sovereignty, modernity developed unilateral institutions to pursue national interests through dyadic relationships with each other in a hazy context of triadic nonsovereign, multilateral institutions.

Humanity now stands at another *conjoncture* with a new set of *mentalités* that includes multiple, robust identities for self, society, and other extending beyond wealth or class. People's identities have become irreversibly "politicized in a way that balks at external processes and attempts to reconnect an idealized past with the vagaries of an uncertain present containing a mix of democratic and undemocratic tendencies."[17] The political process absorbs justice as the ideal of individual equality within and across the many groups that are the sources of people's identities. Establishing boundaries between self and other, institutions form distinct domains for societies while promoting productive, satisfying interactions. Interstate power politics has expanded modernity's legacy into a world of multilateral institutions as the context for political struggle, dyadic governance, and unilateral decisionmaking. Just as transnational corporations have organized dyadic market exchanges on a global scale, global and international political institutions organize and manage dyadic interstate political processes and relationships. What was once an exclusively unilateral activity in dyadic relationships monopolized by a few great powers has become a continuing multilateral project. Led by the forceful American political culture and robust U.S. institutions, globalization has "embarked on an effort to reengineer the human person, reorder basic human relationships, and reconstruct human institutions that have existed for millennia."[18]

Beneath an institutional facade of diplomacy and summitry, global politics has accreted relations among economies and cultures without the mediation of political processes. Beyond power, the extrapolitical networks and patterns of trade, language, religion, ethnicity and culture, commercial alliance, legal conventions and regimes, and others have become legitimate institutions of global politics. Globalization has integrated subnational cultures across national boundaries and created an integrated global economy in a multidimensional web of processes, institutions, and structures. Global politics, however, still occurs among interacting sovereign states that selectively accept global institutions based on political influence and coercive power. "We have no world government, accountable to the people of every country, to oversee the globalization process in a fashion comparable to the way national governments guided the nationalization process. Instead, we have a system that might be called *global governance without global government*."[19]

Global Political Forces

The *conjoncture* of power, fragmegration, institutions, political contagion, and prosperity merges separate streams of global political forces into a turbulent flood threatening to engulf people who are excluded from globalization. One stream has converged around corporations, political parties, and interest groups seeking to use political power for their own purposes outside power politics. This stream comprises business executives, diplomats, bureaucrats, and those people focused on pursuing various self-defined versions of justice or some redistribution of prosperity. Traditional diplomacy and sovereign states form a second political force struggling heroically to maintain global order and preserve the Westphalian political system. The majority of the world's people and states that are excluded from globalization—or even just economic globalization—are slowly congealing into a formidable political force dedicated to changing the current world order. Another stream comprises veto groups dedicated to preventing untoward or undesirable things—sponsored by any of the other streams—from happening. The interactions of these elemental forces in the process-condition of globalization and the institution-system of global governance dominate the political perspective of globalization, despite their proscription from the current agenda of global politics.

After a century of state dominance in the struggle against socialism, communism, fascism, and totalitarianism, globalization is restoring the balance between the individual, society, the corporation, and government. Economic globalization allows business and commerce to avoid governmental interference and ordinary people to obtain goods and services beyond those preferred by a government or offered by local firms. Much of the recent story of globalization is about the hesitant and uneven "spreading of a political culture that is based on individual liberty to areas that have been longing to embrace it for years."[20] Despite the recurring fear that globalization is simply the shift of power from governments to multinationals, most of the forces behind economic globalization—technology, capital, management—as mediated through the market favor individuals and small companies. Although globalization is changing societies and cultures throughout the world, the change is not necessarily towards homogenization, unless individuals choose to be homogenized. When individuals live in an open, globalized society, neither governments nor companies can superimpose their values and interests on those of the individuals who determine the nature of the common good.

GLOBAL GOVERNANCE

"The most fundamental change that is required to make globalization work in the way that it should is a change in governance."[21] Although the processes within the international political system have changed to follow changing human values, the fundamental state-centered structures and processes of international politics remain essentially as they were created several centuries ago. The end of the Cold War, however, misaligned the control mechanisms and destroyed the coherence of the system's structural institutions. As economic forces overcame politics, technology replaced security and the expanding networks of the global economy challenged popular demands for cultural justice. Although the military-political power of the United States remains catastrophically relevant and calls for justice remain strident, the focus of globalization and global governance remains on economic wealth.

Because the emerging processes of global politics refer to no particular, place, the site of governance is literally global, rather than below or above, within or beyond, or even referrent to the state. Global governance floats in hazy patterns of mercurial, global, decisionmaking and structural vacuity: governance without government. Not reducible to local its effects, global governance carries no expectations of simultaneous social or structural realities at every place in the world and does not rely on power to manage processes. "Globalization has constructed new nonterritorial and nonsovereign forms of governance, while simultaneously confirming the sovereign state, transformed from its original historical form as the defining, territorially located site of central and legitimate government, to a new form of local and regional subsidiary government." Relating governmental structures and territorial limits across time and space, global governance emerges and flourishes alongside them as it embraces local politics and cultural histories with native values embedded in them. Beyond governmental structure, the political processes of global governance transform politics "from participating in policymaking to the consumption of policies; from the potential disruption of power as inequality and systemic privilege to the individualism of self-empowerment."[22]

Within the perspectives of people, cities, and states, the scope of government and less-than-global governance comprise solving salient problems, managing current crises, preventing or resolving conflict, sustaining economic growth, and keeping order. State-centered politics and government perceive conflict and growth as problems to solve: by preventing or winning conflict and by generating and sustaining growth. The political controversies involve whether to control, regulate, intervene, or leave things to serendipity, with intermittent embarrassments about justice and morality. Within the global perspective, governance extends beyond problem solving or conflict resolution to transformation of social reality and prefers global initiatives for progress to less-than-global reactions to change or demands for solutions. Beyond a power-based structure of government, global governance is not synonymous with control or good order, which are jealously provided by second-level politics.

Although international politics has contained interstate war within the specter of thermonuclear cataclysm, intrastate and cultural conflicts have exploded in a context of rapid economic growth. The rich, globalized growth-conflict relationship confuses the numbers of states and kinds of groups involved, diverse cultural values and ways of pursuing them, and the nature of the international system. The imponderables of the interactions between these effects of globalization are well beyond the scope and capabilities of *both* international politics *and* state government. Legitimating uses of power and the roles of trade and industry, global governance mediates cultural beliefs about behaviors, expectations about reciprocities and responsibilities, and notions of obligation or privilege. "These sorts of issues have linkages to and among political, economic, commercial, and security issues, and extend into the future and the past through memories, expectations, and aspirations."[23]

How any governance system functions depends on the social, political, and economic processes, structures, relationships, and institutions that it embraces and regulates.[24] Within the global perspective, any system of global governance can emerge only deterministically from the Westphalian legacies of national sovereignty and the Smithian heritage of capitalism. International institutions and political processes, dyadic relationships, structural power polarity, the market economy, and the dynamics of power politics form the context within which governance must operate. Beyond the political-economic legacies, global governance embraces the processes of international law and the structures of nongovernmental organizations as powerful systems of social and cultural interactions without the filters of state power. Although war remains within the political perspective, any global-governance structure prefers peaceful dispute resolution to defer power politics, market confrontations, and cultural frictions to social transformation and progress. Expanding any notion of classical balance of power, the complex politics of global governance struggle with a chronically unstable, quadruple balance: among states; between state and market; between the state and the individual; and between cultures.

Political Community

A precondition for governance at any level is a political community that transcends the functional or ascribed identities that people cherish. Any form of global governance must derive its legitimacy through a shared conviction that the policies and programs proceeding from global institutions represent the perspectives and interests of all members, *both* states *and* people, united in a global political community. Members, or citizens, of political communities may be individuals, groups, or even states, which are themselves political communities. The political community is unique among other types of communities in incorporating some legitimate decision-making authority and is the foundation of stability, continuity, order, and functional efficacy.

In nonauthoritarian political communities, legislators in institutional government initiate governance as inclusive decisions and binding rules for the entire community. Community members agree consensually to accept those decisions and the rules that the government imposes on them and to respect specified rights of other members. This respect for legitimate authority crystallized around the modern state through Thomas Hobbes's social contract and John Locke's ideas of sovereignty.[25] The authoritarian model of political community appeared in Plato's (427–347 B.C.) *Republic*. Aristotle introduced a normative, democratic model in his *Politics*. In various versions, the ideal of a collectivist, secular, egalitarian, political community of individuals united under legitimate rule for their common good has persisted in political thought throughout the world.[26] Although political communities have formed and persisted under authoritarian regimes, democratic and populist political communities with roots in a robust civil society seem to be more stable.[27]

Embedded within every political community is a system: "the interacting set of private associations and governmental institutions involved in the decisionmaking process for the society."[28] Political systems embody "a process of political communication, some machinery for enforcement, and some popular habits of compliance."[29] Each political community creates a common identity as people take active roles in collective efforts, join civic associations, give to community charities, and volunteer their time for the common good.[30] "An active, engaged citizenry is motivated by a shared sense of common purpose that helps people find compromises to difficult issues."[31]

Active partipation in civic organizations creates personal confidence, which political community subtly expands to trust in people whom they do not know. This pseudomoral, communal trust and civic associations are the essential foundation and structures of collective action. Communal trust —Alexis de Tocqueville's self-interest rightly understood—is the precondition for civic engagement, governance, and political community rather than their result.[32] Trusting people are involved in civil society—educational, cultural, and business organizations—and form political communities that embody the processes of governance and legitimate the structures of government.

The shared identity and mutual support within a political community, which have usually been exclusive, define its legal, political, social, and cultural boundaries by ascribing to each member the status of citizenship. Historically, the notion of citizenship has acquired three central propositions as ideals. All citizens are of equal intrinsic worth with equal rights to live under the law. All citizens are able to participate in the political processes for establishing law and policy in a context of procedural governance and institutional government. All citizens have access to public goods, services, and welfare to prevent destitution. As for national political communities, any global political community must embody some operational form of global citizenship carrying legal rights, political privileges, and economic values.[33]

The existing citizens of a trusting, political community prescribe the criteria for membership "in accordance with our own understanding of what membership means in our community and what sort of community we want to have. Membership as a social good is constituted by our understanding; its value is fixed by ourwork and conversation; and then we are in charge (who else could be in charge?) of its distribution."[34] A necessary, but not sufficient, condition for membership in a political community has historically been legal citizenship in an associated state. Beyond moralistic trust, membership is a legal bond of rights and obligations between individual and community. A primary, common purpose of stable, political communities has been to include members of all national subgroups in a political order, a shared identity, and set of common rights and obligations, while excluding all others.[35]

The moral and legal consensus within the political community on identity, purpose, rights, duties, and institutions confers legitimacy on a system of governance and creates solidarity within the community.[36] A political community cannot form or persist at any level of politics in the absence of this consensus.[37] A global political community probably cannot exist without an additional, moralistic, structural foundation that includes the democratic, national state, a global, civil society, and a credible public sphere comprising all of humanity.

Processes of Global Governance

With each transformation of social reality, globalization synthesized all previous political structures, world visions, and value systems into a novel historical system that extended politics a bit deeper into the global perspective. After centuries of efforts to govern bits of the world through mercantilism, empire, colonialism, and suzerainty, by the twentieth century, people could think practicably and operationally about global governance. By the 1960s, globalization had superposed over the clear, rigid structure imposed by the Westphalian system of interstate politics a complex, global political-economic system with neither formal structure nor legitimate operating processes.

Unlike those of domestic and interstate politics, the processes of global politics do not operate in event time but in social time, are not embedded in any stable structures, and do not rest within or upon a robust political community. Global governance occurs at a third level of politics that includes, penetrates, and extends state-level and local-level political processes and institutions of triadic government. Beyond the high politics of power-based governmental politics in pursuing security and the low politics of free-market economics in seeking prosperity, a third level of global governance aspires to justice across humanity and throughout the world.

Third-Level Politics

As Braudel was conceiving his three domains within the economic perspective, globalization transformed the international system into a global social reality with a third political level. At the third, global level, politics began to inspire a sense of progress—rational, pragmatic, or zealous—towards something universal, defined, believed, imagined, or unknown. At a second, social—usually, but not necessarily, national—level, politics either connected individuals to society or isolated them by reifying extrasocial or transborder relationships established by the self. Second-level politics legitimated the connection between individual and society in state government with a civil society and public sphere, in resistance movements, or in nationalism. Politics at the first, individual level *both* provided personal identity *and* allowed individuals to select some font of absolute truth and certainty—God, ethics, law, society, government, self, wealth, justice, some past golden age, or something else.[38]

To obviate the anarchic, Hobbesian war of all against all on the third level, global politics congealed across the three levels of politics around a Rousseauesque *idola tribus*: human compassion. After the Enlightenment transformed premodern acceptance of inequality into modern embarrassment, third-level politics expanded moral repugnance for inequality into salient global political issues. The solidarity of human compassion, which has crystallized gradually since the Renaissance, welds human thought and knowledge into a stable foundation for global politics. Within the primary economic focus of globalization, third-level politics invites the rich to express their human instinct in political urges to improve the material conditions of people in poor countries, but not to a general transfer of wealth from the rich to the poor.

The expansions of perspectives and knowledge carried by globalization ensure that the third-level processes of global governance cannot be limited to politics or even to economics. More than extending national values beyond state boundaries, political globalization creates and legitimates global regimes that operate on the third level through people within national territories that retain state sovereignty. Economic deregulation and transnational legal regimes denationalize territory within a context of third-level legality and global norms enforced by the second-level sovereign state. The rights enforced by the state under global regimes are often beyond those guaranteed under narrow national mandates. Global political processes penetrate national, physical territories and "continue to operate under sovereign regulatory umbrellas, but they do so under new emergent transnational regimes and, often, under circumstances of a denationalizing of national territory."[39] The global symphony of systems is far more complex than a simple canon of national systems.

Triadic Governance

Third-level, global politics legitimates triadic governance as at least an alternative to the traditional dyadic processes of international politics. The primordial unit of human and interstate relations, the dyad is any pattern of direct interaction or exchange between two individuals.[40] The essential structure for dyadic governance lies in the values, knowledge, traditions, and expectancies embedded in culture, which translate chains of sequential, dyadic reciprocity into sociopolitical hierarchies of rights and duties. Premodern, dyadic, governance systems stabilized chains of reciprocal, dyadic relationships into orderly social realities. In dyadic systems, unresolved conflict can destroy the relationship and the system by breaking the dyadic chain of society. Dyadic conflict between or within states resolves around a single, broad unilateral purpose—victory—that pervades the entire family and chronology of crises of confrontation until a conflict ends. Unresolved conflict usually leads to victory for one of the opponents, which destroys the system itself.[41] Over millennia, the stability of dyadic governance congealed into broad platforms of quasi-moral absolute truth protected by all of Bacon's idols.

Rational Enlightenment-modern thought, focusing on rational choice and utility, suggested that dyads were inherently unstable "because each party faces powerful incentives to ignore normative obligations, thereby cheating on the other."[42] Instead, rationalism relied heavily on a triad of two disputants and a dispute resolver or governor as a universal structure for organizing social authority, decisionmaking, and governance in the nation-state. Rooted in the dyad, the state-centered triad guaranteed reciprocity by involving a governor whose interest lay in the stability of the common good and the durability of the dyadic relationships that ensured societal survival. Triadic dispute resolution could be consensual—delegation or mediation—or compulsory —office conferred by a state, adjudication, or arbitration.[43] Governance systems that stabilized triadic dispute resolution, rather than hierarchic dyadic structures, stimulated social progress through transition and transformation, rather than static preservation of traditional values and old knowledge.

Within a context of rational risk assessment, the social logic of triadic governance is one of future individual utility in a context of absolute social benefit. Disputants must believe that the risk of individual loss is lower in delegating power to a governor than in dissolving the chains of dyadic relationships that constitute society. Triadic governance is feasible in future-oriented societies only among individuals who share and value a common identity that embodies some form of trust. Without some minimum levels of social trust and confidence in trustworthiness, individuals can readily perceive the delegation of personal power in the triad as more costly than beneficial.

An early result of globalization within future-oriented societies, state-centered, triadic governance preserved the cultural dyads that formed societies but did not require dyadic chains of political hierarchy or tables of rights and duties to ensure stability. Whereas conflict destroys dyadic systems, it is constitutive of triadic governance, which does not leave conflict unresolved. Triadic governance generates social norms and stable expectations of behaviors while accommodating social transformations in a stable, government-like structure. Through adjudication and legislation, triadic governance not only resolves disputes but "makes rules that are concrete, particular, and retrospective . . . rules of an abstract, general, and prospective nature, . . . [and] clarifies and alters rules comprising the normative structure."[44]

Like dyadic systems, the legitimacy of triadic governance arises in some normative, cultural structure—tradition, institutions, ideology, law, rules, beliefs, or other constraints on behavior in the social community.[45] Operating to reduce the costs of decisionmaking in uncertainty, culture provides the necessary sense of fairness and trust for triadic delegation, just as it does for dyadic reciprocity. Whereas dyadic systems change only through destruction and reestablishment of normative dyadic chains, "triadic governance evolves according to the logic of path dependence, manifested by the increasing dominance of triadic rule making over the content of normative structure."[46] In a profoundly governmental process that dyadic systems inhibit, triadic governance generates and organizes a social discourse—focused in legislative processes—that often merges with cultural trends in *basho* to create new knowledge and launch social innovation. Because the creative, legislative function generalizes the judicial operation of triadic governance, its cultural legitimacy animates politics as a dynamic, normative, cultural structure of the governance system. Although people have not yet created a triadic system of global governance, globalization continues to construct the social norms and stabilize expectations through transformations of social reality.

Cosmopolitan Justice

The global implications of moral issues surrounding poverty, rights, and crime congeal in cosmopolitan justice, which calls for redistribution of wealth and rights *both* among *and* within nation-states "in recognition of the claims many of them make concerning our duties (of justice at least) to others who are not our fellow countrymen."[47] "Mass publics do not consider domestic and international justice as watertight compartments. They support international redistribution more strongly when principles of justice have been institutionalized domestically and when poverty has been tackled at home, and less strongly in the absence of such principles and achievements. . . . Public opinion is in fact considering justice in a global perspective."[48] Proposing that neither nationality nor state boundaries have moral relevance to questions of justice, cosmopolitan justice forms two narrow perspectives: thick and thin.[49]

Within the perspective of *thick* globalism, justice applies primarily to individuals, as the ultimate, legitimate possessors of rights and obligations. Only indirect objects for justice, societies, institutions, and states are the functional agents of people for establishing and enforcing human justice. In contrast, *thin* globalists accept legitimate positions for society, states, associations, and artificial juridical persons as holders of rights and duties, and as *both* objects *and* subjects of justice. For thick and thin alike, cosmopolitan justice balances the universal with the particular on the point that obligations to self and nation coexist with the rights of all other people.

Globalists of both sorts find justice in redistribution of power and wealth from the world's rich to the poor and call for incorporating Asian, Latin, and African ideas, aspirations, and norms into the global political-economy and world law.[50] Challenging use of the world's resources as organized by the global economy, cosmopolitans resent the injustice spread across political-judicial borders as exports of hazards by market or natural forces.[51] Global management of earth's environment and its many nonhuman species must have its foundations in *both* current equity in burden-sharing *and* some concept of intergenerational justice. For globalists, thick and thin alike, cosmopolitan justice can emerge only from rejection of any moral distinction between foreigners and citizens in meeting challenges of refugees, migration, resettlement. Any sort of justice must arise by determining what each person —citizen, foreigner, or displaced—owes all other people and what each can reasonably expect from the others as social, cultural and national obligations.[52]

Third-Level Global Democracy

Historically confined to the nation-states that occupy the entire world, democracy has remained at the local and national levels of politics as a political passenger of globalization instead of the force carrying it. Although the twenty-first century opened with many peoples living in some sort of local democracy, the shallow surge of post–Cold-War democratization has left the triumph of democracy neither complete nor inevitable. Despite diversion of structural democratization into the national level, globalization has expanded the reach of democratic processes beyond these first two political levels. "For the first time, economic conditions and modes of communication make a more global type of interaction and integration a possibility."[53] Expanding human ideals beyond *polis* and the territorial state, third-level democracy equates the *demos*, or *demoi*, with the nonexclusive entirety of humanity and expands democracy from structural government to the processes of governance. More that holding local elections for government officials, democratic governance balances Rousseau's view of human nature as a compassionate desire to avoid harming others with Hobbes's war of all against all.[54]

As political perspectives expanded, the waves of globalization have changed the meaning of democracy imperceptibly but profoundly. Little noticed as national democracy diverged into liberal and social forms was the transformation of individual freedom of political participation into social freedom of access to political influence. Within national polities, robust structural institutions and cultural norms defined and legitimated minimal individual access to influence as inherent in effective social democracy. Although international politics lacks *either* participatory institutions *or* social access to influence, the foundations for extending these norms—participation and access—to the third level lie in national public spheres and an emerging, transnational civil society. The expanding perspectives and universal publicity of globalization carry the promise of democratic process in creating institutions of equal access to influence as a third level of democracy. The emergence of a global democracy is not an intuitive, obvious, logical, or even natural consequence of globalization. The promise of third-level democracy lies in "the legitimation of democratic ideas of governance on a universal basis, the embodiment of these ideas in human rights as specified in global instruments, the democratic implications of nonviolent approaches to resistance and reform, and . . . the deeply democratic convictions of transnational initiatives that have begun to construct the alternative paradigm of a global civil society."[55]

Despite the promise of technology, Bacon's idols, weak institutions, and the social realities of modern civilization present formidable barriers to a third level of democracy. The ambiguous obscurity of global decisionmaking frustrates any structural, institutional, or formal democratic access to influence, either directly or through representation. In a global context of divergent political traditions, exclusive cultural-ethnic identities, and national solidarities, formation of consensus through democratic processes emerges as an intractable dilemma in focusing collective action. "The emergence of a global civil society is an important precondition of democracy at the global level."[56] First- and second-level democratization and the beginnings of populist self-organization into civil society herald the creation of new democratic knowledge that can diffuse into the third level. "Such politicization from below may constitute a major, although not necessarily revolutionary, change in the condition of the emerging world order, and perhaps in a more democratic direction."[57]

Access to Political Influence. Only some feeling of full participation and access to influence allows minorities to accept the will of a majority within democratic systems. Despite equal, structural opportunity to participate, asymmetries of power, resources, and information in first- and second-level democracy deny to citizens any reasonable expectation of influencing political decisions towards individual self-interests. In a global context, the uncertainty of structural democracy requires that the standard for democratic process must be access to political influence within a legitimate process of decisionmaking. All citizens must "be able to avoid being included in decisions over which they have had no influence; moreover, they must be able to avoid being excluded in the sense that their public reasons do not receive effective [consideration] in the course of deliberation."[58] Although first- and second-level democracy, based on the social agreement and legitimacy of *gemeinschaft*, can contain concerns about access in nationalism, patriotism, or social identity, such communal features are not available on the third level.

The dispersal and decentralization of political power inherent in globalization increase *both* the opportunities to exert influence *and* the sources of influence. Paradoxically, although fragmentation of power may offer a functional analogue for structural democracy, it is not a normative equivalent for equality of access. Some notion of equal access to political influence is critical at the third level *both* to provide a global, social agreement *and* to establish the foundation of democratic legitimacy. Any capacity for global governance depends on a dense network of institutions and democratic participation—or at least toleration—for legitimacy. The structural minimum for democratic access to influence seems to be a global civil society and public sphere. Only through equal access to influence in a viable global sphere and civil society does the promise of third-level democracy go beyond functional dispersal of power to public accountability and effective social freedom.

Representation. Although it reduces access to influence to an indirect minimum, the essence of any practicable form of democracy is representation, which provides *both* political participation—a procedural feature—*and* political satisfaction—a psychosocial value. Any notion of fairness in indirect, procedural representation requires as much political participation by any individuals and groups as any others, at all levels of politics, and in every step of the political process. Implicit in any notion of representation is some legitimate identification of groups to be represented. Any putative, global democracy faces the intractable dilemma of representation across the many possible multiple identities across the spectrum of human identities.[59] Citizens whose representatives share a common race, religion, culture, age, occupation, gender often feel better represented than people who are somehow demographically different from their representatives. Analogous concerns arise across economic differences that lead the rich to prefer wealthy representatives and poor people to favor representatives of the common people. Ideological rigidity often forces citizens to seek representation through institutions or individuals with views closest to their own. Politicians seeking ideological votes can all expect to gain votes from both sides of the political spectrum by moving their platforms toward the political center. The consequent overrepresentation for the average citizen imposes underrepresentation on marginal or radical people with political views along the fringes of society.[60]

Despite creative efforts to transform multilateral institutions into representative bodies, few would dispute a significant democratic deficit at the third, global level of politics. Unlike democracy at local or national levels, which can reliably expect to achieve consensus, majority, or at least plurality through direct participation, third-level democracy remains riven by dissent across fundamental values. Global democracy depends less on civil society, open debate, and popular participation than on diplomacy and determined political leadership. Instead of individual voters, the energy of third-level democracy concentrates among parliamentarians, congresses, diplomats, and ministers operating and supervising global political processes and intergovernmental institutions. "Otherwise, endless seminars and conferences will inevitably bog down the process in the name of consensus, and good ideas will become hostage to narrow ambitions."[61] Neither do the spirit and philosophy of democracy bend easily to the Procrustean beds of sovereignty, legislation, and Hobbesian institutional government at the third level.

A pervasive limitation of representative democracy, with profound implications at the global level, is that it cannot be expanded indefinitely. Direct democracy as practiced in the Athenian *polis* is practicably impossible in large societies. Neither is it possible that all of the world's individuals and groups can exert decisive influence on global politics through any demography of representation. One sort of fairness in representation imposes unfairness in other aspects. Although the vision of a global, representative democracy has haunted people for millennia, the formidable paradoxes and practical dilemmas of representation remain strong barriers to globalization of representation.

Political Traditions. Many modern democracies are not rooted in either Christian morality, seen by Alexis de Tocqueville as the essential foundation for acceptance of human equality, or in liberal individualism, the philosophical basis of democracy. Although meeting the structural criteria for democratic behavior, Confucianist democracy or Islamic liberalism can be painfully unequal, unrepresentative, and ruthlessly illiberal. These condensed democracies seem to be fashionable oxymorons that emphasize and obscure foreign unease with Euro-American political, moral, and public traditions.

The intrinsic vulnerability of liberal democracy to contest around all issues and its indeterminacy present philosophical obstacles to agreement on global, democratic institutions and even the fundamental ethos beneath them.[62] The political forces beneath globalization—self-defined visions of justice, redistribution of wealth, preservation of global order, revolutionary change, antiglobalism, democratization, or economic liberalization—are not amenable to democratic decisionmaking. Although globalization is intensifying the debates over democracy, individualism, and modernization, those debates occur largely *within* narrow, liberal perspectives. Nurtured in self-governing, autonomous, territorial communities, liberal traditions are forcing democracy into their own Procrustean beds rather than expanding democracy into a global perspective of progress and new knowledge.

Cultural-Ethnic Identities. Unlike national democracies, global democracy cannot be exclusive; it must be fully inclusive. To claim legitimacy, it must be *both* global *and* democratic, not merely one or the other. Global democracy presupposes a broad consensus on the identities of the *demos* (people) or the many *demoi* (peoples) who are its citizens. Many people create their identities around nationality, tribe, ideology, race, or gender. The world's religions, which provide fundamental foundations for the identities of most of the world's people, pose another challenge to any global democracy. Orthodox and fundamentalist religions all contain a totalizing claim of exclusive rights to the truth. It is at best disingenuous to expect these holders of absolute truth to ally themselves with a global democracy that reflects the opinions of constituents rather than any version of truth. Neither can global democracy expect to displace patriotism and the legitimacy of nation-states that embody the nationalist identities of their citizens. "In an era of multiple and conflicting identities, individuals who come to emphasize one particular facet of their identities at the expense of all others may be all the less willing to enter into democratic dialogue with their fellows."[63]

As globalization fragments individual and social identities, shared common values, which are the foundation of any form of democracy within any perspective, lose solidity and stability. "To the extent [that] citizens begin to tribalize into ethnic or other fixed-identity groups, democracy falters. Any possibility for human dialogue, for democratic communication and commonality, vanishes. . . . Difference becomes more and more exclusivist."[64] Without a sense of common purpose and trust across boundaries and narrow perspectives, any vision of global democracy remains hazy. Without shared identities, democracy cannot address global issues and interests that do not fit neatly into narrow national, religious, cultural, or economic perspectives.

Solidarity. Within the global perspective, the clear realities of national allegiance, global fragmentation, and cultural identity imply an enduring, perhaps permanent role for the nation-state with its baggages of nationalism and patriotism. Although not incompatible with cosmopolitan acceptance and respect towards citizens of other countries, emotional roots and spiritual ties form obstacles to any broad transfer of loyalties to a global polity. Most people remain psychologically unable or unwilling to abandon primary loyalties to their fellow national citizens within broad global identities.

Despite the rarity of global or even international solidarity, people have developed a shallow sense of common interests and concerns about forces that cross national borders—global warming, destruction of the ozone layer, atmospheric and aquatic pollution, or contagious disease. "Progress in addressing such questions has been remarkably uneven, and pursued far more successfully at the national than at the international level."[65] Such transient, *ad hoc* functional harmony is far, however, from the sorts of global solidarity that would sustain any notion of a global *demos* or world citizenship.

A Credible Alternative? Any practicable notion of third-level, global democracy implies a Schumpeterian-Lockeian form of indirect representation and competition for votes among an elite group of leaders.[66] Global democracy would refine traditional notions of political participation, transparency, public accountability, political responsibility, and social freedom. As a system of global governance involving not only states but also other participants, third-level democracy must embody global institutions that create and protect equal access to political influence through a global civil society and public sphere. These must provide a global context for decisionmaking in which effective social freedom extends across all narrow perspectives. Not only the political expression of globalism, third-level democracy is also a normative alternative to state-based, second-level democracy. Unlike second-level democracy that concentrates coercive power to regulate globalization, third-level democracy regulates by dispersing power and distributing influence and social freedom among many sites and sources. Although globalization reinforces the moral imperative for nondemocratic states to conform to democratic standards, it does not diffuse the cultural-political traditions upon which those standards must rest. In the absence of common democratic political traditions and complementary ideologies across the polities of the world, global democracy can be at best a polyarchic patina of constitutional government and multiparty politics in many countries.

Global Public Goods

Governance, at any level, forms the means through which societies deliver public goods—safety and order; an efficient economy; environmental security; access to knowledge and information; some form of justice; and public health and welfare. Politics addresses allocation, use, and distribution of these common resources and public goods, traditionally through use of coercive power. Governance also includes the accompanying need to protect societies against the collective bads—drug trafficking, crime, terrorism, disease, pollution—that emanate from globalization. Provision of global public goods is simply not possible without global governance. "That governance can take different forms—from adequately funded world public institutions, to a concert of understanding among the world's powers, to the participation of civil society groups, or more appropriately a combination of the three."[67]

Providing public goods, however, is neither spontaneous nor costless. Within state jurisdictions, legitimate governments can authoritatively allocate costs across populations. No such possibility exists for global public goods whose consumers are citizens of sovereign states. Societies that distribute power and wealth unevenly have tended to provide public goods even without government as urgency leads the powerful and wealthy to absorb the costs themselves. If large beneficiaries do not allocate disproportionate resources towards providing global public goods, smaller beneficiaries may be unable or unwilling to pay for them individually or through collective efforts.[68]

Although modern international systems for providing global public goods enjoy wide consensus, they rely heavily on wealthy, powerful states in unilateral actions that transfer costs to their own populations. Enjoying less consensus are collective processes that rely on multilateral actions and institutions to provide public goods and distribute costs across users. Within popular consensus, many people persist in exploiting global public goods as *free riders* without contributing to their provision, their costs, or their preservation. Despite political intuition that intergovernmental agreement can provide global public goods efficiently and fairly, popular wisdom recognizes the free-rider problem as especially pernicious among governments.

Any practicable strategy for providing global public goods requires a prominent role for the United States in absorbing costs and in policing free riders, *both sovereign and commercial*. In facing the challenges of providing public goods in a globalizing world, the participation of business and nongovernmental entities is essential. Although governments have historically expected companies to cooperate and comply, the needs of business for public goods are quite as real—albeit often different—as those of governments.

Public Order. Global order comprises diplomatic, military, and economic elements. Extending beyond *both* national security *and* human security, it also includes cultural, ethnic, and religious factors. A legacy for any global approach to order is the commitment of the world's states to peaceful resolution of interstate disputes embodied in the Covenant of the League of Nations and the Charter of the United Nations. "Maintaining regional balances of power and dampening local incentives to use force to change borders provides a public good for many (but not all) countries."[69] People everywhere are coming to believe that all violence—aggression, civil war, genocide, ethnic cleansing or pogroms, religious crusades, terrorism, piracy, crime, or vengeance in the guise of justice—are unacceptable violations of legal and moral codes. Any credible global governance must provide security against all of these and more. The order implicit in effective global governance is a global public good —something that everyone can consume freely without diminishing its value, benefits, and availability to others, nonrivalrous and nonexclusionary.[70]

Global Economy. An open global economy is a necessary, but not sufficient, condition for the local economic growth that can nurture stable, orderly societies. Although many governments manage their own economies effectively, "there is a deficit in the relationship between the *de facto* market-led processes of economic liberalization and integration and the *de jure* state-generated mechanisms that underwrite the international fora for the delivery of collective goods."[71] The current wave of globalization has deepened beyond trade to embrace "intellectual property rights, product standards, internal competition policy, government procurement, and, to a lesser degree, labor and environmental standards. These more complex agreements bring deeper integration . . . and raise new issues concerning the sharing of the gains from trade."[72]   It is clear that the shallow integration of classical free-trade agreements has generated broad global prosperity and growth, which must continue to claim some priority as a global public good in any processes of global governance. The current fashions of deep, behind-the-border economic integration, however, without a parallel deepening of global governance, suggest less a public good than a global public bad. Deeper integration does not intrinsically improve market efficiency or equity, as the imposition of deep integration in the form of colonialism recalls. Neither does it contribute to global order as the many affected domestic political forces expand their local interests and concerns into the global agenda. It is also clear that trade-based globalization has broadened the interstate growth-conflict relationship beyond simple dyadic governance and that technology has deepened it into intrastate conflict and civil war.[73] To accommodate the increasing pressures of deep economic integration, any structure for global governance must at least mediate, if not resolve, the conflicts between the efficiency of shallow integration and the demands for equity raised by deep integration.

Global Commons. Preserving the global commons open to all remains as critical to global governance as it has always been to local government. Beyond freedom of the seas, globalization has expanded the global commons to encompass the climate, the biosphere, nonrenewable resources, outer space, and nonhuman species. Even before the current surge of globalization, many people realized that the environment, energy, air, water, and weather affect the entire world—not just particular states. Problems and conflicts concerning environmental systems and the global public goods that they provide require global solutions emerging through global governance of a global commons. The increasing demands of local economies for raw materials to sustain resource-based growth have extended the growth–conflict relationship from interstate disputes into the global perspective as multilateral competition for access to transnational resources. So dramatic has been the explosion of resource-based growth and environmental conflicts that politics, economics, and science have collaborated in a specialized discipline—sustainable development—to deal with this epiphenomenon. One vision of governance of a global commons involves constructing "myriad small-scale societies organized around commons regimes (which may have significantly differing features across the globe), through a resistance to the globalizing practices of [transnational corporations], states, and international development agencies."[74]

Connectivity. Information technology has created another public good that did not exist in earlier systems of governance: access and interconnectivity. The Internet, which can potentially connect everyone to everyone else, continues to create new systems—political, cultural, and economic—new relationships, and new loyalties that transcend and defy old structures and institutions. It globalizes knowledge creation in vast, persistent, virtual *basho* and diffuses new knowledge and innovation instantaneously. As a public good, with low usage cost, "interconnectivity produces one of the most challenging consequences of this age: contagion—economic, political, social, or security related."[75] Knowledge itself is a privately produced public good, since its consumption by one user does not prohibit its use by another, and it is not inherently excludable. Although intellectual property rights are political-legal measures to privatize this good by making it excludable, access and connectivity offer technical measures to return to knowledge its nature as a public good. The issues of ensuring and providing access and connectivity to knowledge, however, are far more complex, controversial, and difficult than those surrounding security and prosperity or preserving the global commons.

Privatization. The nature of public goods has changed as globalization and political liberalization have divested to private industry responsibility for providing many public goods: water, electricity, communications, transportation, and health care. Technology and the increasing demand for economic efficiency have introduced competition and exclusion into provision of formerly public goods. For at least several generations, until people revise their expectations and perspectives of the public and private sectors, governance at all levels can only struggle with government to resolve the issues of privatization. Beyond the three traditional governmental issues of providing public goods—how much, how to pay for it, and how to answer these two questions—global governance must also accommodate the autonomous decisions and actions of governments in privatizing global public goods. Local privatization shifts to global governance the primary responsibilities for determining how to produce them, how to divide production among all potential producers, and how to balance competition among providers and exclusion of users. Global governance must answer all of these questions in the context of *both* global order *and* market efficiency. Within the economic perspective, the answers may lie in market-based innovations, whereas the political perspective exposes power-based approaches through various political processes and enforcement procedures. Neither narrow perspective, however, provides privatized, global public goods with *both* efficiency *and* equity.

International Law. The essential processes of any system of global governance include international law with the global regimes and judicial institutions to organize and order states' behaviors in domains beyond trade, environment, the sea, and political disputes. At the third level, global law also faces issues of human security and rights; migration and biodiversity; inequality, fairness, and inequity; *ex legis* processes of peaceful dispute resolution, and other controversial human concerns. People look to global governance to address the deepening and expanding links between criminal and terrorist networks within some context of some law. Beyond the adjudication of international law, people expect global governance to stabilize some balance between natural or divine law and positive or human law.

Governance Without Government

Some redefinitions of the political and economic roles of states and governments around a vision of transnational consensus have generated novel notions of nonstate-centered systems of governance without government.[76] Deeper than the state-based structures of intergovernmental politics, this notion expands the systemic processes of agency in making political choices from various versions of the state-centered context to a global level.[77] At any level—local, national, interstate, or global—governance and government alike involve authorities exercising structural power delegated by the public. Like those of domestic government, the critical agency processes of global governance without government are triadic governance, administration of democracy, management of globalization, and provision of all classes of public goods. Whereas most robust, domestic polities have stabilized these processes in constitutional, governmental structures, global politics lacks *both* constitution *and* government. Instead of a global government exercising agency, a hazy pattern of global decisionmaking and mercurial, structural power, a sort of governance without government, or *nébuleuse*, reflects states' reactions to the globalizing influences of technology and the market.[78]

Within the *nébuleuse*, people have created a global, political agenda that converges around three approaches to the politics of technology and development: cooperation, structural power, and contention. Typically sponsored by intergovernmental organizations bound in second-level politics, cooperative agreements address narrowly functional, international solutions to issues that technology and markets have expanded across borders. Diplomacy has expanded from process to structural power to set standards and regulations —access and restrictions—for managing people, money, property, ideas, and technology. Most issues of globalization, however, remain beyond the second-level agenda of the *nébuleuse*, without consensus, and in contention or even conflict among competing state governments. Despite flurries of idealistic rhetoric, much of what global governance has occurred in the *nébuleuse* in the later twentieth century has merely been the exercise of *de facto*, hegemonic, U.S. national power within the traditional, Westphalian perspective.[79]

As political will transforms the *nébuleuse* into *basho*, globalization and new knowledge continue to expand traditional perspectives of governance and government towards some novel form of governance with or without government. "The question of just what the new governance should be is creating a world of unusual intellectual flux, one comparable to the post-1945 era in its quest for some overarching design."[80] Globalization is realigning the forces of interstate politics in a set of structural arrangements in event time that seem only distantly relevant to human aspirations and values about peace, prosperity, justice, and environmental concerns in social time. In experiments with rational relationships and *ad hoc* processes, human political will is actively constructing a new world order. "There is little, or no, normative agency associated with this emergent world order: it is virtually designer-free, a partial dystopia that is being formed spontaneously, and in the process endangering some of the achievements of early phases of statist world order."[81]

Structures of Global Governance

Since the invention of the nation-state, international politics has experimented with remarkably few structures for global governance—empire, balance of power, hegemony, collective security, mutual deterrence, and a few versions of multipolarity. These state-centered structures have linked global order to the ability of the great powers *both* to focus direct power *and* to exert indirect influence on behaviors of lesser states. Within the global perspective, the increasing salience of transnational enterprises, nongovernmental organizations, and economic interdependence is replacing the traditional state-centered regulatory structures with decentralized governance processes.

Complementing the state-centered legacy, ideas of global governance include several structural variations—one world, civil society, society of states, world government, and various forms of polarity. These variants adopt different attitudes towards the state, from accepting nationalist identities and loyalties to absolute blame for all of humanity's problems. Any polar system of governance reflects the interactions among various poles of power in unilateral, bipolar, or multilateral variants. Any society of states would enmesh a robust state in multilateral politics. A world government would assume global sovereignty and derogate the state to a subordinate level of politics. The vision of one world, like classical Marxism, could include a withering away of the state in a context of global community. Governance through civil society would include some administrative role for a less-than-sovereign state. All versions of global governance, however, are hostile to the traditional Westphalian perspective of autonomous, self-centered, state sovereignty.

Balance of Power

The notion of balancing power rests on the premises and perspectives of concentrated political-military power in sovereign states interacting deliberately in global anarchy. Not a community—*gemeinschaft*—and at best an association —*gesellschaft*—the international system of autonomous states has persistently rejected the dominance of a single political state or ethnic nation over others. As globalization has transformed the nature and locus of power, additional possibilities of balancing economic and cultural power have emerged. Within this balance-of-power perspective, global governance among states arises neither in idealistic visions of some common aim nor in pragmatic recognition of emerging trends, but in exercising and resisting state power.

Multipolarity. "A multipolar world could be one in which several hostile but roughly equal states confront one another, or one in which a number of states, each possessing significant power, work together in common."[82] Multipolarity diffuses responsibility for keeping order among several poles—but not all sites—of power committed to preserving a static equilibrium of military-political power. Every multipolar balance-of-power system persists as a loose institutional structure constantly shifting from *ad hoc* diplomacy to permanent alliances, from cooperation to current competition, and from concert to conflict.[83] Neither the structure nor the process of multipolarity require multilateralism —universal political participation by all states and interested parties—either among the power poles or among the lesser participants in international politics. Although economic interdependence stimulates multilateralism, "a far greater likelihood is that a multipolar world would lead to an international system characterized by far more conflict than exists today."[84]

The emergence of a dominant state acting routinely and unilaterally to preserve the global balance of power changes the static structure into a dynamic balancing process through which lesser states maintain local or regional power balances. The dominant power—the unipole—expects lesser states to contain their political or economic ambitions within less-than-global dimensions. Any aspirant state, however, can attempt, "either by relying on its own capabilities or alliance with others, to dislodge the position of the preponderant power."[85] Dynamic regional balancing as a global governance system requires a set of regional great powers—rising, current, or declining—that exercise restraint and geopolitical respect for each other and minimize confrontations through attitudes of coexistence.[86]

Dual Multistate Balance of Power. One theoretical version of a multipolar system balances several multistate poles of power. Several poles of economic power and also particular poles of political-military power would collaborate in a loose, political-economic balance of global governance. Since each power pole—military or economic—would be more than a single country, no country could destroy the multistate balance or dominate the global system. Since the economic balance and the military balance remain distinct, neither functional subsystem could dominate the entire global system. So long as the poles of either military or economic power remained themselves in balance, no single bloc or country could dominate the entire political-economic system.

Economic Multipolarity. Economic globalization conjures neomercantilist visions of an economically multipolar world of power poles that form around transnational enterprises, rather than national governments. Nation-states would mutate into market-states to become political agents of the economic power poles and of global capitalism. They would use political and military power to protect the processes of commercial innovation, capitalism, and market logic that generate national prosperity. governments would provide macroeconomic and monetary infrastructures for market exchanges and regulation to prevent and repair market failures.[87]

Stratified Multipolarity. Modern world system theory suggests a stratified multipolar system of three complementary, interdependent poles of economic function.[88] The rich countries of the world would concentrate into a central political-economic power pole—the core—with the newly industrializing countries loosely formed into a lesser pole of purely economic power—the semiperiphery. A disorganized zone of war, chaos, poverty, crime, and political instability, the periphery would function as a supplier of raw materials and a market for the core. Economic interdependence would preserve system stability as military power degenerated into a global police force.

Cultural Multipolarity. The renascence of culture as a foundation for exclusive individual and social identities conjures another sort of polarity as popular power congeals around cultures. Although some modern civilizations have formed trade blocs, their primary sources of power remain the traditional cultural exclusions, ethnocentric affinity, and religion. Whereas the operation, structures, and processes of any such system of cultural multipolar governance remain speculative, the xenophobic power of cultural identities suggests the intractable difficulties of any transcultural, global governance.

Restricted Multipolarity. Globalization has deepened the conviction that only multilateral action through an institution representing the entire international community can legitimate any use of coercive force to keep global order. The challenges of achieving consensus through multilateral processes of concession and stipulation suggest a narrow multilateralism that empowers a less-than-global community to provide legitimacy for power-based, global governance. Any such narrow community must include the power of the United States as a necessary instrument for keeping order. "The Western alliance [the North Atlantic Treaty Organization] holds out the one real prospect for moderating a dilemma that otherwise promises only to worsen. It is with the states of the alliance that the United States continues to share a community of principle and interest sufficient to bear the onus of the compromises and constraints that multilateralism entails."[89]

Bipolar Mutual Deterrence. The Cold War introduced the power-balanced, bipolarity of mutual deterrence and exclusive economies. Two power poles —the superpowers—constructed blocs of military allies and economic clients around themselves. The system of balanced bipolar power became a zero-sum game in which whatever one bloc lost the other gained. Although bipolarity seemed stable, like a multipolar balance of power, it was rigid and static and could not persist. Although the ideological content of Soviet–U.S. Cold-War bipolarity has lost its potency, the spread of anger, disappointment, and resentment through much of the world could readily re-create an unbalanced bipolar system. Such a bipolar system confronting a unipole and its allies or clients with a loose bloc of angry countries would be inherently unbalanced and dangerously unstable. Like cultural multipolarity, unbalanced bipolarity probably precludes any sort of effective global governance.

Unipolarity

In a logical extension of Hobbes's notion of power concentrated in a leviathan based on a voluntary social contract, classical realist theories of interstate relations suggest seductively that a country should seek to amass as much power as possible. "If a state can establish—and maintain—itself as the only great power in the international system, it will enjoy something very close to absolute security."[90]   Although states uniformly resent economic dependence, and distrust even interdependence, over time, they actively resist the concentration of dominating military power in one hegemonic state.

Unipolarity preserves the form and appearance of hegemony but dissipates some of its content. A hegemon is concerned with everything that occurs within its domain of hegemony and is ready and willing to act to protect its hegemony and its clients by meeting hegemonic responsibilities for order and prosperity. A unipole's concern may be largely rhetorical and even universal but chronically generates action only selectively in response to a narrow range of national interests, cultural values, some sense of morality, and domestic political pressures. Unlike a hegemon, a unipole does not accept hegemonic responsibilities for global order and prosperity and is often either unable or unwilling to act, often for economic or domestic political reasons.

A Hobbesian vision of global governance would include a military leviathan to provide global security: decisive and universal in power projection; precise in targets and effects, and obsessively thorough in multilateralism. A global leviathan would secure the interests of the entire global community and embody the values memorialized in a global social contract, not merely those of its own supporters. Neither classical notions of hegemony nor modern views of social contract suggest any credible global leviathan. It is not enough that one state simply build its own power to global dominance and expand its own national interests to include deterrence of global war, arresting interstate war, and neutralizing those people whom it designates as evil or criminal.

The Threat of Unipolarity. The structural logic of international politics leads through power balancing to conflict. Second-tier powers' fears of abuse of power by a dominant unipole eclipse any concern about providing public goods. The unipole's use of power in pursuit of its own national interests is what lesser states fear most: impetuous, unpredictable, and prone to unilateral coercion of lesser states. The static balancing of a multipolarity discourages conflict except as deliberate challenges to the system's power balancers. The dynamic balancing of unipolarity, in contrast, carries conflict as the necessary accompaniment as economic growth chronically shifts distributions of power and wealth. Whereas multipolarity can often accommodate national economic growth smoothly as a routine shifting of power, unipolarity does not tolerate uneven economic growth to challenge the unipole.

In the balance-of-power generation before World War I, the predominant problem for multilateral global governance was "the appearance of new great powers—mainly Germany and Japan—whose appetites and grievances the existing world order could not accommodate."[91] As economic growth nurtures another group of aspiring great powers in the twenty-first century—China, Korea, Vietnam, India, Germany, or Japan—another great-power conflict seems to threaten U.S. unipolar global governance. In a context of rapid, continuing economic growth fragmented across many power centers, dynamic, unipolar balancing carries the threat of growth-based conflict in the globalized dual growth-conflict relationship. Globalization of knowledge-based growth promises to create a prosperous, multipolar global community through economic integration, whereas expansion of resource-based growth portends another catastrophic struggle for power that may be beyond the capabilities or will of the U.S. unipole.

The Promise of Unipolarity. Another subtle syllogism inspired by E. H. Carr, however, leads to peaceful changes in the "equilibrium of political forces" through globalization "enforced only by the power of the complainant." As the advocate of peaceful change and complainant against power-based balancing, the dominant unipole could enforce and promote globalization, which would become itself a legitimate system of global governance. In a system of globalization enforced by a unipole, "conciliation would come to be regarded as a matter of course, and the threat of force, while never formally abandoned, recede further and further into the background."[92] The threats inherent to the structural pressures of balancing and counterbalancing remain real and formidable even in the context of globalization. The promise, however, of Carr's advice that a dominant unipole could govern changes in global power relations without itself resorting to war is perhaps more compelling as a moral and policy imperative.

To reverse the ominous logic of unipolarity, secondary powers in the globalizing world—China, Russia, Britain, France, Germany, Japan, and even India or Brazil—must be convinced that "any geopolitical challenge to the United States is futile."[93] Negative, strategic cooperation—to prevent war with each other—between the U.S. unipole and the other great powers is the sort of shared commitment to stability and survival that made *both* the classical multipolar balance-of-power systems *and* the bipolar mutual deterrence of the Cold War possible. In such a context of shared commitment, countries and even nonstate entities can seek and make the adjustments and changes that globalization requires of them without resorting to war.

A Society of States

As traders established economic links across their known worlds, political globalizers envisioned replacing the Roman and Chinese empires with an anthropomorphic society whose citizens were nation-states. In the thirteenth century, the Mongols collected polities and tribes into a continental imperium from eastern Europe, Mesopotamia, and Russia in the west to the Pacific Ocean in the east. Although limited initially to the states of Europe, later globalization extended the society of princely states to their colonies and ultimately to the Asian, African, and American peoples. In the natural-law tradition of St. Thomas Aquinas (1225–1274), Francisco Suarez (1548–1617) eloquently globalized the state as the moral, economic, and political unit of global society:

> Although a given sovereign state, commonwealth, or kingdom may constitute a perfect community in itself, consisting of its own members, nevertheless, each one of these states is also, in a certain sense, and viewed in relation to the human race, a member of that universal society; for these states when standing alone are never so self-sufficient that they do not require some mutual assistance, association, and intercourse, at times for their own greater welfare and advantage, but at other times because also of some moral necessity or need.[94]

The intellectual tradition of Hugo de Grotius (1583–1645), Samuel von Pufendorf (1632–1694), and Emer de Vattel (1714–1767) expanded Aquinas and Suarez into the legal structure for a global society of states as political units. By the late twentieth century, the convergence of interdependence and international law recognized that "a society of states (or international society) exists when a group of states, conscious of certain common interests and values, form a society in the sense that they conceive themselves to be bound by a common set of rules of their relations with one another, and share in the working of common institutions."[95]

International Community. Few would dispute the reality and significance of the network of governments, firms, and people that share common interests and values, which has come to be known as the international community. Despite its name, "its connotation of sociability and commitment invites unwise reliance by those who must ultimately fend for themselves."[96] With neither recognizable structure nor reliable processes, the international community lacks any institutions of government analogous to those of states' political communities. Nor is it a proper social community or *gemeinschaft*, since it gives low priorities to any inclusive social justice, individual and communal identities, or moral obligations. For many people, the international community is little more than a club for rich countries using political-military power to combine liberal democracy with capitalist prosperity for their own citizens. Beneath its misnomer, through a series of *conjonctures* and *basho*, people transformed power-based politics and resource-based economics into the vision that states could form and operate a global society of states *and people*. The compelling promise of international community arises in people's efforts to reify its morality and states' efforts to keep global order: "The international community is today less a social fact and more a way to remind nation-states of the common humanity of their citizens and of the essential decencies that must guide relations between nations. It is the single strongest slogan of the liberal value of empathy at a distance, the idea that makes everyone feel obliged to recognize the suffering and needs of all human beings."[97]

An international community, however, is not an embodiment of globalism and does not carry any threat of world government. States still form the structure of global politics around a common acceptance of the system of interstate power-politics, which concentrates power in formal governments to keep domestic order and preserve international order. For any global governance of a society of states "it is this international system and its economic and political norms that again must do the groundwork of keeping order and peace: deepening the ties that bind nations together; coopting failed states such as Afghanistan, potential rogues, and strategic competitors; and isolating, if not destroying, terrorists."[98]

Exclusive Society. Within an exclusive society of states, governance is an interstate process operating through extensions of the state in intergovernmental institutions that blend regulatory regimes to guide the interactions of economies, polities, and societies. Excluded from a society of states yet governed by it, nonstate entities may participate only permissively and incidentally in ways that enhance the predominant patterns of interstate governance. The global perspective expands the scope of governance from interstate exclusivity to global dimensions through phenomena—cultural, environmental, and legal issues—that transcend the geographic boundaries and political constraints of sovereign independence. Globalization of governance reflects the density of relationships, regimes, institutions, and geographic reach of the process, rather than any broader notion of participation. Perhaps anticipating a world government, "the multilateral institutions and their underlying norms, codified in international law, constitute the core of what liberal internationalists refer to as an emerging system of global governance."[99]

The exclusive, global society of states includes an alternative version in a world divided among closed blocs—economic, political, allied—of sovereign autonomous, states. Another alternative allows a global concert of great powers to assume authority for order, justice, prosperity, and progress as the third party in a flexible system of pseudotriadic, interstate governance. Operating through a hierarchic web of power-based, multilateral economic, and security institutions, the concert employs power to govern. Functional, global, or international institutions—the United Nations Security Council, the World Bank, or the Group of Eight—have become *de facto* such informal concerts.

Inclusive Society. Within an inclusive society of states governance refers to the decentralization of political authority to subnational and ethnic groups with concurrent concentration of transferred pseudosovereignty to international or transnational organizations. Drastic reductions in the costs of telecommunication and innovation have "brought new associations and organizations into the political arena, and the efforts of these new entities to obtain external resources or otherwise interact with counterparts abroad have extended the range and intensified the dynamics of world affairs."[100] Political contagion has mobilized many locally organized, globally linked, social movements and interest groups that have mobilized to resist the power-based policies of states and economically driven actions of corporations.[101] Because the scale of the nation-state is too small and too big to meet the diffusing requirements for managing social transformation, global governance emerges spontaneously with a renascence of local government and fragmentation of civil society. As the society of states expands to include nonstates, the process of global governance migrates towards regional and global levels and diffuses concurrently towards local levels and freedom of the individual.[102]

Like the exclusive society of states, the inclusive evolution harbors a latent world government in its emphasis on centralizing, rather than diffusing, the functions of global governance. Such a concentration around the common interests of states, nonstate entities, and people preconditions a collective governance mechanism focused on some common aim. In addition to order or stability among states, globalization seems to be exposing a broadening and deepening consensus around some such common aims as continuing global accumulation of wealth, diffusion of prosperity, and economic development.

Regimes. As the system of sovereign states matured, people established mechanisms for deciding on collective response to international problems or crises. Eventually known as international institutions or regimes, these mechanisms breached the obstacles to cooperation under anarchy as the foundation of global governance in a society of states. Since states retained centrality in political processess, they could react collectively to problems and challenges—economic, environmental, human, or political—without sacrificing sovereignty. The pragmatic realization that cooperation and interdependence were not incompatible with sovereignty led to the normative result that the international system could manage some global problems in addition to conducting interstate relations. The trend of emerging patterns of international regimes suggests that global governance "entails practices which operate at the interstices of the states system, working alongside it, perhaps supplementing it, [and] at times supplanting it."[103]

Expanded Multilateralism. Premodern multilateralism was a formal, even static, state-centric process that complemented bilateral diplomacy and power politics with a preference for peaceful dispute resolution. The multilateralist extension of democracy to a society of states invalidated the principles of power politics and subordinated the interests of the few powerful states to those of the majority of smaller, weaker states. To ameliorate this effect, as modern globalization stimulated the formation of intergovernmental organizations, states developed a political process of functional, selective cooperation. This multilateral system of selective, global governance has comprised the authoritative, power-based activities of diplomats and politicians within the existing, multilateral structures of international governance.

Glolbalization, which also introduced nonstate participants into international politics, shifted the focus of diplomacy and the international political agenda towards political-economic issues and actions. Multilateralism expanded into a globalized variant, "with nongovernmental bodies and assorted political movements and social groups playing an active role in policymaking and policy execution.[104] This expanded multilateralism represents the burgeoning efforts of social movements to construct "a system of global governance from the bottom up."[105] Whereas the old multilateralists expanded geographically and functionally by co-opting more governments in the process of governance, the new multilateralism "tries to change prevailing organizing assumptions of the contemporary global order."[106] Expanded multilateralism involves well-informed individuals—not necessarily officials or politicians—and nongovernmental organizations collaborating to address particular problems outside the public competition of bilateral or domestic politics. Under the umbrella of expanded multilateralism, "technicians can gradually knit the world together in a system of mutually beneficial arrangements, such as the standardization of telephone systems and the exchange of information on diseases and weather."[107] Merging regimes, selective cooperation, and nongovernmental participants, expanded multilateralism invites, but does not require, legitimate, political participation of any interested parties in some discursive process of collective decisionmaking. Within a dominant, but inclusive, society of states, expanded multilateralism promises "a more interactive future [with] no limit to institutional variations."[108]

Mutualism. The idea of mutualism expands the European concept of subsidiarity to the global perspective, accepts the state as the basic political unit, and bases relationships on interests rather than values. Mutualist pluralism tolerates the political choices of others with different values and expects universal toleration of those values. Mutualism expects that "international cooperation is more likely to occur when states exercise responsibility for solving their own problems rather than when solutions are hierarchically imposed by overarching political structures and institutions."[109] Recognizing that different peoples seek different values, mutualist governance relies on the primacy of national interest, rather than convergence or divergence of values or ideologies as the energy for interstate politics.[110] Mutualism does not rely on a hegemon or unipole to impose security but expects different states to act appropriately by intervening to protect their own interests, often through regional structures, which are the foundations of mutualist global governance.

In a world of borderless economies, mutualism replaces Adam Smith's invisible hand, by guiding self-interested people and their states in direct cooperation *within a global economy*. In an inclusive society of states, individual interests, formulated as common national interests *and also narrow, self-centered national interests*, are most likely to be achieved through cooperation rather than in competitive initiatives. The integrated, global economy coopts national and local subsidiarity in a market-led international division of labor, which overrides the growth-conflict relationship by prioritizing the socioeconomic interests of the majority of the world's peoples.

The social dimension of mutualism stresses inclusive national and regional communities within a global community. In triadic national governance systems, governments' welfare responsibilities harmonize conflicting social interests through social subsidies—unemployment insurance, pensions, income support for the indigent, medical care, and educational assistance. To create a global sense of social inclusivity, rich states must pursue their own interests by supporting the social welfare programs of poor states through their participation in regional organizations. Within the society of states, mutualist "development of economically productive and socially cohesive regional communities will improve the prospect of managing a host of international social problems that globalization has exacerbated—migration, environmental decay, drug trafficking, the spread of infectious diseases, and terrorism, among others."[111]

Complex Interdependence. "In the 1970s, the buzzword for globalization was interdependence. . . . Rising interdependence was not only changing international politics but also rendering the nation-state obsolete."[112] Idealizing functional, European integration as the prototype for global integration, this market-based approach to global governance gradually binds states so closely in economic interdependence that they cannot afford to make war on each other. Shared economic interests require political and social integration to preserve security, prosperity, and justice in an inclusive society of states. Unlike the emergent triadic governance of the European Union, the mutualistic vision of interdependent global governance does not include any institutional third-party governor to resolve the disputes among its members.

In a powerful globalizing trend, complex interdependence blends "multiple channels between societies; with multiple actors, not just states; multiple issues not arranged in any clear hierarchy; and the irrelevance of the threat or use of force among states linked by complex interdependence."[113] Beyond traditional liberal separations between politics and economics, complex interdependence exposes a second trend of turbulent duality between the state-centric world and a multicentric, political-economic world: globalization of the growth–conflict relationship. Torn between domestic social demands to sustain growth through self-sufficiency and the attractions of political globalization, countries often seek some compromise between cooperative interdependence and assertive sovereignty. Any deepening interdependence not only creates dependence in transnational corporations on host governments for earnings and resources but shifts the balance of political-economic power and creates novel vulnerabilities in territorial, trading states. "Although ultimately related to growth—or its absence—these can exacerbate any noneconomic international tensions, stimulate competition, and possibly lead to conflict."[114]

A third, complex trend focused through technological progress diffuses destructive power away from states and makes it available to groups beyond the constraints that sovereignty imposes on states. The state-centric world legitimates coercive power to stabilize political institutions and secure populations within territorial boundaries. The multicentric world strives for autonomy outside political institutions and concentrates on nonpolitical problems that people feel are important. Rather than seeking simply to govern effectively with concentrated power as most states have done, nonstate movements, criminal and terrorist organizations, and some corporations often understand their separate interests as opposed to global governance.

The convergence of these three trends in complex interdependence demands a process of global governance that effectively controls globalization and includes *both* engineering *and* politics, *both* economics *and* sociology. Within complex interdependence, global governance relies heavily on extensive and intense economic, social, and environmental interactions through global networks and less on territorial strategies of formal diplomacy or military confrontations. The increased participation in decisionmaking and expansion of issues inherent in complex interdependence do not presage, however, an end to power politics. Despite the salience of wealth and economic growth, destructive, coercive political-military power remains the dominant factor in resolving the asymmetric confrontations among states, nonstate entities, and people. Although complex interdependence has deepened and thickened globalism in all perspectives, it has done so unevenly and has not yet solidified into a sturdy, political, institutional community or infrastructure. Even within the global perspective, the filters of domestic and international politics determine the limits of what is possible in any global arena.

World Government

One logical antidote to state sovereignty and interstate anarchy expands sovereignty and central authority to global dimensions. World government would remove state sovereignty by adding another layer of politics. In the context of a dispersed, decentralized global society, a world government would require a structural concentration of power to establish and exercise governance of globalization. Like a hegemon, a world government would face the need for constant intervention in complex, economic, political, military, cultural, and social processes. Beyond the random and unintended consequences for people's actions, the huge constituency of any world government would constrain any democratic processes or liberal institutions. Although the vision of a world state has become practicable only in modern times, ancient thinkers conceived it in philosophical and theoretical terms.

Ancient Perspectives. Aristotle introduced the notion of combining several similar political entities to form a larger one in his efforts to show the origin and aims of the state and established self-sufficiency, rather than size, as the measure of the ideal state. "The final cause and end of a thing is the best and to be self-sufficing is the end and the best. . . . The proof that the state is a creation of nature and prior to the individual is that the individual, when isolated, is not self-sufficing. . . . A city only comes into being when the community is large enough to be self-sufficing." Although he is not specific,

Aristotle recognized finite limits to the size of states. The state "when composed of too few is not, as the state ought to be, self-sufficing; when of too many, though self-sufficing in all mere necessaries, as a nation may be, it is not a state, being almost incapable of constitutional government." Because of difficulties in communicating between government and the people, Aristotle was skeptical about establishing law and order in very large communities and concluded that any limits to the size of a state must be determined by experience. He offered functional criteria of effectiveness in accomplishing the work of government: military strength and self-sufficiency. "That city which is best adapted to the fulfillment of its work is to be deemed greatest."[115]

St. Augustine (354–430) expanded Aristotle's notion from the city to the entire world. "After the state or city comes the whole world, the third circle of human society—the first being the house, and the second the city."[116] Although Aristotle did not mention it and stressed the ability to wage effective war, St. Augustine was more intensely concerned about peace than self-sufficiency.[117] Within the Augustinian perspective, the work of the state stresses establishing and maintaining peace instead of waging war.

Thomistic Thought. The recognition of a world society by St. Augustine and his earnest concern for peace appear also in the thought of St. Thomas Aquinas as he formally extended Aristotle's hierarchy of social community and Augustine's religious community to a world dimension. St. Thomas adopted an evolutionary attitude towards the state and recognized that the context of social reality might change the nature and details of an adequate or perfect state. He was prepared to regard the entire world as a social community suitable for governance by a single world government. St. Thomas combined peace and self-sufficiency as essential dual characteristics of the perfect community. "The Lord promised his people by the prophets that, as a great favor, He would place them under one head, and that there would be one prince over all. . . . Man is a natural unit, but the unity of a community, which is peace, must be brought into being by the skill of the ruler."[118] St. Thomas finally concluded that "the perfect community is one that does not need the help of another, that is at peace, and that can by its own will and resources remain so. Any other community must be an accidental or inadequate organization of power. It cannot be self-sufficing."[119] Within the Thomistic perspective and even within an Aristotelian perspective, no extant state can claim self-sufficiency in all that is needed *both* to support and maintain its population *and* to ensure peace.

Focusing the broad thought of St. Thomas on government, Dante Alighieri (1265–1321) justified and called for a single global government that would bring unity through law and, in cooperation with the church, restore order to the world. Dante concluded that humanity "is well-ordered on the basis of a single principle, namely, through its governor, God, who is the absolute world-government. Hence we conclude that a single world government is necessary for the well-being of the world."[120]

The Thomistic conclusion that the state can exist as a perfect society only when it can achieve the common good independently of any other civil society implies that any less-than-global state is imperfect. For a society that can attain this end only in collaboration with other societies, collaboration is a moral social duty. The consequence of such morally imperative mutual interdependence is a clear shift of social rights and duties to a new, aggregate society resulting from collaboration. This larger society not only realizes the purposes of individual member-societies but transcends them in the name of the common good of all their citizens. Beyond this duty of existing states to collaborate, St. Thomas is clear that a world government must establish positive, written law and enforce it with coercive power, from both of which it is itself exempt.[121] The necessary human institutions of global law and coercive power would "regulate and control the sovereigns of extant states, who are exempt from the operation of the positive law and who cannot be regulated and controlled by divine and natural law alone."[122]

The Thomistic tradition justifies the state's legal right to sovereignty as the natural right of a people to rule itself in pursuing the common good. Since no less-than-global state can achieve perfection, the only possible perfect community, in Aristotelian, Augustinian, or Thomistic terms, is a world state. Only a world state can be self-sufficient, only a world state can ensure peace, and only a world state can achieve, or even pursue, the common good.

Global Federation. Information technology and rapid transportation have made possible spatial and temporal integration of the world's peoples in a single, universal community united by common interest in pursuing the global common good. A global community comprising *both* individuals *and* states leads almost inevitably to political federation. St. Thomas's requirement for positive law with universal scope and enforced by some global executive permits freedom of individuals and states limited by law only in a federal context. Although St. Thomas does not address the structure of a world state, Thomistic logic concludes that "any world government must be a federal government and must come into existence by consent and not by conquest."[123]

Hegemony. A focus on hegemonic government recalls the realist conviction that any stable world order requires either a global balance of power or hegemony by a single, most powerful state. The responsibilities of the hegemon include mediating the world's conflicts, policing the world to maintain order, and managing a global economy to preserve global prosperity. The realist principle of hegemony, or even a vision of unipolarity, can involve cooperative, multilateral decisionmaking among states with varying levels of power. In a unipolar, but not hegemonic, world, rule making, global politics, and enforcement of world order must be multilateral, collaborative efforts.

A debilitating anomaly of hegemonic stability lies in the powerful advantages of incumbency. Despite any greater competence of an alternate hegemon, a challenger regime, or any doubters, the power of incumbency discourages voluntary cooperation and forces competitors into watchful waiting for a provident opportunity to assume political power. Even if fortune combines with intent to provide an opportunity, the shift from one hegemon to another has always been at best traumatic and often globally catastrophic.

Hierarchy. Concentration of military power and economic influence in hierarchic patterns has historically tended towards stability, peace, and prosperity as more powerful states have tended to exercise governance over weaker states. Competitive empires and balance-of-power politics concentrated power and influence in stable multipolar, hierarchical systems of government, whereas hegemony formed the prototypical unipolar hierarchy.

Hierarchy has historically been a structure that arises to facilitate interactions among states, an institutional setting within which political processes occur. An effective hierarchy provides some foundation for legitimacy and integrity of relationships. Within the traditional realist, Marxist, and structural perspectives, the state is the unit of analysis with authority, control, and hierarchy closely related. In a structure constructed and held together by power, it is power that determines hierarchy. Within other political-economic perspectives—transactional, economic, or behavioral—with the interstate relationship or transaction as the unit of analysis, hierarchic rankings are not synonymous with power or authority. Although a hierarchy generates *de facto* decisionmaking, it need not include a central decision maker and does not include authoritative, political control over states. In a governance system built on self-interest and held together by interactions —interdependence or multilateralism—hierarchic structure determines or constrains power. Neither immutable nor definitive, power is an amorphous result of the hierarchical structure of interstate relationships.

One World

Imprisoned in visions of idealists, philosophers, and dreamers until the emergence of international organizations, the notion of one world is a metaphorical globalization of the family and the nation-state in an ideological globalism. The one-world perspective "recognizes that all the world's people share a common humanity as well as economic needs and dependence on the natural environment. It considers building a sense of community based on social justice as the only path to true, permanent peace."[124]   Within the one-world perspective, community, rather than institutions, forms the structure of governance. The process of globalization embodies tendencies for people to assemble in some universal community—*gemeinschaft*—that each transformation of social reality renders more inclusive than its preceding society or association —*gesellschaft*. "In the *Gemeinschaft* [community], [people] remain essentially united in spite of all separating factors, whereas in the *Gesellschaft* [society] they are essentially separated in spite of all uniting factors."[125]   Process and structure merge in the one-world community of democracy, morality, idealism, politics, economics, and culture, which co-opts representative democracy, civil society, the public sphere, and the structural institutions of government.

Within the one-world perspective, the foundations of global community already exist in "a shared vision of a better world, . . . a sense of common vulnerability in the face of global warming and the threat posed by the spread of weapons of mass destruction. There is the framework of international law, treaties, and human rights conventions. There is equally a sense of shared opportunity, which is why we build common markets and joint institutions such as the United Nations."[126] More prosaic is the global community of public opinion created and sustained by modern telecommunications technology and the graphic, media images that it sends instantaneously around the globe. Such a global community "only emerged when human crises hit the international media, when scenes of misery—whether involving the Kurds, the Rwandans, or the Kosovars—flashed across living room television screens in the developed world."[127]

Democratic Community.   Although it opens the possibility of global democracy, the one-world vision is neither normatively nor structurally equivalent to third-level global democracy. Within the one-world perspective, democratic community displaces political structure and disaggregates the processes of globalization and governance. Although the size, extent, and geographic scope of global humanity precludes equal access to political influence, one-world democracy establishes "possibilities for influence or steering the process at various points. In response to the lack of centralized institutions and effective law at the international level, various decentralized and cooperative solutions to the problem of order have emerged. Such disaggregation provides 'a functional equivalent to democracy.'"[128]

Economic globalization, technology, and the global press media have transformed communal agreements among states and nonstates alike from loose relationships and associations into communal institutions, regimes, and organizations that perform structural roles. Although these institutions cannot control either globalization or politics, through a democratic sort of equal and effective popular freedom they establish normative constraints on power. Rather than the structural controls of representative, democratic agency, these loose institutions of popular politics contain the seeds of some inchoate global democratic community. Rather than affecting either the scope of power or the processes of politics, such nonstructural, communal institutions create democratic accountability and focus regulatory, political influence. Disaggregation presumes, however, the preexistence of some minimally accountable and democratic institutions that people can expand through communal agreements to embrace global governance and globalization. Ironically, the expansion and operation of these institutions lead inevitably to the emergence of civil society, public spheres, and governmental structures that disaggregation seeks to avoid.

Moral Community.   The one-world perspective positions the universal community as a legitimating moral principle that "can shape institutions and inform policy choices. Perhaps this moral meaning is better expressed in the notion of a human community, which exists prior to the sovereign state. . . . The moral reality of the international community is rooted in a shared human nature, and its normative imperative is one of solidarity—a conscious conviction that common humanity sustains a minimal number of moral obligations across cultures, national boundaries, and geographical distances."[129]

Inclusive, moral communities, however, "are not natural: they will have to come from new versions of social solidarity free from bondage to state, nationality, religion, or race before they can produce a confidence in the future of the human race that transcends the persistent differences in religious and political myths that have separated us for a millennium and longer."[130] Although the one-world moral community assumes life more in the meaning to which it aspires than in social reality with which it contrasts, its universal morality generates feelings of "mutual sympathy and loyalties; of we-feeling, trust, and consideration."[131] One-world moralistic trust in people whom one has never met and who are likely to be different in many ways does not depend on any assessment of trustworthiness that can only come through personal experience and does not involve anticipation of reciprocity.[132] These expansive beliefs in a universal moral community stimulate cooperation with strangers, sustained efforts for the common good, and extend human compassion beyond a local community. "Moralistic trust assumes that we do not risk so much when we put faith in people [whom] we do not know, because people of different backgrounds still share the same underlying values. . . . Moralistic trust provides the rational for getting involved with other people and working towards compromises."[133]

Political Community. Moralistic trust, which empowers *both* civil society *and* political community, embodies an optimistic view of the world as a benign place filled with good people, who share some minimum of common moral values and benevolent motives. People who trust others in a moralistic way seek progress actively through joining and participating in political communities, civil society, and other associations. People who rely on this moral dimension of trust readily expand existing social, political, or economic bonds to other people and promote consensus, cooperation, and compromise. While clearly necessary, the democratic and moral communities embedded within the one-world perspective are insufficient foundations for global governance. Only the political community can confer and sustain the legitimacy of either a structure of government or a system of governance. It is the foundation and premise of any political system or form of governance.[134] A one-world community probably cannot stabilize in the absence of *both* the objective *and* the subjective conditions met in a political community. Among these conditions are some common agreement about ethnicity and culture, some form of legitimate, statelike concentration of authority and power, and some common satisfaction with the level of economic development. A global community would also require a legitimate relationship with the other states, groups, and communities in the global system and a reliable process for resolving disputes with them. In an illogical paradox, the sustained interactions between such a community and the other entities in the global political-economy could form a supraglobal collective identity and political community that would enervate the other communities forming it.

Exclusive Communities. Globalism has not yet expanded the one-world metaphor, however, to burst Bacon's idols of exclusive communities and self-centered individualism, which confound any notion of a single, global community. The technological ability of dislocated groups and ephemeral communities to form, dissolve, and recombine at will has created a metastable shadow world of virtual, exclusive communities outside *both* the Westphalian polity *and* the capitalist economy. Shattering Bacon's *idola tribus* that focus the urge to form exclusive groups into a web of confrontations between *us* and *them*, the one-world perspective does not distinguish between *us* and *them*. Governance of a single global population "emphasizes the similarities [that] all humans share and views states as historical artifacts, perhaps now artificial and outdated."[135] Rather than *either* segregating *or* integrating *us* and *them*, one-world global governance is compatible "with a world in which the wishes, and even the needs, of the 'we' will not justify doing harm to the 'they.'"[136] Instead of exclusive nationalism, global governance finds legitimacy in any ideology of symmetrical treatment of *us* and *them*, in nation-states, and across all groups in which people live, work, and play. Global governance invokes universal rules for human interactions, standards of fairness, and questions of what is acceptable to *us* and *them* in any asynchrony of interests.

Universal Education. Within the one-world perspective, human differences appear as learned prejudices that education can replace with new knowledge. For any global society, the salience of universal education as the institutional foundation of transformation and innovation "arises from the purpose of a society to bring or create change in knowledge, perspective, institutions, or even values."[137] Only people with sufficient training to use modern, electronic devices to obtain information can join in designing and transforming social reality. Personal education beyond technological skill is a criterion for entry into the cosmocratic elite of people who operate the globalizing world.

Education as a social or communal institution is paradoxically less than comfortable with globalization. "The role of education as an institution in human affairs embodies efforts to perpetuate a particular society, a community, its perspective on [life and] the universe, its set of institutions, and its values. The power of education as an institution reflects a perspective on the universe that is progressive and optimistic, and engenders a faith in humans that their particular perspectives are correct and useful."[138] For traditional, modern, less-than-global societies and communities, institutional education takes its common form as a communal public good jealously guarded by the state. As one of Bacon's *idola theatri*, national education reinforces local, social purposes of static survival and stability within a narrow perspective that consensus and tradition have crystallized into ideological ritual.

Global Citizenship. Effective governance at any level begins with citizenship, which defines the group for which government exercises agency for political choice, and the political units of society. Among the mélange of states, organizations, commercial enterprises, ethnies, cultures, and individuals that participate in global politics it remains unclear who or what are global citizens and who or what are the units of global society. The claims of organizations to *both* citizenship *and* the rights that states conceived for people have created paradoxical fictions that may overwhelm the ideas of individual citizenship as corporations expand beyond states' regulatory jurisdictions.

Globalization through cultural diasporas over generations has confused any concise definition of individual citizenship. People no longer fit neatly and exclusively into the dichotomous national and foreign categories implicit in Westphalian notions of national citizenship. People who are historically indigenous may not belong to a predominant culture, whereas people who reside outside the country may share ethnic and cultural identity with local residents. The large groups of migrants and refugees throughout the world in all countries are at best political anomalies that obviate residency as the defining criterion for citizenship. The legal principle of *jus sanguinis*, which ascribes citizenship only to the descendants of citizens, prefers ethnic criteria and stresses a predominant national culture. The alternative principle of *jus soli* confers citizenship on individuals born within a territorial jurisdiction. Unicultural groups prefer *jus sanguinis*, whereas multicultural communities tend towards a *jus soli* citizenship and often include increasing ethnic diversity within their communal purposes.

"Globalization has not profoundly challenged the enduring national nature of citizenship. Economic life takes place on a global scale, but human identity remains national."[139] Although globalization may be incubating a germ of universal consciousness, the disjointed unities of technology and markets carry neither collective identity nor solidarity. The world market alone cannot create the inclusive, transnational identity or citizenship that states remain unwilling to endorse.

Any global governance must rest on a definite, global citizenry —individuals or groups—that transcends the awkward balancing between inclusion and exclusion implicit in traditional definitions of citizenship protected by Bacon's idols. Global governance requires a functional relationship—agency, social contract, or something else—between some global citizenry and some global process of choice that functions at least as well as the state and civil society have been doing.

Global Civil Society

The term *civil society* originated in ancient Greece to refer to the state and its government and included a franchised *public sphere* implicit in the direct democratic relationship between people and state. In modern contexts, civil society is the nongovernmental part of a political community, "*the realm of organized social life that is voluntary, self-generating, (largely) self-supporting, autonomous from the state, and bound by the legal order or set of shared rules.*"[140] Despite common usage of the terms as synonymous, civil society is distinct from what has been called the public sphere. Developed, like civil society, in the context of the Hobbesian, central state, the public sphere brings citizens together as a public to engage the public authorities in political confrontation and debate over the general approaches and policies of the government.

Feeding and being fed by globalization, civil society offers an alternative transformation of social reality. Like the public sphere, it cannot expand to the global perspective without effective global governance processes within a consensual, global, normative structure. Any global civil society must rest on a few "basic unarticulated assumptions shared by people concerning the nature of the real world; they are unarticulated because they are so naturally taken for granted."[141]   To complement any institutions and processes of global governance, a global civil society must articulate these assumptions as normative standards of governance monitored by a global public sphere.

Although neither civil society nor the public sphere alone can provide effective governance at any level, other forms of governance seem incomplete, unsatisfying, and ineffective without at least a robust civil society. With the recent wave of globalization, people have rediscovered civil society as the critical third leg that stabilizes global governance around social solidarity and trust, as with the market provides economic prosperity and the state offers political legitimacy. Expanding political-economic perspectives beyond the limits of geography, politics, economics, race, religion, ideology, or culture invites the formation of global, or at least civilizational, civil society as the foundation of global governance. The efficacy of civil-society governance depends on the compatibility of the various strategies not only of states but also of firms, international organizations, and the other elements of civil society that affect political, economic, and social stability.[142]

Rise and Fall of Civil Society. Post-Renaissance globalization supplanted the direct relationship between people and their Hobbesian central states with diffuse, Lockeian civil societies, which were also the carriers of national cultures.[143] As the state expanded the political perspective from a Hobbesian emphasis on life and security to a Lockeian concern also with property and liberty, the agenda of civil society broadened apace. The modern concepts of civil society and a distinct public sphere emerged in Europe during the Enlightenment and modernity. "A host of political theorists and philosophers, from Thomas Paine to Georg Hegel, developed the notion of civil society as a domain parallel to but separate from the state—a realm where citizens associate according to their own interests and wishes."[144]

The Enlightenment-modernity *conjonctures* stimulated separation of civil society from the public sphere in the eighteenth and nineteenth centuries and enlisted other social and political processes in the service of market capitalism. Within the dominant economic perspective of the Industrial Revolutions, the precondition of these infant civil societies was a strong Hobbesian state to establish and enforce the conditions that would ultimately nurture Lockeian civil societies. As an extension of power-based government, the effectiveness of governance emerged from a loose, pseudocausal chain that began with citizenship and civil liberties. Citizen involvement and political participation —including riots, elections, protests, debate, and strikes—continues the chain through civil society, political majorities and minorities, and parties to effective governance. Whereas any general linkages between government policy, structural democracy, and national economic growth are ambiguous, crucial preconditions for effective governance and growth at any level seem to include structural stability, political liberty, and an active civil society.[145]

Including political parties, companies and the market itself, interest groups, labor unions, professional and ethnic associations, churches, and many other groups, civil society in every country comprises a loose diversity of the good, the bad, the irrelevant, and the bizarre. Resting on the state's protection of the rights of free association and free speech, civil society forms "the sphere of institutions, organizations, and individuals located between the family, the state, and the market, in which people associate voluntarily to advance common interests."[146] Many groups within civil society are intensely, even myopically focused on a single issue and have no interest in balancing the public good beyond their ubiquitous economic demands on government or society. Despite this dark, selfish side, however, in holding government accountable in pursuit of common purposes, civil society establishes a common identity and purpose for its members across their various separate interests.[147]

Proliferation and expansion of non- and transgovernmental organizations, however, is neither the nucleus nor a prerequisite for any embryonic, global, civil society. "Many nongovernmental organizations reflect only a tiny segment of the populations of their members' states. They largely represent only modernized countries, or those in which the weight of the state is not too heavy."[148] Although the transnational public is geographically global, it is primarily a narrow-perspective projection of Euro-American domestic interest groups seeking foreign support, not an inchoate global civil society. Moreover, the dark side of civil society is also expanding into foreign societies in the forms of organized interstate crime, terrorism, and other antisocial groups. Globalization converges all of these "spontaneously emergent associations, organizations, and movements that, attuned to how societal problems resonate in the private life sphere, distil, and transmit such reactions in amplified form to the public sphere."[149] In the global context of governance without government, however, the urges to form a global public sphere are just as premature as visions of a global civil society.

The Public Sphere. Whereas civil society may exist with its own agenda or interests, regardless of the form and constitution of the state, the public sphere flourishes only in open, permissive, or democratic societies. Civil society becomes a public sphere only as institutions emerge in which people either organize against the state or appeal to it. Although neither can exist without some statelike, structural government, civil society and the public sphere are both beyond the state-centered venue and institutions in which constitutional political processes generate law and policy. Within the public sphere, private individuals assemble and participate freely and equally in informed discussions of matters affecting the common welfare of the community. Protected by the state but largely self-regulating, the public sphere is the space-time zone in which civil society scrutinizes the state's exercise of power and authority. "The medium of this political confrontation . . . [is] people's public use of their reason (öffentliches Räsonnement) . . . [which] preserves the polemical nuances of both sides: simultaneously the invocation of reason and its disdainful disparagement as merely malcontent griping."[150] Like the openness of civil society, the shared spirit of rational, political confrontation within the public sphere encourages public diversity, self-expression, and civic voluntarism. The narrow agenda of the public sphere concerns the exercise of power under the social contract concerning commodity exchange and social labor and delineates the boundaries between people and state and the limits on each.

The constitutional form of the state and the nature of the social bond among citizens have determined the extent and depth of the public sphere and established rules of access for citizens. As globalization shifts political agendas from primarily national issues to global concerns, the narrow roles of national public spheres lose political relevance. "The emergence of the global public sphere, albeit partial, has an impact on the social bond by modifying the citizens' relationships to their own states, to citizens of other states, and to international organizations. The development of a global public sphere loosens the social bond traditionally defined by the sovereign state."[151] Technological globalization has made possible *both* a civil society that can focus global issues *and* a public sphere that can operate in the global dimensions of social-political relations. Globalization has not, however, created either the state or the community that alone can justify, define, focus, and contain them both.

Civil-Public Merger.   An entire generation of computer users has rejuvenated national civil societies and expanded national public spheres and is heralding the rise of a global civil society from the ashes of decrepit Hobbesian national societies. With emerging features, functions, and effects, these globalizing civil societies are organizing around Anglo-American, Lockeian self-regulating principles and nongovernmental organizations. Floating in the *nébuleuse* of governance without government, these more-than-national, less-than-global civil societies are usurping the traditional function of the public sphere in democracies in a confusing mélange of public and private affairs. In nondemocratic polities they are expanding latent public spheres through communication technologies that transcend political borders.

Economic and technological globalization has formed a drifting, global civil society and an improbable global public sphere despite the absence of any credible forms of *either* global governance *or* world government. By expanding the domains of national civil society and the public sphere and extending participation to any connected individual, people are transforming civil society and the public sphere into global regimes of public accountability and transparency. Although cosmopolitan publicity exposes violators to popular pressures and economic punishments, accountability and transparency do not provide political control or direction. They operate through "the force of public opinion and through democratic institutions that already exist on more local levels."[152] Technology has not yet created a global civil society or public sphere; it has merely weakened traditional national versions.

Civil Society and the World State. Since proliferating uncoordinated social movements can shatter civil society into mutually antagonistic competitors for resources and power, any global civil society must coordinate without centralizing. Just as uncoordinated social movements can quickly become competitive or revolutionary, so also any central civil coordinator can readily become repressive and even suppressive. Without the stability of a world state and its institutions to constrain and protect them, uncoordinated globalist social, cultural, and political movements remain radical and marginal. Any global civil society and public sphere become vulnerable to capture by the mercurial populism of the French Revolution, the idealist despotism of the Bolshevik Revolution, or the opportunism of the Weimar Republic. Although many political structures—the Hobbesian state, as well as many others—can balance despotism and populism, "civil society and the state need each other and, in the best of worlds, they develop in tandem, not at each other's expense."[153] The absence of any robust, global, political structure exposes humanity to the risk of destroying in chaos, competition, or revolution the fundamental *raisons d'être* of any civil society: prosperity, security, and justice.

Civil Society and the Market. Floating between government and market, robust civil society has been a natural partner of a successful market economy, even though neither influenced the other directly. Sharing with government "a sense of things public and a regard for the general good, . . . it was a voluntary, private realm devoted to public goods."[154] Civil society has united the virtues of the private sector—freedom and self-interest—with those of the public sector—social responsibility and concern for the general welfare—in an active, idealistic vision of public good. Instead of concentrating power in government institutions or wealth-based corporate structures, the market-based civil society concentrates the legitimate power of the people.

Within the civil-society vision, the global economy and market capitalism provide the foundations for human progress and development, while civil society would be the locus of global governance, idealism, and cultural efflorescence. Through the power of capitalism guided by civil society's understandings of public good, the market would generate global prosperity. A global civil society would mediate between a global private sector, a vibrant global economy, and residual structure of states in a political space merging voluntary, private, and public actions. Outside the formal governance system, the remaining states would shrink into an administrative bureaucracy with the narrow role of providing security for a global civil society comprising citizens of many cultures and states. The ascendance of civil society would revise state boundaries to accommodate administrative systems of accountability and transparency, political representation, and market-based exchanges.

Cultural Relationships. As globalization and migration have invalidated the social ideal of cultural homogeneity, many states have become multinational and have tended to reify cultural differences and diversity in civil societies. Many multiethnic states allow and expect every ethnic group to install its own autonomous, native authority with its own civil society. The local authority enforces an ethnic version of customary law beneath the state's umbrella of formal, civil, and criminal law. This dual civil-societal relationship—unity in, across, and through diversity—accommodates assimilation into a political community and a national economy through selective acceptance of processes and institutions. Instead, however, of promoting cultural integration through close relationships between civil society and culture, insistence on cultural-ethnic autonomy often precludes a robust national or global civil society.

Although the shared purpose of human unity through diversity may briefly sustain a local political community, it threatens a national community and any nascent global community with irreconcilable disputes about cultural rights and institutions of governance. The rejection of a broader social identity built through cultural integration and embodied in national or global civil society harbors tendencies toward secession, criminal deviance, or revolution. Autonomous local leaders, despite personal dedication to the larger political community, concentrate legitimacy and attract political support away from the consensual institutions of the state and the processes of global governance.[155]

Whether national or subnational, civil society assumes unique context- and culture-specific forms throughout the world. In some contrast to many other aspects of modernity, neither national nor subnational civil societies can export themselves across cultures by any direct process of economic integration of technological globalization. Neither can people expect their own civil societies to expand or merge spontaneously into a global civil society. Neither the substance nor the spirit of civil society is malleable or fertile to foreign sociopolitical engineering, international hectoring and pontificating, or global mentoring. Either a strong, idealistic, civil society will be the indigenous creation of the citizens of an existing, viable *polis* or it will not be created at all. The most that globalization can provide are capability and context, which grow with challenge, learning, and knowledge:

> Civil society is the realm in which those who are disadvantaged by globalization of the world economy can mount their protests and seek alternatives. . . . More ambitious still is the vision of a global civil society in which these social movements together constitute a basis for an alternative world order. In a "top down" sense . . . states and corporate interests . . . [would form an] agency for stabilizing the social an political *status quo* . . . and thus enhance the legitimacy of the prevailing order.[156]

NOTES

1. Václav Havel, "New Year's Address" (January 1990), *Open Letters* (New York: Vintage, 1992), 390–396; 392.

2. David Easton, *The Political System: An Inquiry into the State of Political Science* (New York: Knopf, 1953), 129.

3. See Ferdinand Tönnies, *Community and Association* (originally published as *Gemeinschaft und Gesellschaft*), translated and edited by Charles P. Loomis (East Lansing: Michigan State University Press, [1887] 1957), 65.

4. Joseph E. Stiglitz, *Globalization and Its Discontents* (New York: Norton, 2002), 223.

5. Stephen M. Walt used the metaphor of political contagion in "Fads, Fevers, and Firestorms," by Stephen M. Walt, *Foreign Policy* 121 (November-December 2000): 34–42.

6. Walt "Fads, Fevers, and Firestorms," 41–42.

7. Carl von Clausewitz, *On War*, 3 vols., translated by James J. Graham (London: Routledge and Kegan Paul, 1966), vol. 1, p. 27. See also vol. 1, p. 32; vol. 2, p. 352; vol. 3, p. 10.

8. As one part of the dual relationship between growth and conflict, "resource-based static growth associates high growth with high conflict, and low growth with low conflict, in a direct-positive relationship." William H. Mott IV, *The Economic Basis of Peace: Linkages between Economic Growth and International Conflict* (Westport, Connecticut: Greenwood, 1997), 194.

9. Peter F. Drucker, "The Global Economy and the Nation-State," *Foreign Affairs* 76(5) (September-October 1997): 159–171; 169,

10. Clausewitz, *On War*, vol. 3, p. 121.

11. Stanley Hoffmann, "Clash of Globalizations," *Foreign Affairs* 81(4) (July-August 2002): 104–115; 107.

12. Complex interdependence deteriorates the economic capacity and political will of a classical hegemon to maintain and operate the global political-economic system through power politics. (See Robert Gilpin, *The Political Economy of International Relations* (Princeton: Princeton University Press, 1987), 77–78.). Several related hypotheses about economic integration—Paul Samuelson's theory of factor price equalization—and democratic convergence suggest that the destabilizing economic and political effects of globalization itself "will lead to a change in the international distribution of power, from unipolarity to multipolarity" with consequences of global instability and chronic interstate conflict. (Ethan B. Kapstein, "Does Unipolarity Have a Future?" in *Unipolar Politics: Realism and State Strategies after the Cold War*, edited by Ethan B. Kapstein and Michael Mastanduno, 464–490 (New York: Columbia University Press, 1999), 482. For a summary of convergence theories see James R. Golden, "Economics and National Strategy," in *New Forces in the World Economy*, edited by Brad Roberts, 15–37 (Cambridge: MIT Press, 1996). History suggests that "extreme equality is associated with instability. . . . The inequality of states, although it provides no guarantee, at least makes peace and stability possible" (Kenneth Waltz, *Theory of International Politics* (Reading, Massachusetts: Addison-Wesley, 1979), 132.).

13. Bruce F. Porter, *War and the Rise of the State* (New York: Free Press, 1994), 3.

14. The hypothesis of stress triggering originated in geological theories of plate tectonics in efforts to explain and predict earthquakes. See Ross S. Stein, "Earthquake Conversations," *Scientific American* 288(1) (January 2003): 72–79. See also Tom Parsons, Shinji Toda, Ross S. Stein, Aykut Barka, and James H. Dieterich, "Heightened Odds of Large Earthquakes Near Istanbul: An Interaction-Based Probability Calculation," *Science* 288(5466) (28 April 2000): 661–665.

15. For introduction of the term within the political-economic perspective, see James N. Rosenau, "Global Affairs in an Epochal Transformation," in *The Information Revolution and International Security*, edited by Ryan Henry and C. Edward Peartree, 31–57 (Washington, D.C.: Center for Strategic and International Studies Press, 1998), 37.

16. See David Held, "Democracy and the Global System," in *Political Theory Today*, edited by David Held, 197–235 (Cambridge: Polity, 1991), 207–209.

17. James H. Mittelman, "How Does Globalization Work?" in *Globalization: Critical Reflections*, edited by James H. Mittelman, 229–241 (Boulder, Colorado: Lynne Rienner, 1996), 240.

18. Andrew J. Bacevich, "New Rome, New Jerusalem," *The Wilson Quarterly* 26(3) (Summer 2002): 50–58; 58.

19. Stiglitz, *Globalization and Its Discontents*, 21.

20. John Micklethwaite and Adrian Wooldridge, *A Future Perfect: The Challenge and Hidden Promise of Globalization* (New York: Random House–Crown Business, 2000), 338.

21. Stiglitz, *Globalization and Its Discontents*, 226.

22. John MacLean, "Philosophical Roots of Globalization and Philosophical Routes to Globalization," in *Globalization and Its Critics*, edited by Randall D. Germain, 3–66 (New York: St. Martin's, 2000), 62, 63.

23. Mott, *The Economic Basis of Peace*, 6.

24. See Jonathan Isham, Daniel Kaufmann, and Lant H. Pritchett, "Civil Liberties, Democracy, and the Performance of Government Projects," *The World Bank Economic Review* 11(2) (May 1997): 219–242; 219–220; Ankie Hoogvelt, *Globalization and the Postcolonial World* (London: Macmillan, 1997), 134–149.

25. A precursor of the social contract appeared in the 1215 *Magna Carta*, which pledged the loyalties of English barons in exchange for King John's respect for their rights. In the early seventeenth century, Johannes Althusias formulated a political community around mutual obligations between rulers and ruled. George H. Sabine, *A History of Political Theory*, 4th ed. (New York: Harcourt Brace College Publishers Holt, 1973), 387–390. Hobbes's community arose through the consent of the ruled to surrender their rights, except that of life, to a sovereign ruler who provided order. Thomas Hobbes, *Leviathan*, edited by Crawford B. Macpherson (Harmondsworth: Penguin, [1651] 1968), Book 2, ch. 17, 227. Locke expanded Hobbes's social contract to a commonwealth consisting of a civil society of propertied rights holders and its agent, the government mandated to protect their individual rights to life, liberty, and property. John Locke, *The Second Treatise of Government* (Oxford: Blackwell, [1690] 1976), ch. 7–10, 39–67.

26. See, among others, Sabine, *A History of Political Theory*; Irene Bloom, "Introduction," in *Religious Diversity and Human Rights*, edited by Irene Bloom, J. Paul Martin, and Wayne L. Proudfoot, 1–11 (New York: Columbia University Press, 1996), 4–7.

27. See Juan J. Linz, "Totalitarian and Authoritarian Regimes," in *Handbook of Political Science*, 9 vols., edited by Fred I. Greenstein and Nelson W. Polsby, vol. 3, 175–411 (Reading: Addison-Wesley, 1975), 355.

28. Peter Juviler and Sherrill Stroschein, "Missing Boundaries of Comparison: The Political Community," *Political Science Quarterly* 114(3) (Fall 1999): 435–453; 438. See also David Easton, "An Approach to the Analysis of Political Systems," *World Politics* 9(3) (April 1957): 383–400; 385–386; David Easton, *A Systems Analysis of Political Life*, 2d ed. (Chicago: University of Chicago Press, [1965] 1979) 177, 184–185.

29. Karl W. Deutsch and Sidney A. Burrell, *The Political Community and the North Atlantic Area* (Princeton: Princeton University Press, 1957), 5.

30. See Robert D. Putnam, *Bowling Alone: The Collapse and Revival of American Community* (New York: Simon and Schuster, 2000), ch. 8, 93, 137.

31. Eric M. Uslaner, "Producing and Consuming Trust," *Political Science Quarterly* 115(4) (Winter 2000–2001): 569–590; 569.

32. Alexis de Tocqueville, *Democracy in America*, translated by Henry Reeve, vol. 2 (New York: Knopf [1840] 1945), 108–109, 117, 121.

33. See United Nations, *States of Disarray: The Social Effects of Globalization*, United Nations Research Institute for Social Development Report for the World Summit for Social Development (London: Banson for UNRISD, 1995), 168–169.

34. Michael Walzer, *Spheres of Justice: A Defense of Pluralism and Equality* (New York: Basic Books, 1983), 32. See also Juviler and Stroschein, "Missing Boundaries of Comparison, 446.

35. See Juviler and Stroschein, "Missing Boundaries of Comparison, 446. For a discussion of political community as a form of multiculturalism, see Susan Wolf, "Comment," on "The Politics of Recognition, by Charles Taylor, in *Multiculturalism: Examining the Politics of Recognition*, edited by Amy Gutmann, 75–85 (Princeton: Princeton University Press, 1994).

36. See Deutsch and Burrell, *The Political Community and the North Atlantic Area*, 6, 35; Ernst B. Haas, *The Uniting of Europe: Political, Social, and Economic Forces, 1950–1957* (Stanford: Stanford University Press, 1958), 6; Jack Donnelly, *International Human Rights*, 2d ed. (Boulder: Westview, 1997), 153–159.

37. Refining David Easton's earlier insight, Claus Offe simplifies the formation of a political community in his triple transitions of identity, institutions, and rights. See Easton, *A Systems Analysis of Political Life*, 173–189; Claus Offe, "Capitalism by Democratic Design? Democratic Theory Facing the Triple Transition in East Central Europe," *Social Research* 58(4) (Winter 1991): 865–892; 869.

38. Robert Putnam formalized the idea of levels of politics with his notion of international negotiations as a two-level game, rather than a bilateral government-to-government interaction. In Putnam's view, governments must simultaneously *both* satisfy domestic constituencies *and* meet the demands of a negotiating counterpart government. Robert D. Putnam, "Diplomacy and Domestic Politics: The Logic of Two-Level Games," *International Organization* 42(3) (Summer 1988): 427–460. Jeffrey Knopf expanded the two-level structure into a third level of transgovernmental and cross-level interactions between government leaders, domestic constituencies, and transboundary constituencies that extend beyond state borders. Jeffrey W. Knopf, "Beyond Two-Level Games: Domestic-International Interaction in the Intermediate-Range Nuclear Forces Negotiations," *International Organization* 47(4) (Autumn 1993): 599–628. See also Lee Ann Patterson, "Agricultural Policy Reform in the European Community: A Three-Level Game Analysis," *International Organization* 51(1) (Winter 1997): 135–165.

39. Saskia Sassen, *Globalization and Its Discontents* (New York: New Press, 1998), 200.

40. See Georg Simmel, *The Sociology of Georg Simmel*, translated by Kurt H. Wolff (Glencoe, Illinois: Free Press, 1950), 122–128; George M. Foster, "The Dyadic Contract: A Model for the Social Structure of a Mexican Peasant Village," in *Friends, Followers, and Factions: A Reader in Political Clientelism*, edited by Steffen W. Schmidt, Laura Guasti, Carl H. Landé, and James C. Scott, 15–28 (Berkeley: University of California Press, 1977), 16–18, 27.

41. See Leonard T. Hobhouse, *Morals in Evolution: A Study in Comparative Ethics*, 2d ed. (New York: Holt, 1915), 54–69, 92–102;   Bronislaw Malinowski, *Crime and Custom in Savage Society* (London: Paul, Trench, and Trubner, 1932), 67, 125, 128; Robert R. Sears, "Social Behavior and Personality Development," in *Toward a General Theory of Action*, edited by Talcott Parsons and Edward A. Shils, 465–476 (Cambridge: Harvard University Press, [1951] 1954), 469–472.

42. Alec Stone Sweet, "Judicialization and the Construction of Governance," *Comparative Political Studies* 32(2) (April 1999): 147–184; 149.

43. Official compulsory triads are permanently constituted for a jurisdiction. Dispute resolution is initiated by one party without the consent of the other. Office conferred by the state or other concentration of coercive power replaces *ad hoc* delegation through an initial constitutional act of permanent delegation to an office, not an individual, for the life of the polity. Judicial systems and courts are archetypical forms of constitutional, compulsory triadic dispute resolution. Legislative institutions generalize the triadic paradigm through some political process.

44. Sweet, "Judicialization," 157.

45. See Douglass C. North, *Institutions, Institutional Change, and Economic Performance* (Cambridge: Cambridge University Press, 1990), 3–6, 17, 25; Harry Eckstein, "A Culturalist Theory of Political Change," *American Political Science Review* 82(3) (September 1988): 789–804; 790–792; Aaron Wildavsky, "Choosing Preferences by Constructing Institutions: A Cultural Theory of Preference Formation," *American Political Science Review* 81(1) (March 1987): 3–21; 15–18; James G. March and Johan P. Olsen, *Rediscovering Institutions: The Organizational Basis of Politics* (New York: Free Press, 1989), 22; Michael Taylor, "Structure, Culture, and Action in the Explanation of Social Change," *Politics and Society* 17(2) (June 1989): 115–162; 135–138, 149–152; David M. Kreps, "Corporate Culture and Economic Theory," in *Perspectives on Positive Political Economy*, edited by James E. Alt and Kenneth A. Shepsle, 90–143 (Cambridge: Cambridge University Press, 1990), 111–131.

46. Sweet, "Judicialization," 179.

47. Nicholas Rengger, "Justice in the World Economy: Global, International, or Both?" *International Affairs* 75(3) (July 1999): 469–471; 470. See also Ian Shapiro and Lea Brilmayer, "Introduction," in *Global Justice*, edited by Ian Shapiro and Lea Brilmayer, 1–11 (New York: New York University Press, 1999), 2.

48. Alain Noël and Jean-Philippe Thérien, "Public Opinion and Global Justice," *Comparative Political Studies* 35(6) (August 2002): 631–656; 649.

49. Michael Walzer introduced the dichotomy of *thick* and *thin* in a broadly moral context. Michael Walzer, *Thick and Thin: Moral Argument at Home and Abroad* (Notre Dame: University of Notre Dame Press, 1994).

50. See Hedley Bull, *The Anarchical Society: A Study of Order in World Politics* (London: Macmillan, 1977), 316–317.

51. See Henry Shue, "Exporting Hazards," in *Boundaries: National Autonomy and its Limits*, edited by Peter G. Brown and Henry Shue, 107–146 (Totowa, New Jersey: Rowman and Littlefield, 1981), 114–121.

52. See Walzer, *Spheres of Justice*, 28–30, 59–63, 316–321; Richard Devetak and Richard Higgott, "Justice Unbound? Globalization, States, and the Transformation of the Social Bond," *International Affairs* 75(3) (July 1999): 483–498; 488.

53. Philip Resnick, "Global Democracy: Ideals and Reality," in *Globalization and Europe*, edited by Roland Axtmann, 126–143 (London: Pinter, 1998), 140.

54. See Jean-Jacques Rousseau, "Discourse on the Origins and Foundations of Inequality among Men," in *Collected Writings of Jean-Jacques Rousseau, vol. 3, Discourse on the Origins of Inequality (Second Discourse), Polemics, and Political Economy*, edited by Roger D. Masters and Christopher Kelly, vol. 3, 1–95 (Hanover, New Hampshire: University Press of New England, [1755] 1992), 36–38; Hobbes, *Leviathan*, Book 1, ch. 13, 185–186.

55. Richard Falk, *On Humane Governance: Toward a New Global Politics* (Cambridge: Polity, 1995), 254.

56. United Nations, *Our Global Neighborhood*, Report of the Commission on Global Governance (New York: Oxford University Press, 1995), 39.

57. Stephen Gill, "Globalization, Democratization, and the Politics of Indifference," in *Globalization: Critical Reflections*, edited by James H. Mittelman, 205–228 (Boulder, Colorado: Lynne Rienner), 1996, 217.

58. James Bohman, "International Regimes and Democratic Governance: Political Equality and Influence in Global Institutions," *International Affairs* 75(3) (July 1999): 499–513; 503.

59. For an engaging set of analyses of some of the specific problems associated with representation of minority groups, see "Embattled Minorities Around the Globe" *Dissent*, 43(3) (Special Issue Summer 1996): 6–160; especially Daniel A. Bell, "Minority Rights: On the Importance of Local Knowledge," *Dissent* 43(3) (Summer, 1996): 36–41; 39–40.

60. Harold Hotelling formulated the median-voter paradox in the 1920s to exemplify an economic phenomenon. Arthur Smithies introduced elasticity of demand and Anthony Downs refined it again in the 1950s. Harold Hotelling, "Stability in Competition." *Economic Journal* 39(153) (March 1929): 41–57; 54–55. Arthur Smithies, "Optimum Location in Spatial Competition," *The Journal of Political Economy* 49(3) (June 1941): 423–439; 425–432; Anthony Downs, *An Economic Theory of Democracy* (New York: Harper and Row, 1957), 115–117.

61. Mike Moore, "Multilateral Meltdown, "*Foreign Policy* 135 (March-April 2003): 74–75; 75.

62. See Claude Lefort, *Essais sur la politique, XIXe-XXe siècles* (Paris: Seuil, 1986), 25.

63. Resnick, "Global Democracy," 135.

64. Jean Bethke Elshtain, *Democracy on Trial* (New York: Basic Books, 1995), 74.

65. Resnick, "Global Democracy," 136.

66. See Joseph A. Schumpeter, *Capitalism, Socialism, and Democracy* (New York: Harper & Row, 1976), 291; John Locke, "The Second Treatise of Government: An Essay concerning the True, Original, Extent, and End of Civil Government," in *Two Treatises of Government*, edited by Peter Laslett, 283–446 (Cambridge: Cambridge University Press, 1966), para. 157–158, pp. 390–391; para. 192, p. 412; para. 222, pp. 430–432.

67. Sherle R. Schwenninger, "World Order Lost: American Foreign Policy in the Post-Cold-War World," *World Policy Journal* 16(2) (Summer 1999): 42–71; 51.

68. See Mancur Olson Jr., *The Logic of Collective Action: Public Goods and the Theory of Groups* (Cambridge: Harvard University Press, 1965), 21–36; Michael Mandelbaum, "The Inadequacy of American Power," *Foreign Affairs* 81(5) (September-October 2002):61–73; 66.

69. Joseph S. Nye Jr., "The American National Interest and Global Public Goods," *International Affairs* 78(2) (April 2002): 233–244; 241.

70. For discussion of the difficulties of definition, see Inge Kaul, Isabelle Grunberg, and Marc A. Stern, "Defining Global Public Goods," in *Global Public Goods: International Cooperation in the 21st Century*, edited by Inge Kaul, Isabelle Grunberg, and Marc A. Stern, 2–19 (New York: Oxford University Press, 1999), 9–15.

71. Devetak and Higgott, "Justice Unbound?" 495.

72. Nancy Birdsall and Robert Z. Lawrence, "Deep Integration and Trade Agreements: Good for Developing Countries?" in *Global Public Goods: International Cooperation in the 21st Century*, edited by Inge Kaul, Isabelle Grunberg, and Marc A. Stern, 128–151 (New York: Oxford University Press, 1999), 128.

73. The relationship between resource-based and knowledge-based growth in globalizing economies implies the country's propensity for interstate conflict. "Resource-based static growth associates high growth with high conflict, and low growth with low conflict, in a direct-positive relationship. Knowledge-based dynamic growth associates high growth with low conflict, and low growth with high conflict, in an inverse-negative relationship." Mott, *The Economic Basis of Peace*, 194.

74. Matthew Paterson, "Interpreting Trends in Global Environmental Governance," *International Affairs* 75(4) (October 1999): 793–802; 798.

75. David J. Rothkopf, "Foreign Policy in the Information Age," in *The Global Century: Globalization and National Security*, edited by Richard L. Kugler and Ellen L. Frost, vol. 1, 215–239 (Washington, D.C.: National Defense University Press, 2001), 223.

76. For discussion of the shrinking role of the state and nonstate-centered governance, see, among others, James N. Rosenau, "Governance, Order, and Change in World Politics," in *Governance without Government: Order and Change in World Politics*, edited by James N. Rosenau and Ernst-Otto Czempiel, 1–29 (Cambridge: Cambridge University Press, 1992), 3–8; Oran R. Young, *International Cooperation: Building Regimes for Natural Resources and the Environment* (Ithaca: Cornell University Press, 1989), 229–235; Jan Kooiman and Martin van Vliet, "Governance and Public Management," in *Managing Public Organizations: Lessons from Contemporary European Experience*, edited by Kjell A. Eliassen and Jan Kooiman, 58–72 (London: Sage, 1993), 64–68;   For discussions of neoliberal roles of the state, see, among others, Leo Panitch, "Rethinking the Role of the State in an Era of Globalization," in *Globalization: Critical Reflections, International Political Economy Yearbook, Vol. 9*, edited by James H. Mittelman, 83–113 (Boulder, Colorado: Lynne Rienner, 1996), 103–113.

77. For one perspective on agency in governance see Mahmood Mamdani, "African States, Citizenship, and War: A Case-Study," *International Affairs* 78(3) (July 2002): 493–506.

78. Robert W. Cox introduced the French term *nébuleuse* to describe the political, authority structure for the global political economy and described it as "governance without government." Robert W. Cox, "Global Perestroika," in *New World Order: The Socialist Register 1992*, edited by Ralph Miliband and Leo Panitch, 26–43 (London: Merlin, 1992), 30.

79. See Kenneth N. Waltz, "Globalization and American Power," *The National Interest* 59 (Spring 2000): 46–56; 53–55.

80. Roger Cohen, "Redrawing the Free Market," *New York Times*, 14 November 1998, B9, B11; B9.

81. Richard Falk, "State of Siege: Will Globalization Win Out?" *International Affairs* 73(1) (January 1997): 123–136; 125.

82. Richard N. Haass, "What to Do with American Primacy," *Foreign Affairs* 78(5) (September-October 1999): 37–49; 38.

83. In the seventeenth and eighteenth centuries, the European structure of regional governance was a multipolar system that was balanced in static equilibrium by at least five poles of power committed to preserving the balance through shifting alliances. In the nineteenth century, British dominance expanded the static European balance to global dimensions in a system of imperial balance. The common values shared by the

balancing great powers made cooperation reasonable and usually smooth within their shared perspectives of the world. From 1871 through 1914, this multipolar system deteriorated into an unstable system of dynamic balance as Germany shifted its focus from static balancing to preventing the formation of hostile alliances and Britain began to suffer from overextension. For the classical formulation, see Waltz, *Theory of International Politics*, 117–128. For an explanation of why balance of power occurs, see Michael Doyle, *Ways of War and Peace: Realism, Liberalism, and Socialism* (New York: W.W. Norton, 1997), ch. 5, 169–172, 192. See also Kenneth Waltz,"Evaluating Theories," *American Political Science Review* 91(4) (December 1997): 913–917; 914–915.

84. Robert W. Tucker, "Alone or with Others: The Temptations of Post-Cold-War Power," *Foreign Affairs* 78(6) (November-December 1999): 15–20; 19.

85. Yong Deng, "Hegemon on the Offensive: Chinese Perspectives on U.S. Global Strategy," *Political Science Quarterly* 116(3) (Fall 2001): 343–365; 357.

86. Modern history contains only two great powers that have been able to manage a dynamic system of regional, self-stabilizing balances: Britain from about 1700 through World War I and the United States from the 1940s until the 1960s. Shielded by geography before the technologies of global weapon systems and force-projection capabilities, Britain and the United States implemented global offshore balancing strategies. Each relied on naval—and later, air—power, military assistance, and financial dominance to support allies with interests in regional stability. "Taken together, the experiences of Britain and [the United States] highlight the central feature of the offshore balancing strategy: it allows for burden *shifting*, rather than burden sharing. . . . [When] a predominant power seems to be winning, an offshore balancer can intervene decisively to forestall its victory (as Britain did against Philip II, Louis XIV, and Napoleon), . . . [or] to prevent a single power from dominating a strategically crucial area." Benjamin Schwarz and Christopher Layne, "The Hard Questions, a New Grand Strategy," *The Atlantic Monthly* 289(1) (January 2002): 36–42; 39.

87. See Robert W. Cox, *Production, Power, and World Order: Social Forces in the Making of History* (New York: Columbia University Press, 1987), 253–265.

88. See Immanuel Wallerstein, *The Modern World-System: Capitalist Agriculture and the Origins of the European World-Economy in the Sixteenth Century* (New York: Academic Press, 1974), 349–350.

89. Tucker, "Alone or with Others," 20.

90. Schwarz and Layne, "The Hard Questions," 37.

91. James Fallows, "The Unilateralist, A Conversation with Paul Wolfowitz," *The Atlantic Monthly* 289(3) (March 2002): 26–29; 29. See also Paul Wolfowitz, "American Power—For What? A Symposium," *Commentary* 109(1) (January 2000): 21–47; 47.

92. Edward H. Carr, *The Twenty Years' Crisis: 1919–1939*, 2d ed. (London: Macmillan, [1946] 1961), ch. 13; 219. Quotations are from pp. 214, 218, and 219.

93. William C. Wohlforth, "The Stability of a Unipolar World," *International Security* 24 (1) (Summer 1999): 5–41; 40.

94. Francisco Suarez, *De Legibus*, bk. 2, in *Selections from Three Works of Francisco Suarez*, 3–646 (Oxford: Clarendon, [1612] 1944), ch. 19, para. 9, p. 349.

95. Bull, *The Anarchical Society*, 13.

96. Ruth Wedgwood, "Gallant Delusions," *Foreign Policy* 132 (September-October 2002): 44–46; 44.

97. Arjun Appadurai, "Broken Promises," *Foreign Policy* 132 (September-October 2002): 42–44; 42.

98. Michael Hirsh, "Bush and the World," *Foreign Affairs* 81(5) (September-October 2002): 18–43; 31–41.

99. Robert S. Litwak, "The Imperial Republic After 9/11," *The Wilson Quarterly* 26(3) (Summer 2002): 76–82; 79.

100. James N. Rosenau, *The Study of Global Interdependence* (New York: Nichols, 1980), 1–2.

101. See, among others, Pratap Chatterjee and Matthias Finger, *The Earth Brokers: Power, Politics, and World Development* (London: Routledge, 1994), 6–9; Joshua Karliner, *The Corporate Planet: Ecology and Politics in the Age of Globalization* (San Francisco: Sierra Club Books, 1997), ch. 7.

102. See, among others, James N. Rosenau, *Turbulence in World Politics: A Theory of Change and Continuity* (Princeton: Princeton University Press, 1990), 388–461; Rosenau, "Governance, Order, and Change in World Politics," 13.

103. Paterson, "Interpreting Trends in Global Environmental Governance," 795.

104. See Robert W. Cox, "An Alternative Approach to Multilateralism for the Twenty-first Century," *Global Governance* 3 (January-April 1997): 103–116.

105. Robert W. Cox, ed., *The New Realism: Perspectives on Multilateral and World Order* (Basingstoke: Macmillan, 1997), xxxvii.

106. Devetak and Higgott, "Justice Unbound?" 493.

107. Keith Suter, "People Power," *The World Today* 56(10) (October 2000): 12–14; 13.

108. David T. Twining, *Beyond Multilateralism* (Lanham, Maryland: University Press of America, 1998), xi.

109. Hugh De Santis, "Mutualism: An American Strategy for the Next Century," *World Policy* 15(4) (Winter 1998–1999): 41–54; 44–45.

110. See Hugh De Santis, *Beyond Progress: An Interpretive Odyssey to the Future* (Chicago: University of Chicago Press, 1996), 189–190, 201–202.

111. Hugh De Santis, "Mutualism: An American Strategy for the Next Century," *World Policy* 15(4) (Winter 1998–1999): 41–54; 47–48.

112. Helen V. Milner, "International Political Economy: Beyond Hegemonic Stability," *Foreign Policy* 110 (Spring 1998): 112–123; 120.

113. Robert O. Keohane and Joseph S. Nye, "Globalization: What's New? What's Not? (And So What?)" *Foreign Policy* 118 (Spring 2000)104–119; 115.

114. Mott, *The Economic Basis of Peace*, 225.

115. Quotations are from Aristotle, Politics in The Works of Aristotle, Vol. 2, Great Books of the Western World (Chicago: Encyclopædia Britannica, 1952), I, 2, 1252b35–1253a27, p. 446; II, 2, 1261b13, p. 456; VII, 4, 1326b1–1326b5, p. 530; and VII, 4, 1326a10–1326a15, p. 530. See also VII, 4, 1326b12, p. 539; and II, 7, 1267a20–1267a31, p. 462.

116. St. Augustine, *The City of God* in *The Confessions, The City of God, On Christian Doctrine*, Great Books of the Western World (Chicago: Encyclopædia Britannica, 1952), XIX, 7, p. 515.

117. St. Augustine, *The City of God* in *The Confessions, The City of God, On Christian Doctrine*, Great Books of the Western World (Chicago: Encyclopædia Britannica, 1952), XII, 21, XIX, 17, pp. 522–523; XIX, 26, pp. 528–529.

118. St. Thomas Aquinas, *De Regimine Principum*, in *Aquinas: Selected Political Writings*, translated by J. G. Dawson, 3–83 (Oxford: Blackwell, 1948), bk. 1, ch. 2, p. 13; bk. 1, ch. 15, p. 81; see also bk. 1, ch. 2, p. 9.

119. Robert M. Hutchins, *St. Thomas and the World State* (Milwaukee: Marquette University Press, 1949), 8.

120. Dante Alighieri, *De Monarchia*, translated by Herbert W. Schneider (Indianapolis, Indiana: Bobbs-Merrill, 1957), bk. 1, ch. 7, p. 10. See also Dante Alighieri, "De Monarchia," in *Western Political Heritage*, by William Y. Elliott and Neil A. McDonald, 367–373 (Englewood Cliffs, New Jersey: Prentice-Hall, [1949] 1965), 371.

121. St. Thomas distinguished between divine law, natural law, and positive, human law and included non-monarchic governments with monarchs in the term *sovereign*. See St. Thomas Aquinas, *Summa Theologica*, Vol. 2, Great Books of the Western World (Chicago: Encyclopædia Britannica, 1952), II, q. 90, art. 3, reply obj. 2, p. 207; II, q. 91, art. 2–5, pp. 208–212; II, q. 94–96, pp. 220–235.

122. Hutchins, *St. Thomas and the World State*, 15.

123. Hutchins, *St. Thomas and the World State*, 36.

124. Ann Kelleher and Laura Klein, *Global Perspectives: A Handbook for Understanding Global Issues* (Upper Saddle River, New Jersey: Prentice-Hall, 1999), 180.

125. Tönnies, *Community and Association*, 65.

126. Kofi A. Annan, "Problems without Passports," *Foreign Policy* 132 (September-October 2002): 30–31; 30.

127. Sadako Ogata, "Guilty Parties," *Foreign Policy* 132 (September-October 2002): 39–40; 40.

128. Bohman, "International Regimes and Democratic Governance," 509, quoting from James Rosenau, "Governance and Democracy in a Globalizing World," in *Reimagining Political Community: Studies in Cosmopolitan Democracy*, edited by Daniele Archibugi, David Held, and Martin Köhler, 28–57 (Cambridge: Polity, 1998), 40.

129. J. Bryan Hehir, "The Limits of Loyalty," *Foreign Policy* 132 (September-October 2002): 38–39; 38.

130. John D. Montgomery, "The Next Thousand Years," *World Policy Journal* 15(2) (Summer 1998): 77–81; 81.

131. Deutsch and Burrell, *The Political Community*, 129.

132. This moralistic, generalized trust is in contrast to a strategic, particularized type of trust that depends on some personal relationship, an assessment of trustworthiness, and seems limited to relationships between people who are like each other. Strategic trust is not expansive, whereas moralistic trust includes potentially all of humanity. Whereas moralistic trusters are ready to find common values in shared interests, strategic trusters are wary of people who are different from themselves. See Uslaner, "Producing and Consuming Trust," 571–575, 579.

133. Uslaner, "Producing and Consuming Trust," 572.

134. See Easton, "An Approach to the Analysis of Political Systems," 391.

135. Kelleher and Klein, *Global Perspectives*, 177.

136. Herbert A. Simon, "We and They: The Human Urge to Identify with Groups," *Industrial and Corporate Change* 11(3) (June 2002): 607–610; 608.

137. James Burke, *The Day The Universe Changed* (London: British Broadcasting Corporation, 1985), 13.

138. Burke, *The Day The Universe Changed*, 13.

139. Hoffmann, "Clash of Globalizations," 111.

140. Larry Diamond, "Toward Democratic Consolidation," *Journal of Democracy* 5(3) (July 1994): 4–17; 4.

141. Robert W. Cox, "A Perspective on Globalization," in *Globalization: Critical Reflections*, edited by James H. Mittelman, 21–30 (Boulder, Colorado: Lynne Rienner, 1996), 28.

142. See James N. Rosenau, Governance in the Twenty-First Century," *Global Governance* 1(1) (January-April 1995): 13–44.

143. Thomas Hobbes (1588–1679) introduced the justification for a centralized concentration of power in the state in his *Leviathan*, published in 1651. Hobbes's concept of a social contract among individuals creates a single sovereign with "the use of so much power and strength conferred on him that by terror thereof he is enabled to form the wills of them all, to peace at home, and mutual aid against their enemies abroad." Thomas Hobbes, "Leviathan," in *Great Books of the Western World*, edited by Robert M. Hutchins, vol. 23, 41-283 (Chicago: Encyclopedia Britannica, 1952), 100. John Locke (1632–1689) introduced the concept of civil society: "Those who are united into one body, and have a common established law and judicature to appeal to, with authority to decide controversies between them and punish offenders are in civil society with one another." John Locke, "Concerning the True Original Extent and End of Civil Government," in *Great Books of the Western World*, edited by Robert M. Hutchins, vol. 35, 25–81 (Chicago: Encyclopedia Britannica, 1952), 44.

144. Thomas Carothers, Civil Society: Think Again," *Foreign Policy* 117 (Winter 1999–2000): 18–29; 18.

145. On policy and growth see, among many others, William Easterly and Sergio Rebelo, "Fiscal Policy and Economic Growth: An Empirical Investigation," *Journal of Monetary Economics* 32(3) (December 1993): 417–458; 436; Robert Barro, "Economic Growth in a Cross Section of Countries," *Quarterly Journal of Economics* 106(2) (May 1991): 407–443; 430–432; David Dollar, "Outward-Oriented Developing Economies Really Do Grow More Rapidly: Evidence from 95 LDCs, 1976–1985," *Economic Development and Cultural Change* 40(3) (April 1992): 523–544; 533–536, 540; Bradford De Long and Lawrence H. Summers, "How Strongly Do Developing Countries Benefit from Equipment Investment?" *Journal of Monetary Economics* 32(3) (December 1993): 395–415; 413–414; Dani Rodrik, "Understanding Economic Reform," *Journal of Economic Literature* 34(1) (March 1996): 9–41; 16–17, 21, 25, 31–38. On whether democracy supports economic growth see, among others, Partha Dasgupta, *An Inquiry into Well-Being and Destitution* (Oxford: Clarendon, 1993), 108–121; Seymour M. Lipset, *Political Man: The Social Bases of Politics* (Garden City, New Jersey: Doubleday, 1960), 31–45, 57–58; Eric Weede, "The Impact of Democracy on Economic Growth: Some Evidence from Cross-National Analysis," *Kyklos* 36(1) (March 1983): 21–39; 29–35; Roger C. Kormendi and Philip G. Meguire, "Macroeconomic Determinants of Growth," *Journal of Monetary Economics* 16(2) (September 1985): 141– 163; 154–156; Gerald W. Scully, "The Institutional Framework and Economic Development," *Journal of Political Economy* 96(3) (June 1988): 652–662; 657–661; Kevin B. Grier and Gordon Tullock, "An Empirical Analysis of Cross-National Economic Growth, 1951–1980," *Journal of Monetary Economics* 24(2) (September 1989): 259–276; 271–273; Surjit S. Bhalla, "Freedom and Economic Growth: A Virtuous Cycle," in *Democracy's Victory and Crisis: Nobel Symposium No. 93*, edited by Axel Hadenius, 195–241; 198–205, 226–228 (Cambridge: Cambridge University Press, 1997), 216–219, 226–227; Adam Przeworski and Fernando Limongi, "Political Regimes and Economic Growth," *Journal of Economic Perspectives* 7(3) (Summer 1993): 51–71; 60–66.

146. Barry Smith, "The Concept and Practice of Civil Society" (paper presented at the Tenth Anniversary International Conference of the International Nongovernmental Organization Training and Research Conference, Oxford, United Kingdom, 13–15 December 2001), 3.

147. See Robert M. MacIver, *Community: A Sociological Study*, 2d ed. (London: Macmillan, 1920), 22–38. Although MacIver does not use the term, *civil society*, he clearly has it in mind (26–27) as transcending community and association in his differentiation between society, community, association, and state.

148. Stanley Hoffmann, "Clash of Globalizations," 109.

149. Jürgen Habermas, "Further Reflections on the Public Sphere," in *Habermas and the Public Sphere*, edited by Craig Calhoun, 421–461 (Cambridge: MIT Press, 1996), 453.

150. Jürgen Habermas, *The Structure of the Public Sphere: An Inquiry into a Category of Bourgeois Society* (Cambridge: MIT Press, 1992), 27. See also Jürgen Habermas, *The Theory of Communicative Action, Volume 2, Lifeworld and System: A Critique of Functionalist Reason*, translated by Thomas McCarthy (Boston: Beacon, 1987), 81–82, 346–347.

151. Devetak and Higgott, "Justice Unbound?" 491.

152. Bohman, "International Regimes and Democratic Governance," 507.

153. Carothers, Civil Society: Think Again," 27.

154. Benjamin R. Barber, "Democracy at Risk: American Culture in a Global Culture," *World Policy Journal* 15(2) (Summer 1998): 29–41; 40.

155. See Ted Robert Gurr, "Minorities, Nationalists, and Ethnopolitical Conflict," in *Managing Global Chaos: Sources of and Responses to International Conflict*, edited by Chester A. Crocker and Fen Osler Hampson, with Pamela Aall, 53–77 (Washington, D.C.: United States Institute of Peace Press, 1996), 63–69.

156. Robert W. Cox, "Civil Society at the Turn of the Millennium: Prospects for an Alternative World Order," *Review of International Studies* 25(1) (January 1999): 3–28; 10–11.

6

CULTURAL GLOBALIZATION

Habit and custom have historically been the mundane filling of people's lives in "a pattern of lifeways received among mutually recognized family groups, . . . a relatively autonomous complex of interdependent, cumulative traditions."[1] The addition of a normative set of values—religion, ideology, or ethics—and a few symbols or icons completes the common notion of culture. A legitimate form of inclusive knowledge held in a communal mind, culture "denotes a historically transmitted pattern of meanings expressed in symbolic forms, . . . [by] which men communicate, perpetuate, and develop their knowledge about and attitudes towards life."[2] A primary component of Aristotle's good life, a communal sense of meaning is the nucleus of every culture and the foundation of the beliefs and values with which its members justify their ways of living.[3] Although closely and asymmetrically linked, the terms *culture* and *civilization* are not synonymous. Civilization is the general category, which *both* embraces institutions *and* relates cultures, and culture is the particular. A legacy of history, a context of civilization, and a pattern of values focus an array of forces into meanings, identities, and self-consciousness for *both* societies *and* individuals: their culture.

Premodern cultures found meaning and values beyond human society in cosmic or spiritual metanarratives that superseded the state and the economy as normative foundations for civilizations. The post-Renaissance rise of secular metanarratives—capitalism, liberalism, democracy, socialism—supplanted the universalist values of religion with additional political, economic, and cultural identities. Whereas the Enlightenment sought meaning in universal rationality, the lens of modernity resolved a trinity of individual meanings in utilitarian rationality, a national identity embedded in the sovereign nation-state, and the admixture of industry, technology, and capitalism.[4] Despite the efforts of André Malraux to unify the power of culture with the power of the state in the search for some glorious antidestiny, globalization has threatened each of these fundamental pillars of modern culture and meaning.[5]

Not an ascriptive attribute of citizenship, status, or religion, culture arises from epigenetic experience as a legacy of shared meanings, identities, values, and beliefs about living, "enduring but not immutable."[6] The collective mind of an epigenetic community creates and transforms its culture as an expanding aggregate of individual minds. "When oral tradition is supplemented by writing and the arts, it can grow indefinitely large . . . and even skip generations. But the biasing influence of the epigenetic rules, being genetic and ineradicable, remains the same across all societies and generations."[7]

The Braudelian *conjoncture* of the 1970s released a swarm of ethnic and local cultural movements, each with its own identity and metanarrative of meaning and values. Globalization confronted these fragile cultures not only with neighbors but with an entire world of mature, robust societies. As people perceived threats to delicate identities, confrontation exploded into conflict. "Culture has thus become a new source of conflict and an important dimension of struggle between the global and the local."[8] "The combined pursuit of free markets and democratization has repeatedly catalyzed ethnic conflicts in highly predictable ways, with catastrophic consequences, including genocidal violence and the subversion of markets and democracy themselves."[9]

Unlike static cultures that celebrate equilibrium or fundamentalisms seeking the glorious past, globalization carries its own dynamic future-oriented culture, which converges local cultures into more vigorous cultures as it spreads. Prior waves of cultural globalization Sinicized Southeastern Asia; Romanized Western and Southern Europe; Islamized Central Asia, the Middle East, and Spain; and Russified Eastern and Central Europe. Rather than imposing the legitimacy of a triumphant Anglo-American culture, the current wave of globalization diffuses robust cultures, which retain credibility, without absorbing or destroying them.[10] Cultures that lack robust values or stable institutions paradoxically resist convergence and solidify in defensive antiglobalism. A cultural dichotomy between the global and the local amplifies *both* political-economic tensions across cultures *and* contradictions between local perspectives and the global perspective. Rather than converging, the globalizing metanarratives—liberalism, capitalism, and democracy—coexist in deep, persistent tension with each other and with these static cultures.

CONVERGENCE AND TRANSFORMATION

As new knowledge transforms social reality, it also transforms the cultures that carry it. In contrast to the cognitive knowledge that dominates political and economic transformations, new normative knowledge transforms cultures through diffusion and convergence. Globalization transforms traditional alliances between cultures and political economies into syncretic, dialectical forms that merge or transform cultures in unpredictable ways. Each cultural generation explores the risks and rewards of globalization, isolation, defense, convergence, or cosmocracy in the context of its own time and circumstances.

Cultural Convergence

Early in the nineteenth century, Claude-Henri de Rouvroy, comte de Saint-Simon (1760–1825), noted that industrialization was converging common attitudes toward reason, spreading acceptance of science, and banishing superstition. Recognizing the power of rationality, "The people today accord to the agreed opinions of scientists the same degree of confidence that they gave in the middle ages to the decisions of spiritual power."[11] The spread of this positivism across cultures was shifting the focus of human progress away from the power struggle between church and state. Industrialization had split society into two hostile cross-cultural classes: *les industriels*, the businesspeople, and *les oisifs*, the idlers. Convinced that the historical process assured the triumph of industry, Saint-Simon distilled these trends into a globalizing, humanist philosophy in his final work, *Nouveau Christianisme*.[12]

Refined by his disciple, Auguste Comte, Saint-Simonism informed Émile Durkheim's theories of cultural differentiation.[13] As common behaviors spread, "the collective consciousness must progressively become more weak and abstract in order to encompass intrasocietal diversity."[14] Globalization deteriorated collective commitments to national societies amid populist calls for dismantling political boundaries that hindered integration of a global community around a convergent global culture. Whereas Durkheim saw social differentiation as the negative, fragmenting shadow of globalization, within a different perspective, Max Weber identified purposeful rationalization as a positive, convergent force behind globalization. Weber distilled social relationships into arrangements of instrumental reason and affectual, emotional reactions. These gained meaning only through human purposes, which arose from cultural norms and values. Expansion of relationships beyond rational expediency or affective feelings into mutual orientations of people to each other converged their cultures around instrumental reason.[15]

Inspired by the same social realities that Saint-Simon explained in humanist convergence, Karl Marx's materialism found capitalist exploitation and the historic force of production. Within Marx's visionary globalization of production and consumption as public goods, "the intellectual creations of individual nations become common property. National one-sidedness and narrow-mindedness become more and more impossible, and from the numerous national and local literatures, there arises a world literature."[16] For Marx, unlike *both* Saint-Simonian humanists *and* Weberian rationalists, globalization planted the seeds of cultural convergence through revolution instead of integration. Through his dialectic, the capitalistic convergence of the bourgeoisie into a global social class would coalesce the global proletariat in anticapitalist revolution. Paradoxically, the proletarian triumph would destroy any national and cultural antagonisms that capitalism had put in place. The utopias of humanism, rationalism, and materialism all emerged from the powerful links between production and consumption, which transformed and converged human thought, cultures, and identities in a common global culture.

Through the lens of modernism, progress was the convergence of every society towards a common social reality in two phases: industrialization and globalization. Industrialization differentiated Braudel's global capitalism and market economy from material life through economic specialization. As industrialization urbanized cultures, families specialized in consumption and labor, schools taught work skills and behavioral norms, and bureaucratic governments provided infrastructure to generate economies of scale. While capitalist organizations specialized in efficient production, social institutions sustained a robust class structure and religion promoted supportive moral values. Globalization then spread industrialization from local sources of innovation into other societies and converged them around the same pattern for specialization of roles and institutions. Societies modernized in converging paths towards a universal society and culture operating a global economy.

Talcott Parsons expanded the work of Saint-Simon, Durkheim, and Weber beyond spatial globalization into temporal dimensions. His logic of adaptation —"the capacity of a living system to cope with its environment"—directed societies into a common evolutionary path.[17] Progress became social and cultural adaptation to industrialization. Because industrial societies need to exchange labor, capital, goods, and ideas, their members and products must be interchangeable and interdependent. The adaptation of individualism *and* the interdependence of global universalism converge values towards secular ethics and rationality and local social reality into a convergent global modernity. The Parsonian result—predicted by *both* Saint-Simon *and* Durkheim—is socio-cultural shift from exclusive nationalism towards inclusive universalism.

Through the lens of historicism, Marion Levy resolved Parsons's notions of convergence and individuality into cultural relativity. Whereas Saint-Simon, Durkheim, Weber, and Parsons envisioned universal forces of globalization driving humanity into a modern future, Levy found the motive power for modernization in a neo-Marxian, materialistic motive in every individual to improve. "Once a traditional society is in contact with a modernized society, at least some of its members will want to change it in order to improve their material situation."[18] Progress becomes a process of imitating rich, industrial societies, and globalization is *both* the cause *and* the result of the ensuing changes in social reality. Since historicist progress is inherently reflexive and imitative, globalization spreads *both* stable patterns *and* unstable anomalies as interacting cultures converge. By linking previously isolated individuals and cultural alcoves, globalization *both* contains relative cultural diversity within narrow perspectives *and* creates converging cultural contexts around them.[19]

Cultural Transformation

With the end of the Cold War, people rediscovered that culture and living went beyond *both* Marx's historical materialism *and* Durkheim's division of labor. Notions of convergence faded into images of destroying and re-creating social reality and cultural identity around new normative knowledge within broader perspectives. When confronted with catastrophic events, "cultures are more likely to adjust their institutions so as to better support their ways of life in altered circumstances than to transform themselves into other cultures."[20] Only when the world no longer works the way that culture predicts do people change their cultures.[21] Far deeper than shifting patterns of production or governance, cultural transformation involves epigenetic identities and social values and necessarily includes convergence, since neither human knowledge nor progress can be constrained by political boundaries or economic structures.

Building upon epigenetic legacies, each generation of public institutions and private lives collectively destroys and reconstructs its culture around novel identities for *both* the individual self *and* the larger community. As each generation expands its perspectives beyond tradition and familiar behaviors, "cultural identity that previously enjoyed monopoly power within a country now faces competition. When general consumers find imports more appealing, foreign culture can be charged with supplanting local heritage."[22] Societies and peoples struggling to retain their comfortable identities in current waves of globalization have stressed cultural differentiation while industrialization, trade, and global finance have created pragmatic integration. By the late twentieth century, globalization had effectively transformed culture from the ties that bound people together into identities that kept them apart. Despite the inevitable disappearance of some small, isolated cultures and their identities, the energy of culture is creative destruction through transformation as new knowledge and globalization expand perspectives with every generation.

Cultural transformation begins with *basho*, within which people create new normative knowledge around historic legacy in the context of social reality. New knowledge diffuses through incremental innovation and learning as different cultural norms, new meanings, changed identities, and refined ways of living. Embedded in the reflexivity and relativity of historicism, new knowledge and innovation do not abruptly replace earlier cultures with new ones but refine marginally the ways in which people live with each other and gradually shift the cultural boundaries of social relationships. The epigenetic patterns and biases, which embody the legacies of every culture, ensure that cultural shifts emanate slowly and incrementally from *basho* as people shift their perspectives, create new identities, and find new meanings.

Rejecting the structured, economic patterns of convergence, cultural transformation extends beyond the materialist forces of industrialization and finds the engine of progress in eternal, human creativity. Like *basho*, cultural transformation embraces not only the urgent human struggle for survival and prosperity but also the metanarratives of the eternal past, the aesthetic immortality of art, and inextinguishable drive to know an absolute truth. Just as the Renaissance recovered humankind's metanarratives, the Enlightenment introduced rationality, and modernity prioritized prosperity, twentieth-century globalization has injected art into cultural transformation. Deepening and focusing Benedetto Croce's philosophical aestheticism, André Malraux set about transforming the state into "a bridge between the cultural heritage (including the tradition of the new) and the living nation."[23]

Malraux imagined that the aura of art that created its personal immediacy and awesome majesty expressed and created the meanings of civilization and life itself. Through the lens of historicism, he recognized that artistic creativity emerged in a cultural context of communal ritual. Mechanical reproduction of art and cultural products—radio, recording, or photography—suppressed the communal context and ritualistic content in technology and technique that effectively destroyed the social reality that art expressed. To progress from technical destruction through artistic creativity, Malraux co-opted the state to reconstruct the artistic aura of community and ritual in transforming social reality. The Malrauxist state would resurrect art, the divine faculty of the human soul, as an antidestiny to the chaos of modernization. Government would deepen the bond between community and state into a universal artistic culture, within which people exercise their creativity for the common good in transforming destiny into consciousness. For Malraux and his cultural heirs, artistic culture was the highest expression of human will and liberation from the limits of the human condition.[24] Malraux's historicist vision of aesthetic immortality, ultimately preserved by the state in culture and art, remains adrift in the *nébuleuse* of global governance. His idea of art as integral to conscious identity and justifying life itself has, however, transformed social reality into cultural awareness and human destiny into cultural consciousness.

Cultural Diversity

Although no culture can long resist the modernizing changes forced upon it by global communications and markets, the creative destruction of globalization seems to bring cultural transformation and diversity, not convergence. Instead of ordaining inevitable convergence, electronic telecommunications media not only stimulate cultural interaction and exchange but also act to express and deepen cultural differences and to diversify narrow-perspective societies. "When one society trades a new artwork to another, diversity *within* the receiving society increases (because individuals have greater choice), but diversity *across* the two societies diminishes (the two societies become more alike)."[25] Through the lens of historicism, change within a culture is an important dimension of diversity that replaces equilibrium with the recognition that neither humanity nor any of its cultural groupings have reached a perfection that demands or justifies static preservation. Cultures that require insulation within some narrow perspective to preserve their roots depend for their survival on an absence of the very things that globalization brings: internal cultural diversity, new knowledge, and social transformation. Readiness to exploit and adapt alien knowledge and values remains an essential feature of *basho*, of innovation, of creativity, and of progress.

Like economic development, cultural progress occurs spasmodically and randomly as robust cultures expand and other, fragile ones wither. Isolated societies that remain outside globalization—through geography, protection, or defense—gradually condense the unique features that animate their cultures and make them distinctive into static norms. Unable to sustain themselves in stasis and refusing to change or diversify, these cultures, like unprofitable companies, eventually disappear. Older, narrower cultures must yield to newer, broader ones. Although many people are quick to describe this creative destruction as a tragedy, most cultures in most societies are diverse hybrids—synthetic institutions that people have enlarged under the influences of multiple, changing influences. Few modern cultures can legitimately claim the descriptions *indigenous* or *autochthonous* with their implications of static, insulated societies of tradition-bound artists and workers unable or unwilling to expand perspectives or knowledge. The historicist processes of creative destruction and cultural transformation form a broad dimension of diversity, which excludes the contrary notions of monoculture or convergence.

The Global Village

For millennia, the historical lenses resolved culture into substantive content of norms, values, biases, and patterns of living. For Marshall McLuhan, who famously introduced the *global village*, the fundamental and determining feature of culture was not any substantive content but the medium used by people to transmit it.[26] Since McLuhan's broad concept of media included any means of extending the human senses, his insight seems to have anticipated the technological determinism of post–Cold-War political and economic globalists.[27] McLuhan's stress on media—communications and transportation—naturally separates the world's history of cultural globalization into a tribal or personal epoch and an industrial or literate epoch.

Relying on walking, talking, and the wheel, cultural globalization in the tribal epoch was deeply embedded in place. Human experience in oral, place-based cultures was immediate, personal, and complete. It limited globalization to small, intimate groups, institutional memories, or momentary encounters. Technological advances expanded the media of globalization through writing, printing, and mechanization. People's impersonal interactions became private, fragmented, and even lonely as cultures became literate and tied themselves to familiar places. Globalization stressed sight, and de-emphasized sound, touch, taste, and smell. Distant readers were unengaged and may have had no personal or physical contact. Documents focused thought into obviously connected linear sequences that formed the shape of the cultures that they carried and the structure of the knowledge that people recorded in them.

The powerful technologies of the information age expand human senses beyond local place to allow perception, appreciation, and experience of the world as a whole "globally, instantly interrelating every human experience."

Shattering the linear structures of knowledge and rationality that Bacon's idols celebrate as the primary locus of knowledge creation, the global information media transcend *both* time *and* place. In McLuhan's transformed and converged global village, people experience the world not only globally and instantaneously but chaotically without the structures of place or time. All aspects of experience converge. The present, the past, the future, home, here, and there disappear in simultaneity and synchrony, even while globalization renders them all completely independent. The total experience of living is transformed into the sort of cultural chaos that only the human mind can resolve within its global home. "This is the new world of the global village."[28]

Despite the persistence of goods traders, "globalization is strongest in world information flows. . . . Deterritorialized global networks and global flows dominated by the world core have evolved . . . [around a] principle of global organization of a decontextualized culture."[29] Through a mystical union of convergence and transformation, technological globalization resurrects the self-based, collective cultures of tribalism *without the cornerstone of place* in an expansive global village. The same sense of self-based, local interdependence that formed tribal society exposes the totality of global humanity on every individual who is connected in the global village. The message of the media "is total change, ending psychic, social, economic, and political parochialism. The old civic, state, and national groupings have become unworkable. Nothing can be further from the spirit of the new technology than 'a place for everything and everything in its place.' You can't *go* home again."[30]

The Dilemma of Identity

Whereas premodernity allowed no choice at all, the Enlightenment replaced rigid, ascriptive identities with self-identities. Dichotomous alternatives required rational choices between self and society or between community and prosperity.[31] Modernity tolerated individual autonomy as an intractable paradox that forced people to choose either one identity or the other, although they could switch identities from time to time. In the information age, few people accept this notion of self-sufficient, autonomous individuals who create interchangeable identities by rejecting *both* self *and* society through the power of character. Many, however, accept the Enlightenment logic of Bacon's idols that people cannot split themselves into multiple identities that shift as they pursue their lives. Common wisdom finds dichotomous choices in the global village between universalism and difference, prosperity and community, us and them, homogeneity and diversity, or self and society.

Dual Identities

The dichotomy of identity choices inherent in globalization takes a unique form for each person and for each identifiable group—family, society, culture, or civilization. As cultural identities lose integrity, people turn to technology to replace comfortable relationships between self, place, society, time, and world. Through technology, people have learned to create stable space-time identities in symbolic representations of *both* individuality *and* communality: social character.[32] Many people find a satisfying pair of dual identities with *both* social freedom *and* self-realization in the industrial society of work. Others lose themselves in the paradoxical anonymity of protective isolation and global participation: "a teeming throng whose individual members nevertheless feel themselves to be achingly alone, empty, devoid of purpose or independent meaning."[33] Anonymous participation in huge global events or working for transnational organizations through the impersonal linkages of information technology allows *both* individuality *and* togetherness.

Self or Society? Protected by Bacon's *idola specus*, a narrow, personal identity of self lives in a tiny, private corner of the world that exists only in the brief now and local here as rarified inner-directed individualism. This selfish identity rescues an individual from the soul-numbing anomie that exclusion from, or rejection by, society can readily inflict but also provides welcome shelter from the overwhelming assaults of outrageous majority rule.

Infinitely more than self, a social identity of anonymous other-direction locates the individual in the universal humanity within the global perspective.[34] Not a static, ascriptive status, a shifting, flexible social identity provides comfort in other-directed, fashionable conformity. Beyond the private self of here and now, social identity expands individuality across space and over time. Whereas each individual's self-identity is intensely personal and private, the social identity is protectively anonymous, communal, ethnic, or cultural.

The merger of self and society in a complex, dynamic, dual identity recognizes people's yearning for acceptance in a neat, soul-saving compromise between the constraints of inner-direction, the sycophancy of other-direction, and the rigors of tradition. Through individual exercise of the autonomy idealized by modernity to shift between self and society without making a permanent commitment, globalism offers freedom from *both* the compulsions of fashion *and* the obsessions of idealism. Driven neither by the mindless need to conform nor by the mindless need to rebel, in Buddha-like freedom, the autonomous, dual-identity person enjoys a prospect within which *both* the self *and* society are complementary within the globality of timeless humanity.[35]

Lexus or Olive Trees? Thomas Friedman has famously chosen the Lexus and the olive tree to symbolize this profound dichotomy between self and society. "Dedicated to modernizing, streamlining and privatizing their economies in order to thrive in the system of globalization," the world's connected societies have constructed their identities around the Lexus of consumption.[36] Another, larger part of humanity remains mired in the historic, traditional political-economic struggles of earlier eras about who owns what bit of land with its olive tree of cultural identity and survival.

Friedman's olive trees symbolize all that forms identities in time and space —the joy, pride, and confidence of self; the warmth of family; the intimacy of friendship; and the comfort of home. The security of culture and community in encountering others and the refuge of religion in encountering self are as essential for survival as are the material requirements for sustenance. After expanding their identities for millennia with more, bigger olive trees, people invented the nation-state, "the ultimate olive tree—the ultimate expression of whom we belong to—linguistically, geographically, and historically. You cannot be a complete person alone. You can be a rich person alone. You can be a smart person alone. But you cannot be a complete person alone. For that you must be part of, and rooted in, an olive grove."[37]

Friedman's Lexus symbolizes a dichotomous and equally primal human feature: the search for sustenance and prosperity. In a modern world that has achieved prosperity and even abundance, the Lexus represents the pursuit of higher living standards and new identities through globalization and consumption. Even though most of the world's peoples continue to struggle for survival, the markets and technologies of globalization form the global economy around the pursuit of Lexus-level standards of living.

Globalization and the global village provide the structure for the broad gulf, and the dynamic context of the bitter struggle between those societies pursuing the Lexus and those preserving their olive trees. Most threats to people's olive trees have historically come from other people who sought to destroy or replace homegrown trees with their better, hybrid varieties. Beyond this traditional threat, many olive-tree societies see the greatest threat in globalization itself, in the market forces, information, and Lexus technologies that replace identity with consumerism and displace tradition with new products. Deeper than economic inequality and beyond compromise or balance, the identity gap, or struggle between the Lexus and the olive tree, embodies the primal need to choose between identity and prosperity. Just as people must have *both* self *and* society, they need *both* cultural identity *and* economic prosperity to survive. Economic globalization arises from, around, and for societies with well-rooted, well-watered, mature olive trees, robust cultures, and stable polities that balance and sustain pursuit of the Lexus. To them globalization offers prosperity, further modernization, and stable balance with cultural norms as people transform present identities into new social realities that include taller olive trees and a Lexus in every garage. To weak societies with immature or diseased olive trees, confused identities, or chaotic politics, globalization offers Schumpeterian destruction of inefficiency and convergence with a modern, foreign culture. To them economic development promises creation of national competitiveness, Americanization, and participation in the global economy, but no olive trees and no Lexus.

Cultural and social identities and the Friedmanian olive trees that embody them are essential to human survival.[38] An obsession with one's own olive trees, however, often transforms cultural identities into exclusive, personal disputes over who owns which particular olive trees, bits of land, languages, or even religions. Although many species of olive trees may be shared in a global village with no loss to anyone, territory can only be split, divided, or appropriated exclusively. For peoples whose identities are bound to the land, the logics of identity and territoriality require physical possession, occupation, and residence. Although it may deliver a Lexus, foreign control prevents them from ever going home and destroys not only their olive trees, but also their individual and social identities. Since a homeless life without identity is worse than not living at all, such peoples have no qualms about vicious, venomous struggles to control their homelands where their olive trees are growing. For them, the global village with a new Lexus in every garage has no attraction.

Identities and Addiction

Many people in *both* the Lexus world *and* the olive-tree world fear losing *both* self *and* society in an amorphous, impersonal, homogeneous, global village of good, little Americans. As globalization resettles them in a global village, people lose confidence in their comfortable identities and face uncomfortable choices in refining them. The few, autonomous, undirected freethinkers pursue novelty in surprising Lexus-world combinations of science, fashion, and tradition that avoid convergence. Some, the fundamentalists, cling to olive-tree cultures with their contents of absolute truth—traditions, norms, values, and icons—seek their cultural roots, and define their identities rigidly around tradition-directed, untransformed, cultural content. Others, the pragmatists, like literary ballad-spinners, invent new, inner-directed traditions for old cultures, or transform less new traditions into other-directed, global fashions.

In searching for their identities by avoiding either convergence or transformation, people can readily slide into repetition and cultural addiction: "the influence of the past upon the present, [on which] as in the case of tradition, repetition has a key role."[39] Without the reassurance of a collective past embodied in cultural traditions, anxious individuals and troubled societies readily subvert free choice into mindless repetition. As globalization has persistently diluted traditional culture in societies, individuals' identities also lose the stability of social positions in cohesive, local communities, which are themselves dissolving. Like fundamentalist cultures, people translate some remembered decision or precedent into an *ad hoc* past, which obviates decision making in the chaos of uncertainty and risk that globalization has established as normal. Bacon's idols bound the modern present to the premodern past and focused society fixedly on its own history. So also does the free, rational choice of addictively repeating a single precedent shift people's gaze, interest, and attention fixedly away from the future and contract them into the historical lenses of the past.

Addictive repetition gradually captures people in unwilled identities that they have themselves created. To maintain relevance and credibility of these identities, individuals and communities must re-create transitory self-identities around private storylines or communal metanarratives that differ with each telling. As with physical substances, each repetition and revision deepens the addiction, widens the identity gap, and frustrates *both* individuals *and* societies.

RELIGION

Lashed to the dailiness of survival, primitive peoples explained everything that puzzled them in astonishing varieties of religion as understudies for knowledge. They explained their own existence through metanarratives of creation populated with deistic creatures, a past of vague indeterminacy, and a mythic passage into the present. From the sixteenth century B.C., the defeat of the mother goddess brought a new understanding of the cosmos, nature, and human existence in "three principal ideas that were to inform the age to come: the supremacy of the father god over the mother goddess; the paradigm of the opposition implicit in the deadly struggle between god and goddess; and the association of light, order, and good with the god, and of darkness, chaos, and evil with the goddess."[40] The victory of a solar god over the tellurian goddess transformed *both* religion *and* culture into a new masculine mythology of war and conquest by a heroic archetype of warrior-king-god.

For neolithic cultures, mythological religion celebrated wealth and the stability of local communities in comfortable continuity. The emergence of communal knowledge, with toolmaking or agriculture, marked the climax of domestic civilizations whose myths glorified indigenous origins. In contrast to the mother-goddess parables, myths exalting gods and peoples from far lands as expansive cultural heroes emerged with the spread of agricultural and technical knowledge. The transformation of civilizations between the neolithic period and the Iron Age converted religion from a stable domestic force to a powerful globalizing pressure of cultural meanings that reflected an essential, universal unity of humanity. As knowledge expanded and people learned to think and to answer their own questions, their civilizational narratives congealed into mythic traditions, found their way into scriptures, and formalized into religions. In sophisticated forms, many claimed their places among Bacon's idols and persist as robust, modern institutions.

Fully credible within the historical lenses, Arnold Toynbee's conclusion that a civilization is created around a religion implies that a global civilization cannot form without a global religion. Although each of the world's great, religions contains a totalitarian claim of exclusive rights to the truth, none can credibly claim status as a global religion. Religion has historically formed inclusive communities predisposed to expand by spreading the correct truth through conversion of nonbelievers, often as allies of secular, political-economic structures—mercantilism, empire, colonialism, liberalism, and others. Like ideology, religion provides a solid foundation for social exclusion that has historically discouraged religious diversity and coexistence of alternative truths. The tendency of most modern religions to accept or encourage marriages with converts leads to large, diverse communities of believers in decentralized, physically unconnected localities that transcend political or geographic boundaries. Throughout its institutional evolution, organized religion has projected a dual image of inclusive harmony and cooperation among believers within an exclusive shell of intolerance for the morally feckless outsiders.

Transformation and Modernity

Islam, Protestantism, and technology shattered the geographic constraints that medieval religion used to separate the good, the saved, and the faithful from the evil, the damned, and the infidels. The eighth-century conflict of respective truths between ancient Asian religions, a diasporic Judaism, a maturing, expansive Christianity, and an exuberant, adolescent Islam forced each to transform itself and set them all on different paths into the future. While Islam and Hindu slid into decline and Buddhism stagnated, European transformation stimulated the Protestant Reformation, Jewish migration, and the spurt of globalization that accompanied the Enlightenment and renewed Christianity's universal, apostolic mission.[41] Across the major religions, modernity has transformed religion from the exclusive source of absolute truth into a "convenient language in which to express the community's existing moral rules. . . . This kind of decentralized, instrumental religion is a component of spontaneous order, rather than an alternative for it."[42]

Judaism

In the historical books of the Old Testament, a jealous, national God reigned alone over the chosen people of Israel. With the destruction of the Jewish kingdom for its sins, the Books of the Prophets expanded the God of Israel to a universal dimension, although Israel retained its privilege as the chosen people. The new, universal God embodied assurance of the final reign of justice and peace but gave to Israel the responsibility for establishing the Kingdom of God. With the globalization of the national religion, "Judaism is in the minds of the Prophets a universal monotheism, and the Jewish people are a band of missionaries to spread that teaching, . . . a universal creed which follows from the belief in one God ruling the world, . . . [destined] to prevail not by might but by the peaceful way of proselytism."[43]

The Christianization of the Roman empire and the rise of Islam induced a period of intolerance and persecution that prevented Judaism from pursuing God's mission. Although Christianity included the Judaic, one-world spirit of justice and humanity in its ideals, medieval Christendom exempted interstate politics from any moral law beyond national interests. Until the nineteenth century, when Jews could again participate in the civil life of states, Judaism carried culture, knowledge, and goods in succeeding waves of globalization. The rise of Zionism revived the Messianic mission and transformed it into an internationalized nation, rooted in one place. Now spread across the world, Judaism pursues everywhere its God-given task of reconciling people with the fatherhood of the one true God and the brotherhood of universal man.

Christianity

For medieval Christianity, so long as church—Christendom—and state —the Roman empire and its successors—were consolidated, politics focused on jurisdictional disputes between popes and kings. When the Reformation separated them, the state gained legitimacy from secular sources, cultivated them to enhance its power, and secularized politics. Protestantism shattered the Roman Catholic hierarchy of relationships with God and proclaimed universalism in the possibility of direct, personal relationships between every individual and God. Destroying any notion of global solidarity in universal Christendom, the Reformation split Christianity into a privatized faith and the hierarchical, communal faith preserved by Roman Catholicism. Since any person anywhere could become a Christian simply by an act of faith—either in the Church or in God—the proselytizing mission became an essential and powerful dynamic of the Reformation and Counter-Reformation. Both pieces of Christianity accepted the need to expand the ranks of the faithful and transformed globalization into competition around notions of territorial religions. The Judaic legacy of humanism survived in the idealistic alcoves of both Christian houses as the motive for creating secular, international law.

By the seventeenth century, as European empires were still largely ambitions and global trade was intermittent, the Roman Catholic Church was actively integrating Asia, the Americas, and Africa into a global Christendom centered in Rome. By the nineteenth century, Protestants had consolidated their Euro-American piece of Christianity and were actively expanding individual faith throughout the globe. This privatized Christianity sought not only to recruit nonbelievers but to liberate the morality of public policy and economic commerce from heathen, cultural constraints. Instead of the divinely inspired Roman Catholic ecclesiastics, Protestantism replaced cultural norms and public principles of justice with the consciences of individual decision makers. Protestantism and Catholicism both implicitly presumed that individual Christians had exercised a personal moral calculus in advance of any act whether of fact or of faith. Through this individualization of faith, modern Christianity could condone, justify, or ignore the political-military tragedies and economic exploitations that accompanied globalization.

The Enlightenment shifted perspectives and priorities away from mystical religion and power politics towards material prosperity. Promised power, wealth, and salvation *both* in the Protestant work ethic *and* in the Catholic community, Christians overlooked the crack in Christianity and embraced globalization. Epitomized in Alexis de Tocqueville's work, Christian liberals envisioned their generation as the climax of a great democratic revolution that had been unfolding for at least seven centuries within the hand of God.[44] As the foundations of community shifted from the church to a secular state, modern Christianity "bequeathed the idea of the universal equality of human rights to secular doctrines like liberalism and socialism . . . [and] vastly reduced the density and scope of the shared values mandated by state authority."[45]

As rationality transformed social reality, Christianity struggled heroically to revive an expansive, universal Christendom guided spiritually by the Roman Catholic pope. Although the Vatican Council of 1869–1870 reasserted one-world papal supremacy, the vision of a society of states living in harmony and cooperation *with neither temporal nor spiritual head* prevailed. The ascendance of nationalism and rationalism transformed Christian principle from religious structure to the humanitarian ideas inherited from Judaism. As Judaism internationalized its Messianic mission in its own nationalism, Christianity transformed its latent universalism into humanitarian calls for peace and disarmament. The Covenant of the League of Nations and the Charter of the United Nations reflect Christian success in globalizing its humanist principles of peaceful dispute resolution among states. Despite economic integration and technological compression of time and space, transformed, Christianity calls for the moral revolution upon which human progress depends.

Islam

After the death of Mohammed, Muslim Arabs captured Jerusalem in 638 and swept through Asia, northern Africa, and Southern Europe, as Islam dominated the Middle East, Southern Europe, and Southwestern Asia. Through the twelfth century, Islam extended from Spain and Somalia to Java and Fujian. Despite enormous destruction by *both* Christian armies *and* Mongol hordes, Islam survived in the shadow of a globalizing European civilization. As Islamic civilization declined, it condensed, like Confucianism, Buddhism, and Hinduism, into an exclusive subculture of expanding European Christianity. Unlike Asian religions, by the sixteenth century, Islam had regenerated into three gunpowder empires: the Mughals of India (1526–1857); the Safavids of Persia (1501–1736); and the Ottomans of Anatolia (1301–1923).[46] Embedded in this ecumenical multiculturalism around separate, complementary understandings, Islam lost its future-orientation and slid into the obsession with the past from which Europe was just escaping. Instead of flying into the future on the arrow of time to find God, *Allah*'s eternal tapestry of time wove past, present, and future into a single, timeless design. "The past is ever present . . . [and] the worldly future dimension has been suppressed."[47]

The Enlightenment marked the transformation of Islam from an active, progressive, globalizing civilization into a static culture remembering the glories of *el Andalus* (modern Spain), when Islam was the center of globalization. Napoleon's 1798 invasion of Egypt not only symbolized the obsolescence of Islamic civilization but dropped Islam into a collective psychosis of resentment as Muslims sought to explain their plight by blaming something outside Islam. The successive experience of the Moors, the Arabs, the Mughals, and the Ottoman Turks became a mythology of Islamic suffering under the pressures of secular globalization and the evil power of the infidels. As the collective sense of hopeless persecution spread, Muslim awareness of exclusion from globalization and alienation from the European world brought a vicious spiral of cultural anger, righteous resentment, and helpless rage.

Cosmopolitan Syncretism

Orthodox religions and people of different cultures have often dealt with each other initially as heretics and enemies. Eventually, the great religions suppressed or absorbed local faiths through cosmopolitan cooptation. During post-Reformation Christian globalization, "the [orthodox] Church found ways of alternately coopting and repressing practices considered alien to official ritual and theological acceptability, and found willing accomplices and partners within the indigenous populations."[48] Through asymmetrical, intercultural exchanges, local peoples faced and gradually absorbed the religious patterns brought by the cosmopolitan Christians and Muslims. Under threat of torture or death, heathen converts learned and adopted the ritual behaviors that the powerful European Christians and Arabic Muslims expected in them. Over generations in an insidious process of acculturation, local cultures redefined themselves as distinct variants of Christian and Islamic cultural exports.[49]

The cosmopolitan churches recognized these cultural differences by legitimizing them and "creating mechanisms of accommodation and coexistence, for example by coopting other practices, symbols, and rituals. Inevitably this is a process with a certain power content." This sort of cosmopolitan, cultural globalization with a large power content included *both* homogenization *and* differentiation. The former sort of cultural globalization is glaringly exemplified in Benjamin Barber's concept of McWorld, Marshal McLuhan's global village, or the spread of Islamic fundamentalism. The latter differentiation emerges in "the disembedding of indigenist medical and religious practices, as in Buddhism or New Age, the proliferation of international movements in support of indigenous and ecological survival, [or] the fashion for ethnic styles in music, art, architecture and dress." Within the global perspective, religious confrontation has occurred in a context of asymmetry between cosmopolitan cultural dominance and deep, indigenous, cultural roots. The balance between cosmopolitan, intellectual hegemony and local, spiritual solidarity has led the dominant religions—the Islamic Caliphate or the Roman Catholic Church—"into a multifaceted, often inconsistent, relationship with indigenous cultures and religions, and the result is the syncretism."[50]

Religious Reactions to Globalization

Despite fashionable theories of rational social and political behaviors, the role of religion in global affairs remains significant, even as religion mutates with a Darwinian fervor. The major blocs of orthodox believers—Christians, Jews, Muslims, Buddhists, or Hindus—have reacted to globalization by uniting and concentrating as hardier varieties, or new religious movements, flourish at the fringes of organized religion. Inconveniently for the great faiths, "the world is today as awash in religious novelty, flux, and dynamism as it has ever been."[51] Globalization seems to be privatizing faith through fundamentalism, secularizing society, and separating religious practices in time and space.

Fundamentalism

Secular modernity, with its offer of current prosperity and promise of future growth, handily defeated most efforts to restore the faded patina of a glorious, moral past. Religion compromised with modernity in periodic waves of defensive reform that repaired *both* the religious edifice *and* the faiths that formed religious identities. As religion tardily reacted to the dilemma of identity in the context of globalization and change, a wave of fundamentalist transformation has revitalized the old, universal, monotheistic religions.[52] Societies that could recall a robust set of premodern religious or mythic traditions found it attractive to reject these rational, modernist refinements. Fundamentalists across all faiths accused orthodox religion of destroying *both* the individual *and* the social identities that their scriptures beatifically recalled. Rejecting modernity and postmodernity, many fundamentalists seek to compile social and individual identities, as their ancestors did, from God and nature instead of human rationality. Doing so implicitly and often explicitly restores Bacon's idols to their rightful places as guardians of tradition and identity.

Fundamentalism is the reassertion of absolute truth as presented by ancient scripture and interpreted by culture and tradition in a secular world that demands and accepts only rational reasons based on objective evidence. Applying this absolute truth rigorously across all perspectives—economic, political, and cultural—revitalizes society in God's will and universal understanding of the human condition. Beyond claiming proprietary content of absolute truth, fundamentalism not only rejects rationality but asserts that people cannot live in a rational world of relative truth in which nothing is beyond challenge. With a disturbing tone of estrangement from societies overburdened with *déja vu*, charismatic rhetoricians and venerable pundits use scripts from long ago to lead the retreat from living into absolute truth. Inspired mummers posing as politicians fuse absolute truth—but *not* the secular utility of public interest—with human struggles for power and wealth. With a few innovative refinements, a bit of new language, some compelling slogans, and an ever-changing supply of video clips, for fundamentalists of any faith, God's will remains as it was given in the ancient scriptures.

Every religion with roots in a distant time and place different from those in which most of its followers now live shares a pair of intractable dilemmas. Orthodox religion struggles perpetually in determining which canons God has immutably prescribed for all time and which may vary according to place, century, and human condition. Orthodoxy needs also to determine how the faithful can reconcile acceptance of a body of scientific knowledge that accumulates and changes over time with the doctrine that some statements remain forever valid without change. Fundamentalism slices through these Gordian knots with the absolute truth as revealed in God's word.

Christianity. Fundamentalist Christianity stresses less the hierarchical structures and reforms of orthodoxy than empowering individual believers with the spirit and power of God. Small groups of fundamentalist thinkers or ecumenical demagogues have also entered politics as proponents or opponents of issues that promote or hinder the workings of God's will. Their political versions of religious doctrines, which have secularized and fragmented Christianity, threaten *both* ecumenical religion *and* secular globalization.

Another pluralistic version of Christian fundamentalism spreading through Africa, Asia, and Latin America arises in "a vision of Jesus as the embodiment of divine power, who overcomes the evil forces that inflict calamity and sickness upon the human race."[53] In emulation of Jesus' own incarnation, Christianity has the divine mission to incarnate itself in non-Christian cultures in a generous pluralism with *both* geographic *and* spiritual catholicity.[54] This ecumenical, interfaith Christianity, or the Third Church, is becoming a form of Christianity as distinct as Roman Catholicism and Protestantism.[55]

Islam. After generations of patient expectations, Islam reacted to Euro-American globalization with the resentment of a thousand years of humiliation and cynical disappointment in failed promises. A rejection of modernity and secularism slowly emerged in scattered, fundamentalist calls for a return to first principles. In waging the cosmic struggle between good and evil, the good life emerges from strict dedication to principles presented in sacred texts, and evil grows in countless violations of those principles. With a sense that modern political, social, and economic systems have failed, Islamic fundamentalism seeks human identity in scriptural authenticity in a self-sufficient, unitary ideology for state, church, society, and individual.

Instead of yearning for the return of Islam's golden age, fundamentalists selectively transformed the words of the Prophet into calls for global *jihad* to deliver secular states into an Islamic alternative to nationalism, liberalism, socialism, and capitalism. Some militant sects echo Christian proclamations of the descent of society into *jahiliyya* (pre-Islamic barbarism and ignorance) and consider governments whose legislation and politics are not based on divine law as illegitimate realms of oppression and evil. These societies are the revealed enemy, even though some, or all, individuals living in those countries accept the revealed truth and live religiously by God's commandments.[56]

Although militant Islam tempts Muslims on the margins of society, less dogmatic versions reflect many Muslims' desire for dynamic societies. In contrast to classical Islam and militant fundamentalism, political Islam stresses internal revolution, rather than *jihad*. Political Islam arose in Iran "because the father of the Islamic revolution, Ayatollah Khomeini, had an uncanny ability to build and maintain a broad base of support—including the young and the poor, whom he dubbed the disinherited, and the tradition-minded merchants of the bazaar."[57] In fearful response to the violence of *jihad* and revolution, many middle-class Muslims and Islamic intellectuals form a vague, reformist Islam that insists on freedom to express universal Islamic values in local, pluralist contexts. Middle-class Islam seeks to reorient economics from capitalist-style acquisition towards redistribution, to displace secular law with *sharia*, to purify cultural icons, and to pluralize politics.

Holding the Islamic fundamentalist sects together are calls for Islamization, a reincarnation of a hierarchic, global community of the faithful, *umma*, with a focus of education on holy texts. Islamization campaigns to unify Islam deliberately remind the faithful of "the glories of *al-Andalus* where in Grenada and Cordoba, Muslims ruled what were, a millennium ago, the most civilized places, as measured by artistic and scientific accomplishment, in Europe." For Islamization, the principles of European imperialism are "still said to persist in the vaguer forms of political, cultural, and economic influence."[58] Despite, however, this common theme, Islam—*both* orthodoxy *and* fundamentalism— remains fragmented in dealing with globalization and modernity.

Judaism. Modern Judaism is itself a fundamentalist movement relying on the ancient God-given Messianic mission as the foundation of both religious doctrine and sociopolitical action. Emerging from the tradition of Zionism, the most prominent Jewish fundamentalist movement, *Gush Emunim*, resorts to a single, esoteric reading of the *Torah* to reveal God's will. The movement relies on the mystical utterances of Rabbi Zvi Yehuda Kook the Elder and his son and one of Judaism's 613 *mitzvah*s to settle the entire controversy over the whole land of Israel. Like right-wing Christianity and political Islam, Jewish fundamentalism has sought escape from orthodox doctrine and hierarchy by forming political parties in Israel's *Knesset*. Jewish fundamentalist parties uniformly assert the Jewish right to all of biblical, greater Israel, *Eretz Israel*, and Arab occupation of that land as contrary to God's will.[59]

Asian Fundamentalisms. Asian societies express a loose benevolence for ethnic and religious plurality in a pattern of cultural pluralism rather than the assimilation into a dominant culture preferred by non-Asian cultures. This dominant theme of pluralism enervates most Asian fundamentalist movements so long as economies remain strong and foreign cultures remain content not to assimilate Asian cultures. Only as they feel threatened by non-Asian cultures do most Asian religions either borrow selected features of non-Asian religions or react defensively to protect the fundamentals of their own cultures. Not generally seeking to return to religious fundamentals, "these synthetic Asian variants of fundamentalism select and canonize sacred epics, poems, and other open-ended genres into the stuff of fundamental, inerrant scripture."[60]

Among Asian cultures, Hindu fundamentalism congealed in the International Society for Krishna Consciousness (*Hare Krishna*) movement and the *Vishva Hindu Parishad* (World Hindu Council) in the 1960s. Combining devotion to *Krishna*, Indian nationalism, and globalization in resisting the menacing dominance of Christianity and Islam, fundamentalism sought to rescue the continuity of Hindu identity and recover its proud past. Hinduism determined to reform the Hindu community by borrowing from the enemy the source of its cultural and religious power. In a form of strategic, cultural mimetism, Hindu fundamentalism "has undertaken this mission by imitating the ecclesiastical structure characteristic of the semitic religions, so as more effectively to resist them."[61] The *Hindutva* movement has consciously added theistic, Judeo-Christian-Islamic elements to its fundamentals in the form a Lord Rama as a supernatural patron with his own sacred, earthly places. The monotheistic Sikh sense of apocalyptic expectation that transcends the mundane world of illusion is an open imitation of orthodox Judaism and several Christian movements. Hindu fundamentalism is a fragmented defensive surge of religiocultural conservatism seeking to reverse political trends towards modern secularization and cultural domination by Christianity and Islam.[62]

Within the global community of the devout, the *songha*, several fundamentalist Buddhist movements have emerged in a broad quest for relevance in the modern world of globalization and consumerism. They are broadly oriented towards society and away from the individual and have openly entered local, national, and global politics. Buddhist fundamentalism calls for a broad shift in political power from political-military-economic orthodoxy towards a strong, diverse civil society.[63] Instead of justifying social inequalities in *kharma*, fundamentalism stresses rigid, monastic adherence to discipline and individual moral behavior as a democratic cultural foundation. A managerial alternative to classical Buddhism is built around mass movements and social welfare in a civil-society relationship between church and state. The fundamentalist Japanese Buddhist revival, *Soka Gakkai*, celebrates traditional, rural values, calls for restoration of the state to purge Occidental decadence and materialism, and has become militantly evangelistic. Buddhist fundamentalist movements call for a more dense civil society as part of a cultural revival of Asian individualism within Buddhist reform, embedded in global religious revival and reform. With aspirations to become the world religion that will dominate a war-free future, Buddhist fundamentalism advocates comprehensive disarmament and participates actively in international politics through legitimate global nongovernmental organizations.[64]

Social Secularization and Ecumenicism

As religion shifted from narrative mythologies towards philosophical principles as guides to living, globalization and rationality spawned the social secularization thesis—that humans are outgrowing their belief in the supernatural and their need for religion. In a loose context of fundamentalism, social pragmatism transforms secular humanism into a reinterpretation of the ancient truths that offers spiritual intent rather than textual rigidity as a moral guide. An essential notion embedded in the spirit of social secularization is morality as an integral, self-contained system of globalism that coexists with various communities of religious believers. Although religious moralities are merely localisms constricted within narrow perspectives, universal, secular morality embraces all religions and transcends narrow, orthodox perspectives.

Unlike Christianity, with its hierarchic vision of a global Christendom, Islam and Buddhism offer horizontal, secular views of globalization in the context of pluralistic community. Although the Buddhist *songha* retains much of its mysticism in its growing civil-society role, for Islam, "the objective of building a viable *umma* is inseparable from material progress, constitutional and democratic politics, and the accoutrements of development."[65] The secularization of Islam and Buddhism horizontally from *within* may form the antithesis to the vertical ecumenicism of Christianity and Judaism, which launches Braudel's dialectic transformation of *both* social *and* religious realities.

Faced with several waves of globalization, religions have broadly focused ecumenicism in providing interfaith identities for people and societies beyond both their olive trees and the Lexus. Despite their wide range of doctrinal orthodoxy, most major religions—Bahai, Buddhism, Confucian, Christian, Hindu, Islam, Jain, Judaism, Shinto, Sikh, Zoroastrian, and others—have common convictions that carry a weak, spiritual kinship within a diversity of social customs and religious rituals:

a conviction of the fundamental unity of humanity;
a conviction of the equality and dignity of all human beings;
a sense of the sanctity of the individual person and its conscience;
a sense of value of the human community;
a conviction that love, compassion, selflessness, and spiritual truth have more
    power than hate, enmity, and self-interest;
an obligation to support the poor and oppressed against the rich and oppressors;
a profound hope that good will prevail.[66]

Judaism, Hindu, Confucianism, and Shinto are consolidating their doctrinal positions within traditional, narrow perspectives and expanding through social secularization. Ecumenical Christianity, Islam, and Buddhism, in contrast, are actively involved carriers of globalization through proselyting and conversion. Whereas the former religions seem to have entered the Lexus market, the latter are defending their olive trees.

New Religions

The same pressures beneath social secularization are also initiating "new religious movements, many of which are narrow-minded [and] more hostile to other believers. . . . Human beings cannot survive solely on the physical satisfaction of their needs. [They] have spiritual desires to be fulfilled."[67] With creeds as diverse as their origins, while orthodoxy is reforming and fundamentalism is restoring, new religions are constructing alternative faith-based social systems and immersing believers in supernatural mysticism.

Reformed Religions. As modernity slides into tradition, reformers of the orthodox churches imagine democratizing Christianity, Islam, Hindu, and Judaism into ecumenical institutions freed from bureaucratic hierarchy, superstition, dogma, and corruption. Explicitly rejecting fundamentalism, a new Reformation of Christianity promises social transformations as momentous as those of the first Reformation through the variety of its values and its salience in the fastest-growing populations.[68] Offering radical notions of revelation, instead of interpretation, of God's word, the new Reformation's privatized religion devalues the vast, institutional, clerical communities presiding over Christendom. In league with secular, nationalist reformers, new Christians seek to capture modern technology and prosperity for God and Christians while retaining traditional cultural identities.

A parallel Islamic Reformation is attempting to balance the fundamentalist emphasis on faithful reverence with the popular desire for self-expression. As *jihad* loses appeal, Muslim youth are returning "to a religion that was tolerant and progressive, not one that called for violent displacement of the existing order with utopias."[69] A new generation of Islamist thinkers has begun to address people's demands for a modern, pluralistic society in a context of traditional values by legitimating liberal, democratic concepts through innovative reinterpretation of Islamic texts and doctrines. "Islam did not come with a specific program concerning life. It is our duty to formulate this program through interactions between Islamic concepts and modernity."[70]

Restorative Religions. Rather than reformed, institutional churches or any return to fundamentals, many new religions envision restored churches filled with spiritual power able to alleviate the real tragedies that beset real people —poverty, oppression, loneliness, sickness, natural disaster, or war. Through spiritual healing, intense prayer, and the power of some supernatural patron, the new churches exorcise the demons that make living at best difficult and often unbearable. These religions restore the proper relationship between God and people by replacing religious tradition and clerical hierarchy with a reliance on direct revelation to supplement scriptural authority in establishing individual and social morality. In restoring the simple mysticism of primitive belief, the most successful restorative religions preach a deep, personal faith, communion under God, and unswerving obedience to divine authority exercised through some absolutely governing, earthly source.

Alternative Social Systems. The success of the new religions reflects the spread of industry and the consequent urbanization of developing societies. While tantalizing people with views into the global perspective, globalization perversely excludes most of the world's people from realization of prosperity, security, or justice. For most of the world's excluded peoples, the most visible exclusion is the inadequacy of social welfare provided by their governments. In many industrial centers that lack the infrastructure to support the floods of migrant workers attracted by the promise of jobs, religious communities offer health services, education, and welfare that governments cannot provide.

Most comfortable within fundamentalist or restorative beliefs, these alternative social systems are powerful attractors of mass political support and religious conversion. Often better organized and more effective than government agencies, these religious communities attract foreign aid and humanitarian support from global, nongovernmental organizations and donor governments. In many poor countries, being a member of an active religious movement and its alternative social system can bring more tangible benefits and security than merely being a citizen of an ineffective state.

As globalization has exposed to global audiences the inadequacy of social welfare and public health systems in poor countries, it has raised expectations of local populations of their societies. In many societies, the new religions, with their emphases on healing mind and body before seeking salvation, are displacing inept governments with alternative social infrastructures. Faced with epidemics, exploitation, pollution, drugs, and violence, people outside globalization are looking to religion for health and sanity. The most successful of the new religions have uniformly stressed healing and caring, often with elaborate socioreligious rituals. "Nowhere in the global South do the various spiritual healers find serious competition from modern scientific medicine: it is simply beyond the reach of most of the poor."[71] Although the new, religious, social systems are functionally local and operate to counter the effects of globalization, most are deeply embedded in globalization through *both* their supernatural faiths *and* their supranational functions.

Supernatural and Supranational. Around their supernatural beliefs, the politically fragmented, yet cosmopolitan, centers of the new religions generate supranational visions and relationships that challenge the Westphalian nation-state. Although supranational ideas are flourishing, they are not secular and do not include a replacement for the nation-state. Many new religions envision a modern Christendom, *songha*, or *umma* with some supernatural patron as a global community of people that transcends or ignores political boundaries.

Stimulated and carried by globalization, the success of the new religions "is really about relationships and *not* about religion. What happens is that people form relationships and only then come to embrace a religion."[72] As people project the new relationships generated by globalization backwards into their lives, they form new religions. The demographic centers of orthodox religions, especially Christianity, are diffusing from the Northern Hemisphere —Europe, North America, and China—to Africa, Central and South Asia, the Pacific, and Latin America in the Southern Hemisphere. Continuing migration into Europe and North America accentuate the religious-cultural shift as immigrant communities displace and infiltrate indigenous Euro-American churches with unorthodox religious beliefs and practices of worship.

The new religions have spread through much of the postcolonial world by building expansive communities and relationships that help people deal with the new social and political realities of globalization as it washes over them. New religious movements have succeeded "because they help people *survive*, in all of the ways that people need to survive—social, spiritual, economic, finding a mate. . . . To survive today in Africa, people have to be *incredibly* mobile in search of work. One of the very important things that many of these new religious movements do is [to] create broad transethnic and transnational communities, so that when somebody moves from city to city or country, there is a sort of surrogate family structure in place."[73]

COMMODIFICATION OF CULTURE

Within the economic perspective of a business civilization, globalization promises a prosperous, market-based utopia integrating Braudel's domains —material life, market economy, and capitalism—through the collaboration of instrumental reason and technology. The global market does not, however, trade merely in the goods and services of classical economics but involves the entire scope of human activity and trades in identities, cultures, memories, emotions, and even creativity. Transformation of creativity into instrumental reason focused art and culture on quantifiable, economic goals and transformed artists into laborers with the task of mechanical execution within strict limits. Although the market for culture has overcome Weber's skepticism about a rationalist global culture, globalization has disappointed Parsonian predictions of cultural adaptation towards a rational, global modernity. In a distorted reification of Levy's notion of diversity within a single cultural context, disoriented people struggle to protect their traditional cultures while embracing a vaguely global consumer culture. Built around consumption-based European economic development and deepened by twentieth-century Fordist production technologies, the global market forces transforming culture into products are diversifying cultures as clearly as the consumer culture is homogenizing them.

Culture as Product

The expansion of Braudel's domain of risk-acceptant capitalism into the market economy and the privacy of material life converts cultural symbols and practices—kinship, literature, art, or intellect—into low-risk opportunities. Through information technologies, entrepreneurs transform cultural symbols into products for sale in a global market. Without representational links between cultural icons, social values, and behaviors, *objets d'art* reflect market demand instead of cultural norms. From an economic perspective, "the most important aspect about contemporary culture is not its aesthetic value but the profits [that] it is able to generate for a transnational business class."[74]

Charles Dickens's transformation of Victorian art into standardized commodity with his pioneering introduction of the serial novel exploited modern technologies to integrate the rhythm of commerce with the cycles of literary creation and cadences of daily life. Just as the mechanical clock had expanded seasonal notions of time with durational measures, Dickens transformed people's notions of time beyond the seasons, the religious calendar, or the clock. The instrumental rationality of the weekly installment —Little Nell in the 1850s, Superman in the 1950s, or *Friends* in the 1990s— locked cultural perspectives in a powerful synchrony with tradition—the seven-day living cycle—that remains one of Bacon's most powerful idols.

Strong cultures exploit globalization by transforming production and distribution of cultural products into commercial processes. Not only increasing wealth, commercialization broadens the content of cultural products and expands creative perspectives for artists who invent new traditions for paying audiences. The strong Anglo-American culture exploited technology to refine Dickens's art first into serials and later into television programming. Weak cultures with dwindling populations, however, simply accept technology and gradually succumb to modernity, which slowly transforms their people into consumer-user-audiences. For weak cultures, globalization commodifies traditions and converts cultural contents into passive economic assets. "Tradition that is drained of content, and commercialized, becomes either heritage or *kitsch*—the trinkets bought in the airport store. As developed by the heritage industry, heritage is tradition repackaged as spectacle."[75]

The Cultural Exception

Charles Dickens's entrepreneurial globalization of literature introduced the sociopolitical dilemma of whether trade in culture is normatively, legally, or politically different from trade in goods and services. The 1947 General Agreement on Tariffs and Trade excepted cultural treasures from its provisions. Although the World Trade Organization accepted this cultural exception in 2001, "the doctrine—that culture generally is unlike merchandise and should be protected from commercialization and standardization—has no legal status, and the term does not exist in any agreement or treaty."[76]

Beneath the intent of the political-economic cultural exception to preserve cultures lies a nest of thorny questions about which cultures to preserve and how to preserve them. Historically, the market made such decisions through wealthy collectors and public museums. During the twentieth century, many governments followed Malraux's lead in absorbing cultural institutions and artifacts into their expanding social programs to protect them from the ravages of globalization and free trade. The Cold War brought the notion of using culture as a policy instrument to consolidate national solidarity and pursue national interests in international politics. Despite the cultural exception, the end of the Cold War shifted cultural initiative from governments to local and transnational communities seeking *both* to preserve their identities *and* to increase their prosperities. Exposed to the commercial motives of large corporations, within the global perspective, this cultural dilemma loses the narrow implications of politics, economics, and culture and assumes the formidable aspect of a major challenge for global governance.

Cultural Fragmegration

Commodification of culture leads to *both* integration *and* fragmentation: *fragmegration*. Reifying cultures as products absorbs them into a culture of cultures that promotes "culturally cosmopolitan tastes amongst its consumers through the intermixing of different genres, styles, and types."[77] Pursuit of market advantage fragments cultures to preserve uniqueness and novelty. Commercial fragmentation "involves the stimulation of minor differences of fashion and style as significant, but it also involves a proliferation of a more highly differentiated culture and society in terms of an ever expanding variety and diversity of cultural artifacts, products, and services."[78]

In contrast to integration of political ideologies and economic institutions, the flow of culture across boundaries "does not imply that cultures on each side of those boundaries are coming to resemble each other more and more as cultural complexes."[79] Although homogeneity is a possible result, the migration of products through a global market or transfer of ideas, values, and beliefs through migration is inherently random and erratic. Flows of culture, goods, and people transform each recipient culture in some unique, pseudodialectical pattern that becomes a distinct cultural source in its own right. Such unique, hybrid syntheses of the foreign, the global, and the local stimulate and proliferate heterogeneity and even separation *within* a global culture.[80] Cultural fragmegration embeds local cultures within globalization, which absorbs any fragmentation, and thereby provides humans with a disorienting, dual identity: local, cultural self and global human being.

Cultural Disorientation

Instantaneous, live coverage of events throughout the world juxtaposed with continual, echoing images from the past and bizarre market packages of cultural tokenry disorient people in time and space. Cultural memory and identity disappear into a bewildering collage of music, films, fashion, language, yesterday's news, colorful images of the future, and social behaviors contradicted by the realities of daily living, all periodically recycled by the global media industries. "The proliferation of new information networks may inform us [of] events both spatially and temporally distant from our everyday lives, but what it cannot do is [to] preserve a continuous sense of who we currently are, what we have been in the past, and what we might become in the future."[81] Whereas culture has historically linked past, present, and future in self and society, globalization and commodification have fragmegrated culture, separated self from society, and isolated people in the present.

On the traditional, near side of culture, people have been comfortable and confident in adopting the behaviors, attitudes, ideas, norms, and values of social normalcy. In the premodern, tradition-directed world, no decisions were necessary: Bacon's idols made them all. The retreat of tradition under the assault of globalism supplanted Bacon's idols as the Enlightenment moved people beyond culture into reason and creativity. Globalization exposed people to interaction, discussion, and dialogue with alien cultures, and novel ideas, which required confusing decisions. Modernity simplified things by creating a new set of idols that offered either the powerful inner-direction of personal values and individualistic cultures or the compelling, utilitarian other-direction by society. Although more demanding than the premodern world of tradition, modernity still called for only one decision between the alternative idols of inner-direction and other-direction. People remained on the comfortable, near side of culture under the supervision of Bacon's idols.

As globalization carries people onto the far side of culture, they leave normalcy behind and find themselves within the global perspective without compass, map, or guide. Beyond creativity, social living calls for continuing, complex decisionmaking by every individual in each of Braudel's domains

—material life, the market economy, and capitalist risk taking. Lost on the far side, many people retreat into inner-directed rationality—as the Enlightenment intended—or into utilitarian, other-directed decisionmaking—as modernity suggests. A growing minority of people, especially in less-than-effective modern cultures, withdraw into a fundamentalist past in search of traditional lost identities. A brave few seek progress in cultural renovation, reform, or revolution. With *both* normalcy *and* creativity left on the near side, many individuals and societies are unable to form or recognize their own cultural identities. Without robust linkages between society and the individual or between past, present, and future, culture loses its significance, its temporality, and its spatial orientation. People remain irretrievably lost on the far side trapped by technology in the global village with no way to go home.

Instrumental Reason

The force of technology and the reach of globalization have combined the rational calculability of capitalism and the instrumental efficiency of the free-market economy. Through bureaucratic management, instrumental reason has expanded beyond issues of economic value into all human relationships, especially those that involve attaining goals. From the classical sociology of Max Weber through Taylorism and Fordism to electronic search engines, the growth of expert systems and automated decisionmaking has had broad ordering effects on people's lives and cultures. Although they stifled artistic human creativity, these notions and the prosperity that they brought were immensely seductive. By the 1920s, they had become powerful *idola theatri* in the form of standardization. Managers, experts, and engineers designed work processes, and well-paid laborers did the mindless work. The resulting, mass-produced, standard products reduced prices for consumers, raised profits for producers, increased spending power throughout economies, and raised standards of living for societies of increasingly similar worker-consumers.[82]

McDonaldization

In the global market, technological standardization "drives consumers relentlessly towards the same common goals—alleviation of life's burdens and the expansion of discretionary time and spending power."[83] The conspicuous global success of the McDonald's chain of fast-food franchises through instrumental reason and standardization of every aspect of its business, with a cosmetic touch of local flavor, has branded this process as *McDonaldization*. Far more than a shallow "process of large American multinationals overwhelming foreign markets and getting local consumers addicted to special sauce," McDonaldization applies instrumental reason to every facet of commerce and culture.[84] Globalization penetrates societies with the instrumental reason of McDonaldization: "the process by which principles of the fast-food restaurant are coming to dominate more and more sectors of American society as well as the rest of the world."[85] The basic components of incremental reason are embodied in a few principles of bureaucratic organization: efficiency, quantification or calculability, predictability, and displacement of human labor. The general drift of the current wave of commercial globalization towards efficient commonality beneath cosmetic local diversity pervades not only products but the ways that companies sell, distribute, and price products and operate their businesses.[86] "The result is a new commercial reality—the emergence of global markets for standardized consumer products on a previously unimagined scale of magnitude."[87] Spread across many industries—food production and consumption, hospitals, retailers, and others—the aggregate offers "a smooth, seamless culture with few shocks or surprises; they encourage a kind of stupefied mass conformity."[88]

The McDonald's Culture

Instrumental reason has transformed the supply side of modern commerce, especially the retail industries, into the *McDonald's Culture* or *McWorld*. The McDonald's culture provides efficiency through compressing the time spent and effort expended between consumers' demands and their satisfaction by employing the quickest method possible with minimal personal disturbance. Many activities gain efficiency by shifting labor requirements to the customer through self-service, supermarkets, home-shopping television, and Internet sites. The ultimate efficiency is the elimination of interpersonal relationships. In pursuing the ideal of efficiency, technology creates a culture of distance and indifference by insulating customers from each other and from suppliers.

The McDonald's culture offers services and products that can be counted and measured in local wrappers and languages. Consumers' objective, rational calculations of costs in money, time, and effort as the components of value replace subjective estimates of quality. McWorld offers predictability in psychically comforting uniformity over time and across space and avoids troubling experiences. Instead of unpredictable human labor, McWorld relies on fully predictable automation in production and distribution, standard behavior patterns for workers and management, and minimal interfaces with humans. Controlling people through technology emphasizes using unskilled human workers and tight control of the relationship between company and customer. The cultural results are inflexible menus and product offerings, few options for consumer choice, and minimal person-to-person interfaces.[89]

Although McWorld can convert assertive individuals into docile consumers or compliant employees, outside the narrow economic perspective, people's culturally resistant reactions are often unpredictable and deeply emotional. McDonaldization rationalizes traditional informal, domestic, and individual behaviors by reordering *both* consumption *and* production in a direction of social conformity for common economic benefit. The McDonald's culture "paradoxically both strengthens and undermines the penetration of bureaucratic reason into the far reaches of modern society."[90]

The Consumer Culture

Within the narrow, commercial perspective, the insidious process of instrumental reason focuses standardization ultimately on the final buyer-user of most products: the consumer. The effect of globalization on the demand side of modern commerce is *the consumer culture* as a counterpart to McWorld on the supply side. The heart of the consumer culture is an abundance of mass-produced products, and its blood is advertising carried through electronic arteries and veins. Global media events—from African wars and epidemics through European clothing fashions, popular concerts, American films, Japanese toys, to solar eclipses—form the body of a global consumer culture. Operating through marketing, sales, and distribution channels, the commercial imperative to target particular markets and customers and then to standardize them into larger markets to achieve economies of scale drives its expansion.

Consolidating markets on a global scale brings "sameness and homogeneity everywhere . . . [and exposes] the bland and boring universality and massification in the modernity project."[91] A corollary result unifies societies by making a single, broad set of goods and services available in all places. From its roots in expanding courtly preferences of nineteenth-century elites to the *nouveaux riches*, to the middle classes, and finally to the poor, the consumer culture has expanded possible choices across all cultural patterns.

The consumer culture entails far more than simple consumption, which has been universal across all societies that have adopted money economies.[92] It has deepened into a fragmented source of human meaning and identity as the items consumed have acquired cultural and subjective values beyond their intrinsic, material values. "Under a consumer culture, consumption becomes the main form of self-expression and the chief source of identity."[93] As globalization transforms people into consumers, they alter their self-images and identities, refine their wants and desires towards capitalist norms of accumulation, and seek new meaning in consumption.[94] Far from universal, the consumer culture includes neither tribal peoples too poor to consume nor concerned citizens too civically engaged to shop. Consumerism embraces people who are all equal, as potential customers, with no pretensions to seeking justice through their consumption. Peaceful and reactive rather than forceful or assertive, consumers do not insist on democracy in consuming and are often content to wait in queue or to buy whatever is on sale. Instead of influence or coercion—political power—or wealth, the relevant measure of power and status is the ability to buy. The unique peace without power of the consumer culture "favors the triumph of commerce and consumerism and gives to those who control information, communications, and entertainment ultimate (if inadvertent) control over global culture—and over human destiny."[95] Consumerism is a shallow vessel, quickly filled by some faceless, nameless beings—cosmocrats—operating a global mechanism—cosmocracy—who are better than Bacon's idols at manipulating human behavior.

Meaning

In the consumer culture, advertising, rather than intrinsic value, objective differences, or functional utility, creates meaning for a mass-produced product and transfers that meaning to a consumer. "By adding value to material, by adding meaning to objects, by branding things, advertising performs a role historically associated with religion." Whereas orthodox religion located meaning and value beyond human experience—Heaven, Hell, or Nirvana—consumerism situates meaning firmly in the knowable present and embodies value in consumption. Rather than politics, economics, or self, consumption bestows and preserves identity: people are identifiable as consumers. "As long as goods are interchangeable and in surplus quantities, as long as producers are willing to pay for short-term advantages (especially for new products), and as long as consumers have plenty of disposable time and money so that they can consume both the ad and the product, Adcult [advertising culture] will remain the dominant meaning-making system of modern life. . . . Adcult is the application of capitalism to culture: dollars voting."[96]

The Paradox of Consumerism

Whereas the rationalist controls of McDonaldization implicitly recognize personal autonomy of choice, that same individuality enervates expansion of choice within the consumer culture. Each customer voluntarily chooses to enter McWorld and to fit into the narrow pattern for consumer behavior imposed by instrumental reason. The consumer culture attracts and does not coerce, even as McWorld exerts rigid controls over choice for *both* consumers *and* workers. The consumer culture sends through advertising and fashion the message, which politics allows to be dubious or misleading but not false, that consumers are exercising free choice in accepting McDonaldized constraints.

Within the instrumental rationality of the consumer culture, *both* political issues and participation *and* economic work become standardized items of consumption in a mass illusion that individuals are exercising free choice. The McWorld blend of instrumental reason and its Protean partner of consumer culture in liberal, capitalist, democracy seems logical, natural, and even attractive. As social leaders become media images of issues on a political menu of policy choices presented as rationalized, simplistic packages, individual choice merges democratically into cultural conformity. The globalization of McWorld around a liberal-capitalist-democratic consumer culture offers a credible alternative to the traditional, modern, work-based cultures.

The commodification of culture and, by extension, of society implies the simultaneous atomization and expansion of identities—individual, cultural, social, political, and human. Restructuring human identities subverts the trust, confidence, and risk acceptance that are the sociocultural foundations for the entire edifice of capitalist institutions *and* political liberalism. Beyond eroding the justification for living in Braudel's domain of private life, commodification imposes rigid limits on *both* cultural development *and* economic growth.[97]

With little effect on the direct relationship between resource-based growth and conflict, consumerism carries the threat of exposing knowledge-based growth to the same direct relationship. The McDonald's culture expands the vulnerability of resource-based growth to conflict over capital, labor, and raw materials to global dimensions of sustaining aggregate economic growth. As modernization supplants physical resources and work with knowledge and information as unlimited sources of productivity and market advantage, the consumer culture invites conflict over markets and audiences. In transforming *both* culture *and* knowledge into economic resources and commodities, the consumer-McDonald's culture destroys the splendid duality of the growth–conflict relationship and reverses the shift towards knowledge-based growth that has energized human progress since before the Enlightenment.

CULTURAL IMPERIALISM

Arnold Toynbee spoke with enthusiasm and pride of the expansion of Western culture through political imperialism and economic globalization. "In the course of its expansion, our modern, Western, secular civilization has become literally worldwide and has drawn into its net all other surviving civilizations as well as primitive societies."[98] Equating globalization with expanding geographic reach, Toynbee could not anticipate the shift from political dominance towards cultural imperialism. Neither was it obvious that global capitalism a half century later would have shifted from expanding into unexploited regions towards intensifying in a few concentrated world economic centers: deepening rather than widening.[99]

Beyond economics and politics, the world's civilizations have learned to fear a subtle imperialism embedded in the wisdom that equates development with a particular culture as a precondition for exploiting technology for modernization. The Enlightenment culture launched a poor, backward region —fifteenth-century Europe was primitive in relation to the Chinese, Indian, Ottoman, and perhaps the American empires—on a path that eventually led to world dominance.[100] As also suggested by the more recent experiences of Japan, deliberate adoption of the Enlightenment culture seems to lead through technology to sustainable levels of income and wealth. Although the political-economic push of cultural imperialism may seem irresistible, the cultural pull of a society's conscious choice of modernity seems necessary to garner the benefits of wealth that only technology can provide.

The political-economic push and cultural pull of imperialism neatly complement the instrumental reason of McWorld and the standardization of American consumerism within the narrow perspective of rationalism. These themes relate culture directly to economics, minimize noneconomic influences, and equate capitalism and the American way of living with civilization itself.[101] Although the American culture remains globally dominant, it is not without alternatives and does not preclude the rise of other exporters of culture.[102] The

Asian-Japanese culture is beginning to challenge the cultural fashion for Americanism and has penetrated American culture itself. Whereas the Enlightenment presented rationality, truth, and progress as powerful ideals for transformation, Japanese society uses instrumental rationality, subjective truth, and economic development as techniques to achieve social compromise and order. Unlike exported American culture, which embodies American values of capitalism and individualism within an economic perspective, Japanese cultural exports lack a distinctive ideology or profound deistic, religious faith, and even tend towards an uncertain, inward-looking mysticism.

The Power of American Culture

At the end of the twentieth century, only the American culture could be considered global in any geographic sense. "The United States stands at the epicenter of globalization. This provokes envy and resentment among some other countries."[103] Many people see in globalization the dismaying convergence of their own societies towards the American style of living, whether they like it or not. Although American messianism had a place in U.S. foreign policy throughout the twentieth century, especially during the Cold War, U.S. policy used diplomacy and trade agreements as "vehicles for the spread of democracy and American values."[104] Since the end of the Cold War, "American cultural imperialism, dominated by the big U.S. companies, has simply given way to a form of transnational, corporate, cultural domination under the sway of the big stateless transnationals. . . . U.S. cultural styles and techniques . . . have . . .become transnationalized."[105] Modern technology diffuses American culture quickly and widely even without any official U.S. intent either to disseminate or to contain any particular ideology, culture, or set of values. "Unlike the Cold-War system, globalization has its own dominant culture, which is why it tends to be homogenizing . . . globalization has tended to involve the spread (for better and for worse) of Americanization—from Big Macs to iMacs to Mickey Mouse."[106] Rather than a messianic policy, the post–Cold-War globalization of Americanism is an invisible, coincidental, insidious, and cumulative influence of information technologies, commerce, and telecommunication networks.

The commercialization of Anglo-American culture is changing cultures dramatically and even converging them with itself.[107] The power of American culture operates through its attractiveness to people, rather than any sinister or mercenary intent among Americans. Even as the world deplores the American way of politics, its cultures and societies are following the European lead in embracing "[President] Clinton's conversion to free markets, more free trade, reform of their once-generous welfare systems, privatization of state-owned enterprises, tax cuts, deregulation, and the pursuit of the New Economy."[108] Limiting criticisms to commentary on U.S. policies, many of the world's countries take their security structures, consumer economies and cultures, and technologies directly from the United States. Beyond American products and protection, most countries have also begun borrowing the American way in political fashions, structures, attitudes, and practices.

Commercial Americanization

Historically, people, countries, religions, and cultures have asked whether they were doing good and right by making money, how wealth affected the probability of going to heaven, and whether wealth belonged to society or to people who worked. As the United States matured, the American culture gradually either eliminated or ignored such questions and made the United States "the only country in the world that has a business culture."[109] The ideological and commercial triumphs of the American business and consumer cultures and their current avatar, the McDonald's culture of instrumental reason laid the foundations for what Susan Strange has called the business civilization. The American way of doing business has co-opted globalization into commercial Americanization of and by non-American firms.[110]

After World War II, U.S. companies expanded into foreign markets while seeking some mystical formula for success in Japanese management techniques. While consumerism was capturing Americans' hearts and minds, European, Asian, African, and Latin American firms were quietly and gradually learning, refining, and adopting U.S. business models and practices—the American way. The end of the Cold War, the fall of the Japanese economy, and the spectacular emergence of technology as a critical, commercial advantage replaced any cultural caution with enthusiasm in emulating the Americans. Foreign firms and societies rushed to follow "a herd of American bankers and management consultants who preached privatization and entrepreneurship to populations starved for new ideas as well as for Western consumer goods."[111]

Mass Production. The American culture has never discouraged materialism: Americans enjoy buying, owning, and exchanging things. The remarkable successes of the Industrial Revolution, Fordism, and the McDonald's culture in the United States continue to mass-produce standardized things because American consumers are powerfully attracted to those things and continue to buy them. Most American goods are machine-made parity items, functionally interchangeable with other brands of the same product. They are conceived, designed, and produced for a market of interchangeable consumers. Within a narrow range of interchangeability, often the primary difference between products is the advertising associated with each brand, model, or style. The superfluity of consumer choice created by mass production, standardization, and computerization has created the illusion of choice among interchangeable products without the reality of decision. Many consumer goods that Americans buy have little intrinsic meaning beyond a generic application to survival—food, medicine, clothing, or shelter—or something that is nice to have. What American consumers seem to require is less the objects themselves than the meaning that they may carry for individual lives and identities.

Going Global. The success of U.S. firms in penetrating markets throughout the world relies largely on adding local flavor to a product that has proven successful in home markets: the McDonald's model of globalization. To expand market penetration into commercial success, U.S. firms have uniformly introduced instrumental reason and standardization to integrate those markets into a global economy. Firms that succeed at going global recognize that the American model is as deep as it is broad and as local as it is global. They must learn and adapt to local tastes, identify what appeals to —and offends—local customers, and change cultural and political climates even while standardizing. Managers learn to maintain a delicate balance between acting locally and thinking globally. The American way of globalization reflects the values of the American business culture—entrepreneurship, trust, and innovation—which require a deep understanding of local markets and the cultures, politics, and economics in which they are embedded.

Although some firms resist American business practices (Volkswagen), few obdurately reject Americanization, and most of the world's people share the American dream of universal prosperity. The rules and practices of American business have spread too far and too wide to leave more than isolated pockets where un-Americanized businesses can remain profitable. The abilities of U.S. firms to influence, overwhelm, or displace local cultures generate broad, cultural anti-Americanism as a dark shadow of the American dream. Many firms feel forced to adapt to survive or to penetrate U.S. markets, the largest, most open, and most liquid in the world. Despite resistance, business is unlikely to abandon the American management business culture or ethos. The Russian attitude epitomizes the world's businesses: "Russian business wants to have rules and ethics and be like normal businesses all over the world. Nobody thinks of it as Americanization. We think of it as globalization. We do not fight against what comes from the [United] States."[112]

American Consumerism

Consumption-based economic development, made possible by the abundance of natural resources, formed American consumerism around a European nucleus in the nineteenth century. In the twentieth century, American entrepreneurs constructed a consumption economy in the United States from Fordist mass-production and new communication technologies. The American consumer economy provides the heart, blood, and energy not only of the U.S. economy but of the global consumer culture. Based on mass production and economies of scale, the U.S. economy produces more consumer goods than Americans can absorb. Led by a powerful advertising industry, the U.S. commercial imperative to market expansion carries American consumerism in its train to target particular markets, audiences, and customers, which globalization has expanded beyond the United States and Europe. For Americans, consumption has become a human right expressed reflexively in taste and lifestyle. Beyond the control of civil society or government, the American consumer culture continues to transform traditional social values into trends of fashion that invalidate the political and economic structures that embody those values. Within the American consumer culture, traditional cultural standards crumble into a range of options across the entire spectrum of product choices that consumers can accept or reject.

Advertising. At 5:00 P.M. on 28 August 1922, station WFAF in New York broadcast what may have been the first commercial radio advertisement (for a Queensboro housing development). Since 1922, the rapid advances in communications technology have transformed the American culture by making public broadcast of many messages largely dependent on advertising, which pays the costs of operating many of the telecommunications media. Although radio began as a noncommercial scientific marvel, "television never had a chance to be anything other than the consummate selling machine."[113] Much of what Americans know, share, and value is brought to them "in a plasma of electrons, pixels, and ink, underwritten by multinational advertising agencies dedicated to attracting [their] attention for entirely nonaltruistic reasons."[114] The role of these conglomerates in the consumer economy is not to send messages or carry information—the network operators do both—or to create programming or entertainment—Hollywood, New York, and professional sports do that. The advertising agencies buy space-time in a message, insert advertising, and sell audience attention to a client. Advertising, rather than communications or content, operates the consumer culture.

Cultural Cost Externalization. In contrast to an open-market economy, which thrives on open exchange of information, the consumer economy relies on intense, media-focused beams of entertainment to entice consumers into receiving advertising messages. The foundation of the consumer economy is the American cultural decision to externalize the costs of programming and entertainment and to distribute them through the communications media. Whereas many countries have chosen to absorb those costs as legitimate government expenditures, deregulation in the United States has shifted those costs to the consumer. Americans must pay for communication either with their money or with their time and attention. Rather than spending their money, which they prefer to spend on products, modern Americans have chosen to spend their time paying attention to advertising in exchange for information and entertainment. This externalization of cost energizes the American consumer culture and propels consumerism throughout the world.

America's Youth Culture. The Americans who want and buy the most things are the young. The success of modernity and the Industrial Revolutions managed by their ancestors has provided them amply with time and money. American youths are not merely willing but sincerely eager to spend energy and time to hear a word from the sponsor. Moreover, they have sufficient income to buy the advertised goods. Unlike their parents, they have not yet decided which brands to prefer or even which sorts of things they want to consume. The entrepreneurial spirit of America's business culture sees youth

—American and foreign—as a self-renewing opportunity for selling. Exploitation of this opportunity requires communicating with young buyers by focusing *both* program content *and* advertising on their special interests and unique languages through their preferred media: television and recorded music.

Culture and the Market. With no heritage of social democracy beyond traditional values and current fashions, Americans have blended their consumer culture into government institutions, market structures, social fashion, and speculative capitalism. Responsive to Americans' urge to buy, the forces that activate consumerism operate through mass production and celebrity. The filamentous structure of American consumer culture, woven by commercial advertising, is too costly to allow alternatives that do not involve government funding. American popular culture forms and reforms around U.S. mass-market forces, social pressures towards fashionable conformity, and capitalist motivations to accumulate wealth, which combine to keep American culture shallow and volatile. "The dominance of the economic system over other social spheres helps foster a culture of conformity rather than critique, sensation rather than substance, and technique rather than reflection. . . . American culture carries ideological messages of consumerism and promotes acquisitive behavior in the host and the world population in general."[115] Consumerism is neither new nor American and may have emerged in 1857, when Bradbury & Evans included advertisements for Persian parasols, smelling salts, rubber boots, and patent medicines in Charles Dickens's *Little Dorrit*.

The Japanese Alternative

Japan's frenzied rush into modernity in the nineteenth century adopted the Euro-American model and explicitly accepted the American model after World War II while seeking to preserve the traditional Japanese-Asian culture. The confusing ambiguity cast Japan as a political-economic aggressor, kept Japanese culture obscure to Euro-Americans, and isolated Japan from the rest of Asia as it reconstructed itself. Torn between Euro-American modernity and Asian culture, the Japanese search for national and cultural identity has produced an amorphous, ambiguous paradox that intrigues much of the world.[116] By the late 1980s, Japan had raised its *per-capita* income to such a level that the United States began to perceive Japan as an economic competitor instead of a client. Prosperity, however, exposed "a significant gap between Japan's intellectual ambiguity on the one hand, and its social achievement and economic power in the world on the other."[117] With only a shallow font of national values and a purely rational drive to modernize, Japanese foreign policy shifted smoothly from liberal internationalism to militarist imperialism to political isolation and economic assertiveness during the twentieth century. With only scanty philosophical or ideological foundations, Japanese domestic politics has embraced fascism, liberalism, and democracy for a compromise-oriented society uncommitted to political goals or social good.

A World without Models

Achieving modernity in the 1980s and 1990s has thrust Japan into a world without models. Japanese investigations of cultural pluralism face the dilemma of adopting some other cultural model as a guide or retreating into the unique features of Japanese history to forge a national identity and culture. Modern Japan's broadly egalitarian society is based on cultural sameness and material prosperity, not on equality of rights, and seems hollow as a global alternative to the American way. Enjoying Japanese cultural exports as entertainment products requires no large cultural leap or rapport with Japanese traditions and ambiguities. Japanese instrumental rationality finds no anomaly in commercial cultural symbols that are Western to sell in Japan and Japanese to sell outside Japan. The purely commercial duality that transcends national values, traditions, and even cultures "is part of the genius behind Japanese cultural strength in a global era that has many countries nervous about cultural erosion."[118] Japan has sought to separate modernity from culture, to parallel Euro-American technological achievements and economic prosperity without absorbing or being absorbed by Euro-American culture. Whereas Euro-American culture and society are oriented on the future, Japanese society prefers to avoid sacrificing the real present to the uncertain future.

Differences and Similarities

Despite similar political structures and economic processes, a yawning gap between American ideals of progress and the Japanese spirit of compromise separates the cultures of America and Japan. Whereas Americans entertain global predominance as a national identity and meaning, Japan harbors no cultural desire for national greatness. In contrast to Americans' urge to win, "Japan wishes to enjoy the material benefits of hard work. It wants to be a wealthy and orderly small power, where per capita gross national product and equitable distribution of wealth mean more than aggregate gross national product as a measure of comparative national power."[119]

Successful export of culture requires a solid economic base, even though the national economy itself may not be healthy. The recessions in the U.S. and Japanese economies coincided with surges in their respective exports of culture and stimulated cultural-commercial creativity. Both cultures developed social demographics that favor youth with high disposable income, a reliable demand for luxury and cultural goods, and a solid technological base for national industry. Both cultures have stressed communication technologies, services, and products and have developed extensive media and entertainment industries.

Globalization: Americanization or Japanization?

The predominance of cultural flows towards peripheral cultures from the Anglo-American core "is an ephemeral artifact of America's present lead in communications technologies. It is not a signpost on the road to a universal civilization."[120] After millennia of linear, one-to-one, cultural penetrations carried by trade and war, the spread of computer-mediated interactions carries broad, complex many-to-many interpenetrations. Market-based technology has expanded the Anglo-American cultural base in a powerful one-to-many pattern of penetration, which pushes the commercial icons of American culture into new markets. Also providing new, historically unreachable audiences for exotic, local, art forms, "it equally facilitates this base being constantly influenced from other cultures and societies and being moderated everywhere by local variations."[121] Despite a continuing Japanese cultural insulation, the persistent, instrumental exports of Westernized Japanese culture and products have gradually penetrated every society and culture in the world.

Beyond any cultural transformations or convergence, technological deviations from linear, one-to-many penetration expand all interacting cultures in a many-to-many pattern of mutual interpenetration outside the corporate, media structures of economic and cultural exports. Mutual penetration is increasing sensitivities towards preservation of distinctive, territorial, local, cultural symbols, icons, and artifacts and deliberate efforts to create new cultural cores. Technological penetration of all cultures with foreign, alien influences carries a global result that is less Americanization, Japanization, or global homogeneity than pluralism, diversity, and cultural competition.

Not immune to cultural invasion, the Euro-American culture itself "becomes internally differentiated and gradually more representative of the world as a whole. As the process of Americanization proceeds, it changes such that in time it assumes the features of globalization."[122] While critics reduce Americanization to McDonaldization, the reverse process of Napsterization —an aspect of Japanization—also carries globalization. Through McDonaldization "culture flows from American power, and American supply creates demand."[123] Napsterization brings new cultural symbols, icons—often Asian-Japanese—and products to American consumers through intense contact with cultures outside the United States. Foreign supply creates American demand. Like McWorld, Napsterized culture flows through channels dug by U.S. power and Japanese persistence. Unlike the foreign demand of McDonaldization, Napsterized demand is among rich Americans for entertainment. "The process is highly interactive. Thus, cultural emissions from abroad take root in the United States, in some instances hinting at alternative, that is, non-American, models of modernity."[124]

In contrast, however, to the ease with which the English language diffuses values-based American culture, the Japanese language allows one culture for Japanese only and creates another, exportable Japan for the rest of the world. Whereas the open dynamism of the American culture tends inevitably towards convergence, the plasticity and endurance of Japanese culture allows Japan to absorb and penetrate foreign cultures while still retaining an intact, indigenous culture. Although Japanization transforms foreign cultures, it does not affect the parent Japanese culture, which remains insulated and foreign.

Both cultures balance a flexible, absorptive, salable culture with a domestic, national one. Both have transformed national culture into a product and energized it with a global sales force. The United States and Japan have both learned to create and use soft power to influence other countries, societies, and value systems. Both societies have used commercial forces and technology to pursue and achieve national political and economic purposes in a context of globalization. "There is an element of triviality and fad in popular behavior, but it is also true that a country that stands astride popular channels of communication has more opportunities to get its messages across and to affect the preferences of others."[125] Within their different perspectives of American value-based rationality and Japanese reason-based values, both cultures—albeit in different ways—have become cultural globalizers.

Within his third perspective on values and feelings, Voltaire was too wise, and Max Weber too rational, not to anticipate the powers of Bacon's idols in every cultural context. Neither Japan's instrumental reason nor American liberalism can impose Wilsonian or utilitarian universalism on a multicultural world. Despite its current predominance, the American culture cannot simply replace Bacon's idols with American values. Neither can the Japanese culture bury them beneath rationalism. Globalization must displace them with a newly created social reality. Whether American or Japanese, the vision of a mindless global convergence contradicts millennia of human experience in creating new knowledge and innovating through cultural penetrations and challenges.

NOTES

1. Marshall G. S. Hodgson, *Rethinking World History, Essays on Europe, Islam, and World History* (New York: Cambridge University Press, 1993), 83.

2. Clifford Geertz, *The Interpretation of Cultures* (New York: Basic, 1973), 89.

3. See Michael Thompson, Richard Ellis, and Aaron Wildavsky, *Cultural Theory* (Boulder, Colorado: Westview, 1990), 1–38.

4. For discussion and derivation of this trinity of modernity see Ernest Gellner, *Nations and Nationalism* (Ithaca: Cornell University Press, 1983), 53–58, Eric J. Hobsbawm, *Nations and Nationalism since 1780* (Cambridge: Cambridge University Press, 1990), 18–22, 37–38, 177–183, and Benedict R. O'G. Anderson, *Imagined Communities: Reflections on the Origins and Spread of Nationalism* (London: Verso, 1991), 13–16, 40–49, 141–147 on national identity; and Derek Sayer, *Capitalism and Modernity: An Excursus on Marx and Weber* (London: Routledge, Chapman, and Hall, 1991), 42–53 and 87–95 on modernity and capitalism.

5. For a summary of Malraux's efforts to nationalize French culture, see Herman Lebovics, "Malraux's Mission," *Wilson Quarterly* 21(1) (Winter 1997): 78–87.

6. Ronald Inglehart, *Culture Shift in Advanced Industrial Society* (Princeton: Princeton University Press, 1990), 18.

7. Edward O. Wilson, "Resuming the Enlightenment Quest," *Wilson Quarterly* 22(1) (Winter 1998): 16–27; 24.

8. Douglas Kellner, "Globalization and the Postmodern Turn," in *Globalization and Europe*, edited by Roland Axtmann, 23–42 (London: Pinter, 1998), 35.

9. Amy Chua, "A World on Edge," *Wilson Quarterly* 26(4) (Autumn 2002): 62–77; 74–75. Within a less-than global focus centered on ethnic identity, Chua argues that the two critical conditions that channel liberalization of markets and democratization into ethnic conflict are pervasive poverty and a market-dominant minority.

10. See Jean François Lyotard, *The Postmodern Condition: A Report on Knowledge* (Minneapolis: University of Minnesota Press, [1979] 1997), 37–41.

11. Henri Saint-Simon, *L'Organisateur* in *Œvres de Claude-Henri de Saint-Simon*, 6 vols., vol. 2 (vols. 3 and 4 of *Œvres de Saint-Simon*, edited by E. Dentu (Paris, Enfantin, 1868) (Geneva: Slatkine Reprints, 1977), bk. 5, 1–242; 154.

12. See Saint-Simon, *L'Organisateur* in *Œvres de Claude-Henri de Saint-Simon*, vol. 4, 1–242; 152–166; Henri Saint-Simon, *Cinquième Lettre a Messieurs Les Industriels*, in *Du Système Industriel* in *Œvres de Claude-Henri de Saint-Simon*, 6 vols., vol. 3 (vols. 5, 6, and 7 of *Œvres de Saint-Simon*, edited by E. Dentu (Paris, Enfantin, 1868) (Geneva: Slatkine Reprints, 1977), vol. 6, 1–134; 21–34;   Henri Saint-Simon, *Nouveaus Christianisme* in *Œvres de Claude-Henri de Saint-Simon*, 6 vols., vol. 3 (vols. 5, 6, and 7 of *Œvres de Saint-Simon*, edited by E. Dentu (Paris, Enfantin, 1868) (Geneva: Slatkine Reprints, 1977), vol. 7, bk. 2, 97–192; Sebastien Charlety, *Histoire du Saint-Simonisme* (Paris: Paul Hartman, 1931), 7–26; Frank E. Manuel, *The New World of Henri Saint-Simon* (Cambridge: Harvard University Press, 1956), 246–254.

13. See Émile Durkheim, *The Division of Labor in Society* (London: Macmillan, 1964 [1893]), bk. 1, ch. 5–6, 147–199; bk. 2, ch. 3, 283–303.

14. Malcolm Waters, *Globalization* (London: Routledge, 1995), 5.

15. See Max Weber, *Economy and Society: An Outline of Interpretive Sociology*, edited by Günther Roth and Claus Wittich (New York: Bedminster, 1968), vol. 1, 6–9, 22–31, 40–43, 70–71.

16. Karl Marx and Friedrich Engels, "Manifesto of the Communist Party," in *Great Books of the Western World*, Vol. 50, *Marx*, edited by Robert Maynard Hutchins, 415–434 (Chicago: Encyclopedia Britannica, 1952), 421.

17. Talcott Parsons, "Evolutionary Universals in Society," *American Sociological Review* 29(1) (February 1964): 339–357; 340. See also Talcott Parsons, *Societies* (Englewood Cliffs, Prentice-Hall, 1966), 21–29; Talcott Parsons, *The Evolution of Societies* (Englewood Cliffs, Prentice-Hall, 1977), 230–236.

18. Waters, *Globalization*, 16. See also Marion J. Levy, *Modernization and the Structure of Societies: A Setting for International Affairs* (Princeton: Princeton University Press, 1966), 25–26, 36, 125–126.

19. See Marion J. Levy, *Modernization and the Structure of Societies: A Setting for International Affairs* (Princeton: Princeton University Press, 1966), 790.

20. Charles Lockhart, "Cultural Contributions to Explaining Institutional Form, Political Change, and Rational Decisions," *Comparative Political Studies* 32(7) (October 1999): 862–893; 876.

21. See Thompson, Ellis, and Wildavsky, *Cultural Theory*), 69–93.

22. Robert S. Chase, "The More Things Change . . .; Learning from Other Eras of 'Unprecedented' Globalization," reviewing *Globalization and History: The Evolution of the Nineteenth Century Atlantic Economy*, by Kevin H. O'Rourke and Jeffrey G. Williamson (Cambridge: MIT Press, 1999), *SAIS Review* 20(2) (Summer-Fall 2000): 223–229; 228.

23. Lebovics, "Malraux's Mission," 87.

24. Paraphrased from André Malraux, *Les Voix du Silence* (Paris: Gallimard, 1951), 637–640.

25. Tyler Cowan, "The Fate of Culture," *Wilson Quarterly* 26(4) (Autumn 2002): 78–84; 79.

26. Marshall McLuhan introduced the term *Global Village* in 1989. See Marshall McLuhan, *The Global Village: Transformations in World Life and Media in the 21st Century* (New York: Oxford University Press, 1989).

27. See Marshall McLuhan, *Understanding Media* (London: Routledge, 1964); Marshall McLuhan and Quentin Fiore, *The Medium Is the Massage* (London: Allen Lane, 1967), McKenzie Wark, *Virtual Geography: Living with Global Media Events* (Bloomington and Indianapolis: Indiana University Press, 1994).

28. McLuhan, *Understanding Media*, 368, 93.

29. Zdravko Mlinar and Franc Trček, Territorial Cultures and Global Impacts," in *Globalization and Europe*, edited by Roland Axtmann, 77–92 (London: Pinter, 1998), 80.

30. McLuhan and Fiore, *The Medium Is the Massage*, 16.

31. With temperament and character, identity completes each individual's personality. Temperament refers to the constitutional, physiological determinants of behavior, character is the aggregate of an individual's drives and satisfactions, and identity embodies individual self-awareness or self-consciousness.

32. See David Riesman, with Nathan Glazer and Reuel Denney, *The Lonely Crowd: A Study of the Changing American Character* (New Haven: Yale University Press, [1950] 1967), 4–6.

33. Wilfred M. McClay, "Fifty Years of *The Lonely Crowd*," *Wilson Quarterly* 22(3) (Summer 1998): 34–42; 35.

34. For discussion of inner-direction and other-direction as character types see Riesman, with Glazer and Denney, *The Lonely Crowd*, 9, 13–25.

35. The assertion that individuals can don and remove social character at will rejects a premise of orthodox sociology that appearances of individual autonomy in choosing identities conceal social reality. The fundamental, universal forces that create societies and cultures and bind them together—community, authority, kinship, status, class, religion, and morality—mold the individual into an irretrievably social and heteronomous character that no power of any individual can negate. For orthodox sociology the attractions of psychological autonomy are forever locked in struggle with social necessity. Francis Bacon anticipated modern sociology in his *idola tribus*—human nature—which were, he felt, the most powerful and probably beyond any purely human ability to destroy or even overcome them.

36. Thomas L. Friedman, *The Lexus and the Olive Tree* (New York: Farrar, Straus, and Giroux, 2000), 8.

37. Friedman, *The Lexus and the Olive Tree*, 30–31.

38. In Friedman's symbology, olive trees represent all that forms human identities in worldly time and global space. Friedman, *The Lexus and the Olive Tree*, 31–32.

39. Anthony Giddens, *Runaway World: How Globalization Is Reshaping our Lives* (London: Profile, 1999), 46.

40. Ann Baring and Jules Cashford, *The Myth of the Goddess* (London: Penguin, 1993), 282.

41. The Judaism from which Christianity sprang could not promote globalization because of the notions of God's chosen people and a specific geographic promised land. The Christian syncretism of Judaic monotheism with Greek humanism eventually aligned itself with Roman imperialism and allowed its original proselytizing mission to atrophy through reliance on the Roman state to expand the faith among the heathen.

Until the Protestant Reformation, Christianity approximated a stabilizing, political ideology as much as a universalizing religion. See Norman Bentwich, *The Religious Foundations of Internationalism: A Study in International Relations through the Ages* (London: Allen & Unwin, [1933] 1959), 62, 85–89, 102–106.

42. Francis Fukuyama, *The Great Disruption: Human Nature and the Reconstitution of Social Order* (New York: Free Press, 1999), 238.

43. Bentwich, *The Religious Foundations of Internationalism*, 67.

44. See Alexis de Tocqueville, *Democracy in America*, translated by Henry Reeve (New York: Adlard and Saunders, 1838), xii–xvii.

45. Fukuyama, *The Great Disruption*, 237.

46. See Marshall G. S. Hodgson, *Rethinking World History, Essays on Europe, Islam, and World History* (New York: Cambridge University Press, 1993), 98–101; Marshal G. S. Hodgson, *The Venture of Islam: Conscience and History in a World Civilization*, 3 vols. (Chicago: University of Chicago Press, 1974), vol. 3., bk. 5, 1–162.

47. Ziauddin Sardar, quoted in Carol Ezzell, "Clocking Cultures," *Scientific American* 287(3) (September 2002): 74–75; 75.

48. David Lehmann, "Fundamentalism and Globalism," *Third World Quarterly* 19(4) (1998): 607–634; 609.

49. For analyses of cultural integration and acculturation between Roman Catholicism and indigenous religions in the Spanish American empire, see David Brading, *The First America: The Spanish Monarchy, Creole Patriotism, and the Liberal State* (Cambridge: Cambridge University Press, 1991); Gustavo Gutierrez, *Las Casas: In Search of the Poor of Jesus Christ*, translated by Robert R. Barr (Maryknoll, New York: Orbis, 1993); Enrique Florescano, *Memory, Myth, and Time in Mexico*, translated by Albert G. Bork (Austin: University of Texas Press, 1994), 110–131.

50. Lehmann, "Fundamentalism and Globalism," 610. Expanding an idea introduced in *Atlantic Monthly* in March 1992, Benjamin Barber institutionalized the term *McWorld* in 1995. See Benjamin Barber, *Jihad vs. McWorld* (New York: Times Books, 1995).

51. Toby Lester, "Oh, Gods," *The Atlantic Monthly* 289(2) (February 2002): 37–45; 37.

52. See Roland Robertson, *Globalization: Social Theory and Global Culture* (London, Sage, 1992), 167–177; Bronislaw Misztal and Anson D. Shupe Jr., "Fundamentalism and Globalization: Fundamentalist Movements at the Twilight of the Twentieth Century," in *Religion, Mobilization, and Social Action*, edited by Anson D. Shupe Jr. and Bronislaw Misztal, 3–14 (Westport, Connecticut: Praeger, 1998), 7–14.

53. Philip Jenkins, "The Next Christianity," *The Atlantic Monthly* 290(3) (October 2002): 53–68; 54.

54. See Aylward Shorter, *African Christian Theology. Adaptation or Incarnation?* (Maryknoll, New York: Orbis, 1977), 139–143, 149–155.

55. The term *Third Church* is attributed to Walbert Bühlmann. See Walter Bühlmann, *God's Chosen Peoples* (Maryknoll, New York: Orbis, 1982), 260; Jenkins, "The Next Christianity," 54.

56. See Gilles Kepel, *Muslim Extremism in Egypt: The Prophet and Pharaoh* (Berkeley: University of California Press, 1985), 46–52, paraphrasing the thought of Sayyid Qutb in *Ma'alim fi'l-Tariq* (Signposts) (Dar al-Shourouk: Beirut, 1980), 98–117.

57. "Political Islam: Wave of the Past," *The Economist* 363(8275) (1 June 2002)77–78; 77.

58. "Islam and the West: Never the Twain Shall Meet," *The Economist* 361(8248) (17 November 2001): 17–19; 18.

59. See Jeff Haynes, *Religion in Global Politics* (London: Longman, 1998), 132–136.

60. R. Scott Appleby, "Fundamentalism," *Foreign Policy* 128 (January-February 2002): 16–22; 17.

61. Christophe Jaffrelot, "The Vishva Hindu Parishad: Structures and Strategies," in *Religion, Globalization, and Political Culture in the Third World*, edited by Jeff Haynes, 191–212 (London: Macmillan, 1988), 193; 198–199.

62. See Haynes, *Religion in Global Politics*, 186–187.

63. Kevin Hewison, "Of Regimes, States, and Pluralities: Thai Politics Enters the 1990s," in *Southeast Asia in the 1990s*, edited by Kevin Hewison, Richard Robison, and Garry Rodan, 161–189 (St. Leonard's, England: Allen and Unwin, 1993), 180–181.

64. See Duncan McCargo, "The Politics of Buddhism in Southeast Asia," in *Religion, Globalization, and Political Culture in the Third World*, edited by Jeff Haynes, 213–239 (London: Macmillan, 1988), 219–224, 233–234; Haynes, *Religion in Global Politics*, 191–196, 207–208.

65. Mustapha Kamal Pasha and Ahmed I. Samatar, "The Resurgence of Islam," in *Globalization: Critical Reflections*, edited by James H. Mittelman, 187–201 (Boulder, Colorado: Lynne Rienner, 1996), 199.

66. Hans Küng, *Global Responsibility: In Search of a New World Ethic* (New York: Continuum, 1993), 63.

67. Seizaburo Sato, "Man's Freedom, God's Will," *Civilization* 5(2) (April-May 1998): 54–77; 57.

68. Following the usage by Robert S. Bilheimer in 1947, many Christians equate the term *New Reformation* with the Ecumenical Movement launched by the 1910 World Missionary Conference in Edinburgh, to promote Christian unity. Robert S. Bilheimer, *What Must the Church Do?* (New York: Harper, 1947), 63–64, 80. Michael Pupin introduced the term *New Reformation* in 1927 to refer to the convergence of science and religion in Creative Coordination jointly by God and people around the truth that "the physical and the spiritual realities supplement each other. They are the two terminals of the same realities; one terminal residing in the human soul, and the other in the things of the external world. . . . the two pillars of the portal through which the human soul enters the world where the divinity resides." Michael Pupin, *The New Reformation: From Physical to Spiritual Realities* (New York: Scribner's, 1927), 265. Philip Jenkins has used the term *New Reformation* to stress the profound changes that are occurring in modern Christianity and to predict postmodern global effects analogous to those that occurred as the world modernized in the fifteenth through twentieth centuries. Jenkins, "The Next Christianity," 53–68.

69. Ray Takeyh, "Faith-Based Initiatives," *Foreign Policy* (November-December, 2001): 68–70; 68.

70. Takeyh, "Faith-Based Initiatives," 69; referring to the teachings of Tunisia's Rashid Ghannouchi.

71. Jenkins, "The Next Christianity," 60.

72. Rodney Stark, professor of sociology and comparative religion, University of Washington, in an interview reported in Lester, "Oh, Gods," 42.

73. Rosalind I. J. Hackett, professor of religious studies, University of Tennessee, Knoxville, in an interview reported in Lester, "Oh, Gods," 44–45.

74. Nick Stevenson, "Globalization and Cultural Political Economy," in *Globalization and Its Critics*, edited by Randall D. Germain, 91–113 (New York: St. Martin's, 2000), 91.

75. Giddens, *Runaway World*, 44.

76. Richard S. Kennedy, "Who Is Culture's Keeper?" *Foreign Policy* 133 (November-December 2002): 92–94; 93.

77. Stevenson, "Globalization and Cultural Political Economy," 92.

78. Kellner, "Globalization and the Postmodern Turn," 35.

79. Lehmann, "Fundamentalism and Globalism," 608.

80. For one vivid extreme separation of white religion from black religion, see Albert J. Raboteau, *Slave Religion: The Invisible Institution in the Antebellum South* (New York: Oxford University Press, 1978), 87–92, 295–302. See also Stuart Hall, "The Local and the Global: Globalization and Ethnicity, and Old and New Identities, Old and New Ethnicities," in *Culture, Globalization, and the World-System: Contemporary Conditions for the Representation of Identity*, edited by Anthony D. King, 19–68 (Binghamton: State University of New York Art Department, 1991).

81. Stevenson, "Globalization and Cultural Political Economy," 108.

82. See George Ritzer, *The McDonaldization of Society* (London: Pine Forge, 1996), 9–16; Robert Kanigel, "Frederick Taylor's Apprenticeship," *Wilson Quarterly* 20(3) (Summer 1996): 44–51; 51.

83. Theodore Levitt, "The Globalization of Markets," *Harvard Business Review* 61(3) (May-June 1983): 92–102; 99.

84. Douglas McGray, "Japan's Gross National Cool," *Foreign Policy* 130 (May-June 2002): 44–54; 46.

85. Ritzer, *The McDonaldization of Society*, 1.

86. This trend became significant in the 1960s with the climax of the U.S.-led postwar reconstruction. See Robert D. Buzzell, "Can You Standardize Multinational Marketing?" *Harvard Business Review* 46(6) (November-December 1968): 102–113; 103, 113.

87. Levitt, "The Globalization of Markets," 92.

88. Stevenson, "Globalization and Cultural Political Economy," 95.

89. See Ritzer, *The McDonaldization of Society*, 143–144.

90. Stevenson, "Globalization and Cultural Political Economy," 96.

91. Kellner, "Globalization and the Postmodern Turn," 26.

92. See Mike Featherstone, *Undoing Culture: Globalization, Postmodernism, and Identity* (London: Sage 1995), 73–78.

93. Waters, *Globalization*, 140.

94. See Jonathan Friedman, "Being in the World: Globalization and Localization," in *Global Culture*, edited by Mike Featherstone, 311–328 (London: Sage, 1990), 323–327; Leslie Sklair, *Sociology of the Global System* (Hemel Hempstead: Harvester Wheatsheaf, 1991), 77–81, 129–140, 148–155.

95. Benjamin R. Barber, "Democracy at Risk: American Culture in a Global Culture," *World Policy Journal* 15(2) (Summer 1998): 29–41; 31.

96. James B. Twitchell, "But First, a Word From our Sponsor," *Wilson Quarterly* 20(3) (Summer 1996): 68–77; 71, 77.

97. See Fred Hirsch, *The Social Limits to Growth* (Cambridge: Harvard University Press, 1976).

98. Arnold J. Toynbee, *Civilization on Trial* (New York: Oxford University Press, 1948), 238.

99. See Manuel Castells, *The Rise of the Network Society: The Information Age* (Oxford: Basil Blackwell, 1996), 99–102, 106–115, 145–147; Ankie Hoogvelt, *Globalization and the Postcolonial World* (London: Macmillan, 1997), 216–219.

100. See, among others, William H. McNeill, *The Pursuit of Power: Technology, Armed Force, and Society since A.D. 1000* (Oxford: Basil Blackwell, 1982), 102–117, 143–158; Paul M. Kennedy, *The Rise and Fall of the Great Powers: Economic Change and Military Conflict from 1500 to 2000* (New York: Vintage, 1987), 16–30; Charles C. Mann, "1491," *The Atlantic Monthly* 289(3) (March 2002): 41–53; 49–50.

101. See remarks by U.S. Assistant Secretary of State James Rubin speaking on British television immediately after the attacks on New York and Washington, D.C., in September 2001 that "this was not only a strike against America, but an attack on 'the center of western civilization' itself." Quoted in Toby Dodge, "Space for Dissent, *The World Today* 58(3) (March 2002): 7–8; 7.

102. See Joseph S. Nye Jr., *The Paradox of American Power: Why the World's Only Superpower Can't Go It Alone* (New York: Oxford University Press, 2002), 1, 12–35.

103. Eloise Malone and Arthur Rachwald, "The Dark Side of Globalization," *United States Naval Institute Proceedings* 127/11/1,185 (November 2001): 43.

104. Charlene Barshefsky, deputy U.S. trade representative, quoted in "The Negotiator," by Elsa Welsh, in *The New Yorker* 72(4) (18 March 1996): 86–97; 88. See also Herbert I. Schiller, *Communication and Cultural Domination* (White Plains, New York: Sharpe, 1976), 38–45; Herbert I. Schiller, *Who Knows: Information in the Age of Fortune 500* (Norwood, New Jersey: Ablex, 1981), 5,18–21.

105. Herbert Schiller, *Mass Communications and American Empire*, 2d ed. (Boulder, Colorado: Westview, 1992), 12–13.

106. Friedman, *The Lexus and the Olive Tree*, 9.

107. See Herbert Schiller, *Information Inequality: The Deepening Social Crisis of America* (London: Routledge, 1996), 112–116, 118–121.

108. Martin Walker, "What Europeans Think of America, *World Policy Journal* 17(2) (Summer 2000): 26–38; 36.

109. John Viney, European chairman of Heidrick & Struggles, a New York executive search firm, quoted in "The American Way," by Janet Guyon, 114–120, *Fortune* 144(11) (26 November 2001): 116.

110. For discussion of the business civilization, see Susan Strange, "The Name of the Game," in *Sea Changes: American Foreign Policy in a World Transformed*, edited by Nicholas X. Rizopoulos, 238–273 (New York: Council on Foreign Relations, 1990), 260–265.

111. Guyon, "The American Way," 116.

112. Igor Kostikov, chairman of the Russian securities commission, quoted in "The American Way," by Guyon, 120.

113. Twitchell, "But First, a Word From our Sponsor," 76.

114. Twitchell, "But First, a Word From our Sponsor," 68.

115. Stevenson, "Globalization and Cultural Political Economy," 97.

116. See Kenzaburo Oe, *Aimai na Nihon no Watashi (Ambiguous Japan and Myself)* (Tokyo: Iwanami Shinsho, 1995), 8.

117. Masaru Tamamoto, "The Uncertainty of the Self: Japan at Century's End," *World Policy Journal* 16(2) (Summer 1999): 119–128; 121.

118. McGray, "Japan's Gross National Cool," 50.

119. Tamamoto, "The Uncertainty of the Self: Japan at Century's End," 126.

120. John Gray, *False Dawn: The Delusions of Global Capitalism* (London: Granta, 1998), 60.

121. Michael Talalay, "Technology and Globalization," in *Globalization and its Critics*, edited by Randall D. Germain, 204–222 (New York: St. Martin's, 2000), 211.

122. Mlinar and Trček, Territorial Cultures and Global Impacts," 89.

123. McGray, "Japan's Gross National Cool," 46.

124. Andrew J. Bacevich, "Culture, Globalization, and U.S. Foreign Policy," reviewing *Many Globalizations: Cultural Diversity in the Contemporary World*, edited by Peter L. Berger and Samuel P. Huntington (New York: Oxford University Press, 2002) and *Culture Matters: How Values Shape Human Progress*, edited by Lawrence E. Harrison and Samuel P. Huntington (New York: Basic Books, 2000), *World Policy Journal* 19(3) (Fall 2002): 77–82; 81.

125. Joseph S. Nye Jr., "Soft Power," *Foreign Policy* 80 (Fall 1990): 153–171; 169.

7

THE ECONOMIC PERSPECTIVE

> Because of globalization many people in the world now live longer than
> before and their standard of living is far better. . . .Globalization has reduced
> the sense of isolation felt in much of the developing world and has given
> many people in the developing countries access to knowledge well beyond
> the reach of even the wealthiest in any country a century ago.[1]

What many people have come to understand by globalization is a
"combination of rapid technological progress, large-scale capital flows, and
burgeoning international trade," a purely economic phenomenon.[2] Regardless
of the indicators used, international economic activity—trade, foreign direct
investment, and portfolio investment—has grown at increasing rates over the
last several generations. In parallel with expanding economic liberalization and
trade flows, the responses of states and societies to economic integration seem
to have inspired their success or failure as relevant political and social units.
Economic globalists see "the embrace of globalization as the only route to
economic growth. . . . The Internet is the agent that renders inevitable a
transparent, democratic, decentralized, and market-based society."[3]

Within the economic perspective, the result of globalization would be an
integrated, global economy in which neither distance nor time nor political
borders would impede economic transactions in goods and services. The costs
of transport and communication would be zero, and the barriers between
national political jurisdictions would have vanished.[4] It is, however, too much
to "conclude from the steep growth curves on international economic flows
and policy liberalization that a truly seamless worldwide market is emerging.
. . . Factors such as country size and proximity to neighbors (which have
nothing to do with level of development) have marked bearing on trade
volumes. . . . [Econometric analysis] suggests that the policies governments
pursued with respect to openness or closure to trade and international capital
were essentially uncorrelated with international economic flows." Although

analysis of economic globalization below the surface remains less than conclusive, it is clear that the broad trends of economic globalization are real but that "significant cross-national differences in integration remain."[5]

The historical path of economic globalization is well known, and the process of economic integration has been deeply studied and well documented. Economists and sociologists have demonstrated the differences between current globalization and previous experiences. Less interesting, however, have been the recurring cycles of social stress and conflict around people's struggles to adjust resources, products, and work to increasing demands for prosperity, security, and justice. Economic and sociological orthodoxies still quibble over notions of the historical cycles that "[Nikolai] Kondratieff [1892–1938] had identified (but never explained) and which Joseph Schumpeter [1883–1950] had, in my view, incorrectly associated with the rhythm of major technological innovations."[6] Each cycle, however, coincided with a wave of globalization, an expansion of technology, and a surge of economic growth based on more intense exploitation of resources: resource-based growth.

Within the narrow economic perspective, the late-twentieth-century globalization wave appears as the refurbishment of an edifice of *laissez-faire* free trade, buttressed by capitalism, and resting on a foundation of consumerism. Within the global perspective, globalization has placed political power in thrall to the discipline of global markets and human desires for prosperity. Social stresses are rising in predictable patterns as the global political-economy teeters in a delicate triple balance between states and markets, between the United States and other countries, and between the state and the individual.[7] The virtual hand of technology—especially electronics and information technology—manipulates the balance, just as the invisible hand of resource-based capitalism and the heavy hand of the welfare state manipulated the international economy of the nineteenth and twentieth centuries. The information revolution has begun to replace the power of trade in resources with the power of knowledge in technology transfer.

Within the global perspective globalization is a complex phenomenon that involves not only resources, money, and work but people, their knowledge, their ideas, and their feelings. Within this less fashionable perspective, several noneconomic gaps appear between the rich, growing economies and the poor stagnating economies, which accumulate social stresses. Beneath the increasing productivity of the global economy, complex globalization frustrates Smithian and Marxian expectations of growth as a natural result of uniting markets and sources through Internet-hosted institutions, transactions, and human relationships. The implications of trade-based globalization and resource-based growth include stresses on social solidarity wherever it may exist, on people's ideas about justice, and on people's political struggles for security. Economic globalization presents the challenges of consumerism to cultural, religious, and social values as it carries the economic inequality that seems to follow resource-based capitalism wherever it goes. Offering few prescriptions for social security or individual justice under threat of market failure or geostrategic catastrophe, economic globalization is not a divinely willed feature of human destiny. People choose it deliberately to stress economic well-being.

The experience of the rich, globalized economies suggests that modern economic growth may be the result of deeper, more powerful forces than economic efficiency and material prosperity. The world's most prosperous economies have relied more on knowledge, and less on resources, as the source of growth. The information revolution has produced another source of wealth: knowledge. Knowledge applied to work creates value. Applied to old tasks, it creates productivity; applied to new tasks, the result is innovation. Creating new knowledge, unlike converting resources into utility, creates new value. The United States has created institutions that encourage the creation of new knowledge and radical innovation. European and Asian institutions emphasize continuous, incremental improvement of existing technologies and diffusion of knowledge. These knowledge-based economies and institutions have worked well because they complement each other in expanding people's perspectives. Although Adam Smith's insight probably included knowledge-based growth, in their post–Cold-War exuberance, some modern economists and many political scientists and journalists may have missed it.

RESOURCE-BASED GROWTH

Within the economic perspective famously and compellingly described by Thomas Friedman, globalization seems as inevitable as people's desires for well-being and prosperity. For firms, but also for many governments, globalization is a linear process of "increasing the size of the market and, through it, the division of labor associated with those industries that contribute most to industrial growth."[8] The strategic purpose of globalization is increased income, expressed as national growth or increased corporate profits. For most of the twentieth century, economic growth has captured the attentions of economists, politicians, and many people. In its simplest common sense, economic growth is any aggregate increase in output. In the global political-economic context, the common indicators of growth are gross domestic product (GDP) or *per capita* income (PCI) of a country and corporate earnings per share.

Although every civilization has experienced some economic growth, for premodern peoples, growth was oppressively slow and often little more than hope that one's children would not starve. Annual or generational changes in *per capita* incomes were small, although some eras of sustained growth extended for as many as six centuries in Mayan Yucatán or imperial China.[9] In successive waves of globalization over ninety centuries, the revolutions of trade and commerce expanded this simple growth in some form of material prosperity through the ancient civilizations. The sudden appearance of rapid economic growth in the wake of science and new knowledge in seventeenth-century Europe, however, transformed human life and living irreversibly.

Classical economics explained growth with the premise that economic output depended on inputs—labor and capital—and added growth theories to explain increases in output—resource-based growth. Accumulating resources and combining them to expand production, the first episodes of resource-based growth spanned decades and centuries. Every economy had to provide its own indigenous capital as an engine of growth, although trade provided occasional injections of additional resources. When the attractions of economic growth overwhelmed social, historical, and psychological barriers—Bacon's idols—revolution launched new waves of globalization. With the first Industrial Revolution, expanding trade became the engine of *both* globalization *and* resource-based growth. To transform the chaotic, Hobbesian world of all against all into a tidy system of national sovereignty, governments regulated trade, invested in resource extraction, and accumulated wealth. Energized by technology and trade and insulated by sovereignty, some economies generated rapid, resource-based growth. Economic development seemed to shunt Europe and North America onto a one-way path to prosperity and progress.

As globalization surged again around trade and colonialism in the nineteenth century, liberal capitalism was offering internal, resource-based growth engines in the forms of nationalism, industrialization, and technological innovation. While introducing international organizations into interstate relations reduced the salience of national security regimes and sovereign investment, the novel multinational enterprises provided additional supplies of resources to sustain growth. By the late nineteenth century, the demands of resource-based growth for ever more resources converged smoothly around capitalism as the next wave of globalization merged trade with foreign investment. As social stresses appeared as cracks in the political-economic edifice, the economic progress of industrial countries began to expose political insulation and trade regulation as constraints on resource-based growth. The end of globalization in 1914 brought the interwar turmoil of confused modernity as resource-based growth collapsed into depression and war.

Export-Led Growth and Division of Labor

Built on Adam Smith's invisible hand of the market and David Ricardo's notions of comparative advantage, both focused within national perspectives, trade-based globalization relied on exports to sustain growth and relieve social stress. The imperative of efficiency condensed tightly regulated and costly exports of products and resources to less expensive exports of technologies and capital, which were only loosely regulated. Inconceivable to Smith or Ricardo, knowledge-based globalization expanded national divisions of economic labor into an international structure of production held together by trade and foreign investment. Instead of resources, the ability to operate in the international division of labor became the foundation for export-led, resource-based growth for economies connected to the international trading economy.

In the international world of export-led growth, business was to develop competitive advantage through technology and efficient production techniques. Politics smoothed the path to national prosperity through free markets for goods, services, and labor. Families and societies specialized in consuming indigenous products, and individuals worked for efficient exporters. Bureaucratic governments promoted domestic competition and modernization and provided infrastructure to generate economies of scale. Almost invisibly, the pressures of globalization broadened the division of economic labor into domestic sociopolitical divisions and transformed societies and their economies into commercial and industrial sectors of an international economy. In a context of deepening social stresses, the resurgent imperatives of economic efficiency and resource-based growth gradually co-opted the advances of technology to divide the world into manufacturing economies and resource producers.

A few newly independent countries—the globalizing group—began to export manufactured goods, rather than just raw materials, while most—the stagnating group—tried vainly to expand their primary sectors.[10] As the rich countries developed new technologies and converted their large economies to reliance on service industries for growth, resource-based manufacturing migrated to the poor, developing economies. Demand for land, labor, and capital to sustain resource-based growth shifted to the poorer countries as the rich countries deindustrialized. "An emerging world market for labor and production entailed massive industrial relocation, the subdivision of manufacturing processes into multiple partial operations, major technological innovations, large-scale migratory flows, and the feminization of labor."[11] The emerging division of labor concentrated research, technological development, management, and finance in the rich countries with manufacturing, resource extraction, sales and distribution diffused across the poor countries.[12]

The Fordist division of the world's work into manufacturing countries and resource producers shifted to an equally clear division between countries with high technical capabilities and those with cheap labor and land. The new notion of comparative advantage for export-led growth reflected less any Ricardian concerns about natural resources than consumer demand and availability of markets. Production sharing based on technical capacity and the politics of labor and consumption became the determinant of national prosperity and aggregate growth in the new global economy.

Beyond the processes and outside the structures of international export-led growth, the new global division of labor also affected the informal economic sector that encompasses "traditional artisanal occupations as well as new types of employment in which informal work predominates. The latter [are] closely linked to global market structures and new subcontracting chains, especially in information technology (IT) and the garments and accessories produced in response to emerging fashions. The IT sector has generated both high-paying jobs and lower-remunerated employment, including a variety of services such as medical transcription and Internet and telephone kiosks."[13] Globalization has begun to organize and connect these high-tech home workers in the global economy, *without intermediation of local markets*. The self-centered societies of their isolated, traditional, artisan predecessors, who were neither connected nor included, systematically ignored or exploited them. In stark contrast, globalization focuses the latent social stresses of the connected, informal sector directly on the inadequacies of their less-than-global societies. Establishing global linkages has empowered these people in local and national affairs through a new identity expressed in local political-economic organization and participation in *both* civil society *and* a global collective endeavor.

During the late-twentieth-century wave of globalization, the bulk of resource-based growth occurred in the poor countries as trade shifted from exports of goods for foreign markets towards shipments to foreign subsidiaries or affiliates of multinational firms. "Officially and legally, they are exports. Economically, they are intracompany transfers. They are machines, supplies, and half-finished goods that have been engineered into the production of the plant or affiliate abroad and must be continued, whatever the exchange rate."[14] Export-led growth has matured into visions of aggregate national growth based on full participation in the global division of economic labor through open markets for capital and technology, parallel with those for goods and services.

Bacon's Idols

As if to confirm Francis Bacon's prescient warnings about two especially pernicious idols, this vision of resource-based growth explained globalization with reference to the brief experience of a few turbulent—possibly catastrophic—decades of market dominance. The mechanical conclusion that cheap labor, high technology, and free-market exports drive the movement of capital, which energizes globalization, ignores the profound complexity of the global economy. The increasing importance of financial markets and the continued existence of the international division of labor overlaid on a less formal global pattern of production sharing are forming a deepening, flexible system of global production that remains largely invisible. The reemerging, transnational power of low technology and the continuing regulatory role of the state form an economic legacy that demands recognition. Resource-based growth and export-based globalization conveniently forgot Karl Polanyi's Baconian warning: "To allow the market mechanism to be the sole director of the fate of human beings and their natural environment, indeed, even of the amount and use of purchasing power, would result in demolition of society."[15]

Classical theories of international trade as the engine of resource-based growth, which have assumed a prominent place among Bacon's idols, explain that investment follows trade in goods and, more recently, also trade in services. "But increasingly today, trade follows investment. International movements of capital rather than international movements of goods have become the engine of the world economy."[16] Globalization has also tarnished the Baconian visions of the prosperous, developed economies leading the poor economies in resource-based growth led by exports. In the closing generation of the twentieth century, trade and productivity expanded even while the rich countries lost economic momentum and resource-based growth subsided. Bacon's economic idols of resource-based growth and international trade simply cannot explain what has been happening. Globalization has wrought subtle, important transformations on the economic assumptions and theories that have structured modern, economic reality for decades.

KNOWLEDGE-BASED GROWTH

As post-Renaissance globalization thrust Europe into the industrial age with its rapid, resource-based growth, the Enlightenment was expanding human knowledge beyond the traditional narrow perspectives on life and living. The inspiration to create new knowledge condensed into innovation to reduce the resources required to generate rapid growth. As people experimented with applying innovation to production, knowledge-intensive technologies imperceptibly supplanted resources—land, labor, and capital—as stimulants of growth and factors of production. The knowledge-based, capital-intensive factories that began to replace labor-intensive production in the nineteenth and twentieth centuries increased the contributions of rising productivity to aggregate growth beyond those of additional resources. Knowledge became an alternative to resources as a basis for economic growth.[17]

For individuals living in event time, innovation appeared as startling scientific discovery or the invention of a machine that could increase the productivity of resources. For firms, it usually emerged from a single, large investment in machinery or a dramatic industrialization of production. Countries spread the process of industrialization, with its attendant social stresses, over decades or generations in social time as they transformed their infrastructures, and their firms industrialized at various rates. Progress emerged incrementally through diffusion of a sequence of innovations focused within the constraints of social reality, physical conditions, and the extent of existing knowledge. "How this sequence develops is intimately linked with the process of absorbing those innovations into the economic structure."[18]

Like earlier commercialization, industrialization was an unfamiliar, stressful, triple process of creation, innovation, and diffusion of knowledge. People created new knowledge—not merely learned what someone else already knew—in the conjunctural *basho* that was modernity. Entrepreneurs converted old information into new knowledge and used it rationally to create new economic value through innovation. Companies and countries diffused *both* knowledge *and* value through globalization. Although accumulation of the knowledge created and disseminated in previous waves of commercial globalization provided the foundation, modern industrial globalization has been the result of this triple process. The information revolution, itself a product of knowledge creation and globalization, continues to accelerate the processes, to merge them, and to expand them towards the global perspective.

Within the global perspective, some people can appreciate the increasing order predicted by Kurzweil's law through greater understanding. Within the economic perspective, however, growth and globalization have increased economic uncertainty and chaos. Beyond the logic of the second corollary, "the explanation, in large part, is that knowledge has replaced the economists' 'land, labor, and capital,' as the chief economic resource. Knowledge, mainly in the form of the training methods and philosophies developed in the United States during World War II, exploded the axiom that low wages mean low productivity."[19] Orthodox economics has gradually expanded understandings of growth by including human capital as a factor of production in the form of "new knowledge gleaned from scientific discovery and technological progress—in short, innovation. In this scheme of things, innovation accounts for any growth that cannot be explained by increases in capital and labor."[20]

Few philosophers or economists would quibble about the assertion that accumulating knowledge is a proximate source of economic growth, and many politicians champion innovation as the most important element in any modern or modernizing economy. Nor would many disagree with a conclusion that steady economic growth would require steady accumulation of knowledge. The notion of a steady rate of knowledge accumulation, however, contradicts much of history and overlooks the structural changes, social stresses, and political conflict that have historically accompanied economic growth. Rapid, aggregate, economic growth in national or global prosperity has often brought periods of local turmoil in societies, economies, and polities. This turmoil is not, however, an anomaly or an economic inconvenience. It reflects the prominent and turbulent influence of knowledge on the process of economic growth across different perspectives. As globalization intrudes uncertainties and chaos into the narrow, economic perspective, Bacon's idols allow only fleeting glimpses of the vast prospect within the global perspective. Deepening the need for new understanding and new knowledge, the idols preserve the difficulties for people in abandoning their traditional perspectives and expanding to new, unfamiliar vistas. Although economics, resources, and growth are important features of economic reality, they do not, and cannot, dominate social reality within the global perspective.

MODERN ECONOMIC GROWTH

The Industrial Revolution brought what Simon Kuznets has distinguished from the simple growth of ancient civilizations as modern economic growth (MEG).[21] "This restricted concept includes high growth rates of both population and *per capita* product, with the necessary result of enormous increases in aggregate product."[22] Through several stages, MEG transforms an economy from resource-based to knowledge-based growth as people transform social reality across all perspectives. In most economies, MEG has begun abruptly as economic production and population both began to grow slowly, often stimulated by trade-based globalization, with little change in standards and conditions of living. Societies shifted traumatically towards industrial production as capitalism imported additional resources and generated resource-based growth by applying more resources in a static production function. Most modern civilizations, countries, and peoples have experienced this slow, resource-based, parallel growth of populations and production as the first stage of MEG and faced the unprecedented social stresses that it brought.

After some delay until population growth stabilized and industrialization began to affect productivity, *per capita* income began to grow significantly when indigenous innovation induced knowledge-based growth. This second stage of MEG actually improved living conditions of the entire society by increasing *per capita* income even as population also grew. In these first stages of MEG, resource-based growth has brought wrenching changes in productive capabilities, capital assets, and economic, social, and political institutions. In later stages of MEG, knowledge-based growth has accompanied rapid expansion of knowledge and new political beliefs that overturned tradition, shattered Bacon's idols, and demanded new sets of cultural values and social norms. The social stresses of both types of growth contain the germs of interstate war and domestic strife, and all societies that have experienced MEG have concurrently experienced violent conflict.

Perspectives on Modern Economic Growth

Within the traditional perspective of classical, resource-based economics, knowledge appears within an economy's production function as technology. Growth is a natural consequence of the operation of resource-based capitalism within a free-market economy. Capitalism accumulates and concentrates the right proportions of physical and human resources within a national economy and uses them efficiently for production. Since a free market reallocates resources as the economy expands and contracts, resource-based growth is self-sustaining upon a foundation of *sufficient resources, efficient capitalism,* and *unconstrained market processes* and appears as change in gross national product. This modern view that MEG reflects higher efficiency or greater factor productivity across an expanded production function—land, capital, labor, and technology—is well known.[23] Within the neoclassical perspective, knowledge appears *both* as an externality—rational foreign and domestic policy—*and* a factor of production—technology—for resource-based growth. Within these perspectives, the demand for ever more resources to sustain growth has led historically to conflict over supplies of critical resources.

In a context of interdependence, economic growth is only one aspect of modernization, and MEG seems necessarily to entail increasing foreign trade and investments.[24] Interdependence transforms production "to meet changing demands and to make more productive use of technology."[25] Modern economic growth relies on deliberate policies to coordinate domestic growth with global growth. Simply generating indigenous resource-based growth is not enough. Through innovation and knowledge creation, society—usually a government— corrects market failure and capitalist inefficiency to reallocate resources to meet social demands. Knowledge-based policy assumes a primary role in generating growth based on *both* resources *and* knowledge. This dual growth appears as material improvement in living conditions and changes in *per capita* income. The persistent salience of resource-based growth within this perspective contains in economic dependence the seeds of conflict over resources.

The lens of historicism extends the economic perspective beyond policy, resources, technology, and growth to embrace *both* innovation *and* creation of new knowledge as primary bases of growth. Whereas measurements of growth provide useful information to policymakers and technical planners, the focus of historicism lies on social transformation and progress. Aggregate measures necessarily obscure the details of knowledge creation in *basho*, conversion and diffusion of knowledge within *conjonctures*, and incremental innovation as engines of progress. Seeking human welfare through material prosperity, classical economics found good explanations and policy prescriptions for resource-based growth in consolidating economic interactions into macroeconomic principles for resource-based capitalism. Orthodox economics rightly celebrates and stimulates the power of resource-based capitalism to generate wealth and prosperity. Within the narrow economic perspective, however, the even greater power of knowledge-based capitalism to generate knowledge remains constrained within an economy's production function. Within the global perspective, the essence of capitalism lies not in aggregate growth, but in the details of the spectacular creations of new knowledge and incremental innovation that carry progress. The knowledge creation and innovation inherent in knowledge-based capitalism are the heart and soul of the social transformations through which people create human progress.

Types of Modern Economic Growth

Disjunction of growth into two types—static, resource-based and dynamic, knowledge-based—shifts the focus from local measures of resources and rates to the effects of knowledge within the global perspective. The shift from static to dynamic growth also emphasizes the differences between the need of a resource-based society to absorb and accumulate social stresses and the ability of a knowledge-based society to relieve them through transformation. The prevalence of conflict among societies experiencing static growth reflects the difficulties faced by resource-based societies in relieving social stress.

Static Growth

As insulated, premodern economies become able to increase their resources and use them for economic production, MEG begins abruptly as static resource-based growth. At some point, domestic production can be expected to saturate domestic markets and force expansion into foreign markets to sustain aggregate growth. This intrinsic feature of static growth has historically coincided with waves of commercial trade-based globalization as growing economies struggled to sustain growth through inputs of more resources. History leaves no doubt that economies that expand through trade can prosper. Expansion of resource-based growth beyond a national economy requires society to become a net exporter and has universally demanded internal political and economic reforms. Sustaining static growth through trade requires other countries to be willing buyers with open markets. Trade liberalization cannot be unilateral if national static growth is to continue.

Efforts to sustain static, resource-based growth in an international economy, whether through conquest or through trade, ultimately generate economic disagreements that have often expanded to political conflict. Whereas many countries have been ready to sell, fewer countries, including sellers, have been willing to buy. Traded resources needed to sustain growth in a home economy would necessarily be products or raw materials from a foreign economy and would not be available to support resource-based growth in the foreign economy. The flows of resources and products to sustain static growth portend increasing social stresses in all of the economies involved.

"It is well known that the simple Solow growth model predicts long-run convergence, at least for countries with similar savings rates, population growth rates, and other fundamentals. It is equally well known that the data in the Penn World Tables show no unconditional convergence for the world as a whole. . . . Different countries have different investment, education, and population growth rates, and thus are converging to different steady states." The augmented Solow model of resource-based growth includes knowledge, in the form of human capital, as a factor of production beyond labor and capital. It remains unclear whether growth is "conditional on attitudes towards thrift, commitments to education, quality of institutions, geographic location, and demographic preferences." The open-economy model of resource-based growth predicts "convergence among those countries that have adopted open trading policies, but not among countries that have remained protectionist."[26]

A paradox of Ricardian comparative advantage obviates *both* sustained resource-based growth *and* convergence of trading economies, even while maximizing current welfare in both countries. Only where two economies are fully and broadly matched in their respective resource requirements (imports) and products (exports) could people expect them to converge on shared prosperity through trade. Only when they remain complementary through even, static growth would trade sustain resource-based growth in each country, which would probably be at different rates. In the more common situations of incompatible comparative advantages, divergence of trading economies, even when both are growing, is more likely to generate pervasive social stresses and political conflict than shared prosperity. In contrast to the prospect within national perspectives, the global political and economic perspectives across multiple national economies expose static, resource-based growth as ultimately not sustainable, except possibly within a fully integrated global economy.

Static growth has been common over time and across economies as societies have increased available resources through conquest, trade, colonialism, diplomacy, and foreign investment—Victorian Britain, France, or Hong Kong. Planned economies—the Soviet Union, the People's Republic of China, or Cuba—have preferred to shift factor intensities and mobilize unused domestic resources. So long as planners or traders can continue to increase allocations of resources, static growth can continue. When quantity or quality of resources or political power to mobilize them deteriorates, *both* planned economies *and* trading economies grind to a halt. The world's most prosperous economies—the United States, Japan, Europe, or Southeast Asia—have uniformly shifted factor intensities and managed foreign trade in response to political forces, rather than relying on markets for allocation decisions. These more prosperous economies have deliberately used foreign investment and technology transfer, rather than trade, to overcome factor shortages. They have used political power to decrease dependence on labor-intensive production and policy to stimulate technological innovation. As social stresses have accumulated to nearly explosive pressures, these societies have deliberately transformed their social realities through learning, innovation, and new knowledge to relieve stresses. The uniform result over several generations has been an effective, gradual shift to knowledge-based dynamic growth.

Dynamic Growth

Unlike simple and static growth, which have occurred frequently throughout history, dynamic growth has appeared only since the Enlightenment. As industrialization introduced innovation to static-growth economies, technology diffused through societies that were also gaining knowledge from other sources and through indigenous learning by doing. Industrializing societies gradually learned to relieve social stresses through transformation instead of conflict. Beyond increasing productivity, new knowledge induced sociopolitical, cultural, and structural transformation as technology eventually became a legitimate factor of production.

Industrialization also added technology and risk management to capitalism. Rationality shifted the risk associated with Braudel's domain of high-risk global capital from the realm of divine will and whimsy to calculable human decisions. Capitalism began to expand from its foundations on solid resources to a less tangible reliance on technology. The hesitant emergence, adolescent confidence, and mature stability of knowledge-based capitalism carried aggregate economic growth along with it from resource-based growth to dynamic, knowledge-based growth. Capitalism's first incremental innovation towards knowledge-based growth was little more than learning by doing: direct technology transfer as a supplement to trade. Later, in the nineteenth century, came foreign direct investment (FDI) and, in the twentieth century, intellectual property rights and venture capital. Although each of these innovations in capitalism created traumatic social stresses, knowledge-based capitalism has relieved them with new knowledge created in *basho*, expanded across multiple perspectives, and applied in transforming social reality. In transforming itself, capitalism energized economic transitions from resource-based growth through technology-based growth to knowledge-based growth as an engine of progress *both* within the economic perspective *and* towards the global perspective.

Learning through Technology Transfer. During preindustrial waves of trade-based globalization, technology transfer occurred primarily through local reverse engineering of imported technically advanced products, since FDI was rare outside the political-military protection of empire or colonial suzerainty. Industrialization transformed FDI into an alternative for trade and its parent, global enterprise, into a critical and powerful carrier of globalization. Relying on indigenous innovation to sustain local, dynamic growth, industrial economies sustained resource-based growth through regulated trade and shifted further towards knowledge-based growth through unregulated FDI. Economies that had not yet begun MEG "could easily rely on an external engine of growth provided by foreign direct investment and technology transfer from multinational enterprises."[27]

Instead of simply using imported technology to sustain export-led growth, capitalists and entrepreneurs molded it to their purposes through embodiment in processes and devices—learning through innovation. A basic human force, innovation not only refined transferred technology but also increased the stocks of human knowledge, which energized dynamic growth in a context of capitalism.[28] "Technology-intensive operations replaced capital-intensive or labor-intensive production, and eventually technology became the growth-limiting resource."[29] Unlike simple learning, innovation could occur only in a context of prior, existing knowledge. Without such a foundation, imported technology has been little more than a material resource that quickly became a constraint to static growth unless new technology was also forthcoming.

Technology-Based Growth. Beyond overcoming shortages of labor or capital as factors of production, this transitional, technology-based growth increased *both* production *and* productivity and brought noticeable improvements in standards of living. It contained the germ of dynamic, knowledge-based growth in *both* learning by doing *and* the innovative learning that energizes incremental progress. Developing high-technology national industries within a capitalist system, rather than simply importing production technologies, stimulated indigenous innovation as a precursor of dynamic growth.

Although some modern foreign-aid programs also include a knowledge content, the predominant medium for learning through technology transfers and knowledge diffusion has become FDI. Beyond sustaining static growth through direct transfers of technology and expertise, FDI also increases knowledge indirectly through training, education, and example. The introductions of tacit knowledge, novel management styles, and global business practices through FDI have routinely stimulated technology-based growth, indigenous innovation, and even creation of new knowledge in international epistemic communities and global *basho*.[30]

As most economists agree, trade, portfolio investment, and FDI are complements rather than substitutes in *both* generating aggregate growth *and* deepening economic integration.[31] Although their contributions seem smaller, international portfolio investment and economic policy are positive factors.[32] "Foreign direct investment is the only case in which economists universally endorse the basic, neoclassical approach to market integration." In contrast to the other facets of economic globalization—trade and portfolio investment— "there is little dispute in the economics community that the effects of FDI are unambiguously positive from the standpoint of economic growth."[33]

Creating New Knowledge. History suggests that current social reality imposes rigid constraints on the ability of a society to learn and on the rates with which it can absorb knowledge, whether through learning or innovating. Dynamic growth and MEG require a substantial basic stock of knowledge, which humanity has accumulated only in modern times and in a few places. Recent increases in that stock seem also critical, since "it is generally believed that there may be increasing returns to knowledge, *i.e.* that knowledge gained today facilitates the acquisition of further knowledge tomorrow."[34]

Instead of simply creating economic value or acquiring wealth, dynamic growth creates new resources. Beyond the Solow growth model, knowledge-based growth is based on creating new knowledge and using it to create value. For MEG, technology is not simply a factor of production; "technology is knowledge, and knowledge provides the capability for doing new things."[35] The shift from resource-based to technology-based to knowledge-based growth as trade condenses to FDI and learning expands to epistemic communities is not mere semantics. Neither synonymous with technology nor limited to a role as an economic resource, knowledge has unique capabilities for creation and innovation that function best within a capitalist system.

General Education. Intuition suggests that education—accumulation and dissemination of knowledge—is an important contributor not only to growth but also to convergence of *per capita* incomes. Shallow investigation of the North Atlantic economy before World War I confirms the well-known lesson of Ricardian trade theory: free trade benefits all societies with open markets. Within the narrow perspective of aggregate economic growth, Euro-American development unfolded just as Bacon's idols of trade suggested that it should: countries with liberal policies of economic openness enjoyed rapid aggregate growth. Within the global perspective, however, something deeper than static growth was happening: resource-based growth was shifting to knowledge-based growth. The same investigation of the same economic history "confirms that education was positively associated with growth and that [economic] convergence conditional on initial education is stronger than unconditional convergence."[36] As the Euro-American economies shifted in tandem, global migration and capital flows explained more than half of their growth and convergence. The effect of trade was positive but uniformly low. Despite intuition that expansion of knowledge should bring convergence, education contributed less to convergence than to divergence. "Good and bad schooling help explain convergence and divergence around the European periphery a century ago, but they help explain these patterns only in Scandinavia and Iberia, and in only one case, Iberia, do they explain very much."[37]

Although the simple accumulation and dissemination of knowledge —through technology transfer, general education, or focused training—clearly stimulates economic growth, it seems inadequate to expand prosperity beyond a national economy. As societies shift towards dynamic growth, something more than education itself is needed to converge their economies towards some vision of global, or even shared, prosperity. Although it seems a necessary precondition for knowledge-based, dynamic growth, education also seems less than sufficient for launching the social transformations that bring progress.

Unbounded Growth. In 1983, Paul Romer elaborated knowledge-based growth to four discrete factors of production—economic capital, unskilled labor, human capital, and intellectual capital—and the dynamic of investment. In a spiral of unbounded growth, capital investment elicits or generates new knowledge, which increases productivity, which reduces the risk of investment. Sustained investment can lead to sustained growth, with knowledge as the dynamic mediator between capital, labor, and output. The Romer model of knowledge-based growth incorporates global diffusion of knowledge into explanations of different growth rates in different countries: *ceteris paribus*, closed economies grow more slowly than open ones. It also predicts that lack of human capital (education, innovation, or intellectual freedom) could prevent growth even with heavy investment in physical and economic capital.[38]

Dynamic, knowledge-based growth in a context of capitalism may have been what Kenichi Ohmae and Thomas Friedman had in mind—but neglected to mention—in their descriptions of globalization.[39] In contrast to the self-interest that energizes static growth with an incentive to trade, the foundation of dynamic growth is diffusion of knowledge through education with an incentive to learn. Also increasing stocks of knowledge and intellectual capital through knowledge creation, dynamic growth enhances the functional or productive capacities of an individual, society, region, or the entire world. Dynamic growth is positive-sum, since it converts noneconomic factors and resources into economic products and profits, and since additional resources are newly created knowledge, not products from some other economy. In contrast to the finite limits on resource-based, static growth, which must ultimately end, dynamic growth has arisen from innovation and seems limited only by capacities of the human intellect to create new knowledge.

Transformations and Transition

Of more relevance than measurements of aggregate growth are the transformations of social reality that occur during modern economic growth. Each transformation can occur within a Braudelian *conjoncture* between social time and event time as the foundation for continuing innovation, knowledge conversion, and accumulation in incremental progress. Historically generated by knowledge creation in *basho*, these transformations, the order of their occurrence, and the ability of a society to manage them orchestrate the transition from static to dynamic growth:

> Two political transformations that (1) link politics responsively to domestic economic influences and (2) to global cultural and social forces; these transformations establish the domestic stability for rapid, static growth and introduce the specter of resource-based, interstate conflict;
>
> A social revolution that loosens traditional linkages between political status, social position, economic wealth, and personal attributes; this transformation establishes the linkages of knowledge with wealth and power that are the essential determinants of dynamic growth;
>
> A series of economic revolutions that (1) distribute productive labor across the entire population; (2) increase the intensities of capital and technology, and decrease that of labor, in an economy's production function; and (3) shift the intensity of production from physical resources to knowledge and intellectual capital; these transformations introduce the stimuli for domestic, civil conflict, reduce the threats of interstate war, and moderate interstate conflict into multilateral competition and cooperation.[40]

People observe resource-based growth and aggregate economic growth in event time in the context of current social reality and experience. Modern economic growth and the shift to knowledge-based growth occur in social time in the context of a series of transformations. Through the historicist lens, social time remains the basic time unit for MEG, although event time seems to compress as people accumulate knowledge and expand their perspectives.[41]

To generate rapid aggregate growth, several modernizing economies have pursued deliberate, unilateral growth strategies to compress the stages of MEG in a rapid shift from static growth to sustained dynamic growth. The most successful—Japan, South Korea, Taiwan, Malaysia, Thailand, and others—have combined FDI with other domestic efforts to expand the national knowledge base and stimulate indigenous innovation. Within the global perspective, however, such domestic efforts seem less critical for shifting to dynamic growth as globalization expands human knowledge and perspectives independently of policy. The double dynamics of FDI and globalization seem to reinforce each other in stimulating the shift towards dynamic growth and social transformation. For societies that can manage the necessary transformations of social reality and avoid their destructive effects, globalization may replace simplistic, unilateral growth strategies.

Nothing inherent in MEG, however, suggests that the transition from static to dynamic growth is inevitable or irreversible or that a society will accomplish these transformations smoothly, at all, or ever. Although resource-based industrialization seems to invite progress from static growth to knowledge-based dynamic growth, the transition includes human will, the possibility of alternative political decisions, and the intrusion of unpredictable social and cultural effects. Although globalization has forced social revolution on most of the world's societies, only about a third of the world's national economies have begun MEG. Fewer than half of these have linked knowledge with either wealth or power and begun to operate as knowledge-intensive economies. Fewer still of the world's polities have established the responsiveness to domestic forces that is the foundation for political legitimacy and stability. The global economy has not even entered MEG; none of these transformations have occurred in a global context. The pervasive reliance on resources for growth across the world's economies leaves most of the world's societies deeply vulnerable to interstate and civil conflicts over resources.

Dual Growth

Although static growth has usually preceded dynamic growth, both types have regularly occurred simultaneously within most economies during the transtion from resource-based to knowledge-based growth. Aggregate growth seems to involve brief periods of rapid, intense resource-based growth, sustained between and through those periods by incremental shifts towards dynamic growth. The shifts have occurred with enough consistency to form a reliable pattern of evolutionary growth and sociopolitical progress. The historically common pattern of aggregate growth reflects *both* static *and* dynamic factors of production, with knowledge and innovation gradually supplanting capital and labor as the foundations of sustained prosperity.

For most of history, dual economic growth has occurred with accumulation of knowledge in societies in various combinations of learning by doing and learning through innovation. Learning by doing seems to be a universal experience for all people in all epochs of the *longue durée* and within all perspectives. Brief spurts of knowledge-creation in *basho* punctuate the *longue durée* of continuous, slow, aggregate growth of *both* human prosperity *and* human knowledge and mark units of social time. These spurts of creativity have generally occurred within a narrow, functional perspective—natural science, religion, art, politics, or economics—and launched long periods of learning the implications and diffusing applications of newly created knowledge. Although the immediate contributions of new knowledge to aggregate growth have historically been minor, diffusion and application of that knowledge have incrementally shifted production functions towards knowledge-based growth. During these long periods, people have generated aggregate growth by improving old production methods through learning by doing and introducing new applications through entrepreneurial innovation, which often creates new knowledge. Rather than new knowledge directly, the gradual learning diffusing from bursts of creativity has been the primary engine of incremental progress and aggregate economic growth as dynamic growth gradually supplanted static growth.

Within a context of dual growth, resource-based growth across multiple industries and economic sectors remains the largest contributor to aggregate growth. Even in the world's most advanced economies and sophisticated societies, random, opportunistic learning by doing and gradual accumulation of knowledge through diffusion seem persistently associated with aggregate growth. Largely concentrated and focused within narrow perspectives or even proprietary, corporate contexts on local, immediate growth or profit, innovation may also be an indirect catalyst for sustained, aggregate growth.[42] Dual economic growth has stimulated the process of globalization through accumulation of knowledge—learning by doing—and incremental innovation, as growth has shifted from static towards dynamic and the economic returns to knowledge have increased. Within the global perspective, dual growth is an autogenous, reflexive part of the condition of globalization in *basho* and in the transition from resource-based to knowledge-based growth as the economic perspective expands. The essence of globalization as an eternal condition of human living seems concentrated in creating new knowledge continuously through learning and innovation, and most powerfully through *basho*.

KNOWLEDGE, TRADE, GROWTH, AND GLOBALIZATION

Orthodox trade theory and analysis did not include a significant role for knowledge, except incidentally as specialized, technical labor embodied in products, since economic agents had no way to appropriate the benefits of innovation.[43] Evolutionary trade analyses in a context of globalization either accord a central role to technology as a source for economies of scale or recognize knowledge and learning as essential resources of human capital that add value to either products or processes.[44] Beyond the value added to products by knowledge, intuition quickly suggests the importance of learning as a stimulant to international trade and economic globalization.[45] Learning by doing and learning through innovation tend to occur primarily within national or local contexts of dual growth.[46] Diffusion of knowledge within national contexts and across industries expands growth beyond the resource-based contributions of products' technological contents into a positive, significant impact on the trade balance. Expanding international trade across the export shares of several industries embodies a shift from resource-based increases in value to knowledge-based increases in trade volume. The deeper effect of knowledge diffusion is to stimulate progressive change and a shift to dynamic growth within an economy.

Intuition also suggests that international trade can be the basis for learning by interaction, which emerges through diffusion among suppliers, producers, and users. "Surely firms can learn from experience in other countries, though perhaps not as well as they can from other domestic firms."[47] Historical and economic analyses are, however, unclear about the effects of international technological linkages or diffusion of knowledge on either trade or growth.[48] "While domestic linkages appear to play a positive role on the trade balance in several sectors, this is not the case for foreign linkages. Foreign linkages or international spillovers seem to have no impact on the trade balance in most sectors." Domestic linkages and diffusion seem intuitively more important than international relationships for *both* the shift from static to dynamic growth *and* integration of the global economy through trade. Beyond speculation and polemic, however, "it is difficult to conclude whether international linkages just matter less or whether they do not matter at all."[49]

The implications of the relationships between trade, knowledge, and globalization suggest that domestic conditions for growth—the balance of static and dynamic growth and stage of MEG—matter. The ability and propensity of a society to expand learning by doing and by interaction into innovation and knowledge creation determine not only rates of economic growth but also patterns of trade. The prevalent role of domestic social relationships and technological linkages in forming trade patterns and balances suggests the critical importance of national elements in diffusing knowledge and exploiting it as technology.[50] A robust web of supplier-producer-user interactions is a critical stimulus to the transition from static to dynamic growth.

Globalization is a result, rather than a carrier, of economic growth and modernization. Economic integration and expanding trade seem to emerge as products of modern economic growth as a society transforms its indigenous growth from static to dynamic. The expansion of society's perspectives from internal learning through innovation to creating new knowledge within some domestic industrial revolution seems to be the economic stimulant for a country to globalize. Globalization begins within each individual country; it is not brought or imposed from outside. Without indigenous modern economic growth and a domestic stimulus for dynamic growth in the form of new knowledge, globalization—even with large flows and stocks of FDI—can only remain alien, possibly exploitative, and probably oppressive.

SHIFTING PATTERNS OF CONFLICT

A second critical pattern around dual growth is the relationship between economic growth and interstate conflict wherein the determinant is the type of growth. "Resource-based static growth associates high growth with high conflict, and low growth with low conflict, in a direct-positive relationship. Knowledge-based dynamic growth associates high growth with low conflict, and low growth with high conflict, in an inverse-negative relationship."[51] The relationship between static and dynamic growth in growing economies implies the country's propensity for interstate conflict. Globalization and contagion have transformed this dual relationship between conflict and growth into a contagious mutant that infects not only interstate conflict but also intrastate civil war. Although globalization and economic interdependence seem to have enervated traditional economic and cultural immunities, each society's type of growth—static, dynamic, or dual—determines its susceptibility.

Traditional Interstate War

As globalization introduced more economies to modern resource-based economic growth, market-based competition for resources and interstate struggles for power deepened and intensified. In an industrial context of rising political expectations of sustained economic growth, the demands for ever more material resources translated uneven growth into interstate tensions and domestic social stress. Constrained by the threat of escalation to catastrophic, nuclear war, the power politics of international relations, with its batteries of realist and liberal control mechanisms, suppressed interstate conflict reasonably well. Globalization and interdependence adjusted war to the realities of the global economy but have done little to replace interstate conflict as an efficient relief for the social stresses that they generate.

A half century of aggregate, global growth built on U.S. knowledge-based economic performance seems to offer an alternative to interstate war. The U.S. experience suggests the novel "possibility for states to avoid inevitable decline by promoting those investments that provide the underlying conditions for [continuing] national innovation. . . . education, research, and infrastructure."[52] These actions, which are functions of *domestic* politics without foreign involvement, stimulate a shift from static, resource-based growth to knowledge-based, dynamic growth. The U.S. dominance of the world's investments in these drivers of globalization—innovation, technology, education, human capital—seems to present a new sort of unipolar, knowledge-based capitalism that avoids the repetitive cycles of multipolarity, hegemony, and interstate war. Although U.S. unipolarity is not coercive, the fundamental imperative of the common good, which Americans claim to respect, limits state actions through imposing a moral and economic prohibition on interstate war.

Intrastate Civil War

Globalization has exposed the social stress, which is often the source of war and conflict, not "as an exogenous force that acts on states and societies from without; it derives rather from within them."[53] "Although the interdependence resulting from globalization appears to have reduced the occurrences of interstate conflict, we are seeing increased fragmentation in the less affluent nations, with intrastate conflict [increasing]. There remain large discrepancies in wealth and growth between and within nations, which act as potential sources of instability and catalysts for conflict."[54] The variations in rates of static, resource-based growth, not surprisingly, have generated conflict *both* among *and* within societies as globalization emphasized differences across political borders. Since international politics has no effective control mechanisms to resolve internal conflicts, such conflicts often generate the brutal civil wars that invite foreign military and political intervention.

Global Civil War

The end of the Cold War brought few changes in global governance, rates of growth, balances of power, or distribution of wealth. Neither did it relax "other sources of tension and conflict often based on need or greed. . . . Poverty is rife and the divisions between the haves and the have-nots are all too plain to see. The trends of globalization and fragmentation are exacerbated by the worsening inequalities of wealth, and the poorer countries are being increasingly marginalized in world affairs."[55] The dominance of geostrategic and political concerns delayed and contained any relief for the accumulating socioeconomic stresses in every society. Its end did, however, accelerate the processes of economic integration and diffusion of power towards a global civil war "fought among competing groups for authority in and over an administrative or political unit, in this instance the global village. . . . The struggle will be between the haves and the have-nots, between relatively privileged and those who perceive themselves to be underprivileged. It will be a war about the rule of law, about justice, about human rights and individual freedoms—concepts [that] are neither universally accepted nor . . . altogether objective in content. It will, also, inevitably be about wealth and power."[56]

In some contrast to *both* the interstate wars *and* the national civil wars of modernity, the engine of the global civil war is less political than economic. Stimulated by quarrels over food, water, resources, and the environment, many societies have been nurturing resentment over their respective shares of the relevant economic and political results of globalization—wealth and power. Focusing resentment into a deep hostility, the global information revolution has made it impossible for those excluded from globalization to ignore the prosperity of others. Although the immediate targets are often their own tainted regimes, often the excluded perceive those regimes as clients sustained in power and supported in wealth by capitalist Europe and the United States.

Within the global perspective of an economic, global civil war, the dichotomies across *both* types *and* rates of growth become critical determinants of peace and prosperity. As poor economies rely more on high resource-based, static growth to launch modern economic growth, they become susceptible to the historic, direct relationship between static growth and conflict. The slow shift towards dynamic, knowledge-based growth exposes prosperous societies to the constraining burdens of new investment in information technologies on aggregate growth rates. Exposing both rich and poor to growth-based conflict, these historic patterns of dual growth converge in global civil war as globalization deepens and broadens the economic gulf between them.

The common, economic wisdom of globalization prescribes deeper and broader integration to utilize resources effectively, share burdens, shift sacrifices, and focus strategic effort in fighting the global civil war. Deepening resentment and anger, however, suggest that "tighter integration among the prosperous societies of the primarily Christian West is bound to exacerbate the sense of division in the world. . . . It is an illusion to say that [the] current prosperity [of the rich countries] can, in decades to come, simply be extended to include the currently dispossessed." Although expanding global markets will create much new wealth, it will be concentrated in the already rich economies. Since a long global civil war will neither expand prosperity nor dissipate global inequality, "the impatience of the poor can only increase. It is hard to see how [the rich] can evade the need for a significant transfer of wealth from the developed to the underdeveloped world. . . . something very different from overseas aid and a good deal more painful for the donors."[57]

Although transfer of wealth through foreign aid, charity, humanitarian assistance, or investment brings donors good feelings, to many recipients loans and gifts represent "not the compassion and generosity of the West, but rather its imperialistic or paternalistic tendencies. Moreover, the aid provided is sometimes so meager that it is seen as an insult. . . . Aid agencies represent the lack of will of Western governments to intervene in a more constructive and decisive way. . . as part of a duplicitous and uncaring international system."[58]

The Growth–Conflict Relationship

The insulated, resource-based growth of the industrializing European economies and the direct growth–conflict relationship that it embodied are no longer necessary, clearly impractical, and probably not possible.[59] In contrast to visions of market-based economic integration around the law of one price, global social reality exposes a complex collection of national economies struggling between interdependence and self-sufficiency. Instead of spreading peace and prosperity, globalization seems to nurture resentments that generate conflicts and fragment growth as predicted by historic patterns of dual growth. "The lowering of various barriers celebrated by [Thomas] Friedman, especially the spread of global media, makes it possible for the most deprived or oppressed to compare their fate with that of the free and well-off. These dispossesssed then ask for help from others with common resentments, ethnic origin, or religious faith. Insofar as globalization enriches some and uproots many, those who are both poor and uprooted may seek revenge and self-esteem in terrorism."[60] The visible contradictions to the Enlightenment image of globalization—misery, injustice, humiliation, cultural pride, aspiration to more than prosperity—provoke resistance, revolt, and social conflict.

Even, however, as economic integration makes countries vulnerable to exogenous stresses and shocks, globalization expands political will and people's determination to manage crises. Despite any resilience to external economic shocks, however, globalization tends not only to create indigenous social stresses but also to diffuse the stresses of other interdependent countries. Through the interdependence of economic integration, these social stresses are virulently contagious within triggering zones and shadows that conform closely to those of civil wars, political conflict, and cultural tensions. The same contagious, stress-triggering dynamic that has nourished political contagion has intensified and amplified the effects of economic growth. In adapting to the global political-economy and its knowledge-based institutions, the growth–conflict relationship has mutated into a powerful carrier of *both* growth *and* conflict *and also* the relationship between them. Economic integration seems to have developed the dual growth-conflict relationship (GCR) into a politically contagious mutant that infects not only interstate conflict but also intrastate conflict and any nascent global civil war.

Instead of isolated and random, economic growth is contagiously interactive across societies. A mutant of the dual growth–conflict relationship spreads *both* growth *and* conflict. Maintaining the same distinction between static and dynamic growth, the mutated relationship expands their dramatically different effects through contagion. Since conflict has traditionally relieved the stresses of resource-based growth, the mutant GCR activates static-growth triggering within a stress triggering zone of political-economic interdependence. Because transformation of social reality has more often relieved those social stresses generated by knowledge-based growth, dynamic growth casts a growth shadow over a different set of interdependent economies.

Growth Triggering

The congruity of political and economic triggering zones and the close relationships between political tension and economic inequality in a context of globalization suggest the virulence of this mutated growth–conflict relationship. Globalization diffuses *both* social stresses *and* resource-based growth into other societies through political contagion, economic interdependence, and cultural convergence. Within triggering zones of interdependent economies, *either* resource-based growth *or* conflict might relieve at least some of the domestic social stresses that globalization gradually concentrates within economic, political, or cultural perspectives.

Since the international system does not tolerate interstate conflict, the stresses of static growth can find relief only in sustained growth, intrastate civil war beyond the controls of international politics, or in contagious diffusion within a triggering zone. Resource-based growth can continue only so long as domestic resources augmented by trade, foreign investment, and foreign aid increase. When flows of foreign resources fail to sustain growth, contagious diffusion becomes the only relief. Cultural idiosyncracies and unique resource dependencies quickly expand subtle stresses in one society into cataclysmic pressures for growth in another. While relieving domestic social stress, contagious triggering by resource-based growth in one economy can explode trivial market adjustments into the triggers of civil war elsewhere in the trigger zone. The contagion inherent in resource-based growth triggering across distinctive cultures suggests *that the probability of consequent, related conflict or growth spread through interdependence can change abruptly and drastically.*

Growth Shadows

Although diffusing the stress of resource-based growth increases the probabilities of conflict or growth in some interdependent societies, the same relationship also generates sympathetic reductions of social stress in other, also interdependent societies. Transformation of domestic social reality not only relieves internal stress and increases stress in other resource-based economies within some stress-triggering zone but also relieves stress within some stress shadow. Since globalization diffuses knowledge so much more readily than resources, the mutant growth–conflict relationship reinforces knowledge flows through learning, technology transfer, and even conversations between *basho*. A shift towards knowledge-based growth in one economy actively generates a parallel shift within some growth shadow. These contagion-induced social transformations in shadowed societies seem to be, like all knowledge-based growth, self-sustaining, and actively relieve social stresses. The mutated growth–conflict relationship seems to strengthen the contagion of knowledge-based growth, rather than simply relieving social stresses and discouraging conflict. The globalized result of knowledge-based, dynamic growth is "a powerful inverse relationship between growth and conflict, and the splendid paradox that the source of high economic growth and general prosperity may be the same as the source of low international conflict and relative peace."[61]

Growth Fatigue

Whereas stress fatigue in political triggering zones and shadows ensures that stress rates diminish over time, growth shadows stimulate the same type of growth that originates them. Sympathetic, resource-based growth in triggering zones can continue in Solow's steady state so long as the host economy—or the international economy—provides additional resources. Knowledge-based growth in shadow zones, however, escapes from the Solow model and can continue at rates that need not diminish with time. Not limited by either globalization or interdependence, shadowed economies infected by knowledge-based growth can sustain *both* growth *and* social transformation at rates set within the society. In *both* parent *and* triggered societies, the rate of resource-based growth immediately falls but gradually recovers as each economy adjusts its resources flows to the growth of its labor force. Although parent dynamic-growth societies need not lose the momentum of knowledge-based growth, like triggered societies, shadowed economies experience a brief fall in aggregate growth rates. As incremental innovation and diffusion of new knowledge permeate the society with new values and attitudes, growth accelerates. Although globalization and interdependence determine the patterns of triggering and shadowing, it is the type of growth that determines duration, extent, and effects of stress fatigue.

Assault on Orthodoxy

The virulent, globalized relationship between growth and conflict is inconsistent with the monistic level-of-analysis principle beneath classical realism's systemic anarchy. The dual influences of the type of growth through triggering and shadowing on conflict and the power of foreign direct investment to carry knowledge-based globalization compromise any realist notion of monistic causality.[62] Neither do trigger and shadow zones fit smoothly into the materialistic or revolutionary corners of Marxism-Leninism. Not inconsistent with liberal dedication to democratic peace and free trade as antidotes to conflict, stress triggering suggests that resource-based trade and globalization are neither ideal nor complete as remedies or prescriptions.

The abilities of societies to choose their growth paths by changing their social institutions and structures destroy the inevitability of technological globalization, the determinism of mercantilism, and the spontaneity of self-determination. Contagion of disjunct growth through stress triggering and shadowing subtly refines the nondeterminism of interdependence into identifiable pressures of globalization. Through politically willed action to transform social reality, societies can deflect, absorb, or resist globalization.[63] "States can choose their paths for political-economic development, balance costs and benefits, violate the law of uneven growth, and choose between the logic of the trading state and the imperatives of the territorial state."[64]

GLOBAL POLITICAL-ECONOMY

The twentieth-century waves of globalization have begun to restructure a global political-economy around "new players, new capabilities, and new alignments—but no new rules."[65] The expansion of people's perspectives through knowledge-based globalization has begun to merge the economic and political perspectives into a hyphenated, global, political-economic perspective. As states become more aggressive in manipulating economic processes in seeking growth, companies and nongovernments become adept at influencing political processes in their search for power.

Institutions

Although in the context of the Westphalian power-based political system the fundamental institutional structures embodied the sovereign state and intergovernmental organizations, the global political-economy has expanded to embrace additional institutions. Converging politics with the neoclassical capitalist economic system, the 1970s wave of globalization, interdependence, and privatization confirmed the transnational enterprise as a legitimate global institution concentrating resources and wealth. Despite government resistance to their penetration into politics, these huge concentrations of economic power, with their powerful dynamics of FDI and intrafirm trading, are *de facto* prominent influences on the global political-economy.[66] In the global political-economy, *both* sovereign national states *and* transnational enterprises have and exercise political and economic power. The twentieth century introduced the nongovernmental organization as a legitimate global institution that focuses popular power, distinct from *both* political power *and* economic wealth.

States remain the dominant political-military institutions and provide a stable legal structure for the global economy and remain the focus of national security. "Despite globalization and transgovernmentalism, . . . the nation-state preserves a monopoly on the legitimate use of force."[67] Resisting the pressures of economic globalization to make borders more porous, people seem unready to eliminate states completely and remain ready to defend them with military power and force. Neither has globalization changed the aims and practice of interstate diplomacy or the institutional foundations—military and police operations, legislation and adjudication, or social welfare—of the state. Within an emerging context of additional institutions and their processes—the *nébuleuse*—the international political system remains a system of states, whereas the global political-economy is not a system of only states.

Power

The progress of economies into and through MEG over the last two centuries has irreversibly transformed the nature of power. As physical resources lose salience as stores of value, information, knowledge, and human skills become *both* sources of power *and* indicators of wealth. The balance of power between the state and the market has shifted relentlessly towards the market.[68] Persistent intrusions of commerce, economics, and popular priorities for prosperity into traditional models of political-military high politics have recast national power as a political-economic attribute exercised by *both* firms *and* governments. Through transnational firms, FDI, interpersonal communication, and intercultural exchanges, globalization has redefined power resources and redistributed power. By disjoining the process of economic growth, globalization has spread it contagiously to the entire world in the company of interethnic conflicts and civil wars.

With the 1990s surge of privatization and deregulation and mutation of the growth–conflict relationship, government spending is no longer the primary stimulus for growth. Neither are large companies the focus for technical innovation. Rather than stripping governments of sovereignty, however, globalization has confirmed that states have never had the powers that global markets seem to be exercising. Operating through governments, markets, companies, and people, knowledge-based capitalism has become the source and structure for economic growth and the engine of social progress.

Foreign Direct Investment

Within the global perspective, the special importance of FDI is implicit in the disjunction of modern economic growth and complex interdependence. Not only does FDI carry the power to accelerate the transition from static to dynamic growth, but it can shift the results of the mutated growth–conflict relationship from triggered conflict to shadowed growth. Globalization increases the opportunities for governments to attract FDI and reduces the costs of hosting investors. Conversely, the intensely competitive global market penalizes countries for failing to provide investment opportunities for domestic funds. Although many governments include this dichotomy as a high priority in policymaking, paradoxically, most investment is still financed from domestic savings and single economic units—local companies, funds, or personal wealth.

Globalization, whether as a process or as a condition, reinforces FDI in all that it does, *both* within *and* beyond the narrow economic perspective with its focus on aggregate growth. The alliance of FDI and globalization may even be able to force Bacon's idols to release humanity from the current obsession with trade and resource-based growth to pursue its own destiny into knowledge-based progress within the global perspective.

Growth Is Not Enough

The triumph of trade-based globalization and resource-based growth in a global economy seemed to confirm that "adherence to the principles of free enterprise offers the most efficient means for generating wealth."[69] For most of the world's peoples, however, imbalances in the distribution of resource-based wealth have obscured aggregate global growth beneath the social stresses of economic inequality. Despite—or, perhaps, because of—the intolerance of international politics for interstate conflict, people have continued their resource-based, political struggles with each other within and beyond their states in related forms of intrastate and global civil war.

The additional institution—transnational enterprise—of the global political-economy and its knowledge-based dynamic—FDI—have poised humanity for global take-off into modern economic growth. People's effectiveness in creating, managing, and sustaining flows of FDI, trade, capital, people, and knowledge will energize any global shift from resource-based to knowledge-based growth. Knowledge-based capitalism *within effective global governance* may be even more critical than traditional balances of political-military power in achieving and sustaining acceptable levels of peace and prosperity. Whereas the several waves of modern globalization have loosely spread the effects of resource-based growth to all peoples of the world, globalization of dynamic growth presents the real possibility of *both* global security *and* human prosperity, *both* olive trees *and* a Lexus.

NOTES

1. Joseph E. Stiglitz, *Globalization and Its Discontents* (New York: Norton, 2002), 4.

2. Michael Pettis, "Will Globalization Go Bankrupt?" *Foreign Policy* (October 2001): 52–59; 52.

3. Barry Eichengreen, "One Economy, Ready or Not: Thomas Friedman's Jaunt through Globalization," reviewing *The Lexus and the Olive Tree*, by Thomas L. Friedman (New York: Farrar, Straus, and Giroux, 1999), *Foreign Affairs* 78(3) (May-June 1999): 118–122; 120.

4. See Martin Wolf, "Will the Nation-State Survive Globalization?" *Foreign Affairs* 80(1) (January-February 2001): 178–190; 178.

5. Geoffrey Garrett, "The Causes of Globalization," *Comparative Political Studies* 33(6–7) (August-September 2000): 941–991; 949–954. See also Dani Rodrik, "How Far Will International Economic Integration Go?" *Journal of Economic Perspectives* 14(1) (Winter 2000): 177–186; 178–180; Robert Wade, "Globalization and Its Limits," in *National Diversity and Globalization*, edited by Suzanne Berger and Robert Dore, 60–88 (Ithaca: Cornell University Press, 1996), 76–78, 85–88; J. Michael Finger, Merlinda D. Ingco, and Ulrich Reinecke, *The Uruguay Round, Statistics on Tariff Concessions Given and Received* (Washington, D.C.: World Bank, 1996), 67.

6. Walt Whitman Rostow, "The Marshallian Long Period," in *Pioneers in Development* edited by Gerald M. Meier and Dudley Seers, 227–261 (Washington, D.C.: Oxford University Press for the World Bank, 1984), 253–254. The first Kondratieff cycle spanned the first Industrial Revolution in the eighteenth century. The second opened the American West in the nineteenth century, and the third opened Canada, Australia, Argentina, and Ukraine before World War I. The fourth cycle opened Middle Eastern oil to production as the global economy developed into the automobile and airplane ages in the twentieth century. The current, fifth Kondratieff cycle began in the 1970s with the information revolution.

7. For three patterns with similar predictions of rising social stresses as the prelude to major social transformation, see Craig N. Murphy, *International Organization and Industrial Change: Global Governance since 1850* (Cambridge: Polity, 1994), 26–45; Antonio Gramsci, *Selections from the Prison Notebooks of Antonio Gramsci*, edited and translated by Quintin Hoare and Geoffrey Nowell Smith (New York: International, 1971), 158–175, 242–245, 275–276; Karl Polanyi, *The Great Transformation: The Political and Economic Origins of Our Time* (New York: Rinehart, 1944).

8. Craig Murphy, "Globalization and Governance: A Historical Perspective," in *Globalization and Europe*, edited by Roland Axtmann, 144–163 (London: Pinter, 1998), 145.

9. See Lloyd G. Reynolds, *Economic Growth in the Third World: 1950–1980* (New Haven: Yale University Press, 1985).

10. See Giovanni Arrighi and Jessica Drangel,"The Stratification of the World Economy: An Exploration of the Semiperipheral Zone," in *Review, Volume 10*, edited by James O. Hoge, 9–74 (Charlottesville: University Press of Virginia), 55–56; Gary Gereffi, "Paths of Industrialization: An Overview," in *Manufacturing Miracles: Paths of Industrialization in Latin America and East Asia*, edited by Gary Gereffi and Donald L. Wyman, 3–31 (Princeton: Princeton University Press, 1990), 8–9; World Bank, *World Development Report 1989* (New York: Oxford University Press, 1989), 148–150.

11. James H. Mittelman, "The Dynamics of Globalization," in *Globalization: Critical Reflections, International Political Economy Yearbook, Vol. 9*, edited by James H. Mittelman, 1-19 (Boulder, Colorado: Lynne Rienner, 1996), 4.

12. See Andrew Pollack, "Technology without Borders Raises Big Questions for the U.S." *New York Times* 1 January 1992, p. 1, 48.

13. Ratna Sudarshan and Jeemol Unni, "When Home-Based Workers Raise Their Voices: An Indian Perspective," *SAIS Review* 21(1) (Winter-Spring 2001): 109-115; 112.

14. Peter F. Drucker, "The Global Economy and the Nation-State," *Foreign Affairs* 76(5) (September-October 1997): 159-171; 166,

15. See Karl Polanyi, *The Great Transformation: The Political and Economic Origins of Our Time* (Boston: Beacon Press, [1944] 1957), 73.

16. Drucker, "The Global Economy and the Nation-State," 166.

17. See David S. Landes, *The Unbound Prometheus: Technological Change and Industrial Development in Western Europe from 1750 to the Present* (London: Cambridge University Press, 1969), 41-43; Maxine Berg, *The Age of Manufacturers: 1700-1820* (New York: Oxford University Press, 1985), 23-24.

18. J. Stanley Metcalfe, "Technology Policy in an Evolutionary World," paper presented at the second International Conference on Science and Technology Policy Research of the National Institute of Science and Technology Policy (24-26 January 1991: Oiso, Japan) *What Should Be Done? What Can Be Done? Science and Technology Policy Research: The Proceedings of the NISTEP Second International Conference on Science and Technology*, edited by Sogo Okamura, Kenichi Marakami, and Ikujiro Nonaka (Tokyo: Mita Press, 1991), 109-121; 109.

19. Drucker, "The Global Economy and the Nation-State," 166.

20. "Thanksgiving for Innovation," *The Economist Technology Quarterly*, inserted between pages 50 and 51, in *The Economist* 364(8291) (21 September 2002): 13-14; 13.

21. This section refines and draws heavily on the concepts that I introduced in my earlier book: William H. Mott IV, *The Economic Basis of Peace: Linkages between Economic Growth and International Conflict* (Westport: Greenwood, 1997), ch. 4, 107-170 and ch. 5, 171-192.

22. Mott, *The Economic Basis of Peace*, 116.

23. See Moses Abramovitz, "Resource and Output Trends in the United States since 1870," *Occasional Paper 52* (New York: National Bureau of Economic Research, 1956); Robert M. Solow, "Technical Change and the Aggregate Production Function." *Review of Economics and Statistics* 39 (August 1957): 312-320; Odd Aukrust and Juul Bjerke, "Real Capital and Economic Growth in Norway, 1900-56," in *The Measurement of National Wealth*, International Association for Research in Income and Wealth, Income and Wealth, Series VIII, edited by Raymond Goldsmith and Christopher Saunders, 80-118 (Chicago: Quadrangle Books, 1959); Edward F. Denison, *The Sources of Economic Growth in the United States and the Alternatives Before Us*, CED Supplementary Paper No. 13 (New York: Council on Economic Development, 1960); John W. Kendrick, *Productivity Trends in the United States* (Princeton, New Jersey: National Bureau of Economic Research, 1961); World Bank, *The East Asian Miracle* (New York: Oxford University Press, 1993). But see also Angus Maddison, *Economic Growth in the West* (New York: Twentieth Century Fund, 1964) for a dissenting view. Maddison (p. 88) suggests that "in modern conditions there cannot be widely varying degrees of technical advance due to differences in technical knowledge." Variations in growth are due to more or less capital per employee and differing age structure of capital. In analyzing the

period 1870-1933, when U.S. advantage was in superior natural resources and rapid population growth, Maddison (pp. 88-90) argues that from about 1913, European investment was reduced due to World War I and its consequences. Variations in growth occurred because assets have a longer life where relative labor costs are rising more slowly. Differences in European and American growth were determined by macroeconomic circumstances affecting entrepreneurial attitudes toward risk and reinforced by the momentum of the economy. Government policy was primarily responsible for setting this momentum.

24. Simon Kuznets, *Modern Economic Growth* (New Haven: Yale University Press, 1966), 498.

25. Hollis B. Chenery, Sherman Robinson, and Moshe Syrquin, *Industrialization and Growth* (New York: Oxford University Press, 1986), 13. See also Simon Kuznets, "Findings and Questions," in *Postwar Economic Growth: Four Lectures, Simon Kuznets* (Cambridge: Belknap Press of Harvard University Press, 1964), 120.

26. Kevin H. O'Rourke and Jeffrey G. Williamson, *Globalization and History: The Evolution of a Nineteenth-Century Atlantic Economy* (Cambridge: MIT Press, 1999), 283. Robert Solow developed a model of growth in potential economic output around varying combinations of capital and labor based on a constant marginal propensity to save and an exponential growth rate of the labor force. Solow's model predicts steady-state growth with a fixed production function and increasing growth with improving technology. Alpha C. Chiang , *Fundamental Methods of Mathematical Economics*, 3d ed. (New York: McGraw-Hill, 1984), 496-500.

27. Mott, *The Economic Basis of Peace*), 195.

28. See Simon Kuznets, "Findings and Questions," in *Postwar Economic Growth: Four Lectures, Simon Kuznets* (Cambridge, Massachusetts: Belknap Press of Harvard University Press, 1964), 109. Although Kuznets recognized the ability of innovation to accelerate growth, it was only in the 1980s that the concept of decomposition of growth into resource-based and knowledge-based components emerged. Rosenberg and Birdzell differentiated between "growth associated with an expansion of trade and economic resources and economic growth primarily attributable to innovation." Nathan Rosenberg and Luther E. Birdzell, *How the West Grew Rich* (New York: Basic Books, 1986), 328.

29. William H. Mott IV, *The Economic Basis of Peace: Linkages between Economic Growth and International Conflict* (Westport: Greenwood, 1997), 179.

30. See Ronald Findlay, "Relative Backwardness, Foreign Direct Investment, and the Transfer of Technology," *Quarterly Journal of Economics* 92(1) (February 1978): 1-16; 5-6, 13-15; and Eduardo Borenzstein, Jose De Gregario, and Jong-Wha Lee,"How Does Foreign Direct Investment Affect Economic Growth?" *Journal of International Economics* 45(1) (June 1998): 115-135; 116, 124-128, 134.

31. See World Trade Organization, *Annual Report: 1996* (Geneva, Switzerland: World Trade Organization, 1996), 53-55.

32. See Garrett, "The Causes of Globalization," 952-953.

33. Garrett, "The Causes of Globalization," 960, 966.

34. Paul Geroski and Mariana Mazzucato, "Learning and the Sources of Corporate Growth," *Industrial and Corporate Change* 11(4) (August 2002): 623-644; 630.

35. Herbert A. Simon, "Forecasting the Future or Shaping It?" *Industrial and Corporate Change* 11(3) (June 2002): 601-605; 602.

36. O'Rourke and Williamson *Globalization and History*, 272. For a summary of the orthodox interpretation of this study focused on aggregate growth and lessons to be learned, see Robert S. Chase, "The More Things Change . . .; Learning from Other Eras of 'Unprecedented' Globalization," *SAIS Review* 20(2) (Summer-Fall 2000): 223–229; 225–226.

37. O'Rourke and Williamson *Globalization and History*, 273.

38. See Paul Romer, "Endogenous Technical Change," *Journal of Political Economy* 98 (1990): S71-S102; Paul Romer, *Are Nonconvexities Important for Understanding Growth?* (Cambridge, Massachusetts: National Bureau of Economic Research, 1990). Refinement of Romer's theory suggests that the rate of growth of knowledge is a critical determinant of an economy's growth rate. Where population growth is faster than growth of knowledge, demands for consumption, energy, and resources increase apace population, but enhancements to national capacities to meet demand are constrained by lagging knowledge. Such an economy must rely on increasing its material factors of production through exploration, conquest, trade, economies of scale, or fiscal policy to meet demand. When knowledge expands faster than population, enhancements to national capacities proliferate, availabilities of resources, energy, and goods for consumption increase beyond the demands of society. Increases in productivity through invention, innovation, automation, or rationalization increase the aggregate and *per capita* wealth of society.

39. See Robert Gilpin, *The Political Economy of International Relations* (Princeton, New Jersey: Princeton University Press, 1987); Rosenberg and Birdzell, *How the West Grew Rich*; Kenichi Ohmae, *The Borderless World* (New York: HarperCollins, 1990), 30-31 and ch. 8; Friedman, *The Lexus and the Olive Tree*, 8–9.

40. In Europe the political, social, and first economic revolutions occurred over the seventeenth, eighteenth and nineteenth centuries; the second economic revolution occurred as the Industrial Revolution in the nineteenth century; and the third economic revolution began in the last half of the twentieth century. In North America, these same transformations began a few generations later but proceeded faster. Uncolonized Asia (Japan, Thailand, and China) began even later and suffered several major interruptions. Colonial Asia, Africa, and Latin America were powerfully focused in their beginnings of growth by their various metropoles (Britain, France, Netherlands, Belgium, Portugal, and the United States), and have stalled or accelerated accordingly. See Rudolf von Albertini, *Decolonization: The Administration and Future of the Colonies, 1919-1960* (London: Holmes and Meier, 1982), for lucid discussions of their respective fates without the expected burden of polemic.

41. It is easy to forget that annual growth of 0.8% was seen as virtually impossible in the seventeenth century. Historical comparisons suggest that countries that began modern economic growth in the presence of other countries that had already grown have grown faster than their predecessors. The first country to experience MEG, Britain shifted toward dynamic growth over more than two centuries. After a century of annual growth at about 0.3%, from 1780 Britain took 58 years to double real income *per capita* and led the Industrial Revolution (1830-1910) with annual growth of about 1.2%. In 1820, as the United States was entering MEG before industrial expansion, GDP *per capita* in the United States was about three-quarters that of Britain. Annual growth of the American economy from 1830 to 1910 was about 1.6% (GDP grew at 4.2%, but population also grew rapidly). From 1839 the United States took only 39 years to double income *per capita* at about 1.8% annually and by the 1890s was the

world's richest country. After the Meiji reforms, from 1885, with increasing influences from the advanced countries of the time, Japan took 34 years to double GDP *per capita* at an annual rate of about 2%. From 1966 South Korea, with deliberate solicitation of FDI, took 11 years to double GDP *per capita* at about 6.3% annual growth.

42. These suggestions differ to the point of contradiction with the conventional wisdom about corporate and national economic growth, which argues that innovation is the primary driver of economic growth. Research and investigation into the aggregate effects of changing mixes of static and dynamic growth and into the different results of learning by doing and innovation are at best shallow, narrow, unsophisticated, and controversial. At worst, they are flawed, ill specified, and even wrong. "It is possible to be slightly uneasy about using annual growth rates to assess performance, and it is possible that their relatively high volatility might contain an unusually large number of measurement errors or reflect the effects of noisy events (like strikes)." Geroski and Mazzucato, "Learning and the Sources of Corporate Growth," 641.

43. See Bertil G. Ohlin, *Interregional and International Trade* (Cambridge: Harvard University Press, 1933), 84–86, 517–520; Ronald W. Jones, "The Structure of Simple General Equilibrium Models," *Journal of Political Economy* 73(6) (December 1965): 557–572; 558–559, 567–572.

44. Paul R. Krugman, "The Narrow Moving Band, the Dutch Disease, and the Competitive Consequences of Mrs. Thatcher: Notes on Trade in the Presence of Dynamic Scale Economies," *Journal of Development Economics* 27(1–2) (October 1987): 41–55; 43–44; Gene M. Grossman and Elhanan Helpman, *Innovation and Growth in the Global Economy* (Cambridge: MIT Press, 1991), 6–18, 122–130, 336–342.

45. See Michael V. Posner, "International Trade and Technological Exchange," *Oxford Economic Papers* 13(3) (October 1961): 323–341; 325, 334–337; Gary C. Hufbauer, "The Impact of National Characteristics and Technology on the Commodity Composition of Trade in Manufactured Goods," in *The Technology Factor in International Trade*, edited by Raymond Vernon, 145–231 (New York: Columbia University Press, 1970), 172–176, 184–189, 193–197.

46. See Staffan B. Linder, *An Essay on Trade and Transformation* (Stockholm: Almqvist and Wiksell, 1961), 88–90.

47. Krugman, "The Narrow Moving Band," 43.

48. Some analyses find that the effects of domestic innovation and international technology diffusion are broadly substitutable determinants of total factor productivity and growth: Jonathan Eaton and Samuel Kortum, "Trade in Ideas: Patenting and Productivity in the OECD," *Journal of International Economics* 40(3–4) (May 1996): 251–278; 270–276; Eaton and Kortum, "Engines of Growth: Domestic and Foreign Sources of Innovations," *Japan and the World Economy* 9(2) (May 1997): 235–259; 236–238, 254; Bart Verspagen, "Estimating International Technology Spillovers Using Technology Flow Matrices," *Weltwirtschaftliches Archiv* 133(2) (June 1997): 226–248; 242–246; Rakesh Basant and Brian Fikkert, "The Effects of R&D, Foreign Technology Purchase, and Domestic and International Spillovers on Productivity in Indian Firms," *Review of Economics and Statistics* 78(2) (May 1996): 187–199; 187–188, 196–197; and David T. Coe and Elhanan Helpman, "International R&D Spillovers," *European Economic Review* 39(5) (May 1995), 859–887; 871–875. Other analyses find potent trade-related international spillovers of technology: Hans-Jürgen Engelbrecht, "International R&D Spillovers, Human Capital, and Productivity in OECD Economies: An Empirical Investigation," *European Economic Review* 41(8) (August 1997), 1479–1488; 1484–1487;

Frank R. Lichtenberg and Bruno van Pottelsberghe de la Potterie, "International R&D Spillovers: A Comment," *European Economic Review* 42(8) (September 1998), 1483–1491; 1487–1490. Yet other studies conclude that foreign linkages stimulate trade less than domestic ones: Maury Gittleman and Edward N. Wolff, "R&D Activity and Cross-Country Growth Comparisons," *Cambridge Journal of Economics* 19(1) (February 1995): 189–207; 203–205.

49. Keld Laursen and Valentina Meliciani, "The Relative Importance of International *vis-à-vis* National Technological Spillovers for Market Share Dynamics," *Industrial and Corporate Change* 11(4) (August 2002) 875–894; 888, 889. See also Keld Laursen and Valentina Meliciani, "The Importance of Technology-Based Intersectoral Linkages for Market Share Dynamics," *Weltwirtschaftliches Archiv* 136(4) (December 2000): 702–723; 715–719.

50. Still perceived by orthodox trade and growth theory as an anomolous special case, this suggestion is congealing into the foundations of evolutionary theories of trade and growth. See Richard R. Nelson and Sidney G. Winter, *An Evolutionary Theory of Economic Change* (Cambridge: Harvard University Press, 1982), 231–233, 262–272, 400–404.

51. Mott, *The Economic Basis of Peace*, 194.

52. Ethan B. Kapstein, "Does Unipolarity Have a Future?" in *Unipolar Politics: Realism and State Strategies After the Cold War*, edited by Ethan B. Kapstein and Michael Mastanduno, 464–490 (New York: Columbia University Press, 1999), 483. This possibility is an expansion of Raymond Vernon's product-cycle theory to global politics. See Raymond Vernon, "International Investment and International Trade in the Product Cycle," *Quarterly Journal of Economics* 80 (1966): 190–207.

53. Bruce F. Porter, *War and the Rise of the State* (New York: Free Press, 1994), 3.

54. Glenn L. Torpy, "Future British Operations," *Royal United Services Institute Journal* 146(1) (February 2001): 8–12; 8.

55. Charles Guthrie, "British Defence—The Chief Of Defense Staff's Lecture, 2000—," *Royal United Services Institute Journal* 146(1) (February 2001): 1–7; 1–2.

56. Michael Alexander, "A Global Civil War," *RUSI Journal* 146(6) (December 2001): 12–15; 12.

57. Alexander, "A Global Civil War," 14.

58. Mark Cutts, "Prime Targets," *The World Today* 54(8–9) (August-September 1998): 220–221; 221.

59. As the direct part of the dual growth–conflict relationship, "resource-based static growth associates high growth with high conflict, and low growth with low conflict, in a direct-positive relationship." Mott, *The Economic Basis of Peace*, 194.

60. Stanley Hoffmann, "Clash of Globalizations," *Foreign Affairs* 81(4) (July-August 2002): 104–115; 111–112.

61. Mott, *The Economic Basis of Peace*, 196.

62. See Jürg Martin Gabriel, *Worldviews and Theories of International Relations* (New York: St. Martin's, 1994), 7.

63. Interdependence theory holds that *both* the distribution of political-military capabilities *and* trade explain the incidence of conflict and that the relationship between trade and the frequency of war is inverse. Edward D. Mansfield, *Power, Trade, and War* (Princeton: Princeton University Press, 1994), 233. See also Jacob Viner, "Peace as an Economic Problem," in *International Economics*, by Jacob Viner, 247–267 (Glencoe, Illinois: Free Press, 1951), 249, 258–261, 264–267; Robert O. Keohane and Joseph S.

Nye Jr., *Power and Interdependence: World Politics in Transition* (Boston: Little, Brown, 1977), 11–19; Robert O. Keohane and Joseph S. Nye Jr., *"Power and Interdependence Revisited," International Organization* 41 (4) (Autumn 1987): 725-753; 728–731, 737–738, 746; Richard N. Rosecrance, *The Rise of the Trading State: Commerce and Conquest in the Modern World* (New York: Basic Books, 1986), 22–43, 212–214; Joseph S. Nye Jr., "Neorealism and Neoliberalism," *World Politics* 40 (2) (January 1988): 235-251; 250).

64. Mott, *The Economic Basis of Peace*, 223. See also Kuznets, *Modern Economic Growth*, 155–159, 466–468, 472; Robert S. Gilpin, *War and Change in World Politics* (Cambridge: Cambridge University Press, 1981), 223–228. Rosecrance, *The Rise of the Trading State*, 43, 162, 211–214.

65. Richard N. Haass, "Paradigm Lost," *Foreign Affairs* 74(1) (January-February 1995): 43–58; 43.

66. The United States continues to lead the resistance to transnational firms through extraterritoriality, discriminatory taxation, economic sanction against various countries, and antitrust legislation, Many countries also invoke tort law, product liability codes, technical and product-content standards, and also various legislative proscriptions and definitions of corruption.

67. John Micklethwaite and Adrian Wooldridge, *A Future Perfect: The Challenge and Hidden Promise of Globalization* (New York: Random House–Crown Business, 2000), 160.

68. See, among others, Walter B. Wriston, *The Twilight of Sovereignty: How the Information Revolution is Transforming Our World* (New York: Scribners, 1992), 3–4, 7–8, 19, 34–39, 135–138, 170–176.

69. Andrew J. Bacevich, "New Rome, New Jerusalem," *The Wilson Quarterly* 26(3) (Summer 2002): 50–58; 58.

8

THE DOUBLE MOVEMENT: GLOBALIZATION AND ANTIGLOBALISM

In 1944, Karl Polanyi conceived his well-known double movement of orchestrated social forces creating and extending a liberal, market society and those seeking protection from the commodification of land, labor, and ideas.[1] The expansion of self-regulating markets to global dimensions seemed to generate sharp, social countermovements to restrict the reach of globalization and government policies to mitigate its human and environmental costs. Polanyi probably realized that the double movement was not new but had been operating since people confronted the rational efficiency of liberal economics with the rational force of liberal politics. From the dawn of modernity, technology and conquest have expanded the political and economic relationships through which Bacon's idols operated the double movement. Often eclipsed by the power of liberty and the visibility of prosperity, the populist forces of culture, art, philosophy, faith, and ideology have also expanded their effects on people and their social arrangements. Beyond physical, technological capabilities, in some ontological sense, globalization may not only activate the double movement but be integral to it.

By the 1930s, modernization had created new liberal forces—populist and economic—that operated in global dimensions as carriers of globalization. The double movement had also created new forms of the state—the New Deal, the Third Reich, social democracy, socialism, or fascism—as populist and political barriers to control the apparently natural and universal forces of globalization. Within the global perspective, the lens of historicism resolves this double movement into a conjunctural dialectic. With the carriers on one side and the barriers that antiglobalism constructs in their path on the other, what balances the double movement in social transformation is the power of the people. Populism confronts globalization as *both* carrier *and* barrier. Whereas the carriers are identifiable as particular groups of people pursuing progress through various institutions, the barriers are more elusive in the forms of attitudes, movements, crusades, and campaigns. Moving largely in the global economy, the carriers struggle to develop consilience between politics and economics, partnership between government and business, and synergy between culture and consumption. Largely passive, the barriers managed by Bacon's idols constrain people's understanding within narrow, cultural, and functional perspectives and often present new knowledge as treacherous.

CARRIERS OF GLOBALISM

Beyond the momentum of the process itself, a few groups of people seem to be the primary carriers of globalism. The well-organized executives of global business and the interested, but insulated, politicians and institutions of progressive governments form an increasingly coherent global cosmocracy. The commercial entertainment, or *pop*, culture continues to Americanize every corner of the world with expansion of the Internet. A growing audience of attentive, analytical scholars and intellectuals of a self-defined global intelligentsia is concentrating in a network of interconnected epistemic communities. Another loose group of idealistic individuals and fragmented nongovernmental organizations of transnational popular movements seems dedicated to creating and operating through a global civil society. Whereas few global revolutionaries offer a robust alternative, all are ready to destroy the current unsatisfactory system of global governance. The often tragic immigrants and refugees from economic and political misfortune are generally beset with personal tragedy and necessarily focused on individual survival.

None of these groups of people seem well suited for governing a globalizing world. Commercial interests focus narrowly on making money, whereas politicians are tied to the chimeric volatility of public opinion and centers of local power. Bureaucrats and institutions are chronically pursuing the stability of the familiar and comfortable. Entertainers seem self-satisfied so long as they have audiences, and intellectuals are content with criticizing and explaining. Idealists and revolutionaries are obsessed with their particular visions and involved in thousands of single-issue movements.

Living in the global economy, these globalizers—especially cosmocrats—look to Wall Street, Silicon Valley, or Hollywood for guidance and leadership just as their parents relied on Washington, Moscow, Peking, Paris, and London in their respective polities. Neither does this new generation of people "feel guilty about professing a doctrine of self-interest which it pursues strenuously in its own economic activities." Whereas the high politics of interstate conflict and deterrence and the high finance of balancing capital and current accounts obsessed Westphalian internationalists, post–Cold-War globalizers have other interests. Imbued with the ethics of meritocracy, "this generation is subject to being seduced by the idea of riskless global relations as compensation for the intense competitiveness of its private lives. In this environment, the belief comes very naturally that the pursuit of economic self-interest will ultimately and almost automatically produce global political reconciliation and democracy."[2]   Schooled to the conviction that global war is no longer a significant danger and inured to the chronic nuisance of disputes among petty polities not yet globalized, cosmocrats and idealists alike find common cause with progressive politicians. Together, these globalizers shape foreign policies around expanding capitalism and instructing the rest of the world in the liberal virtues of globalization. Perhaps the greatest challenge for all globalizers is focusing the power of people on some still hazy vision of the global good.

Global Cosmocracy

Before modern democracy, politics and business were affairs for a coherent elite of well-educated people who generally shared similar views about the things that mattered. This elite formed a social-economic-political ruling class —the aristocracy—that bore the broad responsibilities for governance, government, industry, and commerce in a society of states. The elite that Karl Marx positioned as the enemy was a sinister cabal of omnipotent capitalists and financiers struggling with aristocracy for control of the state. Cecil Rhodes imagined a clique of clean-cut British heroes who bound the English-speaking world to London, whereas H. G. Wells and the Webbs invented a global ruling class of modern, Platonic guardians. Like Saint-Simon and Marx, Max Weber conceived these social classes as arrayed against other social classes within the nation-state in struggles for control of the rewards of modernity.

Nationalism, liberalism, and democracy have swept most of these national social-class elites from political power and restricted modern elites to economic functions—commerce, science, management, scholarship, diplomacy, law, or medicine. Revolution and social transformation marginalized the power struggle between elite social classes—aristocracy and church. Industrialization refocused class struggle across a capitalist upper class, a bourgeois middle class, and a lower class of workers and peasants as modernization constrained national elitism to economics. Capitalism co-opted the obsolescing elites of rich countries into a loose international bureaucracy and international consciousness that stimulated development of statelike, international governing structures within a society of states. The League of Nations, the United Nations, and a series of regional intergovernmental organizations emerged to make the society of states safe and comfortable for capitalism.

Deepening into normative internationalism across trade and production, this same international consciousness socialized labor from national classes into an international family of national organizations and classes.[3] Balanced by international labor, business, and classes, the international bureaucratic-capitalist elite assumed responsibility for managing and maintaining the international division of labor as the foundation of an international political economy. Although most of the world's countries are trapped in the capitalistic, production-based international division of labor, people who can connect directly to globalization are often able to escape, physically by migration or virtually by instantaneous telecommunication. People with skills and knowledge can flee into globalization and find class mobility. Others simply join the growing, international lower class of unskilled migrants.

The intersection of globalization and technology has created a conspicuous elite of people who operate the global economy, conduct global business and diplomacy, govern the process of globalization, and carry cosmopolitan ideas back and forth around the world. This cosmocracy, which excludes most of the world's lower and middle classes, comprises managers of states and companies, banks and international institutions, populist movements and nongovernmental organizations, and a few globally visible individuals. Among the cosmocrats are politicians, diplomats, bureaucrats, entertainers, athletes, and interventionist opinion makers. As the *de facto* officials and operators of global governance, these people carry a trend towards centralizing power in multilateral institutions to establish global rules for national policymaking. A central tenet of cosmocracy, derived paradoxically from Fabian Keynesianism, is that the private sector is far more able to solve the world's—or anybody else's—problems than any government or civil society could be. Despite many rivalries and conflicts, the cosmocracy is collectively committed to a Protean, inchoate ideology that values strengthening the global political-economy in patterns that include *both* global capitalism *and* the market economy.[4]

Some twenty million cosmocrats form a new meritocratic ruling class, primarily Anglo-American in values and heritage but culturally pluralistic and cosmopolitan in personal tastes. About 40% of cosmocrats live in the United States, although they are not all U.S. citizens, and the cosmocratic elite is actively recruiting people from Asia, Latin America, and Africa. Cosmocrats ardently declare themselves global citizens, apparently willing to abandon the specific identities of national citizenships. "Unlike more idealistic and cosmopolitan shifts in loyalty, which in the past have been associated with the advocacy of world government, this new type of global citizenship is pragmatic, and has grown up without accompanying feelings of regional or global solidarity of the sort associated with a sense of community."[5] With no intrinsic commitment to a community or state, the cosmocratic orientation arises in practical calculation of self-interest reinforced by global capitalism. As the cosmocracy creates its own insulated world within the world, its citizens secrete themselves among themselves in a secession of the successful.[6]

The cosmopolitan meritocracy has little respect for age, race, gender, or any of the traditional discriminators between people. Cosmocracy has globalized a narrow set of what originated as American values into a universal secular morality: higher education and an advanced degree, personal dignity, managerial simplicity, transaction speed, and a disdain for bureaucracy. "Cosmocrats are forever eliminating barriers, overcoming limits, removing rigidities, [and providing global solutions]."[7] The fragile porosity of national boundaries, which limits cultural mixing only by the human imagination, is shifting humanity's sense of identity from traditional kinship and nationalism towards an inchoate global cultural reflexivity. Although globalization carries human uncertainty and cultural fragmentation, the global cosmocracy carries global acceptance of human differences, discursive amalgamation of different traditions, and novel concepts of identity within the global perspective.[8]

The bulk of the cosmocracy comprises the employees and retainers of multinational firms, although many are entrepreneurs. Most diplomats and officials of international organizations are official cosmocrats, at least so long as they remain in office. Another sector of cosmocracy includes intellectuals and scholars—on sabbatical, presenting papers, or with generous research grants—dedicated more to undiscovered truth than to education. Within the offices of every government are global bureaucrats who assemble in Tokyo, Washington, London, and other exotic capitals routinely to solve the problems of the benighted governments that cannot afford to send delegates. Although many well-educated cosmocrats are neither European nor American, all speak American—or at least English—and several other languages with fluency. Exercising an interpretive cultural receptivity to alien cultures and norms, these sophisticated intellectuals and mobile knowledge workers are creating their own cosmopolitan society with its own culture, identity, and citizenry.[9]

Cosmocratic firms pride themselves on using local people to operate their offices. Like colonial or religious syncretism, cosmocracy assimilates its recruits and transforms them. While local in demographics, they become cosmopolitan in taste, opinions, morals, and intellect. This inevitable transformation just as inevitably persuades the cosmocrats who monitor local operations that they are rightly the elite and probably deserve to rule at a safe distance from local populations. As young cosmocrats mature, the merit, intelligence, and spirit that brought them into the cosmocracy seem likely to congeal into the same arrogance of power that ultimately infected traditional elites.

All of the traditional aristocratic elites felt some responsibility for *their* people among whom they lived as patronal leaders. In poignant contrast, cosmocrats generally are not connected to any group that they can call *their people*. Their meritocratic success, their peripatetic lifestyle, and the superficiality of their work combine to prevent any attachment to place or people. Politics—especially democracy—remains robustly local, and cosmocrats have neither the time nor the interest to become involved in local initiatives, campaigns, or elections. The companies, agencies, and organizations that are the structure of cosmocracy are learning to disregard and de-emphasize traditional national or territorial loyalties. As cosmocracy slowly secedes from the Westphalian world, *both* cosmocrats *and* the organizations that they serve arouse hostility for their disdain of national values and law, their contempt of citizens, and their revolt "against the constraints of time and place."[10]

Whereas traditional elites were property owners and hereditarily bound to their lands, cosmocrats "owe their positions to information and expertise, which flow easily across borders. Their loyalties . . . are international rather than local and calculating rather than emotional. They are far more concerned with the smooth operation of the system as a whole than with the health of any particular part of it." Just as traditional elites had deficiencies and degenerated in a self-satisfaction, the global cosmocracy has glaring weaknesses, beyond its domination by an insecure Anglo-American plurality. Cosmocratic sophistication is rarely deep or based on experience. Although cosmocrats are "often better traveled than even the most wizened sailor that Joseph Conrad could invent . . . [their exposure to peoples and societies is often limited to the airport and a few hotels]; cosmocrats have no Conradian depth."[11]

Commercial Globalization

In what Susan Strange has called the business civilization, commercial enterprise performs, beyond its profit-making function, a critical *mission civilatrice* in carrying global extensions of Adam Smith's invisible hand.[12] In the neoliberal-Marxist, business civilization, market forces analogous to universal, natural forces beyond politics form the structures of relationships and provide the dynamics of globalization. The primary commercial carriers of globalism have been multinational enterprises with their growing populations of cosmocrats and government officials that support them—the cosmocracy. At the heart of twentieth-century globalism and commercial globalization is the information revolution, which has made possible the global distribution of labor and expansion of markets to global dimensions. Several industries—especially electronics, computers, and information technologies—have exploited the information revolution to create technical networks that integrate specialized industrial clusters into global production networks. Encircling the world through interconnections among networks, commerce has carried globalization wherever firms can find markets and sources.

Multinational Enterprise

Dominating global trade, production, and distribution in *both* the resource-based *and* the knowledge-based sectors, multinational enterprise divides the world's work among firms and polities. Although Adam Smith did not forecast the modern, global economy, he understood the principle of division of labor, which is its foundation. In national, resource-based economies, Smith's principle operates in firms and industries. In the global, knowledge-based economy it operates across economic activities—research, design, and development; sourcing and supply; finance and investment; labor and production; or transportation and communications. Transcending *both* national borders *and* company boundaries, these activities occur within dense, global patterns of *both* political *and* economic specialization by *both* firms *and* polities. Firms doing international or global business operate around and through regional, sociopolitical business centers, which are themselves global enterprises.[13] While multinational firms concentrate capital and knowledge, the global cities concentrate assets and infrastructure related to particular industries. These regional centers are linked through a few thousand multinational firms, each with its own global intrafirm networks that link the respective regional specialties. Within the global perspective, multinational enterprise includes *both* firms *and* cities.

The Firm. As an industry expands towards the global perspective, it forms a narrow-perspective oligopoly of a few firms using interdependent strategies to produce and sell in a global market. Even the smallest multinational firms develop mobile, expert teams within the company who work and live in the cosmocracy and interconnect with teams from other companies. These novel structures and practices in multinational firms create economies of scale not at the local, production level but at the corporate, global, managerial level. With global markets and sources, many multinational firms are gradually developing into stateless, transnational firms whose executives and managers are responsible to corporate owners that are dispersed around the world. The pull of economic globalization "is weakening the connections that bind companies to their communities," as they become corporate citizens of the world.[14]

Built firmly on networks among various business functions and economic activities, multinational firms build competitive advantage on intangible assets —intellectual property, flexible organization, or brand names. Responding to the needs of customers throughout the world "multinational corporations do not compete so much on scale, although they are large, but on their ability to coordinate international activities. Such coordination also includes transferring knowledge on how to organize for manufacturing, research, and sales from one country to the next."[15] In the global, knowledge-based economy, "competition is no longer about richly endowed firms battling against poorer ones: It is also a contest to develop strategies and learn new skills . . . in terms of the intensity of managers' imagination."[16] Innovations in strategy and process, rather than in product, are the heart of growth for multinational firms.

The Global City. Within the global economy, a few cities are the focal points for the specialization of work, economies of scale, and the dynamic technologies that guide the global distribution of labor. The ready availability of the resources of production, living, and wealth creation, and the concentration of demand for consumption forms the infrastructural underside of globalization in the global cities. Electronically interconnected cities often specialize in a broad type of business operation within the functional division of the work of the global economy. Global cities conceal the useful functions of globalization behind an urban facade that conceals the details of operating globalization from the underside. Much of the cosmocracy, and probably most people, are blithely unaware of the intricate urban collaborations and processes that operate this underside of globalization. For the user, globalization is transparent; for the global city, it is daily business routine. The immobile resources of these global cities form "a dense network of specialized, often small, independent enterprises that supply crucial inputs and are difficult to replicate elsewhere."[17] Many multinational firms have become dependent on such immobile concentrations of labor, innovation, and physical infrastructure.

In contrast to traditional priorities for facilities and people in the home countries, many multinationals prefer the rich processes of innovation and global infrastructures in megacities to nationalistic notions of patriotic duty.

The Enterprise. Although the practice of financial arbitrage is well known, multinational enterprise involves arbitrage of two other factors of production —labor and knowledge—and the transformation of land into infrastructure *outside the firm.* Within the global perspective, this knowledge arbitrage occurs within and through the infrastructures of global cities, often in entrepreneurial conversion and diffusion of knowledge between firms and cities. The salience of knowledge arbitrage is a definitive feature of multinational enterprise, which is not captured by traditional definitions of the firm in terms of ownership, structures, relationships, and location. Neither do classical notions of the polity in terms of citizenry, institutions, and territoriality involve the extra- and transpolitical knowledge creation in the context of political-economic multinational enterprise. Within the global perspective, "a firm is viewed as a repository of valuable knowledge that can be exploited either through new productions or through the dissemination of existing products to new locations. This knowledge consists not just of what an individual employee knows but of collective information on how people, machines, and technology are best organized and directed."[18] This collective knowledge resides not exclusively within the firm, but *socially across the global city.*

As a partnership-combination of the firm and the city, the political-economic multinational enterprise is a powerful carrier of globalism. "A firm can be world-class in behavior without being global in its asset disposition, provided it has a global perspective, a global information base, and the necessary imagination to strive for continuous improvement and adapt to shifting circumstances."[19] It is the global city that provides the infrastructure to support world-class firms. The multinational enterprise of firms and cities with its web of technical, commercial, and infrastructural networks is the archetype of doing either global or local business in the business civilization.

Technical-Industrial Networks

In traditional, resource-based economies and industries the communities, structures, and networks of any technical exchanges or learning are primarily inside companies. The firm is the optimal organization for creating and transferring knowledge and technological know-how among individuals and internal groups in controlled technical networks.[20] As the complexity of technology increases and firms seek to penetrate foreign markets, "cooperation between organizations tends to develop. One of the most important reasons for industrial networks is the need for firms to be able to share and combine elements of know-how. Similar networks may, for the same reasons, be formed between research teams and laboratories."[21] Economic globalization has stimulated firms to develop and expand internal technical networks across political boundaries in technology transfers as they expand their markets.

The infrastructures of transnational technical networks are communities of engineers, technicians, and scientists with similar educations—typically in U.S. universities—with social-technical connections among complementary industrial clusters. Within these fluid, technical-industrial community-networks, diffusion of knowledge is smooth and rapid through personal relationships or the movements of individuals between and among firms.[22] Although most transnational technical networks developed from U.S. exports of capital and technology in the 1960s and 1970s, by the 1990s, reciprocal flows of skills and management were supplanting these one-way flows. Beyond technology transfers, the most effective technical networks expanded into cosmopolitan social arrangements and professional collaborations among investors, entrepreneurs, small businesses, divisions of large firms, venture capitalists, and professional-technical associations—primarily cosmocrats.

Technical-industrial networks connect and integrate the infrastructures and work of regional industrial clusters, despite gradual deterioration of local advantages—cheap labor, resources, favorable laws and regulations, or location. Transnational arbitrage across market, financial, or technical opportunities links centers of specialization and cross-regional partnerships to each other and to the network's core—usually a cluster in the United States. Government policymakers, corporate executives, and other cosmocrats rely tacitly, and often exclusively, on the smooth operation of these "dense professional and social networks that keep them close to state-of-the-art technical knowledge and leading-edge markets in the United States [and throughout the world]."[23]

The Silicon Valley-Hsinchu Prototype. An early technical network in the information-technology industry is the Silicon Valley-Hsinchu network, which has become one prototype for technical-industrial globalization. Distinguished from the Chinese diaspora—overseas Chinese—by personal technical identities and a communal homeland in Taiwan rather than mainland China, this network carries deep integration into *both* Silicon Valley *and* Hsinchu.

As globalization confronted information technology, the Silicon-Valley industrial cluster fragmented its division of labor in nested, horizontal, international networks of specialized designers, producers, and distributors. The horizontal business structure obviated the classical, auction-style price competition, common in vertically integrated national markets, which relies on the law of one price and open competition. Instead, the fragmented system of horizontal technical networks came to rely on coordination through social structures, technical networks, and professional institutions.[24] In Silicon Valley, the growing community of Taiwanese technical immigrants formed social networks to overcome the cultural isolation of living in American communities and working in U.S. firms. Gradually, these evolved into a technical-professional network that transcended company structures, which were deteriorating into the loose, decentralized model of Silicon-Valley entrepreneurship. As they absorbed the norms of the entrepreneurial culture, which was rapidly expanding from Silicon Valley across the United States, immigrants discovered the value of solidarity in launching entrepreneurial ventures. "The most successful Chinese businesses in Silicon Valley today are those that draw on ethnic resources, at least initially, while integrating over time into the mainstream technology and business networks."[25]

As the first generation of Taiwanese students found jobs in Silicon Valley in the 1970s, Taiwanese policymakers recognized their value as a national asset, established formal connections, and promoted an indigenous information-technology industry of small firms. With technology from the United States, Taiwan created a U.S.-linked venture-capital industry and an information-industrial cluster in the Hsinchu Science-Based Industrial Park, as the Asian end of the Silicon Valley–Hsinchu technical-industrial network.[26] The Taipei government sponsored frequent advisory meetings and technical interactions between Taiwanese engineers, entrepreneurs, executives, and bureaucrats in Taiwan and in the United States. Perhaps originally unintended, a consequence of Taiwan's aggressive, outward-looking technological development strategy was a powerful transpacific technical community and industrial network that, by the second generation, had become self-sustaining.

The mid-1980s reversed the Taiwan-U.S. flow of engineers as opportunities in Taiwan, which earlier Taiwanese in Silicon Valley had created, complemented cultural, patriotic, and family influences in drawing U.S.-educated Taiwanese engineers back home. In 1989, the Silicon Valley–Hsinchu technical-industrial network became a formal international business association, the Monte Jade Science and Technology Association, to promote Taiwan-U.S. cooperation, investment, and technology transfer through Silicon Valley and Hsinchu. Such networks are not, of course, unique to either Taiwan or the United States and are common within the cosmocracy. They have also emerged in Israel, India, and China as local engineers, technicians, and entrepreneurs have developed networks with U.S. and European technical communities and expanded them into stable, self-sustaining financial, social, cultural, and even political relationships.

Local Globalization. Localization—economic, technological, or cultural—is not antiglobal. The Silicon Valley–Hsinchu connection integrates local sociocultural structures and technical-industrial perspectives within the global perspective on research, development, commerce, and production. "The multinational corporation may no longer be the advantaged or preferred organizational vehicle for transferring knowledge or personnel across national borders. An international technological community provides an alternative and potentially more flexible and responsive mechanism for long-distance transfers of skill and know-how—particularly between very different business cultures or environments."[27] Focused technical-industrial networks allow distant businesses to specialize locally and collaborate globally through routine communications and cooperation. The best contexts for such networks are matched or complementary sets of decentralized industrial, commercial, political, and cultural systems. Beyond technology transfer, the globalization of trust, local knowledge, and individual identities not only creates global competitiveness but transforms global markets and societies as network-mediated relationships deepen. Through technical-industrial networks, localization and globalization reinforce each other in a new social reality that includes, yet transcends, *both* the local *and* the global. These networks allow firms, people, and even countries to become global by localizing.

Epistemic Communities

Beyond the purely commercial contexts of technical-industrial networks, the foundation of transnational social-cultural-political communities on which they form is an essential, if invisible, carrier of modern globalization.[28] As they expand narrow cultural and political attitudes into the global perspective, the technology, trust, and values shared in technical-industrial networks readily evolves into knowledge-creating *basho*. Beyond the cosmocrats who form technical-industrial networks, the notion of an epistemic community describes a broad coalition of scientists, scholars, students, politicians, and others who develop a common understanding of the knowledge surrounding an issue.

Perhaps the first formal epistemic community emerged in the voluminous and regular secretarial correspondence of Henry Oldenburg (1615–1677), first secretary of the English Royal Society, with the *Académie Française* and more than seventy scientists around the world.[29] Refining Oldenburg's handwritten letters into Internet chat rooms, modern epistemic communities connect professional concerns and needs for information in dealing with global issues —the environment, population growth, migration and refugees, crime, drugs, or disease. Beyond creating or diffusing knowledge, an epistemic community expands the narrow perspective of a technical network beyond industrial issues to its political-economic implications and policy requirements.[30] Each epistemic community develops an inclusive, knowledge-based approach to professional challenges that establishes and legitimates its political influence. Common understanding of arcane science and interpretive flexibility of new knowledge secure the knowledge-policy nexus through continuing commitment of the political members as the policy agenda changes over time.

Members of epistemic communities are mutually engaged in doing things together, maintaining mutual relationships, and often form an operating *basho* for creating new knowledge in a consensually determined context. Consciously sharing a common history of learning, members negotiate diversity among themselves around a community-wide code of practice and some regime of mutual accountability. With no systemic pressure towards agreement on policy, epistemic communities focus on creating and diffusing the scientific and technological knowledge of an issue and developing the implications across various perspectives. More than simple coordination mechanisms for common practices, epistemic communities of professionals within every perspective effectively socialize and globalize knowledge "through routines and repeated interactions, rather than encrypted in rules or in an organizational design."[31]

Translation of knowledge into application and policy occurs necessarily in a particular political-economic context that contains epistemic communities as influences. Epistemic communities generate several types of effects: creation of new knowledge, innovative policy options, and political influence. Collaborative research papers and reports—intramural and extramural—are the vehicles for expressing new knowledge. Although epistemic communities rely on the traditional academic peer-review process to validate new knowledge, the presence of nonacademic members permits direct, rapid dissemination of ideas to policymakers. Innovative policy options often enter the policymaking process through research organizations and institutions as new concepts, novel approaches, or creative interpretations of equivocal information and facts. Epistemic communities also exploit powerful media imagery to sell policy options to the broad public and politicians who respond to public opinion.

Disciplinary Networks

Rather than economic exchanges or political decisions, the interests of professionals in many disciplines lie in obtaining information to explain events in more detail and depth than commercial media provide. Scholars, professionals, and analysts "need information that is timely, reliable, and comparable. Uncertainty and false information are the enemies of stability whether in the social, political, or economic arena."[32] Although the Internet allows direct communication between scholars and professionals, only active collaboration can convert the data provided by direct observations into useful information about events and knowledge of what to do about them and why.

Developed spontaneously within many scholarly disciplines and professions, these networks connect scholars and professionals sharing, disseminating, and collecting information, ideas, and knowledge. Connected selectively through global conferences, letters, satellite and cable telecommunications, and computer networks, scholars and professionals use these loose networks without formal network managers. Instead of respecting rules and hierarchies prescribing channels of communication or methods of interaction, any participant in a disciplinary network communicates freely and directly with any or all nodes of the network. Although even the Internet is not global in extent or electronic connectivity, the disciplinary networks that use it extensively are literally global in their reach. For many networks, however, the Internet presents a perverse threat of deglobalization in the tendency of connected nodes to exclude the unconnected nodes of the network from communications, as traditional communication channels lose favor.

Despite disparities in size, capability, and resources, disciplinary networks cohere around most professional and academic disciplines and operate through a common base of disciplinary knowledge. All of the nodes and the people who operate them share a common intellectual foundation or professional curriculum in relevant fields. Because many scholars, professionals, and bureaucrats remain in their posts for long periods, network interactions often involve exchanges of tacit knowledge and develop into close personal relationships around trust and confidence. Some professions have developed their networks around their own common languages, standards, norms, and practices that transcend political systems, economic relationships, and cultural idiosyncrasies. "In the final analysis, the defining test of the existence of a global [disciplinary] network is the shared belief in a set of common attitudes and characteristics. The existence of such a set would define and bind together official statisticians [or other professionals] regardless of where they are."[33]

Educational Convergence

In the context of globalization, the end of the Cold War stimulated colleges and universities throughout the world to introduce multidisciplinary, liberal-education curricula and pedagogical styles of small classes, dialogue, and critical thinking. Unlike the formal U.S. and European programs—Institute for International Education, Fulbright Programs, Rhodes Scholarships, and others—the initiative and commitment to a global, liberal curriculum have arisen among people transforming and designing their societies. Although a third of foreign students study in the United States, an educational diaspora is pursuing joint degrees between universities in their home societies and U.S.-European partner-schools through satellite campuses throughout the world.

Although commercialization threatens the quality of education, the global liberal-education curricula converge around multidisciplinary scholarship and knowledge-sharing across political, economic, and cultural boundaries. Most of the societies providing most of the students "share a new emphasis on civil society and the nurturing of more democratic institutions. And there is an awareness that older methods of education are inappropriate for free-market economies."[34] Despite the continuing struggle between proponents of liberal education and pragmatists who call for career-related, cost-effective training, the global educational community accords prestige to the liberal education.

Beyond the formal U.S.-European programs, local liberal-education initiatives in many Central European cities have spawned a host of local *invisible colleges* that do not offer degrees or send students abroad. Instead, they enhance existing state education systems with focused training and emphasis on independent thinking through intensive, dialogue-style, discursive instruction, *explicitly to prepare students for liberal study abroad*. They provide "extra courses, a closely regulated tutorial system, . . . psychological consulting, and a substantial stipend. . . . individualized planning of students' professional and intellectual development and weekly tutorials and consultations."[35] Invisible colleges rely on nonstate institutions and charity for support and stress multidisciplinary programs across the humanities, since the formal exchange-student programs focus on natural sciences, politics, and economics. Many reflect a pragmatic interest in maintaining local peace and promoting the cultural and economic revival of parent societies in a liberal context. From a loose foundation of formal, U.S.-European programs, visible, local initiatives, and invisible, pseudoentrepreneurial projects, the next generation of cosmocrats is converging around the collegiality of liberal education.

Cooperative Technical Organizations

These organizations exchange technical information, set standards, and make decisions for specific technological applications. Alternatively known as working groups, standards bodies, technical committees, task forces, and interest groups, these organizations may have formal structures or simply be *ad hoc* meetings. Although membership includes firms, governments, scientists, and scholars, the sizes of cooperative technical organizations are generally limited explicitly to invited individuals. Small memberships permit detailed information exchange, consideration, and discussion of technical options and constraints among well-informed, or expert, individuals who can make and institutionalize technical decisions in standards or position papers.[36] Although information technology extends potential participation to arbitrarily large communities, the need for consensus in collective decisionmaking remains a constraint on the executive functions of these organizations.

Cooperative technical organizations often establish, or reflect, the institutional dynamics among the member organizations that form the parent technical-industrial community. Often necessary catalysts in creating public legitimacy for immature technologies, cooperative technical organizations expand the institutional foundations of an industry as the technology expands into the global economy. The individuals who form cooperative technical organizations are often active cosmocrats who participate in several such organizations across related technical communities and industries. These multidimensional connections promote diffusion of knowledge across technical, disciplinary, political, and organizational boundaries. Cooperative technical organizations form the institutional core and hub of "an overlay network of interorganizational relationships. . . . This multiplicity of ties, taken together, constitutes a knowledge network in which firms are embedded."[37]

Transgovernmental Networks

The end of the Cold War brought the possibility of global networks organized and sponsored by international organizations around disciplinary networks or technical organizations. Exemplifying these carriers of globalism, one of the early networks—the global statistical system—intended to reinforce the connectivity of the world's economies, has expanded into other global concerns. Like most official networks, it offers access to nongovernmental participants, the primary core of the global statistical system comprises the national statistical offices of the U.N. member countries. Varying widely in size, organization, and structure, at one extreme lie those countries with a single chief statistician. Limited to producing economic aggregates, this individual is responsible for collecting and producing the entire range of national statistical data. Able to compile extended accounts of microeconomic data, "the United States represents the other end of the scale with no one directly responsible for more than a [portion] of the official statistical [database] and coordination of the system assigned to the Chief Statistician in the Executive Office of the President."[38] On 14 April 1994, the United Nations Statistical Commission, to focus the existing disciplinary network, adopted a code of ten fundamental principles for official statistics across political boundaries. The global statistical system is a network whose nodes include

> national statistical offices; statistical offices of international agencies—the International Monetary Fund, the Organization for Economic Cooperation, the United Nations [U.N.], and the World Bank—the Regional Economic and Social Commission of the United Nations; specialized agencies of the U.N. system—the International Labor Organization and the World Health Organization; and the statistical office of the European Union, Eurostat. In addition, the International Statistical Institute is a member. Increasingly, central banks, nongovernmental organization, and private-sector interests are becoming important to this network and are potential future nodes. . . . Within the large network are essentially two subnetworks. The first comprises the national statistical offices and the second, the international agencies and others.[39]

Comprising nodes that have not accepted the U.N. principles for official statistics, the secondary network shares the professional discipline of the primary network. The bond across both networks is a common commitment to public service through developing and implementing voluntary international statistical standards and norms. Like the disparities among national capabilities, the structural differences among intergovernmental and nongovernmental organizations tend to weaken the networks' cohesion and stability.

Beyond the need for accurate, complementary data, many global problems do not have national solutions—pollution, disease, weather, or biodiversity. To deal with these, governments must act together through technical-industrial and disciplinary networks or suffer separately. The densest transgovernmental networks connect the bureaucracies of the modern regulatory states. The routine bureaucratic work that deals with global problems is done by dozens of specialized intergovernmental bodies—the World Health Organization, the United Nations Environmental Program, or the United Nations Children's Fund. Although these networks promulgate their own rules, they do not aspire to exercise power but seek to broaden the state's abilities to enforce its own laws.[40] The interconnecting networks within epistemic communities fade into a continuing process of global, functional cooperation: "getting experts to work together out of the public eye. Technicians can gradually knit the world together in a system of mutually beneficial arrangements."[41]

Popular Globalization

Populists articulate a view of globalization that places people, rather than corporations or governments, at the center of the global perspective. Built directly on people power, populism calls on two of Bacon's idols—*idola specus* and *idola tribus*—to emphasize personal emotion and human love in mobilizing the power of the people. The populist carriers of globalism comprise idealistic movements built around people power; autonomous, nongovernmental organizations; and domestic civil-societies struggling for global relevance. Beyond offering opportunities for people to participate in building a better world, these populist carriers publicize global issues through glimpses into the global perspective. Despite global visions, the most successful idealists have been those addressing local, functional, or national concerns. As their success expands beyond local concerns, they either evolve into nongovernmental organizations or fade into irrelevance. Not remarkably successful at recruiting volunteers of time or donors of resources to address the broad concerns that appear only within the global perspective, nongovernmental organizations often focus on specific, narrow issues. Concentrations of wealth in businesses and power in governments focus civil society on national interests and constrain globalist idealism to the resources of philanthropy, personal wealth, and volunteers. The political right accuses populism of irresponsibility while the left berates idealistic donors for wasting resources on undeserving projects. Although idealistic people power remains fickle, fragmented, and underfunded, some corporations and a few governments have begun to recognize its expansion beyond annual shareholder meetings and periodic national elections.

Populist Movements

Like cosmocrats, many local people are disenchanted with politics and bureaucrats who seem unresponsive or impotent in addressing the problems advertised by the global news media. Spontaneous expressions of people power often consolidate into larger movements of popular feeling, *ad hoc* action groups, or coalitions around single issues. Without the advertising or propaganda budgets of corporations and governments, populists have learned to use the mass media to influence global audiences. Increasingly effective in shifting the focus of public opinion and politics towards their own concerns, "it [is] all done cheaply by Internet, e-mail, word of mouth, and graffiti."[42]

As a form of Polanyi's double movement, populist movements throughout the world have responded to expansion of the consumer culture with a perverse sort of globalism against consumerism. As consumerism expands, people are influencing governments and companies more effectively through the amounts and kinds of consumer goods that they buy than through political processes and elections or protests and strikes. In response to the persistent attacks of populist movements on their brands through local retailers, transnational corporations have begun to sell *fair-trade* or *fair-labor* products. "By choosing products from companies with fair-trade supplier policies in developing countries, and boycotting others seen as less ethical, . . . consumers are effectively casting votes that will influence corporate behavior, and eventually the livelihoods of people in poor producer countries."[43] Spontaneous local populism and the growing experience of populist organizers have begun to converge as carriers of political and cultural globalism, despite their narrow, shared intent of opposing expansion of the consumer culture.

Nongovernmental Organizations

Populists promote nongovernmental organizations to give people a voice in undemocratic decisionmaking processes that are beholden to corporate or political interests. The nongovernmental organization matured in the twentieth century as a legitimate institution that focuses popular power, distinct from *both* political power *and* economic wealth, within the global perspective. Influencing governments indirectly, these autonomous entities also influence social behaviors directly through extragovernmental collaboration in populist movements or by forming public opinion. Through many channels, they form expansive epistemic communities of *both* shapers *and* users of information.

Nongovernmental organizations have invaded political domains that the Westphalian system had reserved for governments, political parties, or politicians and also economic regions dominated by corporations. With resources that dwarf those of some companies and many states in which they operate, these entities are shifting the focus of global politics and molding the shape of the global economy. Using technologies not available outside the Internet world and huge, global subscriber lists, many of these groups enthusiastically promote universal human rights, protection of nature, global equality, or some other universal ideal. The growing salience of these concentrations of popular power raises the specter of bizarre coalitions of government bureaucrats, corporate lawyers, demagogic radicals, and sincere believers combining politics, business, and people in global governance.

Civil Society

Civil society has been part of experiments in governance for several millennia and is growing quickly within the global perspective even while disintegrating within national perspectives. Most salient within the economic perspective, the initial "globalization of civil society involves resistance from disadvantaged strata in a changing division of labor. The losers in global restructuring seek to redefine their role in the emerging order."[44] Responding to domestic pressures, populist movements have expanded the agendas of national civil societies to gain control over the remote forces of globalization.

As globalization attenuates the grips of national communities on their states, national civil societies weaken and lose vitality as national social and cultural bonds erode. People clamor for global political engagement through institutions that engage a global civil society across traditional boundaries. In the absence of a global civil society, populist social movements, cosmocrats, and nongovernmental organizations mingle to engage global governance on issues of accountability and transparency. The expansion and coalescence of eroding domestic civil-society into global antiglobalist movements form a perverse globalizing reaction to the antisocial effects of globalization.

Although technology has made possible a civil society that can address global issues within the global perspective, globalization has not created either the state or the community that can justify, define, focus, and contain it.

Globalization has launched into the *nébuleuse* of global governance a drifting mass of incoherent, popular power, which floats aimlessly between government and market. Within and across innumerable organizations, associations, networks, and private foundations, people from all countries debate and comment not only on matters of civil concern or issues of exercising power, but on anything, including the meaning of life.

Revolutionary Globalization

Revolutionary leaders seek to foment or export a particular sort of revolution—usually ideological—throughout the world. After Karl Marx envisioned a revolution of workers across the world, "Lenin did not want to spark Marxist revolution only in Russia, but throughout the world. Mao [Tse-tung] in China and Che [Guevarra] and [Fidel] Castro in Latin America sought to spread Marxist revolution in their regions and beyond. [Gamal Abdel] Nasser was not content to lead an Arab nationalist revolution in Egypt, but hoped to effect revolutionary change throughout the Arab world. . . . The Ayatollah Khomeini did not want Islamic revolution just for Iran, but for the entire Muslim world."[45] Beyond local particulars, global revolutions have all glimpsed at least a bit of the one-world perspective from a vantage point of human misery, resentment, and rage. Beyond the one-world perspective is the revolutionary obsession with distinguishing good from evil, with isolating *us* from *them*, and ultimately with destroying *them* completely. Revolutionary global governance would not face the challenge of symmetry between *us* and *them* but would deal with a homogeneous population of *us* joined by a reformed, repentant *them* who had adopted *our* version of absolute truth.

Revolutionary globalization depends on a specific strategy devised by its leader to suit the mood of the era, the content of the revolution, and the context of people or regions targeted. History's attempts at global revolution were driven by a resentment of something foreign: authoritarian rule, colonial domination, overbearing foreign influence or presence, economic exploitation, even rejection of a religion. Revolutionary disciples were convinced that foreign interests were imposing unjust oppression through either direct foreign rulers or an installed puppet regime to subjugate local people.

In a perverse political-economic globalization to prevent revolutionary globalization, the contemporary political powers and global corporations have always joined ranks to crush, or at least to oppose, global revolution. Global, antirevolutionary suppression strategies have included military intervention, political and economic containment, conquest or partition, world war, economic warfare through consumerism, and psychological warfare through propaganda and media campaigns. While companies have saturated and boycotted markets and deposed governments, states have suppressed and criminalized revolutionary parties and movements, imposed diplomatic isolation, and launched counterinsurgency and counterterrorism campaigns.[46]

Despite visions of global utopia, the implications of revolution within the one-world perspective have never overcome the persistent nationalist struggles, bitter ethnic rivalries, and introspective self-interest bequeathed by the Westphalian system. Instead of submerging local differences and national preferences in revolutionary alliance, revolutionary regimes and movements have exploited revolution for local benefit and advantage and even cooperated with the *status-quo* powers. Instead of uniting the peoples of the world in a transcendent global community, revolutionary zeal survives in many peoples as demands for independence from *both* their oppressors *and* the revolution.

Although revolution has not globalized any ideology or creed, the spirit of revolution spans the globe and appeals to humanity through the lowest common denominator of the human condition: misery. Although people can expect more waves of revolution, they can also expect them probably to fail. Neither globalization nor the future rides on these waves. Any success that global revolution has had lies not in the direct, explicit results of any particular revolution but rather in revolution's perverse power of integration. The specter of revolution mobilizes privileged and connected polities, economies, and societies of the world to oppose it. Integrating to preserve the *status quo* paradoxically reinforces the process of globalization by integrating the rest of the world's peoples in support of the revolution. *Both sides of the paradox are globalization.* If people so will it and can agree on which revolution to pursue, globalization can realize Osama bin Laden's revolutionary vision of a global caliphate or the equally revolutionary visions of Immanuel Kant and Adam Smith of a permanent global peace and a global invisible hand.

Migration and Globalization

Embedded in larger social, economic, and political processes as vital globalizing forces, "migrations do not just happen; they are produced. And migrations do not involve just any possible combination of countries; they are patterned."[47] Constitutive processes of globalization, migration patterns and flows form an alternative social reality beneath and within the formal, visible patterns of liberal, capitalist, democratic globalization. "Globalization also has its own demographic pattern—a rapid acceleration of the movement of people from rural areas and agricultural lifestyles to urban areas and lifestyles more intimately linked with global fashion, food, markets, and entertainment trends."[48] Although migration is a demographic and social process, a prominent pattern of migration is economic. As hypermobile capital seeks optimal returns, labor—not necessarily all people—becomes mobile in pursuit of prosperity, which economic globalization promises. More deeply than economic integration, migration has generated the fashionable, urban multiculturalism that is as much a part of globalization as are global finance and international trade. Refugees from catastrophe, in contrast, are seeking stability, security, and justice, which globalization does not promise.

Economic Globalization through Migration

Economic integration and inequality have channeled migration broadly into the transatlantic economic system that prospered during the nineteenth and twentieth centuries. Several globalizing economic processes—offshore production, foreign investment, internationalization of cities, and the international division of labor—continue to rely heavily on migration. For economists, migration reflects differences in countries' wage levels and demands for workers and is an unremarkable accompaniment to economic integration. Countries with higher wages and demands attract *both* transient, unskilled workers *and* permanent, skilled technicians or professionals. For economists, national regulations and laws to control immigration—legal or illegal—are artificial impediments to efficient operation of the global market. For government legislators and policymakers, multilateral cooperation in managing migration is rational adaptation of politics and economics to the power of globalization, whereas unilateral controls on emigration and immigration often reflect efforts to exploit globalization for national interests.

For poor countries, internal migration and urbanization often present intractable problems for weak, unstable governments, whereas emigration to rich countries is a beneficent result of globalization. Popular disappointment with urbanization generates emigration to foreign countries and cultures, where migrants add to their poverty the pressures of cultural and personal estrangement. The allure of better living conditions and rich countries' demands for skilled workers and professionals draws the best and brightest away from the local challenges of national development. The effects of migration on poor countries are extremely complicated and often costly or dysfunctional for national development efforts.

For rich, industrial countries, immigration has been an intuitively obvious response to increasing demands for cheap, low-skilled labor in the resource-based sectors of their economies. It is also, however, providing many of the skilled professionals necessary for their growing knowledge-based economies, which domestic education systems are increasingly failing to meet. Although the United States was the preferred destination in the 1980s and 1990s, "European countries are also beginning to enter the competition to attract skilled resources from India, China, South Africa, Malaysia, Nigeria, and elsewhere. This global battle for brains can only intensify."[49]

The collapse of the Soviet bloc and the failure of several emerging countries created a wave of low-skilled immigrants—legal and illegal—from Africa and Asia seeking better lives in Europe and the Americas. The 1990s surge in migration reflected increased awareness of opportunities in other countries through global telecommunication systems and migrant networks. Pragmatic participants in the global economy, these new immigrants have established "new partnerships [and mastered] the culture of capitalism while reinforcing traditions of long-distance [home-country] traditions. They have staked out individual space in a market culture while engaging in the cooperative economics dictated by [their religions] and by long-standing [home-country] commercial practices. They have adjusted to the unfamiliar stresses of big-city life in [their new countries] while reaffirming their [home-country] identities."[50] With families in home countries, most are torn between family allegiances, relationships with colleagues in their new countries, material necessity, and economic opportunity. Many rely on religious communities to provide health care and education, since the host-country welfare system excludes them. Even more than their better educated and more demanded high-tech compatriots, these people *both* carry *and* participate in globalization. "Migration should therefore not be seen as a process caused simply by the political or economic deficiencies of sending states: it is very much a product of the pressures of economic globalization, as well as the intensification of cultural and social links between sending and receiving countries."[51]

Cultural Globalization through Migration

In contrast to nineteenth-century immigration, which was predominantly permanent, the modern transportation and communication technologies allow frequent visits home, constant contact with relatives and friends around the world, and creation of cultural ghettoes with native-language television and radio, ethnic foods and clothing, and even tourists from the parent country. The continuing flow of migration around the world is creating a new class of people with hyphenated nationalities through a shallow ethnic homogenization that is intuitively related to the globalization of consumerism. The proliferation of significant immigrant communities throughout the world and the official fashions of nondiscrimination are spawning a global multiculturalism, or at least cultural pluralism. High birth rates within these immigrant communities are expanding these groups rapidly and extending multiculturalism deep into increasingly defensive national cultures. "Up to a third . . . of the population of western European countries, America, and even to a smaller extent Japan, will be composed of [immigrant] populations, . . . who will be socially, economically, and often politically excluded."[52]

The pursuit of prosperity through economic migration and individual participation in the global economy challenges traditional links between identity and nationality. Although most people of most nationalities want more economic integration with more prosperous economies, they are equally keen to retain their own cultures, national identities, and societies. Growing populations of immigrant workers exacerbate this clash between the desire for prosperity and the need for individual and social identity and deepen it by globalizing identities and cultures across *both* polities *and* economies.

Cultural globalization through various forms of migration has introduced the notion that a single individual, in contradiction of Westphalian doctrines of sovereignty and territoriality, can be a citizen of several countries. As its focus shifts from the duties of loyalty to a territorial state to the rights provided by a welfare state, the meaning of citizenship is fading into the *nébuleuse* of global governance. Many countries allow their citizens to claim citizenship also in other countries and permit naturalized citizens to retain their original citizenship. The eligibility of millions of people to vote in several countries' elections is introducing an unfamiliar—possibly uncomfortable—global element into national democracy.

National Security and Migration

Whereas emigration may seem intuitively obvious for people seeking better lives, for those societies that are seeking to protect their own good lives, the intuitive response has been to restrict the legal channels of immigration. Since the 1960s, destination societies have recognized an increasing threat as migration has expanded under the pressures of military conflict, violent crime and political insecurity, economic inequality and deprivation, disease, and natural disasters. Beyond the overt threats of criminality and terrorism, recipient societies often find psychological and social threats in immigration. Increasing flows of migrants—legal immigrants, illegal aliens, refugees, or asylum seekers—"not only pose internal security concerns but may encourage xenophobia and conflict, as traditional work opportunities appear threatened. . . . Mass movement may bring with it the possibility of infectious diseases affecting both people and livestock."[53] Although migration stimulates economic and cultural globalization, recipient-society reactions often generate political antiglobalism in a complex, dynamic counter-balancing effect.

Migrant Trafficking. Most governments identify migrant trafficking as a primary threat to national security and the national economy, but increasingly also to some vague notion of global security. Europeans and Americans have reacted to the threat with efforts to reduce migrant flows through restrictive national control measures as globalization accelerated. Even as recipient states tightened and closed legal channels, new irregular channels appeared to carry the increasing flows of migration, which slowly became illegal. The rising pressures to emigrate stimulated migrant trafficking as a growth enterprise in the business of globalization through migration. Trafficking organizations, like drug traffickers and global terrorists, are transnational carriers of globalism with bases and operators in countries of origin, along their particular routes, and at their destinations. "They are frequently linked to other types of organized crime, particularly drug and arms smuggling and prostitution, [and maximize] profits by using the same routes and networks for different illegal activities."[54] In perversely paradoxical reactions to the globalizing threats of migration, many countries spend huge amounts on physical barriers and border controls while disregarding the global causes and sources of migration.

International Cooperation. The 1980s brought increasing awareness that these defensive sorts of security measures could be effective only in a context of interstate cooperation. By the 1990s, as globalization began to assume policy salience and political credibility, threatened countries—led by the European Union—began to propose comprehensive, antiglobalizing cooperation with source countries to reduce flows.[55] Initiatives to remove the causes of migrant flows have stressed legal harmonization and coordination of penalties in recipient countries. Recipients have sought police cooperation in countries of origin and transit, enforcement of human rights, and cooperation between national judicial and intelligence systems. Although most governments recognize that individual states alone cannot deal effectively with the threat of migration, few are inclined to put migration—or even illegal trafficking—in a context of globalization. Within the global perspective, theorists and visionaries can readily assert the obvious wisdom of expanding, instead of restricting, migration, although within national perspectives the idea seems irrational, uneconomic, politically insupportable and culturally irresponsible. The pragmatism of international and domestic politics suggests, however, that the initiative will remain with recipient countries with a focus on interstate police and judicial action and national border controls.

Prosperity or Security?

As migration continues to increase, and accelerate, the global perspective exposes significant conflicts between the defensive immigration policies of recipient states and their aggressive economic policies. While insulating themselves from foreign people, most countries advertise their fashionable commitments to globalizing trade and investment through open borders.[56] Moreover, the readiness in the knowledge-based economies to extend permanent residence or citizenship to high-tech, high-skill, well-educated immigrants, while restricting low-skill laborers appears at best disingenuous. "As a distinct, exogenous force, economic globalization renders national controls on immigration untenable with increasing integration of international capital and services markets and shifts the locus of immigration policy from states to international institutions, bilateral agreements, and multinational arrangements. . . . Within the global perspective, states' resistance to diminution of sovereignty creates an unstable tension between the increasingly free movement of services, people, capital, and goods and the persistence of political limits on the movement of workers."[57]

Despite legislative and police restrictions, the influx of immigrants into the rich countries—the United States, Canada, Australia, the European Union, South Korea, and Japan—continues. The dual nature of migration, as a carrier of globalism and a stimulant for national insulation, presents every state and its people another face of globalization. They face the uncomfortable choice between prosperity and security or the sacrifice of a bit of national sovereignty to global institutions to pursue both in the company of the rest of the world.

BARRIERS TO GLOBALIZATION

Many antiglobalists feel that the collapse of the third ministerial meeting of the World Trade Organization in Seattle in 1999 marked the birth—or at least the christening—of antiglobalism. Although people have probably resisted globalization for millennia, as a social movement antiglobalism was born in the nineteenth-century double movement of forces opposing the commodification of land, labor, and ideas. Labor unions, Jacobins, Owenites, Luddites, conservative reformers—Edmund Burke, Benjamin Disraeli, or Prince Otto von Bismarck—and imperial businesses seeking protection from foreign competition became the first antiglobalists. Like most contemporary antiglobalists, these earlier protest movements perceived globalization as largely an economic matter and resisted any expansion of liberal markets.

Although globalization extends well beyond economics and technology, antiglobalism remains firmly rooted in economic disappointment and inequity. Fed by desire, inspired by electronic images of the good life elsewhere, and watered by hope, antiglobalism begins with the premise that inequality and poverty are ethically wrong and morally evil. Realization that technology has made global prosperity a real possibility somply broods resentment. "An international system in which all things are left to the unfettered market will further heighten political, social, and economic inequality. The role of politics is to mitigate this tendency by pursuing the goals of social justice and the common good."[58]

Resting on the broad *raison d'être* of resisting the current form of economic globalization and repairing the failings of global governance, the chaotic energy of antiglobalism is more a *mood* than a movement or ideology. As neoliberal hubris overcame official inertia and expansive economic integration became policy, antiglobalism expanded from economic protest to political opposition and social dissent. Bacon's idols have crystallized people's political, economic, and cultural reactions into narrow-perspective barriers and linked them into a passive, antiglobalist screen of human obstacles. relying on people's persistant preferences for what is familiar and comfortable.

Resistance to globalization emanates from diverse sources and concerns within narrow perspectives. The obvious targets for active reform or revolution are the state with its concentration of power, the intergovernmental organization with its transferred sovereignty, and the transnational firm with its concentration of wealth. Across its ecumenical diversity, the most prominent orientations of antiglobalism are radical ideas and populist thought. Obsessively focused on economics, radical thought dismisses political concerns as driven by economics. Radical movements are often associated with the political left and revolution, although some right-wing radicals also advocate violent confrontation with globalization. Usually more subjective and emotional and less materialistic, populism stresses social, cultural, and environmental anxieties and is most comfortable in the political center.

Passive Barriers

Recalling the good old days of local living and personal relationships, Bacon's *idola theatri* have merged democratization and liberation movements with ethnonationalism and hyperpatriotic statism in clamoring for stability, order, and honesty in government. The *idola fori* insist that global governance cannot, and should not, exist because it is too complicated and beyond human understanding. The *idola tribus* insist that globalization is unnatural, that people are, and should be, self-concerned even while universally compassionate. Neither is it human nature to meddle with nature by integrating, liberalizing, or modernizing. The *idola tribus* and *idola specus* are collaborating in a broad reaction to the globalization of familiar identities into uncomfortable new ones. This dual stratagem is coalescing in an antiglobalist counterttrend towards regionalization, "a search for meaning in an era when, in Europe, the nation-state has become less relevant than it once was."[59]

Beyond these passive barriers to globalization, the idols have channeled antiglobalist thought into three identifiable flows or movements. The *idola theatri* dominate the crusade to resurrect the nationalism, local community, and independence that are the poltical victims of globalization. The *idola tribus* and *idola specus* mobilize radical antiglobalist thinkers to preserve human identities, freedoms, and societies from the monolithic homogeneity of consumerist, economic globalization. The *idola fori* present the populist face of antiglobalism with its human compassion and concern that people are losing control of globalization and becoming its objects instead of its operators.

Nationalism

With the help of Bacon's idols, modernity transformed the world into a mosaic of exclusive national cultures, each with its unique nationalism that harnessed the irrational-emotional-spiritual forces of ethnicity to the rational-legal state. In sovereignty, nationalism provided the ideological, cultural, and psychological basis for the conjunction of national community, the political-legal state, and an administrative government.[60] As the world's dominant political ideology and cultural token, "nationalism offers a time-honored, often uncontested idea of a person's location in the world and place in its flow of history."[61] Despite the inward-focused perspective of nationalism, globalization penetrated its shell of sovereignty and inexorably expanded people's perspectives and knowledge beyond the nation. By the end of the twentieth century, the anomalous had become the norm, and most societies were multicultural hybrids. Despite, however, a global economy, international politics, and a diverse cultural traffic, the permanence and durability of nationalistic cultures reflect humanity's primal, ethnic communities.

Facing globalization, nationalism offers a stable focus for people's primal need to form and belong to groups, to have personal place within a group, and to transfer loyalty: Bacon's *idola tribus*. A powerful barrier to globalization, the group loyalty concentrated in nationalism creates "a strong tendency to evaluate events and prospects in terms of whether they are good or bad for 'our' group, whatever their effects on others. We divide the world into 'we' and 'they,' and when the outcomes for 'we' and 'they' diverge, we have little hesitation in choosing the outcomes favorable for 'us,' whatever may be the detriment to 'them.'"[62] This notion of exclusive identity—we and us, including I and me, but not they or them—built on collective memory-myths and focused by nationalism has emotional resonance throughout the world.[63] While protectively compassionate among us, nationalism is ready to harm or even destroy them, if we believe that doing so will protect us, or achieve our goals.

One of the most powerful of Bacon's idols concentrates people's exclusive identity around the territoriality of the state and common destiny-ideals in state-centered nationalism. The Westphalian merger of state and nation sealed the alliance between Bacon's idols around state-centered, exclusive nationalism and legitimated the state's expectation of every citizen's ultimate loyalty, which was not transferrable or expandible to the global perspective. Modern nationalists have discovered or invented national traits that allow nationality and the state to transcend time and space independently of history or geography. In direct antithesis of any global community, nationalism imparts a collective solidarity to the exclusive nation often with racial or hereditary standards for citizenship in the state.[64] Although globalism and humanism continue to erode nationalism, it remains a formidable barrier to globalization

The expansion of human compassion to the global perspective, however, exposes a distressing paradox and dilemma of nationalism. Nearly all people, of every nationality, are ready to decry war for the human misery that it entails. Most people, who are also nationalists, find circumstances that create a moral obligation for the nation to wage war and a personal duty to participate in it. Many people, especially in modern, wealthy countries, "feel considerable guilt about some of the actions our loyalties lead us to, and also helplessness about doing anything to change the situations that produce our guilt. Helplessness, when we are torn between feelings of a need for change and feelings of our inability to be instrumental in producing change, turns us to the kinds of actions we call 'expressive.'"[65] Instead of doing something to change the contradictions of human nature and nationalism, people follow Bacon's nationalistic idols to war in expectation of victory and pray that peace will prevail on earth in satisfaction of their hopes and wishes.

Ethnic Autonomy

As an alternative to the state as the source of human identities, Bacon's *idola tribus* and *idola specus* have taught people to recognize cultural-ethnic and other demograpphic groups. Many of these ethnic groups can offer challenges the nationalistic loyalties expected by traditional nation-states. Ethnicity embodies a sense of common ancestry, language, religion, and culture among people but is as exclusive as nationalism in its political or economic implications. Derived from Woodrow Wilson's notion of self-determination, ethnic autonomy envisions participation and representation of separate ethnies in the processes and structures of governance and government. Despite the improbability of comprehensive personal relationships throughout the group, the psychological bonds of ethnicity may be sufficiently strong to form the cultural foundation for the identity and legitimacy of a political community. Political nationalism extends it further into the goal of forming, operating, and sustaining a separate, autonomous, ethnic-political community and legal state.[66]

Both ethnic autonomy *and* a derived, political nationalism erect nationalistic barriers to globalization in the forms of robust, exclusive, less-than-global, individual and social identities.

By replacing the individuality of liberalism with the cultural right of ethnic self-determination within the global perspective, autonomous, ethnic communities fragment any global, human community into insulated cultural-ethnic groups. The focus on ethnic autonomy creates a profound social, political, and psychological struggle of conflicting loyalties between state-centered nationalism, ethnic identity, self, and universal human community. Ethnic autonomy and nationalism based on cultural identities, politics, and economics present persistent, dissonant barriers to developing *both* state-centered, nationalistic cultures *and* humanistic, global communities.

In reviving ethnicity and pluralizing humanity into cultural niches and ethnic identities, globalization paradoxically erodes its own coherence. In contrast to robust ethnies that are syncretically transforming identities into global forms, ethnic nationalism recedes into tradition to rediscover the certainty of the past and resurrect its primal, exclusive foundations and roots. The clash between the symbolic icons of the cultural past and the fluid pragmatism of daily living forces people to choose between past and present, between tradition and progress, or between culture and reality.[67] Although progressive ethnicity can be a powerful carrier of globalism, the more fashionable ethnic nationalism is an equally formidable barrier to globalization.

Radical Thought

For radical thinkers passionately dedicated to their causes, globalization has not improved people's lives significantly or brought much progress. It has reformulated the same, old divisions between righteous believers and heathen infidels, between oppressors and oppressed, between the ignorant and the enlightened, or between rich and poor. Since the first Industrial Revolution, radicals have found in globalization a source of this polarization that would eventually explode into social revolution. As globalization expands economic crises into people's lives and the earth's environment, radicals work to reverse or hinder the process. While some radicals deplore the accelerating shift of resources from productive investment to financial speculation as a falling-domino process to global collapse, others proclaim the rise of a new, revolutionary, world order.[68] While globalist radicals struggle against governments, socialist and labor parties urge them to take the politically unacceptable decisions to reflate the world economy before global capitalism collapses under its own weight.[69]

Radical Fragmentation

The radical movements are riven with dissent between nationalist groups seeking to cripple globalization from below and globalist factions opposing it from above. Although the aim is shared, globalists expand their programs

—terrorism, protests, crime, or cyberwar—throughout the world as nationalists wage local or regional campaigns against local regimes. The visionary elements of the radical, globalist left tend to accept the broad patterns of global interdependence with their promises of freedom from conventional warfare based on economic integration. Pragmatic, nationalistic skeptics of the radical right, however, reject liberal inferences of a global democratic peace and note the prevalence of antagonism and conflict, despite economic integration.

Across global, international, and national levels of political-economic interactions, radical movements collect either on the political left or the right. "Whereas the left argues more from economic and sociological bases, the right points to the governmental and regulatory aspects of globalization as threats to national sovereignty. The left wants greater democracy. The right wants to secure national independence, identity, and security. The left worries about the rights of man, whereas the right worries about preserving nationalistic tradition and culture."[70] While the radical left protests globalization for its economic inequities, the right notes the gradual increase in international terrorism and the high concentration of small civil and interstate wars among the world's poorer countries. The left and the right agree that the remarkable increase in international peacekeeping operations and the continuing salience of military operations other than war describe a less benign world than that predicted by globalists. Often in opposition on other issues, in an unexpected antiglobalist convergence, the radical right condemns the ideology of globalism, which justifies the process of globalization protested by the left.

Although radical thought is dynamically disparate and impossibly complex, it tends to converge in several broad approaches to antiglobalism. Two major leftist strands—neo-Marxism and the New Left—display some continuity, ideological coherence, and organizational structure in focused antiglobalism. The amorphous radical right floats around various forms of less-than-global statism in a society of states. A few lesser movements and various *ad hoc*, functional idealists range from single-issue movements to opportunist allies of any antiglobal movement. Although radical thinkers differ on many other issues, they converge in their opposition to globalization as a diversion on the path of progress towards truth in a better world.

Neo-Marxism

Beneath any focus on truth and behind every vision of a better world lies in every radical a socialist heart, the legacy of Karl Marx. Within every radical thought lurks a conviction of increasing polarization between a poor, working class, an affluent middle class, and an elite of a society's rich and powerful. As the heart and mind recovered from the Soviet collapse after a few years of recrimination and blame casting, radical thinkers began to dismiss claims of liberal victory. The rich remained rich, the poor remained poor, the North-South gap continued to widen, the United States remained in charge, and the rest of the world remained in thrall to global capitalism and American consumerism. Recalling U.S.-Soviet nuclear chauvinism, military spending dominated government budgets, power and wealth remained unequally distributed, the ignorant remained unenlightened, the heathen and infidel threats were ubiquitous and increasing. In effect, nothing had changed.[71]

Radical neo-Marxism has found little difficulty in translating liberalism and McDonaldization into cultural imperialism and neocolonialism. Even though global revolution had receded beyond sight into the future, opposition to capitalist globalization, McDonaldization, and exported liberalism remained not only strategically attractive but ideologically and morally imperative. With a broad focus on *both* consumers and the workers, Marx's historical materialism and Lenin's antiglobalization remain solid barriers to globalization. Despite the collapse of Soviet communism, revolution, not globalization, remains the only path to a beatific future of prosperity, security, and justice. With its new consumer-friendly face, revolutionary neo-Marxism is slowly regaining its former credibility as an alternative to *both* idealistic, liberal ideas *and* pragmatic, conservative policies.

Dependency Theory

Sufficiently flexible to embrace a broad spectrum of views, dependency theory begins with the premise that the global political-economy enslaves the poor economies by making them politically and economically dependent on the rich economies. The result of globalization is economic growth in the rich economies as they exploit the poor ones. "Some countries (the dominant ones) can expand and can be self-sustaining, while others (the dependent ones) can do this only as a reflection of that expansion, which can have either a positive or negative effect on their immediate development."[72] Economic globalization began to create dependency as colonial imperialism in the eighteenth century and deepened it as the international distribution of labor of the Industrial Revolutions. The post–Cold-War wave of financial-industrial globalization has created permanent dependency through the global networks of transnational banks and corporations and their connections between rich and poor states. The pernicious combination of technology transfer, foreign direct investment, official development aid, and commercial-sovereign loans has transformed globalization from the path to progress into an avenue of exploitation.

A number of dependency theorists have called for dependent countries to withdraw from the global political-economy and reject globalization. Since development for poor countries was inconsistent with integration into the global economy, dependency theory has called for socialist models of insulated development, state control, and socialism. Reversing the process of capitalist globalization would set poor countries on an independent path to progress. Many social and political movements have found common cause with neo-Marxists in preferring ideological mass movements to reverse globalization. More sophisticated than dogmatic Leninist calls for violent revolution, dependency movements favor antiglobalism to change not only the dynamics of the global political-economy but to replace the structures of global capitalism. Deep, neo-Marxist, dependency-theoretic antiglobalism demands actions by intergovernmental organizations to redistribute wealth and power from rich countries to poor people. Less radical prescriptions have included import substitution to ameliorate the effects of globalization in self-sufficiency.

The New Left

The antiglobal, anticapitalist New Left appeared as a recognizable, flow of radical thought in 1989 as the Berlin Wall fell and joined neo-Marxism in its focus on historical materialism and the economic struggle between rich and poor. With the evolution of the New Left, the anticapitalism of orthodox Cold-War radicalism has mellowed into antiglobalism. "The notion that globalization is merely an external manifestation of the internal struggles that doom capitalism—and that globalization is also, in essence, the capitalist exploitation of weak nations—provides an explanation linking the two phenomena that resonates among the idealist young on the left. Capitalism, they argue, seeks globalization to benefit itself, and, in the process, harms others abroad."[73] This already complex relationship is rendered nearly incoherent by the admixture of various versions of anti-Americanism.

What the New Left shares with violent, neo-Marxist revolutionaries, pacifist idealists, and populist protesters is the basic premise that capitalism and globalization are bad. Forming the nucleus of this hostility of the New Left is Jagdish Bhagwati's "trilogy of discontents about the idea of capitalism, the process of globalization, and the behavior of corporations."[74] Generally too young to have experienced the rapture of Cold-War radical idealism, the ideologues of the New Left see in *both* global capitalism *and* Westphalian sovereignty degenerate systems ignoring human concerns about social justice.

New Leftists agree with globalists that globalization rests on two pillars: communication and the market. They see communication not as a technical process but as a McLuhanesque merger of media and message that displaces progress with communication as the prime mover for humanity. The New Left accuses globalists of raising the significance of the market in replacing social cohesion as the ideal structure and reason as the leading dynamic of human affairs. "Since ancient times, humanity has known two great organizing principles: the gods, and then reason. From here on out, the market succeeds them both."[75] The New Left generally observes that capitalism has prospered as technology has expanded communications and that economic globalization and the information revolution have accelerated over the last few generations. Since "social ills have worsened, then the former phenomena must have caused the latter. . . . While globalization may be economically benign in the sense that it increases overall wealth, it is socially malign in terms of its impact on poverty, literacy, gender equality, cultural autonomy, and diversity."[76] Since the market cannot, or will not, address these social issues, it is the moral duty of people to reverse globalization and replace the market with human will.

A Nietzsche-esque nihilism implicit in impotent rage against the machine and an idealistic urge to control transformation often led the New Left to ideological chaos and moral anarchy. Distinct from Marxism, the philosophical and theoretical roots of the New Left penetrate deeply into the French *engagé* tradition from Émile Zola and Jean-Paul Sartre to Viviane Forrester.[77] Consciously rational, the New Left "sees in capitalism and globalization a malign conjunction that disempowers citizens everywhere, privileges corporations, and reduces democracy to an ever more hollow sham. [The prophets of the New Left] are cartographers of the many terrains occupied by the protesters against globalization."[78] Although continental Europe takes the New-Left seriously, Britain and North America are less inclined towards this sort of antiglobalism, which claims to be *both* revolutionary *and* reformist.

The Reformist Perspective. A growing group of *engagé* thinkers of the New Left sympathizes with reformist attitudes that avoid the abrupt, revolutionary approaches of Marxism-Leninism and do not condone violent action. This suffused body of thought rejects radical change and prefers gradual, partial change to ameliorate current injustices and inequalities. In a perversely anomalous and bewildering self-image, most reformists see themselves as the only true defenders of globalization against *both* isolationist calls for reversing the process *and* ultraliberal insistence on pure, open-market capitalism.

The reformist approach influences not only antiglobal groups—labor unions, faith groups, charities, and humanists—but also many institutions of globalization. "The reformists act within current political systems and advocate gradualism and peaceful change. Most accept a role for the market, but believe [that] it must be better regulated and managed in order to achieve socially just and sustainable [results]."[79] Although its center of intellectual gravity lies in the New Left, reformism spans many currents of antiglobalism. Many reformers of the New Left have accepted the permanence of capitalism and "concluded that working with the market can produce results, and are willing to swallow their skepticism and work alongside corporations."[80]

The Communitarian Perspective. A *potpourri* of Gramscian social ideas, Gandhian economics, and Rawlsian politics occludes the communitarian perspective. The ultimate good resides in tight, independent communities of like-minded people who balance moral and civic virtues with a deep suspicion of market economics.[81] Oriented towards the anticorporate, antigovernment, left, communitarians find in globalization a primal foe of social life and human values. Although some communitarian thought includes creating a global community, the focus is on local community and resurrecting traditional civil societies. "Believing that globalization is ultimately unsustainable because of its devastation of the environment, many communitarians advocate return to a world of self-sufficient, closed communities."[82]

The Humanitarian Perspective. A powerful humanist thrust of radical thought stresses the debilitating effects of capitalist globalization on people: increasing inequality and economic polarization.[83] Like communitarianism, this humanitarian strand of thought rejects Smithian invisible-hand arguments about capitalist institutions that produce the public good. The humanitarian soul of the New Left is torn between "empathy for the misery of a distant elsewhere and an inadequate intellectual grasp of what can be done to ameliorate that distress. The resulting tension then takes the form of unhappiness with the capitalist system within which we live and anger at its apparent callousness."[84] This humanism of the New Left not only challenges liberal, capitalist, democratic systems but finds a kindred spirit in fashionable concern that global deregulation has increased the gap between the rich and the poor.[85] Generous compassion and sensitivities to human misery generate calls for a revolutionary new world order, protectionism, government action, drastic reform, or individual protest, all within the humanitarian perspective.

The Political Perspective. Although the New Left tends to accept the current dominance of the market, Bacon's idols are actively rebuilding opposition and resistance to economic globalization in the cracks between the nationalist, dependency, and humanitarian movements. The political New Left proposes globalization of democracy, public transparency, constitutional change, universal health care, trade unionism, and environmental management at national and global levels. The broad scope of action suggests a pragmatic opportunism focused on nothing any more substantial than opposing globalization in whatever form it appears.

Not abandoning the proletariat, oppressed by globalization, and beginning to act spontaneously as predicted by Marx, the New Left recognizes the mediation of self-awareness and group identities between production and society. The political left is expanding its call for antiglobal reactions into the consumer culture, the world's segmented workforces, and any emerging, global civil society. Embracing McDonaldized workers, farmers, shopkeepers, technicians, and small businesses, the political left resists the logic of global capitalism in globalizing them into a world without frontiers, where capital's only loyalty is to its shareholders.[86] With some success in mobilizing this disparate force of the threatened, the New Left is struggling to shift from simply opposing globalization to promoting an alternate global governance.

Beyond Radicalism

Globalization's collision with radical thought and determined opposition has left people and societies vulnerable and exposed. On one side, Bacon's *idola theatri* and *idola specus* offer prosperity through the enticing, totalitarian logic of the market. On another, the heartless logic of materialism and reason seems irresistible. On yet another, the mindless demagogy of perfect, divine truth invites people to experience perfection.[87] Although the fragmented, radical movements have yet to develop any consensus, or even a common view, on globalization, a growing, small group of radicals is finding, and occupying, new political spaces, especially in Europe. Deepening economic globalization invites them to a new global "social democratic third way between a highly dynamic but politically unacceptable American-style liberal capitalism and a moribund Soviet-style communism."[88] For many radical thinkers, the drama and dynamism of global revolution are mellowing into a sort of global Fabianism that is finding expression through traditional leftist-moderate party platforms in Britain, France, Japan, Australia, and Latin America.

The Statist Movements

The statist focus on national government as *both* a barrier *and* the solution to globalization is visibly split between the political left and the political right. Dominated by social-democratic and isolationist tendencies, labor parties and social-welfare movements stress economic statism in rich and poor countries alike. The statist left stresses the role of the state in managing economic conditions for the benefit of the masses. The statist right recalls the preglobalization era of its own relevance in proposals for state-based global governance, an exclusive hypernationalism, international power politics, and deference to identity-based politics in a passive civil society.

Economic Statism

Interpreting globalization as a political-economic disaster, the statist left finds the solution to humanity's economic miseries in reversing globalization and rebuilding national social structures. With no ideology or even mythology beyond broad, humanistic socialism, economic statism resolves into a nebulous, social-democratic, civil-society defense of the welfare state against the forces of globalization. Statism has refined and strengthened the Keynesian consensus that the state can better manage people's affairs than can the market or the people. Statists extend the responsibility of the state from President Roosevelt's New Deal and European social democracy of merely providing welfare for the destitute to managing the aggregate prosperity of the nation.

With a narrow, domestic, economic focus, statist left movements in the rich countries reject liberalization of trade and call for restoration of sovereign state powers to protect domestic industries from unfair trade practices, cheap imports, and export of jobs. Statists in poor countries tend to reject global institutions on the premise that globalization is creating the worst of all possible worlds and call for reversal of globalization to recover state sovereignty and autonomy. Beyond its stress on national prosperity, the statist left retains a strong sense of classical interstate politics in a society of states.

Political Statism

Less focused on economics than the left, the statist right suggests that the state remains powerful, even dominant in politics, although it is no longer the *only* participant. Even in a world completely globalized into a single market, "there are still opportunities for the development of governance mechanisms at the level of the international economy that neither undermine national governments nor hinder the creation of national strategies for international control. . . . the world of markets remains susceptible to conscious intervention."[89] In this spirit of statism, Bacon's idols confuse globalism with internationalism and transform globalization into national interest. Classical diplomacy and staaatist power politics converge in an antiglobalist return from cooperative multilateralism to the autonaomous, unilateral state. Instead of global or transnational governance, the statist right offers a diplomatic, balance-of-power approach to interstate politics modified by sovereign interactions with nonsovereign entities within a society of states.

With tasteful regard for globalism, the rightist return to the state has deepened with diffusion of political authority, unilateralism, and intervention. In the context of European Union, political statism gained momentum from the Amsterdam summit to the 2001 intergovernmental conference in Nice as authority devolved from the Commission to the Council of Heads of State. The United States has shown this antiglobalist tendency in its return to unilateral approaches to global warming, counterterrorism, criminal justice, and opposition to multilateral global financial and anticriminal regulation.

The same antiglobalist tendencies toward rediscovery of the efficacy of national, unilateral policy generate strident calls for reform of the ponderous structures of multinational or global politics within the United Nations. The history of U.N.-sponsored interventions presents a vivid image of rightist antiglobalism in operation. During the 1990s the world has

> seen two cycles in the realm of U.N. interventions. First [was] a boom and a bust, from the Gulf War to Rwanda and Bosnia. Then, subsequently [was] a boomlet, with the oblique Kosovo and the direct East Timor and Sierra Leone mandates, and within [the boomlet] the very various and different executions, respectively in those cases [that] many take to be a sort of *bustlet*. . . . Implications of these trends are registered in repeated questions about how to deal with a blocked U.N. process in the face of urgent need to act; in pragmatic listing of modalities; and [in] the emergence of the [unilateral] *framework* or [single-country-led] *mixed model* [of U.N.-sponsored intervention].[90]

The Dark Faces of Globalization

Globalization presents several bright faces of material benefit, wealth creation, new knowledge, and progress to the rich democracies, cosmocrats, and the world's connected people. To the world's poor, oppressed, and excluded, however, it presents darker faces filled with tribulations, confusion, trauma, and destruction of what little wealth that they may have. Instead of presenting golden opportunities for progress, globalization poses grim barriers to survival. Instead of understanding, Bacon's idols expand its dark faces into asymmetric wars of resistance, terrorism, and global crime. "Today's terrorist fanatics often harbor a loathing towards the spread of Western secular, consumer values and the declining power of their own traditional elites. They perceive these developments to be byproducts of globalization, and they identify the United States as the symbol and epitome of globalization."[91]

Deconstructivism

"Professor John Gray of the London School of Economics, has recently been arguing that the dark, deconstructing aspects of globalization are becoming rapidly more evident than the bright, cohering ones [that] fascinated people so much in the early years of the *interregnum* at the end of the Cold War."[92] Within the dark, deconstructivist shadow, globalization is absolutely wrong and is leading people blindly towards a nonexistent dream-world. To understand the truth of social reality requires deconstructing globalization by first stopping it, then reversing it, and ultimately by shattering Bacon's idols to expose its many faces. Anticapitalist, antimoralist, and antiglobalist, deconstructivism demands radical, egalitarian redistribution of everything from political rights and moral obligation to meaning and money.

Economic Predominance

Another dark face of globalization is the specter of unipolar economic dominance by a single country—usually envisioned as the United States. Whereas fewer radical, antiglobal thinkers have devoted much attention to the clear U.S. preponderance in military power since the end of the Cold War, concern about economic predominance permeates the entire body of antiglobalist thought. The absolute size and predominance of the U.S. economy and market ensure that any weakness in American demand will be exported, as reductions "in spending by American consumers and businesses hurt demand for foreign-made goods. The great danger is that [although the United States] can weather a downturn, the developing countries cannot. Poverty, especially outside China, has been increasing, the growth of the 1990s has turned into stagnation and recession, and what growth has occurred has largely accrued to the wealthy."[93] Instead of constructing a bright, integrated global economy as promised, the process of globalization has created a collection of weak national economies that are all critically dependent on the huge U.S. market and its demand for foreign goods and services.

Destructive Creation

A particularly dark face of globalization presides over creating a few large winners who increase their wealth and a host of economic losers who increase their poverty. "Along with traditional [U.S.] allies in Europe and Japan, U.S. citizens have experienced unprecedented prosperity and freedom that [have] allowed [them] to enjoy wealth, power, and a sense of democratic superiority."[94] The disposition of global capitalism to balance this generation of wealth with creation of poverty recalls what Joseph Schumpeter celebrated as the *dual process of creative destruction*, the entrepreneurial engine of economic growth. As Marx predicted, however, at the global level the same zero-sum balancing process reverses and splits into *separate effects* of *destruction* and *creation*. Instead of recycling destroyed assets, people, and firms into a newly created social reality as growth, *destructive creation* accumulates separate stocks of wealth and poverty. "The winners and losers of this phase of globalization are not predetermined by either the logic of technology or the political will of the powerful. The outcome will also depend on human beings continuing to make history by pursuing their passions and their interests —both by those who side with power and those who resist it."[95]

This blackest face of globalization presides over the clashes between antiglobalist, nationalist—and even radical—thought of poor, premodern societies with the globalizing values of liberal, capitalist democracies. Unable to compete with capitalist economies and to provide the political governance that modernizing populations require, many loser communities retreat into their own traditional, spiritual, and political orthodoxies. As retreat becomes defense of cultural values, meanings, and identities, these losers turn to asymmetric warfare in the forms of terrorism and crime to resist globalization.

Creative Alternatives

Non-Marxist thinkers generally concentrate initially on building small-scale alternatives to global politics and economics in faith that their examples will be irresistible to people of goodwill, who will join in resisting globalization. As ecologists tend organic gardens, environmentalists protest corporate power, entrepreneurs struggle to destroy global brands, or Zapatistas advertise their own marginalization, these thinkers create alternatives to globalization. With the blessings of this brightest of globalization's dark faces, these alternatives rely on creativity and human will to transform globalization into progress. Stubbornly defending their private, cultural, political, and economic spaces, these creative alternatives defy market penetration, political encroachment, or cultural pollution of their beliefs and heritages. The collective effect, however, extends beyond antiglobal destruction to creation of alternative, new social realities and new knowledge in a broadening and deepening *conjoncture-basho*.

Populist Antiglobalism

Focused on people, rather than economics or politics, populism finds in the corporate power of wealth and the political power of coercion not the means to prosperity and security but the sources of human misery. The state and capitalism have not only diverted progress from human purposes but also threatened earth's environment. Perhaps more damaging than the direct effects of industry and government is the absence of global governance to balance economics and politics with people and nature. Populism joins radicalism in using *idola theatri* to castigate business and government for ignoring or even suppressing people. More effectively than radicals or statists, populism has focused Bacon's *idola fori* through visual imagery against globalization. In a perverse paradox, populist movements routinely use the technologies and mechanisms of globalization and the mass media to oppose globalization.

Although most movements focus on single issues, populists share the theme that the problem of political-economic globalization is incompatible with protecting human rights and the environment.[96] "Speaking the language of opposition, their discourse reflects a greater commitment to the questions of justice, accountability, and democracy."[97] Disillusioned with politics, globalization's losers take responsibility for their own survival and begin to make socioeconomic choices that reflect their own interests.[98] At the heart of civil society, nongovernmental organizations actively focus social choices in populist initiatives opposing privatization and deregulation.[99] One pervasive articulation of populist antiglobalism is the movement for new protectionism "to put governments at a local, national, and regional level back in control of their economies, and to relocalize and rediversify them."[100]

After decades of disorganized dissent, the focused street mobilizations in Seattle in November 1999 launched a better coordinated series of well-publicized populist actions.[101] The global intensity and persistence of protest began to shift the attention of political and economic leaders to the recurring populist themes. "Some of them are anarchists, but a lot of them have some very legitimate complaints."[102] The increasing, nonviolent power of the powerless, living in truth with their own ethic of responsibility, balances their apparent powerlessness against violence by denying the right of the powerful to exist.[103] Although active populism has gained a responsive audience, it has not yet articulated a credible, people-based, normative alternative to resource-based globalization.[104] As populism shifts from radicalism to responsibility, efforts to use people power to arrest the process of globalization converge in three channels: economic, environmental, and most recently political.

Economic Populism

In the wonderful world of consumerism, the global firms and speculators seeking open markets, cheap labor and materials, and low-risk opportunities present one of the darker faces of globalization. Studiously disinterested in the noneconomic affairs of host communities, these commercial carriers of globalization earn the denunciation of citizens more as parts of their problems than as solutions. Many people-power movements have learned "how to tap into the growing worries that people in many countries have about economic globalization."[105] Finding any solutions at all beyond the reach of local government or civil society, disillusioned consumers, stockholders, and voters noisily resort to people power to regain control over their lives. The obvious targets are the institutions of McWorld, the global corporations. Echoing popular rumblings, many small governments—and politicians in larger countries—have targeted big corporations as the same monolithic instrument of unwanted social transformation that the medieval church had been.

Despite its anarchic fringe and synergy with the New Left, the core of populism is neither revolutionary nor reformist. Economic populism seeks to make global capital and corporations accountable not only to shareholders in home countries but to stakeholders—employees, customers, or suppliers—in the countries where they buy and sell, and to global humanity. Most important is not ending global capitalism but convincing multinational enterprises to impose some level of ethics and moral responsibility on their activities.

Focused on redistributive economics, unaffordable politics, and environmentally unsustainable development schemes, the first loose generation of economic populism informally adopted the antiglobalism of the New Left in the 1980s. As economic populism shifts its *raison d'être* away from redistribution towards antiglobalization, transnational firms are becoming more comfortable with populist programs in home countries and host countries alike. Although they rarely react favorably to populist initiatives through unions or governments to control operational decisions, most provide safe working environments, opportunities for promotion, and health programs. After failure of the first generation of economic populists to achieve redistribution, and tentative success in gaining responsivity to local communities, a third generation of economic populism seems to be on the verge of abandoning antiglobalism. Some economic populists are recognizing that many victims of globalization suffer from too little globalization—political trade barriers, few foreign-operated factories, low foreign investment—rather than from too much.

Environmental Populism

The broadly antiglobal Green movement has become a sophisticated political force since Rachel Carson launched it in 1961 with her *Silent Spring*. Embedded in the economic crises of the 1970s, Green populism adopted "an ecological concern that the planet was reaching the limits of its capacity to sustain human settlement under prevailing conditions of production, resource-depletion, and attendant pollution."[106] Although humanity has not yet experienced the end of history, ecological reality of the twenty-first century depicts "a society living after the end of nature. Few aspects of the physical world . . . are any longer just natural—unaffected by human intervention."[107]

The foundation of environmental populism is the truism that business of all sorts, in all places, and at all times is dirty, consumes resources, and deprioritizes people and the natural environment. The ultimate objects of concern are the interactions of people with other forms of life and with the life-sustaining substances that permeate the biosphere—the thin film in which life flourishes that envelops the planet from the seabeds to the upper atmosphere. Environmentalism portrays globalization—especially technological and economic—as an irresponsible, uncontrolled vehicle for capitalistic exploitation of the biosphere. Crucial to environmentalist concerns is "an implicit, and very strict, idea of sustainability, which in effect denies that natural resources can often be replaced or augmented by manmade ones."[108]

In league with economic populism, global environmentalism has achieved some modest success in influencing the local operations of global firms. Populism has brought firms to recognize that dirty, unhealthy factories in poor countries lose customers in rich markets and that economies of scale reduce the costs of compliance with unilateral, environmental, and labor regulations. Like economic populists, Green populists are also beginning to recognize that "far from being caused by unfettered capitalism, environmental damage is often caused by exactly the opposite. . . . Globalization sometimes directly benefits the environment by promoting things such as trade in pollution control technology and the privatization of state-owned companies, which become less polluting as they are restructured."[109]

Political Populism

"Before the liberating technology was available, companies were hierarchical organizations, and democratic societies were organized through representation. Now citizens who live in representative democracies have the power to decentralize radically and to evolve into direct democracies."[110] Political populism rests on a literal interpretation of majority rule through decentralized initiative-and-referendum or direct democracy and a conviction of the goodwill and ability of the people to govern. Patronizingly tolerant of structural, representative democracy, political populism finds no value in elites —elected, appointed, or self-selected. In contrast to liberalism, populist thought rejects constitutional limits, electoral constraints, or party systems that frustrate the ascendance of dominant, popular majorities. Instead of the individual rights and rationalism that animate liberalism, the "guiding principle is that all politics tends to come down to a conflict between the people and the interests. . . . Populists see politics not so much in terms of class, but as a matter of relations between the overwhelming mass of the people as a whole and a small number of vested interests marked by a strong tendency toward conspiratorial action."[111]

Less visible that either economic or environmental populism, the political dimension of populism finds expression in "the 'politics of antipolitics.' Populists who come to power through democratic elections govern in an authoritarian style justified by continual attacks on traditional political elites and established institutions."[112] For political populists, the corrupted political process itself is the primary barrier to human freedom, which can be realized only when government is utterly subservient to the people.

On the right, political populism has forged alliances with protectionists, environmentalists, and statists and on the left with organized labor and socialism. Across these alliances, populism accuses free trade, multinational corporations, and international organizations of causing global disaster. With the precedent established by Alberto Fujimori in Peru in the 1990s, political populism has also begun to expand into local, antiparty politics.[113] Antiglobal populism continues to seek and find in the world's political institutions and among the directors of global corporations the corruption, ineptitude, and criminality that justify depoliticization of global politics and politization of global economics. Just as Fujimori dismantled many of Peru's constitutional institutions and political parties on the argument that the people had lost faith in them, antiglobal populism demands that international organizations limit their activities to administration and economics, not politics.

DEGLOBALIZING GLOBALISM?

Despite the media's celebration of globalization, the pressures of antiglobalism have wrought profound transformations in the social reality that people accept as normal. After more than a century of repeated radical attempts at revolution and reform, the 1970s wave of globalization has been profoundly influenced by the antiglobalist power of the people through populist movements. Within the greater context of expanding global political-economic governance, antiglobalism has expanded global attention to issues of justice and increased the relative priorities of economic issues in the processes of global politics. Corporations have come to recognize some notion of corporate social responsibility as a legitimate business concern.

The Power of the People

Despite the common pride of populists and radicals in their lack of formal leadership and structure, radical successes and revolution continue to retreat into memory, while populism accumulates credibility and even legitimacy. It is clear that populism has become more than a noisy public nuisance and has generated some significant, progressive changes in the global political-economic establishment. Although most populist protests fade invisibly into history after a few days of entertaining, live television coverage, they have captured some portions of the global political agenda. The steady pressure of populism is achieving some success in fracturing cosmopolitan consensus about the virtues of globalization. When the 1996–1997 Asian financial crisis exposed the flaws in the global financial structure, civil-society populism quickly placed the blame on corruption and cronyism as radicals called for revolution. Populist antiglobalists joined statists, however, in pointing to multinational insensitivity to local conditions and retorted that "the East Asian countries had been forced to globalize prematurely."[114] After intensive and extensive investigation of the facts, economics, and policies involved by official inquiries supported by populist pressures, it later became clear that "we were overemphasizing the benefits of free movement of capital and underemphasizing the risks."[115] Globalist policymakers and development economists quietly recognized the validity of populist-statist wisdom and retired the orthodox, global-capitalist consensus on free capital movement.

Populist antiglobalism is deeply skeptical about the universal benefits of free trade and recognizes the close relationships between human economics and the rest of nature. Populism suggests that, beyond simply increasing economic inequality, free trade creates social and environmental problems that have important effects on people, even though they are beyond the scope of market economics. Many of the world's liberal governments recognize and share civil society's concerns about "unequal trade relations and financial speculation that bring entire economies to the brink of ruin."[116] Supporting civil-society wisdom and populist sentiment, statist economic research indicates that "the countries that do best . . . do not simply fling open their markets and wait for trade to work its magic. They use trade as part of a homegrown strategy that includes building sound political and legal institutions."[117]

Although radical thought had introduced them earlier as revolutionary ideas, many changes that were already forming in the late 1980s found their ways into the 1990s protests of populists and environmentalists. The persistence of populist activism—environmentalists, statists, and civil society, as well as antiglobalists—has forced onto the international political agenda such controversial issues as labor relations and working conditions, environmental degradation, terms of trade, debt relief, and human rights. Public visibility of these issues has significantly increased the influence of the large nongovernmental organizations and interests groups—World Wide Fund for Nature, OxFam, the Sierra Club, and others. Faced with unruly populist protesters and consumer boycotts, "firms and governments are suddenly eager to do business with the respectable face of dissent."[118]

Antiglobal Globalization

Primarily through nongovernmental organizations and civil society, political institutions and corporations have prioritized antiglobalists' concerns about justice within their political and economic perspectives. Cosmocracy has not only developed a formidable base of knowledge about people's feelings, behaviors, and concerns but has created significant new knowledge across economic, political, and cultural perspectives. The huge masses of relevant information and the consequent need for antiglobalist organizations and movements to specialize in particular efforts continue to increase the impacts of antiglobalism on specific features of globalization. Antiglobalism seems increasingly comfortable in several broad perspectives of living.

People: The Material Life

Antiglobalist strategies focused on people—Braudel's domain of material life—seek to empower families and individuals with the economic capacity to overcome dislocations brought by globalization. Historically calling for redistribution of wealth by state governments, the appeal of this approach to *both* statism *and* populism also focuses cosmocracy on a society of states or a world government. This sort of antiglobalism has historically stressed state income support to insulate people from catastrophic change, job loss, or disability, and to protect and stabilize the national environments in which they live. Within the global perspective. "alternatively, and more innovatively, it could mean ensuring the provision of the kinds of health, leisure, and community-related services [that] serve as anchors for stable communities."[119] Antiglobalist movements with this human-welfare focus calling for transfer of resources, accountability, and responsibility for these services from central state authorities find common cause with one-world global humanists.

Regionalism

Within the broader perspective of the market economy—Braudel's second domain—economic antiglobalism has opened a regional, macroeconomic path to expand national economies beyond the political constraints of national borders. Exemplified in the European Union, regional antiglobalism creates less-than-global, extranational spaces for transparent, competitive markets protected against disruptions of speculative, global capitalism—Braudel's third domain. Statist regionalism prefers a deeper political and institutional structure. State governments use targeted, microeconomic, fiscal policies and local tax privileges to stabilize social systems or limit global capitalist penetrations into the regional market economy. Populism calls for regional, public-owned community banks and insurance programs across decentralized welfare states. Statists and populists support each other's demands for export-promotion subsidies to strengthen local finance and production networks and insulate local markets from the extraregional pressures of economic globalization.

Humanizing Governance

Politicians—global, international, and domestic—have clearly recognized and accepted the need and legitimacy of responding to public concerns. "When there are genuine doubts in the minds of policymakers, a comparatively small number of demonstrators can have a disproportionate political impact."[120] Beneath this shift in the attitudes of the institutions of global governance has been a noticeable trend in public opinion, led by the persistent, if inconsistent and mercurial, global news media. Real-time television pictures of military intervention, massive bombing campaigns, and police brutality generate sympathetic populist and radical political actions throughout the world. Populations sensitive to the environment have demanded the increasing availability of organic, fair-trade, recyclable, or sustainable products and more restrictions on pollution, industrial wastes, or resource consumption. The combination of media coverage and the consumer culture has shifted public opinion ponderously towards humanist antiglobalism and populist anticapitalism. After a half century of promoting capitalism and globalization as foundations of the market economy and national prosperity, governments throughout the world are struggling with the micro- and macroeconomic aspects of *both* domestic *and* global governance.

Antiglobal Global Community?

The dawn of the twenty-first century exposed the structure of global political-economy and the process of globalization in a joint crisis of legitimacy within the condition of globalization. Much of the world no longer regarded transnational corporations, the global financial and goods markets, the political systems of liberal democracy, or U.S. military predominance as legitimate, credible, or good. As the illusion of a global community of liberal-capitalist-democratic interests splintered, an antiglobalist global community began to reassemble the shards during the 2001–2002 World Social Forum in Pôrto

Alegre, Brazil. The Pôrto Alegre process provided the forum and focus for the diverse antiglobal movements, concentrated the people power of antiglobalism, and organized the debate over designing an alternative world order.

The global community forming spontaneously around the spirit of Pôrto Alegre subordinates the rational efficiency of the market and the social contract of the Hobbesian polity to security, equity, and justice. Embedding politics and economics in society, Pôrto Alegre humanism rescues people from the control of the collective polity and the impersonal economy, This humanist community calls on antiglobalism to transform global governance for control, rather than promotion, of globalization. Rather than a regime that imposes the rules of one model of living on all people, global governance must decentralize institutional power and wealth in a pluralistic system. "Only in such a global context—more fluid, less structured, more pluralistic, with multiple checks and balances—will the citizens of the South and North find ways to develop based on their own unique values, rhythms, and strategies."[121]

A Human Face for Globalization

Historically, profound political-economic change of the sort envisioned by most of the antiglobalists has been created by the great powers and wealthy countries. The raw material and stimuli for change emerged from world war and global economic collapse in a process of globalization. Significant change in the apparatus of global governance has been rigidly dependent on perceptions of global order and security, not on human concerns about justice or even prosperity. Despite its tentative achievements in reminding global politics of the existence of people, any sustained success of either antiglobalism or globalization will probably depend on popular perceptions of security and the great-power debate on keeping global order. The antiglobalist movement of movements has developed from a vexing barrier into a legitimate, active participant in global politics and globalization. Antiglobalism will remain at least a latent prod to global decisionmakers to expand the perspective of global politics to include people. Within the human perspective, the global political agenda and the process of globalization prioritize people's concerns for security and prosperity. The condition of globalization, however, also recognizes their concerns about justice and their political-economic visions into the global perspective.

Humanity is probably unwilling, although not unable, to reverse, halt, or even slow the process of globalization by erecting impenetrable barriers within and across various perspectives. Billions of resentful, angry people throughout the world, however, are likely to maintain a continuous threat to the agents and carriers of globalization unless it assumes a softer and gentler guise. "It may have to adopt more culturally sensitive and economically inclusive approaches that can help bridge the gap between winners and losers. Sharing is a cornerstone of Western civilization that may be handy in the new world order. An emphasis on sharing may create a sense of inclusiveness and hope among those who today feel left behind. If globalization is to be distinguishable from old-time colonialism, it has to be welcomed by all participants, who must see themselves as partners rather than vassals. If globalization is to represent real progress, we must give it a human face."[122]

NOTES

1. See Karl Polanyi, *The Great Transformation: The Political and Economic Origins of Our Time* (New York: Rinehart, 1944), 130–134.

2. Henry A. Kissinger, *Does America Need a Foreign Policy?* (New York: Simon and Schuster, 2001), 30.

3. See Kees van der Pijl, "The International Level," in *The Capitalist Class: An International Study*, edited by Tom Bottomore and Robert J. Brym, 237–266 (New York: New York University Press, 1989), 243–258.

4. For a discussion of the financial community and transnational enterprises as the nucleus of a privileged, transnational, ruling class, see Stephen Gill, *American Hegemony and the Trilateral Commission* (Cambridge: Polity, 1990), 37, 89–95.

5. Richard Falk, "State of Siege: Will Globalization Win Out?" *International Affairs* 73(1) (January 1997): 123–136; 129.

6. Robert Reich, *The Work of Nations: Preparing Ourselves for 21st- Century Capitalism* (New York: Alfred A. Knopf, 1991), 252–261, 268–280, 282–300.

7. John Micklethwaite and Adrian Wooldridge, *A Future Perfect: The Challenge and Hidden Promise of Globalization* (New York: Random House–Crown Business, 2000), 232.

8. See Nick Stevenson, "Globalization and Cultural Political Economy," in *Globalization and its Critics*, edited by Randall D. Germain, 91–113 (New York: St. Martin's, 2000), 109.

9. See Ulf Hannerz, *Cultural Complexity: Studies in the Social Organization of Meaning* (New York: Columbia University Press, 1992), 217–265, esp. 252–255.

10. Christopher Lasch, *The Revolt of the Elites and the Betrayal of Democracy* (New York: W. W. Norton, 1995), 47, 33.

11. Micklethwaite and Wooldridge, *A Future Perfect*, 232, 241.

12. See Susan Strange, "The Name of the Game," in *Sea Changes: American Foreign Policy in a World Transformed*, edited by Nicholas X. Rizopolous, 238–273 (New York: Council on Foreign Relations, 1990), 260–265.

13. Known variously as megacities, microregions, global cities, or region-states, such centers have formed around Hong Kong and southeastern China; Singapore, Brunei, western Indonesia, and southern India; Vancouver and Seattle; Toronto, Detroit, and Cleveland; Palo Alto and San Francisco; the port cities of the Baltic, Stuttgart, London, and other locations.

14. Micklethwaite and Wooldridge, *A Future Perfect*, 306.

15. Bruce Kogut, "International Business: The New Bottom Line," *Foreign Policy* 110 (Spring 1998): 152–165; 160.

16. John Stopford, "Multinational Corporations," *Foreign Policy* 113 (Winter 1998–1999): 12–24; 15.

17. Stopford, "Multinational Corporations," 12.

18. Kogut, "International Business," 160.

19. Stopford, "Multinational Corporations," 17.

20. See Bruce Kogut and Ugo Zander, "Knowledge of the Firm and the Evolutionary Theory of the Multinational Corporation," *Journal of International Business Studies* 24(4) (Fourth Quarter 1993): 625–646; 631–632, 636, 639.

21. Björn Johnson, Edward Lorenz, and Bengt-Åke, "Why All the Fuss about Codified and Tacit Knowledge?" *Industrial and Corporate Change* 11(2) (April 2002): 245–262; 251.

22. See Anna Lee Saxenian, *Regional Advantage: Culture and Competition in Silicon Valley and Route 128* (Cambridge: Harvard University Press, 1994), 30–57.

23. Anna Lee Saxenian and Jinn-Yuh Hsu, "The Silicon Valley-Hsinchu Connection: Technical Communities and Industrial Upgrading," *Industrial and Corporate Change* 10(4) (December 2001): 893–920; 898.

24. See Masahiko Aoki, *Innovation in the Governance of Product-System Innovation: The Silicon Valley Model*, Stanford Institute for Economic Policy Research, Policy Paper no. 00-003, October 2000, cited in Saxenian and Hsu, "The Silicon Valley-Hsinchu Connection," 899.

25. Saxenian and Hsu, "The Silicon Valley-Hsinchu Connection," 904.

26. See Saxenian and Hsu, "The Silicon Valley-Hsinchu Connection," 905. Constance S. Meaney, "State Policy and the Development of Taiwan's Semiconductor Industry," in *The Role of the State in Taiwan's Development*, edited by Joel D. Aberbach, David Dollar, and Kenneth L. Sokoloff, 170–192 (London: Sharpe, 1994), 174–180; Chung Yuan Liu, "Government's Role in Developing a High-Tech Industry: The Case of Taiwan's Semiconductor Industry," *Technovation* 13(5) (July 1993): 299–309; Pao Long Chang, Chintay Shih, and Chiung Wen Hsu, "The Formation Process of Taiwan's IC Industry—Method of Technology Transfer," *Technovation* 14(3) (April 1994): 161–171; Pao Long Chang, Chiung Wen Hsu, and Chien Tzu Tsai, "A Stage Approach for Industrial Technology Development and Implementation—The Case of Taiwan's Computer Industry," *Technovation* 19(4) (February 1999): 233–241.

27. Saxenian and Hsu, "The Silicon Valley-Hsinchu Connection," 901.

28. See Alejandro Portes, "Global Villagers: The Rise of Transnational Communities," *American Prospect* 7(25) (March-April 1996): 77–90.

29. See Alice Stroup, *A Company of Scientists: Botany, Patronage, and Community at the Seventeenth-Century Parisian Royal Academy of Sciences* (Berkeley: University of California Press, 1990), 202–203; Lisa Jardine, *Ingenious Pursuits: Building the Scientific Revolution* (New York: Doubleday, 1999), 277, 313–316, 348–353.

30. Peter Haas introduced the concept of the epistemic community to explain the increasing political influence of such groups. Peter Haas, "Introduction: Epistemic Communities and International Policy Coordination," *International Organization* 46(1) (Winter 1992): 1–36; 2–4, 16–20.

31. Bernard Ancori, Antoine Bureth, and Patrick Cohendet, "The Economics of Knowledge: The Debate about Codification and Tacit Knowledge," *Industrial and Corporate Change* 9(2) (June 2000): 255–288; 278.

32. Hermann Haberman, "The Global Statistical System: What It Is and Why Should We Care?" *Chance* 12(2) (Spring 1999): 39–42; 42.

33. Haberman, "The Global Statistical System," 40.

34. Susan H. Gillespie, "Opening Minds: The International Liberal Education Movement," *World Policy Journal* 18(4) (Winter 2001–2002): 79–89; 81.

35. Peter Darvas, *Institutional Innovation in Central European Higher Education* (Vienna: Institute of Human Sciences, 1996), 18.

36. See Joseph Farrell and Garth Saloner, "Coordination through Committees and Markets," *RAND Journal of Economics* 19(2) (Summer 1988): 235–252; 239–240, 249–251; Howard E. Aldrich and Toshihiro Sasaki, "R&D Consortia in the United States and Japan," *Research Policy* 24(2) (March 1995): 301–316; 307–314; von Hippel, "Cooperation between Rivals," 292, 301–302; Rogers, *Diffusion of Innovations*, 17–19, 286–293, 304–313.

37. Rosenkopf and Tushman, "The Coevolution of Community Networks and Technology," 338.

38. Haberman, "The Global Statistical System," 40.

39. Haberman, "The Global Statistical System," 39.

40. See Anne-Marie Slaughter, "The Real New World Order," *Foreign Affairs* 76(5) (September-October 1997): 183–197; 189–192.

41. Keith Suter, "People Power," *The World Today* 56(10) (October 2000): 12–14; 13.

42. Suter, "People Power," 13.

43. Carol Kennedy, "Riding Out the Storm," *Director* 55(2) (September 2001): 56–59; 58, referring to comments by Andrew Wilson, director of the British Ashridge Centre for Business and Society.

44. James H. Mittelman, "The Dynamics of Globalization," in *Globalization: Critical Reflections*, edited by James H. Mittelman, 1–19 (Boulder, Colorado: Lynne Rienner, 1996, 10.

45. Mark N. Katz, "Osama bin Laden as Transnational Revolutionary Leader," *Current History* 101(652) (February 2002): 81–85; 81.

46. For a brief summary of western counterrevolutionary efforts during the Cold War see Katz, "Osama bin Laden as Transnational Revolutionary Leader," 82–83.

47. Saskia Sassen, *Globalization and Its Discontents* (New York: New Press, 1998), 56.

48. Thomas L. Friedman, *The Lexus and the Olive Tree* (New York: Farrar, Strauss, Giroux, 2000), 12.

49. Jean-Pierre Lehmann, "Developing Economies and the Demographic and Democratic Imperatives of Globalization," *International Affairs* 77(1) (January 2001): 69–82; 79–80.

50. Paul Stoller, "Trading Places: Muslim Merchants from West Africa Expand their Markets to New York City," *Natural History* 111(6) (July-August 2001): 48–55; 52–53.

51. Christina Boswell, "Desperate Measures," *The World Today* 57(11) (November 2001): 25–27; 26.

52. Immanuel Wallerstein, "Member, Dismember, Remember," *Civilization* 5(2) (April-May 1998): 54–77; 68–69.

53. Robert Hall and Carl Fox, "Rethinking Security," *NATO Review* 49(4) (Winter 2001–2002): 8–11; 8.

54. Boswell, "Desperate Measures," 25.

55. The Tampere conference of the European Union Council on Justice and Home Affairs in October 1999 used language intended to imply that the European Common Foreign and Security Policy should target European foreign aid to address the causes of emigration from recipient countries. See Boswell, "Desperate Measures," 27.

56. See Christian Joppke, "Immigration Challenges in the Nation-State," in *Challenge to the Nation-State*, edited by Christian Joppke, 1–46 (Oxford: Oxford University Press, 1998), 13, 17; Zig Layton-Henry, "Britain: The Would-Be Zero-Immigration Country," in *Controlling Immigration: A Global Perspective*, edited by Wayne A. Cornelius, Philip L. Martin, and James F. Hollifield, 274–295 (Stanford: Stanford University Press, 1994),

293;   Gary P. Freeman, "Britain, the Deviant Case," in *Controlling Immigration: A Global Perspective*, edited by Wayne A. Cornelius, Philip L. Martin, and James F. Hollifield, 297–300 (Stanford: Stanford University Press, 1994), 299–300;   Randall Hansen, *Citizenship and Immigration in Postwar Britain* (Oxford: Oxford University Press, 2000), 248–250, 259–264; Saskia Sassen, "The *de facto* Transnationalizing of Immigration Policy," in *Challenge to the Nation-State*, edited by Christian Joppke, 49–85 (Oxford: Oxford University Press, 1998), 53–69.

57. Randall Hansen, "Globalization, Embedded Realism, and Path Dependence," *Comparative Political Studies* 35(3) (April 2002): 259–283; 261–262; Gary P. Freeman, "The Decline of Sovereignty? Politics and Immigration Restriction in Liberal States," in *Challenge to the Nation-State*, edited by Christian Joppke, 86–108 (Oxford: Oxford University Press, 1998), 89–93; Sassen, "The *de facto* Transnationalizing of Immigration Policy," 69–71; Saskia Sassen, *Losing Control* (New York: Columbia University Press, 1996), 67–75, 88–99.

58. Duncan Green and Matthew Griffith, "Globalization and Its Discontents," *International Affairs* 78(1) (January 2002): 49–68; 65.

59. Robert E. Hunter, "Global Economics and Unsteady Regional Geopolitics," in *The Global Century: Globalization and National Security*, edited by Richard L. Kugler and Ellen L. Frost, vol. 1, 109–125 (Washington, D.C.: National Defense University Press, 2001), 112.

60. See Eric J. Hobsbawm, *Nations and Nationalism since 1780: Programme, Myth, Reality*, 2d ed. (Cambridge: Cambridge University Press, 1992), 188.

61. Ann Kelleher and Laura Klein, *Global Perspectives: A Handbook for Understanding Global Issues* (Upper Saddle River, New Jersey: Prentice-Hall, 1999): 177.

62. Herbert A. Simon, "We and They: The Human Urge to Identify with Groups," *Industrial and Corporate Change* 11(3) (June 2002): 607–610; 607.

63. See Anthony D. Smith, "Towards a Global Culture," in *Global Culture: Nationalism, Globalization, and Modernity*, edited by Mike Featherstone, 171–191 (London: Sage, 1990); Zygmunt Bauman, "Soil, Blood, and Identity," *Sociological Review* 40(4) (November 1992): 675–701; Anthony D. Smith, "The Problem of National Identity: Ancient, Medieval, and Modern," *Ethnic and Racial Studies* 17(3) (July 1994): 375–399; Anthony D. Smith, *Nations and Nationalism in a Global Era* (Cambridge, Massachusetts: Polity, 1995), 148–159.

64. See Malcolm Waters, *Globalization* (London: Routledge, 1995), 135.

65. Simon, "We and They," 608.

66. See Walker Connor, "A Nation Is a Nation, Is a State, Is an Ethnic Group, Is a . . .," in *Ethnonationalism: The Quest for Understanding*, by Walker Connor, 90–117 (Princeton: Princeton University Press, 1994), 100–103; Peter Juviler and Sherrill Stroschein, "Missing Boundaries of Comparison: The Political Community," *Political Science Quarterly* 114(3) (Fall 1999): 435–453; 450; Ernest Gellner, *Nations and Nationalism*, 2d ed. (Ithaca: Cornell University Press, 1993), 1.

67. See Waters, *Globalization*, 137.

68. See Leo Panitch and Colin Leys, *The End of Parliamentary Socialism: From New Left to New Labour* (London: Verso, 1997), 262–263, 268–271.

69. See William Greider, *One World, Ready or Not: The Manic Logic of Global Capitalism* (London: Penguin, 1997).

70. William B. Sorens, "Capital Ideas," *Letters to the Editor, Foreign Affairs* 81(3) (May-June 2002): 182–183; 183.

71. See Noam Chomsky, *Deterring Democracy* (London: Verso, 1992); Robert W. Cox with Timothy J. Sinclair, *Approaches to World Order* (Cambridge: Cambridge University Press, 1996), 34; Immanuel Wallerstein, "The Interstate Structure of the Modern World-System," in *International Theory: Positivism and Beyond*, edited by Steve Smith, Ken Booth, and Marysia Zalewski (Cambridge: Cambridge University Press, 1996); Immanuel Wallerstein, ed., *The Capitalist World-Economy* (Cambridge: Cambridge University Press, 1979); Robert Wade, "Winners and Losers," *The Economist* 359(8219) (28 April 2001): 72–74; Andrew Sayer and Richard Walker, *The New Social Economy: Reworking the Division of Labour* (Oxford: Oxford University Press, 1992).

72. Theotonio Dos Santos, "The Structure of Dependence," *American Economic Review, Papers and Proceedings of the Eighty-Second Annual Meeting of the American Economic Association*, New York, 28–30 December 1969, 60(2) (May 1970): 231–236; 231.

73. Jagdish Bhagwati, "Coping with Antiglobalization: A Trilogy of Discontents," *Foreign Affairs* 81(1) (January/February 2002): 2–7; 4.

74. Bhagwati, "Coping with Antiglobalization," 2.

75. Ignacio Ramonet, "Let Them Eat Big Macs," in "Dueling Globalizations: A Debate between Thomas L. Friedman and Ignacio Ramonet," *Foreign Policy* 116 (Fall 1999): 110–127; 126.

76. Bhagwati, "Coping with Antiglobalization," 5.

77. For some contemporary French ideas, see Viviane Forrester (*L'Horreur Economique*, (Paris: Fayard, 1996)). This *engagé* strand of the New Left is represented in North America by the Canadian Naomi Klein. *No Logo: Taking Aim at the Brand Bullies* (New York: Picador, 2001). See also the American Thomas Frank. *New Consensus for Old: Cultural Studies from Left to Right* (Chicago: Prickly Paradigm, 2002).

78. John Lloyd, "Britain's Lonely Left," reviewing *Captive State: The Corporate Takeover of Britain*, by George Monbiot (London: Macmillan, 2000), *Foreign Policy* 126 (September-October 2001): 82–84; 82.

79. Green and Griffith, "Globalization and Its Discontents," 55.

80. Green and Griffith, "Globalization and Its Discontents," 57.

81. See Dani Rodrik, *Has Globalization Gone Too Far?* (Washington, D.C.: Institute for International Economics, 1971), 2.

82. Robert S. Gilpin, *The Challenge of Global Capitalism: The World Economy in the 21st Century* (Princeton: Princeton University Press, 2000), 298. See also Richard Falk, *Economic Aspects of Global Civilization: The Unmet Challenges of World Poverty*, World Order Studies Program Occasional Paper no. 22 (Princeton: Princeton University Center of International Studies, 1992), 1.

83. See Wade, "Winners and Losers," 72–74; Elmar Altvater and Birgit Mahnkopf, "The World Market Unbound," *Review of International Political Economy* 4(3) (Autumn 1997): 448–471; Andrew Hurrell and Ngaire Woods, "Globalization and Inequality," *Millennium* 24(3) (1995): 447–470; Julian Suarin, "Globalization, Poverty, and the Promises of Modernity," *Millennium* 25(3) (1996): 657–680.

84. Bhagwati, "Coping with Antiglobalization," 3.

85. See Ronen Palan, *Underconsumptionism and Widening Income Inequalities: The Dynamics of Globalization*, Newcastle Discussion Papers in Politics, no. 4, September 1993. Unpublished.

86. See Cox with Sinclair, *Approaches to World Order*, 191–197; "Global Economy, Local Mayhem," *The Economist* 342(8000) (18 January 1997): 15–16.

87. See Benjamin Barber, *Jihad vs. McWorld* (New York: Times Books, 1995), 6–7.

88. Michael Cox, "Radical Theory and the International Disorder after the Cold War," in *The New World Order*, edited by Birthe Hansen and Bertel Heurlin, 197–216 (London: Macmillan, 2000), 203. Bogdan Denitch, *The End of the Cold War: European Unity, Socialism, and the Shift in Global Power* (London: Verso 1990), 3–14.

89. Michael Cox, "Radical Theory and the International Disorder after the Cold War," in *The New World Order*, edited by Birthe Hansen and Bertel Heurlin, 197–216 (London: Macmillan, 2000), 205. For a contrasting view of the political impact of globalization, see Kenichi Ohmae, *The End of the Nation-State: The Rise of Regional Economics* (London: HarperCollins, 1996), 99, 115, 136, 142.

90. Gwyn Prins, "Thinking about Intervention: An Essay Reflecting Upon the State of the Policy Debate in Early 2001," *RUSI Journal* 146(4) (August 2001): 12–17; 14–15.

91. Eloise Malone and Arthur Rachwald, "The Dark Side of Globalization," *United States Naval Institute Proceedings* 127/11/1,185 (November 2001): 43.

92. Prins, "Thinking About Intervention," 13–14.

93. Joseph E. Stiglitz, "Globalization: You Have to Walk the Talk," *Fortune* 144(11) (26 November 2001): 88.

94. Malone and Rachwald, "The Dark Side of Globalization," 43.

95. Sanjib Baruah, "Globalization—Facing the Inevitable?" *World Policy Journal* 16(4) (Winter 1999–2000): 105–112; 111.

96. See Cecilia Lynch, "Social Movements and the Problem of Globalization," *Alternatives* 23(2) (April-June 1998): 149–173; 154.

97. Richard Devetak and Richard Higgott, "Justice Unbound? Globalization, States, and the Transformation of the Social Bond," *International Affairs* 75(3) (July 1999): 483–498; 494.

98. See Fantu Cheru, *The Silent Revolution in Africa: Debt, Development, and Democracy* (London: Zed-Anvil, 1989), 19–20; James C. Scott, *Weapons of the Weak* (New Haven: Yale University Press, 1985), 182–183, 239–240, 255–273, 301–303.

99. See Devetak and Higgott, "Justice Unbound?" 493–495.

100. Colin Hines, "The New Protectionism: What It Is—Why It Is Coming," 10 November 1995, first published as *Employment and the Culture of Insecurity: Time to Protect Jobs*, Economic Report 9, no. 5 (London: Employment Policy Institute, June 1995), note 30. See also Colin Hines and Tim Lang, *The New Protectionism, Protecting the Future against Free Trade* (New York: New Press, 1993).

101. After the Seattle protest in November 1999, major populist protest operations have occurred in Davos (January 2000), Bangkok (February 2000), Washington, D.C. (April 2000), Göteborg and Bologna (June 2000), Salzburg (July 2000), Prague and Melbourne (September 2000), Seoul (October 2000), Pôrto Alegre (January 2001), Naples (March 2001), Montreal (April 2001), Honolulu (May 2001), and Genoa (July 2001).

102. Madeleine Albright, comments at the New Future Conference, sponsored by *Fortune* magazine in Aspen, Colorado, summer 2001, quoted by Jerry Useem in "Globalization," *Fortune* 144(11) (26 November 2001): 76–84; 78.

103. See Václav Havel, "The Power of the Powerless," in *Living in Truth*, edited by Jan Vladislav, 316–324 (London: Unwin Hyman, 1989); Raimo Väyrynen, "Violence, Resistance, and Order in International Relations," in *Global Transformation: Challenges to the State System*, edited by Yoshikazu Sakamoto, 385–411 (Tokyo: United Nations University Press, 1994), 395–399.

104. See Lynch, "Social Movements and the Problem of Globalization," 161–167.

105. Suter, "People Power," 13.

106. Robert W. Cox, "A Perspective on Globalization," in *Globalization: Critical Reflections, International Political Economy Yearbook, Vol. 9*, edited by James H. Mittelman, 21–30 (Boulder, Colorado: Lynne Rienner, 1996), 24.

107. Anthony Giddens, *Runaway World: How Globalization Is Reshaping Our Lives* (London: Profile, 1999), 43.

108. "Economics Focus: Treading Lightly," *The Economist* 364(8291) (21 September 2002): 74.

109. John Micklethwaite and Adrian Wooldridge, "The Globalization Backlash," *Foreign Policy* (September-October 2001): 16–26; 18.

110. John Naisbitt, *Global Paradox* (New York: William Morrow, 1994), 273.

111. James P. Young, *Reconsidering American Liberalism: The Troubled Odyssey of the Liberal Idea* (Boulder, Colorado: Westview, 1996), 139.

112. Forrest Colburn, "Fragile Democracies," *Current History* 101(652) (February 2002): 76–80; 79.

113. Fujimori dissolved Peru's Congress in 1992—the *fujimorazo*—with the justification that the legislators were all corrupt and inept.

114. Useem, "Globalization," 80.

115. Jagdish Bhagwati, Columbia University, quoted in "Globalization," by Useem, 80.

116. German Chancellor Gerhard Schröder, quoted in "Globalization," by Useem, 78.

117. Useem, "Globalization," 80, referring to research by Dani Rodrik, Harvard University, and Joseph E. Stiglitz, Columbia University.

118. "Anticapitalist Protests: Angry and Effective," *The Economist* 356(8189) (23 September 2000): 85–87; 86.

119. Randall D. Germain, "Globalization in Historical Perspective," in *Globalization and its Critics*, edited by Randall D. Germain, 67–90 (New York: St. Martin's, 2000), 84.

120. Green and Griffith, "Globalization and Its Discontents," 61.

121. Walden Bello, "Battling Barbarism," *Foreign Policy* 132 (September-October 2002): 41–42; 42.

122. Malone and Rachwald, "The Dark Side of Globalization," 43.

9

THE GLOBAL PERSPECTIVE

Any credible explanation of globalization must expand all of the fashionable, narrow perspectives—economic, political, cultural, or other—into the global perspective. It must also expand the historical horizon of past and present into the future. Within the global perspective, globalization not only compresses time in space but also transforms modern social reality beyond fashionable extrapolations of the present into the future. Rather than carrying people smoothly into a new and better, but comfortable and familiar, world, the most recent waves of globalization have deposited them on the far side of progress with only their wits and hearts to create any new world.

By expanding the scope—or raising the level—of human consciousness, globalism embodies all of people's perspectives without diminishing their local, narrow priorities, interests, or circumstances. Global understanding embraces not only aggregate humanity but also individuals and societies. Through the lens of historicism, globalization appears as *both* a permanent human condition *and* a recurrent, temporal process with a beginning and an end. The process of globalization reintroduces people as the particular, local, and timely focus of living in a humanized reality as part of the condition of globalization. The condition of globalization does not, however, require people to choose between humanism and rationality. Instead, globalization invites people to recover the premodern legacy of humanism and integrate it into modern rationality. The exact sciences and innovative technologies of modernity have laid the infrastructure of globalization. By humanizing rationality, human will can erect the structure that houses both the particular and the universal. Only within the global perspective can people create the new knowledge of a social reality built solidly on both, not balanced precariously between them.

Globalization has transformed the relationship between economic growth and political conflict from a linear political-economic process into a complex, nonlinear phenomenon that remains beyond the competence of global governance. Expanding the economic perspective exposes the wekaneses of capitalism and the failures of socialism without disclosing a clear third way. Expanding the cultural perspective exposes the vacuity of orthodox approaches to self and society. Expanding the political perspective exposes global governance as a critical challenge for people everywhere well into the future.

GLOBALIZATION: EXPANDED PERSPECTIVES

Globalization goes by many names—internationalization, interdependence, integration, imperialism, and others—within a few narrow perspectives to refer to *a tendency for the economic significance of political boundaries to diminish.*[1] Within a purely economic perspective, transnational corporations are the primary carriers of globalization in a process of integrating markets. The political perspective perceives the same process as integrating economic systems across political boundaries under the leadership of governments through international organizations. Within the cultural perspective, populist and radical movements congeal as the balancing force in Polanyi's double movement. Although globalization, especially in its common sense of economic integration, refers to a process, it also refers to the historicist context of that process and even, for some people, the goal or purpose of the process. Whereas within a particular narrow-perspective, process—economic integration or internationalization—implies an end, the condition of globalization within the global perspective and through the lens of historicism is endless, timeless, and universal. The essence of globalization is expansion of human understanding towards the unknown, not yet created future, energized and guided by human will. As narrow perspectives contract into memory, the global perspective expands human knowledge into the future.

Beyond the security, prosperity, and society stressed by Hobbes, Locke, Smith, Rousseau, or Weber, globalization has indiscriminately broadened people's perspectives to embrace culture, art, justice, and the rest of their global interests. Technology and globalization have extended understanding beyond the multiple narrow perspectives of rational modernity and dragged people, despite themselves, into the humanistic global perspective conceived during the Enlightenment. As modern civilizations have matured, people have, for the first time in history, gained the technical ability to construct a novel, complex, historical system as the foundation of a global civilization.

Expansion into the global perspective exposes four primary focal points of hierarchically nested social reality: the individual; national societies; some current, international system; and humanity itself as a global, timeless whole. For most individuals, societies, and international systems, the focus of living is on and through people's own immediate senses, decisions, and collective interests within one or a few narrow perspectives. For aggregate humanity, social reality comprises a broad spectrum of spirit, thought, and action that transcends the here and now, merges all other perspectives, and defines itself in terms of knowledge and knowledge creation. The essence of the global perspective is complexity, in contrast to the simple patterns of life idealized within the multiple narrow perspectives of modernity or the single perspective of Enlightenment rationality. The global perspective offers understanding not only of novel emerging patterns of politics, history, economics, political-economy, and culture but recognizes transcendent and historicist patterns that do not exclude irrationality, chaos, or uncertainty.

Globalization has exposed the composite, global context around Braudel's triple political-economic perspective, while eroding the political order of the politics of sovereignty and destabilizing the social order of stratified inequality. The narrow, unidimensional perspectives—humanity, economics, politics, culture, nature, living, and others—of modernity have proven barren of resolutions for the recurring crises of humanity. Although the Enlightenment and modernity created the seeds and instruments of progress in new knowledge, people must sow and cultivate those seeds in the mire of historical crisis across the broad terrain exposed within the global perspective.

Global Consciousness: Globalism

The end of the Cold War and the information revolution legitimated the notion of a global—rather than an international—system that embraces economic, political, communal, and cultural activities, past, present, and future. While the globalization process compresses time and space in the here and now, the historicist condition of globalization deepens with "the intensification of consciousness of the world as a whole, . . . both concrete global interdependence and consciousness of the global whole."[2] The notion of global consciousness, which clearly gained salience and intensity in the 1990s, is little more or less than perceiving life from and living within the global perspective. A holistic, global consciousness includes the individual self of each person, the relationships between various national societies and their citizens, and the social identity of each individual as an example of humanity. Carried by modern technology, in the aggregate, global consciousness expands people's narrow perspectives to a pseudoideological globalism and a semireligious historicism. Within the global perspective, it is a minor excursion from globalism to the perception and conviction that all humans everywhere and forever possess some inherent set of inclusive features and rights that does not allow exclusivity, differentiation, or discrimination.

Far more than using global media to participate in global mass events, communicate, or conduct—or resist—global consumerism, globalism redefines human issues in global terms and locates them within the global perspective. Globalism establishes a global context for understanding the several elements of social reality—politics, economics, culture, the physical world, the individual, and humanity itself—in relation to each other. Political-military issues appear in a context of world order, not national interests. Economic concerns reflect the operation of the global economy, not local prosperity or pockets of poverty. Religious issues involve ecumenism, not absolute truth, evil, or salvation. Citizenship and civil society assume their proper places in a context of universal human rights and duties, not national constitutions. Pollution, purification, and biodiversity unfold as threats to the planet, not as economic costs or elements of cultural heritage. Globalism humanizes the individual self as a complete, whole organic to inclusive humanity rather than as a component or citizen of any exclusive local group.

Beyond exploiting lessons learned from history to avoid mistakes in the present or make policy for the future, global historicism extends the global perspective from space into time. Present social reality carries the legacy of the eternal past and chooses the path into the unknowable, path-dependent future. Operating in event time, world order and the global economy converge in social time and merge in the *longue durée*. Culture and morality, science and art, memory and imagination, faith and certainty find each other in Braudelian *conjonctures* and flow through *basho* along the path of progress. Human consciousness expands beyond the narrow perspectives of nationalism, prosperity, and religion towards recognition of the future and past of the earth as parts of the present social reality of humankind.

Global Civilization

Within the global perspective, the unit of analysis for any understanding of globalization is civilization itself. "A civilization is first of all a space, a cultural area, . . . a locus which may be more or less extensive, but is never too confined. . . . If to this spatial coherence can be added some sort of a temporal permanence, then I would call civilization or culture the totality of the range of attributes."[3] Like Plato's *polis*, which did not equalize or homogenize people but created equal opportunity, any inchoate society of states would be more than a political base of power, an economic unit, or a social context, but still less than a civilization. This discrepancy between civilization and community does not appear in less-than-global perspectives that do not recognize any civilization as "constituting mankind through the consciousness of representative humanity."[4] Any global civilization would embody a self-conscious, global community, an identifiable, global culture, and create a robust set of dual identities—private and social—for every person.

Beyond a sense of community across all of humanity, a global civilization would provide universal political-military order, a cultural context, and a sense of personal and social meaning. Any civilizational foundation would embrace *not only* Braudel's domains of material life, market economy, and capitalism in a global structure of economic prosperity *but also* Ibn Khaldun's concept of social organization and Kantian notions about ethical-moral standards. Previous generations of humanity have created historical civilizations within their narrow, less-than-global perspectives, each broader than its parent.

The technologies of globalization have empowered humanity to construct a global *polis*—an inclusive community comprising state, economy, society, religion, and culture—as a novel historical system of social reality but can do no more. For Ibn Khaldun's science of civilization, the concepts of global governance, global politics, and a global economy can have real, profound meaning only in a civilizational context. Aristotelian thought links the individual to the *polis* in Plato's insight that "the city is the soul writ large."[5] In a later era, Ibn Khaldun expanded Plato's *polis* into the necessary social organization that provided the foundation for human civilization.[6]

On a civilizational scale, globalization is transforming the soul writ large into a global commonwealth or even community (*oikomene*), Marshall McLuhan's global village, which embraces every individual human being, tribe, clan, city, state, or country, in a broad human civilization.[7] Within the global perspective, the concept of a global civilization resolves the paradox of fragmegration into a universal dual existence for individuals and humanity itself. Like the individual, humanity and civilization are multidimensional along the same uniquely human dimensions. When not politically or economically excluded from globalization, individuals share with humanity the dynamism that creates civilizations and transforms social realities. Not merely the *polis* but civilization itself are, indeed, the soul writ large.

By expanding perspectives across all humanity, globalization locates the individual in a global context with an inclusive sense of cosmopolitan participation. An emergent, global civil society and public sphere empower people by identifying them within a global community. Across the spectrum of human spirit, thought, and action, globalization merges the many, broad dimensions of individuality and communality—existence, rationality, *modus operandi*, purpose, and result. Through the power of perspective and the medium of technology, every individual identity can manifest itself not only in a city, a tribe, a country, or a culture, but in the nascent global civilization that globalization has made credible and possible.

Although technological, economic globalization broadens and expands people's relationships, it does not carry homogenization or even convergence. Creating new knowledge deepens and intensifies human relationships around various epistemic communities. The global perspective suggests a global civilization that encompasses many civilizations. "A full modern world may have as many, or more, civilizations as did the premodern world because a civilization is not just a matter of democracy, science, and capitalism, but of ritual, manners, literature, pedagogy, family structure, and a particular way of coming to terms with what Christians call the four last things: death, judgment, heaven, and hell. Modernity will not change or remove the human condition, to which each culture provides its own distinct answers."[8]

The global perspective exposes plurality in many forms through inclusive participation in global politics, decentralized economic production, or various versions of multiculturalism across and within multiple civilizations. Within the global perspective, modernity is only one metanarrative that may provide legitimacy for the knowledge of a civilization: people may take diverse and even diverging paths in search of truth. Technological-economic globalization has effectively mired modernity in a Braudelian *conjoncture* that people have not yet resolved into a transformed civilizational reality. Bacon's idols ensure that the traditional narrow perspectives and the basic limits of logic, ethics, and thought remain within the global perspective. Globalization allows humanity to transcend them by expanding beyond rationality and justice, beyond religion and culture, and beyond prosperity and security into and through civilizational *basho* to transform present social reality into the future.

Global Culture

As globalization penetrates deeper into the shell of sovereign territoriality, the traditionally nation-centered, cultural perspectives lose credibility and legitimacy in multicultural states. As cultural insulation becomes convergence, any global identity for twenty-first-century people expands into a matter of cultural interchange, not political transformation and not economic integration. Young people are now instinctive, trained, rather than idealistic, globalists, at ease with the idea of crossing frontiers, working, or studying in other countries, and not preoccupied with any need either to preserve old values or to build a new world. For the world's aspiring, young cosmocrats, multiculturalism is the cultural norm, not an uncomfortable exception.

For the Malrauxist cosmocracy of culture, the focus for managing globalization is to expand cultural perspectives to deal with multiculturalism. How can any global state construct any degree of community and artistic aura with so many competing sources of cultural identity? When society leaves culture to the commercial, private sector—as in Europe, Japan, and the United States—its media reify culture as entertainment or products and transform the citizenry into the shallow, media-based suburbs of Marshall McLuhan's global village.[9] State intervention to rescue the national heritage—France during Malraux's tenure as minister of cultural affairs (1959–1969) or the underfunded U.S. National Endowment for the Arts—erodes its own legitimacy by *both* its failures *and* its successes. The Malrauxist dilemma in constructing an inclusive global culture around which to form a global community and reweave ties of social solidarity seems hopelessy deepened by the absence of a world state.

Although globalization has crystallized modernity around rationality within the economic perspective, the expanding cultural perspective paradoxically offers opportunities to escape from rigid rationality. Arising from trade and foreign aid in the global economy and the political contacts of conquest, migration, intervention, and terrorism, new strains of hybrid multicultures are maturing and combining in unpredictable patterns. The global perspective exposes these new cultural forms as new social and collective knowledge that embodies the histories of internationalism and globalism.

Also within the global perspective, a global culture that remembers but neither perpetuates nor legitimates the legacies of the colonial past is emerging from and within the bandwidth the carries globalization. In the *conjoncture* of the current wave of globalization, visionary people and busy cosmocrats have created another *basho* on the underside of globalization. Replacing political hierarchies and economic rationality, a nascent civil society is learning to share power with political institutions and the market. Globalization ensures that this inchoate global culture will not be subject to the caprices or interests of any one group of people, states, or firms. Instead, governments, corporations, and communities are shaping the legacies of the past into *both* the cultures *and* the museums of the future. Expanding from the invisible, structural underside of globalization into the global perspective, the *nébuleuse* of global governance without government includes people living everywhere in a social reality that they all create. Although its scope and content are far from clear, an identifiable global culture borrows heavily from local norms and social patterns of interactions. Like its origin, its features are unequivocally American: individualistic, innovative, materialistic, industrious, often crude and sometimes uncouth, compassionate, and always practical. With significant traces of European and Asian values in legalism and societal concerns, the values that form its foundation are also conspicuously American: freedom, equality and fairness, tolerance, and moral dualism.

GLOBALIZATION: PROCESS AND CONDITION

Within the global perspective, living in social time is the continuing, dynamic condition of expanding perspectives, gaining new understanding, and making progress—globalization. Although few individuals can claim to have perceived the global perspective, the human aggregate has been living within the global perspective since people discovered how to think and began to understand. For most people, living in event time outside the global perspective, globalization appears a process linking the remembered past through the urgent present to the impenetrable future. Within *both* global *and* narrow perspectives, the sedulous attendant of globalization—condition or process—is the uncertainty that exposes the ineptitude of Bacon's idols and institutional tradition in managing unprecedented circumstances.

Despite the fashionable hyperbole that the information revolution is more intense, extensive, and profound than anything in history, the condition of globalization has persistently accompanied humanity through its entire progress. The origin, engine, and process of the current wave of globalization have been constantly evolving since the dawn of human thought. More than a confusing economic, political, or cultural process, globalization is an enduring human condition. As *both* a process *and* a condition, the pattern of globalization has always reflected contemporary social reality, the level of technology, the breadth of people's perspectives, and depth of their knowledge.

Globalization: The Process

Throughout history, people have created new knowledge and applied it to solving some annoying, current social problem. Acting along three temporal dimensions, the process created by these solutions has operated *not only* in event time *but also* in social time and the *longue durée*. As they mastered successive technologies, people changed their ways of living and thinking, expanded into broader perspectives, created new knowledge, and invented innovative organizations, institutions, and management techniques in event time. Although science and technology have been significant in every wave of globalization, more important has always been the ever-changing process of expanding knowledge. People's ability to use technology to transform social reality in social time and create new knowledge has repeatedly energized the next wave of globalization. As a process of expanding interdependence mediated through long-distance telecommunication networks, the current wave of globalization is a modern temporal-spatial phenomenon with ancient origins. This wave, however, is unique in carrying the physical and technological capability to transform social reality into a progressive, global civilization for the first time in history. The legacies that inform the current wave of globalization do not minimize the profound, current transformation of social reality, which is, and has always been, a part of globalization.

Through the historical lenses, globalization appears to have occurred in a series of discrete waves parallel with political and economic development. As societies expanded their perspectives from a premodern focus on survival to multiple modern perspectives on understanding, they also learned the rudiments of resource-based growth and political rationality. The modern waves of globalization and development have brought capitalist economics and general prosperity, rational-legal structures of authority, centralized institutions, and decentralized, democratic politics. Like previous waves, they have also brought shifts in cultural values and norms as people repeatedly transformed contemporary societies into broader and deeper social realities and expanded understanding towards the global perspective.

Through the lens of historicism, rather than a self-reproducing, homeostatic process with a beginning and an end, globalization not only rises and falls in waves. It is a dynamic type of creative environment—*basho*—that is immanent in social time for all human knowledge, will, thought, behaviors, institutions, and relationships. Enabled by technology, historicist globalization is something that people will and do eternally, not something that they experience briefly in the here and now. Not mechanistically done to them, globalization is a strategy for creating the future, not a present reality. Not simply "an independent variable that affects the nation-state and its policy capabilities," it transcends and includes *both* politics *and* economics, *and also human living itself.*[10] In every aspect of social existence, humanity is continually willing and transforming the social reality of the present into something new through the creation of new knowledge. Although the process of globalization has stressed various narrow perspectives in succeeding waves, the essence of globalization remains, today as it has always been, an expansion of people's perspectives through new knowledge. The heart, soul, and mind of globalization merge in people's creation of new knowledge.

Although the waves of globalization have historically been correlated with economic growth, the global perspective forces noneconomic concerns into people's attentions and priorities. Despite the modern obsession with political-military power globalization expands politics into transnational and global issues that transcend power. People can understand the active participation of nontraditional groups in global politics only within the global perspective. As the process of globalization has broadened human perspectives and shifted values, modernization has accompanied globalization, although it is not clear that any stable, causal linkage makes either dependent on the other.[11] Neither can humanity yet infer that globalization, modernity, and postmodernity are, or are not, related. The information revolution has drastically changed economics and politics but has not brought a corresponding revolution within the cultural perspective in the human heart or mind. Economists and politicians cannot resolve this paradox, since it springs from the important difference between globalization as a process and globalization as a condition.

Globalization: The Condition

Although the information revolution, like the commercial and industrial revolutions before it, has profoundly changed the process and conduct of globalization, the nature of globalization as a human condition remains much as it was in the mists of prehistory. As a central force and spirit behind human progress, the condition of globalization displays a powerful set of features that separate it clearly from the globalization process:

Globalization has been a stable condition of living since people realized that they were alive; the globalization process has been unique with each wave.

Within the global perspective, the condition of globalization embraces *both* rationality *and* spirituality *and also* irrational, temporal emotionality.

The destructive creativity of the globalization process transforms social reality; it does not replace it; the eternal and constant condition of globalization preserves social reality for another transformation.

Although the process of globalization is intrinsically nondeterministic and ambiguous, the condition of globalization is path-dependent on the legacies of previous social realities and people's deliberate choices.

As a condition, globalization embraces all narrow perspectives, merges some, mixes others, but expands them through creating and diffusing knowledge.

Although people can choose to forget the past in the globalization process, the condition of globalization includes all of the corners of collective memory, dark ones hidden in shame and regret, and bright ones lighted by pride.

The condition of globalization rejects any notion of economic equilibrium, recurring cycles, political balance, or cultural stasis. Every social reality differs from any that preceded it. Within the global perspective, "the most important insight that it is possible to gather from knowing and understanding the past is that what is should not be construed as what has always been, nor what necessarily must be, nor as what can be."[12] Despite common wisdom that the latest wave of globalization is fundamentally different from anything that people have experienced before, the nature of globalization in the twenty-first century differs only in degree and detail from that experienced by forgotten Asian travelers thirty centuries ago. Globalizing people are expanding their perspectives towards the global perspective through new knowledge. The ways that people actually conduct globalization, the technologies that they use, their cultural styles, and their institutions have changed repeatedly and will always change to suit current social reality. These instruments of the process, however, are incidental details within the condition of globalization as an eternal human quest to understand.

THE UNDERSIDE OF GLOBALIZATION

Often obscured in celebrating the benefits of globalization and denouncing its imperfections is the subterranean infrastructure of the process and the psychological substructure of the condition. Even globalization cannot encompass the world without the extensive set of physical facilities—often invisible even to dedicated cosmocrats—that carry electronic flows and manage distributions of goods around the world. Neither would globalization be able to transform people's ideas, identities, behaviors, and social realities unless they believed deeply in it.

The Infrastructure of Connectivity

Like other human interactions, globalization embodies a struggle for economic wealth and political power. Within the traditional, resource-based perspectives of life and living, the struggle was for access to the sources and beneficial results, power, and profits of living itself and the legitimate authority to make the rules of human justice for the future. As knowledge-based globalization deterritorializes the world, information technology concentrates the sources of prosperity, security, and even justice beyond political boundaries and economic resources. The fashionable celebration and denunciation of the hypermobility of capital and the decentralization of politics implicit in globalization quickly obscure their deep, solid foundations in several physical places scattered across the world's national jurisdictions. Despite the reality of electronic networks, the Internet, mobile capital, and migrant voters, the global, infrastructural *infosphere* of virtual space through and over which globalization flows requires physical, strategic sites.

Expanding through a dense web of cross-border flows and networks, the political-economic struggle for power and wealth now "includes access to the infosphere, to financial markets, to materials (of which information is one), to the means of production, and to the market population."[13] Globalization shifts the focus of the struggle from control of territory and populations to access to knowledge—information, data, technology, skills, experience, and innovation—markets, and resources. Just as traditional military forces could deny access to territory and resources, modern corporations and governments can use information technology to delay, disrupt, distort, or deny access to the infosphere. In a globalized world, the ability to ensure access to knowledge through connection to the infrastructure assumes strategic priorities over military force structures optimized to exert control.

The complexity of every global operation or connection concentrates people, resources, skills, and knowledge that are immovably located in national territories. This territorial underside of spatially dispersed globalization exposes the concrete processes and physical facilities located in specific places. The emergence of global cities, megacities, and other nonstate, noncorporate sites for the struggles of global politics and commerce displaces the focus of globalization from economics and economics to global interactions between people. Penetration to the physical underside of globalization shifts attention from the power of the state and the wealth of the corporation to the prosaic activities, social processes, and untidy infrastructure beneath globalization. A global geography of strategic places where complex social interactions occur has transformed social reality into a world order that involves nation-states, transnational firms, cities, cultures, and ordinary people as active, essential participants in the struggle. This social reality operates through global markets, local wars, interstate diplomacy, migration, cultural diffusion, and other transactions between people. These various sorts of strategic sites and processes mediate the complex interactions and indirect relationships among the various sorts of participants: "Distances mean little and direction means even less. Relative location is more important than absolute location in a tightly connected and integrated world. . . . What is more important as markets, societies, cultures, and governments are becoming more connected is whether one is connected, how far one is from other places in time not in absolute distance, and how one is connected with other places."[14]

Beneath their role as an amorphous global venue for the political-economic struggle for connection, the panorama of strategic sites, their infrastructures, and the broad spectrum of participants form an emergent global commons. From its underside, globalization appears as a global geography of knowledge-based networks and epistemic communities linking concentrations of resources and people across their narrow-perspective visions of social reality. "Globalization can then be seen as embedded and dependent on these linkages and strategic concentrations and material infrastructure. To a considerable extent, global processes are this grid of sites and linkages."[15]

The Psychology of Connecting

For preglobal societies, the prospects of expanding political participation and economic transactions, of universal enlightenment, or of discussion among people who did not know each other were radically controversial and idealistic and possibly mad. These notions demanded a new kind of politics, not associated with the demographic homogeneity of the Westphalian nation-state, and a new kind of economics that did not depend on personal trust: a new kind of global thinking. Historicist, knowledge-based globalization reaches into the heart and structure of human living with the opportunity to relieve personal and social stress and the means for transforming social reality and human identities.

The Tyranny of Distance

Lying deep with the etiology of a global psychology, globalization's radical compression of distance—physical, social, economic, intellectual, cultural, and political—"imposed, even for its proponents, a frightening tolerance for political uncertainty. But it was the outline, at least, of a universal, diverse, and discursive politics."[16] Distances—physical, social, economic, or cultural—had always been factors to calm ideological passions into deliberate political action and spontaneous personal desires into rational market exchanges. The tyranny of distance and its temporal dimension had carried people from emotional crisis and uncertainty to rational, deliberation, action and confident decisions. The technologies that have submerged the pragmatic deliberacy of distance beneath instantaneous policymaking have wrapped globalization in the specter of technological inevitability that is often a source of political passivity and resignation. Neither Westphalian, sovereign territoriality nor Newtonian, sequential time any longer constrain people in moving, exchanging, or transferring themselves, their goods, their money, their ideas, their hatreds, or their bombs anywhere in the world. A coherent theme running through all of the various concepts of globalization is the erosion of the tyranny of distance.[17]

For many people, globalization has meant "the intensification of worldwide social relations which link distant localities in such a way that local happenings are shaped by events occurring many miles away."[18] Others relate globalization to society as "a social process in which the constraints of geography on social and cultural arrangements recede."[19] Within this narrow, individual perspective on globalization, "distance is defined less by geography than by psychology, and information is [instantly] available to anyone with a television, [radio, telephone], or computer."[20]

As technological globalization continues to erode the tyranny of distance, the psychologies of the *foreign* and the *other* are losing their grips on societies and individuals. "Because strangeness or foreignness works as a bar to much of social interaction, technology encourages the practice of globalization by helping to foster a wider feeling of familiarity and a less geographically bound conception of the local."[21] Not only are icons of foreign cultures penetrating political borders, but also individuals' personal territories—the bits of the world that contain their olive trees—are expanding to encompass many areas neither contiguous nor geographically close to home. As foreign others encroach and individual territories expand, everyone's olive trees become vulnerable. The ultimate paradoxical dilemma of the psychology of global thinking lies in the soul-rending search for personal identity among one's own olive trees in the morass between individual autonomy and global anonymity.

The Connection: Globalism

Globalism is positioning itself as the antithesis to modernity—in its forms of socialism, nationalism, capitalism, and liberalism—to activate the conjunctural dialectic of time into a new, more nearly global, social reality with three levels. At the global level, globalism replaces modern certainty with a sense of progress—rational, pragmatic, or zealous—towards something defined, believed, imagined, but unknown. At a social—usually, but not necessarily, national—level, globalism connects individuals to society or isolates them by reifying some relationship that each self establishes for itself. Globalism legitimates that relationship in government, in civil society, in resistance movements, or in universality and justifies any derivative rights and duties. At the individual level, de Tocqueville saw no contradictions or conflicts between private individualism and social or humanitarian compassion. Globalism *both* provides personal identity *and* allows individuals to select some font of absolute truth and certainty—God, morality, ethics, law, self, wealth, justice, some historic golden age, or something else.

Across the three levels, the solidarity of human compassion for other people, which has crystallized gradually since the Renaissance, welds globalism into a tangible structure for global politics and economics. Although globalism has not yet resolved the swarm of paradoxes that the historicist lens exposes within the global perspective, globalism—in contrast to liberalism, nationalism, or socialism—prioritizes people's need to do so.

HUMANIZING GLOBALIZATION

The modern waves of globalization replaced the experiential philosophy of premodern humanism with well-formulated theories of the scientific method. Splitting people's purposes and ideals between the search for justice and the search for truth also split humanism and science into separate, mutually exclusive perspectives. The union of globalism with historicism redeems philosophy and science by reconnecting them both to the humanist foundations of life and living. To maintain the connection within the global perspective, "the techniques of seventeenth-century rationalism will not be enough: from this point on, all the claims of theory—like those of nationhood—must prove their value by demonstrating their roots in human practice and experience."[22]

Science and Humanism

Since Descartes's *Discourse on Method* spawned a mechanistic and self-conscious *natural philosophy* based exclusively on theory and a certainty borrowed from geometry, globalization has gradually transformed the natural sciences as the scientific method mellowed. Not only are the twenty-first-century sciences heavily reliant on direct observation, experience, will, and insight, but their results are vulnerable to crippling criticism of *both* human impacts *and* rational truth. Scientists and humanists alike have learned to balance the Platonist-Cartesian drive towards universal truth with an Aristotelian-Rousseauesque focus on the here and now, the human contexts of events, and the implications of scientific truth for the human future. During the last generation, globalization has stretched the line between the moral and technical dimensions of science tighter until it is approaching the breaking point, as the practical challenges of living overwhelm the distinctions between *facts* and *values*. For many people—scientists and humanists—globalization has made the quality of living as important as biological-scientific life. Governments, companies, and people no longer perceive nature as a stock of resources provided by God for the exploitation, benefit, and comfort of humans. They recognize—at least implicitly—that nature is humanity's only home. The lens of historicism reassembles science, technology, nature, and people within the global perspective as the essence of living.

In enervating Bacon's idols separating science and rationality from inspiration and insight, globalization blurs the modern distinction between theoretical, pure science and practical, applied technology with humanist feelings. Through knowledge-based capitalism as a human institution, science reconciles the rational exactitude of Newtonian mechanics with the humanism of Francis Bacon's syllogisms. As globalization occludes Bacon's idols, the context of managing knowledge shifts from the search for truth to human relevance. Instead of preserving traditional wisdom and adding incremental novelties to keep people's intellectual instruments polished and sharp in pursuit of ultimate truth through technical excellence, people find it better to use those instruments for human good. Just as war became too important to be left to generals, wealth has become too important to concentrate with capitalists, and knowledge is too important to be left to the scholars. Globalization expands science and technology from the pursuit of excellence on the narrow path of truth through a global political-economy towards priorities that are relevant to people who are not connected.

Those unconnected people are willfully transforming modern societies and civilizations by humanizing the rational legacy of modernity into a new, inchoate social reality: a humanist future. While focusing on the universal and the eternal, the global perspective redirects attention to the practical, local, transitory issues locked in narrow-perspective contexts that *formed the global perspective of the premodern humanists*. The condition of globalization shifts the focus for life and living away from the *stability* of the Westphalian state, the *equilibrium* of the market economy, and the *certainty* of rational science. The lens of historicism calls attention to the *diversity* of global governance, the *dynamism* of growth, and the *adaptability* of human will. The process of globalization ensures that stability, certainty, and equilibrium are self-contradictions. The condition of globalization provides recursive *basho* and the new knowledge that creates new institutions, processes, values, and attitudes to transform contradictions into progress.

Ethics and Values

For millennia, people have found their values, norms, biases, and ethics by looking inward into themselves, their societies, their cultures, and their gods. Since their origins in antiquity, civilizations have offered universal values in cosmic metanarratives to explain everything from the operation of nature to the structure of society to the meaning of individual lives. Global interdependence calls for people to extend their narrow-perspective values beyond the microlevel of interpersonal relationships and the mesolevel of institutions, nation-states, and cultures. Modern rationality has shifted perspectives and priorities away from mystical religion and absolute truth towards prosperity and security. "Those values that are shared by a modern liberal democracy as a whole increasingly tend to be political rather than religious in character."[23] The process of globalization erodes the cultural roots —religion, superstition, or images of beauty—of human values and exposes people's relationships to rational, ethical, and moral considerations at a macrolevel within the global perspective. The condition of globalization demands a global ethic that resolves values through the lens of historicism within the global perspective.

A Global Ethic

A global ethic that begins not with truth or good but with humanity and a moral imperative to the progress of the human community provides a normative foundation for progressive and beneficial use of knowledge, wealth, and power. Unlike learning, innovation, wealth, or power, which emerge from and after new knowledge, people create values as they create knowledge. Through creating new knowledge in *basho*, globalization develops ethical values that are as universal as the knowledge that embraces them. Created collectively by multiple minds in many contexts in *basho*, new global values create new social contracts between the individual and society, between the state and society, and between science and society.[24]

Like those of any narrow culture, the values of a global ethic establish the roles and relationships of knowledge, technology, art, faith, people, society, economics, and politics. Although people have found their values in religion and expressed them in art for millennia, only recently has rationality begun to explore the human soul. Like art and faith, knowledge and science are not value-free and have deep social foundations. Especially in liberal, capitalist democracies, social and economic priorities energize and sustain much scientific endeavor.[25] The moral responsibilities of scientists and engineers extend beyond projecting the trends and capabilities of technology and technique into the future and creating devices simply because they can make them work. "The important moral duty, which is shared by scientist and nonscientist alike, is to devote effort to fostering the benficial uses of knowledge, old and new alike, and opposing its harmful uses."[26]

In many capitalist societies, the socioeconomic "value placed on acquiring" —not necessarily creating—"new knowledge exceeds that placed on how best to apply existing knowledge."[27] A global ethic would supplant useful applications with a moral imperative to progress. Globalism values the balance across creating new knowledge, aquiring knowledge through learning, and also applying it to beneficial human progress. "Science cannot be focused solely on acquiring new knowledge. It must also examine the ethical implications of the application of such knowledge in an international context in order to form legitimate public policy and promote ways to ameliorate the miserable conditions in which the majority of the world's people live."[28]

Global Values

The historicist *mentalité* of the global perspective recognizes economic problems and development, good governance and global order, people with their many concerns, and human progress as all immanent within a single, complex, interdependent universe. A system of global values establishes the priorities and orderings for human will and action in dealing with this universe. Globalization invites people to explore the links across and within the many perspectives of reality, past, present, and future and to understand their effects and implications. A global ethic provides the fundamental values and structure for creating the new knowledge to transform the here and now into progress. Although such a global ethic remains airily floating in the *nébuleuse* of global governance, some seers claim to discern its shape in the values that it embodies.

Human Life. All civilizations, cultures, and societies, have evinced—at least in rhetoric—some *respect for human life*. This value emerges from the ubiquitous, traditional religious belief that people are made in the image of God. Beyond the narrow perspectives of culture, nationalism, economics, or politics, within the global perspective, this value expresses the fundamental unity of humanity. Extending beyond and beneath liberalism, individualism, socialism, or communalism, people have been consistent in their rejection of homicide as morally, ethically, and legally unacceptable. Despite people's chronic predilections to ignore this value, it retains a broad global consensus.

Universal Ethics. Rejecting the view that ethical principles are relative to particular cultures, globalism accepts the existence of *universal ethical principles* that transcend culture, embrace all people. This value expresses a deep, broad, and powerful sense of the value of the human community within the cosmos of life. Continuing controversy revolves around "the observed differences in moral behavior accepted as the norm in different societies (descriptions of what is), and universal principles that represent an attempt to provide, through critical reasoning, justification of universal norms (prescriptions of what ought to be).[29] Globalism recognizes that "considerations of context are essential aspects of moral reasoning in the application of universal principles within specific situations, and this process does not entail supporting the moral relativism that would make all local practices legitimate."[30]

Human Rights. Although all people have accepted the rhetoric of *human rights*, consensus on the substance of those rights has not emerged. "The application of human rights must extend beyond civil and political rights to include social, cultural, and economic rights and their close integration with the reciprocal responsibilities to ensure that rights are honored and basic needs met. Just as the concept of political citizenship requires nondiscriminatory enfranchisement of all, so the concept of social citizenship requires access to the basic requirements of survival and potential flourishing."[31] Extending beyond the rhetoric of universal human rights, individual self-interest, or personal freedom, this global value includes corresponding individual duties, social justice and rights, and global interdependence. The Hobbes-Locke social contract allows people to balance between duties and rights; Kant's moral imperative disallows such a balance. Neither globalism nor historicism resolves the issue. It is only in *basho* that people will create the new values to resolve the controversies around balancing individual duties and societies' rights.[32]

Equity. Whereas few globalizers advocate equality across all people, various notions of *equity*, or fairness, appear in every salient personal, social, cultural, or civilizational ethic. Most definitions of equity in a social context include "provision of equal shares for equal needs, or the allocation of unequal shares for unequal needs as long as proportionality is maintained. However, proportionality is difficult to assess because of incommensurability. Some inequalities in wealth, health, and disease are inevitable aspects of life. Eliminating all inequalities is not possible. In addition, not all inequality is inequitable. Inequity refers to those inequalities that are considered to arise from unfairness."[33] An indirect approach rejects equity as an end in itself and embeds it in a larger concept of social justice and a sense of obligation to support the poor and oppressed against the rich and oppressors. "This approach emphasizes the concept of agency and well-being (defined as having the capabilities that a person can achieve) and the freedom to pursue one's life.

THE PARTICULAR, THE LOCAL, AND THE TIMELY

Globalization has gradually revitalized the premodern technique of casuistry, or applying the particular ethics of a situation, as universal, abstract rationalism proved itself inadequate in understanding issues of moral philosophy. Although early modernism self-consciously scorned medieval case ethics, globalism inverts the search for explanation and understanding into the details embodied in the casuist tradition. Globalization inhibits the relevance of general, abstract theories to the problems that face people and enhances the credibility of a focus on particular situation. The very particularity of human concerns about globalization, living, and the future challenges the modernist insistence on generalizing to universality.

Within the global perspective, with its porous, indistinct boundaries between disciplinary and functional perspectives, Descartes's factual realms of knowledge—history, ethnography, or anthropology—converge in human nature. Neither have these social sciences nothing to contribute to the natural sciences. Although the postmodern *reductio ad absurdum* finds in such cross-disciplinary fluidity the implications that all people, societies, and cultures are equally good in their own ways, the historicist lens resolves such absolute relativism into convergence around human knowledge and will. Globalism appeals to multiperspective insights to clarify actual human approaches to *both* morality *and* rationality in particular cultural, historical contexts. Historicist, global recognition of traditions, cultures, and ways of living denies Descartes's approach of ignoring traditional notions in preference for the clarity and definition of rational ideas that made them moral universals. Whereas modernity sought to reduce cultural idiosyncrasies to differences in fact, globalization unites questions of fact with questions of faith.

Rather than retreating from the universal and returning to the local and particular, globalism expects each science to pursue its own special excellence within its own narrow perspectives and to preserve the polish and cutting edge of its own intellectual instruments. Each discipline develops and masters its own proper techniques, knowledge, art, and methods adapted to its own special standards and truths within its own perspectives as Aristotle's *techne* (mastery of art and skill). Globalism redirects scientific practice from deciphering absolute truths of universal application (Aristotle's notion of theoretical truth, *episteme*) to devising particular codes that focus the complexities of nature on the particularities of people. Modernity institutionalized this redirection within narrow disciplines as the universal scientific method that begins with a human problem. The lens of historicism obscures scientific mastery of a permanent, universal order in nature within "a substantive ability to discover the local, temporary relations embodied in one specific aspect of nature, here and now, in contrast to another, elsewhere."[34] Beyond modernity, science, humanism, economics, politics, art, and philosophy retain relevance through expanding into, and accepting new knowledge from, other perspectives. Globalization merges particular technical excellence and local human relevance in the here and now in *conjonctures* of the legacies of the past, resolves the contradictions between them in *basho*, and transforms them through human will into the future.

Globalization broadens the modern focus of technology, science, philosophy, art, and knowledge from the narrow search for absolute truth to encompass human concerns whose rational significance is nearer than eternity and arises in the timeliness of practical solutions. Within the global perspective, the technological applications of science and knowledge are scientific arts performed effectively only by people with *both* extensive experience and insight in living *and* rational, scientific knowledge. The lens of historicism resolves Aristotle's notions of *episteme*, *techne*, and the wisdom to use them in addressing human problems (*phronesis*) into Plato's hope of discovering general truths of *both* nature *and* humanity. Science, art, and humanism converge smoothly in people who take wise action willed within the context of the global perspective. Broader and deeper than cosmocrats, these people enter *basho* not only to solve timely human problems but also to understand the universals of the environmental survival, human ethics, justice, or the unanswerable questions beyond rationality. Although the epistemological focus for modern thinkers was Plato's demand for *episteme* in his *Republic*, globalism rests on Aristotle's *phronesis*, practical wisdom. Instead of the stability of human understanding of absolute truth, the global perspective offers the adaptability of human truth. Although knowledge links them to the timeless past and the eternal future, people live always in the present, where they define human truth through human will.

THE GROWTH–CONFLICT RELATIONSHIP

Economic globalization in a context intolerant of interstate conflict has created around each national economy zones of stress triggering and shadowing that resonate with growth and conflict in the home society. Globalization and complex interdependence have transformed the dual relationship between domestic growth and interstate conflict into a contagious variety that seems immune to the orthodox cures of diplomacy. The mutant version triggers intrastate civil wars, political conflict, and cultural tensions not only at home but *in other, interdependent societies.* As in national economies, the type of growth influences how contagion affects a triggered or shadowed society. In some preglobalization world, each society determined how and when it would launch its economy into modern economic growth and whether it would follow a path of resource-based growth or knowledge-based growth. "The critical selection of either the path from growth toward conflict or that toward cooperation occurs when a nation both determines to extend its capabilities further outside its own boundaries, and selects a mode or style of international behavior for doing so."[35] Globalization has, however, co-opted this national social decision in interdependence. In the global economy, the decision of the market determines the type of growth that an economy may expect and, consequently, the social stresses that its society may need to relieve.

A Conjecture

The common, global-market decision to stress less sophisticated economies as sources of labor and resources suggests that the virulent, globalized growth–conflict relationship spreads not only growth but conflict across interdependent societies. Relegation to a primary role as a source and market for resource-based trade may stimulate such economies to pursue resource-based growth *rather than shifting to knowledge-based growth* through continuing the transition of modern economic growth (MEG). The single-economy, growth–conflict relationship generates social stresses within these economies that international politics no longer allows the society to relieve in direct interstate conflict. Instead, relief comes as stresses migrate to interdependent, triggered societies, carrying a possible epidemic of civil conflict in several societies consequent to resource-based growth in one home economy.

From the moment of contagion, continued static growth *in any of the interdependent triggered economies or in the home economy* through resource-based trade increases the probabilities of conflict *until a society shifts to the dynamic-growth path* and activates the inverse growth–conflict relationship. To shift, a society would need not only to overcome the pressures of globalization but also to refine *both* the balance of its production function *and* the content of its national strategy. "Static growth continues, but loses its urgency as dynamic growth accelerates to maintain high aggregate growth rates. Efficient trade continues to provide enough resources; intensity of production shifts from muscle power to human capital; returns to capital increase even though amounts of capital may not; national capabilities can easily become threatening; political conflict remains a possibility."[36]

Neither this shift in factor intensity and type of growth, nor *the essential social and strategic policies* are likely to emerge from an international division of labor established by global markets. It requires willed action by the people of a society to transform their own social reality by containing the virulence of the growth–conflict relationship. Whatever they do must also reinforce the clear relationship between prosperity, peace, and knowledge creation that is the heart of progress. The market-led integration of globalization and FDI may compress the evolution of MEG into a single-generation transformation built on new knowledge, learning, and innovation, but it cannot energize the process of MEG. Although trade-based macroeconomic policy reforms in the early stages of MEG are essential, they are insufficient to *navigate the transition to knowledge-based growth* and to *contain the growth–conflict relationship*. Accelerated by FDI, the social, economic, and political transformations of MEG occur in a context of globalization that is beyond the control of most societies but lies within the reach of *both* policy *and* civil society. More progressive than growth itself, transformations *require* willed, civil-societal action; sensitive, focused, economic policy to shift the production function; and an intense strategic focus on the dual growth–conflict relationship.

Some Global Concerns

Although globalism presupposes *both* interdependence *and* the economic-industrial foundations of national power and influence, *both* practical globalization *and* theoretical globalism stress aggregate growth with little notice of *type of growth*. The globalized growth–conflict relationship suggests, however, a critical influence for type of growth and a significant role for foreign direct investment, *which may be independent of national military-political power*. More than merely a powerful linkage between growth and conflict, stress triggering emerges as a potentially powerful force behind globalization mediated by knowledge-based growth. Triggered, or shadowed, dynamic growth need not rely on an autonomous, indigenous engine to carry an economy into modern economic growth. Interdependence, *when moderated by domestic political will*, extends the liberal economic perspective to include developmental market capitalism *without the often unwelcome baggage of the liberal political perspective*. Stress triggering and shadowing include hierarchic, paternal government with significant intervention by parent and recipient governments in economic affairs and in providing human security.

In the context of triggering or shadowing, the close relationship between dynamic growth and foreign direct investment exposes an apparent paradox reminiscent of Raymond Vernon's "obsolescing bargain."[37] Beyond economic interdependence between trading societies, dynamically growing countries experience another mutual dependency between multinational enterprises, foreign investors, and governments, which is also triggered in recipient economies. Sustaining resource-based growth requires only more resources, whereas the technology-based growth that energizes the transition to dynamic growth requires continuing supplies of foreign technology through foreign direct investment. The foreign investors that stimulate dynamic growth come to rely on aggregate growth—static and transitional—for earnings, markets, and profits. This unfamiliar dimension of interdependence brings *both* governments *and* investors to compete for either receiving or providing not only resources but also foreign direct investment for growing economies. Although competition among firms is resolved in the market, competition among governments has historically been a prelude to interstate conflict or war, which are no longer tolerated in the international political system. The results of competition for flows of investment and resources among *both* governments *and* firms seem to extend through the globalized growth–conflict relationship to triggered social stresses or foreign civil wars.

Kenneth Waltz's three images of international relations probably reflected the preglobalized world as it existed and operated in the early and mid-twentieth century. The globalized growth–conflict relationship suggests a different—perhaps a fourth—image for the global political-economy of the twenty-first century. "In addition to Man, the State, and the System, the world now responds to a powerful Market, with its own actors—firms, corporations, multinational enterprises—that involve, affect, include, and exclude the actors and processes in each of Waltz's images. The most powerful of these new actors—the multinational enterprises—and the process that can accompany them—dynamic growth—are exogenous to, yet penetrate into, each of the three images. Nor is war still the most significant relationship among global actors; economic growth has assumed primacy for many actors in each of Waltz's images."[38] The confident predictions of the nonvirulent growth–conflict relationship in an international context of autonomous economies carried the credibility of experience. Those of the contagious, globalized relationship seem profoundly different. As globalization and interdependence expand social relationships beyond economic transactions, the dual foci of societies on *inter*national affairs (diplomay and war) and *non*state business (trade, investment, or litigation) broaden to *trans*- and *extra*national relationships and actions. In this emerging system of diverse relationships that seem to carry stress triggering and shadowing among interdependent societies, conflict depends not on the incidence or absence of growth but on its type. Neither state government nor global governance, perhaps not even society itself, has yet learned to manage this contagious growth–conflict relationship.

GLOBAL GOVERNANCE

The notion of global governance invokes a vision of order, rather than the visions of power evoked by state-centered government. Deep in prehistory, people discovered two primary sorts of order in their lives: natural order, which Classical Greece called *cosmos*, and human order, called *polis*. The *cosmos* arranged seasons, tides, time, the stars, and all beyond human control in a knowable, not random, order. The *polis* arranged cities, roads, collective projects, and everything under human control in a coherent, cohesive fabric of society. Many civilizations sought and created connections between *cosmos* and *polis* in some universal harmony, from China's celestial mandate through numerology, necromancy, and deism to modern, secular rationality. The formal fusion of *cosmos* and *polis* into *cosmopolis* probably appeared first among the Greek Stoic philosophers in their notion of a single order expressed as the reason that bound all things and actions together. Monotheism simplified Stoicist notions into a spiritual moral order of divine law embossed on a natural order also embraced within God's will. Limited to *polis* expressed as morality, people concentrated power in the sovereign state explicitly to keep order among themselves. The role of human will was to avoid clashes between the power-based *polis* of human government with the *cosmos* of God's will and natural order, which remained beyond human knowledge. For people, the state provided security and social order; for the state, sovereignty was its own reward; God's will and natural order remained eternal and inscrutable.

As modern globalization expanded human perspectives and perceptions of order beyond the *polis* with the rational urges to know the *cosmos* as absolute truth, people recognized the narrow focus of state-centered, power-based government. Expanding knowledge gradually confronted the pragmatic need for local, political order among people and societies with the ancient *cosmopolitan* conviction that actions were right only if they were also natural, and thereby moral. Succeeding waves of modern globalization intensified the demand for *both* morality *and* rationality. Progress seemed to require people to fuse them *both* within themselves *and* across humanity in a global governance that transcended everything from the universe itself to the *sanctum sanctorum* of the human heart. The process of globalization created the human need for consciousness of the condition of globalization.

Within the global perspective where state sovereignty is no longer its own reward, globalization *both* diffuses political power and legitimate authority *and* extends them to broader functions. Expansion to the global perspective implies that politics "is determined less and less from domestic processes operating *within* relatively autonomous and hierarchically organized structures called states, and more and more from transnational processes operative *across* states."[39] Extending beyond power-based government within a bordered *polis*, global governance embraces inter-, non-, and subgovernmental organizations; multinational enterprises and financial institutions; terrorist and criminal groups; and individuals. Globalism deepens governance into processes, structures, and institutions that address people's social, political, and economic concerns that lie beyond the rational *polis* of state-centered government.

By adapting power and authority congruently to local particularities *and also* to global universality, people's willed actions create the nonstate, non-national, and multistate institutions that shape global living and thought in the legacy context of state-centered government. Instead of its traditional concentration in states, "power resides in *both* macro- *and* microinstitutions; it is more complex than ever, with new configurations of global, national, regional, and more properly local forces and relations of power, generating new conflicts and sites of struggle."[40] Global governance introduces the possibilities of novel forms of global citizenship that include *both* diversity, difference, and otherness *and* homogeneity, unity, and self-identity.[41] Complex interdependence seems to be one stage in human political-economic development towards some concept of global citizenship for countries, governments, economies, societies, companies, and people.

Structure and Institutions

Instead of hierarchical concentration, effective global governance demands responsivity and decision at remote places throughout the world. Neither a power-based coercive system nor a wealth-based inducive system, global governance can rely only on the power of human knowledge for either efficiency or credibility. Not only smaller and faster than the modern world, the disintermediated, dislocated world is flatter with less need for institutions, social structures, interpretations of information, or governments and companies. Despite inexperience with either *cosmopolis* or global governance, several trends of globalization converge in a still unclear image that excludes much of the institutional context of state-centered systems.

Acceleration: Revolutionary technologies in information, manufacturing, management, and transportation move things and ideas faster than ever before in human history.

Asymmetry: New technologies allow individuals or small groups to exercise power that the state-centered system reserved to governments and classical capitalism concentrated in large corporations.

Amplification: A single incident can generate a global reaction with consequences that neither democratic politics nor market economics can control.

Volatility: Public interest and political attention follow the networks from crisis to crisis, and public opinion forgets yesterday's tragedy as the global press corps and mobile media cover today's celebration.

Power Transition: The foundations of wealth and power are no longer territory, resources, and inhabitants but information and knowledge. The availability of new technological instruments redistributes power in a knowledge-intensive world to individuals and groups who could have no such power in a property-based capitalist world. In a complicated triple transition, huge transnational corporations are concentrating economic power even as political power is dissipating and the power of knowledge is growing.

Disintermediation: As technology enables people to deal directly with any other people, companies, or institutions anywhere in the world, they no longer need, or want, brokers, traders, managers, broadcasters, newspapers, television networks, ambassadors, diplomats, or even bureaucrats.

Dislocation: Within the global perspective, political and economic borders are unwinding from each other as states and companies face the threats that transient groups of nonaffiliated individuals in cyberspace can pose implement to sovereign states and wealthy corporations.

Cooperation from Discord: "Alongside the necessary but imperfect interstate institutional framework, there is developing an informal political process that supplements the formal process of cooperative relations among states."[42] Cooperation and formation of regimes both arise from discord and a common belief that reciprocity and adjustment—albeit painful—are better than rigid confrontation.[43]

Global Civil Society: An incipient global civil society is evolving into *de facto* pluralistic, if not democratic, structure of global governance.

Although theorists and idealists can readily design various systems of global governance that accommodate these trends, any technical or institutional solution can be compelling only within the global perspective. While Bacon's idols sequester people within their narrow perspectives, they can be expected to resist transforming the familiar into the unknown without the new knowledge that they must themselves create. Without *both basho and* incremental innovation, global governance can only drift with political and economic tides within its own *nébuleuse*. Risk-averse people remain cautiously reluctant to expand their perspectives, transform the world, and reform its institutions. Since the effects of interdependence and globalization appear differently in each narrow perspective, any contrived conjunction, compromise, or convergence of global governance is likely to be fragmented, chaotic, untidy, and satisfying to neither rationalists nor humanists.

Governance of Globalization

Any vision or structure of global governance embodies regulating the effects of interdependence and governing the process of globalization. Interdependence presumes "that changes or events in any single unit of the system will produce some reaction from, or have some significant consequence on, other units of the system—*whether they like it or not*. The images of the global village, the spaceship earth, and the shrinking planet are all derived from this idea of interdependence and its two different dimensions, *sensitivity* and *vulnerability*."[44] Increasingly sensitive to each other, states and firms alike typically react to globalized threats unilaterally to decrease their vulnerabilities. "Sensitivity and vulnerability often go together, but do not necessarily correlate."[45] Their preferred responses—barriers to trade and immigration, coercive intervention, policy adjustments, strategic aliances, or competitive balancing—often act reflexively. Within triggering zones, they appear as counterthreats to the initial threat, whereas within shadow zones defensive responses often stimulate new threats. To mediate this reflexivity, many societies unilaterally transform *both* their respective states *and* their firms into "the means to resist and reshape the pressures generated by globalization."[46]

Since societies persistently pursue their own narrow interests, commerce and politics alternate spasmodically between cooperation and conflict in deepening and broadening of both into the paradox of pervasive, complex interdependence. The result is *neither* the shift towards Immanuel Kant's vision of a democratic peace *nor* the extension of Adam Smith's invisible hand around the entire globe. With neither the visible hand of power-based government to impose *polis* nor divine, natural order to impose *cosmos*, an increasingly urgent challenge for any version of global governance remains the control of globalization.

Global governance merges the legacy of Kant's democratic peace neatly with Smith's invisible hand in peaceful dispute resolution as a primary institution for governing the untoward effects of globalization. The social integration of economic globalization and political consensus lead to the absence of even the consideration of using force or coercion to resolve disputes among members of a global, or international, community. For an integrated, interdependent world, global governance generalizes the norm of peaceful dispute resolution in a war-peace system to a global, stable peace, which inspired the expanding *zones of peace* in the 1990s.[47]

One paradoxical result of peaceful dispute resolution as a behavioral norm of global governance is that it may destroy any *purely rational* reason for states to integrate beyond security communities to deeper ones involving economics or culture. If peaceful dispute resolution within security communities can also bring economic prosperity and some acceptable version of justice, it would be rational to avoid the greater costs of deeper integration. The European effort to integrate the security community of the North Atlantic Treaty Organization into the European Union is the world's first test of this paradox.

International Law?

An unnoticed result of modern globalization has been the hesitant emergence of a vague set of global constitutional structures of governance beyond the diplomacy, treaties, and precedent of international law. Economic interdependence requires states and peoples to recognize, accept, and meet their responsibilities towards their neighbors and trading partners in a global extension of *pacta sunt servanda*. People everywhere are beginning to recognize the existence of a legal, international society of states that features legal rules applicable to all states, regardless of power or wealth, without their specific consent to those rules. In a revolutionary departure from the foundations of domestic law in power-based enforcement by the state, this docrine of *jus cogens* includes the notion of *collective self-enforcement*.

Globalization of the doctrine of *jus cogens* no longer permits states to opt out of a common nucleus of interstate legal rules, which includes peaceful dispute resolution and minimum standards for protecting people. A powerful expansion of the idealistic notion of collective security, the related *erga omnes* effect implies that all states have a legal interest in ensuring that all other states comply with these same rules. "Through the concept of serious breaches of obligations under peremptory norms of general international law, the international community as a whole is moving towards common action at the state level against violations of these rules."[48] The still controversial doctrine of legal universality threatens all violators with criminal prosecution by any state acting as an agent of the unwritten global constitution and exercising jurisdiction on behalf of the entire global community.

Global Sovereignty?

A globalist political-legal system would reject the exclusive nationalism that is the ideological foundation for sovereignty, deny the right of a state to set its boundaries by force, and would place the entire phenomenon of migration in controversy. Globalism suggests that national sovereignty may be the fundamental barrier to managing transnational and global issues. Within the global perspective, the image of sovereignty expands from its doctrinal domain in the nation-state to a borderless realm of law and order, rights and duties, and an open set of sovereign institutions. A socially constructed bundle of features whose composition and priorities shift over time and across space, global sovereignty comprises autonomy, control, and authority, which people can attach to various social institutions, not just states. People can reconfigure sovereignty with different understandings of themselves, the law, their rights and obligations, and how they prefer to manage them.[49] The broadening of sovereignty beyond the nation-state and the many nonstate interests clamoring for political participation concurrently stimulate the global civil society that must organize the structures and processes of global governance.

Transformation or Creation?

The socereignty and territoriality of Westphalian government, protectively managed by Bacon's idols, constrain the structure and processes of politics beyond and among nation-states. To realize the promise of either an international society of states or a Gaian global community requires people to create global structures, processes, and institutions in transnational arenas for *both* citizenship *and* sovereignty. To expand to the global perspective, the atavistic and euphemistic international community must "transform itself into an instrument of global governance. This objective cannot be achieved by stretching the current liberal visions of international law and a common humanity to accommodate more countries and points of view. Rather, new ideas about global governance are a prerequisite for tackling the problem of inclusion."[50] Although it remains unclear how or whether people will govern either globalization or themselves within the global perspective, any surprises that history brings will inevitably occur in a context of expanding knowledge, expanding perspectives, and deliberate human creation of new knowledge. As in any period of profound, social transformation, the challenge of global governance is not merely to predict the results of globalization; historians will do that in clear retrospect. We active participants must learn to cope with —and try to manage—transformation and transition and understand the consequences or reactions to them.

FOREIGN POLICY AND GLOBALIZATION

Since recognizing interdependence, the world's great powers and many other countries have accepted active roles in global politics and adopted a global—or at least international—perspective for foreign policy. Despite the accelerating tendency of businesses and international organizations to take a global perspective on what they do, nation-states still focus their power through inward-looking foreign policy and national strategy. Most countries retain the classical, Westphalian self-regarding focus for defining and pursuing national interests, dealing with the rest of the world, and looking after themselves and their populations. Even within an international perspective, foreign policy is premised upon some mutually exclusive relationship between *us* and *them*: their concept of nationalism. Most people in most of the world's countries rely staunchly on nationalism in defining themselves politically, although they find no anomaly in defining themselves in anthropological terms as citizens of the world or in ethnic or cultural terms as members of a transnational community. Embedded in this paradox is the dilemma of integrating a country into the global political-economy through foreign policy: national globalization strategy.

As countries look beyond their own borders for approaches and solutions to globalization, their various strategies reflect their geographic locations but seem to cluster in two broad categories: linkage and autonomy. Countries that adopt linkage strategies—Mexico, Poland, Canada, Mongolia, Switzerland, Ukraine, and others—are clearly influenced by geography and relationships with dominant countries, and link foreign policies, economies, and political roles to their more powerful neighbors. In contrast, a strategy of autonomy includes a relatively closed economy, a role of clear regional leadership or deference, and a global political role that is often disruptive or opposed to the positions of the great powers.

Linking Strategy

Countries that adopt linking strategies seek rapid economic growth as an important national priority. A linking strategy includes foreign trade and portfolio investment with a few countries as a primary engine of economic growth and actively promotes exports of a substantial portion of national income (gross domestic product). Linking strategies seek to shift an economy from agriculture towards industry and services in a coordinated Ricardian relationship with dominant, economic neighbors. A country that adopts a linkage strategy tends to have been historically dependent on one powerful country and seeks to convert economic dependency into political-economic interdependence. Economic linkages with a wealthy and powerful neighbor seem to generate a wide range of other linkages on noneconomic issues.

A linkage strategy places a high priority on partnership with a particular powerful partner and shapes a country's entire foreign policy around that partnership, which can generate instability, or at least volatility, in foreign policy. Beyond trade and economics, a linkage strategy often positions a country as a bridge between the powerful partner and other countries in the region to carry particular aspects of globalization—human rights, democracy, free trade, or stability—into the region. Through a linkage strategy a globalizing country assists and promotes globalization not as a regional leader but as a carrier and projection of the power of the dominant partner. Policy itself remains focused around particular issues of interest either to the country's own population or to the greater power, and policy decisions tend to be made by bureaucrats using technical criteria. With narrow, restrained aims for globalizing, the success of linkage strategies tends to be focused on economic criteria and domestic economic growth linked to the prosperity of the wealthy partner. Linkage strategies tend to become irreversible as economies and polities become hopelessly integrated.

Autonomy Strategy

National strategies of autonomy accept slower domestic growth of exports and industry but stress diverse foreign trade and foreign direct investment, rather than the portfolio investment that linking strategies seek. An autonomy strategy not only eschews large trading relationships with a single country but maintains total foreign trade as only a small portion of national income and supports multilateral trade agreements. Even a successful autonomy strategy, however, faces the chronic domination of a regional hegemon and the global great powers. Some autonomy strategies have expanded into aspirations to regional hegemony and even global great-power status.

In seeking active roles in regional and global politics, an autonomy strategy does not hesitate to balance or oppose the policies of regional or global great powers but does not readily become an adversary of a more powerful country. Deliberately developing bargaining power for dealing with more powerful countries, an autonomy strategy demands a diversified foreign policy that may include a single primary relationship with a powerful partner. Any primary relationship, however, does not dominate or restrict foreign policy, and the autonomous globalizing country retains the ability either to support or to oppose and even to change positions. Instead of acting as a projection of another country's power, the autonomous strategy prefers a partnership with a greater power in dealing with regional issues. An autonomy strategy tends to generate a stable, predictable foreign policy that supports a preferred position and role in global politics that go beyond specific issues and seek a major influence in managing global affairs. Policy decisions within an autonomous strategy reflect domestic politics around a popular consensus that the country deserves a major role in global affairs.

The ambitious aims of autonomy strategies often extend beyond economic growth and interdependence to avoid the constraints on any political role imposed by scarcity of resources. Diversion of attention and resources to establishing a diverse global political role necessarily deprives domestic social and economic problems of the attention and resources to address them quickly or effectively. Since economic growth has a lower priority than developing a global political role, an autonomy strategy remains vulnerable to domestic pressures to protect economic competitiveness. Paradoxically, in many autonomous globalizing countries, despite political consensus on building a global role, internal disarray and dissatisfaction with social welfare prevent any credible expansion of global political roles.

The Strategic Dilemma

National cultures, histories, and self-images are critical in choosing one or the other type of globalizing strategy. Some countries—Mexico, Canada, Ireland, many former colonies, Vietnam, Mongolia, or Korea—have been far less concerned about their places in the world than with their relationships with powerful neighbors. Other peoples—Brazil, Argentina, Nigeria, Egypt, Iran, India, or Japan—have felt entitled to a significant role among the great powers in global politics.[51]

The dilemma of choosing between a unilateral, autonomous—often confrontational—policy and a multilateral—often deferential—linkage strategy remains intractable for all but the global powers. So long as a government can maintain domestic political-economic stability, either strategy can successfully integrate a country into the global political-economy. Deliberate, focused, and increasing pressure on other countries to cooperate with it can achieve *both* economic integration *and* a global political role without transforming the institutions of the classical, power-based nation-state system.

CHAOS OR DESIGN?

The long pageant of history depicts humanity's persistent search for truth, understanding, and order. Globalization has been the process of expanding human understanding of reality and reducing chaos to order. Superimposed on globalization has been the capacity to exploit chaos in improving the human condition. Less-than-global segments of humanity continue to thrive on chaos as prior civilizations have done since antiquity. Modern globalization has penetrated deeply enough into the global perspective to convince people that they can, and should, design the future instead of merely learning to exploit it. Whatever people decide to do, however, globalization will continue to expand people's perspectives and carry them along a path to progress.

Thriving on Chaos

Although policy coordination among states remains difficult, global trade is thriving and flourishes in multinational enterprises across cities and firms alike. Individual businesses and global corporations may expand or fail and governments may generate economic growth and political development or stagnation and chaos. Globalization, however proceeds regardless of the residue left in its wake. Even as they sell their olive trees for above-market prices, people still want their Lexus and those who have one cherish it.

Adam Smith argued in the eighteenth century that states and people were steered towards prosperity not by the firm hand of governments but by the invisible hand of enlightened self-interest and the force of individual enterprise. Governments prescribe the rules for economic and social interactions in terms of political realities and preferences and maintain an infrastructure—law, national defense, public services, and welfare—to provide some stability. Even in centrally planned Marxist economies, policy must be executed ultimately by individuals seeking to increase their own prosperity, security, and justice within *both* national political-economies *and* a larger global system. Although states change their rules periodically, resources become cyclically scarce or plentiful, markets boom or crash, and countries go to war or form alliances, interdependent and self-reliant individuals everywhere adapt and prosper. Adam Smith would probably approve enthusiastically of this chaotic process of globalization and fragmentation. While Karl Marx or Frederick Taylor might simply shake their heads in dismay, modern cosmocrats and high-tech idealists might resolve to design and build a better future.

Designing the Future

The global perspective does not predict or reveal the future. Rather, it offers a broad understanding of the present and the past. The lens of historicism expands history beyond the past to encompass the present and the future and links them with *both* change *and* continuity. It also reveals that the *conjoncture* in which people are now living is global in dimension and extent. The destinies of every culture, society, and civilization are now inextricably linked to the condition of all people everywhere by human will. Neither arbitrary nor inevitable, whatever will happen in the future will be contingent on decisions and choices that other people have already made and those that we make today. The global perspective expands people's perspectives beyond the urgency of reacting in event time into social time through the deliberacy of incremental progress and through catastrophic transformation into the *longue durée*. Although people cannot yet design the details of the future, globalization has enormously increased the collective power of humanity to shape the processes that lead into the future.

Within the global perspective, humanity comprises heroes and heroines who, simply by existing, determine the future. Modernists laid the infrastructure and foundations of the future. Cosmocrats, globalists, humanists, and idealists set themselves the initial task of designing the future as a sustainable and acceptable world for people. The succeeding task is to transform modern social reality into that designed, future world. A major task in deliberately designing and building the future is discovery of some way for broad and fair sharing of human creations—wealth, income, products, ideas, or services. Establishment of democracy or devolution of power do little more than deepening the hold of Bacon's idols on people's minds without adapting power *both* to the needs of local citizens *and* to the promise of a global future shared by all people. Political recognition of human rights, multilateral diplomacy, and peaceful dispute resolution are little more than rhetoric without sharing. Whereas the process of globalization has often simply extended political rule, the condition of globalization replaces the very notion of rule with that of sharing. The operation of a market—free, open, planned, or any other sort—is little more than a caricature of social interaction that ignores all moral, ethical, or compassionate issues of sharing. Any global future must include legitimate institutions at *all* levels of human interactions: local, subnational, national, non-national, international, transnational, and global.

Globalism rejects technology as the determinant of the future and subjects knowledge to human will in responding to the primal human needs and desires that have animated humanity since the first *homo sapiens* recognized its first thought. People still want enough to eat and drink in comfortable places to live, warm relations with some other people, some pleasant and intellectually challenging things to do, and freedom from pain and fear. Globalist positivism asks whether technology provides "the means to reach the kind of future we would like, or is it at the root of the problems we must solve? . . . Surely, the answer is some of both. . . . technology is not metal and glass and plastic molded to our human purposes; technology is knowledge, and knowledge provides the capability for doing new things."[52] People decide to which purposes it will be put and which new things it will do—good things and bad things. Instead of destroying the foundations of future life on earth, humanity must use technology to husband natural resources and recognize the humanity is a part of nature, not its master.

Rather than simply enjoying material comfort, people must discover or invent some way to live at peace not only with people but with all of nature and choose deliberately to live that way. The future is for humanity to design, choose, and construct, not merely to experience or predict. Although constructing the future depends heavily on the technology brought by innovation, designing it requires not technological applications but the new knowledge that people create in *basho*. Choosing the future demands neither technology nor knowledge, but the human will that people express in social transformation and creation of that values that focus action. Regardless of technology and even scientific knowledge, it remains the powerful alliance of moral values and human will that design the future and guide globalization in constructing it. We can still shape our destiny. Human will transforms globalization into opportunities as new knowledge exposes its threats as less menacing.

NOTES

1. David Henderson, "International Economic Integration: Progress, Prospects, and Implications," *International Affairs* 68(4) (October 1992): 633–653; 633.

2. Roland Robertson, *Globalization: Social Theory and Global Culture* (London, Sage, 1992), 8.

3. Fernand Braudel, "The History of Civilizations: The Past Explains the Present," in *On History*, edited by Fernand Braudel, 177–218 (Chicago: University of Chicago Press, 1980), 202.

4. Eric Voegelin, *Order and History, Volume 2: The World of the Polis* (Baton Rouge: Louisiana State University Press, 1957), 15, 14–23.

5. Plato, *The Republic*, translated by Alan Bloom (New York: Basic Books, 1948), 368–369.

6. See Ibn Khaldun, *The Muqaddimah: An Introduction to History*, translated by Franz Rosenthal, 3 vols (New York: Pantheon, 1958), vol. 1, 89.

7. See Marshall McLuhan, *The Global Village: Transformations in World Life and Media in the 21st Century* (New York: Oxford University Press, 1989).

8. David R. Gress, "The Drama of Modern Western Identity," *Orbis* 41(4) (Fall 1997): 525–544; 526.

9. See McLuhan, *The Global Village*.

10. Roland Axtmann, "Globalization, Europe, and the State: Introductory Reflections," in *Globalization and Europe*, edited by Roland Axtmann, 1–22 (London: Pinter, 1998), 18.

11. See Ronald Inglehart, *Modernization and Postmodernization: Cultural, Economic, and Political Change in 43 Societies* (Princeton: Princeton University Press, 1997).

12. Martin van Creveld, *Technology and War: From 2,000 B.C. to the Present* (New York: Free Press, 1989), 6.

13. Sam J. Tangredi, "Beyond the Sea and Jointness," *U.S. Naval Institute Proceedings* 127/9/1,183 (September 2001): 60–63; 63.

14. Stanley Brunn and Thomas R. Leinbach, eds., *Collapsing Space and Time: Geographic Aspects of Communications and Information* (London: HarperCollins, 1991), xvii.

15. Saskia Sassen, *Globalization and Its Discontents* (New York: New Press, 1998), 214.

16. Emma Rothschild, "Globalization and the Return of History," *Foreign Policy* 115 (Summer 1999): 106–116; 115.

17. See Geoffrey Blainey, *The Tyranny of Distance*, rev. ed. (Melbourne: Sun Books, 1983), 338–343.

18. Anthony Giddens, *Modernity and Self-Identity: Self and Society in the Late Modern Age* (Cambridge: Polity, 1991), 64.

19. Malcolm Waters, *Globalization* (London: Routledge, 1995), 3.

20. Richard W. Mansbach, *The Global Puzzle: Issues and Actors in World Politics*, 3d ed. (Boston: Houghton Mifflin, 2000), 17.

21. Michael Talalay, "Technology and Globalization," in *Globalization and Its Critics*, edited by Randall D. Germain, 204–222 (New York: St. Martin's, 2000), 210.

22. Stephen E. Toulmin, *Cosmopolis: The Hidden Agenda of Modernity* (New York: Free Press, 1990), 180.

23. Francis Fukuyama, *The Great Disruption: Human Nature and the Reconstitution of Social Order*, (New York: Free Press, 1999), 237.

24. See Michael Gibbons, "Science's New Social Contract with Society," *Nature* 402(6761) (2 December 1999, supplement): C81–C84.

25. See United States, National Academy of Sciences, National Academy of Engineering and Institute of Medicine, *On Being a Scientist* (Washington, D.C.: National Academy Press, 1995), 6–8.

26. Herbert A. Simon, "Forecasting the Future or Shaping It?" *Industrial and Corporate Change* 11(3) (June 2002): 601–605; 603.

27. Solomon R. Benatar, Abdallah S. Daar, and Peter A. Singer, "Global Health Ethics: The Rationale for Mutual Caring," *International Affairs* 79(1) (January 2003): 107–138; 110. See also Nicholas Maxwell, *The Comprehensibility of the Universe: A New*

Conception of Science (Oxford: Clarnedon, 1998), 6–19.

28. Benatar, Daar, and Singer, "Global Health Ethics," 110–111.

29. Benatar, Daar, and Singer, "Global Health Ethics," 118.

30. Benatar, Daar, and Singer, "Global Health Ethics," 108–110. See also Tom L. Beauchamp, "The Role of Principles in Practical Ethics," in *Philosophical Perspectives on Bioethics*, edited by L. Wayne Sumner and Joseph Boyle, 79–95 (Toronto: Toronto University Press, 1996), 91–93.

31. Benatar, Daar, and Singer, "Global Health Ethics," 119.

32. Any consideration of minority rights adds another level of complexity to any global ethic concerning rights. Beyond inclusive human rights, minority rights are exclusive and involve some source of right other than simply humanity.

33. Benatar, Daar, and Singer, "Global Health Ethics," 121.

34. Toulmin, *Cosmopolis*, 204.

35. William H. Mott IV, *The Economic Basis of Peace: Linkages between Economic Growth and International Conflict* (Westport, Connecticut: Greenwood, 1997), 183.

36. Mott, *The Economic Basis of Peace*, 184.

37. Progressive obsolescence of the bargain on foreign direct investment between a multinational firm and a host government reduces the benefits and increases the costs of the project for the country. Fixed capital invested by the company becomes sunk and hostage to the host government. As risk decreases when production begins, and as technology matures, becomes available on the open market, and loses value, power shifts. The host government gains technological and managerial skills that reduce the relative values of those of the company. The company's bargaining power decreases as management of the enterprise by host-country citizens becomes practicable. (See Raymond Vernon, *Sovereignty at Bay: The Multinational Spread of U.S. Enterprises* (New York: Basic Books, 1971), 47; Raymond Vernon, "The Obsolescing Bargain: A Key Factor in Political Risk," in *The International Essays for Business Decision Makers*, vol. 5, edited by Mark B. Winchester, 281–286 (Houston: Center for International Business, 1980), 283. If the host society chooses to shift to dynamic growth, "the country starts to move up a learning curve that leads from monitoring industry behavior to replicating complicated corporate functions." Theodore H. Moran, *Multinational Corporations and the Politics of Dependence: Copper in Chile* (Princeton: Princeton University Press, 1974), 164.

38. Mott, *The Economic Basis of Peace*, 226.

39. Philip G. Cerny, "Restructuring the Political Arena: Globalization and the Paradoxes of the Competition State," in *Globalization and its Critics: Perspectives from Political Economy*, edited by Randall D. Germain, 117–138 (New York: St. Martin's, 2000), 118. (Italics in original.)

40. Douglas Kellner, "Globalization and the Postmodern Turn," in *Globalization and Europe: Theoretical and Empirical Investigations*, edited by Roland Axtmann, 23–42 (London: Pinter, 1998), 37.

41. Roland Axtmann, "Collective Identity and the Democratic Nation-State in the Age of Globalization," in *Articulating the Global and the Local: Globalization and Cultural Studies*, edited by Ann Cvetkovich and Douglas Kellner, 33–54 (Boulder: Westview, 1997).

42. Robert O. Keohane and Joseph S. Nye Jr., *Power and Interdependence*, 3rd. ed. (New York: Longman, 2001), 261. See also Robert O. Keohane and Joseph S. Nye, Jr., "Transgovernmental Relations and International Organizations," *World Politics* 27(1) (October 1974): 39–62; 42–50; Anne-Marie Slaughter, "The Real New World Order,"

Foreign Affairs 76(5) (September-October 1997): 183–197; 185–189, 195–197.

43. See Robert O. Keohane, *After Hegemony: Cooperation and Discord in the World Political Economy* (Princeton: Princeton University Press, 1984), 54–55.

44. Harvey Starr, *Anarchy, Order, and Integration: How to Manage Interdependence* (Ann Arbor: University of Michigan Press, 1997), 17. See also Robert O. Keohane and Joseph S. Nye, *Power and Interdependence*, 2d ed. (Glenview, Illinois: Scott, Foresman, 1989), 12–13.

45. Steven L. Spiegel and Fred L. Wehling, *World Politics in a New Era*, 2d ed. (Fort Worth, Texas: Harcourt Brace, 1999), 192.

46. Helen V. Milner, "International Political Economy: Beyond Hegemonic Stability," *Foreign Policy* 110 (Spring 1998): 112–123; 121.

47. For a brief analysis of the democratic peace, see Starr, *Anarchy, Order, and Integration*, 77–79, ch. 7, 111–137. For his seminal work on social integration into security communities, see Karl W. Deutsch, *Political Community and the North Atlantic Area: International Organization in the Light of Historical Experience* (Princeton: Princeton University Press, 1957), 28–42, 58–59, 70–116. Kenneth Boulding later globalized Deutsch's work into social war-peace systems. See Kenneth E. Boulding, *Stable Peace* (Austin: University of Texas Press, 1978), 31–49.

48. Marc Weller, "Undoing the Global Constitution: U.N. Security Council Action on the International Criminal Court," *International Affairs* 78(4) (October 2002): 693–712; 693.

49. See, among others, Karen T. Litfin, "The Greening of Sovereignty: An Introduction," in *The Greening of Sovereignty in World Politics*, edited by Karen T. Litfin, 1–27 (Cambridge: MIT Press, 1998), 5–9; Karen Litfin, "Sovereignty in World Ecopolitics," *Mershon International Studies Review* 41(2) (November 1997): 167–204; 194–196.

50. Arjun Appadurai, "Broken Promises," *Foreign Policy* 132 (September-October 2002): 42–44; 43.

51. For a comparative analysis of a country that has adopted a Linking strategy for globalization—Mexico—and Brazil, which has adopted an Autonomy strategy, see Peter Hakim, "Two Ways to Go Global," *Foreign Affairs* 81(1) (January-February 2002): 148–162.

52. Herbert A. Simon, "Forecasting the Future or Shaping It?" *Industrial and Corporate Change* 11(3) (June 2002): 601–605; 602

SELECTED BIBLIOGRAPHY

Aberbach, Joel D., David Dollar, and Kenneth L. Sokoloff, eds. *The Role of the State in Taiwan's Development*. London: Sharpe, 1994.

Abramovitz, Moses. "Resource and Output Trends in the United States since 1870," *Occasional Paper 52*. New York: National Bureau of Economic Research, 1956.

Aquinas, St. Thomas. "De Regimine Principum." In *Aquinas: Selected Political Writings*, translated by J. G. Dawson, 3–83. Oxford: Blackwell, 1948.

———. *Summa Theologica, Vol. 2*, Great Books of the Western World. Chicago: Encyclopædia Britannica, 1952.

Albertini, Rudolf von. *Decolonization: The Administration and Future of the Colonies, 1919-1960*. London: Holmes and Meier, 1982.

Aldrich, Howard E. and Toshihiro Sasaki. "R&D Consortia in the United States and Japan." *Research Policy* 24(2) (March 1995): 301–316.

Alexander, Michael. "A Global Civil War." *RUSI Journal* 146(6) (December 2001): 12–15.

Alighieri, Dante. *De Monarchia*, translated by Herbert W. Schneider. Indianapolis, Indiana: Bobbs-Merrill, 1957.

———. "De Monarchia." In *Western Political Heritage*, by William Y. Elliott and Neil A. McDonald, 367–373. Englewood Cliffs, New Jersey: Prentice-Hall, [1949] 1965.

Alt, James E. and Kenneth A. Shepsle, eds. *Perspectives on Positive Political Economy*. Cambridge: Cambridge University Press, 1990.

Altvater, Elmar and Birgit Mahnkopf. "The World Market Unbound." *Review of International Political Economy* 4(3) (Autumn 1997): 448–471.

Ancori, Bernard, Antoine Bureth, and Patrick Cohendet. "The Economics of Knowledge: The Debate about Codification and Tacit Knowledge." *Industrial and Corporate Change* 9(2) (June 2000): 255–288.

Anderson, Benedict R. O'G. *Imagined Communities: Reflections on the Origins and Spread of Nationalism*. London: Verso, 1991.

Annan, Kofi A. "Problems without Passports." *Foreign Policy* 132 (September-October 2002): 30–31.

"Anticapitalist Protests: Angry and Effective." *The Economist* 356(8189) (23 September 2000): 85–87.

Aoki, Masahiko. *Innovation in the Governance of Product-System Innovation: The Silicon Valley Model*, Stanford Institute for Economic Policy Research, Policy Paper no. 00–003, October 2000. Unpublished.

Appadurai, Arjun. "Broken Promises." *Foreign Policy* 132 (September-October 2002): 42–44.

Appleby, R. Scott. "Fundamentalism." *Foreign Policy* 128 (January-February 2002): 16–22.

Archibugi, Daniele and Jonathan Michie. *The Globalization of Technology: Myths and Realities*, University of Cambridge Research Papers in Management Studies, 1992–1993, no. 18. Cambridge: University of Cambridge, 1993.

Archibugi, Daniele, David Held, and Martin Köhler, eds. *Re-imagining Political Community: Studies in Cosmopolitan Democracy*. Cambridge, Massachusetts: Polity, 1998.

Arendt, Hannah. *Between Past and Future: Six Exercises in Political Thought*. New York: Viking, [1954] 1961.

Aristotle. "Politics." In *The Works of Aristotle*, vol. 2, Great Books of the Western World. Chicago: Encyclopædia Britannica, 1952.

Aron, Raymond. *Introduction à la Philosophie de l'Histoire*. Paris: Gallimard, 1938.

Arrighi, Giovanni and Jessica Drangel. "The Stratification of the World Economy: An Exploration of the Semiperipheral Zone." In *Review, Volume 10*, edited by James O. Hoge, 9–74. Charlottesville: University Press of Virginia.

Aubrey, John. *Minutes of Lives*, edited as *Aubrey's Brief Lives* by Oliver L. Dick. Ann Arbor: University of Michigan Press, [1813] 1957.

Augustine, St. "The City of God." In *The Confessions, The City of God, On Christian Doctrine*, Great Books of the Western World. Chicago: Encyclopædia Britannica, 1952.

Aukrust, Odd and Juul Bjerke. "Real Capital and Economic Growth in Norway, 1900-56." In *The Measurement of National Wealth*, International Association for Research in Income and Wealth, Income and Wealth, Series VIII, edited by Raymond Goldsmith and Christopher Saunders, 80-118. Chicago: Quadrangle Books, 1959.

Axtmann, Roland. "Collective Identity and the Democratic Nation-State in the Age of Globalization." In *Articulating the Global and the Local: Globalization and Cultural Studies*, edited by Ann Cvetkovich and Douglas Kellner, 33-54. Boulder, Colorado: Westview, 1997.

———. "Globalization, Europe, and the State: Introductory Reflections." In *Globalization and Europe*, edited by Roland Axtmann, 1–22. London: Pinter, 1998.

———. ed. *Globalization and Europe*. London: Pinter, 1998.

Babbitt, Irving. *Democracy and Leadership*. Indianapolis, Indiana: Liberty Classics, [1924] 1979.

———. *Rousseau and Romanticism*. Austin: University of Texas Press, 1977.

Bacevich, Andrew J. "Culture, Globalization, and U.S. Foreign Policy." *World Policy Journal* 19(3) (Fall 2002): 77–82.

———. "New Rome, New Jerusalem." *The Wilson Quarterly* 26(3) (Summer 2002): 50–58.

"Back to the Classics." *The Economist* 339(7966) (18 May 1996): 85–87.

Bacon, Francis. *The Letters and Life of Francis Bacon, Including All His Occasional Works*, edited by James Spedding, 7 vols. London: Longman, Green, Longman, and Roberts, [1862–1874] 1890.

———. *Selected Writings: Essays, Advancement of Learning, New Atlantic*. Franklin Center, Pennsylvania: Franklin Library, 1982.

———. *The Works of Francis Bacon*, edited by James Spedding, Robert L. Ellis, and Douglas D. Heath, 15 vols. Cambridge, Massachusetts: Riverside Press, 1870.

Baldacchino, Joseph F., Jr. "The Value-Centered Historicism of Edmund Burke." *Modern Age* 27(2) (Spring 1983), 139–145.

Barber, Benjamin R. "Democracy at Risk: American Culture in a Global Culture." *World Policy Journal* 15(2) (Summer 1998): 29–41.

———. *Jihad vs. McWorld*. New York: Times Books, 1995.

Baring, Ann and Jules Cashford. *The Myth of the Goddess*. London: Penguin, 1993.

Barro, Robert. "Economic Growth in a Cross Section of Countries." *Quarterly Journal of Economics* 106(2) (May 1991): 407–443.

Baruah, Sanjib. "Globalization—Facing the Inevitable?" *World Policy Journal* 16(4) (Winter 1999–2000): 105–112.

Basant, Rakesh and Brian Fikkert. "The Effects of R&D, Foreign Technology Purchase, and Domestic and International Spillovers on Productivity in Indian Firms." *Review of Economics and Statistics* 78(2) (May 1996): 187–199.

Bauman, Zygmunt. *Modernity and Ambivalence*. Cambridge, Massachusetts: Polity, 1991.

———. "Soil, Blood, and Identity." *Sociological Review* 40(4) (November 1992): 675–701.

Beauchamp, Tom L. "The Role of Principles in Practical Ethics." In *Philosophical Perspectives on Bioethics*, edited by L. Wayne Sumner and Joseph Boyle, 79–95. Toronto: Toronto University Press, 1996.

Beck, Ulrich. *Risk Society*. London: Sage, 1992.

Bell, Daniel A. "Minority Rights: On the Importance of Local Knowledge." *Dissent* 43(3) (Summer 1996): 36–41.

Bello, Walden. "Battling Barbarism." *Foreign Policy* 132 (September-October 2002): 41–42.

Benatar, Solomon R., Abdallah S. Daar, and Peter A. Singer. "Global Health Ethics: The Rationale for Mutual Caring." *International Affairs* 79(1) (January 2003): 107–138.

Bentwich, Norman. *The Religious Foundations of Internationalism: A Study in International Relations through the Ages*. London: Allen & Unwin, [1933] 1959.

Berg, Maxine. *The Age of Manufacturers: 1700–1820*. New York: Oxford University Press, 1985.

Berger, Suzanne and Robert Dore, eds. *National Diversity and Globalization*. Ithaca: Cornell University Press, 1996.

Bergson, Henri. *Essai sur les Donnés Immédiates de la Conscience*, 144th ed. Paris: Presses Universitaires de France, [1927] 1970.

Bertalanffy, Ludwig von. *General System Theory: Foundation, Development, Applications*. New York: Braziller, 1968.

Best, Steven. *The Politics of Historical Vision*. New York: Guilford, 1995.

Bhagwati, Jagdish. "Coping with Antiglobalization: A Trilogy of Discontents." *Foreign Affairs* 81(1) (January/February 2002): 2–7.

Bhalla, Surjit S. "Freedom and Economic Growth: A Virtuous Cycle." In *Democracy's Victory and Crisis: Nobel Symposium No. 93*, edited by Axel Hadenius, 195–241. Cambridge: Cambridge University Press, 1997.

Bilheimer, Robert S. *What Must the Church Do?* New York: Harper, 1947.

Birdsall, Nancy and Robert Z. Lawrence. "Deep Integration and Trade Agreements: Good for Developing Countries?" In *Global Public Goods: International Cooperation in the 21st Century*, edited by Inge Kaul, Isabelle Grunberg, and Marc A. Stern, 128–151. New York: Oxford University Press, 1999.

Blainey, Geoffrey. *The Tyranny of Distance*, rev. ed. Melbourne: Sun Books, 1983.

Bleich, Erik. "Integrating Ideas into Policymaking Analysis: Frames and Race Policies in Britain and France." *Comparative Political Studies* 35(9) (November 2002): 1054–1076.

Bloom, Irene. "Introduction." In *Religious Diversity and Human Rights*, edited by Irene Bloom, J. Paul Martin, and Wayne L. Proudfoot, 1–11. New York: Columbia University Press, 1996.

———, J. Paul Martin, and Wayne L. Proudfoot, eds. *Religious Diversity and Human Rights*. New York: Columbia University Press, 1996.

Bohman, James. "International Regimes and Democratic Governance: Political Equality and Influence in Global Institutions." *International Affairs* 75(3) (July 1999): 499–513.

Boorman, Scott A. "Island Models for Takeover by a Social Trait Facing a Frequency-Dependent Selection Barrier in a Mendelian Population." *Proceedings of the National Academy of Sciences* 71(5) (May 1974): 2103–2107.

Borenzstein, Eduardo, Jose De Gregario, and Jong-Wha Lee, "How Does Foreign Direct Investment Affect Economic Growth?" *Journal of International Economics* 45(1) (June 1998): 115–135.

Boswell, Christina. "Desperate Measures." *The World Today* 57(11) (November 2001): 25–27.

Bottiglia, William F., ed. *Voltaire: A Collection of Critical Essays*. Englewood Cliffs, New Jersey: Prentice-Hall, 1968.

Bottomore, Tom and Robert J. Brym, eds. *The Capitalist Class: An International Study*. New York: New York University Press, 1989.

Boulding, Kenneth E. "The Boundaries of Social Policy." *Social Work* 12(1) (January 1967): 3–11.

———. *Stable Peace*. Austin: University of Texas Press, 1978.

Bowles, Samuel and Herbert Gintis. *Democracy and Capitalism: Property, Community, and the Contradictions of Modern Social Thought*. New York: Basic Books, 1986.

Bramson, Leon. *Robert MacIver on Community, Society, and Power: Selected Writing*. Chicago: University of Chicago Press, 1970.

Braudel, Fernand. *Capitalism and Material Life, 1400–1800*, translated by Miriam Kochan. New York: Harper & Row, 1963.

———. *Civilization and Capitalism, 15th–18th Century, Vol 3, The Perspective of the World*, translated by Siân Reynolds. London: Collins/Fontana, 1984.

———. "The History of Civilizations: The Past Explains the Present." In *On History*, edited by Fernand Braudel, 177–218. Chicago: University of Chicago Press, 1980.

———, ed. *On History*. Chicago: University of Chicago Press, 1980.

Bronowski, Jacob. *Science and Human Values*. New York: Harper Colophon, [1956] 1975.

Brown, Peter G. and Henry Shue. *Boundaries: National Autonomy and Its Limits*. Totowa, New Jersey: Rowman and Littlefield, 1981.

Brunn, Stanley and Thomas R. Leinbach, eds. *Collapsing Space and Time: Geographic Aspects of Communications and Information*. London: HarperCollins, 1991.

Buckley, Walter. *Sociology and Modern Systems Theory*. Englewood Cliffs, New Jersey: Prentice-Hall, 1967.

Bühlmann, Walter. *God's Chosen Peoples*. Maryknoll, New York: Orbis, 1982.

Bull, Hedley. *The Anarchical Society: A Study of Order in World Politics*. New York: Columbia University Press, 1977.

Burckhardt, Jacob. *Reflections on History*. Indianapolis, Indiana: Liberty Fund, 1979.

Burke, Edmund. *Reflections on the Revolution in France*. Indianapolis, Indiana: Hackett, [1790–1792] 1987)

———. *The Works of Edmund Burke*. London: Bohn's Standard Library, 1886.

Burke, James. *The Day The Universe Changed*. London: British Broadcasting Corporation, 1985.

Burns, Edward M. *Western Civilizations*. New York: Norton, 1969.

Buzzell, Robert D. "Can You Standardize Multinational Marketing?" *Harvard Business Review* 46(6) (November-December 1968): 102–113.

Calhoun, Craig, ed. *Habermas and the Public Sphere*. Cambridge: MIT Press, 1996.

Carothers, Thomas. "Civil Society: Think Again." *Foreign Policy* 117 (Winter 1999–2000): 18–29.

Carr, Edward H. *The Twenty Years' Crisis: 1919–1939*, 2d ed. London: Macmillan, [1946] 1961.

Carroll, Lewis. *Through the Looking Glass and What Alice Found There*. New York: Random House, 1946.

Casey, Edward S. *The Fate of Place: A Philosophical History*. Berkeley: University of California Press, 1997.

Castells, Manuel. *The Rise of the Network Society: The Information Age*. Oxford: Basil Blackwell, 1996.

Castiglione, Baldesar. *The Book of the Courtier*, tr, Leonard E. Opdycke. New York: Scribner's, [1528] 1903.

Cerny, Philip G. "Restructuring the Political Arena: Globalization and the Paradoxes of the Competition State." In *Globalization and Its Critics*, edited by Randall D. Germain, 117–138. New York: St. Martin's, 2000.

Chace, James. "Voltaire's Coconuts—and Ours." *World Policy Journal* 16(2) (Summer 1999): 147–148.

Charlety, Sebastien. *Histoire du Saint-Simonisme*. Paris: Paul Hartman, 1931.

Chase, Robert S. "The More Things Change . . .; Learning from Other Eras of 'Unprecedented' Globalization." *SAIS Review* 20(2) (Summer-Fall 2000): 223–229.

Chatterjee, Pratap and Matthias Finger. *The Earth Brokers: Power, Politics, and World Development*. London: Routledge, 1994.

Chenery, Hollis B., Sherman Robinson, and Moshe Syrquin. *Industrialization and Growth*. New York: Oxford University Press, 1986.

Cheru, Fantu. *The Silent Revolution in Africa: Debt, Development, and Democracy*. London: Zed-Anvil, 1989.

Chiang, Alpha C. *Fundamental Methods of Mathematical Economics*, 3d ed. New York: McGraw-Hill, 1984.

Chomsky, Noam. *Deterring Democracy*. London: Verso, 1992.

Chua, Amy. "A World on Edge." *Wilson Quarterly* 26(4) (Autumn 2002): 62–77.

Chung, Yuan Liu. "Government's Role in Developing a High-Tech Industry: The Case of Taiwan's Semiconductor Industry." *Technovation* 13(5) (July 1993): 299–309.

Clausewitz, Carl von. *On War*, 3 vols. translated by James J. Graham. London: Routledge and Kegan Paul, 1966.

Coe, David T. and Elhanan Helpman. "International R&D Spillovers." *European Economic Review* 39(5) (May 1995), 859–887.

Cohen, Roger. "Redrawing the Free Market." *New York Times*, 14 November 1998, pp. B9, B11.

Cohen, Saul B. *Geography and Politics in a World Divided*. New York: Random House, 1963.

Cohendet, Patrick and W. Edward Steinmueller. "The Codification of Knowledge: A Conceptual and Empirical Exploration." *Industrial and Corporate Change* 9(2) (June 2000): 195–210.

Colburn, Forrest. "Fragile Democracies." *Current History* 101(652) (February 2002): 76–80.

Collier, Paul and Anke Hoeffler. "On Economic Causes of Civil War." *Oxford Economic Papers* 50(4) (October 1998): 563–573.

Condorcet, Marie-Jean-Antoine-Nicolas de Caritat. *Outlines of an Historical View of the Progress of the Human Mind*. London: J. Johnson, 1795.

Connor, Walker. *Ethnonationalism: The Quest for Understanding*. Princeton: Princeton University Press, 1994.

Coricelli, Fabrizio and Giovanni Dosi. "Coordination and Order in Economic Change and the Interpretive Power of Economic Theory." In *Technical Change and Economic Theory*, edited by Giovanni Dosi, Christopher Freeman, Richard R. Nelson, Gerald Silverberg, and Luc Soete, 124–147. London: Pinter, 1988.

Cornelius, Wayne A. Philip L. Martin, and James F. Hollifield, eds. *Controlling Immigration: A Global Perspective*. Stanford: Stanford University Press, 1994.

Cowan, Tyler. "The Fate of Culture." *Wilson Quarterly* 26(4) (Autumn 2002): 78–84.

Cox, Michael. "Radical Theory and the International Disorder after the Cold War." In *The New World Order*, edited by Birthe Hansen and Bertel Heurlin, 197–216. London: Macmillan, 2000.

Cox, Robert W. "An Alternative Approach to Multilateralism for the Twenty-first Century." *Global Governance* 3 (January-April 1997): 103–116.

——. "Civil Society at the Turn of the Millennium: Prospects for an Alternative World Order." *Review of International Studies* 25(1) (January 1999): 3–28.

——. "Civilizations, Encounters, and Transformations." *Studies in Political Economy* 47(2) (Summer 1995): 7–31.

——. "Global Perestroika." In *New World Order: The Socialist Register 1992*, edited by Ralph Miliband and Leo Panitch, 26–43. London: Merlin, 1992.

——. "A Perspective on Globalization." In *Globalization: Critical Reflections, International Political Economy Yearbook, Vol. 9*, edited by James H. Mittelman, 21–30. Boulder, Colorado: Lynne Rienner, 1996.

——. *Production, Power, and World Order: Social Forces in the Making of History*. New York: Columbia University Press, 1987.

——, ed. *The New Realism: Perspectives on Multilateral and World Order*. Basingstoke: Macmillan, 1997.

—— with Timothy J. Sinclair. *Approaches to World Order*. Cambridge: Cambridge University Press, 1996.

Creveld, Martin van. *Technology and War: From 2,000 B.C. to the Present*. New York: Free Press, 1989.

Croce, Benedetto. *Aesthetic*, 2d. rev. ed. London: Macmillan, 1922.

Crocker, Chester A. and Fen Osler Hampson with Pamela Aall, eds. *Managing Global Chaos: Sources of and Responses to International Conflict.* Washington, D.C.: United States Institute of Peace Press, 1996.

Cutts, Mark. "Prime Targets." *The World Today* 54(8–9) (August-September 1998): 220–221.

Cvetkovich, Ann and Douglas Kellner, eds. *Articulating the Global and the Local: Globalization and Cultural Studies.* Boulder, Colorado: Westview, 1997.

Cyert Richard M. and James G. March. *A Behavioral Theory of the Firm.* Englewood Cliffs, New Jersey: Prentice-Hall, 1963.

Danilevskyi, Nikolai I. *Russland und Europa.* Osnabruck: Otto Zeller, [1888, 1920] 1965.

Darvas, Peter. *Institutional Innovation in Central European Higher Education.* Vienna: Institute of Human Sciences, 1996.

Darwin, Charles. *On the Origin of Species.* New York: Heritage, [1859] 1963.

Dasgupta, Partha. *An Inquiry into Well-Being and Destitution.* Oxford: Clarendon, 1993.

Davies, Paul. "The Mysterious Flow." *Scientific American* 287(3) (September 2002): 40–47.

Dawson, Jane I. *Eco-Nationalism: Anti-Nuclear Activism and National Identity in Russia, Lithuania, and Ukraine.* Durham: Duke University Press, 1996.

De Long, Bradford and Lawrence H. Summers. "How Strongly Do Developing Countries Benefit from Equipment Investment?" *Journal of Monetary Economics* 32(3) (December 1993): 395–415.

Deng, Yong. "Hegemon on the Offensive: Chinese Perspectives on U.S. Global Strategy." *Political Science Quarterly* 116(3) (Fall 2001): 343–365.

Denison, Edward F. *The Sources of Economic Growth in the United States and the Alternatives Before Us*, CED Supplementary Paper No. 13. New York: Council on Economic Development, 1960.

Denitch, Bogdan. *The End of the Cold War: European Unity, Socialism, and the Shift in Global Power.* London: Verso 1990.

De Santis, Hugh. *Beyond Progress: An Interpretive Odyssey.* Chicago: University of Chicago Press, 1996.

———. "Mutualism: An American Strategy for the Next Century." *World Policy* 15(4) (Winter 1998–1999): 41–54.

Deutsch, Karl W. *Political Community and the North Atlantic Area: International Organization in the Light of Historical Experience.* Princeton: Princeton University Press, 1957.

——— and Sidney A. Burrell. *The Political Community and the North Atlantic Area.* Princeton: Princeton University Press, 1957.

Devetak, Richard and Richard Higgott. "Justice Unbound? Globalization, States, and the Transformation of the Social Bond." *International Affairs* 75(3) (July 1999): 483–498.

Diamond, Larry. "Toward Democratic Consolidation." *Journal of Democracy* 5(3) (July 1994): 4–17.

Dodge, Toby. "Space for Dissent. *The World Today* 58(3) (March 2002): 7–8.

Dollar, David R. "Outward-Oriented Developing Economies Really Do Grow More Rapidly: Evidence from 95 LDCs, 1976–1985." *Economic Development and Cultural Change* 40(3) (April 1992): 523–544.

—— and Edward N. Wolff. *Competitiveness, Convergence, and International Specialization.* Cambridge: MIT Press, 1993.

Donnelly, Jack. *International Human Rights,* 2d ed. Boulder, Colorado: Westview, 1997.

Dos Santos, Theotonio. "The Structure of Dependence." *American Economic Review, Papers and Proceedings of the Eighty-Second Annual Meeting of the American Economic Association,* New York, 28–30 December 1969, 60(2) (May 1970): 231–236.

Dosi, Giovanni. "The Nature of the Innovative Process." In *Technical Change and Economic Theory,* edited by Giovanni Dosi, Christopher Freeman, Richard R. Nelson, Gerald Silverberg, and Luc Soete, 221–238. London: Pinter, 1988.

—— and Luigi Marengo. "Some Elements of an Evolutionary Theory of Organizational Competences." In *Evolutionary Concepts in Contemporary Economics,* edited by Richard W. England, 157–178. Ann Arbor: University of Michigan Press, 1994.

——, Christopher Freeman, Richard R. Nelson, Gerald Silverberg, and Luc Soete, eds. *Technical Change and Economic Theory.* London: Pinter, 1988.

Downs, Anthony. *An Economic Theory of Democracy.* New York: Harper and Row, 1957.

Doyle, Michael. *Ways of War and Peace.* New York: W. W. Norton, 1997.

Drucker, Peter F. "The Global Economy and the Nation-State." *Foreign Affairs* 76(5) (September-October 1997): 159–171.

——. *Post-Capitalist Society.* New York: HarperCollins, 1993.

Durant, Will and Ariel Durant. *The Story of Civilization,* vol. 6, *The Age of Reason Begins.* New York: Simon and Schuster, 1961.

Durkheim, Émile. *The Division of Labor in Society.* London: Macmillan, 1964 [1893].

Easterly, William and Sergio Rebelo. "Fiscal Policy and Economic Growth: An Empirical Investigation." *Journal of Monetary Economics* 32(3) (December 1993): 417–458.

Easton, David. "An Approach to the Analysis of Political Systems." *World Politics* 9(3) (April 1957): 383–400.

——. *The Political System: An Inquiry into the State of Political Science.* New York: Knopf, 1953.

——. *A Systems Analysis of Political Life,* 2d ed. Chicago: University of Chicago Press, [1965] 1979.

Eaton, Jonathan and Samuel Kortum. "Engines of Growth: Domestic and Foreign Sources of Innovations." *Japan and the World Economy* 9(2) (May 1997): 235–259.

——. "Trade in Ideas: Patenting and Productivity in the OECD." *Journal of International Economics* 40(3–4) (May 1996): 251–278.

Eckstein, Harry. "A Culturalist Theory of Political Change." *American Political Science Review* 82(3) (September 1988): 789–804.

"Economics Focus: Treading Lightly." *The Economist* 364(8291) (21 September 2002): 74.

Eichengreen, Barry. "One Economy, Ready or Not: Thomas Friedman's Jaunt through Globalization." *Foreign Affairs* 78(3) (May-June 1999): 118–122.

Eldridge, Niles. *Life in the Balance: Humanity and the Biodiversity Crisis.* Princeton: Princeton University Press, 1998.

Eliassen, Kjell A. and Jan Kooiman, eds. *Managing Public Organizations: Lessons from Contemporary European Experience.* London: Sage, 1993.

Eliot, Thomas S. *Selected Essays.* New York: Harcourt, Brace, 1960.

Elshtain, Jean Bethke. *Democracy on Trial*. New York: Basic Books, 1995.

Engelbrecht, Hans-Jürgen. "International R&D Spillovers, Human Capital, and Productivity in OECD Economies: An Empirical Investigation." *European Economic Review* 41(8) (August 1997), 1479–1488.

England, Richard W. ed. *Evolutionary Concepts in Contemporary Economics*. Ann Arbor: University of Michigan Press, 1994.

"Evolution: The Grand View." *The Economist* 365(8302) (7 December 2002): 82.

Ezzell, Carol. "Clocking Cultures." *Scientific American* 287(3) (September 2002): 74–75.

Falk, Richard. *Economic Aspects of Global Civilization: The Unmet Challenges of World Poverty*, World Order Studies Program Occasional Paper no. 22. Princeton: Princeton University Center of International Studies, 1992.

———. *On Humane Governance: Toward a New Global Politics*. Cambridge: Polity, 1995.

———. "State of Siege: Will Globalization Win Out?" *International Affairs* 73(1) (January 1997): 123–136.

Fallows, James. "The Unilateralist, a Conversation with Paul Wolfowitz." *The Atlantic Monthly* 289(3) (March 2002): 26–29.

Farrell Joseph and Garth Saloner. "Coordination through Committees and Markets." *RAND Journal of Economics* 19(2) (Summer 1988): 235–252.

Faulkner, Wendy. "Conceptualizing Knowledge Used in Innovation." *Science, Technology, and Human Values* 19(4) (Autumn 1994): 425–458.

Featherstone, Mike. *Undoing Culture: Globalization, Postmodernism, and Identity*. London: Sage 1995.

———, ed. *Global Culture: Nationalism, Globalization, and Modernity*. London: Sage, 1990.

Findlay, Ronald. "Relative Backwardness, Foreign Direct Investment, and the Transfer of Technology." *Quarterly Journal of Economics* 92(1) (February 1978): 1–16.

Finger, J. Michael, Merlinda D. Ingco, and Ulrich Reinecke. *The Uruguay Round, Statistics on Tariff Concessions Given and Received*. Washington, D.C.: World Bank, 1996.

Fischer, David Hackett. *The Great Wave: Price Revolutions and the Rhythm of History*. New York: Oxford University Press, 1996.

Florescano, Enrique. *Memory, Myth, and Time in Mexico*, translated by Albert G. Bork. Austin: University of Texas Press, 1994.

Forgacs, David, ed. *The Antonio Gramsci Reader*. New York: Schocken, 1988.

Forrester, Viviane. *L'Horreur Economique*. Paris: Fayard, 1996.

Foster, George M. "The Dyadic Contract: A Model for the Social Structure of a Mexican Peasant Village." In *Friends, Followers, and Factions: A Reader in Political Clientelism*, edited by Steffen W. Schmidt, Laura Guasti, Carl H. Landé, and James C. Scott, 15–28. Berkeley: University of California Press, 1977.

Foster, John. "Economics and the Self-organization Approach: Alfred Marshall Revisited." *Economic Journal* 103(419) (July 1993): 975–991.

Foucault, Michel. *Power/Knowledge: Selected Interviews and Other Writings 1972–1977*, edited and translated by Colin Gordon. New York: Pantheon, 1980.

Frank, Thomas. *New Consensus for Old: Cultural Studies from Left to Right*. Chicago: Prickly Paradigm, 2002.

Freeman, Gary P. "Britain, the Deviant Case." In *Controlling Immigration: A Global Perspective*, edited by Wayne A. Cornelius, Philip L. Martin, and James F. Hollifield, 297–300. Stanford: Stanford University Press, 1994.

———. "The Decline of Sovereignty? Politics and Immigration Restriction in Liberal States." In *Challenge to the Nation-State*, edited by Christian Joppke, 86–108. Oxford: Oxford University Press, 1998.

Friedman, Jonathan. "Being in the World: Globalization and Localization." In *Global Culture*, edited by Mike Featherstone, 311–328. London: Sage, 1990.

Friedman, Milton. *Essays in Positive Economics*. Chicago: University of Chicago Press, 1953.

Friedman, Thomas L. *The Lexus and the Olive Tree*. New York: Farrar, Straus, and Giroux, 2000.

Fukuyama, Francis. *The End of History and the Last Man*. New York: Free Press, 1992.

———. *The Great Disruption: Human Nature and the Reconstitution of Social Order*. New York: Free Press, 1999.

———. *Our Posthuman Future: Consequences of the Biotechnology Revolution*. New York: Farrar, Straus, and Giroux, 2001.

Gabriel, Jürg Martin. *Worldviews and Theories of International Relations*. New York: St. Martin's, 1994.

Garrett, Geoffrey. "The Causes of Globalization." *Comparative Political Studies* 33(6–7) (August-September 2000): 941–991.

Gates, Bill. *The Road Ahead*. New York: Viking, 1995.

Geertz, Clifford. *The Interpretation of Cultures*. New York: Basic Books, 1973.

Gefter, Amanda. "Throwing Einstein for a Loop." *Scientific American* 287(6) (December 2002): 40–41.

Gellner, Ernest. *Nations and Nationalism*. Ithaca: Cornell University Press, 1983.

Gereffi, Gary. "Paths of Industrialization: An Overview." In *Manufacturing Miracles: Paths of Industrialization in Latin America and East Asia*, edited by Gary Gereffi and Donald L. Wyman, 3–31. Princeton: Princeton University Press, 1990.

——— and Donald L. Wyman, eds. *Manufacturing Miracles: Paths of Industrialization in Latin America and East Asia*. Princeton: Princeton University Press, 1990.

Germain, Randall D. ed. *Globalization and Its Critics*. New York: St. Martin's, 2000.

———. "Globalization in Historical Perspective." In *Globalization and Its Critics*, edited by Randall D. Germain, 67–90. New York: St. Martin's, 2000.

Geroski, Paul and Mariana Mazzucato. "Learning and the Sources of Corporate Growth." *Industrial and Corporate Change* 11(4) (August 2002): 623–644.

Gibbons, Michael. "Science's New Social Contract with Society." *Nature* 402(6761) (2 December 1999, supplement): C81–C84.

———, Camille Limoges, Helga Nowotny, Simon Schwartzman, Peter Scott, and Martin Trow. *The New Production of Knowledge*. Beverly Hills, California: Sage, 1994.

Giddens, Anthony. *Modernity and Self-Identity: Self and Society in the Late Modern Age*. Cambridge: Polity, 1991.

———. *The Consequences of Modernity*. Cambridge: Polity, 1990.

———. *Runaway World: How Globalization Is Reshaping Our Lives*. London: Profile, 1999.

Gill, Stephen. *American Hegemony and the Trilateral Commission*. Cambridge: Polity, 1990.

——. "Globalization, Democratization, and the Politics of Indifference." In *Globalization: Critical Reflections, International Political Economy Yearbook, Vol. 9*, edited by James H. Mittelman, 205–228. Boulder, Colorado: Lynne Rienner, 1996.

—— and James H. Mittelman, eds. *Innovation and Transformation in International Studies*. Cambridge: Cambridge University Press, 1997.

Gillespie, Susan H. "Opening Minds: The International Liberal Education Movement." *World Policy Journal* 18(4) (Winter 2001–2002): 79–89.

Gilpin, Robert S. *The Challenge of Global Capitalism: The World Economy in the 21st Century*. Princeton: Princeton University Press, 2000.

——. *The Political Economy of International Relations*. Princeton: Princeton University Press, 1987.

——. *War and Change in World Politics*. Cambridge: Cambridge University Press, 1981.

Gittleman, Maury and Edward N. Wolff. "R&D Activity and Cross-Country Growth Comparisons." *Cambridge Journal of Economics* 19(1) (February 1995): 189–207.

Gladwell, Malcolm. *The Tipping Point: How Little Things Can Make A Big Difference*. Boston: Little, Brown, 2000.

"Global Economy, Local Mayhem." *The Economist* 342(8000) (18 January 1997): 15–16.

Goffman, Erving. *Frame Analysis: An Essay on the Organization of Experience*. Cambridge: Harvard University Press, 1974.

Golden, James R. "Economics and National Strategy." In *New Forces in the World Economy*, edited by Brad Roberts, 15–37. Cambridge: MIT Press, 1996.

Goldsmith, Raymond and Christopher Saunders, eds. *The Measurement of National Wealth*, International Association for Research in Income and Wealth, Income and Wealth, Series. Chicago: Quadrangle Books, 1959.

Gordon, John Steele. "Pioneers Die Broke." *Forbes* 170(13) (23 December 2002): 258–264.

Gould, Stephen Jay. "Bacon, Brought Home." *Natural History* 108(5) (June 1999): 28–33, 72–78.

——. "Branching through a Wormhole." *Natural History* 108(2) (March 1999): 24–27, 84–89.

——. "On Embryos and Ancestors." *Natural History* 107(6) (July-August 1998): 20–22, 58–65.

——. *The Mismeasure of Man*. New York: Norton, 1996.

——. "Pillars of Wisdom." *Natural History* 108(3) (April 1999): 28–34, 87–89.

——. "The Sharp-Eyed Lynx, Outfoxed by Nature." *Natural History* 107(5) (June 1998): 23–27, 69–73.

Grafton, Anthony. "Descartes the Dreamer." *The Wilson Quarterly* 20(4) (Autumn 1996): 36–46.

Gramsci, Antonio. *Selections from the Prison Notebooks of Antonio Gramsci*, edited and translated by Quintin Hoare and Geoffrey Nowell Smith. New York: International, 1971.

Granovetter, Mark S. "Economic Action and Social Structure: The Problem of Embeddedness." *American Journal of Sociology* 91(3) (November 1985): 481–510.

——. "The Strength of Weak Ties." *American Journal of Sociology* 78(6) (May 1973): 1360–1380.

Grant, Robert M. "Toward a Knowledge-Based Theory of the Firm." *Strategic Management Journal* 17 (Special Issue) (Winter 1996): 109–122.

Gray, John. *False Dawn: The Delusions of Global Capitalism.* London: Granta, 1998.

Green, Duncan and Matthew Griffith. "Globalization and its Discontents." *International Affairs* 78(1) (January 2002): 49–68.

Greenstein, Fred I. and Nelson W. Polsby, eds. *Handbook of Political Science,* 9 vols. Reading, Massachusetts: Addison-Wesley, 1975.

Greider, William. *One World, Ready or Not: The Manic Logic of Global Capitalism.* London: Penguin, 1997.

Gress, David R. "The Drama of Modern Western Identity." *Orbis* 41(4) (Fall 1997): 525–544.

Grier, Kevin B. and Gordon Tullock. "An Empirical Analysis of Cross-National Economic Growth, 1951–1980." *Journal of Monetary Economics* 24(2) (September 1989): 259–276.

Grossman Gene M. and Elhanan Helpman. *Innovation and Growth in the Global Economy.* Cambridge: MIT Press, 1991.

Guerrieri, Paolo. "Technological and International Trade Performance of the Most Advanced Countries." Berkeley Roundtable on the International Economy working paper no. 49. Berkeley, California, 1991.

Gurr, Ted Robert. "Minorities, Nationalists, and Ethnopolitical Conflict." In *Managing Global Chaos: Sources of and Responses to International Conflict,* edited by Chester A. Crocker and Fen Osler Hampson with Pamela Aall, 53–77. Washington, D.C.: United States Institute of Peace Press, 1996.

Guthrie, Charles. "British Defence—the Chief of Defense Staff's Lecture, 2000—." *Royal United Services Institute Journal* 146(1) (February 2001): 1–7.

Gutierrez, Gustavo. *Las Casas: In Search of the Poor of Jesus Christ,* translated by Robert R. Barr. Maryknoll, New York: Orbis, 1993.

Guyon, Janet. "The American Way." *Fortune* 144(11) (26 November 2001): 114–120.

Haas, Ernst B. *The Uniting of Europe: Political, Social, and Economic Forces, 1950–1957.* Stanford: Stanford University Press, 1958.

Haas, Peter. "Introduction: Epistemic Communities and International Policy Coordination." *International Organization* 46(1) (Winter 1992): 1–36.

Haass, Richard N. "Paradigm Lost." *Foreign Affairs* 74(1) (January-February 1995): 43–58.

———. "What to Do with American Primacy." *Foreign Affairs* 78(5) (September-October 1999): 37–49.

Haberman, Hermann. "The Global Statistical System: What It Is and Why Should We Care?" *Chance* 12(2) (Spring 1999): 39–42.

Habermas, Jürgen. "Further Reflections on the Public Sphere." In *Habermas and the Public Sphere,* edited by Craig Calhoun, 421–461. Cambridge: MIT Press, 1996.

———. *The Structure of the Public Sphere: An Inquiry into a Category of Bourgeois Society.* Cambridge: MIT Press, 1992.

———. *The Theory of Communicative Action, Volume 2, Lifeworld and System: A Critique of Functionalist Reason,* translated by Thomas McCarthy. Boston: Beacon, 1987.

Hadenius, Axel, ed. *Democracy's Victory and Crisis: Nobel Symposium No. 93.* Cambridge: Cambridge University Press, 1997.

Hakim, Peter. "Two Ways to Go Global." *Foreign Affairs* 81(1) (January-February 2002): 148–162.

Hall, Robert and Carl Fox. "Rethinking Security." *NATO Review* 49(4) (Winter 2001-2002): 8–11.

Hall, Stuart. "The Local and the Global: Globalization and Ethnicity, and Old and New Identities, Old and New Ethnicities." In *Culture, Globalization, and the World-System: Contemporary Conditions for the Representation of Identity*, edited by Anthony D. King, 19–68. Binghamton: State University of New York Art Department, 1991.

Hannerz, Ulf. *Cultural Complexity: Studies in the Social Organization of Meaning*. New York: Columbia University Press, 1992.

Hansen, Birthe and Bertel Heurlin, eds. *The New World Order*. London: Macmillan, 2000.

Hansen, Randall. *Citizenship and Immigration in Postwar Britain*. Oxford: Oxford University Press, 2000.

———. "Globalization, Embedded Realism, and Path Dependence." *Comparative Political Studies* 35(3) (April 2002): 259–283.

Harvey, David. *The Condition of Postmodernity: An Enquiry into the Origins of Social Change*. Oxford: Blackwell, 1989.

Havel, Václav. "Faith in the World." *Civilization* 5(2) (April-May 1998): 51–53.

———. "New Year's Address" (January 1990). *Open Letters*. New York: Vintage, 1992, 390–396.

———. "The Power of the Powerless." In *Living in Truth*, edited by Jan Vladislav, 316–324. London: Unwin Hyman, 1989.

Hayek, Friedrich A. von. "Economics and Knowledge." *Economica* 4(NS 13) (February 1937): 33–54.

———. "The Use of Knowledge in Society." *American Economic Review* 35(4) (September 1945): 519–530.

Haynes, Jeff, ed. *Religion, Globalization, and Political Culture in the Third World*. London: Macmillan, 1988.

———. *Religion in Global Politics*. London: Longman, 1998.

Hehir, J. Bryan. "The Limits of Loyalty." *Foreign Policy* 132 (September-October 2002): 38–39.

Held, David. "Democracy and the Global System." In *Political Theory Today*, edited by David Held, 197–235. Cambridge: Polity, 1991.

———, ed. *Political Theory Today*. Cambridge: Polity, 1991.

———, David Goldblatt, Anthony McGrew, and Jonathan Peraton. *Global Flows, Global Transformations: Concepts, Theories, and Evidence*. Cambridge: Polity, 1997.

———. "The Globalization of Economic Activity." *New Political Economy* 2(2) (July 1997): 257–277.

Helleiner, E. N. "Braudelian Reflections on Globalization: The Historian as Pioneer." In *Innovation and Transformation in International Studies*, edited by Stephen Gill and James H. Mittelman, 90–104. Cambridge: Cambridge University Press, 1997.

Henderson, David. "International Economic Integration: Progress, Prospects, and Implications." *International Affairs* 68(4) (October 1992): 633–653.

Henry, Ryan and C. Edward Peartree, eds. *The Information Revolution and International Security*. Washington, D.C.: Center for Strategic and International Studies Press, 1998.

Hewison, Kevin. "Of Regimes, States, and Pluralities: Thai Politics Enters the 1990s." In *Southeast Asia in the 1990s*, edited by Kevin Hewison, Richard Robison, and Garry Rodan, 161–189. St. Leonard's, England: Allen and Unwin, 1993.

——, Richard Robison, and Garry Rodan, eds. *Southeast Asia in the 1990s.* St. Leonard's, England: Allen and Unwin, 1993.

Hines, Colin. "The New Protectionism: What It Is—Why It Is Coming." 10 November 1995, first published as *Employment and the Culture of Insecurity: Time to Protect Jobs,* Economic Report 9, no. 5. London: Employment Policy Institute, 1995.

—— and Tim Lang, *The New Protectionism: Protecting the Future against Free Trade.* New York: New Press, 1993.

Hippel, Eric von. "Cooperation between Rivals: Informal Know-How Trading." *Research Policy* 16(6) (December 1987): 291–302.

——. *The Sources of Innovation.* Oxford: Oxford University Press, 1988.

Hirsch, Fred. *The Social Limits to Growth.* Cambridge: Harvard University Press, 1976.

Hirsh, Michael. "Bush and the World." *Foreign Affairs* 81(5) (September-October 2002): 18–43.

Hobbes, Thomas. "Leviathan." In *Great Books of the Western World,* edited by Robert M. Hutchins, vol. 23, 41–283. Chicago: Encyclopædia Britannica, 1952.

——. *Leviathan,* edited by Crawford B. Macpherson. Harmondsworth: Penguin, [1651] 1968.

Hobhouse, Leonard T. *Morals in Evolution: A Study in Comparative Ethics,* 2d ed. New York: Holt, 1915.

Hobsbawm, Eric J. *Nations and Nationalism since 1780: Programme, Myth, Reality,* 2d ed. Cambridge: Cambridge University Press, 1992.

Hodgson, Marshall G. S. *Rethinking World History, Essays on Europe, Islam, and World History.* New York: Cambridge University Press, 1993.

——. *The Venture of Islam: Conscience and History in a World Civilization,* 3 vols. Chicago: University of Chicago Press, 1974.

Hoffmann, Stanley. "Clash of Globalizations." *Foreign Policy* 81(4) (July-August 2002): 104–115.

Holbach, Paul Henri Thiery. *Common Sense: or Natural Ideas Opposed to Supernatural.* New York: N.p. 1795.

Hoogvelt, Ankie. *Globalization and the Postcolonial World.* London: Macmillan, 1997.

Hotelling, Harold. "Stability in Competition." *Economic Journal* 39(153) (March 1929): 41–57.

Hufbauer, Gary C. "The Impact of National Characteristics and Technology on the Commodity Composition of Trade in Manufactured Goods." In *The Technology Factor in International Trade,* edited by Raymond Vernon, 145–231. New York: Columbia University Press, 1970.

Hunter, Robert E. "Global Economics and Unsteady Regional Geopolitics." In *The Global Century: Globalization and National Security,* edited by Richard L. Kugler and Ellen L. Frost, vol. 1, 109–125. Washington, D.C.: National Defense University Press, 2001.

Huntington, Samuel P. *The Clash of Civilizations and the Remaking of World Order.* New York: Simon and Schuster, 1996.

Hurrell, Andrew and Ngaire Woods. "Globalization and Inequality." *Millennium* 24(3) (1995): 447–470.

Hutchins, Edwin. *Cognition in the Wild.* Cambridge: MIT Press, 1995.

Hutchins, Robert M. *St. Thomas and the World State.* Milwaukee: Marquette University Press, 1949.

Ibn Khaldun. *The Muqaddimah: An Introduction to History*, translated by Franz Rosenthal, 3 vols. New York: Pantheon, 1958.

Inglehart, Ronald. *Culture Shift in Advanced Industrial Society*. Princeton: Princeton University Press, 1990.

———. *Modernization and Postmodernization: Cultural, Economic, and Political Change in 43 Societies*. Princeton: Princeton University Press, 1997.

"Islam and the West: Never the Twain Shall Meet." *The Economist* 361(8248) (17 November 2001): 17–19.

Isham, Jonathan, Daniel Kaufmann, and Lant H. Pritchett. "Civil Liberties, Democracy, and the Performance of Government Projects." *The World Bank Economic Review* 11(2) (May 1997): 219–242.

Jaffrelot, Christophe. "The Vishva Hindu Parishad: Structures and Strategies." In *Religion, Globalization, and Political Culture in the Third World*, edited by Jeff Haynes, 191–212. London: Macmillan, 1988.

Jardine, Lisa. *Ingenious Pursuits: Building the Scientific Revolution*. New York: Talese, Doubleday, 1999.

Jenkins, Philip. "The Next Christianity." *The Atlantic Monthly* 290(3) (October 2002): 53–68.

Johnson, Björn, Edward Lorenz, and Bengt-Åke Lundvall. "Why All the Fuss about Codified and Tacit Knowledge?" *Industrial and Corporate Change* 11(2) (April 2002): 245–262.

Johnson, Chalmers. *MITI and the Japanese Miracle*. Stanford: Stanford University Press, 1982.

Jones, Ronald W. "The Structure of Simple General Equilibrium Models." *Journal of Political Economy* 73(6) (December 1965): 557–572.

Juviler, Peter and Sherrill Stroschein. "Missing Boundaries of Comparison: The Political Community." *Political Science Quarterly* 114(3) (Fall 1999): 435–453.

Joppke, Christian, ed. *Challenge to the Nation-State*. Oxford: Oxford University Press, 1998.

———. "Immigration Challenges in the Nation-State." In *Challenge to the Nation-State*, edited by Christian Joppke, 1–46. Oxford: Oxford University Press, 1998.

Kanigel, Robert. "Frederick Taylor's Apprenticeship." *Wilson Quarterly* 20(3) (Summer 1996): 44–51.

Kant, Immanuel. *Perpetual Peace and Other Essays*, translated by Ted Humphrey. Indianapolis: Hackett, 1983.

Kapstein, Ethan B. "Does Unipolarity Have a Future?" In *Unipolar Politics: Realism and State Strategies after the Cold War*, edited by Ethan B. Kapstein and Michael Mastanduno, 464–490. New York: Columbia University Press, 1999.

——— and Michael Mastanduno, eds. *Unipolar Politics: Realism and State Strategies after the Cold War*. New York: Columbia University Press, 1999.

Karliner, Joshua. *The Corporate Planet: Ecology and Politics in the Age of Globalization*. San Francisco: Sierra Club Books, 1997.

Katz, Mark N. "Osama bin Laden as Transnational Revolutionary Leader." *Current History* 101(652) (February 2002): 81–85.

Kaul, Inge, Isabelle Grunberg, and Marc A. Stern, eds. *Global Public Goods: International Cooperation in the 21st Century*. New York: Oxford University Press, 1999.

Keen, Benjamin. *Essays in the Intellectual History of Colonial Latin America.* New York: Westview, 1998.

Keiji, Nishitani. *Nishida Kitarō,* translated by Yamamoto Seisaku and James W. Heisig. Berkeley: University of California Press, 1991.

Kelleher, Ann and Laura Klein. *Global Perspectives: A Handbook for Understanding Global Issues.* Upper Saddle River, New Jersey: Prentice-Hall, 1999.

Kellner, Douglas. "Globalization and the Postmodern Turn." In *Globalization and Europe,* edited by Roland Axtmann, 23–42. London: Pinter, 1998.

———. *Television and the Crisis of Democracy.* Boulder, Colorado: Westview, 1990.

Kendrick, John W. *Productivity Trends in the United States.* Princeton, New Jersey: National Bureau of Economic Research, 1961.

Kennedy, Carol. "Riding Out the Storm." *Director* 55(2) (September 2001): 56–59.

Kennedy, Paul M. *The Rise and Fall of the Great Powers: Economic Change and Military Conflict from 1500 to 2000.* New York: Vintage, 1987.

Kennedy, Richard S. "Who Is Culture's Keeper?" *Foreign Policy* 133 (November-December 2002): 92–94.

Keohane, Robert O. *After Hegemony: Cooperation and Discord in the World Political Economy.* Princeton: Princeton University Press, 1984.

——— and Joseph S. Nye Jr. "Globalization: What's New? What's Not? (And So What?)" *Foreign Policy* 118 (Spring 2000): 104–119.

———. *Power and Interdependence: World Politics in Transition.* Boston: Little, Brown, 1977.

———. *Power and Interdependence,* 2d ed. Glenview, Illinois: Scott, Foresman, 1989.

———. *Power and Interdependence,* 3d ed. New York: Longman, 2001.

———. "*Power and Interdependence* Revisited." *International Organization* 41(4) (Autumn 1987): 725-753.

———. "Transgovernmental Relations and International Organizations." *World Politics* 27(1) (October 1974): 39–62.

Kepel, Gilles. *Muslim Extremism in Egypt: The Prophet and Pharaoh.* Berkeley: University of California Press, 1985.

Khong, Yuen Foong. *Analogies at War.* Princeton: Princeton University Press, 1992.

Kissinger, Henry A. *Does America Need a Foreign Policy?* New York: Simon and Schuster, 2001.

Kitarō, Nishida. *Fundamental Problems of Philosophy: The World of Action and the Dialectical World.* Tokyo: Sophia University Press, 1970.

———. *An Inquiry into the Good.* New Haven: Yale University Press, [1921] 1990.

———. *Last Writings: Nothingness and the Religious Worldview,* translated by David A. Dilworth. Honolulu: University of Hawaii Press, 1987.

Klein, Naomi. *No Logo: Taking Aim at the Brand Bullies.* New York: Picador, 2001.

Kline, Stephen J. "Innovation Styles in Japan and the United States: Cultural Bases; Implications for Competitiveness," The 1989 Thurston Lecture, Report INN-3. Stanford: Department of Mechanical Engineering, Stanford University, 1990.

Knopf, Jeffrey W. "Beyond Two-Level Games: Domestic-International Interaction in the Intermediate-Range Nuclear Forces Negotiations." *International Organization* 47(4) (Autumn 1993): 599–628.

Kogut, Bruce. "International Business: The New Bottom Line." *Foreign Policy* 110 (Spring 1998): 152–165.

——— and Ugo Zander. "Knowledge of the Firm and the Evolutionary Theory of the Multinational Corporation." *Journal of International Business Studies* 24(4) (Fourth Quarter 1993): 625–646.

Kooiman, Jan and Martin van Vliet. "Governance and Public Management." In *Managing Public Organizations: Lessons from Contemporary European Experience*, edited by Kjell A. Eliassen and Jan Kooiman, 58–72. London: Sage, 1993.

Kormendi, Roger C. and Philip G. Meguire. "Macroeconomic Determinants of Growth." *Journal of Monetary Economics* 16(2) (September 1985): 141–163.

Krasner, Stephen D. "Sovereignty: An Institutional Perspective." *Comparative Political Studies* 21(1) (February 1988): 66–94.

Kreps, David M. "Corporate Culture and Economic Theory." In *Perspectives on Positive Political Economy*, edited by James E. Alt and Kenneth A. Shepsle, 90–143. Cambridge: Cambridge University Press, 1990.

Krugman, Paul R. "The Narrow Moving Band, the Dutch Disease, and the Competitive Consequences of Mrs. Thatcher: Notes on Trade in the Presence of Dynamic Scale Economies." *Journal of Development Economics* 27(1–2) (October 1987): 41–55.

Kugler, Richard L. and Ellen L. Frost, eds. *The Global Century: Globalization and National Security*. Washington, D.C.: National Defense University Press, 2001.

Küng, Hans. *Global Responsibility: In Search of a New World Ethic*. New York: Continuum, 1993.

Kurzweil Ray. *The Age of Spiritual Machines*. New York: Viking Penguin, 1999.

Kuznets, Simon. *Economic Growth of Nations: Total Output and Production Structure*. Cambridge: Belknap, Harvard University Press, 1971.

———. *Modern Economic Growth*. New Haven: Yale University Press, 1966.

———. *Postwar Economic Growth: Four Lectures, Simon Kuznets*. Cambridge: Belknap Press of Harvard University Press, 1964.

———. "Two Centuries of Economic Growth: Reflections on U.S. Experience." *American Economic Review* 67(1) (February 1977): 1–14.

Landes, David S. *The Unbound Prometheus: Technological Change and Industrial Development in Western Europe from 1750 to the Present*. London: Cambridge University Press, 1969.

———. *The Wealth and Poverty of Nations*. New York: Little, Brown, 1998.

Lang, Tim and Colin Hines. *The New Protectionism: Protecting the Future Against Free Trade*. New York: New Press, 1993.

Langlois, Richard N. "Systems Theory, Knowledge, and the Social Sciences." In *The Study of Information: Interdisciplinary Messages*, edited by Fritz Machlup and Una Mansfield, 581–600. New York: Wiley, 1983.

Lasch, Christopher. *The Revolt of the Elites and the Betrayal of Democracy*. New York: W. W. Norton, 1995.

Latsis, Spiro J. ed. *Method and Appraisal in Economics*. Cambridge: Cambridge University Press, 1976.

Laursen, Keld and Valentina Meliciani. "The Importance of Technology-Based Intersectoral Linkages for Market Share Dynamics." *Weltwirtschaftliches Archiv* 136(4) (December 2000): 702–723.

———. "The Relative Importance of International *vis-à-vis* National Technological Spillovers for Market Share Dynamics." *Industrial and Corporate Change* 11(4) (August 2002): 875–894.

Lawrence, Bruce B. *Defenders of God: The Fundamentalist Revolt against the Modern Age*. San Francisco: Harper and Row, 1989.

Layton-Henry, Zig. "Britain: The Would-Be Zero-Immigration Country." In *Controlling Immigration: A Global Perspective*, edited by Wayne A. Cornelius, Philip L. Martin, and James F. Hollifield, 274–295. Stanford: Stanford University Press, 1994.

Lebovics, Herman. "Malraux's Mission." *Wilson Quarterly* 21(1) (Winter 1997): 78–87.

Lefort, Claude. *Essais sur la politique, XIXe-XXe siècles*. Paris: Seuil, 1986.

Lehmann, David. "Fundamentalism and Globalism." *Third World Quarterly* 19(4) (1998): 607–634.

Lehmann, Jean-Pierre. "Developing Economies and the Demographic and Democratic Imperatives of Globalization." *International Affairs* 77(1) (January 2001): 69–82.

Lester, Toby. "Oh, Gods." *The Atlantic Monthly* 289(2) (February 2002): 37–45.

Levi, Margaret. "A Model, a Method, and a Map: Rational Choice in Comparative and Historical Analysis." In *Comparative Politics: Rationality, Culture, and Structure*, edited by Mark I. Lichbach and Alan S. Zuckerman, 19–41. Cambridge: Cambridge University Press, 1997.

Levinthal, Daniel and Jennifer Myatt. "Coevolution of Capabilities and Industry: The Evolution of Mutual Fund Processing." *Strategic Management Journal* 15 (Special Issue) (Winter 1994): 45–62.

Levitt, Theodore. "The Globalization of Markets." *Harvard Business Review* 61(3) (May-June 1983): 92–102.

Levy, Marion J. *Modernization and the Structure of Societies: A Setting for International Affairs*. Princeton: Princeton University Press, 1966.

Lichbach, Mark I. and Alan S. Zuckerman, eds. *Comparative Politics: Rationality, Culture, and Structure*. Cambridge: Cambridge University Press, 1997.

Lichtenberg, Frank R. and Bruno van Pottelsberghe de la Potterie. "International R&D Spillovers: A Comment." *European Economic Review* 42(8) (September 1998), 1483–1491.

Lindblom, Charles E. *Politics and Markets: The World's Political-Economic Systems*. New York: Basic Books, 1977.

Linder, Staffan B. *An Essay on Trade and Transformation*. Stockholm: Almqvist and Wiksell, 1961.

Linz, Juan J. "Totalitarian and Authoritarian Regimes." In *Handbook of Political Science*, 9 vols., edited by Fred I. Greenstein and Nelson W. Polsby, vol. 3, 175–411. Reading, Massachusetts: Addison-Wesley, 1975.

Lipset, Seymour. *Political Man*. Garden City, New Jersey: Doubleday, 1960.

Litfin, Karen T. "The Greening of Sovereignty: An Introduction." In *The Greening of Sovereignty in World Politics*, edited by Karen T. Litfin, 1–27. Cambridge: MIT Press, 1998.

———, ed. *The Greening of Sovereignty in World Politics*. Cambridge: MIT Press, 1998.

———. "Sovereignty in World Ecopolitics." *Mershon International Studies Review* 41(2) (November 1997): 167–204.

Litwak, Robert S. "The Imperial Republic After 9/11." *The Wilson Quarterly* 26(3) (Summer 2002): 76–82.

Lloyd, John. "Britain's Lonely Left." *Foreign Policy* 126 (September-October 2001): 82–84.

Loasby, Brian J. *Knowledge, Institutions, and Evolution in Economics*. London: Routledge, 1999.

Locke, John. "Concerning the True Original Extent and End of Civil Government." In *Great Books of the Western World*, edited by Robert M. Hutchins, vol. 35, 25–81 Chicago: Encyclopedia Britannica, 1952.

———. *The Second Treatise of Government*. Oxford: Blackwell, [1690] 1976.

———. *Two Treatises of Government*, edited by Peter Laslett. Cambridge: Cambridge University Press, 1966.

Lockhart, Charles. "Cultural Contributions to Explaining Institutional Form, Political Change, and Rational Decisions." *Comparative Political Studies* 32(7) (October 1999): 862–893.

Londoño, Juan Luis. *Poverty, Inequality, and Human Capital Development in Latin America, 1950–2025*. Washington, D.C.: World Bank, 1996.

"Lots of It About." *The Economist* 365(8303) (14 December 2002): 62–63.

Lyell, Charles. *Principles of Geology*, 10th ed. London: John Murray, 1867.

Lynch, Cecilia. "Social Movements and the Problem of Globalization." *Alternatives* 23(2) (April-June 1998): 149–173.

Lyotard, Jean-François. *La Phénoménologie*. Paris: Presses Universitaires de France, 1967.

———. *The Postmodern Condition: A Report on Knowledge*. Minneapolis: University of Minnesota Press, [1979] 1997.

Machlup, Fritz and Una Mansfield, eds. *The Study of Information: Interdisciplinary Messages*. New York: Wiley, 1983.

MacIver, Robert M. "The Primacy of Community." reprinted from *Community: A Sociological Study*, 3d ed. London: Macmillan, 1936), 22–36. In *Robert MacIver on Community, Society, and Power: Selected Writing*, edited by Leon Bramson. Chicago: University of Chicago Press, 1970.

Mackinder, Halford J. *Democratic Ideals and Reality*. New York: Holt, [1919] 1942.

MacLean, John. "Philosophical Roots of Globalization and Philosophical Routes to Globalization." In *Globalization and Its Critics*, edited by Randall D. Germain, 3–66. New York: St. Martin's, 2000.

Maddison, Angus. *Economic Growth in the West*. New York: Twentieth Century Fund, 1964.

Malinowski, Bronislaw. *Crime and Custom in Savage Society*. London: Paul, Trench, and Trubner, 1932.

Malone, Eloise and Arthur Rachwald. "The Dark Side of Globalization." *United States Naval Institute Proceedings* 127/11/1,185 (November 2001): 43.

Malraux, André. *Les Voix du Silence*. Paris: Gallimard, 1951.

Mamdani, Mahmood. "African States, Citizenship, and War: A Case-Study." *International Affairs* 78(3) (July 2002): 493–506.

Mandelbaum, Michael. "The Inadequacy of American Power." *Foreign Affairs* 81(5) (September-October 2002): 61–73.

Mann, Charles C. "1491." *The Atlantic Monthly* 289(3) (March 2002): 41–53.

Mansbach, Richard W. *The Global Puzzle: Issues and Actors in World Politics*, 3d ed. Boston: Houghton Mifflin, 2000.

Mansfield, Edward D. *Power, Trade, and War*. Princeton: Princeton University Press, 1994.

Manuel, Frank E. *The New World of Henri Saint-Simon*. Cambridge: Harvard University Press, 1956.

March, James G. and Johan P. Olsen. *Rediscovering Institutions: The Organizational Basis of Politics*. New York: Free Press, 1989.

Marshall, Alfred. *Industry and Trade*. London: Macmillan, 1898.

——. *Principles of Economics*, 9th ed. London: Macmillan, 1961.

Marx, Karl and Friedrich Engels. "Manifesto of the Communist Party." In *Great Books of the Western World*, vol. 50, *Marx*, edited by Robert M. Hutchins, 415–434. Chicago: Encyclopedia Britannica, 1952.

Maxwell, Nicholas. *The Comprehensibility of the Universe: A New Conception of Science*. Oxford: Clarnedon, 1998.

McCargo, Duncan. "The Politics of Buddhism in Southeast Asia." In *Religion, Globalization, and Political Culture in the Third World*, edited by Jeff Haynes, 213–239. London: Macmillan, 1988.

McClay, Wilfred M. "Fifty Years of *The Lonely Crowd*." *Wilson Quarterly* 22(3) (Summer 1998): 34–42.

McGray, Douglas. "Japan's Gross National Cool." *Foreign Policy* 130 (May-June 2002): 44–54.

McLuhan, Marshall. *The Global Village: Transformations in World Life and Media in the 21st Century*. New York: Oxford University Press, 1989.

——. *Understanding Media*. New York: McGraw-Hill, 1964.

—— and Quentin Fiore. *The Medium Is the Massage*. New York: Bantam, 1967.

McNeill, William H. *The Pursuit of Power: Technology, Armed Force, and Society since A.D. 1000*. Oxford: Basil Blackwell, 1982.

Meaney, Constance S. "State Policy and the Development of Taiwan's Semiconductor Industry." In *The Role of the State in Taiwan's Development*, edited by Joel D. Aberbach, David Dollar, and Kenneth L. Sokoloff, 170–192. London: Sharpe, 1994.

Meek, Ronald L. ed. and tr. *Turgot on Progress, Sociology, and Economics*. Cambridge: Cambridge University Press, 1973.

Meier, Gerald M. and Dudley Seers, eds. *Pioneers in Development*. Washington, D.C.: Oxford University Press for the World Bank, 1984.

Merleau-Ponty, Maurice. *Phénoménologie de la Perception*. Paris: Gallimard, 1945.

Metcalfe, J. Stanley. "Institutions and Progress." *Industrial and Corporate Change* 10(3) (September 2001): 561–586.

——. "Technology Policy in an Evolutionary World." Paper presented at the second International Conference on Science and Technology Policy Research of the National Institute of Science and Technology Policy (24–26 January 1991: Oiso, Japan) *What Should Be Done? What Can Be Done? Science and Technology Policy Research: The Proceedings of the NISTEP Second International Conference on Science and Technology*, edited by Sogo Okamura, Kenichi Marakami, and Ikujiro Nonaka, 109–121. Tokyo: Mita Press, 1991.

Micklethwaite, John and Adrian Wooldridge. *A Future Perfect: The Challenge and Hidden Promise of Globalization*. New York: Random House–Crown Business, 2000.

——. "The Globalization Backlash." *Foreign Policy* (September-October 2001): 16–26.

Miliband, Ralph and Leo Panitch, eds. *New World Order: The Socialist Register 1992*. London: Merlin, 1992.

Mill, John Stuart. *Utilitarianism*. Indianapolis, Indiana: Hackett, [1861] 2001.

Milner, Helen V. "International Political Economy: Beyond Hegemonic Stability." *Foreign Policy* 110 (Spring 1998): 112–123.

Misztal, Bronislaw and Anson D. Shupe Jr. "Fundamentalism and Globalization: Fundamentalist Movements at the Twilight of the Twentieth Century." In *Religion, Mobilization, and Social Action*, edited by Anson D. Shupe Jr. and Bronislaw Misztal, 3–14. Westport, Connecticut: Praeger, 1998.

Mittelman, James H. "The Dynamics of Globalization." In *Globalization: Critical Reflections, International Political Economy Yearbook, Vol. 9*, edited by James H. Mittelman, 1–19. Boulder, Colorado: Lynne Rienner, 1996.

———. "How Does Globalization Work?" In *Globalization: Critical Reflections, International Political Economy Yearbook, Vol. 9*, edited by James H. Mittelman, 229–241. Boulder, Colorado: Lynne Rienner, 1996.

———, ed. *Globalization: Critical Reflections, International Political Economy Yearbook, Vol. 9*. Boulder, Colorado: Lynne Rienner, 1996.

Mlinar, Zdravko and Franc Trček. "Territorial Cultures and Global Impacts." In *Globalization and Europe*, edited by Roland Axtmann, 77–92. London: Pinter, 1998.

Mokyr, Joel. *The Lever of Riches*. Oxford: Oxford University Press, 1990.

Montgomery, John D. "The Next Thousand Years." *World Policy Journal* 15(2) (Summer 1998): 77–81.

Moran, Theodore H. *Multinational Corporations and the Politics of Dependence: Copper in Chile*. Princeton: Princeton University Press, 1974.

Morley, David and Kevin Robbins. *Spaces of Identity*. London: Routledge, 1995.

Mott, William H., IV. *The Economic Basis of Peace: Linkages between Economic Growth and International Conflict*. Westport, Connecticut: Greenwood, 1997.

Murphy, Craig N. "Globalization and Governance: A Historical Perspective." In *Globalization and Europe*, edited by Roland Axtmann, 144–163. London: Pinter, 1998.

———. *International Organization and Industrial Change: Global Governance since 1850*. Cambridge: Polity, 1994.

Murray, Gilbert. *Essays and Addresses*. London: G. Allen and Unwin, 1921.

Naisbitt, John. *Global Paradox*. New York: William Morrow, 1994.

Nelson, Richard R. "Assessing Private Enterprise: An Exegesis of Tangled Doctrine." *The Bell Journal of Economics* 12(1) (Spring 1981): 93–111.

———, ed. *National Innovation Systems: A Comparative Analysis*. New York: Oxford University Press, 1993.

———. "A Retrospective." In *National Innovation Systems: A Comparative Analysis*, edited by Richard R. Nelson, 505–523. New York: Oxford University Press, 1993.

———. "National Innovation Systems: A Retrospective on a Study." *Industrial and Corporate Change* 2(2) (June 1992): 347–374.

——— and Sidney G. Winter. *An Evolutionary Theory of Economic Change*. Cambridge: Harvard University Press, 1982.

Nielsen, Michael A. "Rules for a Complex, Quantum World." *Scientific American* 287(5) (November 2002): 67–75.

Nightingale, Paul. "A Cognitive Model of Innovation." *Research Policy* 27(7) (November 1998): 689–709.

Noël, Alain and Jean-Philippe Thérien. "Public Opinion and Global Justice." *Comparative Political Studies* 35(6) (August 2002): 631–656.

Nonaka, Ikujiro. *Chishiki-Souzou no Keiei* [A Theory of Organizational Knowledge Creation]. Tokyo: Nihon Keizai Shimbun-sha, 1990.

————. "Managing Innovation as an Organizational Knowledge Creation Process." Paper prepared for *Tricontinental Handbook of Technology Management*. Tokyo: Institute of Business Research, Hitotsubashi University, 1992.

———— and Hirotaka Takeuchi. *The Knowledge-Creating Company*. New York: Oxford University Press, 1995.

———— and Noboru Konno. "The Concept of Ba: Building a Foundation for Knowledge Creation." *California Management Review* 40(3) (Spring 1998): 40–55.

———— and Ryoko Toyama. "A Firm as a Dialectical Being: Towards a Dynamic Theory of a Firm." *Industrial and Corporate Change* 11(5) (November 2002): 995–1009.

————, Ryoko Toyama, and Akiya Nagata. "A Firm as a Knowledge-Creating Entity: A New Perspective on the Theory of the Firm." *Industrial and Corporate Change* 9(1) (March 2000): 1–20.

Nordhaus, William and James Tobin. *Economic Growth*. New York: National Bureau of Economic Research, 1972.

North, Douglass C. *Institutions, Institutional Change, and Economic Performance*. Cambridge: Cambridge University Press, 1990.

Nye, Joseph S. Jr. "The American National Interest and Global Public Goods." *International Affairs* 78(2) (April 2002): 233–244.

————. "Neorealism and Neoliberalism." *World Politics* 40(2) (January 1988): 235-251.

————. *The Paradox of American Power: Why the World's Only Superpower Can't Go It Alone*. New York: Oxford University Press, 2002.

————. "Soft Power." *Foreign Policy* 80 (Fall 1990): 153–171.

Oakeshott, Michael. *The Voice of Liberal Learning*. New Haven, Connecticut: Yale University Press, 1989.

Oe, Kenzaburo. *Aimai na Nihon no Watashi (Ambiguous Japan and Myself)*. Tokyo: Iwanami Shinsho, 1995.

Offe, Claus. "Capitalism by Democratic Design? Democratic Theory Facing the Triple Transition in East Central Europe." *Social Research* 58(4) (Winter 1991): 865–892.

Ogata, Sadako. "Guilty Parties." *Foreign Policy* 132 (September-October 2002): 39–40.

Ohlin, Bertil G. *Interregional and International Trade*. Cambridge: Harvard University Press, 1933.

Okamura, Sogo, Kenichi Marakami, and Ikujiro Nonaka, eds. *What Should Be Done? What Can Be Done? Science and Technology Policy Research: The Proceedings of the NISTEP Second International Conference on Science and Technology*. Tokyo: Mita Press, 1991.

Olson, Mancur, Jr. "Dictatorship, Democracy, and Development." *American Political Science Review* 87(3) (September 1993): 567–576.

————. *The Logic of Collective Action: Public Goods and the Theory of Groups*. Cambridge: Harvard University Press, 1965.

Ohmae, Kenichi. *The Borderless World*. New York: HarperCollins, 1990.

————. *The End of the Nation-State: The Rise of Regional Economics*. London: HarperCollins, 1996.

O'Rourke, Kevin H. and Jeffrey G. Williamson. *Globalization and History: The Evolution of a Nineteenth-Century Atlantic Economy*. Cambridge: MIT Press, 1999.

Palan, Ronen. *Underconsumptionism and Widening Income Inequalities: The Dynamics of Globalization*, Newcastle Discussion Papers in Politics, no. 4, September 1993.

Panek, Richard. "And Then There Was Light." *Natural History* 111(9) (November 2002): 46–51.

Panitch, Leo. "Rethinking the Role of the State in an Era of Globalization." In *Globalization: Critical Reflections, International Political Economy Yearbook, Vol. 9*, edited by James H. Mittelman, 83–113. Boulder, Colorado: Lynne Rienner, 1996.

—— and Colin Leys. *The End of Parliamentary Socialism: From New Left to New Labour*. London: Verso, 1997.

Pao, Long Chang, Chintay Shih, and Chiung Wen Hsu. "The Formation Process of Taiwan's IC Industry—Method of Technology Transfer." *Technovation* 14(3) (April 1994): 161–171.

——, Chiung Wen Hsu, and Chien Tzu Tsai. "A Stage Approach for Industrial Technology Development and Implementation—The Case of Taiwan's Computer Industry." *Technovation* 19(4) (February 1999): 233–241.

Parkinson, James. *Organic Remains of a Former World: An Examination of the Mineralized Remains of the Vegetables and Animals of the Antediluvian World, Generally Termed Extraneous Fossils, the First Volume; Containing the Vegetable Kingdom*. London: J. Robson, 1804.

Parsons, Talcott. *The Evolution of Societies*. Englewood Cliffs, Prentice-Hall, 1977.

——. "Evolutionary Universals in Society." *American Sociological Review* 29(1) (February 1964): 339–357.

——. *Societies*. Englewood Cliffs, New Jersey: Prentice-Hall, 1966.

—— and Edward A. Shils, eds. *Toward a General Theory of Action*. Cambridge: Harvard University Press, [1951] 1954.

Parsons, Tom, Shinji Toda, Ross S. Stein, Aykut Barka, and James H. Dieterich. "Heightened Odds of Large Earthquakes Near Istanbul: An Interaction-Based Probability Calculation." *Science* 288(5466) (28 April 2000): 661–665.

Pasha, Mustapha Kamal and Ahmed I. Samatar. "The Resurgence of Islam." In *Globalization: Critical Reflections, International Political Economy Yearbook, Vol. 9*, edited by James H. Mittelman, 187–201. Boulder, Colorado: Lynne Rienner, 1996.

Paterson, Matthew. "Interpreting Trends in Global Environmental Governance." *International Affairs* 75(4) (October 1999): 793–802.

Patterson, Lee Ann. "Agricultural Policy Reform in the European Community: A Three-Level Game Analysis." *International Organization* 51(1) (Winter 1997): 135–165.

Penrose, Edith T. *The Theory of the Growth of the Firm*. Oxford: Blackwell, 1959.

Pettis, Michael. "Will Globalization Go Bankrupt?" *Foreign Policy* (October 2001): 52–59.

Pierson, Paul. "When Effect Becomes Cause: Policy Feedback and Political Change." *World Politics* 45(4) (July 1993): 595–628.

Pijl, Kees van der. "The International Level." In *The Capitalist Class: An International Study*, edited by Tom Bottomore and Robert J. Brym, 237–266. New York: New York University Press, 1989.

Plato. *The Republic*, translated by Alan Bloom. New York: Basic Books, 1948.

Pleskovic Boris and Joseph E. Stiglitz, eds. *Annual World Bank Conference on Development Economics 1998*. Washington, D.C.: World Bank, 1999.

Polanyi, Karl. *The Great Transformation: The Political and Economic Origins of Our Time*. Boston: Beacon Press, [1944] 1957.

——. *The Great Transformation*. New York: Rinehart, 1944.

"Political Islam: Wave of the Past." *The Economist* 363(8275) (1 June 2002): 77–78.

Pollack, Andrew. "Technology without Borders Raises Big Questions for the U.S." *New York Times* 1 January 1992, pp. 1, 48.

Pollard, Sidney. *The Idea of Progress.* New York: Basic Books, 1968.

Porter, Bruce F. *War and the Rise of the State.* New York: Free Press, 1994.

Portes, Alejandro. "Global Villagers: The Rise of Transnational Communities." *American Prospect* 7(25) (March-April 1996): 77–90.

Pope, Alexander. *An Essay on Man*, edited by Maynard Mack. London: Routledge, [1733] 1950.

Posner, Michael V. "International Trade and Technological Exchange." *Oxford Economic Papers* 13(3) (October 1961): 323–341.

Prahalad, Coimbatore K. and Gary Hamel. "The Core Competence of the Corporation." *Harvard Business Review* 68(3) (May-June 1990): 79–91.

Prins, Gwyn. "Thinking about Intervention: An Essay Reflecting upon the State of the Policy Debate in Early 2001." *RUSI Journal* 146(4) (August 2001): 12–17.

Przeworski, Adam and Fernando Limongi. "Political Regimes and Economic Growth." *Journal of Economic Perspectives* 7(3) (Summer 1993): 51–71.

Pupin, Michael. *The New Reformation: From Physical to Spiritual Realities.* New York: Scribner's, 1927.

Putnam, Robert D. *Bowling Alone: The Collapse and Revival of American Community.* New York: Simon and Schuster, 2000.

———. "Diplomacy and Domestic Politics: The Logic of Two-Level Games." *International Organization* 42(3) (Summer 1988): 427–460.

Quigley, Carroll. *The Evolution of Civilizations: An Introduction to Historical Analysis.* Indianapolis, Indiana: Liberty Fund, 1961.

Raboteau, Albert J. *Slave Religion: The Invisible Institution in the Antebellum South.* New York: Oxford University Press, 1978.

Rajaee, Farhang. *Globalization on Trial: The Human Condition and the Information Civilization.* West Hartford, Connecticut: Kumarian, 2000.

Ramonet, Ignacio. "Let Them Eat Big Macs." In "Dueling Globalizations: A Debate between Thomas L. Friedman and Ignacio Ramonet." *Foreign Policy* 116 (Fall 1999): 110–127.

Reich, Robert B. *The Work of Nations: Preparing Ourselves for 21st Century Capitalism.* London: Simon and Schuster, 1991.

Reich, Simon. *The Fruits of Fascism: Postwar Prosperity in Historical Perspective.* Ithaca: Cornell University Press, 1990.

Rengger, Nicholas. "Justice in the World Economy: Global, International, or Both?" *International Affairs* 75(3) (July 1999): 469–471.

Resnick, Philip. "Global Democracy: Ideals and Reality." In *Globalization and Europe*, edited by Roland Axtmann, 126–143. London: Pinter, 1998.

Reynolds, Lloyd G. *Economic Growth in the Third World: 1950–1980.* New Haven: Yale University Press, 1985.

Riesman, David with Nathan Glazer and Reuel Denney. *The Lonely Crowd: A Study of the Changing American Character.* New Haven: Yale University Press, [1950] 1967.

Ritzer, George. *The McDonaldization of Society.* London: Pine Forge, 1996.

Rizopoulos, Nicholas X. ed. *Sea Changes: American Foreign Policy in a World Transformed.* New York: Council on Foreign Relations, 1990.

Roberts, Brad, ed. *New Forces in the World Economy*. Cambridge: MIT Press, 1996.

Robertson, Roland. *Globalization: Social Theory and Global Culture*. London, Sage, 1992.

Rodrik, Dani. *Has Globalization Gone Too Far?* Washington, D.C.: Institute for International Economics, 1971.

———. "How Far Will International Economic Integration Go?" *Journal of Economic Perspectives* 14(1) (Winter 2000): 177–186.

———. "Understanding Economic Reform." *Journal of Economic Literature* 34(1) (March 1996): 9–41.

Rogers, Everett M. *Diffusion of Innovations*, 4th ed. New York: Free Press, 1995.

Romer, Paul. *Are Nonconvexities Important for Understanding Growth?* Cambridge, Massachusetts: National Bureau of Economic Research, 1990.

———. "Endogenous Technical Change." *Journal of Political Economy* 98 (1990): S71–S102.

Rorty, Richard. "Against Unity." *Wilson Quarterly* 22(1) (Winter 1998): 28–38.

Rosecrance, Richard N. *The Rise of the Trading State: Commerce and Conquest in the Modern World*. New York: Basic Books, 1986.

Rosenau, James N. "Global Affairs in an Epochal Transformation." In *The Information Revolution and International Security*, edited by Ryan Henry and C. Edward Peartree, 31–57. Washington, D.C.: Center for Strategic and International Studies Press, 1998.

———. "Governance and Democracy in a Globalizing World." In *Re-imagining Political Community: Studies in Cosmopolitan Democracy*, edited by Daniele Archibugi, David Held, and Martin Köhler, 28–57. Cambridge: Polity, 1998.

———. "Governance in the Twenty-First Century." *Global Governance* 1(1) (January-April 1995): 13–44.

———. "Governance, Order, and Change in World Politics." In *Governance without Government: Order and Change in World Politics*, edited by James N. Rosenau and Ernst-Otto Czempiel, 1–29. Cambridge: Cambridge University Press, 1992.

———. *The Study of Global Interdependence*. New York: Nichols, 1980.

———. *Turbulence in World Politics: A Theory of Change and Continuity*. Princeton: Princeton University Press, 1990.

——— and Ernst-Otto Czempiel, eds. *Governance without Government: Order and Change in World Politics*. Cambridge: Cambridge University Press, 1992.

Rosenberg, Nathan. *Inside the Black Box: Technology and Economics*. Cambridge: Cambridge University Press, 1982.

——— and Luther E. Birdzell. *How the West Grew Rich*. New York: Basic Books, 1986.

Rosenkopf, Lori and Michael L. Tushman. "The Coevolution of Community Networks and Technology: Lessons from the Flight Simulation Industry." *Industrial and Corporate Change* 7(2) (June 1998): 311–346.

Rostow, Walt Whitman. "The Marshallian Long Period." In *Pioneers in Development* edited by Gerald M. Meier and Dudley Seers, 227–261. Washington, D.C.: Oxford University Press for the World Bank, 1984.

———. *Perspectives on Technology*. Cambridge: Cambridge University Press, 1976.

Rothkopf, David J. "Foreign Policy in the Information Age." In *The Global Century: Globalization and National Security*, edited by Richard L. Kugler and Ellen L. Frost, vol. 1, 215–239. Washington, D.C.: National Defense University Press, 2001.

Rothschild, Emma. "Globalization and the Return of History." *Foreign Policy* 115 (Summer 1999): 106–116.

Rothwell, Roy. "Successful Industrial Innovation: Critical Factors for the 1990s." *R&D Management* 22(3) (July 1992): 221–239.

Rousseau, Jean-Jacques. *Collected Writings of Jean-Jacques Rousseau, vol. 3, Discourse on the Origins of Inequality (Second Discourse), Polemics, and Political Economy*, edited by Roger D. Masters and Christopher Kelly, vol. 3, 1–95. Hanover, New Hampshire: University Press of New England, [1755] 1992.

Rowe, Constance. *Voltaire and the State.* New York: Columbia University Press, 1955.

Ruef, Martin. "Strong Ties, Weak Ties, and Islands." *Industrial and Corporate Change* 11(3) (June 2002): 427–449.

Rueschemeyer, Dietrich and Theda Skocpol, eds. *States, Social Knowledge, and the Origins of Modern Social Policies.* Princeton: Princeton University Press, 1996.

Ryn, Claes G. "Defining Historicism." *Humanitas* 11(2) (Spring-Summer 1998):86–101.

———. *Will, Imagination, and Reason: Babbitt, Croce, and the Problem of Reality.* New Brunswick, New Jersey: Transaction, 1997.

Sabine, George H. *A History of Political Theory*, 4th ed., revised by Thomas L. Thorson. New York: Harcourt Brace College Publishers Holt, 1973.

Saint-Simon, Claude-Henri de. *Cinquième Lettre a Messieurs Les Industriels.* In *Du Système Industriel* in *Œvres de Claude-Henri de Saint-Simon*, 6 vols. vol. 3 (vols. 5, 6, and 7 of *Œvres de Saint-Simon*, edited by E. Dentu. Paris, Enfantin, 1868), vol. 6, 1–134. Geneva: Slatkine Reprints, 1977.

———. *L'Organisateur* in *Œvres de Claude-Henri de Saint-Simon*, 6 vols. vol. 2 (vols. 3 and 4 of *Œvres de Saint-Simon*, edited by E. Dentu. Paris, Enfantin, 1868) bk. 5, 1–242. Geneva: Slatkine Reprints, 1977.

———. *Nouveau Christianisme* in *Œvres de Claude-Henri de Saint-Simon*, 6 vols. vol. 3 (vols. 5, 6, and 7 of *Œvres de Saint-Simon*, edited by E. Dentu. Paris, Enfantin, 1868), vol. 7, bk. 2. Geneva: Slatkine Reprints, 1977.

Sakamoto, Yoshikazu. *Global Transformation: Challenges to the State System.* Tokyo: United Nations University Press, 1994.

Sassen, Saskia. "The *de facto* Transnationalizing of Immigration Policy." In *Challenge to the Nation-State*, edited by Christian Joppke, 49–85. Oxford: Oxford University Press, 1998.

———. *Globalization and Its Discontents.* New York: New Press, 1998.

———. *Losing Control.* New York: Columbia University Press, 1996.

Sato, Seizaburo. "Man's Freedom, God's Will." *Civilization* 5(2) (April-May 1998): 54–77.

Saxenian, Anna Lee. *Regional Advantage: Culture and Competition in Silicon Valley and Route 128.* Cambridge: Harvard University Press, 1994.

——— and Jinn-Yuh Hsu. "The Silicon Valley-Hsinchu Connection: Technical Communities and Industrial Upgrading." *Industrial and Corporate Change* 10(4) (December 2001): 893–920.

Sayer, Andrew and Richard Walker. *The New Social Economy: Reworking the Division of Labour.* Cambridge, Massachusetts: Blackwell, 1992.

Sayer, Derek. *Capitalism and Modernity: An Excursus on Marx and Weber.* London: Routledge, Chapman, and Hall, 1991.

Scarre, Geoffrey. *Utilitarianism.* London: Routledge, Chapman, and Hall, 1996.

Schiller, Herbert I. *Communication and Cultural Domination*. White Plains, New York: Sharpe, 1976.

———. *Information Inequality: The Deepening Social Crisis of America*. London: Routledge, 1996.

———. *Mass Communications and American Empire*, 2d ed. Boulder, Colorado: Westview, 1992.

———. *Who Knows: Information in the Age of Fortune 500*. Norwood, New Jersey: Ablex, 1981.

Schmidt, Steffen W. Laura Guasti, Carl H. Landé, and James C. Scott, eds. *Friends, Followers, and Factions: A Reader in Political Clientelism*. Berkeley: University of California Press, 1977.

Schumpeter, Joseph A. *Capitalism, Socialism, and Democracy*. New York: Harper and Brothers, 1942.

———. *History of Economic Analysis*. New York: Oxford University Press, 1954.

———. *The Theory of Economic Development*. Cambridge: Harvard University Press, [1911] 1934.

Schwarz, Benjamin and Christopher Layne. "The Hard Questions, a New Grand Strategy." *The Atlantic Monthly* 289(1) (January 2002): 36–42.

Schwenninger, Sherle R. "World Order Lost: American Foreign Policy in the Post-Cold-War World." *World Policy Journal* 16(2) (Summer 1999): 42–71.

Scott, James C. *Weapons of the Weak*. New Haven: Yale University Press, 1985.

Scully, Gerald W. "The Institutional Framework and Economic Development." *Journal of Political Economy* 96(3) (June 1988): 652–662.

Sears, Robert R. "Social Behavior and Personality Development." In *Toward a General Theory of Action*, edited by Talcott Parsons and Edward A. Shils, 465–476. Cambridge: Harvard University Press, [1951] 1954.

Senker, Jacqueline. "Tacit Knowledge and Models of Innovation." *Industrial and Corporate Change* 4(2) (June 1995): 425–447.

Shackle, George L. S. *Decision, Order, and Time in Human Affairs*, 2d ed. Cambridge: Cambridge University Press, 1969.

Shapiro, Ian and Lea Brilmayer, eds. *Global Justice*. New York: New York University Press, 1999.

———. "Introduction." In *Global Justice*, edited by Ian Shapiro and Lea Brilmayer, 1–11. New York: New York University Press, 1999.

Shaw, Martin. "The State of Globalization: Towards a Theory of State Transformation." *Review of International Political Economy* 4(3) (Autumn 1997): 497–513.

Shermer, Michael. "The Captain Kirk Principle." *Scientific American* 287(6) (December 2002): 39.

———. "Digits and Fidgets." *Scientific American* 288(1) (January 2003): 35.

Shorter, Aylward. *African Christian Theology. Adaptation or Incarnation?* Maryknoll, New York: Orbis, 1977.

Shue, Henry. "Exporting Hazards." In *Boundaries: National Autonomy and its Limits*, edited by Peter G. Brown and Henry Shue, 107–146. Totowa, New Jersey: Rowman and Littlefield, 1981.

Shupe, Anson D., Jr. and Bronislaw Misztal, eds. *Religion, Mobilization, and Social Action*. Westport, Connecticut: Praeger, 1998.

Simmel, Georg. *The Sociology of Georg Simmel*, translated by Kurt H. Wolff. Glencoe, Illinois: Free Press, 1950.

Simon, Herbert A. "Forecasting the Future or Shaping It?" *Industrial and Corporate Change* 11(3) (June 2002): 601–605.

———. "From Substantive to Procedural Rationality." In *Method and Appraisal in Economics*, edited by Spiro J. Latsis. Cambridge: Cambridge University Press, 1976, 129–148.

———. "Organizing and Coordinating Talk and Silence in Organizations." *Industrial and Corporate Change* 11(3) (June 2002): 611–618.

———. "We and They: The Human Urge to Identify with Groups." *Industrial and Corporate Change* 11(3) (June 2002): 607–610.

Sklair, Leslie. *Sociology of the Global System*. Hemel Hempstead: Harvester Wheatsheaf, 1991.

Slaughter, Anne-Marie. "The Real New World Order." *Foreign Affairs* 76(5) (September-October 1997): 183–197.

Smith, Adam. *The Wealth of Nations*. New York: Modern Library, [1776] 1994.

Smith, Anthony D. *Nations and Nationalism in a Global Era*. Cambridge, Massachusetts: Polity, 1995.

———. "The Problem of National Identity: Ancient, Medieval, and Modern." *Ethnic and Racial Studies* 17(3) (July 1994): 375–399.

———. "Towards a Global Culture." In *Global Culture: Nationalism, Globalization, and Modernity*, edited by Mike Featherstone, 171–191. London: Sage, 1990.

Smith, Steve, Ken Booth, and Marysia Zalewski, eds. *International Theory: Positivism and Beyond*. Cambridge: Cambridge University Press, 1996.

Smithies, Arthur. "Optimum Location in Spatial Competition." *The Journal of Political Economy* 49(3) (June 1941): 423–439.

Snow, Charles P. *The Two Cultures and the Scientific Revolution*. New York: Cambridge University Press, 1959.

Solow Robert M. "Technical Change and the Aggregate Production Function." *Review of Economics and Statistics* 39 (August 1957): 312-320.

Sombart, Werner. *Quintessence of Capitalism*. New York: Dutton, 1915.

Sorens, William B. "Capital Ideas." *Letters to the Editor, Foreign Affairs* 81(3) (May-June 2002): 182–183.

Spengler, Oswald. *The Decline of the West*, 2 vols. New York: Knopf, [1926, 1928] 1973.

Spiegel Steven L. and Fred L. Wehling. *World Politics in a New Era*, 2d ed. Fort Worth, Texas: Harcourt Brace, 1999.

Spragens, Thomas, Jr. *Understanding Political Theories*. New York: St. Martin's, 1976.

Spykman, Nicholas J. *America's Strategy in World Politics: The United States and the Balance of Power*. New York: Harcourt, Brace, 1942.

———. *The Geography of the Peace*. New York: Harcourt, Brace, 1944.

Starr, Harvey. *Anarchy, Order, and Integration: How to Manage Interdependence*. Ann Arbor: University of Michigan Press, 1997.

Stein, Ross S. "Earthquake Conversations." *Scientific American* 288(1) (January 2003): 72–79.

Stern, Marc A. "Defining Global Public Goods." In *Global Public Goods: International Cooperation in the 21st Century*, edited by Inge Kaul, Isabelle Grunberg, and Marc A. Stern, 2-19. New York: Oxford University Press, 1999.

Stevenson, Nick. "Globalization and Cultural Political Economy." In *Globalization and Its Critics*, edited by Randall D. Germain, 91–113. New York: St. Martin's, 2000.

Stiglitz, Joseph E. *Globalization and Its Discontents*. New York: Norton, 2002.

———. "Globalization: You Have to Walk the Talk." *Fortune* 144(11) (26 November 2001): 88.

———. "Knowledge for Development: Economic Science, Economic Policy, and Economic Advice." In *Annual World Bank Conference on Development Economics 1998*, edited by Boris Pleskovic and Joseph E. Stiglitz, 9–58. Washington, D.C.: World Bank, 1999.

Strang, David and John W. Meyer. "Institutional Conditions for Diffusion." *Theory and Society* 22(4) (August 1993): 487–511.

Strange, Susan. "The Name of the Game." In *Sea Changes: American Foreign Policy in a World Transformed*, edited by Nicholas X. Rizopoulos, 238–273. New York: Council on Foreign Relations, 1990.

Stroup, Alice. *A Company of Scientists: Botany, Patronage, and Community at the Seventeenth-Century Parisian Royal Academy of Sciences*. Berkeley: University of California Press, 1990.

Stoller, Paul. "Trading Places: Muslim Merchants from West Africa Expand their Markets to New York City." *Natural History* 111(6) (July-August 2001): 48–55.

Stopford, John. "Multinational Corporations." *Foreign Policy* 113 (Winter 1998–1999): 12–24.

Suarez, Francisco. *De Legibus*, bk. 2. In *Selections from Three Works of Francisco Suarez*, 3–646. Oxford: Clarendon, [1612] 1944.

Suarin, Julian. "Globalization, Poverty, and the Promises of Modernity." *Millennium* 25(3) (1996): 657–680.

Sudarshan, Ratna and Jeemol Unni. "When Home-Based Workers Raise Their Voices: An Indian Perspective." *SAIS Review* 21(1) (Winter-Spring 2001): 109–115.

Sumner, L. Wayne and Joseph Boyle, eds. *Philosophical Perspectives on Bioethics*. Toronto: Toronto University Press, 1996.

Surowiecki, James. "A Virtuous Cycle." *Forbes* 170(13) (23 December 2002): 248–256.

Suter, Keith. "People Power." *The World Today* 56(10) (October 2000): 12–14.

Sweet, Alec Stone. "Judicialization and the Construction of Governance." *Comparative Political Studies* 32(2) (April 1999): 147–184.

Takeyh, Ray. "Faith-Based Initiatives." *Foreign Policy* 127 (November-December 2001): 68–70.

Talalay, Michael. "Technology and Globalization." In *Globalization and Its Critics*, edited by Randall D. Germain, 204–222. New York: St. Martin's, 2000.

Tamamoto, Masaru. "The Uncertainty of the Self: Japan at Century's End." *World Policy Journal* 16(2) (Summer 1999): 119–128.

Tangredi, Sam J. "Beyond the Sea and Jointness." *U.S. Naval Institute Proceedings* 127/9/1,183 (September 2001): 60–63.

Taylor, Charles. "The Politics of Recognition." In *Multiculturalism: Examining the Politics of Recognition*, edited by Amy Gutmann, 75–85. Princeton: Princeton University Press, 1994.

Taylor, Michael. "Structure, Culture, and Action in the Explanation of Social Change." *Politics and Society* 17(2) (June 1989): 115–162.

"Thanksgiving for Innovation." *The Economist Technology Quarterly*, inserted between pages 50 and 51, in *The Economist* 364(8291) (21 September 2002): 13–14.

Thompson, Michael, Richard Ellis, and Aaron Wildavsky. *Cultural Theory.* Boulder, Colorado: Westview, 1990.

Titmuss, Richard M. *The Gift Relationship: From Human Blood to Social Policy.* New York: Random House, 1971.

Tocqueville, Alexis de. *Democracy in America*, translated by Henry Reeve. New York: Knopf [1840] 1945.

Toffler, Alvin. *Powershift, Knowledge, Wealth, and Violence at the Edge of the 21st Century.* New York: Bantam, 1991.

Tönnies, Ferdinand. *Community and Association* (originally published as *Gemeinschaft und Gesellschaft*), translated and edited by Charles P. Loomis. East Lansing: Michigan State University Press, [1887] 1957.

Torpy, Glenn L. "Future British Operations." *Royal United Services Institute Journal* 146(1) (February 2001): 8–12.

Toulmin, Stephen E. *Cosmopolis: The Hidden Agenda of Modernity.* New York: Free Press, 1990.

Toynbee, Arnold J. *Civilization on Trial.* New York: Oxford University Press, 1948.

———. *Civilization on Trial* and *The World and the West.* New York: Meridian, 1948.

———. *A Study of History*, 10 vols. London: Oxford University Press, 1934.

Trow, Martin. *The New Production of Knowledge.* Beverly Hills, California: Sage, 1994.

Truxillo, Charles A. *The Sword and The Cross.* Westport, Connecticut: Greenwood, 2001.

Tucker, Robert W. "Alone or with Others: The Temptations of Post-Cold-War Power." *Foreign Affairs* 78(6) (November-December 1999): 15–20.

Turgot, Anne-Robert-Jacques. "A Philosophical Review of the Successive Advances of the Human Mind." In *Turgot on Progress, Sociology, and Economics*, edited and translated by Ronald L. Meek, 41–59. Cambridge: Cambridge University Press, 1973.

Twining, David T. *Beyond Multilateralism.* Lanham, Maryland: University Press of America, 1998.

Twitchell, James B. "But First, a Word from our Sponsor." *Wilson Quarterly* 20(3) (Summer 1996): 68–77.

United Nations. *Our Global Neighborhood.* Report of the Commission on Global Governance. New York: Oxford University Press, 1995.

United States, National Academy of Sciences, National Academy of Engineering and Institute of Medicine. *On Being a Scientist.* Washington, D.C.: National Academy Press, 1995.

Useem, Jerry. "Globalization." *Fortune* 144(11) (26 November 2001): 76–84.

Uslaner, Eric M. "Producing and Consuming Trust." *Political Science Quarterly* 115(4) (Winter 2000-2001): 569–590.

Väyrynen, Raimo. "Violence, Resistance, and Order." In "International Relations." In *Global Transformation: Challenges to the State System*, edited by Yoshikazu Sakamoto, 385–411. Tokyo: United Nations University Press, 1994.

Vernon, Raymond. "International Investment and International Trade in the Product Cycle." *Quarterly Journal of Economics* 80 (1966): 190–207.

———. "The Obsolescing Bargain: A Key Factor in Political Risk." In *The International Essays for Business Decision Makers*, vol. 5, edited by Mark B. Winchester, 281–286. Houston: Center for International Business, 1980.

———. *Sovereignty at Bay: The Multinational Spread of U.S. Enterprises*. New York: Basic Books, 1971.

———, ed. *The Technology Factor in International Trade*. New York: Columbia University Press, 1970.

Verspagen, Bart. "Estimating International Technology Spillovers Using Technology Flow Matrices." *Weltwirtschaftliches Archiv* 133(2) (June 1997): 226–248.

Viner, Jacob. *International Economics*. Glencoe, Illinois: Free Press, 1951.

Vladislav, Jan, ed. *Living in Truth*. London: Unwin Hyman, 1989.

Voegelin, Eric. *Order and History, Volume 2: The World of the Polis*. Baton Rouge: Louisiana State University Press, 1957.

Voltaire, François Marie Arouet de. *Voltaire: Political Writings*, edited by David Williams. Cambridge: Cambridge University Press, 1994.

Wade, Robert. "Globalization and Its Limits." In *National Diversity and Globalization*, edited by Suzanne Berger and Robert Dore, 60–88. Ithaca: Cornell University Press, 1996.

———. "Winners and Losers." *The Economist* 359(8219) (28 April 2001): 72–74.

Walker, Martin. "What Europeans Think of America." *World Policy Journal* 17(2) (Summer 2000): 26–38.

Wallerstein, Immanuel. "The Interstate Structure of the Modern World-System." In *International Theory: Positivism and Beyond* edited by Steve Smith, Ken Booth, and Marysia Zalewski. Cambridge: Cambridge University Press, 1996.

———. "Member, Dismember, Remember." *Civilization* 5(2) (April-May 1998): 54–77.

———. *The Modern World-System: Capitalist Agriculture and the Origins of the European World-Economy in the Sixteenth Century*. New York: Academic Press, 1974.

———. "The Prospect of Politics." *Civilization* 5(2) (April-May 1998): 70–77.

———, ed. *The Capitalist World-Economy*. Cambridge: Cambridge University Press, 1979.

Walt, Stephen M. "Fads, Fevers, and Firestorms." *Foreign Policy* 121 (November-December 2000): 34–42.

Waltz, Kenneth N. "Evaluating Theories." *American Political Science Review* 91(4) (December 1997): 913–917.

———. "Globalization and American Power." *The National Interest* 59 (Spring 2000): 46–56.

———. *Theory of International Politics*. Reading, Massachusetts: Addison-Wesley, 1979.

Walzer, Michael. *Spheres of Justice: A Defense of Pluralism and Equality*. New York: Basic Books, 1983.

———. *Thick and Thin: Moral Argument at Home and Abroad*. Notre Dame: University of Notre Dame Press, 1994.

Waters, Malcolm. *Globalization*. London: Routledge, 1995.

Weber, Max. *Economy and Society: An Outline of Interpretive Sociology*, edited by Guenther Roth and Claus Wittich. New York: Bedminster, [1924] 1968.

Wedgwood, Ruth. "Gallant Delusions." *Foreign Policy* 132 (September-October 2002): 44–46.

Weede, Eric. "The Impact of Democracy on Economic Growth: Some Evidence from Cross-National Analysis." *Kyklos* 36(1) (March 1983): 21–39.

Weller, Marc. "Undoing the Global Constitution: U.N. Security Council Action on the International Criminal Court." *International Affairs* 78(4) (October 2002): 693–712.

Welsh, Elsa. "The Negotiator." *The New Yorker* 72(4) (18 March 1996): 86–97.

West, Jonathan. "Limits to Globalization: Organizational Homogeneity and Diversity in the Semiconductor Industry." *Industrial and Corporate Change* 11(1) (February 2002): 159–188.

White, Lynn T. Jr. *Medieval Technology and Social Change.* Oxford: Clarendon, 1962.

White, Thomas E. "The Army Is Dedicated to Delivering Victory." *Army* 52(10) (October 2002): 15–22.

Wildavsky, Aaron. "Choosing Preferences by Constructing Institutions: A Cultural Theory of Preference Formation." *American Political Science Review* 81(1) (March 1987): 3–21.

Wilkins, Edward J. "The Mind Electric." *Sextant: The Journal of Salem State College* 10(2) (Spring 2000): 40–43.

Wilson, Edward O. "The Bottleneck." *Scientific American* 286(2) (February 2002): 82–91.

——. *Consilience, The Unity of Knowledge.* New York: Knopf, 1998.

——. "Resuming the Enlightenment Quest." *Wilson Quarterly* 22(1) (Winter 1998): 16–27.

Winchester, Mark B. ed. *The International Essays for Business Decision Makers*, vol. 5. Houston: Center for International Business, 1980.

Wittgenstein, Ludwig. *Tractatus Logico-Philosophicus.* London: Routledge and Kegan Paul, [1921] 1961.

Wohlforth, William C. "The Stability of a Unipolar World." *International Security* 24(1) (Summer 1999): 5–41.

Wolf, Martin. "Will the Nation-State Survive Globalization?" *Foreign Affairs* 80(1) (January-February 2001): 178–190.

Wolfe, Alan. *The Limits of Legitimacy: Political Contradictions of Contemporary Capitalism.* New York: Free Press, 1977.

Wolfowitz, Paul. "American Power—For What? A Symposium." *Commentary* 109(1) (January 2000): 21–47.

World Bank. *The East Asian Miracle.* New York: Oxford University Press, 1993.

——. *World Development Report 1989.* New York: Oxford University Press, 1989.

World Trade Organization. *Annual Report: 1996.* Geneva, Switzerland: World Trade Organization, 1996.

Wriston, Walter B. *The Twilight of Sovereignty: How the Information Revolution Is Transforming Our World.* New York: Scribners, 1992.

Young, James P. *Reconsidering American Liberalism: The Troubled Odyssey of the Liberal Idea.* Boulder, Colorado: Westview, 1996.

Young, Oran R. *International Cooperation: Building Regimes for Natural Resources and the Environment.* Ithaca: Cornell University Press, 1989.

AUTHOR INDEX

SUBJECT INDEX

ABOUT THE AUTHOR

WILLIAM H. MOTT IV is a Predoctoral Tutor at the Fletcher School of Law and Diplomacy at Tufts University. He has spent all of his adult life in public service as a military and diplomatic officer, and as a teacher and scholar. In a 30-year career in the U.S. Army with dual foci on Command and Military Diplomacy, he observed, analyzed, and managed behaviors of governments and people under stress and in control in both Europe and Asia. He completed his postgraduate work at Fletcher School of Law and Diplomacy.